ELEMENTS OF FUNCTIONAL PROGRAMMING

INTERNATIONAL COMPUTER SCIENCE SERIES

SELECTED TITLES IN THE SERIES

PROLOG Programming for Artificial Intelligence *I Bratko*

Parallel Programming *R H Perrott*

The Specification of Computer Programs *W M Turski and T S E Maibaum*

Concurrent Programming *N Gehani and A D McGettrick* (eds.)

Functional Programming *A J Field and P G Harrison*

Comparative Programming Languages *L B Wilson and R G Clark*

Distributed Systems: Concepts and Design *G Coulouris and J Dollimore*

Software Prototyping, Formal Methods and VDM *S Hekmatpour and D Ince*

C Programming in a UNIX Environment *J Kay and R Kummerfeld*

An Introduction to Functional Programming through Lambda Calculus *G Michaelson*

Clausal Form Logic: An Introduction to the Logic of Computer Reasoning *T Richards*

Software Engineering (3rd Edn.) *I Sommerville*

High-Level Languages and their Compilers *D Watson*

Interactive Computer Graphics: Functional, Procedural and Device-Level Methods *P Burger and D Gillies*

Software Development with Modula-2 *D Budgen*

Program Derivation: The Development of Programs from Specifications *R G Dromey*

Programming in Ada (3rd Edn.) *J G P Barnes*

Programming for Artificial Intelligence: Methods, Tools and Applications *W Kreutzer and B J McKenzie*

Common Lisp Programming for Artificial Intelligence *T Hasemer and J Domingue*

Object-Oriented Programming with Simula *B Kirkerud*

ELEMENTS OF FUNCTIONAL PROGRAMMING

Chris Reade

Brunel University

ADDISON-WESLEY
PUBLISHING
COMPANY

Wokingham, England · Reading, Massachusetts · Menlo Park, California
New York · Don Mills, Ontario · Amsterdam · Bonn
Sydney · Singapore · Tokyo · Madrid · San Juan

Cover designed by Crayon Design of Henley-on-Thames
and printed by The Riverside Printing Co. (Reading) Ltd.
Typeset by Times Graphics, Singapore.
Printed and bound in Great Britain by T.J. Press (Padstow) Ltd., Cornwall.

First printed in 1989. Reprinted in 1991, 1993 and 1995.

British Library Cataloguing in Publication Data
Reade, Chris
Elements of functional programming
1. Computer systems. Functional programming
I. Title.
005.1

ISBN 0–201–12915–9

Library of Congress Cataloging in Publication Data
Reade, Chris
Elements of functional programming/Chris Reade.
p. cm.
Bilbliography: p.
Includes index.
ISBN 0–201–12915–9
1. Functional programming (Computer science) I. Title.
QA76.6.R4 1989 89–36
005.1'1—dc19 CIP

Preface

This book is intended to introduce the reader to concepts and techniques used in functional programming today. It gives particular emphasis to the use of modern programming techniques based on abstraction and strong polymorphic type systems.

The book is predominantly concerned with practical functional programming and aims to give plenty of useful examples rather than to provide just a rigorous development of the subject from first principles. However, the theoretical underpinnings and use of formal methods in design and analysis are developed alongside the examples and covered in greater detail in the later chapters.

Although most readers are likely to be familiar with some conventional programming in procedural languages such as C, Pascal, Ada, FORTRAN, COBOL, Modula, Simula, Clu, this is not a strict prerequisite. Anyone familiar with older functional or functional-related languages such as LISP or APL may also benefit from reading about how the new developments in languages can be used to enhance functional programming methods.

Notation

The notation adopted in the book is that of Standard ML (SML) (Harper *et al.*, 1986). However, the book is not concerned with a single functional language, but rather with the concepts and techniques of functional programming, generally. The examples can be adapted for other functional languages, most notably Hope (Burstall *et al.*, 1980), Miranda (Turner, 1985 – Miranda is a trade mark of Research Software Ltd), Ponder (Fairbairn, 1982) and Lazy ML (Augustsson, 1984) with relative ease.

We have taken some liberties with SML notation, using special symbols such as → and α instead of the SML convention of using -> and 'a which can be typed on a keyboard. The following table summarizes the special symbols used:

Symbol	*SML convention*
$\rightarrow$	->
$\Rightarrow$	=>
$\times$	*
α	'a
β	'b
γ	'c
$\alpha^{=}$	''a
$\beta^{=}$	''b
$\gamma^{=}$	''c
“	"
”	"
$\leqslant$	<=
$\geqslant$	>=
=	=
$\circ$	o

Bold font has also been used for keywords in SML.

About the book

The book is based on lecture courses given at Brunel University at both introductory and advanced levels. The introductory courses benefited a great deal from the availability of an interactive functional language (SML). The automatic type inference/checking provided by this language also helped a great deal with the early detection of errors in students' programs. It was particularly useful to have some of the abstract types (pictures and generation for the game of life) as well as a library of general purpose functions (which are introduced throughout the book) compiled in advance. This enabled students to use them and become familiar with their behaviour before learning how they were implemented.

Chapters 1–9 and 14 are suitable for an introduction to the subject, while Chapers 10, 11, 12 and 13 contain material on more advanced topics. A brief synopsis of the chapters is given below.

The first two chapters introduce the fundamental concepts used throughout the rest of the book. Chapter 3 introduces lists as a major structured type for general purpose programming and Chapter 4 develops the use of lists and higher order functions with some extended examples. Chapter 5 is a long chapter which shows how new types can be defined and used in functional programming and Chapter 6 develops a longer example involving the use of new types. The role of types in programming is taken still further in Chapter 7 where abstract types are introduced.

The burning issue of whether lazy or non-lazy functional languages are better for programming is tackled in Chapters 8 and 9. Although brief mention of this subject is given earlier, the tools and examples developed in the first seven chapters are useful for both forms of language, so it is not until Chapter 8 that the divergence becomes apparent. Chapters 10, 11, 12 and 13 are more technical in nature and cover more advanced theoretical aspects of functional programming. Chapter 10 on denotational semantics provides a detailed mathematical treatment of the data objects used in programming and forms the framework for establishing further proof techniques. Chapter 11 discusses polymorphic type checking and includes a (functional) algorithm for automatic type inference. Chapter 12 gives some basic definitions and results concerning the lambda calculus – the fundamental functional language. This material is used to introduce various language implementation techniques in Chapter 13. However, a detailed study of the many approaches to functional language implementation is beyond the scope of this book. The final chapter gives an overview of current developments and looks at prospects for functional programming in the future.

Acknowledgements

I would like to thank all those friends and colleagues who encouraged me while writing this book. I am also indebted to many other researchers and practitioners of functional programming who have helped to develop the subject and whose work is described here. I would particularly like to thank Peter Landin whose early work in this area inspired my interest, and Mike Fourman for many interesting examples and advice on practical functional programming with Standard ML.

Finally, I would like to thank my wife, Diane, for being so patient with me during the many years I worked on this book.

Contents

Chapter 1
Functional Programming Concepts

In this chapter the main ideas underlying functional programming are introduced along with some notation for writing functional programs. For the most part, we adopt the notation of a particular language, namely Standard ML (Harper *et al.*, 1986), for the examples. However, the book is not concerned with a single functional language, but rather with the concepts and techniques of functional programming. The examples can be adapted for other functional languages, most notably Hope (Burstall *et al.*, 1980), Miranda (Turner, 1985a), Ponder (Fairbairn, 1982) and Lazy ML (Augustsson, 1984) with relative ease. These languages exemplify some of the most recent advances in functional language design. There is an appendix giving a brief résumé of Standard ML and some collected examples from the text. We also show some of the examples written in Miranda in another appendix.

1.1 Programming and languages

In order to answer the question *what is functional programming* we should first consider what we understand by *programming* and *program* generally. One, rather narrow, view is that a **program** is a sequence of instructions for a machine. We hope to show that there is much to be gained from taking the much broader view that programs are descriptions of values, properties, methods, problems and solutions. The role of the machine is to speed up the manipulation and evaluation of these descriptions to provide solutions to particular problems. A **programming language** is a convention for writing descriptions which can be evaluated.

1.1.1 Procedural languages

Conventional programming languages (such as FORTRAN, COBOL, ALGOL 60, ALGOL 68, Pascal, C, Clu, Modula and Ada) make essential use of assignment statements as the basic construct, around which are built the control abstractions of sequencing, branching and looping, etc. Such languages are called **imperative** or **procedural** because of the way programs are based on the idea of instructions to be carried out like a recipe. These instructions incrementally transform a store (made up of cells) by updating the contents of the cells to achieve some overall effect. For example, an assignment such as:

```
X := X + 1
```

is usually thought of as an instruction to update the contents of the storage cell associated with storage variable X by adding 1 to the current contents.

Procedural languages have evolved as abstractions from a von Neumann model of sequential machines and their control mechanisms have arisen as abstractions from the use of a program counter to locate the next instruction and to perform jumps (by updating the program counter).

The main consequence of having variables which refer directly to storage cells is that the programmer has the task of organizing their use and re-use to hold different values, and of distributing large values across many cells (e.g. by using arrays). The programmer is having to do several things at the same time, namely:

(1) describe what is to be computed;
(2) organize the computation sequencing into small steps;
(3) organize memory management during the computation.

1.1.2 Separation of concerns

Ideally, the programmer should be able to concentrate on the first of the three tasks (describing what is to be computed) without being distracted by the other two, more administrative, tasks. Clearly, administration is important but by separating it from the main task we are likely to get more reliable results and we can ease the programming problem by automating much of the administration.

The separation of concerns has other advantages as well. For example, program proving becomes much more feasible when details of sequencing and memory management are absent from the program. Furthermore, descriptions of what is to be computed should be free of such detailed step-by-step descriptions of how to do it if they are to be evaluated with different machine architectures. Sequences of small changes to a data object held in a store may be an inappropriate description of how to compute something when a highly parallel machine is being used with thousands of processors distributed throughout the machine and local rather than global storage facilities.

Automating the administrative aspects means that the language implementor has to deal with them, but he/she has far more opportunity to make use of very different computation mechanisms with different machine architectures. In particular the implementor may wish to use as much parallelism as possible when it is available and draw the right balance between shared access to data versus copying data. There is a trade-off between the programmer's ability to control efficient use of storage space for a particular program and the possibilities for automatic discovery of other efficiencies for all programs. Sometimes, a well written compiler can do better than a programmer in finding optimizations, especially when it is not tied down by unnecessary and inappropriate detail in the program.

From this point of view, it is argued that the assignment statement is considered harmful in high-level languages, just as the 'goto' statement was considered harmful for structured programming in the sixties (Dijkstra, 1968). Note that it is the use of assignments that takes most of the blame for not allowing separation of concerns when programming. Even within most procedural languages, a certain degree of freedom from explicit control and storage details can be seen in the way expressions are used (usually on the right-hand side of assignment statements). As an example, let us consider the following expression which, incidentally, describes the sum of the integers between two given integers m and n:

```
((m + n) * (abs (m − n) + 1)) div 2
```

The expression describes the application of several functions as well as referring to data values (integers) m, n, 1 and 2. The functions involved are *addition*, *multiplication*, *subtraction* and integer *division* (represented by the operators +, *, − and div respectively) as well as abs which we assume calculates the absolute (non-negative) value of an integer (which may be positive, negative or zero). In the expression, we see an absence of certain details, such as where the intermediate results are stored. We can also see the potential for several different orders of evaluation, including parallel evaluations of subexpressions such as (m + n) and (abs (m − n) + 1). Another important point is that the occurrences of m and n in the expression stand for integer values rather than cells in which values may be placed. This is in contrast to the use of identifiers for storage variables on the left-hand side of assignment statements). For example in:

```
X := X + 1
```

the first occurrence of X is taken to denote a storage cell and not the integer contents of the cell, whereas the second occurrence of X is taken to denote an integer (the contents of the same cell). In ordinary expressions, the emphasis is on the data values themselves and not the machine administration concept of cell location.

1.1.3 Declarative (applicative) languages

The very high-level languages which we will be looking at here are based far more closely on expressions, and come under the various headings of applicative/declarative/descriptive languages. Their design is not so much influenced by particular machine details but rather by a clear mathematical understanding of descriptions. Of course, declarative languages are not just imperative languages with certain facilities (like assignment statements) removed; they involve alternative means for describing data values and calculations.

Consider the desiderata for a language which is to support the descriptive, high-level view of programming rather than the machine controlling view. The language should be **expressive** so that descriptions of problems, situations, methods and solutions are not too difficult to write. On the other hand it should have a simple, uniform basis so that it is not difficult to understand. This suggests that it should be **extensible**, allowing the user to extend the language easily from a simple basis to suit particular needs rather than having a large collection of primitive constructs. The language should also **protect** users from making too many errors as far as possible (for example, by not allowing inconsistent uses of descriptions). It should be possible to write programs with the language which run efficiently on currently available machines. Finally, it should be mathematically **elegant** in order to allow for mathematical support in the major programming activities. More specifically, analysis, design, specification, implementation, abstraction and especially reasoning (derivations of consequences and properties) are becoming more and more formal activities. Declarative languages are usually generated from mathematical principles. After all, a large part of mathematical activity has been centred on describing and reasoning about complex objects and it would be unwise to ignore this legacy of notations and concepts when programming.

The move towards a more declarative approach to programming is also bridging the gap between the notion of program and specification. The two notions begin to blur into a single spectrum where any executable specification is a program and there are varying degrees of efficiency associated with specifications. It is becoming more feasible to generate efficient programs by transforming specifications to get the required degree of efficiency. A collection of general purpose transformation tools can be built up for use alongside a compiler (which is just another transformation tool) to assist the programmer.

There are two specific classes of declarative language in current use, namely **functional languages**, which focus on data values described by expressions (built from function applications and definitions of functions) with automatic evaluation of expressions, and **logic languages** (such as PROLOG) which focus on logical assertions describing relationships between data values and automatic derivations of answers to questions from the assertions. In both cases programs can be viewed as descriptions declaring information about values rather than instructions for the computation of values or of effects.

Logic languages will be mentioned again in Chapter 14 where comparisons are made between the different types of declarative language. (Further details may be found in Kowalski (1979), Clocksin and Mellish (1981), Hogger (1984).) In this book we concentrate on the functional programming languages which emphasize the central role of functions for building programs and reasoning about computations. Sometimes, the term **functional** is used only for those languages with a total absence of explicit procedural (storage-control) features, in which case languages like Standard ML and most variants of LISP would not be considered functional since they do support some procedural features (e.g. assignments). Many of the benefits of the functional approach to programming are lost when these features are introduced, so in most of this book we restrict our attention to the purely applicative forms and also use the terms functional and applicative synonymously.

In the next section we discuss the role of functions in programming.

1.2 Functions

1.2.1 The mathematical notion of function

In mathematics, the concept of **function** has become fundamental. Informally, a function is seen as a correspondence between argument values and result values. This correspondence must associate at most one result value (output) for each possible argument value (input). For example, the function double associates the result value 6 with argument value 3 and, in general, associates the value 2 * n with each integer argument n. We say that double maps argument n to result 2 * n or that double produces 2 * n when applied to n. Similarly, the function even associates the value true with the integers which are exactly divisible by 2 and associates false with the others. So, even maps 6 to true and 5 to false (for example). In the usual set-theoretic formulation of functions, each function has a specified set of values from which argument values may be chosen (the **source** set) and a specified set of values in which all possible results lie (the **target** set). The function double has the set of integers {..., −2, −1, 0, 1, 2, 3, ...} as both its source and target set and the function even has the set of integers as its source and the set {true, false} of **boolean** (or truth values) as its target. Note that a function must map each element in the source to at most one element of the target, but several elements of the source can be mapped to the same element of the target (as in the case of even) and some elements of the target may not have any element of the source mapped to them (as in the case of double).

A function is called **total** if it associates exactly one element in the target with each element in its source. A **partial** function may or may not associate an element in the target with each element in the source and is said to be undefined for those arguments which it does not map to a result. Usually, when mathematicians speak about functions they mean total functions, but here we will use *function* to mean *partial function* which includes the possibility of being total (defined for all arguments). Although we would much rather deal with just total functions, we will be looking at several functions which are not naturally defined for all arguments to which they may be applied.

Some less trivial examples of functions (some of which are clearly not total for the indicated source set) are suggested in the box diagrams of Figure 1.1. The functions are depicted as boxes with input and output wires to suggest that they *process* arguments (entering on the input wire) to produce results (leaving on the output wire).

A function can be described **intensionally** by a rule describing the association, but it can also be viewed **extensionally** as a set (usually infinite) of associated pairs of the form (*argument*, *result*) called the graph of the function. For example, the graph of the function double contains pairs such as (3, 6), (2, 4), (1, 2), (0, 0), (−1, −2) and so on. Similarly

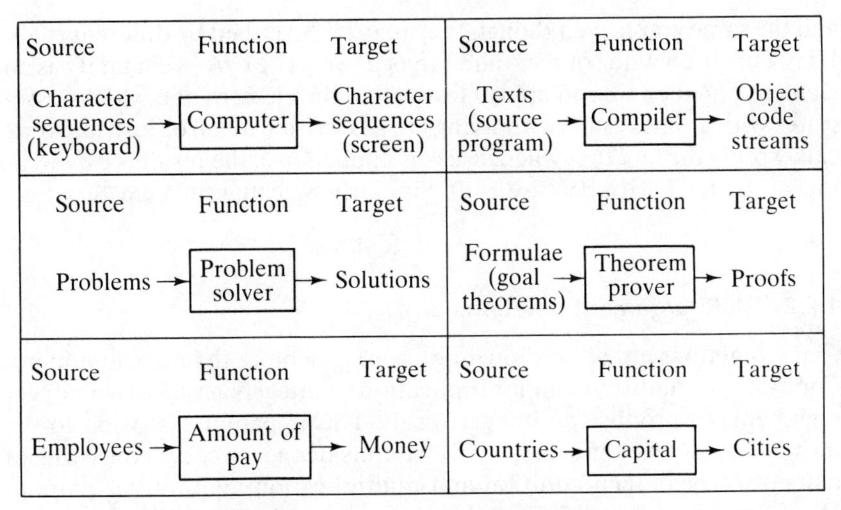

Figure 1.1 Box diagrams of functions.

the graph of the function even contains pairs such as (0, true), (1, false), (2, true), ...

An intensional description of a function emphasizes the process by which the result is found for given arguments. The extensional view is extremely important since it abstracts away from the details of the process and focuses on the external behaviour. Functional programming combines these two aspects of functions. When we write down a function definition in a functional program we need to pay attention both to the way the function works as a rule for calculation (i.e. as an algorithm) and also to its overall (external) behaviour as represented by its graph. However, when a function comes to be used, only its external behaviour is significant and the rule used in calculations becomes invisible. For example, in any context in which the function double is used, the same behaviour should result when using the rule that n maps to n * 2 or the rule that n maps to n + n. The ability to abstract away from the details of how a function is built and consider only the external behaviour of the function when using it gives us a fundamental encapsulation mechanism for building large systems. This facility for abstraction is one of the most powerful features of functional programming. It enables us to interchange components of programs which have the same behaviour even when they have been built in quite different ways. This in turn allows us to have an algebra of programs and transformations based on substitutions and replacements of equivalent components. We will give examples of this later.

Mathematically, we regard two functions f and g as being equal (writing f = g) when they have the same source set, the same target set and the same graph even though they may be described by different rules. If f is a function with source A and target B, we write f : A → B, and if a is an element of A then we can apply f to a to find the element of B which f associates with a. The result of applying f to a is written as f(a) or just f a. So we can express the fact that when double is applied to 3, the result is 6 by writing: double (3) = 6 (or double 3 = 6). Similarly we can write even (8) = true.

1.2.2 Multi-argument functions

Many functions are often thought of as having more than one argument. For example, addition and multiplication of integers require two integer arguments to produce an integer result. This apparent extension to the idea of function is not necessary. If we consider a source set consisting of pairs of integers then addition and multiplication map integer pairs to integer results. Thus by regarding pairs as single data objects, we can include addition and multiplication as ordinary (single argument) functions. The familiar way of writing the application of a function like (+) to the pair (2, 3) is with infix notation as in 2 + 3, but we regard this as just an abbreviation for the rather clumsy (+) (2, 3). In either case, the symbol + represents the addition function and it is being applied to the argument pair (2, 3). For sets A and B, we usually write $A \times B$ (the cartesian product of A and B) to denote the set of all pairs that can be formed with a first component from A and a second component from B. For a function f which is defined to have as argument a pair consisting of an element from A and an element from B and giving results in C we can write f : $A \times B \rightarrow C$. Similarly, triples of the form (a_1, a_2, a_3) where a_1 is in A_1, a_2 is in A_2 and a_3 is in A_3, will be elements of the cartesian product $A_1 \times A_2 \times A_3$. In general, $A_1 \times A_2 \times \cdots \times A_n$ denotes the set of n-tuples that can be formed with i^{th} component from A_i (for $i = 1, \ldots, n$ and $n \geq 2$) and we might have f : $A_1 \times A_2 \times \cdots \times A_n \rightarrow B$. Tuples are discussed in more detail when we look at types in Section 1.3.

We will continue to speak of multi-argument functions when we really mean a function with a cartesian product source set and draw box diagrams with several input wires as in Figure 1.2.

1.2.3 Expressions, composition and equality

When we write an expression we can combine several functions, composing them by making the result of one application an argument in another application. Thus even(45 * 30) combines the functions even and *. The combination can be pictured by connecting up output wires to input wires as in Figure 1.3. The combination (without the explicit arguments 45 and 30) can also be regarded as a new function (a com-

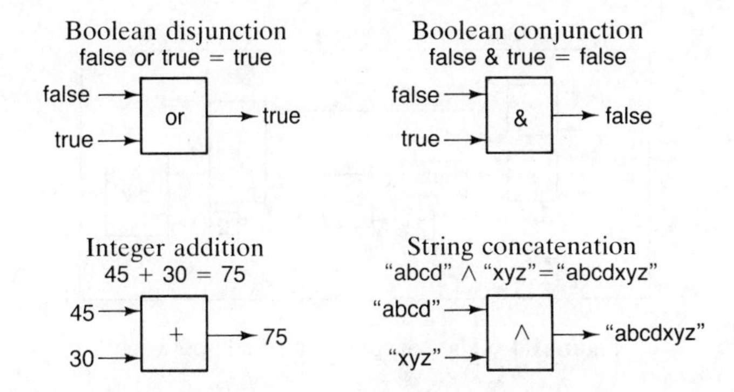

Figure 1.2 Box diagrams of some (multi argument-) function applications.

position of even and ∗) which we shall call evenprod (see Figure 1.3). This new function has the property that for any integers x and y:

evenprod (x, y) = even (x ∗ y)

and, in particular:

evenprod (45, 30) = even (45 ∗ 30) = even (1350) = true

Any composition of functions described by an expression is guaranteed to be a function. The more complicated expression describing the sum of integers between n and m (given in an example in Section 1.1.2) can be regarded as a description of the effect of a function sumbetween on arguments m and n such that

sumbetween (m, n) = ((m + n) ∗ (abs (m − n) + 1)) div 2

This composition is depicted in Figure 1.4.

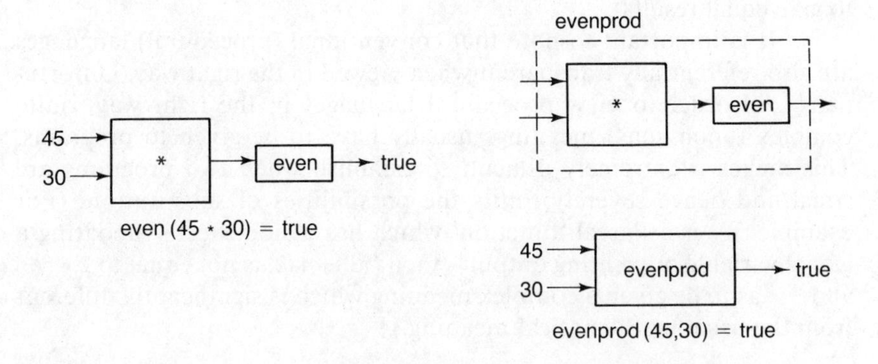

Figure 1.3 Combining functions by composition.

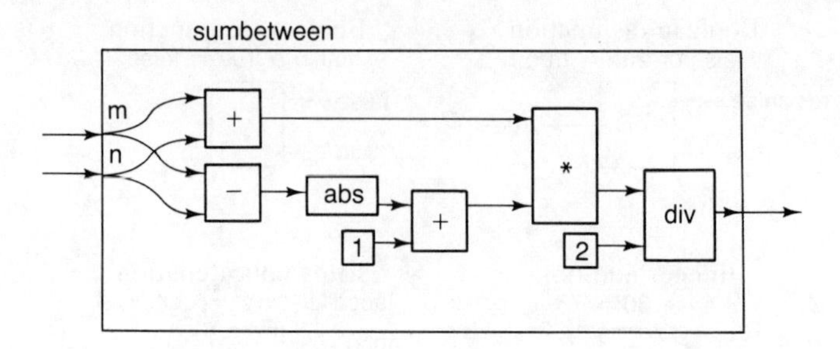

Figure 1.4 The composition of sumbetween.

The essence of functional programming is that all values produced in subcalculations are communicated to other parts of a program only by the use of function application (i.e. as arguments and results of functions). This is in contrast to the communication mechanism used in imperative languages whereby global storage variables are updated and parts of programs make use of the storage location of such values to share the effect of an update. It is common practice for programmers using some languages (such as Lisp) to use both mechanisms, but this is not functional programming.

It is the adherence to a strict applicative style that enables us to use simple substitutions of equal expressions in reasoning about, designing and evaluating programs (i.e. expressions). This facility derives from the fairly direct notation used, where meanings of expressions depend in a simple way on the meanings of the immediate components of the expression (and nothing else). The phrase **referentially transparent** is used to describe notations where only the meaning (value) of immediate component expressions (sentences/phrases) is significant in determining the meaning of a compound expression (sentence/phrase). Since expressions are equal if and only if they have the same meaning, referential transparency means that substitutivity of equality holds (i.e. equal subexpressions can be interchanged in the context of a larger expression to give equal results).

It is important to note that conventional (procedural) languages are also referentially transparent when viewed in the right way. Unfortunately, in order to view procedural languages in the right way, quite complex (unobvious) meanings usually have to be given to programs. This makes it extremely difficult to establish when two programs are equal and hence severely limits the possibilities of substitution. (For example, if f is a Pascal 'function' which has a side-effect – updating a global variable or printing output – then f (3) + f (3) is not equal to 2 * f (3) and + has to be given a complex meaning which is significantly different from the usual mathematical meaning.)

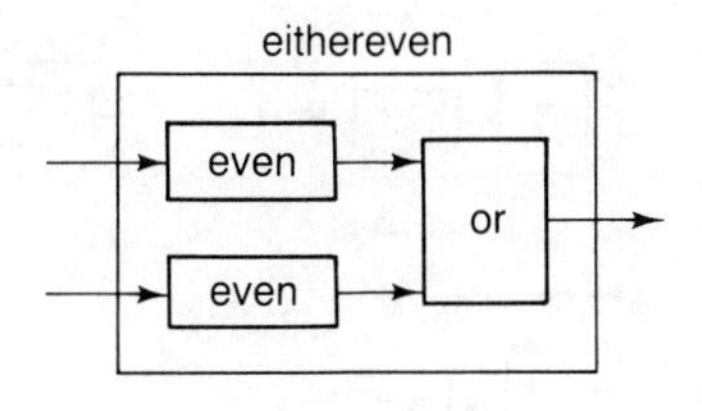

Figure 1.5 The function eithereven = evenprod.

We will frequently have many different ways of describing the same function. For example, consider a function eithereven which is defined as a composition of the function even and the boolean disjunction (or), such that for any integers x and y:

eithereven (x, y) = (even x) or (even y)

(see Figure 1.5). With a little thought, it is easy to see from the definitions that for any integers x and y,

eithereven (x, y) = (even x) or (even y) = even (x * y) = evenprod (x, y)

and hence eithereven and evenprod describe the same function (because they have the same external behaviour). Remember, we write eithereven = evenprod to indicate that they describe the same value (function) even though the descriptions are quite different. (This equivalence may need to be qualified further depending upon the way we choose to treat undefined expressions. We look into this further in Chapters 8, 9 and 10.) Some further simple equivalences are depicted in Figure 1.6, where some more functions are introduced. The function (^) concatenates a pair of strings to form a single string, while size produces the length of a string. In addition to the boolean operations or and &, we also have not which maps true to false and false to true. The function I, which we discuss in more detail later, is the identity function which, when applied to a boolean argument, returns the argument as the result. Although I effectively does nothing, it is useful in expressing equivalences and simplifications (rather like 0 in arithmetic).

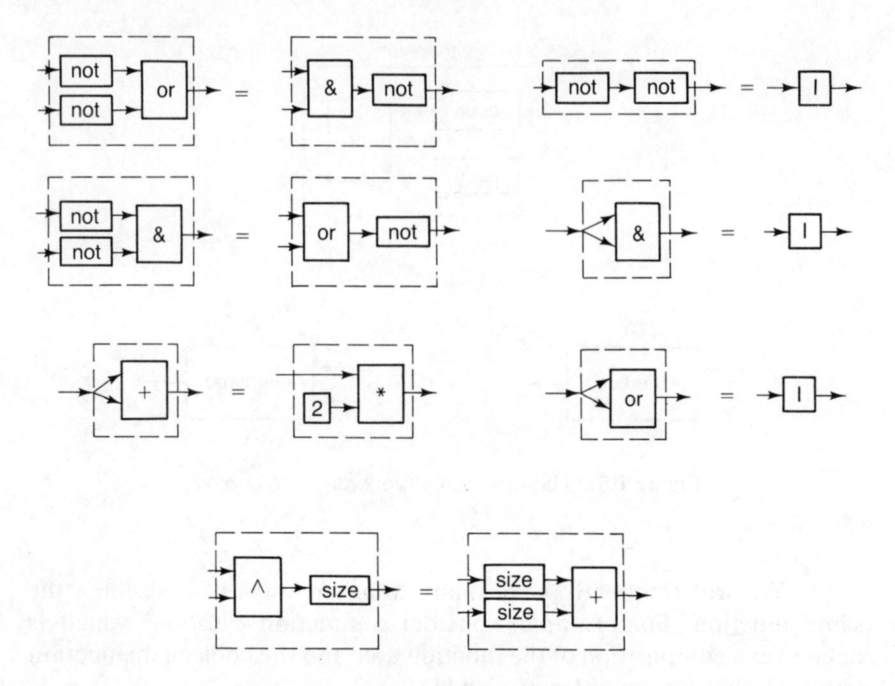

Figure 1.6 Some simple equivalences.

1.3 Types

1.3.1 The need for types

Anyone who is involved in giving precise descriptions of complicated constructions and situations (in particular, anyone who is involved in programming) is likely to appreciate the need for some form of protection against accidental error. A good programming language can help a programmer a great deal by finding as many errors as possible as soon as possible. However, some errors cannot be discovered automatically without an independent description of the intent of a programmer. A surprisingly large number of errors can be discovered by classifying data values according to how they are supposed to be used and then checking that no values are misused. This classification technique is known as **typing** the data.

In a typed programming language, each value that we deal with in a program has an associated type which determines how the value can be used. For example, the values $\cdots, -1, 0, 1, 2, \cdots$ have type int (integers) and true and false have type bool (boolean or truth values). The operations (functions) $+$, $-$, $*$, div are defined to operate on pairs of values of type int, but not on pairs of values of type bool. Similarly the operations & and or are defined only for application to pairs of values of type bool (returning a result of type bool). A function like even (mentioned earlier) would be applicable to arguments of type int only and would return results of type bool only. Programs and program components need to be checked for type correctness so that data values such as integers, booleans, functions, etc., are used in a consistent way within a program and erroneous computations, such as subtracting a truth value from an integer, do not pass by unnoticed.

Automatic type checking is highly desirable for the production of reliable software since manual type checking is likely to be just as error prone as writing programs. A programming language which performs type checking and thus ensures that type errors do not lead to erroneous computations is said to be **strongly typed**. If the types of program components can be determined before evaluation, the time and space penalty introduced by type checking during evaluation can be removed. This is known as **static type checking** and it also enables many programming mistakes to be caught much earlier during program development. Many modern programming languages are strongly typed with static type checking.

What constitutes a type is necessarily restricted by the requirement of static checking, and this restriction can reduce the flexibility of a language. However, as Milner (1978) has shown, an extremely general type system can be provided for functional languages without the programmer having to specify the types of newly defined values. Milner's **polymorphic** type system has been extended and used in several recent programming languages (including Standard ML) and we base the types used in this book on it.

We will impose an important restriction on ourselves when we introduce functions and other values in the examples presented in this book – namely that they have a well defined type. Although we could choose arbitrary sets as sources and targets of functions, we will restrict ourselves to sets associated with types which can be formed within the type system we are using. Thus, for example, we will not assume a separate primitive type for natural numbers $\{0, 1, 2, \cdots\}$ since these values are already associated with type int. Any function which would naturally have just the natural numbers as a source set will be extended (by making it only partially defined if necessary) to have all values of type int as the source set.

The restriction being imposed is not too severe, since the type system we are using is quite rich. We will show how the type of a newly defined value can be inferred from the types of the components so, provided we know the types of the primitive values we start with, additional specification of a value's type is not usually necessary (but it is often useful for documentation purposes). We defer a full description of the type system until the next chapter, but introduce some of the types and rules as we need them.

We should point out that it is perfectly possible to construct programs (functional or otherwise) in programming languages without type systems. However, as pointed out in Cardelli and Wegner (1985), programmers then have to create an implicit type system (consciously or otherwise). Types are an organizational mechanism which are indispensable for the construction of reliable software on a large scale. In this book we are concerned with modern functional programming methods and we regard polymorphic type systems as an important advance in this area.

1.3.2 A type system

We begin with a small collection of **primitive types** (along with some associated **primitive operations** and **constants**). These primitive types include int, bool and string. (Although Standard ML includes the type real as well, we do not make use of real numbers in any of the examples given here.) The constants true and false denote the only values of type bool. The values of type int are the integers but we will adopt the convention of writing negative integers with the tilde symbol (~); thus we write ~5 rather than -5 in order to avoid overloading the subtraction symbol ($-$). (*Overloading* means using the same symbol for different things in the hope that the context will provide sufficient information to avoid ambiguity.) Values of type string will be denoted by character sequences enclosed in double quotation marks ("). Again, we adopt the Standard ML convention for escape sequences in order to include non-printable, control characters as well as the double-quote symbol itself in strings. This convention uses \ to indicate that the next character is to be treated specially. The only examples we use here are: \n standing for the newline (control) character, \" standing for the double-quote symbol and \\ standing for the back-slash symbol. Thus, for example, "abc\\de\"fg\nhi" is a string with size 12 containing the 9 alphabetic characters "abcdefghi", one back-slash, one double-quote and one newline character. Further types can be built from these primitive types using **type operators** (described below).

If T_1 and T_2 are types, then $(T_1 \rightarrow T_2)$ is the type of function whose source consists of values of type T_1 and whose target consists of values of type T_2. So, for example, double would have type int → int and even would have type int → bool. A tuple will have a (cartesian) product type formed from the types of the components of the tuple. For example, the pair (3, true) has type int × bool since 3 has type int and true has type bool. Similarly ((3, "ab"), false, 6) has type (int × string) × bool × int since it is a triple whose last two components are a boolean and an integer, respectively, and whose first component is a pair consisting of an integer and a string. In general, if E_1 is an expression with type T_1, E_2 is an expression with type T_2, $\cdots$ and E_n is an expression with type T_n, ($n \geq 2$), then $(E_1, E_2, \ldots, E_n)$ is an expression (denoting a tuple) of type $T_1 \times T_2 \times \cdots \times T_n$.

The product type formers ($\_ \times \_ \times \_ \cdots \times \_$) and the function type former ($\rightarrow$) are called type operators since they produce new types from old. They can be combined to form more and more complicated types as we shall see later. As an example, the type of the function (^) which concatenates strings is string × string → string since it is a function whose argument is supposed to be a pair of strings and whose result is a string.

The fundamental rule for ensuring type correctness is the following:

> IF E is an expression describing a function with type $T_1 \rightarrow T_2$
> AND E' is an expression describing a value of type T_1
> THEN the application of E to E' (written $E\ E'$ or $E(E')$) is correctly typed and will have type T_2.

From now on, we will write $E : T$ to mean that expression E is correctly typed with type T so the rule can be more succinctly expressed as:

$$\text{(type rule for application)} \qquad \frac{E : T_1 \rightarrow T_2 \qquad E' : T_1}{E\ E' : T_2}$$

We will frequently use this way of representing a rule, where the statement below the line (in this case $E\ E'$ has type T_2) follows from the statements above the line. As another example, we express the rule which determines the types of tuples from the types of the components:

$$\text{(type rule for tuples) } n \geq 2 \qquad \frac{E_1 : T_1 \quad E_2 : T_2 \cdots E_n : T_n}{(E_1, E_2, \ldots, E_n) : T_1 \times T_2 \times \cdots \times T_n}$$

Table 1.1 shows the types of some functions we have already mentioned and some other primitive functions for use with types int, string and bool (which we will use in subsequent examples). Those marked as infix will be written between the components of the argument pair when they are applied and the higher the precedence number, the tighter they group with their arguments. (Such precedence conventions help to reduce the number of parentheses in expressions. For example, 3 + 2 * 4 groups as 3 + (2 * 4) because of the higher precedence given to the multiplication operator.) We also assume that association is to the left when several operators of equal precedence are combined without parentheses and that normal application of a function which is not infix (non-fix) binds tighter than any infix application (thus 3 − 2 − 4 groups as (3 − 2) − 4 and not false or true groups as (not false) or true). Those listed

Table 1.1 Some simple functions used in Chapter 1.

Function		*Type*	*Fixity*	*Precedence*
+	:	int × int → int	infix	6
−	:	int × int → int	infix	6
*	:	int × int → int	infix	7
div	:	int × int → int	infix	7
mod	:	int × int → int	infix	7
<	:	int × int → bool	infix	4
≤	:	int × int → bool	infix	4
>	:	int × int → bool	infix	4
≥	:	int × int → bool	infix	4
~	:	int → int		
abs	:	int → int		
not	:	bool → bool		
^	:	string × string → string	infix	6
size	:	string → int		
chr	:	int → string		
ord	:	string → int		
I	:	(see later)		
=	:	(see later)	infix	4
&	:	bool × bool → bool	infix	3
or	:	bool × bool → bool	infix	2
even	:	int → bool		
double	:	int → int		
evenprod	:	int × int → bool		
eithereven	:	int × int → bool		
sumbetween	:	int × int → int		

from + to ord are predefined in Standard ML (but some of the symbols are overloaded; standing for functions over reals as well as integers). We will give formal definitions of the others later in the chapter. The new functions which may need some explanation are: mod which gives the remainder after integer division (e.g. 17 mod 5 = 2 and n mod 0 is undefined for all integers n); ord and chr which encode and decode between characters and integers according to the ASCII code (American Standard Code for Information Interchange). ord gives the number associated with (the first character of) a string and chr decodes an appropriate integer to give a character (as a string of size 1). For example, chr 48 = "0", chr 65 = "A", ord "Z" = 90 and ord "a" = 97.

In Figure 1.6, a function I was used with type bool → bool, but in fact we will define it with a much more general type (a *polytype*) later. Similarly, the type of = is quite subtle. For any type T for which it is possible to compare values for being equal, we should be able to use = with type $T \times T \rightarrow$ bool. In particular, we can test for equality of integers, equality of strings, equality of booleans and equality of tuples of such values (when the tuples being compared have the same type). We discuss

...ypes and the types of these functions in more detail in the next ...hapter.

It is important to note that we distinguish between the use of the operator '=' (which indicates a function for calculating whether or not two values are equal) and the use of '=' to assert that two values are equal when we reason about programs (as in evenprod = eithereven). This distinction is necessary because we can sometimes establish that, for example, two functions are equal by reasoning about their behaviour, but no general algorithm exists for calculating exactly which functions are equal. For this reason, we never use '=' in expressions to compare functions.

In the next section we look at the ways in which functions and other values can be defined. Such definitions (and groups of definitions) constitute functional programs and they will be presented using Standard ML syntax for the most part. Since this syntax is relatively transparent, the definitions can usually be adapted for other functional languages without too much effort.

1.4 Definitions

In this section we show how definitions and expressions can form a basis for programming. Writing expressions is facilitated by the ability to define new functions and other values so, by means of definitions, we can build up a stock of useful functions to use in expressions or further definitions. A functional program requires no other command-like constructs embedded in it. Even commands such as read and write became unnecessary if both input and output are considered to be single data objects (e.g. strings or character streams) and an interactive program can be regarded as a function of type input → output. (We postpone a look at how this can be achieved until Chapter 8 because it requires some deeper analysis of evaluation techniques. However, we can do a great deal without using special input and output.)

We can think of any expression (with associated definitions of any names used in the expression) as a program. Sometimes we will refer to a single function or just a collection of definitions as a program as well and hope that this does not cause confusion. Later we will see how definitions and expressions can be unified under one framework, so this apparent laxity is not misleading.

1.4.1 Names, bindings, environments and scope

Definitions allow us to associate a name with a value; the name is said to be **bound** to the value by the definition. For example:

```
val codeof0 = ord "0"
val codeof9 = codeof0 + 9
```

introduces two names (codeof0 and codeof9) and binds them to the integer values 48 and 57 respectively (since we specified that ord produces the ASCII code number of characters and 48 is the ASCII code for the character 0). The keyword **val** is just the Standard ML convention for introducing definitions (of value names). The choice of the symbol = to separate the name from the expression denoting the value to be bound to the name is significant. We choose = because in the context of the definitions, the name and the corresponding expression are equivalent and therefore interchangeable when we reason with or evaluate expressions. For example, we can calculate that:

```
codeof9 = codeof0 + 9 = ord "0" + 9 = 48 + 9 = 57
```

Here is another example, where we give a name to a pair of integers:

```
val thepair = (size "abc", size "abcdef")
```

Note that the expression on the right-hand side has type int × int and is equivalent to (3, 6) since we are assuming that size is defined to be the function producing the size of a string, so we can assert that thepair = (size "abc",size "abcdef") = (3, 6) and that thepair has type int × int.

As we introduce larger groups of definitions for subsequent use by ourselves or others and find we have to write expressions in various different contexts, it is important to keep track of which names are bound to which values. A collection of bindings (of names to values) is called an **environment**. Definitions extend or modify environments, and any expression we write down can only be evaluated in the context of an environment where all the names in the expression are bound to values.

When writing (sequences of) expressions and definitions (for example, as programs or just for discussion), we sometimes use the phrase **scope of a definition** to mean the textual context of the definition; that is, the expressions and other definitions which are to be regarded as within the context of the given definition. For example, the scope of most of the definitions introduced in this text can be taken to be the rest of the book (beyond the definition) or, in case we re-use a name to stand for something else, up to the point where the name is redefined. Later we will introduce notation for limiting the scope of a definition when we wish to regard it as local or temporary.

Sometimes we will use the term **variable** synonymously with **name** but it is important to note that we are not talking about the storage variables found in procedural languages. This is the mathematical use of the word variable as standing for an arbitrary value which is fixed by a definition. (This use is more akin to the use of constants in constant definitions in many procedural languages.)

1.4.2 Defining functions

Names can similarly be given to new functions which are defined in terms of other functions. However, in most cases it is convenient to describe a function by means of a rule describing the mapping with a **parameter**. A parameter is just a (temporary) name taken to stand for an arbitrary argument value to which the function might be applied and the result is described in terms of this argument name. For example:

```
fun double x   = x + x
fun treble x   = x * 3
fun sixtimes x = double (treble x)
```

are three definitions of functions with type int → int (called double and treble and sixtimes) and in each definition, the name x has been used to stand for the argument. (The keyword **fun** is used instead of **val** in Standard ML to indicate a definition with parameters but it is possible to introduce function names with **val**. We will see examples where functions are defined without parameters later.) The parameter is introduced temporarily and is said to have scope extending up to the end of the expression on the right-hand side of a definition. Thus the x used in each definition is unrelated to the x used in the other definitions. In the context of these definitions, we know that the following rules hold:

```
for any x : int   double x = x + x
for any x : int   treble x = x * 3
for any x : int   sixtimes x = double (treble x)
```

which, once again, explains the use of '=' in such definitions. When we come to reason with and evaluate expressions in the context of such definitions, we can substitute any expression of the appropriate type for the parameter x in the rule. (Once again, we may need to qualify this depending on our treatment of undefined expressions, as we discuss in later chapters.) Thus we can calculate that:

```
sixtimes 2 = double (treble 2)   (by the definition of sixtimes)
           = double (2 * 3)      (by the definition of treble)
           = double 6            (by the definition of *)
           = 6 + 6               (by the definition of double)
           = 12                  (by the definition of +)
```

Parameters (which we also refer to as variables or bound variables) are particularly useful when more complex compositions (combinations) are to be described and they can be thought of as labels for the input wires in the box diagrams we used to depict functions in the previous section. Here are some more examples of simple function definitions:

```
fun even n          = (n mod 2 = 0)
fun digit d         = ord d ≥ codeof0 & ord d ≤ codeof9
fun uppercase s     = ord s ≥ ord "A" & ord s ≤ ord "Z"
fun lowercase s     = ord s ≥ ord "a" & ord s ≤ ord "z"
fun letter s        = lowercase s or uppercase s
fun charofdigit n   = chr (n + codeof0)
```

The types of the functions introduced can be inferred from the knowledge of the types of the functions and values used on the right-hand side. For example, even : int → bool because, firstly, mod : int × int → int is applied to the argument pair (n, 2) implying that the argument n must have type int. Also, = is being used with type int × int → bool to compare integers so the overall result type is bool. Thus even maps n : int to a bool (the bool is true if the remainder after dividing n by 2 is 0, i.e. if n is exactly divisible by 2). The next four functions are predicates on strings (having type string → bool – any function with result type bool will be called a **predicate**). They use ord : string → int, ≤, ≥ both of type int × int → bool and &, or both of type bool × bool → bool. The function digit returns true if the first character of the argument is one of the characters 0, 1, 2, 3, 4, 5, 6, 7, 8, 9; uppercase returns true if the first character of the argument is an upper case letter (A, B, . . . , Z); lowercase returns true if the first character of the argument is a lower case letter (a, b, . . . , z); and letter returns true if the first character of the argument is either an upper or a lower case letter. The last function charofdigit : int → string, when applied to an integer between 0 and 9, returns the corresponding string "0","1", "2" · · · or "9". For integers n other than 0 to 9, charofdigit n may or may not produce a string depending upon whether chr is defined for n + 48 (chr m is defined for 0 ≤ m ≤ 127).

1.4.3 Argument tuples

So far we have only defined functions with simple arguments. The following examples take argument pairs; the parameters are *patterns* consisting of a pair of variables:

```
fun evenprod (x, y)     = even (x * y)
fun eithereven (x, y)   = even x or even y
fun sumbetween (m, n)   = ((m + n) * (abs (m − n) + 1)) div 2
fun avepair (x, y)      = (x + y) div 2
```

```
fun fst (x, y)        = x
fun snd (x, y)        = y
fun sumdiff (x, y)    = (x + y, abs (x − y))
```

The functions evenprod and eithereven (both of type int × int → bool), and sumbetween of type int × int → int were discussed in the previous section, while avepair : int × int → int just returns the average of a pair of integers. For example:

avepair (3, 5) = (3 + 5) div 2 = 8 div 2 = 4

The function fst and snd select the first and second components of a pair, respectively. They have polymorphic types which we will see later, and they can be applied to any pair. (In particular, if they are applied to a pair of integers they return an integer.) The final example sumdiff : (int × int) → (int × int) is particularly interesting because it returns a pair as the result (namely the sum and absolute difference of the integer arguments). Thus sumdiff (3, 5) = ((3 + 5, abs (3 − 5)) = (8, abs (~2)) = (8, 2). Since we regard pairs and other tuples as data objects, the possibility of having tuples as results of functions is quite natural. It is perhaps less obvious that the following expressions can be written, making use of the fact that we have defined thepair : int × int with value (3, 6):

Expression	Evaluation
avepair thepair	= avepair (3, 6) = 4
sumdiff thepair	= sumdiff (3, 6) = (9, 3)
snd (sumdiff thepair)	= snd (9, 3) = 3
avepair (sumdiff thepair)	= avepair (9, 3) = 6
(thepair = sumdiff thepair)	= ((3, 6) = (9, 3)) = false

In the last example, the expression involves a comparison of two pairs using the operator = so the whole expression has type bool and should evaluate to true or false. In this case, the pairs are different so evaluation produces false.

1.4.4 Conditional expressions

Other notation for function definition is frequently used in mathematics, such as case analysis, as in the following description of minpair : int × int → int:

$$\text{minpair}(x, y) = \begin{cases} x & \text{if } x < y \\ y & \text{otherwise} \end{cases}$$

We will use a conditional construct **if** ··· **then** ··· **else** ··· for such definitions by case analysis, and see later how the construct can be regarded as a function application. The above definition will be expressed as:

```
fun minpair (x, y) = if x < y then x else y
```

In general, given three expressions E_1, E_2 and E_3 such that E_1 has type bool and E_2 and E_3 both have the same type (T, say), then **if** E_1 **then** E_2 **else** E_3 constitutes an expression with type T as well. Written as a rule, this appears as:

$$\text{(type rule for conditionals)} \quad \frac{E_1 : \mathsf{bool} \quad E_2 : T \quad E_3 : T}{\textbf{if } E_1 \textbf{ then } E_2 \textbf{ else } E_3 : T}$$

One of the strong typing restrictions is that the branches (E_2 and E_3) of the conditional cannot have incompatible types, for otherwise the conditional expression could not be given a type without prior evaluation of the test E_1 (i.e. the type of the conditional would depend on the value of the test). The other important facts we need to know about the conditional expression are that:

$$\textbf{if } \mathsf{true} \textbf{ then } E_2 \textbf{ else } E_3 = E_2$$
$$\textbf{if } \mathsf{false} \textbf{ then } E_2 \textbf{ else } E_3 = E_3$$

and that if E_1 is undefined, then **if** E_1 **then** E_2 **else** E_3 is also undefined. These properties can be used to reason about and evaluate conditionals. They answer questions such as: What is the value of **if** E_1 **then** E_2 **else** E_3 when E_2 is undefined but E_1 = false?

We can evaluate an application of minpair as follows:

```
minpair (3, 6) = if 3 < 6 then 3 else 6    (by definition of minpair)
               = if true then 3 else 6     (since 3 is less than 6)
               = 3                         (by the properties of the
                                            conditional)
```

In order to illustrate an alternative approach, we choose to define maxpair indirectly as follows:

```
fun minmaxpair (x, y) = if x < y then (x, y) else (y, x)
fun maxpair anypair   = snd (minmaxpair anypair)
```

This introduces minmaxpair : (int × int) → (int × int) which orders a pair of integers and maxpair : int × int → int which selects the second (i.e. larger) of the ordered pair of its arguments. In the second definition, we have chosen to use a parameter anypair to stand for the whole of the argument pair rather than use a pattern parameter of the form (x, y) since we do not need to refer to the individual components of the pair in the definition.

Conditional expressions can, of course, be used as arbitrary subexpressions (and not just immediately on the right-hand side of a definition), so we can nest conditional expressions to allow multi-way branches. The following are examples of expressions with conditionals as subexpressions (assuming n, m stand for arbitrary integers and s1, s2 stand for arbitrary strings). These particular expressions can be greatly simplified, but we leave this as an easy exercise:

```
m + (if m = 0 then n else n − m)
if m = n then m else if m < n then avepair (m, n) else (m + n) div 2
size (if s1 = s2 then s1 ^ s2 else s1 ^ s1)
```

1.4.5 Pattern matching definitions

As an alternative to using conditional expressions, we will sometimes give several cases when defining a function, allowing particular constants in argument patterns. For example, we define the boolean functions not, & and or by considering the cases for an argument being true or false:

```
fun not true     = false
|   not false    = true
fun true or b    = true
|   false or b   = b
fun true & b     = b
|   false & b    = false
```

In these definitions, two cases are given for each function (separated by '|') and some of the arguments are constants (rather than variables). When one of the functions is applied, the value of the actual argument of the application should be matched against the argument patterns in the definition to find the appropriate case to use. We can regard each case as a property of the function so, for example, not true = false is an equivalence and for any b : bool, false or b = b is an equivalence. These properties can be used to evaluate expressions, as in:

```
(not true) or false = false or false = false
```

Recall that we have regarded infix notation as an abbreviation, so the definition of or in non-fix form would appear as:

```
fun or (true, b) = true
|   or (false, b) = b
```

which shows that we have used an argument pattern consisting of a pair of a constant and a variable. In general, we may use any combination of constants, tuples and variables in a pattern and any number of cases in a definition, but with the following restrictions:

(1) The patterns in each case should have compatible types and the right-hand sides should all have compatible types.

(2) The cases should be exhaustive (with patterns to cover every possible argument).

(3) There should be no ambiguity as to which case applies in any instance.

To avoid ambiguity, we will assume the cases are ordered top to bottom so that if more than one pattern matches with an argument, the earliest case is the one chosen. (We will also avoid repeated variables in patterns since this is an implicit test for equality which we prefer to write explicitly.) Thus if we define:

```
fun safediv (m, 0) = 1000
|   safediv (m, n) = m div n
```

then the application safediv (6, 3 − 3) matches the left-hand side in both cases (since 6 matches m, 3 − 3 = 0 and 0 matches both 0 and n) so the first case applies and the result is 1000. Later, we will extend the use of patterns and give a more precise description of the matching process.

We can also use patterns in value definitions like this:

```
val (three, six) = thepair
```

Since thepair was defined earlier with value (3, 6), the left-hand side has an appropriate form and we are effectively binding the name three to the value of the first component of thepair (i.e. 3) and binding the name six to the value of the second component of thepair (i.e. 6).

1.5 Recursive definitions

An extremely powerful facility for describing values is to allow a description to refer to the object being described (i.e. self referentially). A definition of a value is **recursive** if the name being defined appears in the body of the definition (the expression describing the value to be bound to the name). To anyone who is not familiar with the use of recursion in programming, this may seem to be a bizarre idea which needs careful explanation.

1.5.1 The meaning of recursive definitions

We will study a particular example to begin with and show several quite different ways of looking at the idea of recursion. We will give a recursive definition of a function called stringcopy : int × string → string which is designed such that for integer n ≥ 0 and string s, stringcopy (n, s) produces a concatenation of n copies of s thus:

```
stringcopy (n, s) = s ^ s ^ s · · · ^ s   (n copies)
```

In particular, stringcopy (3, "xyz") = "xyzxyzxyz". The following definition is recursive because the function stringcopy is used in the description on the right-hand side:

```
fun stringcopy (n, s) = if n = 0
                        then ""
                        else stringcopy (n − 1, s) ^ s
```

This is pictured as a box diagram in Figure 1.7 where a copy of the box stringcopy appears inside the outer box labelled stringcopy. If we were to look inside the inner box, it would appear exactly like the outer box, containing yet another copy inside. This nesting of copies goes on forever (like a picture containing a smaller version of itself). Thus, one way of understanding a recursive definition is as an abbreviation for an infinitely deep expression.

However, we really need an understanding of recursion which helps us to reason about recursive definitions, to see how they might be evaluated and also to see how and when to use them in designing programs. Table 1.2 shows how the recursive definition might be used in an evaluation (by hand), by regarding it as an equation satisfied by the function it defines. Treating the recursive definition as an equation allows us to expand an instance of the left-hand side by an appropriate instance of the right-hand side as and when we need to in simplifying an expression. The calculation by hand illustrates how evaluation is related to deduction. We deduce, by simple substitutions and algebraic rules, that:

```
stringcopy (2, "xyz") = "xyzxyz"
```

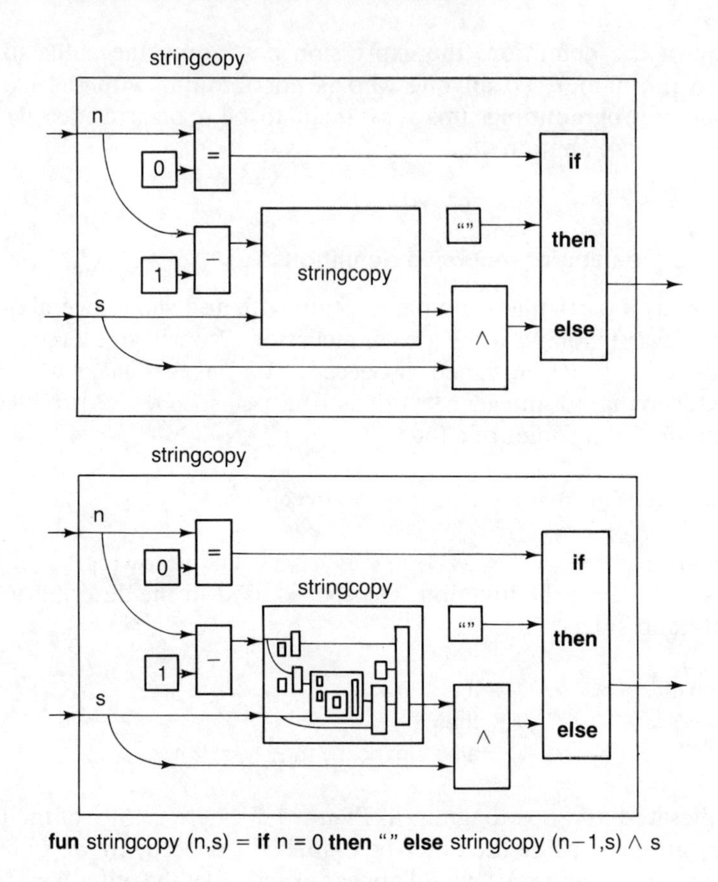

Figure 1.7 A recursive description of stringcopy.

Table 1.2 Evaluation using a recursive definition.

```
stringcopy (2, "xyz")
= if 2 = 0 then " " else stringcopy (2 − 1, "xyz") ^ "xyz"
= if false then " " else stringcopy (1, "xyz") ^ "xyz"
= stringcopy (1, "xyz") ^ "xyz"
= (if 1 = 0 then " " else stringcopy (1 − 1, "xyz") ^ "xyz") ^ "xyz"
= (if false then " " else stringcopy (0, "xyz") ^ "xyz") ^ "xyz"
= (stringcopy (0, "xyz") ^ "xyz") ^ "xyz"
= ((if 0 = 0 then " " else stringcopy (0 − 1, "xyz") ^ "xyz") ^ "xyz") ^ "xyz"
= ((if true then " " else stringcopy (0 − 1, "xyz") ^ "xyz") ^ "xyz") ^ "xyz"
= (" " ^ " xyz") ^ "xyz"
= "xyz" ^ "xyz"
= "xyzxyz"
```

We can also deduce more general consequences of definitions. For example, using 'proof by induction' (described later) along with substitution it can be shown that for any m, n ≥ 0 we have:

```
stringcopy (m + n, s) = stringcopy (m, s) ^ stringcopy (n, s)
```

and indeed:

```
stringcopy (m * n, s) = stringcopy (m, stringcopy (n, s))
```

Evaluation is really a special case of deduction which is so straightforward that we can entrust it to be done automatically by a machine. The more sophisticated forms of deduction require some human guidance, in general, and this is an important aspect of programming. We may consider many properties of functions and use many equivalences to specify a function and to derive a final program.

A recursive definition can be regarded as an indirect specification of a function which can be used for automatic evaluation. The definition describes properties of a function (a recurrence relationship) and we assume that the properties uniquely specify the function. In this case, we read the definition as: Let stringcopy be a function such that:

```
for any n : int, and for any s : string
   stringcopy (n, s) = if n = 0 then "" else stringcopy (n − 1, s) ^ s
```

or, equivalently:

```
for any s : string,
   stringcopy (0, s) = ""
for any n : int (n ≠ 0), and any s : string,
   stringcopy (n, s) = stringcopy (n − 1, s) ^ s
```

In general, the properties may not constrain the function sufficiently for a unique solution, so we need to know what function we have actually defined when several functions satisfy a property or if no functions satisfy a property. We shall see later that at least one (partial) function satisfies the properties in a recursive definition, and there is a natural choice if more than one function satisfies the properties. (This choice is the least defined function among the possible choices and it is natural because it assumes no other properties except those forced by the definition. It also produces the same results we get when we evaluate applications by unfolding the definition as we did above.)

1.5.2 Designing recursive definitions

So far we have discussed the form and meaning of recursive definitions, but we have not discussed their pragmatics (i.e. how to go about the design of a function with a recursive definition). We will look at how the definition of stringcopy can be arrived at by considering the informal description given at the beginning. First of all, we note that the description says nothing about what the function should produce for negative integers, so we concentrate on the non-negative integers. Later, we will discuss some alternative ways of dealing with unspecified cases. The non-negative integers are frequently classified into two groups, namely {0} and the rest, where those in the latter group are each the successor of another non-negative integer (i.e. equal to $n + 1$ for some non-negative n). Consequently we will frequently consider the two cases separately and look for a recurrence relationship in the second case. This is a basis for both recursive definitions and inductive proofs as we will see later.

For the example at hand, we observe that a concatenation of 0 copies of a string is naturally taken to be " " which gives us the property stringcopy (0, s) = " ". (Beware! Many mistakes arise in programming when such degenerate cases are not considered carefully enough.) When we consider the cases for $n > 0$, we look for a relationship between stringcopy (n, s) and stringcopy (m, s) for any m such that $0 \leq m < n$ (usually we try $m = n - 1$ but not always). For the example, we see that for any $n > 0$ (and any s : string):

$$
\begin{aligned}
\text{stringcopy}(n-1, s) &= s \wedge s \wedge \cdots s && (n-1 \text{ copies})\\
\text{stringcopy}(n, s) &= s \wedge s \wedge \cdots s \wedge s && (n \text{ copies})\\
&= \text{stringcopy}(n-1, s) \wedge s
\end{aligned}
$$

and this recurrence is used to construct the definition. Since we have only considered non-negative integers, the definition of stringcopy is incomplete. We will look at its completion in the next subsection but, meanwhile, the reader is encouraged to think about the consequences of allowing n to be negative in the definition (as it stands).

There are many ways to describe functions, so it is perhaps surprising to learn that any function which can be computed can be described recursively (according to Church's thesis (1941)). As another example, consider the following problem. We are given a function $g : int \rightarrow int$ which we assume is fully defined for non-negative arguments. We are asked to provide a function sumg which calculates the sum of the results of applying g to a range of integers from 0 up to some limit $n \geq 0$. More precisely, we want (for $n \geq 0$):

$$\text{sumg}(n) = \sum_{i=0}^{n} g(i)$$

We use a similar analysis to the one in the previous example, assuming only non-negative values of n and observing that for n > 0:

```
sumg (n − 1) = g 0 + g 1 ··· + g (n − 1)
sumg (n)     = g 0 + g 1 ··· + g (n − 1) + g n
             = sumg (n − 1) + g n
sumg (0)     = g 0
```

which gives us the definition (assuming that a particular function g has been defined – we resolve the problem of such dependencies in the next chapter):

```
fun sumg 0 = g 0
|   sumg n = sumg (n − 1) + g n
```

(We have used a pattern match to single out the zero case, but we could just as well have used a conditional instead. We have also assumed $n \geq 0$ in the second case but have not yet put in a check for this.)

1.5.3 Undefined cases and partial functions

Both stringcopy (n, s) and sumg (n) are naturally defined when n is a non-negative integer, but we include all integers as values of type int. When the (integer) argument is negative, the definitions only specify that stringcopy (n, s) = stringcopy (n − 1, s) ^ s and sumg n = sumg (n − 1) + g n which are not sufficient to determine the results for negative arguments. In such cases, we take this to mean that the function is partial and undefined when it is not sufficiently specified. This is compatible with the operational view of the definition which suggests that in order to calculate stringcopy (~1, s), one must first calculate stringcopy (~2, s) and in order to calculate stringcopy (~2, s), one must calculate stringcopy (~3,s) and so on. So any calculation with negative arguments for stringcopy (by unfolding the definition) is non-terminating, and leads to an infinite regression with no final answer being produced.

In Chapter 8 we will see that non-terminating evaluations need not mean that the function is undefined since an infinite output may be being produced in stages. In these examples, there is no progression towards a final output, so the functions are undefined for negative integers. Frequently in the sequel, we will define a (partial) function with argument type int (and hence source set equal to the set of all values of type int) because that is our chosen basic numeric type, even though the *natural* source of the function is some subset of the integers (such as the non-negative integers).

It is clearly a dangerous practice to produce a definition after only considering some of the argument cases and having no protection from the possibility of the other cases arising. It is particularly dangerous when the other cases can lead to fruitless, non-terminating computations. Thus we consider how the definitions can be extended by the programmer in a sensible way. The specifications only tell us what is wanted for non-negative arguments, so we must first ask what we wish to produce for negative arguments and then implement it. There are three possibilities:

(1) Produce some sensible default result of the appropriate type (e.g. "" for stringcopy and 0 for sumg).
(2) Allow an arbitrary result or non-termination (based on what falls out of the recursive definition for the natural argument cases).
(3) Make the function explicitly undefined (reporting an error rather than allowing non-termination by an infinite calculation).

All three possibilities have their place, but we choose the last one in preference to the others as recommended practice in most cases. Some people may prefer the first choice since this gives more flexible functions, but when a default result is used, errors are much harder to find (and may go undiscovered). The second choice seems irresponsible, but sometimes it is forced on us (for example when it is unknown for which arguments a function is undefined). In order to adopt the third choice, we introduce a primitive function error which takes a string as argument and produces no result. Although error is totally undefined, we assume it is implemented so that an evaluation of error s causes computation to cease and the string s to be reported as an error message. We will endeavour to make robust versions of functions by using error to abort computations when a function is applied to arguments for which it is not defined. (Such an error is not predefined in ML but the language has a rich exception mechanism. The appendix on Standard ML explains how programmers can implement error for themselves.)

We can complete the definition of stringcopy in several ways introducing a test and an error message for negative integers. If we just add a conditional test like this:

```
fun stringcopy (n, s) = if n < 0
                        then error "stringcopy with neg int"
                        else if n = 0
                        then ""
                        else stringcopy (n − 1, s) ^ s
```

the test is repeated over and over again when we evaluate recursive applications. It is better to perform the test once and then use the unsafe definition when the argument is known to be non-negative. If we rename the function in the original definition, calling it stringcopy0, the name stringcopy can be used for the safe version which uses stringcopy0 as an auxiliary function:

```
fun stringcopy0 (n, s) = if n = 0
                         then ""
                         else stringcopy0 (n − 1, s) ^ s
fun stringcopy (n, s)  = if n < 0
                         then error "stringcopy with neg int"
                         else stringcopy0 (n, s)
```

Thus when stringcopy is applied to (n, s) a check is made to see if n is negative. When n is not negative, stringcopy0 is used to calculate the result without further tests for negative arguments. A similar modification can be done for the definition of sumg (which we leave as an exercise).

Sometimes, it is useful to have a dangerous (non-robust) auxiliary function even when the main function is total. In the following example, the main function is stringofint : int → string which produces a string of the standard decimal notation for an integer (e.g. stringofint (~133) = "~133"). The auxiliary function stringofnat : int → string only works properly for non-negative arguments. (It is considered dangerous because it may return erroneous answers rather than just being undefined for negative arguments.) stringofnat n describes a string (for n ≥ 10) in terms of the string for n div 10 (i.e. stringofnat (n div 10)) which should contain all but the last character. The expression n mod 10 is used to provide the last character. Thus for n = 213 we have n div 10 = 21 from which we eventually obtain the string "21" by a recursive calculation and n mod 10 = 3 from which we obtain the string "3" using charofdigit. The result for stringofnat 213 is then "21" ^ "3" = "213":

```
fun stringofnat n = if n < 10
                    then charofdigit n
                    else stringofnat (n div 10) ^ charofdigit (n mod 10)
fun stringofint n = if n < 0
                    then "~" ^ stringofnat (~n)
                    else stringofnat n
```

The following example shows why it is useful to have recursive definitions which do not explicitly prevent non-terminating computations. We are provided with a function p : int → bool which we know nothing about except that it is total. We are asked to find the smallest integer n ≥ 0 such that p (n) = true. To calculate the required integer, we search for a value satisfying the definition starting with 0. For each value n which we try, we see whether or not p (n) holds. If it does hold then n is the required value otherwise we try again using n + 1 and so on. We will define the searching function leastp which makes use of p in searching for this integer, but which will continue searching forever if p (n) = false for all $n \geq 0$. The argument for leastp is a number from which we begin the search and will initially be 0. (It is frequently the case that the description of a function or other value is made easier by first defining a more general function so that the original value can be seen as a special case. Thus, we generalize the search from 0 to a search from n.) Now consider the properties of leastp. We have that for any n : int:

IF p (n) = true THEN leastp n = n
IF p (n) = false THEN leastp n = leastp (n + 1)

which suggests the definitions (dependent on a definition of p):

```
fun leastp n = if p (n) then n else leastp (n + 1)
val answer  = leastp 0
```

Thus, for example, if p (n) = (n > 2) the calculation of answer proceeds as follows:

```
answer = leastp 0
       = if 0 > 2 then 0 else leastp (0 + 1)
       = leastp 1
       = if 1 > 2 then 1 else leastp (1 + 1)
       = leastp 2
       = if 2 > 2 then 2 else leastp (2 + 1)
       = leastp 3
       = if 3 > 2 then 3 else leastp (3 + 1)
       = 3
```

If p were undefined for some arguments, then the definedness of leastp would also depend upon whether or not any of the undefined cases were encountered before a value returning true was found in the search. Of course, if we analyse the definition of p, we may well come up with a direct calculation of the answer, but without knowledge of p, we cannot simplify the search or even be sure the search is going to terminate. In the next chapter we show how p can be made a parameter of the definition, so that leastp becomes least p and the generalized function least will work for any predicate p which need not be defined in advance. Such a general searching function as least would be impossible to define if we were forced to guarantee termination. Note that it is possible that when given the definition of p, no amount of analysis helps us to shortcut the search.

We should also remark that there are recursively describable functions for which no one knows the arguments on which the function is undefined (if any). For example, it is not known if strange n = 1 for all n > 0 where:

```
fun strange 1 = 1
  | strange n = if even n
                then strange (n div 2)
                else strange (n * 3 + 1)
```

1.5.4 Inductive proofs and recursive definitions

The reader may have observed the close correspondence between the technique used for designing a recursive definition and the technique for proving statements about the non-negative integers by mathematical induction. This is no coincidence. If P (n) is a statement about an integer n, and we wish to prove that for all n ≥ 0, P (n) is true, simple mathematical induction tells us that it is sufficient to show that:

(1) P (0) is true.

(2) For any n > 0, P (n) follows from the assumption that P (n − 1) is true.

We can use induction to justify our recursive definition of stringcopy0 taking P (n) to be:

$$P(\mathsf{n}) = \begin{cases} \text{For any s : string} \\ \text{stringcopy0 (n, s) correctly produces a} \\ \text{concatenated string of n copies of s} \end{cases}$$

We need only observe that:

(1) For any s : string, stringcopy0 (0, s) correctly produces a concatenated string of 0 copies of s, and

(2) If we assume that for any s : string, stringcopy0 (n − 1, s) correctly produces a concatenated string of n − 1 copies of s, then it follows that for any s : string, stringcopy0 (n, s) correctly produces a concatenated string of n copies of s (since stringcopy0 (n, s) is equal to stringcopy0 (n − 1, s) ^ s which is the concatenation of n − 1 copies and 1 copy).

By induction, it follows that stringcopy0 (n, s) is defined and correct for all strings s and for all integers n ≥ 0.

Sometimes, the relationship between a recursive definition and an inductive proof is a bit more subtle. We often need to use a more general form of induction which is applicable to many sets (not just non-negative integers). Some recursive definitions of functions with integer argument n will involve a recurrence between n and integers between 0 and n − 1. This is justified by a generalization of simple induction over the non-negative integers which allows one to assume all of $P(0)$, $P(1)$, $\cdots$, $P(n-1)$ in establishing $P(n)$ (and not just $P(n-1)$).

The next example shows how some careful analysis of a problem can lead to a simple but subtle function definition (which is not at all obvious without the analysis). After we derive our definition, we will show how its correctness can be established formally using the more general form of induction.

The problem is to produce a recursive definition of the greatest common divisor function. This will be a function posgcd : int × int → int such that for any two positive integers m and n, posgcd returns the largest integer which exactly divides both m and n. We first note that for any positive integers m and n, posgcd (m, n) is defined and lies somewhere in the range 1 ··· k (where k is the minimum of m and n) having value 1 when there are no other common divisors. Thus, we could just search to see which of the numbers 1 ··· k has the properties of being a common divisor and of being larger than any of the other common divisors. Such an expensive search can be avoided by taking account of the following observations concerning the function, some of which are obvious, but some of which are not. The third property, in particular, was observed by Euclid (circa 400 BC) and he used it to construct an algorithm as we hope to do here. (It can be proved from basic properties of division and subtraction but we will not go into this.)

for any integers m > 0 and n > 0	posgcd (m, n) = posgcd (n, m)
for any integer n > 0	posgcd (n, n) = n
for any integers m > n > 0	posgcd (m, n) = posgcd (m − n, n)

We note that the third property gives us a recurrence relationship between the argument (m, n) and another argument pair (m − n, n). The important point to note is that the latter pair is simpler than the pair (m, n) and both components are still positive (provided m > n > 0). More accurately, the maximum of the components is decreased but stays positive. The case when n = m allows the recursion to terminate and this must be reached sooner or later if the integer arguments are always positive while their maximum is decreased.

We still have to work out what to do if n > m. The first property listed allows us to swap arguments at any stage and also to derive symmetric counterparts to the other properties such as:

for any integers n > m > 0 posgcd (m, n) = posgcd (m, n − m)

The definition we choose is thus:

```
fun posgcd (m, n) = if m = n then n
                              else
                    if m > n then posgcd (m − n, n)
                              else posgcd (m, n − m)
```

Our informal understanding for why this definition ensures a terminating computation for any pair of positive integers is the following (assuming $m, n > 0$):

(1) For the recursive cases ($m \neq n$) the result is defined in terms of the result for a pair with a strictly smaller maximum.

(2) For the same cases, the application of posgcd is to a pair of positive integers again.

Thus the pair (1, 1) gives a lower bound and only a finite number of decreases to the maximum is possible (without producing pairs with non-positive components).

We will formalize this reasoning and define the method of **complete induction** which we use in the proof. The formalization is somewhat technical, and can be omitted on a first reading.

1.5.5 Complete induction

The first step in introducing complete induction is to generalize from the non-negative integers which are totally ordered by $<$ to arbitrary sets which are partially ordered (by $\prec$, say).

Definition

We say that a set S with a (binary) relation $\prec$ is a **partial order** (PO) if $\prec$ satisfies the following two properties:

(1) (transitivity) for all $x, y, z \in S$, $x \prec y$ and $y \prec z$ implies $x \prec z$.

(2) (anti-symmetry) for all $x, y \in S$, $x \prec y$ implies that not $y \prec x$.

Total orders are special cases of partial orders where for each pair of elements $x, y \in S$, either $x \prec y$ or $y \prec x$ or $x = y$. Here are some examples of partial orders:

(1) S is the set of non-negative integers and $x \prec y$ is defined to mean $x < y$. This is a total order.

(2) S is the set of integers and $x \prec y$ is defined to mean $x < y$. This is also a total order.

(3) *S* is the set of integers and x < y is defined to mean abs x < abs y. This is not a total order. (Why?)

(4) *S* is the set of pairs of integers and (a, b) < (a′, b′) is defined to mean a < a′ or (a = a′ and b < b′). This is called **lexical order** and it is total.

(5) *S* is the set of pairs of non-negative integers with the same ordering as in the previous example.

(6) *S* is the set of pairs of integers and (a, b) < (a′, b′) is defined to mean maxpair (a, b) < maxpair (a′, b′).

(7) *S* is the set of pairs of non-negative integers with the same ordering as in the previous example.

Definition

A partial order (S, <) is said to be **well founded** if there are no infinite decreasing chains, that is there are no infinite sequences of elements from *S* $\{x_0, x_1, \cdots\}$ such that $x_{i+1} < x_i$ for all $i \geq 0$. Only the examples 1, 3, 5 and 7 above are well founded, since infinite decreasing chains can be found for the other examples.

Definition

The **principle of complete induction** says that if (S, <) is a well founded partial order, and *P* (s) is a statement about elements s ∈ S (which is either true or false), then in order to show that *P* (s) is true for all s ∈ *S* it suffices to show that (for any s ∈ *S*):

> *P* (s) follows from the assumption that *P* (t) is true for all t < s

The assumption *P* (t) for all t < s is called the **induction hypothesis**. Note that there may be s ∈ S with no t < s. For such elements the principle says we must show *P* (s) with no assumptions. These are called the **base cases** of the proof (and the other cases are often called the **step cases**).

We now apply this to show the correctness of posgcd for positive pairs of integers. We take as our well founded partial order, the set of positive pairs of integers with the same ordering as in example 7 above. We define

$$P(m, n) = \begin{cases} \text{postgcd (m, n) is defined and equal to the greatest} \\ \text{common divisor of m and n.} \end{cases}$$

Let (m, n) be any pair of positive integers. By the principle of complete induction we must show that P (m, n) follows from the assumption P (m′, n′) for all positive pairs (m′, n′) whose maximum is less than the maximum of m and n. We consider three separate cases:

(1) *Either* m = n in which case posgcd (m, n) = n which is the correct result so P (m, n) is true;

(2) *Or* m > n in which case posgcd (m, n) = posgcd (m − n, n) and the latter is defined and equal to the greatest common divisor of m − n and n by the assumption P (m − n, n). Appealing to the properties claimed for greatest common divisors, this is also the greatest common divisor of m and n, so P (m, n) holds;

(3) *Or* m < n in which case the result follows by a symmetrical argument to the previous case.

Later, we will show some specializations of complete induction for specific data types (this is also called **structural induction**).

We finish this section by completing the function posgcd with a definition of gcd which produces the greatest common divisor for any pair of integers which have one. In fact, since 1 divides every integer, every integer divides 0 and 0 only divides 0, gcd is defined for all pairs except possibly (0, 0). The following additional properties are observed for gcd:

for any integer n > 0	gcd (n, 0) = n
for any integer n < 0	gcd (n, 0) = ~n
for any integers m, n	gcd (m, ~n) = gcd (m, n)
for any integers m > 0, n > 0	gcd (m, n) = posgcd (m, n)

leading to the definition:

```
fun gcd (0, 0)   = error "gcd undefined for (0, 0)"
  | gcd (0, n)   = abs n
  | gcd (m, 0)   = abs m
  | gcd (m, n)   = posgcd (abs m, abs n)
```

which ensures that gcd performs the checks and conversions for the cases when (m, n) are not both positive and only makes use of posgcd with positive pairs of arguments (for which posgcd is defined and correct). Note that we have taken gcd (0, 0) to be undefined because every integer divides 0 so there appears to be no greatest common divisor of 0. However, there is a good argument for making gcd (0, 0) = 0 (see Exercise 1.17).

1.6 Local definitions and control of scope

1.6.1 Scope revisited

When a name is introduced in a definition, we say that this is a **binding occurrence** of the name and that the definition (or more accurately the binding occurrence of the name introduced) has a certain textual scope. Other occurrences of names are called **applied occurrences** and (usually) can be associated with an appropriate binding occurrence (determined by the scopes of binding occurrences). Any name which cannot be associated with a binding occurrence is called **free** and those which can be associated with binding occurrences are said to be **bound**. Usually, when we write down an expression to be evaluated or as part of another definition, we assume all the names occurring in it are bound, but we make an exception for certain primitives (like $+$, $*$, $\cdots$) which we assume are predefined. (The only time we did not adhere to this was in discussing sumg which depended upon some arbitrary g being defined (i.e. g was free) and leastp which depended upon some arbitrary p being defined (i.e. p was free).) We now look at the concept of **scope** more closely and at how it may be limited.

So far we have introduced names in two ways: with definitions using **val** or **fun**; and by using parameters in **fun** definitions. A name introduced as a parameter constitutes a binding occurrence, and the scope of the parameter is limited to the right-hand side of the definition in which it appears. In contrast, the main name introduced by a definition has a potentially unbounded scope, in general. More accurately, the scope continues to the end of the context in which the definition occurs, which may be to the end of a program or the end of the input of an interactive session or the end of this book, excluding any scope which is covered by a (more recent) overriding (re-)definition of the same name. Furthermore, the exact beginning of a scope needs to be made precise to avoid possible ambiguities. The convention in Standard ML is that definitions using just **val** are not recursive, so the scope of the definition begins after the end of the definition (the name is not bound to the defined value within the definition). Conversely, names introduced by **fun** are assumed to be recursive by default which means that the scope of the definition includes the right-hand side of the definition. One consequence of these conventions is that only functions can be defined recursively. We will show later (in Chapter 8) that recursive definitions of other sorts of data objects are not only meaningful, but highly desirable for functional programming. For the time being, however, we will only define functions recursively and adopt the Standard ML conventions. We also make use of **and** to introduce a group of bindings simultaneously rather than one at a time. This enables us to define several (*mutually recursive*) functions which are defined in terms of each other, as in:

```
fun f x = ··· g ···
and g y = ··· f ···
```

For **val** definitions:

val $V_1 = E_1$ **and** ··· **and** $V_n = E_n$

is just another way of writing **val** $(V_1, \ldots, V_n) = (E_1, \ldots, E_n)$. (Several other equivalences are pointed out in the exercises and in later chapters.)

1.6.2 Local definitions

Another language feature which benefits safe programming style is a mechanism for simple control over the scope of definitions. It is frequently convenient to introduce specialized auxiliary functions which solve subproblems when defining a main function or set of functions. If the auxiliary functions are not of general use, we may feel the need to limit the scope of their definitions, making them local to the main definition(s). Furthermore, we may well introduce non-robust auxiliary functions with the knowledge that all applications of these functions in the main definition(s) are safe. In this case, it is important to be able to limit the scope of the auxiliary definitions to guard against accidental mis-use of the non-robust functions. A simple scheme to achieve this in Standard ML is to use the **local** construct which has the form:

local D_1 **in** D_2 **end**

Here, D_1 and D_2 are (groups of) definitions and the construct introduces the same bindings of names to values that D_2 introduces. The bindings introduced by D_1 are assumed temporarily within the definitions D_2, but subsequently hidden. This ensures that anything defined in D_1 is unavailable beyond the **end** and cannot be used accidentally.

For example, when we introduced stringcopy0 in order to define stringcopy, we noted that the former was not robust. We could make the non-robust function local as in the following group of definitions:

```
local fun stringcopy0 (n, s) = if n = 0
                               then ""
                               else stringcopy0 (n − 1, s) ^ s
in    fun stringcopy (n, s) =  if n < 0
                               then error "stringcopy with neg int"
                               else stringcopy0 (n, s)
end

fun spaces n   = stringcopy (n, " ")
fun newlines n = stringcopy (n, "\n")
```

This is a sequence of three definitions (counting the local part as a single definition) introducing stringcopy, spaces and newlines into our current working environment but not stringcopy0. The definitions of stringofnat and posgcd can similarly be made local to the corresponding definitions of the robust versions stringofint and gcd (but this is left as an exercise).

In addition to having some definitions local to other definitions, we also want to allow definitions to be made local to expressions. This allows us to break up complicated expressions by naming subexpressions and introducing temporary functions within subexpressions. This facility is particularly important since it also allows us to indicate common subexpressions by naming them. For example, in the definition of digit, which we gave earlier, we saw a repeated subexpression (ord d):

```
fun digit d = ord d ≥ codeof0 & ord d ≤ codeof9
```

This suggests that the calculation of ord d (when a particular argument d is supplied) is repeated. Such a repeated calculation is never necessary because the same result will be returned both times for a functional language. Astute human beings and compilers may well spot the repeated subexpression and see that it is only necessary to calculate this once for each argument when digit is applied. A programmer should not have to rely on this astuteness, and may wish to give an explicit indication that the same value of ord d is needed twice. Standard ML provides a **let** construct for such situations with the form:

let *D* **in** *E* **end**

This forms an expression (not a definition as in the **local** case), with value equal to the value of *E* (the **main** expression) except that the bindings introduced by the **auxiliary** definitions *D* are assumed to hold up to the **end**. The definitions *D* are thus temporary and local to *E*. This allows us to write:

```
fun digit d = let val n = ord d
              in n ≥ codeof0 & n ≤ codeof9
              end
```

As another example, we give a definition of a function windowint : int × int → string. This function is designed so that windowint (w, n) finds the string representation of n (as does stringofint), but fits the string into a window size of w. This is done by padding with spaces on the left to get a string of the appropriate length. A string of stars is produced if the window size is not large enough, but a negative window size is an error and the result is undefined in this case.

```
fun windowint (w, n) = let
                          val intrep = stringofint n
                          val intwidth = size intrep
                       in
                          if w < intwidth
                          then stringcopy (w, "*")
                          else spaces (w - intwidth) ^ intrep
                       end
```

Here, the definitions of intrep and intwidth have been made local to the main conditional expression. To see what the alternative would look like, we substitute for the local names throughout the scope of their definitions. We first remove the definition of intrep and substitute stringofint n for the two occurrences of intrep in the subsequent definition and main expression. We then remove the definition of intwidth similarly to obtain (for the right-hand side of the definition):

```
if w < size (stringofint n)
then stringcopy (w, "*")
else spaces (w - size (stringofint n)) ^ stringofint n
```

Such substitutions provide a means of evaluation as well (see the exercises). Figure 1.8 shows how the local definitions can be depicted as labels for shared wires in a box diagram. Naturally, functions can be made local to expressions with expressions of the form:

```
let fun ··· in ··· end
```

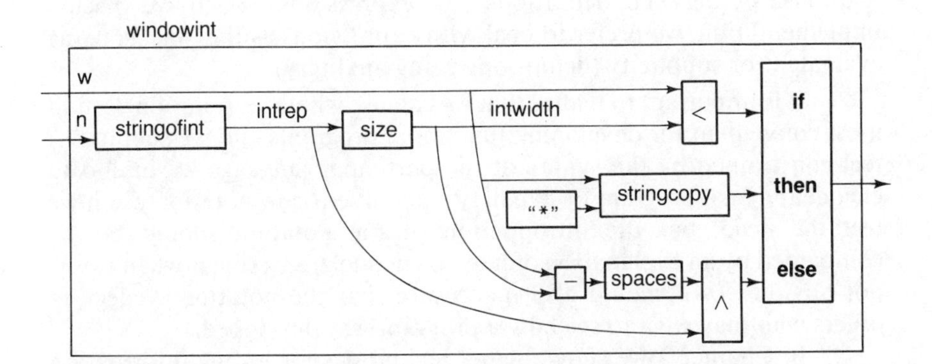

Figure 1.8 Local definitions correspond to shared subexpressions (i.e. shared intermediate values intrep and intwidth).

1.6.3 Notation and programs

There are many syntactic variations for introducing local definitions. Miranda makes use of expressions with a where clause so that the local definitions follow rather than precede the main expression. (This gives a more top-down flavour to the description.) Semantically, E where D is equivalent to **let** D **in** E **end** and we shall sometimes use the former notation in developing programs even though occurrences would have to be transcribed into the latter form for a Standard ML encoding.

Miranda also assumes the collection of definitions which form a program (called a **script**) are simultaneous and mutually recursive at the top level whereas the definitions and expressions entered in an interactive ML session are compiled incrementally, building on the current environment.

One may be tempted to ask 'What does a complete functional program look like?' Is it

(1) a collection of definitions which are self contained with no free variables other than those defined in an initial context (i.e. primitives)? Or is it

(2) an expression with no free variables (other than primitives again)?

From a theoretical point of view, it does not really matter which alternative one takes, because it is easy to convert from one form to the other. For example, suppose D represents a collection of definitions which we regard as a program, and we use them to create an environment in which expressions $E_1, \ldots, E_n$ are to be evaluated. We could just as well consider each of the individual expressions **let** D **in** E_1 **end**, . . ., **let** D **in** E_n **end** to be the programs being evaluated. Later, we will show some further relationships between definitions and expressions. When we discuss implementation, we prefer to deal with expressions as the objects being evaluated for simplicity (definitions being auxiliary).

It is important to realize that we can use whatever notation we find most convenient for developing functional programs and we should not feel constrained by the syntax of the particular language we intend to encode the final program in. We may even invent new notation when we feel the need, but the introduction of the notation should be accompanied by an explanation of how to encode/transcribe it when this is not obvious. (We should also make sure that the notation is clear to others who may wish to see how a program was developed.)

In Chapter 7 we show further techniques for hiding information and dealing with programs on a larger scale. Table 1.3 summarizes the syntax used in the examples so far, and the exercises explore some equivalences.

Table 1.3 A summary of the syntax used for expressions and definitions (abbreviations for infix applications are omitted).

Meta-symbols:

$V, V_1, \ldots$	for variables (= names)	
$C, C_1, \ldots$	for constants (of type bool, int or string)	
$P, P_1, \ldots$	for patterns	
$E, E_1, \ldots$	for expressions	
$D, D_1, \ldots$	for definitions	
$VB, VB_1, \ldots$	for value bindings (in **val** definitions)	
$FB, FB_1, \ldots$	for function bindings (in **fun** definitions)	
Forms of definition (D)	**val** VB	(value definitions)
	fun FB	(parameterized definitions)
	$D_1\ D_2$	(sequence of definitions)
	local D_1 **in** D_2 **end**	(local definitions)
Forms of expression (E)	V	(variables)
	C	(constants)
	$E_1\ E_2$	(applications)
	$(E_1, E_2, \ldots, E_n)$	(tuples ($n \geq 2$))
	if E_1 **then** E_2 **else** E_3	(conditionals)
	let D **in** E_1 **end**	(qualified expressions)
	(E_1)	(bracketed expressions)
Forms of pattern (P)	V	(variable patterns)
	C	(constant patterns)
	$(P_1, P_2, \ldots, P_n)$	(tuple patterns ($n \geq 2$))
	(P_1)	(bracketed patterns)
Forms of value binding (VB)	VB_1 **and** $VB_2 \cdots$ **and** VB_n	(simultaneous bindings ($n \geq 2$))
	$P = E$	(simple bindings)
Forms of function binding (FB)	FB_1 **and** $FB_2 \cdots$ **and** FB_n	(simultaneous bindings ($n \geq 2$))
	$V\ P_1 = E_1 \mid \cdots$ $\cdots \mid V\ P_n = E_n$	(function binding with pattern match ($n \geq 1$))

EXERCISES

1.1 Define abs using a conditional expression.

1.2 Suggest some 'reasonable' answers for what n mod m might produce when n or m is negative. Do the same for n div m and then consider what relationships hold between div and mod (and *

and +). Can you find an 'elegant' solution with 'clean' relationships (no ugly special cases)?

1.3 Redefine sumbetween in terms of sumdiff.

1.4 Given that for all n : int, n + n = 2 * n and for all m, n, k (: int) with m ≥ 0, n > k ≥ 0, ((n * m) + k mod n = k), prove that for all n : int, even (double n) = true, using the definitions of even and double.

1.5 Simplify the expressions at the end of Section 1.4.4.

1.6 Give an alternative description of size (stringcopy (n, s)) for n ≥ 0.

1.7 Use the definition of sumg at the end of Section 1.5.2 to expand sumg 4.

1.8 Give a recursive definition of the factorial function fact and go through a step-by-step evaluation of fact 4. If you have not already done so, make the function robust by using error for negative arguments.

1.9 By analogy with the definition of stringofint, define binrepint : int → string which produces a string showing the binary representation of an integer (e.g. binrepint 13 = "1101").

1.10 Define a robust version of charofdigit.

1.11 Define power : (int × int) → int recursively (using multiplication) so that for n ≥ 0, power (m, n) = m^n.

1.12 Define a function to compute the product of the integers between n and m (n ≤ m) inclusive. Use this function to define the factorial function on non-negative integers.

1.13 Redefine sumg to take a lower and upper bound of values over which to sum rather than assuming 0 as the lower bound.

1.14 Assuming functions g : int → int and h : int → int have been defined, give a recursive definition of minvalgh where (for any x : int) minvalgh (x) is the minimum value of g (x, y) for y between 0 and h (x). Discuss how the values for which minvalgh is defined depend on g and h.

1.15 Construct a more efficient version of gcd using the following fact: For any integers m > n > 0, gcd (m, n) = gcd (m mod n, n). (Be careful in dealing with zero and negative cases since m mod n may be 0.)

1.16 Prove by induction that for all integers m, n ≥ 0 and strings s:

stringcopy (m + n, s) = stringcopy (m, s) ^ stringcopy (n, s)

and hence that:

stringcopy (m * n, s) = stringcopy (m, stringcopy (n, s))

1.17 Why is the following purported equivalence not true for the definitions given in this chapter?

even x & even y = even (gcd (x, y))

Consider an alternative interpretation of the word 'greatest' in 'greatest common divisor' so that m is greater than n if n divides m exactly and m ≥ 0 and m ≠ n (rather than just m > n). What consequences should this have for the definition of gcd and the above purported equivalence?

1.18 Why does the definition of windowint in Section 1.6.2 make it undefined for negative window sizes?

1.19 Define windowL : (int × string) → string which justifies a string to the left in a given window size, that is, for n ≥ size s, windowL (n, s) is a string of size n beginning with s and possibly followed by spaces. (The result is undefined if n < size s.) Similarly, define windowR which justifies a string to the right of a window and windowC which centrally justifies the string (slightly to the left if the window size and string size are not both even or both odd).

1.20 Redefine windowint with windowR.

1.21 Ackerman's function is defined as follows:

```
fun  ack (0, m)  = m + 1
|    ack (n, 0)  = ack (n − 1, 1)
|    ack (n, m)  = ack (n − 1, ack (n, m − 1))
```

This function is well known to grow at an enormous rate, but it is fully defined for any pair of non-negative integers n, m. Use complete induction to show that it is defined for such arguments. (Hint, consider a lexical ordering of the argument pairs.)

1.22 Go through some of the steps in an evaluation of windowint (3, 12) trying both a full evaluation of the locally defined values before substitution and also a substitution to remove the local definitions before the expressions are evaluated.

1.23 The positive integer square root of a non-negative integer is given by the function introot such that if introot m = n, then n is the largest integer such that n^2 is less than or equal to m. Give a recursive definition of introot. (Hint, search for an appropriate n starting with 0 for $m \geq 0$.)

1.24 Using div, to find a midpoint between two integers, rewrite the product function of Exercise 1.12 so that for $n < m$ it recursively finds the products of the integers from n up to the midpoint of n and m and also from the midpoint + 1 to m. This is called a binary chop technique and can greatly reduce the number of recursive applications of a function.

1.25 Use a similar binary chop technique to that of the previous exercise to improve the power function (Exercise 1.11). Hint, consider the relationships (for $n \geq 2$):

$$m^{2*n} = \text{square}(m^n)$$
$$m^{2*n+1} = \text{square}(m^n) * m$$

1.26 Define a function to compute ${}^nP_r$ where

$${}^nP_r = \frac{n!}{(n-r)!} = n * (n-1) * (n-2) * \cdots * (n-r+1)$$

when $n \geq r \geq 1$

1.27 More local (nested) definitions of a variable override less local definitions throughout their (inner) scope, thus making a hole in the scope of the outer definition. Using this convention, match applied occurrences of variables with their binding occurrence (i.e. the defining occurrence or parameter) in the following definitions:

```
fun g (x) = let val x = x + 1 in x * x end

fun f (x, y) =
  let val x = x + y in
    if let val x = y div 2 and y = x + y in x > y end
    then let val z = x * x in x * z end
    else x + y
  end
```

(Note that obscure programs can be written in any notation!)

1.28 What are the values of:

```
let fun f x = x * 2 val a = 2
in f (let val x = a + 3 in x * x end) end
```

```
let fun f x = x - 1 val a = 2 in
let val x = let val x = a+3
            in x * x end
in f x end end
```

1.29 What are the scopes of the definitions of V_1 and V_2 in the following, where you may assume E, E_1, E_2 do not contain nested redefinitions of the variables:

(a) **let val** $V_1 = E_1$ **in let val** $V_2 = E_2$ **in** E **end end**
(b) **let val** $V_1 =$ **let val** $V_2 = E_2$ **in** E_1 **end in** E **end**
(c) **let val** $V_1 = E_1$ **and** $V_2 = E_2$ **in** E **end**
(d) **let fun** $V_1 (V) = E_1$ **and** $V_2 (V) = E_2$ **in** E **end**
(e) **let val** $V_1 = E_1$ **in let fun** $V_2 (V) = E_2$ **in** E **end end**
(f) **let fun** $V_1 (V) = E_1$ **in let val** $V_2 = E_2$ **in** E **end end**
(g) **let fun** $V_1 (V) =$ **let val** $V_2 = E_2$ **in** E_1 **end in** E **end end**
(h) **let val** $V_1 =$ **let fun** $V_2 (V) = E_2$ **in** E_1 **end in** E **end**
(i) **let fun** $V_1 (V) = E_1$ **in let fun** $V_2 (V) = E_2$ **in** E **end end**
(j) **let fun** $V_1 (V) =$ **let fun** $V_2 (V) = E_2$ **in** E_1 **end in** E **end**

What happens in each case if any of the names V_1, V_2, V are the same?

1.30 Suppose E_1, E_2, E_3 are expressions, possibly involving free occurrences of f, g, h, so that the definitions:

fun f x = E_1 **and** g y = E_2 **and** h z = E_3

are mutually recursive. Now suppose we want to introduce f and g as above but 'hide' h. We could write:

```
fun f x  = let fun h z = E3
           in E1 end
and g y  = let fun h z = E3
           in E2 end
```

but this duplicates the definition of h. Can you find a way to avoid the duplication? (Remember each E_i may refer to f, g and h.)

1.31 Which of the following equivalences are true for all cases or under certain restrictions?

(a) **let** D_1 D_2 **in** E **end**
  $\equiv$ **let** D_1 **in let** D_2 **in** E **end end**

(b) **local** D_1 D_2 **in** D **end**
  $\equiv$ **local** D_1 **in local** D_2 **in** D **end end**

(c) **let local** D_1 **in** D_2 **end in** E **end**
$\equiv$ **let** D_1 **in let** D_2 **in** E **end end**

(d) **let local** D_1 **in** D_2 **end in let** D_1 **in** E **end end**
$\equiv$ **let** D_1 **in let** D_2 **in** E **end end**

(e) **let local val** $V_1 = E_1$ **in val** $V_2 = E_2$ **end in** E **end**
$\equiv$ **let val** $V_2 =$ **let val** $V_1 = E_1$ **in** E_2 **end in** E **end**

Chapter 2
Support for Abstraction

In this chapter we look at some important features of modern functional languages which help us to write more robust (and/or more sophisticated) programs with greater ease. In particular, they all provide support for greater abstraction in programming. We introduce topics which will be studied at greater depth in the subsequent chapters.

First, we discuss the notion of polymorphic types and summarise the type system which we will be extending in Chapters 5 and 7. Types play an important role in structuring and designing programs on a large scale.

We then look at the treatment of functions as data objects and at the higher order approach to programming that this allows. Higher order functions are used extensively in subsequent examples and this is probably the main feature of the functional approach to programming.

The chapter is concluded with a consideration of the way programs are evaluated and a brief look at the strictness of functions. This is related to the important technique of *lazy evaluation*. The implications for and importance of lazy evaluation for further abstraction are studied at greater depth in Chapter 8.

2.1 Polymorphism

2.1.1 General purpose functions

We have referred to certain functions as being **polymorphic** and we will now explain what this means, beginning with the example of the identity function I. The definition of I is simply **fun** I x = x and the function returns its argument as result. This suggests that the function is quite general and could be applied to objects of any type (int, bool, string, int × string, etc.). So what is the type of I? When applied to an integer, it returns an integer (e.g. I 5 = 5) and when applied to an int × string it returns an int × string (e.g. I (5, "xyz") = (5, "xyz")). In general, if T is a type then I should be applicable to objects of type T returning objects of type T, which suggests I should have type $T \rightarrow T$ for all types T. With the types we have introduced so far (the so-called **monotypes**), we cannot express a unique type for I. Most strongly typed programming languages (e.g. Pascal, ALGOL 68, Ada) only allow monotypes (i.e. they have **monomorphic** type systems), and general purpose functions like I are thus disallowed. This can be a tremendous restriction for programming, forcing the programmer to introduce several versions of functions like I with the same definition but with different types.

We do not wish to split functions like I into many versions nor do we want to consider I to be an overloaded name denoting many different functions (because it has a single definition); instead, we consider I to be **polymorphic** with a single definition and a more general type or type **schema**.

2.1.2 Introducing type variables and polytypes

We are led to an extension of the type system which will allow us to express general purpose types or **polytypes** representing type schemas like $T \rightarrow T$ *for all types* T. We introduce type variables α, β, γ, $\cdots$ which can stand for any type in a type description and allow us to form new types like $\alpha \times$ int $\rightarrow$ int $\times \beta$ and $\alpha \rightarrow \alpha$. The type variables in such a (poly-)type stand for any type but in a consistent way. For example, $\alpha \rightarrow \alpha$ will be the type of a function like I which can take a value of any type α as argument, but always returns a result with the same type as the argument. Table 2.1 gives the most general (poly-)types which can be inferred for some polymorphic functions (some of which we have already introduced).

The functions fst, snd and swappair take arbitrary pairs as arguments and the types of the two components of the pairs are independent. Thus we use two type variables α and β to range independently over all possible types and $\alpha \times \beta$ represents all possible types of pairs. The result

Table 2.1 Some polymorphic functions.

Definition	*Inferred type*
fun I x = x	I : $\alpha \rightarrow \alpha$
fun fst (a, b) = a	fst : $(\alpha \times \beta) \rightarrow \alpha$
fun snd (a, b) = b	snd : $(\alpha \times \beta) \rightarrow \beta$
fun swappair (a, b) = (b, a)	swappair : $(\alpha \times \beta) \rightarrow (\beta \times \alpha)$
fun K5 x = 5	K5 : $\alpha \rightarrow$ int

type for fst is the same type as the first component (namely α) and so the type of the function is $(\alpha \times \beta) \rightarrow \alpha$. The statement of the type should be read as: for all types α, for all types β, fst : $(\alpha \times \beta) \rightarrow \alpha$.

Similarly, snd returns a value with the same type as the second component and swappair returns a pair where the first and second components have the same types as the second and first components of the argument, respectively. The function K5 is a constant function which always returns the integer 5. Since the definition suggests no constraint for the type of the argument (x), the function has the polytype $\alpha \rightarrow$ int.

2.1.3 Principal types and instances

The introduction of type variables allows us to express the type of general, polymorphic expressions with a single polytype. We should observe, however, that an *instance* of a polytype may also be associated with an expression. For example, it makes sense to write 3 + fst (5, true), so in this expression, fst : (int $\times$ bool) $\rightarrow$ int. The type (int $\times$ bool) $\rightarrow$ int is an instance of the type $(\alpha \times \beta) \rightarrow \alpha$, where int has been substituted for all occurrences of α and bool has been substituted for all occurrences of β. In general, an instance of a type is obtained by (consistent) substitutions of further types for the type variables. We allow the substituted types to contain variables as well. So, for example, $(\gamma \times \gamma) \rightarrow \gamma$ is a also an instance of $(\alpha \times \beta) \rightarrow \alpha$, obtained by substituting γ both for α and for β. In type checking an expression, names which have polytypes can appear anywhere a value with an instance of the type makes sense. (We will describe the processes of type checking and type inference more formally in Chapter 11.) For example, in the following expressions I appears with the indicated type instances:

Expression	*Type of* I (an instance of $\alpha \rightarrow \alpha$)
I (3 + 5)	int $\rightarrow$ int
I (true, 6)	(bool $\times$ int) $\rightarrow$ (bool $\times$ int)
I (double)	(int $\rightarrow$ int) $\rightarrow$ (int $\rightarrow$ int)

The last example involves a higher order use of I with a function as argument (and result). We discuss higher order functions in the next section.

The most general type that we associate with a name is called the **principal** type of the name, and the type of any occurrence of the name should be an instance of the principal type. It will always be the case that an expression has a principal type in our examples and it is always possible to infer this principal type from the types of the names used in the expression and the context. The inference method is explained in detail in Chapter 11, but informal inferences can usually be carried out by hand for most examples. As an illustration, we consider the type of minpair given by:

```
fun minpair (a, b) = if a < b then a else b
```

From the form of the left-hand side of the definition, it is clear that minpair is a function taking an argument pair, so we conjecture, initially, that its type is $(\alpha \times \beta) \rightarrow \gamma$ which assumes no further constraints. Furthermore, we are assuming a : α and b : β which we bear in mind when we come to analyse the right-hand side. We recall that the branches of the conditional have to be of the same type, so in this case α and β must have the same type giving the constraint $(\beta = \alpha)$. The type of the whole conditional must be the type of the result of minpair and also the same as the type of the branches, giving $(\gamma = \alpha)$. Finally, the type of the test must be bool which is compatible with < : (int × int) → bool but this also requires that a : int and b : int (i.e. $\beta = \alpha =$ int). No further information can be gleaned from the expression, so we deduce that minpair : (int × int) → int. (With practice, one can handle the type information more efficiently to arrive at the principal type more quickly. However, it is useful to have an implementation for automatic type inference, like the one provided for Standard ML and Miranda, in order to have such informal reasoning checked.) In future examples, we will explicitly state the principal type of functions we introduce (except sometimes when they are just auxiliary and local). It is not always possible to deduce types automatically when names are overloaded and this is why we have chosen to avoid overloading names in the examples. Note the difference between polymorphism and overloading. We said that **overloading** means using the same name (in the same context) ambiguously for two or more different values which may have totally different definitions and types. On the other hand, the value denoted by a polymorphic name (like I, say) has one definition and its types are all the instances of some principal type. (The distinction was made by C. Strachey (1967) who referred to polymorphism and overloading as (respectively) parametric polymorphism and *ad hoc* polymorphism.)

2.1.4 The type of equality tests

One important problem remains to be resolved, and that is the type of =. It is not obvious whether = should be regarded as polymorphic or overloaded. If we say it is polymorphic ($= : (\alpha \times \alpha) \to \text{bool}$) then we allow all types (α) to have an equality test as an operation (this is the approach taken in Miranda). The problem is, it is not possible to implement this for all types, so it would occasionally be undefined. Another approach is to make = overloaded but applicable to a large class of types. This can prevent us from using = freely in defining general purpose functions. The Standard ML approach, which we adopt here, is to distinguish the class of types with equality, and introduce special type variables for this class. We will use $\alpha^=, \beta^=, \gamma^=, \cdots$ to stand for any type for which an equality test is available, and then we can be more explicit about the generality of a function defined in terms of =. The type of = is simply $(\alpha^= \times \alpha^=) \to \text{bool}$.

The primitive types int, bool, string and unit are all equality types and any types we build up from equality types using product type operators ($\_\times\_\times \cdots \times\_$) are also equality types. On the other hand, any type involving a function type ($T_1 \to T_2$) is not an equality type. For example, int × (string × string × bool) is an equality type and is therefore a possible instance type for $\alpha^=$ (as well as for α). Whereas, int × (string → bool) is not an equality type and cannot be an instance type for $\alpha^=$ (but can be an instance type for α). Similarly $\alpha^= \times$ int is an equality type, but $\alpha \times$ int is not (even though some instance types of $\alpha \times$ int will be).

2.1.5 A summary

We summarize the polymorphic type system (introduced so far) in Table 2.2. There is a basic type unit mentioned there which we have not yet described. The type unit has only one proper value which is written as ( ) and can be regarded as an empty tuple (it will come in useful later). So we have tuples with n components for $n = 0$ and $n > 1$. Tuples with 1 component are redundant, and we identify them with the component itself.

The arrow (→) and crosses (×) are known as **type operators**, since they form new types from given types according to the rules shown in the table. In the next chapter, we introduce another type operator (list) and in Chapter 5 we discuss how the type system can be extended by allowing new constant types and type operators to be introduced into programs by the programmer.

Table 2.2 Polymorphic types.

type constants	(int, string, bool, unit)
type variables	$(\alpha, \beta, \gamma, \cdots)$
equality-type variables	$(\alpha^{=}, \beta^{=}, \gamma^{=}, \cdots)$

$$\frac{T \text{ is a type constant}}{T \text{ is a type}} \qquad \frac{T \text{ is a type variable}}{T \text{ is a type}} \qquad \frac{T \text{ is an equality-type variable}}{T \text{ is a type}}$$

$$\frac{T_1 \text{ is a type} \quad T_2 \text{ is a type}}{T_1 \rightarrow T_2 \text{ is a type}} \qquad \frac{T_1 \text{ is a type} \quad T_2 \text{ is a type} \cdots T_n \text{ is a type}}{T_1 \times T_2 \times \cdots \times T_n \text{ is a type}} \ (n > 1)$$

$$\frac{T \text{ is a type constant}}{T \text{ is an equality-type}} \qquad \frac{T \text{ is an equality-type variable}}{T \text{ is an equality-type}}$$

$$\frac{T_1 \text{ is an equality-type} \quad T_2 \text{ is an equality-type} \cdots T_n \text{ is an equality-type}}{T_1 \times T_2 \times \cdots \times T_n \text{ is an equality-type}} \ (n > 1)$$

2.2 Higher order functions

An essential feature of modern functional programming languages is a facility to treat functions as data objects which can be used in programs like other data objects. Functional programming goes beyond just the simple view of programs and program components as mathematical functions. It involves the use of functions to manipulate, create and generalize other functions. This in turn provides for a higher level approach to program creation.

2.2.1 Functions as data objects

So far, we have emphasized the definitions of functions and their application to arguments. If functions are to be treated as data objects, we should also allow:

(1) functions to be arguments for other functions,

(2) functions which produce functions as results (and therefore expressions describing functions),

(3) data structures (such as tuples) with functions as components.

A language with these possibilities is usually called **higher order** and we also refer to functions which take functional arguments and/or produce functional results as higher order functions.

Allowing functions to be components of data structures is quite natural, and saves us from having to make exceptions for expressions like (double, true). According to the rule given earlier for forming tuples, we deduce that since double : int → int and true : bool the tuple is a valid expression with type (int → int) × bool. We can write this deduction as an instance of the rule as follows, with the premises above the horizontal line and the conclusion below:

$$\frac{\text{double} : \text{int} \rightarrow \text{int} \qquad \text{true} : \text{bool}}{(\text{double, true}) : (\text{int} \rightarrow \text{int}) \times \text{bool}}$$

The expression (double, true) describes a pair whose first component is a function and whose second component is a boolean. (Incidentally, when such an expression is evaluated in ML, the system responds in the usual way by reporting both the value and the type. However, function values cannot be displayed in a canonical way, so the value is shown as (**fn**, true). Since we distinguish between functional values and the user's description of functional values (in definitions), it is not considered appropriate for the system to display a name when a functional value is produced. We will see later that functions can also be described without using a name, so there may be no obvious canonical description in general.) It follows from the above example that we should be able to form a meaningful expression with just a function name (without an argument expression). The expression (double) describes a function value of type int → int since it is not being applied to any arguments. Similarly, the following expressions show that we can locally describe functions which can then be delivered as the value of the expression:

```
let fun dbl x = x + x in dbl end
let fun dbl x = x + x and trbl x = x * 3 in (dbl, trbl) end
```

The value described by the first of these two expressions is a function of type int → int which doubles its argument. The function is given a local name (dbl) in the description, but it is anonymous in the wider context of the whole expression. Similarly, the value of the second expression is a pair of functions (each of type int → int) which are described locally in terms of dbl which doubles integers and trbl which trebles integers.

2.2.2 Higher order functions

The type of a higher order function will typically involve an arrow (→) nested within the T_1 or T_2 of some type $T_1 \rightarrow T_2$. For example, (int → int) → (int × bool) is the type of a higher order function which expects as argument a function of type int → int, and bool → (int → int) is the type of a higher order function which when applied to a value of type bool returns a function of type int → int.

In the previous section, we wrote the expression I (double) showing that the identity function could be applied to functions (returning the same function as result), and, in this instance, it has the higher order type (int → int) → (int → int). In fact I can be used on any function, and we can even apply it to itself (i.e. I (I)). In the expression I (I) the second occurrence of I has its most general type $(\alpha \rightarrow \alpha)$, which means that the first occurrence needs to have type $(\alpha \rightarrow \alpha) \rightarrow (\alpha \rightarrow \alpha)$ in order for the application to be type correct. This is perfectly possible, since the latter type is indeed an instance of the principal type of I (with $\alpha \rightarrow \alpha$ substituted for α).

Another example of a higher order function is the composition operator, frequently used by mathematicians. Given two functions f and g, the expression f ∘ g denotes the function formed by composing f and g. That is, for any argument x, (f ∘ g) (x) = f (g x). The symbol (∘) is being used to denote a higher order function-composition operator, and this gives us a direct way of combining functions without having to use parameters. For instance, we could define:

```
val sixtimes = double ∘ treble
```

instead of **fun** sixtimes x = double (treble x). (Note the use of **val** since there are no parameters in the definition even though it is a function being defined.) The type of ∘ is rather complicated but very interesting. First, we note that it combines a pair of functions to produce a function, so it should have a type with the form $((T_1 \rightarrow T_2) \times (T_3 \rightarrow T_4)) \rightarrow (T_5 \rightarrow T_6)$. However, there are constraints since not all functions can be composed and the type of the result is not independent of the types of the arguments. For f ∘ g to make sense, it is necessary that the result type of g matches the argument type of f (i.e. $T_4 = T_1$). Furthermore, the result type will be the same as that of f (i.e. $T_6 = T_2$) and the argument type of the composition will be the same as that of g (i.e. $T_5 = T_3$). This gives us the principal type:

$$\circ : ((\alpha \rightarrow \beta) \times (\gamma \rightarrow \alpha)) \rightarrow (\gamma \rightarrow \beta)$$

The operator ∘ is predefined in ML and in Miranda (written as ".") because it is particularly useful when working with functions, although it is a simple matter for a programmer to define it (see the next subsection).

When we have introduced a few more higher order functions we hope to show the power of expression they introduce into programming and why they are considered to be an essential ingredient of functional languages.

2.2.3 Curried functions

We will introduce a notation for defining higher order functions below, but we must first consider some new forms for expressions. Suppose f is defined with type int → (int → int), then it makes sense to write f 5 (an application of f to 5) which denotes a function of type int → int. The application of this latter function to 3 also makes sense, and we would write it as (f 5) 3. This is an example of an application where the function is represented by a compound expression rather than just a name. In fact, this will occur so frequently when we work with higher order functions that it is convenient to assume left association for applications so that the parentheses can be dropped. Thus f 5 3 is read as (f 5) 3 and in general $E_1\, E_2 \cdots E_n$ is read as $(\cdots ((E_1\, E_2)\, E_3 \cdots)\, E_n)$. Bearing this convention in mind, we introduce a generalization for writing definitions, allowing sequences of parameters when we wish to introduce a higher order function. Thus:

```
fun plus   m n = m + n
fun times  m n = m * n
```

introduces functions plus : int → (int → int) and times : int → (int → int). When we apply plus successively to two arguments, the result is the sum of the arguments, and similarly for times we get the product. For example:

```
plus 3 5 = 3 + 5
times 3 5 = 3 * 5
```

The definitions appear to give us just another way of writing additions and multiplications. However, we get more than that because we can now write down expressions like times 3 which denotes a function which multiplies arguments by three. This expression can be used in any context where such a function makes sense, e.g.

```
val treble = times 3
```

Note that this example is a definition of a function (treble : int → int) which does not use parameters. From the definitions of treble and times, it follows that for any integer argument (x):

```
treble x = times 3 x = 3 * x
```

Similarly, we can write expressions like double ∘ (plus 6). This expression describes a function of type int → int which is the composition of a function which adds 6 to its argument and a function which doubles its argument (i.e. it first adds 6 and then doubles the argument). Conventional uses of the operators + and * force us to provide both the integers making up the argument pair when we wish to apply the function (but see Exercise 2.16).

The additional notation is not strictly necessary when we can produce functions as results of expressions (using **let**). For example, the following (less readable) definition introduces plus, by describing the function which is produced after the first integer argument is supplied:

```
fun plus n = let fun addnto m = n + m
             in addnto end
```

This variation requires us to name the intermediate function (addnto) but its definition is within the scope of the parameter n introduced by the main definition. The dependence of addnto on the value of n can be clearly seen and different intermediate functions must be constructed for different values of n whenever plus is applied. For example:

```
plus 6 = let fun addnto m = 6 + m in addnto end
plus 3 = let fun addnto m = 3 + m in addnto end
plus 3 5 = (let fun addnto m = 3 + m in addnto end) 5 = 3 + 5
```

Since we regard functions as programs, examples like plus can be viewed as programs which dynamically create programs. The appropriate function described locally as addnto is created as a result of an evaluation of an application of the higher order function (plus).

Functions which are defined to expect arguments one at a time so that they can be supplied at different points in a computation or program are called **curried functions**. This terminology is derived from the mathematician and logician H.B. Curry who used higher order functions extensively in the study of **combinatory logic** (Curry and Feys, 1958), although it was Schonfinkel (1924) who first used them to replace tupled argument functions. Any tuple-expecting function f (of type $(\alpha_1 \times \alpha_2 \times \cdots \times \alpha_n) \rightarrow \beta$, say) has a corresponding curried version curryf (say) of type $\alpha_1 \rightarrow (\alpha_2 \rightarrow \cdots (\alpha_n \rightarrow \beta) \cdots)$ and vice versa. Any expression of the form f $(E_1, E_2, \ldots, E_n)$ can thus be replaced by curryf $E_1\, E_2 \cdots E_n$ and vice versa. We will frequently say that the curried function has n arguments (bending terminology a little since all functions really have one argument), and we adopt the convention that arrows associate to the right. Thus we can write curryf : $\alpha_1 \rightarrow \alpha_2 \rightarrow \cdots \alpha_n \rightarrow \beta$ in preference to curryf : $\alpha_1 \rightarrow (\alpha_2 \rightarrow \cdots (\alpha_n \rightarrow \beta) \cdots)$ which blends well with the convention for writing curried applications in the form curryf $E_1\, E_2 \cdots E_n$ where $E_i : \alpha_i$.

Curried functions do turn up frequently in mathematical texts, but they are usually disguised by making one of the parameters an index.

Thus, one is more used to seeing notation like $\log_{10}(x)$ rather than log 10 x. An obvious definition of the infix symbol ($\circ$) also disguises the fact that it is partly curried:

```
fun (f ∘ g) x = f (g x)     (definition in infix form)
fun ∘ (f, g) x= f (g x)     (definition in nonfix form)
```

Thus $\circ$ is curried for two arguments, but the first argument is a pair (of functions). The result of composing the pair of functions is described as a function which acts on the second argument (x) to produce the result f (g x). Later, we will make use of a fully curried version of this function which is traditionally called B:

```
fun B f g x = f (g x)
```

and has the type $(\alpha \to \beta) \to (\gamma \to \alpha) \to \gamma \to \beta$.

We will make heavy use of curried functions from now on, since they are more flexible than their uncurried (tuple-expecting) counterparts. We will still use tuples as compound data objects which may be formed as results of functions, but we will also introduce a curried version of the tuple constructors (at least for pairs) so that they can be built in stages when necessary:

```
fun pair x y = (x, y)
```

This makes pair : $\alpha \to \beta \to (\alpha \times \beta)$. We leave it as an exercise for the reader to go back and define curried versions of functions introduced in Chapter 1, but we indicate a special consideration that needs to be made for the argument order. We prefer to define:

```
fun lessthan x y = y < x
```

(which appears to be the wrong way round) for the following reason: The partial application (lessthan 3) can be regarded as a predicate which asks if an integer is less than 3. Thus (lessthan 3 5), which is an application of (lessthan 3) to 5, should produce false.

2.2.4 Generalizing with higher order functions

Frequently, quite specific functions can be seen as special cases of much more general functions or as applications of higher order functions to particular arguments. A very simple example of this is the function k5 defined in the previous section to produce the result 5 whenever it is applied to an argument. Obviously, there are many variations on this (k6, ktrue, $\cdots$) and we can summarize these by defining a constant-function creator K : $\alpha \rightarrow \beta \rightarrow \alpha$ as follows:

```
fun K x y = x
```

When K is given a first argument (x), it forms a function (K x) which returns that first argument whatever (y) it is applied to. Thus, for example K 5 7 = 5 and K true 8 = true. Clearly, the constant function k5 can be expressed as K 5 (an instance of the more general function K). To show a less obvious use of K, we express an equivalence with it:

```
even ∘ double = K true
```

This is another way of saying that for any x : int, even (double x) = true, but the equivalence is expressed between two functions without using a variable to stand for an arbitrary argument. (We will see in Chapter 8 why this equivalence need not always be true. This is related to *lazy evaluation.*) The equivalence says that the composition of functions even and double is the same as the function which constantly returns true. Strictly speaking, we should restrict the equivalence to the common type, since the right-hand side has a much more general type ($\alpha \rightarrow$ bool) than the left-hand side (int $\rightarrow$ bool), and can therefore be applied to arguments which cannot be given to the left-hand side. In future we assume that when we write $E_1 = E_2$ we mean that the expressions are equal at any types common to both sides.

We can similarly employ extra parameters in generalizing some earlier examples where certain dependencies were stated rather informally. In Chapter 1 we introduced a function sumg which summed the results of a function g over a range of integers. At the time, we indicated that the definition assumed that g had been defined, but we did not want to specify what that g was (since it was supposedly a general description of the summing process). Allowing higher order functions means that we can make g an explicit parameter in the definition. The dependence then becomes quite formal and general and we can indicate which function we are summing by a simple application. We define the general purpose operation sum as follows:

```
fun sum g 0 = g 0
  | sum g n = sum g (n - 1) + g n
```

(we assume that $n \geq 0$, leaving the definition of a robust version as an exercise). The type of sum in this definition is (int $\rightarrow$ int) $\rightarrow$ int $\rightarrow$ int, so any function g of type int $\rightarrow$ int can be supplied as first argument and used in the summing process. For $n \geq 0$, sum g n will be g 0 + g 1 + $\cdots$ g n so if square is the function which squares integers:

```
sum square 3 = square 0 + square 1 + square 2 + square 3
             = 0 + 1 + 4 + 9
```

In Chapter 1, we also described a function leastp, assuming some unspecified p : int → bool had been defined. We rewrite this definition as well, with p as a proper parameter:

```
fun least p n = if p n then n else least p (n + 1)
```

so that least has type (int → bool) → int → int.

Drawing box diagrams to represent higher order functions is non-trivial because functions can be both active processing agents (boxes) and passive data values (associated with wires) within the same context. One useful technique for partly alleviating this problem is to make all functions passive data except for one primitive higher order function apply. This function is defined by:

```
fun apply (f, x) = f x
```

and any expression of the form $E_1\ E_2$ can be converted to apply (E_1, E_2). An attempt to draw the internal description of apply is given in Figure 2.1 along with an example function where apply is used in the description.

We discuss diagrams for curried functions and show how diagrams are related to expression graphs in the exercises.

2.2.5 Higher order functions as control constructs

The **control constructs** of procedural languages **(loops, branching** and **sequencing)** correspond to particular higher order operations. We will

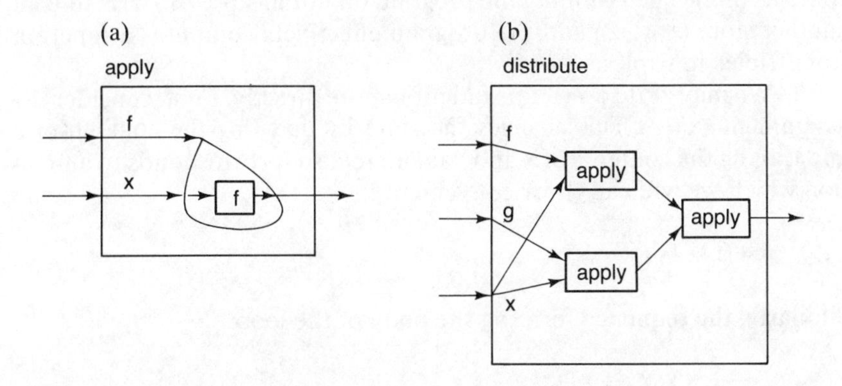

Figure 2.1 (a) A picture for **fun** apply (f, x) = f x, and (b) a picture for function distribute defined by **fun** distribute (f, g, x) = (f x) (g x).

illustrate this correspondence in a moment, but first we consider how a simple procedural computation can be converted to a functional form. We use the following fragment of a procedural program as our example and convert it into a function definition using recursion to replace loops and explicitly describing the piece of program as an operation on stores:

```
Prog : BEGIN Z := 1;
             WHILE X ≤ Y DO
             BEGIN
                Z := Z * X;
                X := X + 1
             END
       END
```

This program calculates the product of all the numbers between two given numbers. More specifically, if X and Y are assigned initial integer values (x and y, say) and x ≤ y then the program terminates with the value x * (x + 1) * · · · * y assigned to (stored in) Z.

In Chapter 1 we mentioned an important difference between this style of program description and the functional style, in the use of program variables (X, Y, Z). These are being used to denote (integer) storage locations (unlike our use of x and y to denote the actual integers contents of the storage locations at a particular point in a computation). This piece of program transforms the initial store into a final store by re-assigning new values to the locations denoted by the program variables in a sequence of steps. For simple programs like this, the store at any particular point in the computation can be characterized by the contents associated with each of the variables used in the program. In Prog, only X, Y and Z are used, so a store may be represented as a triple of values (x, y, z) (x being the contents of X, y being the contents of Y and z being the contents of Z). Then running the program on initial store (x, y, z) results in another store (x′, y′, z′) and the program effectively computes a function from triples to triples.

We may write down this function more directly. First, consider the assignment Z := 1. This changes the store by updating the contents of Z and leaving the contents of X and Y unaltered, so it corresponds to a function which we will call f1 for convenience:

```
fun f1 (x, y, z) = (x, y, 1)
```

Similarly, the sequence forming the body of the loop:

```
Z := Z * X; X := X + 1
```

changes the store in two stages, so it can be associated with a function (called body) which is the composition of two functions f3 and f2:

```
fun f2 (x, y, z) = (x, y, z * x)
fun f3 (x, y, z) = (x + 1, y, z)
val body         = f3 ∘ f2
```

In fact body could be directly defined by:

```
fun body (x, y, z) = (x + 1, y, z * x)
```

The test of the loop (X ≤ Y) returns true or false depending on the store at the time it is evaluated, so we will represent it as a predicate on stores:

```
fun test (x, y, z) = x ≤ y
```

The while-loop itself can be expressed using a recursively defined function:

```
fun loop (x, y, z) = if test (x, y, z)
                     then loop (body (x, y, z))
                     else (x, y, z)
```

Here loop is defined to apply test to the store first and if this produces false, the same store is returned unchanged. If the test returns true, the body of the loop is performed by applying body to the store and loop is recursively applied to the resulting store (thus repeating the loop). Finally Prog corresponds to function prog where:

```
val prog = loop ∘ f1
```

and the whole definition can be simplified to:

```
local
   fun loop (x, y, z) = if x ≤ y
                        then loop (x + 1, y, z * x)
                        else (x, y, z)
in
   fun prog (x, y, z) = loop (x, y, 1)
end
```

We leave further improvements as an exercise (note that the initial z parameter for prog is redundant and loop does not affect the y component although its behaviour depends on it). From this example, we can derive some useful higher order functions which capture the way the components are put together once and for all. Clearly, we already have a higher order function corresponding to the sequencing of commands (C_1; C_2) namely ($\circ$). We note also that a while-loop repeats an operation on data values while some condition on the data values is satisfied. Given a predicate test and a function body acting on data values and representing the action of the body of a loop, we could define a higher order function loopwhile as follows:

```
fun loopwhile test body s = if test s
                            then loopwhile test body (body s)
                            else s
```

Here, s represents the store contents, but some type analysis will show that s has an arbitrary type (α) with test : $\alpha \to$ bool and body : $\alpha \to \alpha$. The function loopwhile therefore has the type:

$$(\alpha \to \text{bool}) \to (\alpha \to \alpha) \to \alpha \to \alpha$$

and constructs a loop function (of type $\alpha \to \alpha$) when supplied with an appropriate test and body. Before seeing an application of loopwhile, we take time out to look at a slight variation in the description of the (same) function. An alternative way to describe the function emphasizes the intermediate loop function which is built before the initial store s is supplied:

```
fun loopwhile test body
    = let fun loop s = if test s
                       then loop (body s)
                       else s
      in loop end
```

The equivalence can be seen more readily when one observes that loop is being introduced to stand for the expression loopwhile test body. To obtain the second form from the first, we note that the subexpression loopwhile test body appears twice (once on each side of the definition), and introduce the name loop to stand for this. Thus we might write as an intermediate (non-standard ML) form:

```
fun loopwhile test body s = loop s

                            where

                            fun loop s = if test s
                                         then loop (body s)
                                         else s
```

We then observe that a definition of the form **fun** loopwhile test body s = loop s is equivalent to **fun** loopwhile test body = loop. (Note that saying E_1 s = E_2 s (for any s) is equivalent to saying the functions represented by E_1 and E_2 are the same and that $E_1 = E_2$ (provided that s does not occur free elsewhere in E_1 and E_2). In this example, E_1 is the expression loopwhile test body and E_2 is the expression loop.) The alternative version is then obtained by simply rewriting the locally defined loop using the standard **let** construct in ML (replacing *E* where *D* by **let** *D* **in** *E* **end**).

We will not declare any particular preference for the different ways of writing these functions, but the reader should become familiar with such conversions so that equivalences may be spotted more readily. It may well be that the first form looks easier to read, but the second is more efficient for some language implementations.

Let us now return to an example application of loopwhile. We will redefine the function least, using loopwhile:

```
fun least p y = let fun test x = not (p x)
                    fun next x = 1 + x
                in loopwhile test next y end
```

Note that in the expression loopwhile test next y, the initial store contents are represented by a single integer value (the value of y). The test function returns true only when p is false for a given integer, and next increments an integer to provide the next value (store) to be tried (when the test gives true).

We can be more succinct in our description of least if we describe test and next more directly with higher order functions. Noting that (not ∘ p) x = not (p x) and plus 1 x = 1 + x, we can replace test by not ∘ p and replace next by plus 1. This gives:

```
fun least p y = loopwhile (not ∘ p) (plus 1) y
```

We could also *cancel* the occurrences of y in the definition since the parameter is redundant. In future, we will usually take such opportunities to cancel parameters when they are not essential for a definition. So watch out for definitions like:

```
fun least p = loopwhile (not ∘ p) (plus 1)
```

where the sequence of parameters in the definition is shorter than the sequence of arguments you might find in full applications of the function.

Let us now define another higher order function which turns out to have quite general use. This function corresponds to simple procedural **for**-loops (which do not make an explicit reference to a counter) used as in

FOR 32 DO X := X + X · · · . (See Exercise 2.19 for a discussion of loops with loop counters.) This time we supply an integer n as argument to describe the number of loop iterations wanted, and again use body to represent the action of the body of the loop. We first introduce repeatpos which applies a given function (body) a given number of times (n) to an initial value s, returning s if n < 1:

```
fun repeatpos n body s = if n < 1
                         then s
                         else repeatpos (n − 1) body (body s)
```

Thus when $n \geq 1$, body is applied to s once to form a new store and repeatpos (n − 1) is applied (with the same body) to the new store (body s). The following function repeat is just a safe version which is undefined and complains (reports an error) if n is negative (but repeat 0 s = s). Note that we have dropped two parameters in the definition of this version:

```
fun repeat n = if n < 0
               then error "negative argument for repeat"
               else repeatpos n
```

The types of the functions repeat and repeatpos are the same (despite the different numbers of parameters used to describe them), namely:

$$\text{int} \rightarrow (\alpha \rightarrow \alpha) \rightarrow \alpha \rightarrow \alpha$$

Once again, the argument representing the state (s) can be of any type (α), so the functions are much more general than the procedural construct from which they are derived. To illustrate this, we will use repeat to build a data object. More precisely, we will redefine the function stringcopy (which produced strings) using repeat rather than via a direct recursive definition.

The function stringcopy was defined so that stringcopy (n, s) produced a concatenation of n copies of the string s (for $n \geq 0$). The recursive definition showed how the final string could be constructed by concatenating s (n times), beginning with an empty string. Thus we conclude that the operation we want to repeat is the concatenation of s; n is the number of times we want to repeat the operation and "" is the initial data value. We make use of a curried version of the string concatenation operator (^) in the definition:

```
fun concat s1 s2 = s1 ^ s2
fun stringcopy (n, s) = repeat n (concat s) ""
```

Now, for example:

```
stringcopy (2, "abc")
  = repeat 2 (concat "abc") ""
  = repeatpos 2 (concat "abc") ""
  = repeatpos 1 (concat "abc") (concat "abc" "")
  = repeatpos 1 (concat "abc") "abc"
  = repeatpos 0 (concat "abc") (concat "abc" "abc")
  = repeatpos 0 (concat "abc") "abcabc"
  = "abcabc"
```

We will show a number of similarly useful higher order functions after introducing lists in Chapter 3.

We conclude this section on higher order functions with a brief look at some additional notation. This notation is not introduced for use in practical examples where we will avoid it. It is, however, important from a theoretical point of view and helps us to see some further equivalences and a simplicity underlying the wealth of notation introduced already.

2.2.6 Abstractions

Let us look once again at a definition of a simple non-recursive function such as:

```
fun double x = x + x
```

It is the name double which is being bound to a value by this definition, and the name (parameter) x serves as an aid in the description of the functional value. We introduce the following alternative way of writing this:

```
val double = fn x => x + x
```

Although this seems less readable, it shows that double is the name being bound to a value which is described on the right-hand side of the definition and that x is part of the value's description. The expression **fn** x ⇒ x + x is called an **abstraction** and can be read as *the function which maps* x *to* x + x. Thus it provides a description of an anonymous function (the name double is bound to this function after the description is completed). In an abstraction of the form **fn** x ⇒ E, the parameter x is sometimes referred to as the **bound variable** of the abstraction and E is called the **body** of the abstraction. The abstraction notation is derived from Church's λ(lambda)-calculus (Church, 1941) which was developed to study computation with functions before there were any modern computers or programming languages. (We discuss this important theoretical tool in Chapter 12.)

Descriptions of anonymous functions using abstractions need not be confined to the right-hand side of a definition, because the function being described can immediately be applied or made part of a data structure. Thus we could write an expression like:

```
(fn n ⇒ n + n) 5
```

which is an application of the function whose rule is n ⇒ n + n to actual argument 5 and simplifies to (5 + 5). (This simplification is obtained by substituting 5 (the argument) for n (the parameter) in the result of the rule (i.e. in the body of the abstraction) n + n.) Similarly, the expression (3, **fn** n ⇒ 6 + n) describes a pair with type int × (int → int).

The notation is also useful if one wishes to do evaluations by hand, because it helps in describing intermediate values. For example, consider the expression **let fun** f x = 3 + x **in** f 5 **end**. This is an application of a function (locally named f) to argument 5, where f is defined as adding 3 to its argument. A formal evaluation could proceed as follows:

```
let fun f x = 3 + x in f 5 end
  = let val f = fn x ⇒ 3 + x in f 5 end   (converting fun to val)
  = (fn x ⇒ 3 + x) 5                      (substituting for f)
  = (3 + 5)                               (substituting for x)
  = 8
```

In general, if a function definition is given in curried form (again assuming it is simple – without pattern matching or recursion), there is an equivalent **val** definition with nested abstractions. For example, **fun** plus x y = x + y is equivalent to:

```
val plus = fn x ⇒ (fn y ⇒ x + y))
```

We must take care, however, if a function name is used recursively, because we assumed that **val** was non-recursive whereas **fun** was recursive by default. Accordingly, we introduce **rec** so that we can express a recursive definition like **fun** f x = **if** x = 0 **then** 1 **else** x * f (x − 1) as:

```
val rec f = fn x ⇒ if x = 0 then 1 else x * f (x − 1)
```

For completeness, we should allow for abstractions where the rule is expressed with pattern matching and cases. Thus the most general form for an abstraction is **fn** *MATCH* where *MATCH* has the form:

$$P_1 \Rightarrow E_1 \mid P_2 \Rightarrow E_2 \mid \cdots \mid P_n \Rightarrow E_n$$

The earlier examples were special cases where n was 1 and the pattern P_1 was a variable.

As we stated earlier, we do not propose to use this notation in future definitions, but we will use it to explain some correspondences between expressions. (We also use it when we consider language implementation techniques in Chapter 13.) One correspondence is an equivalence between conditional expressions and a particular form of abstraction. We claim that the following two expression forms mean the same thing:

if E_1 **then** E_2 **else** E_3
(**fn** true $\Rightarrow E_2 \mid$ false $\Rightarrow E_3$) E_1

The second expression is an application of the function which maps true to E_2 and false to E_3 to the argument E_1. In both forms, the value of E_1 determines the value of the whole expression as follows:

if E_1's value is true then the final value is that of E_2
if E_1's value is false then the final value is that of E_3
if E_1 is undefined then the whole expression is undefined.

Another important correspondence forms a link between local definitions and applied abstractions. Consider the values of expressions with the following forms:

let val $V_1 = E_1$ **in** E_2 **end**
(**fn** $V_1 \Rightarrow E_2$) E_1

Once again, we see an equivalence when we consider that both forms describe the value of E_2 but in a context where the name V_1 stands for the value of E_1. Unfortunately, there are occasions when the latter form may not be a type correct expression with the polymorphic type system we are using even though the corresponding first form is type correct. So, we should say that they are equivalent when they are both well formed, type correct expressions. More general type systems have been proposed so that if one form is type correct then so is the other and the stated equivalence always holds. (Such an extension is implemented for Ponder (Fairbairn, 1982).) The equivalence is important because it relates the concept of local definitions with simple function applications and suggests that local definitions could be handled in the same way as function applications when a functional language is implemented.

We also note in the exercises that once we have a way to represent abstractions with box diagrams, then we can represent all higher order functions and expressions (see Exercises 2.24, 2.25 and 2.26). From now on, we will rarely draw box diagrams for functions but later we will make use of the corresponding graphs as indicated in the exercises.

In the next section, we discuss a possible ambiguity implicit in the way we have been referring to the value of an expression. This ambiguity turns out to have important consequences for programming which we discuss in detail in Chapter 8.

2.3 Evaluation (lazy and eager)

So far, we have not been very explicit about how expressions can be evaluated. We have also not discussed how functions should behave when their arguments are undefined (assuming an undefined result is not necessarily the only sensible option open to us). These questions are related, and we will briefly mention some different possibilities.

Up to now, we have assumed that expressions can be evaluated simply by expanding definitions and calculating the results of primitive function applications. We have only described this process informally as a special form of deduction, that is an evaluation of E is rather like a deduction (from properties of primitive functions and definitions) that $E = N$ where N is some simplest or **normal form** representing the value.

The restricted form of deduction where definitions are only used as left to right *rewrite rules* to obtain a normal form is usually called **reduction**. When a normal form exists for an expression, we would expect it to be unique (otherwise there is ambiguity about the value of the expression) and we would hope that it could be discovered automatically by a functional programming system. In some of the example evaluations we gave, there were usually several choices of what to simplify next although we did not discuss these at the time (but see Exercise 1.1). It is often clear that the choice makes no difference to the final result, as we see in the following example:

```
let val x = 3 * 2 in (x + x) - (4 * 2) end
```

If we simplify 3 * 2 first and then substitute the result for x in the main expression we get (5 + 5) − (4 * 2). The simplification of 4 * 2 to 8 could have preceded or followed this step or even have been done simultaneously to get (5 + 5) − 8 and eventually 2. A less obvious order might have been to substitute 3 * 2 for x at the start and then to calculate (3 * 2 + 3 * 2) − (4 * 2), but most people would try to avoid the repeated calculation of 3 * 2 that this produces. One could draw a diagram for the expression with arrows to indicate the common subexpression so that its evaluation could be delayed but done at most once:

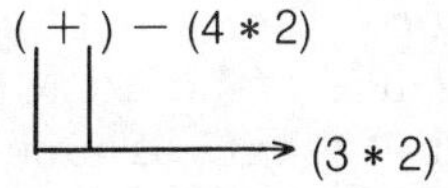

```
(+) − (4 * 2)
 ||
 ||________→ (3 * 2)
```

This latter technique forms the basis of what is called **lazy evaluation** which we study in later chapters.

The important question which remains to be answered is: Does it matter in which order the simplifications are done so long as we get a result? A fundamental property of functional languages is that such results are unique and do not depend on the evaluation (simplification) order. On the other hand, the evaluation order *can* affect whether or not a result is obtained (as well as affecting efficiency of evaluation). We could, for example, expand a recursive definition over and over again without attempting to simplify any applications. As another example, consider the following expression where we assume that n div 0 is undefined for any integer n:

```
(3 = 3) or ((5 div 0) = 4)
```

If we ignore the right-hand component of the argument for the function or, we could calculate that 3 = 3 is true. We might then deduce that true or ((5 div 0) = 4) = true according to the rule true or x = true in the definition of or. By postponing evaluation of the second argument component, we find that its value is not needed but we may also fail to notice that it is undefined. An attempt to evaluate both argument components before using the definition of the function would pick up the undefined subexpression. The question is now whether the whole expression is defined and equal to true or whether the expression is simply undefined? There are many other expressions where a similar problem arises. For example, is K 5 (5 div 0) equal to 5 or undefined? Our answers must be related to the way we choose to understand function definitions when undefined arguments are considered, and the choice affects the choice of correct evaluation orders that are open to us.

Functions which can give defined results even when arguments are undefined are called **non-strict** whereas functions which are always undefined with undefined arguments are called **strict**. So the choice is whether to understand definitions in the strict sense or the non-strict sense (when either is possible). Languages supporting the non-strict interpretation (like Miranda, Ponder, Lazy ML) are based on lazy evaluation methods. Such languages turn out to be much more flexible when it comes to treating input and output functionally. They also support simpler descriptions of functions and other infinitary data objects. Unfortunately, not enough is understood about the time and space efficiency for lazy languages nor about how efficiency can be controlled by the programmer. Consequently, such languages have not yet been used to develop a great deal of production software, but this may well change as research progresses. Languages like Standard ML and others with procedural features are usually non-lazy (i.e. assume strict functions). They use applicative order evaluation where arguments to functions are always fully evaluated before the function is applied. These languages are usually implemented in similar ways to conventional procedural languages and have similar performance characteristics.

For most of the examples up to Chapter 8, the choice between lazy and non-lazy (non-strict or strict) will make no difference to the results for the arguments we consider and we will assume the latter (strict) interpretation for definitions for the time being. This means that expressions which are defined with this convention will also be defined in a non-strict interpretation (with the same value). In contrast, when we come to consider lazy languages in Chapter 8, we will make a great deal of use of expressions which would not be defined under the strict interpretation. We will also look at techniques for overcoming some of the limitations of non-lazy languages.

EXERCISES

2.1 Describe in English the sorts of object to which a function with type $(\alpha \times \alpha) \rightarrow (\text{int} \times \alpha)$ can be applied. Give an example of a function with this type.

2.2 Deduce (informally) principal types for the functions f and g defined by:

```
fun f (a, b, 0)  = a
 |  f (a, b, n)  = if b then a else a ^ f (a, b, n - 1)
fun g (a, h, 0) = a
 |  g (a, h, n) = h (a, g (a, h, n - 1))
```

State the assumptions and facts you use at each step of the deduction.

2.3 By carefully using the rules which describe what constitutes a type (Table 2.2) prove that:

$$((\text{int} \rightarrow \alpha) \rightarrow \text{bool}) \rightarrow (((\beta \rightarrow \alpha) \times \text{int}) \rightarrow \alpha)$$

is indeed a type. Note that you can draw a tree to show the proof by combining instances of rules as in the following:

$$\dfrac{\dfrac{\alpha \textbf{ is a type variable}}{\alpha \textbf{ is a type}} \quad \dfrac{\text{int} \textbf{ is a type constant}}{\text{int} \textbf{ is a type}}}{\alpha \times \text{int} \textbf{ is a type}}$$

2.4 Another type inference rule for polymorphic types allows us to deduce instances of types from more general types:

$$\frac{E : T}{E : T'} \text{ where } T' \text{ is an instance of type } T$$

The following proof tree puts inference rules together to show the deduction of a type for I (double) from the premisses that I : $\alpha \to \alpha$ and double : int → int:

$$\cfrac{\cfrac{\mathsf{I} : \alpha \to \alpha}{\mathsf{I} : (\mathsf{int} \to \mathsf{int}) \to (\mathsf{int} \to \mathsf{int})} \quad \mathsf{double} : \mathsf{int} \to \mathsf{int}}{\mathsf{I}\ (\mathsf{double}) : \mathsf{int} \to \mathsf{int}}$$

This combines a use of the instance rule with the rule for function application. Draw similar trees deducing the types of (a) double (I 5), (b) I (double 5, not true), (c) I (I) (assuming appropriate principal types for I, double, not, 5, true).

2.5 Use (simple) induction to show that sum I n = sumbetween (0, n) for all n ≥ 0 where sum was defined in Section 2.2.4 and sumbetween was defined in Section 1.4.3. Similarly, use induction to show that sum double n = double (sum I n) for all n ≥ 0.

2.6 Define a general function sigma so that sum g n = sigma g 0 n for n ≥ 0 and sumbetween (m, n) = sigma I m n.

2.7 Express the equivalences in Figure 1.6 as equivalences between functions. You will need to define auxiliary functions to operate on pairs in some cases, e.g.

(&) ∘ (both not) = not ∘ (or)

where **fun** both f (x, y) = (f x, f y). (Note that (&) and (or) are infix operators so we use parentheses to avoid ambiguity when their arguments are missing. In SML these should be written as **op** & and **op** or. (See also Exercise 2.16.)

2.8 Is there a function f which makes (swappair ∘ f = f) true where f has argument type α? Are there any different functions which also make this equivalence true?

2.9 In Chapter 1 a definition of answer which described the least integer (greater than or equal to zero) satisfying a particular predicate (p) depended on the definition of leastp which in turn depended on p? How should this be modified using least to make the dependence on p explicit?

2.10 Derive a general definition of minval based on the description of minvalgh in Exercise 1.14 with g and h as parameters.

2.11 Redefine sum in terms of loopwhile.

2.12 Consider the following definition of a function to do multiplication of non-negative integers using addition. It uses a technique called **binary chop** to express multiplication by n in terms of multiplication by n div 2.

```
fun mult (0, m) = 0
|   mult (n, m) = let
                    val halfans = mult (n div 2, m)
                  in
                    if even n
                    then plus halfans halfans
                    else plus m (plus halfans halfans)
                  end
```

Check that this works correctly when n = 1. How many times would plus be applied in a calculation of mult (20, m) for some m? Redefine the function stringcopy following the structure of this mult definition as closely as possible. Can you generalize from these two definitions to produce a general purpose binary chop algorithm binchop such that:

```
mult       = binchop (plus, 0)
stringcopy = binchop (concat, "")
```

2.13 Corresponding to any pair of functions with a common argument domain there is a unique single function which returns the pair of results that the two former functions return individually (for any element of the common argument domain). Conversely, corresponding to any function returning a pair, there is a unique pair of functions with a common argument domain which return the separate components of the pair returned by former function. Can you express these facts as a correspondence (**isomorphism**) between two types? Can you define higher order conversion functions (in each direction) to obtain the pair of functions from the single function and vice versa? What are the types of these conversion functions?

2.14 Define a fully curried function C which switches the order of the first two arguments of curried functions (i.e. (C f) does for curried functions f what (g ∘ swappair) does for functions g which expect pairs).

2.15 If f : $\alpha \times \beta \rightarrow \gamma$ then we claimed that there is a corresponding curryf : $\alpha \rightarrow \beta \rightarrow \gamma$ such that f (a, b) = curryf a b. Define an operation curry so that curry f = curryf and describe its type. Similarly define its inverse uncurry so that uncurry curryf = f.

2.16 Bird (1984b) has argued for the use of *sections* to combine advantages of curried functions and infix notation. If we write an infix operator with only one of its arguments (using parentheses to ensure that this is not ambiguous) we will understand this as a partially applied curried version of the infix operator. Thus the section (3*) means the function which when applied to argument x produces 3 * x. That is:

(3*) = (**fn** x ⇒ 3 * x)

Similarly:

(3 div) = (**fn** x ⇒ 3 div x)

and also

(div 3) = (**fn** x ⇒ x div 3)

so we can curry the arguments in either order to get different partial applications. Furthermore, we sometimes want to denote the function corresponding to an infix operator itself without either of its arguments. Again, using parentheses, we can ensure that this is not ambiguous so, for example:

(+) = (**fn** (x, y) ⇒ x + y)

This facility is often needed when (+) is supplied as an argument to another (higher order) function. (The Standard ML convention is to write **op** + for argumentless uses of infix operators, but other forms of section are not possible.) Write down the various alternative notations introduced for $E_1 + E_2$ using sections as well as curry, uncurry and plus. Do you foresee any problems with sections for (−)?

2.17 Improve the final definition of prog (the functional counterpart of the procedural program segment Prog) by making loop a function on (x, z) pairs and removing the z parameter from prog.

2.18 Define higher order functions cond1 and cond2 which correspond to conditional command constructs with one and two branches respectively, that is corresponding to constructs like:

IF B THEN C FI
IF B THEN C_1 ELSE C_2 FI

for B a boolean expression (possibly involving storage variables) and commands C, C_1 and C_2. Redefine loopwhile using cond1.

2.19 Usually, loop constructs in procedural languages introduce a loop-counter variable which can be referred to in the body of the loop:

```
FOR I = N TO M DO . . . I . . . END
```

Assume that such references to the counter (I) in the loop body cannot update the variable (which is incremented automatically) and assume that the variable is local to the loop (unlike in Pascal). Can you suggest a higher order function corresponding to such loops? How does your function have to be changed if the variable is global and its residual value can be accessed in subsequent computations? Can you model cases when the variable I can be updated in the loop, thus affecting control of the loop?

2.20 Define higher order, functional counterparts for procedural loop control constructs like Pascal's REPEAT · · · UNTIL P and Ada's LOOP · · · ; EXITWHEN P; · · · ENDLOOP. Can you define these in terms of loopwhile?

2.21 What is the relationship between K and fst (where K was defined by **fun** K x y = x)?

2.22 Describe the type and behaviour of the function K I.

2.23 Use abstraction notation to formally derive 8 from the expression:

(**let fun** f x = 3 + x **in** f **end**) (5)

2.24 By using the equivalence apply (g, E) = g E, find a way to draw a box diagram for the function f, where:

fun f x = **let fun** g x = x + x **in** g (g (x − 1)) **end**

2.25 Invent box diagrams for abstractions with simple parameters and single cases. Extend this for the general case and find a way to represent pattern matching and curried definitions. Invent suitable abbreviations for representing curried/uncurried and mixed function applications and tuple formation.

2.26 The previous two exercises suggest that we could draw box diagrams for all the examples given so far. Such diagrams would be closely related to expression trees which describe the subexpression structure of an expression. Through the use of equivalences, we could reduce the complexity of the diagrams to some standard form. For example, local definitions and parameters introduce

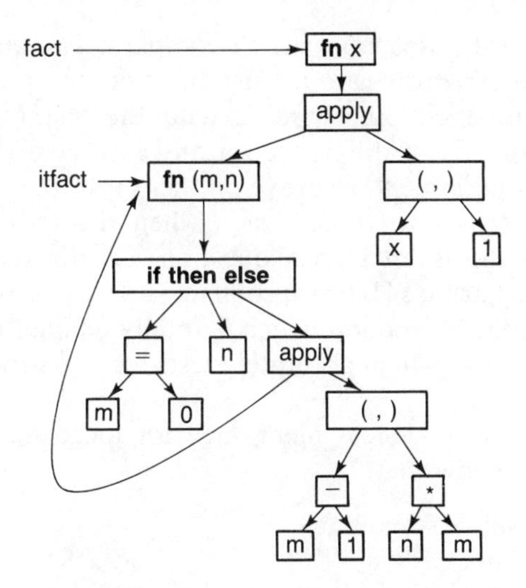

Figure 2.2 Example graph for Exercise 2.26.

shared subexpressions so we have graphs rather than trees. Furthermore, recursion could introduce cycles into the graphs. Figure 2.2 is an example graph for the definition:

```
fun fact x = let fun itfact (m, n) = if m = 0
                                      then n
                                      else itfact (m − 1, n * m)
             in itfact (x, 1) end
```

In the graph, we have reversed the direction of arrows so that they point towards subexpressions rather than in the direction of data flow as in the previous box diagrams. Boxes contain primitive functions and parameter names as well as abstractions. Recursion in the definition of itfact is replaced by a cycle with a pointer back to the beginning of the graph for itfact. The exercise is to draw similar graphs for other examples from the first two chapters and to experiment with variations. For example, one can use apply nodes with pointers to the function and argument graphs along with special tuple-forming nodes (with pointers to the components of the tuples) so that primitive functions need only appear in boxes at leaf nodes. Furthermore, tuples can be replaced by applications of curried tuple formers like pair, so only apply and abstraction formers need be used at internal (non-leaf) nodes of the graph, i.e.

$$(E_1, E_2) = \text{pair } E_1\ E_2 = \text{apply (apply (pair, } E_1\text{), } E_2\text{)}$$

(One could also replace 'parameter' leaves – like m, n in the diagram – by arrows back to the **fn** parameter where they are introduced.)

2.27 Define a test posequalfun which compares two functions of type int → int and reports false if they differ on any positive argument but is undefined otherwise. Extend the test to define equalfun which looks for a difference on any integer argument. Do you think it is possible to improve on these tests to sometimes return true or use error to report cases when the result is undefined? (Careful – this is not a trivial question. The limits are dictated by a variant of Turing's Halting problem which establishes that there is no computable function which is totally defined for fully defined arguments and which accurately tests for equality of functions.)

2.28 Using the equivalences mentioned for local definitions and abstractions, show that:

```
let val x = 3 + 2
    fun f x = x + 2
in  f (6 − x)   end
```

is equivalent to:

```
(fn x ⇒ ((fn f ⇒ f (6 − x)) (fn x ⇒ x + 2))) (3 + 2).
```

2.29 Why should the expression **if** 3 = 4 **then** 3 div 0 **else** 3 equal 3 rather than be undefined?

2.30 Standard ML introduces the constructs **orelse** and **andalso** (which are not primitive functions), such that for boolean expressions B_1 and B_2, (a) evaluation of the expression B_1 **orelse** B_2 delays evaluation of B_2 until after B_1 has been evaluated and found to be false, and (b) evaluation of the expression B_1 **andalso** B_2 delays evaluation of B_2 until after B_1 has been evaluated and found to be true. What conditional expressions are B_1 **orelse** B_2 and B_1 **andalso** B_2 equivalent to? Describe any changes in behaviour you would get by replacing applied occurrences of or and & by these constructs in the definitions given up to now.

2.31 Consider the possibility of replacing the conditional construct (**if** · · · **then** · · · **else** · · ·) by a function cond defined by:

```
fun cond true x y = x
  | cond false x y = y
```

Why will this cause problems in a strict language? Would this cause any problems in a lazy language?

Chapter 3
Programming with Lists

A very important concept in mathematics is that of a sequence or list of values. Lists also play a major role in functional programming so we devote a chapter to discussing lists and list operations. This chapter introduces lists using basic functions and concepts which will be used and developed further in subsequent chapters.

3.1 Introducing lists

The central importance of lists stems from the fact that they provide a simple way of grouping together a collection of items (of the same type) as a single data object (where the number of items may vary for each such collection). (Note that 'lists' in some untyped languages (such as LISP) which have mixed sorts of elements do not correspond to the sequences we are using here. LISP-style lists are more closely modelled by the binary trees which we consider in Chapter 5.)

Although *sets* are taken to be the fundamental concept concerning collections of items in mathematics, sequences turn out to be more useful from a computational point of view. This is because the items in a collection nearly always need to be dealt with and presented in some specific order and it is therefore important to have direct control over the order. A sequence is essentially a collection presented in a particular order with a first item, second item, and so on to the last item (for a finite sequence). Another important difference between sets and sequences is the fact that the same item can appear several times in a sequence, whereas we do not distinguish different *occurrences* of items in a set. (An item is either in a set or not in a set.)

It is difficult to see how sets can be described and manipulated in an effective computational way without introducing some bias towards a sequential representation. Later, in Chapter 7, we will discuss this problem and see how the more abstract notion of set can be approximated as a data object. Meanwhile, we present the (computationally) simpler notion of sequence, or list, below.

We will be introducing quite a large number of relatively simple operations on lists in this chapter. In order to appreciate some more extensive applications of lists in functional programming, the reader is encouraged to glance ahead to Chapter 4.

3.1.1 List types and constructors

A list will be a value (data object) consisting of an arbitrary number of items, all of the same type. For the moment, we assume that the number of items in a list is finite (which is the natural assumption for a strict interpretation), but we relax this constraint in Chapter 8.

If T is a type then we write T list for the type of lists of items of type T. As a new type rule we express this as:

$$\frac{T \textbf{ is a type}}{T \text{ list } \textbf{is a type}}$$

which introduces list as a new type operator. This allows us to make use of types such as:

int list	(integer lists)
(bool × string) list	(lists of boolean-string pairs)
(int list) list	(lists integer lists)
(int → string) list	(lists of functions from integers to strings)
int → (string list)	(functions from integers to lists of strings)
α list	(lists of values of type α for any type α)

(The convention in ML is that type operators like list which operate on a single argument type (T) to produce a new type are written after the argument in postfix form. (Hence T list rather than list T.) We will assume that list binds tighter than × and that × binds tighter than → to cut down on the need for parentheses in type expressions.)

We will frequently write lists like this:

[5, 6, 3, 2, 8]	(a value of type int list)
[true, true, false]	(a value of type bool list)

An expression such as [not false, 3 < 5, 3 = 5] describes a value which is a list (a bool list in this case) and this value can also be expressed by the simplified expression [true, true, false]. Note that we do not allow, for example:

    [5, true, 3, 0]

which has components of different types (but a method for defining mixed lists and the more general sorts of lists found in LISP will be shown in Chapter 5). The empty list (with zero items) is simply written as [ ] (pronounced 'nil') and we have that:

    [ ] : α list

since [ ] polymorphically denotes an empty list of any type.

The left-hand end of a list is regarded as the front of the list and we use a special infix operator (denoted :: and pronounced 'cons') to add a new element to the front so that, for example:

    5 :: [6, 3, 2, 8] = [5, 6, 3, 2, 8]

The operator :: is assumed to be right associative with precedence 5. The type of the operator is given by:

    :: : α × α list → α list

This ensures that we can only add an item to a list if it is of the same type as existing items in the list. In fact, every list we construct can be built up entirely through the use of just :: and [ ]. The previous notation we used for lists is assumed to be an abbreviation, so that the following are all equivalent:

```
[5, 6, 3, 2, 8]
5 :: [6, 3, 2, 8]
5 :: 6 :: [3, 2, 8]
5 :: 6 :: 3 :: [2, 8]
5 :: 6 :: 3 :: 2 :: [8]
5 :: 6 :: 3 :: 2 :: 8 :: [ ]
```

(Note in particular that [*E*] is equivalent to *E* :: [ ].)

3.1.2 The dual role of constructors

We will in fact define many other operations on lists, but :: and [ ] play a special role. They are called **list constructors** (list constructing operators). Values of type *T* list can be expressed in terms of these list constructors along with representations for the values of type *T*. Thus $t_1 :: t_2 :: \cdots t_n :: [\ ]$ might denote a fully simplified value of type *T* list (but we will usually abbreviate this as $[t_1, t_2, \ldots, t_n]$). The list constructors therefore provide both (a) *names for operations* (or rather an operation and a constant value) and also (b) *notation for canonical representations of values* (with list types). They do not themselves have definitions. An attempt to define :: and [ ] would involve us in describing a representation for lists in terms of other types, but we prefer to regard the constructors as primitives and to regard list types as distinct new types. More formally, we specify that (for any type *T*):

(1) Values of type *T* list are *generated* by the list constructors :: and [ ] (from values of type *T*).

(2) Lists are *uniquely constructed* by :: and [ ] which means that [ ] is not equal to any list constructed with :: and a :: x = b :: y if and only if a = b and x = y.

It follows from (1) and (2) and the types of :: and [ ] that a value of type *T* list is either empty (constructed by [ ]) or it is constructed from an item of type *T* (the head or first element of the list) and some other object of type *T* list (the tail or rest of the list) by means of ::. This is a recursive description of the objects of type *T* list because it says that a non-empty list has another list as a component and this recursive pattern will reappear in many of the operations we define on lists.

3.1.3 Hiding storage details

Notice that the decision about how data objects are to be stored in the machine can be handled automatically in a functional language implementation and hidden from the user. Structured data objects like tuples and lists can be thought of as just data values which happen to have components. They do not need to be described in terms of storage structures which detail how the values are to be distributed into locations. This is an important distinction because the process of updating a component of a record in Pascal, say, is strictly a storage operation and it would not make sense to talk of destructively updating a component of the purely mathematical (i.e. non-storage-dependent) data values we are using. The idea of changing a component of a data object still makes sense as long as we understand that we are creating a new data object which will exist alongside the original object but which differs in the value of some of the components. That is, *change* does not mean *update destructively* but rather *form a modified version.* It is only because we have rejected side affecting procedures (and assignments) that it is possible to hide details of which components are pointed to rather than stored directly as part of a storage structure and whether subcomponents are shared among several data objects rather than copied. With side-effects, we would need to know these details because they could give rise to different behaviour.

3.2 Example list operations

Before discussing definitions of functions involving lists and applications of lists, we introduce a collection of simple operations described informally via examples. These are listed in Table 3.1. The examples do not completely specify the functions, but they give a flavour of the intended behaviour and the types indicate how general each function is. As an exercise, the reader is invited to write down other expected properties of, and relationships between, these functions as they are introduced. Many combinations of the functions make sense, but there are some elegant equivalences to be discovered.

The infix operator @ (pronounced 'append') joins two lists of the same type to produce a single list. As special cases we note that [ ] @ x = x @ [ ] = x and that [a] @ x = a :: x (for x : α list and a : α). Furthermore, @ is associative so that (x @ y) @ z = x @ (y @ z) and we may safely omit the parentheses, writing x @ y @ z without introducing ambiguity. (We will,

Table 3.1 Example list operations.

$@ : \alpha$ list $\times$ α list $\rightarrow$ α list (infix)
$[a_1, a_2, \ldots, a_n]$ @ $[b_1, b_2, \ldots, b_m] = [a_1, a_2, \ldots, a_n, b_1, b_2, \ldots, b_m]$

rev : α list $\rightarrow$ α list
rev $[a_1, a_2, \ldots, a_n] = [a_n, \ldots, a_2, a_1]$

explode : string $\rightarrow$ string list
explode "astring" = ["a", "s", "t", "r", "i", "n", "g"]

implode : string list $\rightarrow$ string
implode $[s_1, s_2, \ldots, s_n] = s_1 \wedge s_2 \cdots \wedge s_n$
(e.g. implode ["this","and","that"] = "thisandthat")

link : (α list) list $\rightarrow$ α list
link $[x_1, x_2, \ldots, x_n] = x_1$ @ $x_2 \cdots$ @ x_n
(e.g. link [[1, 2], [1], [2, 3, 4], [ ], [3, 6]] = [1, 2, 1, 2, 3, 4, 3, 6])

length : α list $\rightarrow$ int
length $[a_1, a_2, \ldots, a_n] = n$

hd : α list $\rightarrow$ α
hd $[a_1, a_2, \ldots, a_n] = a_1$

tl : α list $\rightarrow$ α list
tl $[a_1, a_2, \ldots, a_n] = [a_2, \ldots, a_n]$

null : α list $\rightarrow$ bool
null $[a_1, a_2, \ldots, a_n]$ = false   null [ ] = true

upto : int $\times$ int $\rightarrow$ int list (infix with precedence 4)
m upto n = $[m, m + 1, \ldots, n - 1, n]$

sumlist : int list $\rightarrow$ int
sumlist $[a_1, a_2, \ldots, a_n] = a_1 + a_2 \cdots + a_n$

prodlist : int list $\rightarrow$ int
prodlist $[a_1, a_2, \ldots, a_n] = a_1 * a_2 \cdots * a_n$

doublelist : int list $\rightarrow$ int list
doublelist $[a_1, a_2, \ldots, a_n] = [2 * a_1, 2 * a_2, \ldots, 2 * a_n]$
(e.g. doublelist [1, 3, 4, 2] = [2, 6, 8, 4])

copy : int $\rightarrow$ α $\rightarrow$ α list
copy 6 10 = [10, 10, 10, 10, 10, 10]
copy 2 true = [true, true]
copy 0 10 = [ ]
copy 3 (copy 1 8) = [[8], [8], [8]]

member : $\alpha^=$ list → $\alpha^=$ → bool
member [9, 8, 121, 66, 15] 8 = true
member [9, 8, 121, 66, 15] 7 = false

---

however, assume precedence 5 for @. In Standard ML, operators of equal precedence associate to the left except for :: which associates to the right. Thus a :: b :: c @ d @ e :: f :: g groups as ((a :: (b :: c)) @ d) @ (e :: (f :: g)).)

The function rev simply reverses lists and there are two notable equivalences relating to combinations of rev with itself and with @. (These are left as a simple exercise.)

A string can be exploded into a list of the individual characters (using explode) which gives us a way to take strings apart in order to inspect them a bit at a time. This operation needs to be predefined since it cannot be defined in terms of the other string operations we have introduced (for building strings and finding the size). The complementary function implode joins a list of strings into one string and thus generalises the concatenation operator (^).

Note that we will regard characters as a special case of strings of size 1 and not a separate type. In some lazy languages such as Miranda the type string is identified with character lists where char is a primitive (built in) type. This makes explode redundant because list operations can be applied directly to strings. Other functions like ^ can be identified with the corresponding list operation (@ in this case). However, following the ML convention, we must explode strings to perform list operations on them, and use implode to compact lists of characters (or longer strings) back to single strings. Although this is slightly more cumbersome, it has the advantage of saving space in the representation of strings.

A 'list of lists' counterpart for implode which we call link generalizes @ to allow several lists to be appended. The function length calculates the number of items in a list (counting repetitions) and is the list counterpart to size. In fact, for any string s, size s = length (explode s).

The functions hd and tl return the head (first item) and tail (all but the first item) of a non-empty list, respectively. They are called **selectors** (selection operators) since they select the immediate components used to construct a list with :: . The selectors act as partial inverses for the constructor ::, but they are undefined on the empty list, that is hd (a :: x) = a, tl (a :: x) = x, and both hd [ ] and tl [ ] are undefined. When values of a data type can be constructed with more than one constructor, we often have **predicates** to tell us which variant a value has. For lists, we have the predicate null which simply tells whether or not a list is empty (nil). Hence for any a : α and x : α list, null (a :: x) = false and null [ ] = true.

The next four functions involve integer lists. The infix operator upto produces the increasing list of integers in the indicated range (m upto n is undefined if n < m); sumlist and prodlist produce the sum and product of a list of integers respectively; and doublelist doubles all the integers in a list. These latter three functions are defined for [ ], but we leave it to the reader to work out what the natural results would be for this argument.

The curried function copy generates a list where all the items are the same. More specifically, given argument n (a non-negative integer) and any value a (of any type), copy n a is a list with length n and all items equal to a.

Finally, member when applied to a list x and value a determines whether or not the value a occurs as an item in x. The items need not be integers, but since the check for an occurrence requires a comparison of items in x with a (using =), the items (and of course a) must be of a type for which there is an equality test. Hence the principal type involves occurrences of $\alpha^=$ rather than α.

We will give complete definitions of these functions in the following sections (apart from explode which we assume as a primitive string operation and upto which is left as an exercise. (The first four functions in Table 3.1 are predefined in ML along with map which is described later.) We will introduce many other functions in addition to the ones listed so far. Although those listed form a rich collection with which to work, we will need to generalize functions like sumlist, prodlist and doublelist. We will show techniques for doing this in a moment.

Some of the infix operators will often be needed in partially applied forms. There is a notational device called *sections* (see Exercise 2.16) which would allow us to write (a ::) for the function which 'conses' a onto arguments and (:: x) for the function which conses arguments onto x. Since sections are not part of standard ML notation, we will instead introduce curried versions of (::) to express these functions along with a curried version of @:

```
fun cons a x       = a :: x     (cons : α → α list → α list)
fun consonto x a   = a :: x     (consonto : α list → α → α list)
fun append x y     = x @ y      (append : α list → α list → α list)
```

Then (a ::) is written cons a and (:: x) is written consonto x. An alternative definition for consonto, namely **val** consonto = C cons, shows that it is just the argument reversal of cons where C f x a = f a x. We have not introduced a swapped version of append (we will write C append if we ever need it), but we should take care to remember which way append works. A partial application like append x represents a function which appends its argument after x (i.e. append x should be read as 'append after x' and not as 'append x after').

There are usually many different ways in which to define further functions by combining the functions already introduced. For example, if we wanted to define a function consr : $\alpha \rightarrow \alpha$ list $\rightarrow \alpha$ list which puts items on the back of lists (e.g. consr 3 [1, 5, 4] = [1, 5, 4, 3]), we might introduce it as:

```
fun consr a x = rev (a :: rev x)
```

This reverses the list, places the item on the front of the reversed list and then reverses the result. Alternatively, we might define the same function more directly like this:

```
fun consr a x = x @ [a]
```

which appends a singleton list constructed from the item. Quite succinct definitions can often be obtained by using appropriate higher order functions as well. For example, a function drop : int → α list → α list which removes a given number of items from the front of a list can be very neatly described by:

```
fun drop n = repeat n tl
```

So for a list x, drop n x = repeat n tl x and if x has at least n items ($n \geq 0$) this repeats the tl operation n times to obtain the nth tail of x. In fact, we will also use repeat to define copy later.

Many operations which have list arguments could be defined in terms of the predicate null which distinguishes the two types of list (empty or non-empty) along with the selectors hd and tl which take a non-empty list apart. This is the form of definition to be found in many LISP programs. A function f with argument x representing a list would usually be described with a definition of the form:

```
fun f x = if null x
          then (expression for the [ ] case)
          else (expression possibly involving hd x and tl x)
```

However, there is a particularly convenient way of describing such operations and that is by pattern matching the argument.

3.3 Pattern matching with lists

3.3.1 Simple list patterns

Since all lists must be either [ ] or of the form a :: x for some unique a and x, we can define a function on lists by describing what it does in each of the cases for the argument. We thus extend patterns to allow the constructors [ ] and :: to appear (with appropriate arguments in the latter case). Many functions can be simply introduced with two cases for the definitions as in Table 3.2. In each case the parameter used in the definition is a pattern of constructors and variables which will either *match* an actual argument or not. One of the cases must match a well defined argument of the correct type. The pattern for the non-empty case also allows us to introduce names standing for the head and tail of the argument.

Thus in evaluating (sumlist [5, 6]) or equivalently (sumlist (5 :: 6 :: [ ])), the actual argument matches the pattern in the first case associating (binding) 5 with a and 6 :: [ ] with x so the value is the same as 5 + sumlist (6 :: [ ]). Similarly sumlist (6 :: [ ]) = 6 + sumlist [ ] = 6 + 0 = 6.

The following definition of sumlist should be compared with the one given in Table 3.2 to see how patterns help to keep definitions clear:

```
fun sumlist x = if null x then 0 else hd x + sumlist (tl x)
```

Sometimes, cases are considered to be undefined (as for hd and tl). Rather than omit such cases, we will explicitly state that they are undefined using the function error. An attempt to apply hd or tl to an expression which evaluates to [ ] will be a runtime error (and not a type error since it cannot, in general, be detected at compile time). In the last example (the definition of @), one of the arguments is pattern matched in the definition while the other is not. Strictly speaking, we should say that the first component of the parameter pair is a list pattern while the second component is a simple variable. The function therefore applies to pairs of lists and the case is chosen according to the form of the first of the pair. The second of the pair will match with y in either case.

3.3.2 More complex patterns

We may also have functions operating on lists defined with more than two cases. For example, the function alternate : α list → α list returns a list of every second item in the list supplied as argument. Its definition includes separate cases for the empty list, lists with one item and lists with two or more items:

```
fun alternate (a :: b :: x) = b :: alternate x
  | alternate [a]           = [ ]
  | alternate [ ]           = [ ]
```

The first case will match any argument which is a list of length two or more and a will be bound to the head of such an argument, b will be bound to the second element (head of the tail) and x will be bound to the rest (tail of the tail). The second case will only match arguments which

Table 3.2 Some definitions using pattern matching with lists.

```
fun null (a :: x) = false
|   null [ ]      = true

fun hd (a :: x) = a
|   hd [ ]      = error "hd of [ ]"

fun tl (a :: x) = x
|   tl [ ]      = error "tl of [ ]"

fun length (a :: x) = 1 + length x
|   length [ ]      = 0

fun sumlist (a :: x) = a + sumlist x
|   sumlist [ ]      = 0

fun prodlist (a :: x) = a * prodlist x
|   prodlist [ ]      = 1

fun (a :: x) @ y = a :: (x @ y)
|         [ ] @ y = y
```

are lists with one item (i.e. with tail equal to [ ] since [a] abbreviates a :: [ ]). As an illustration, we calculate alternate [1, 2, 3]. Since [1, 2, 3] is an abbreviation for 1 :: 2 :: 3 :: [ ], the argument will match with the first pattern binding the variable a to the value 1, b to 2 and x to 3 :: [ ]. The right-hand side is thus 2 :: alternate (3 :: [ ]). The expression alternate (3 :: [ ]) now matches the second case (binding a to 3 returning [ ]) so the final result is 2 :: [ ] or [2].

For completeness, here is the general definition of **pattern**:

> A pattern is either a variable or a constant or a constructor applied to an argument pattern or a tuple of patterns. We also assume that the same variable does not appear more than once in a pattern.

We can simplify this definition to allow only constructors and variables in patterns by regarding constants as just constructors taking no arguments and regarding tuples as applications of constructors to a sequence of the appropriate number of arguments. For example, (P_1, P_2) = Tup2 P_1 P_2 and (P_1, P_2, P_3) = Tup3 P_1 P_2 P_3, etc. where Tup2, Tup3, . . . are constructors for tuples of the indicated size. (We will continue to describe tuples with parentheses and commas for the sake of legibility in future. We just note that they can be regarded as abbreviations for these applied constructors.)

Naturally, the constructors and variables in pattern matching definitions must occur in type consistent ways in each case of a definition. (If the same variable is introduced in patterns for different cases, the occurrences are assumed to be independent and the scope of a variable introduced in the pattern is just that particular case of the definition in which it occurs.)

We can combine constructors in a pattern to give even more specific cases as in the following example:

```
fun firsttrue ((false, n) :: x) = firsttrue x
  | firsttrue ((true, n) :: x)  = n
  | firsttrue [ ]               = 0
```

Before revealing what firsttrue does, let us calculate its type. The function expects a list as argument since the parameters are of the form $P_1 :: P_2$ (where P_1 and P_2 are patterns) or just [ ]. Furthermore, the elements of this list are expected to be pairs since the patterns for the heads are of the form (P, P') and the first item of each pair should be of type bool since the patterns contain constants of that type. Further analysis of the definition shows that the result is an integer (by the third case) so n must stand for an integer in the second case and hence the second item of each pair should be an integer. We deduce that the function firsttrue has type (bool × int) list → int. For an argument list of pairs x, firsttrue searches for the first pair in x for which the boolean is true and returns the corresponding integer in the pair. It returns 0 if no such pair is found.

Patterns may also be used in curried definitions:

```
fun member (a :: x) b = if a = b then true else member x b
  | member [ ]      b = false
(member: α= list → α= → bool)

fun front 0 x = [ ]
  | front n (a :: x) = a :: front (n − 1) x
  | front n [ ]      = error "front n [ ]"
(front: int → α list → α list)
```

The definition of member simply pattern matches against one of the curried arguments (note the polymorphic use of = in this definition). In contrast, the definition of front mixes the matching of both curried arguments. The function returns the front n items of a list x when applied to arguments n and x by consideration of three cases. The first case applies if the integer is 0 (for any list). The second case applies provided that the list is not empty and that the first case does not apply (i.e. the integer is non-zero). The third case covers all other possibilities ([ ] could be replaced by a variable in this case). (As an exercise, the reader should work out what front n x does when $n \leq 0$ and when $n >$ length x.)

Warning

A word of warning may be necessary here. We note that we will never introduce constructors by means of ordinary definitions. This means that when we define, for example, cons as a curried version of the list constructor :: then cons cannot be used in patterns as a constructor (it is not a constructor itself but a function defined in terms of a constructor). The constructors introduced so far are limited to constants of types bool, int and string along with [ ], :: (and those for forming tuples). A method for introducing further constructors along with new types into a program is given in Chapter 5.

We could go on to define many more basic list operations but, in the spirit of functional programming, we would do better to introduce some more powerful and general purpose functions and derive further operations from these.

3.4 Higher order list operations

The following higher order functions enable us to encapsulate the recursive processing of lists so that most other functions can be built directly with these without involving further recursion. This often leads to clearer definitions and better programming style.

3.4.1 Map

Frequently, we will want to do the same thing (apply the same function) to all the items in a list. The higher order function map takes care of the administration of this task. All we need to do is supply the function to be applied to items and the list of items the function is to be applied to. Thus map takes as (curried) arguments a function f and a list, returning the list of values f a as a ranges over the items in the argument list (see Figure 3.1(a)), for example:

$$\text{map f } [a_1, a_2, \ldots, a_n] = [\text{f } a_1, \text{f } a_2, \ldots, \text{f } a_n]$$

The higher order function is simply defined by:

```
fun map f [ ]      = [ ]
|   map f (a :: x) = f a :: map f x
(map : (α → β) → α list → β list)
```

and has the indicated principal type which allows $\alpha \to \beta$ as the most

(a) map

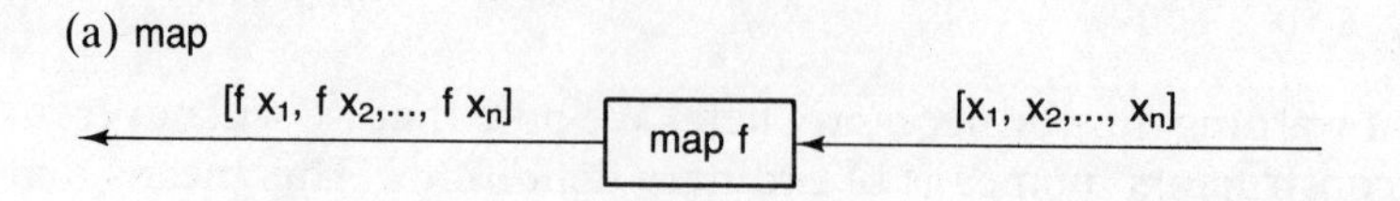

(b) filter, exists, all

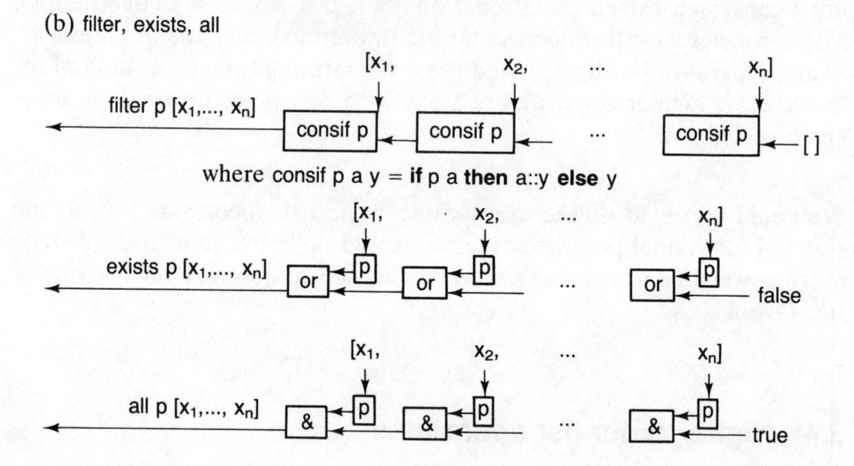

(c) zip

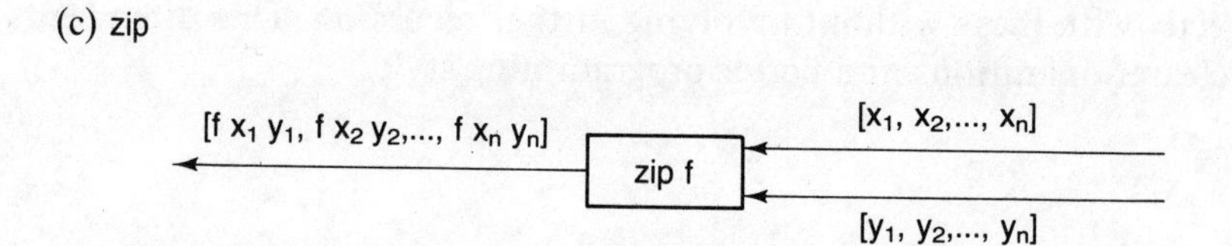

(d) accumulate and reduce

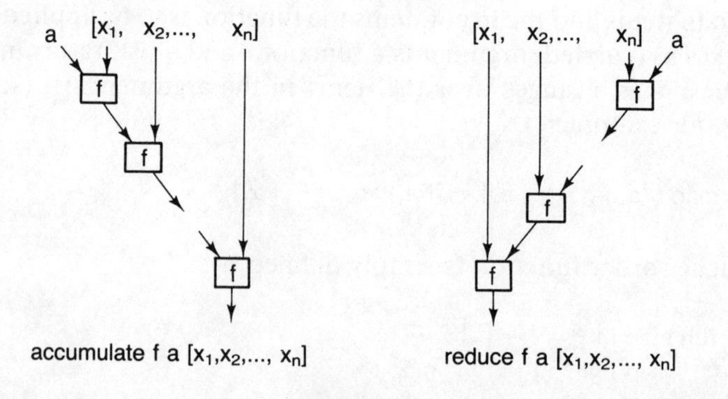

Figure 3.1

general type that can be assumed for any function supplied as first argument. This constrains the items of the argument list to be of type α and the items of the resulting list to be of type β.

Here are some simple applications of map. If we wished to define doublelist which doubles the integers throughout a list we could simply write:

```
val doublelist = map double
```

then, for example:

```
doublelist [1, 5, 6, 3] = map double [1, 5, 6, 3]
                        = [double 1, double 5, double 6, double 3]
                        = [2, 10, 12, 6]
```

and, from the definition and the types of double and map, we can deduce that doublelist has type int list → int list.

To add two throughout an integer list x we could write map (plus 2) x and to convert the list of integers to their decimal representations as strings, we can write map stringofint x. For example:

```
map (plus 2) [1, 5, 6, 3]
   = [plus 2 1, plus 2 5, plus 2 6, plus 2 3]
   = [3, 7, 8, 5]

map stringofint (8 upto 12)
= ["8", "9", "10", "11", "12"].
```

The function map is used a great deal in later examples. A useful equivalence involving map states that if we map one function (f, say) across a list x and then map g across the result, the overall effect is the same as mapping the composition g ∘ f across the list, that is:

```
map g (map f x) = map (g ∘ f) x
```

or equivalently: (map g) ∘ (map f) = map (g ∘ f).

We also have

```
map I x = I x = x
```

We will look at proofs of such equivalences later, but regard them as intuitively obvious for the time being.

3.4.2 Filter, exists and all

This next group of functions work with predicates and lists. They each take an argument (p) of type $\alpha \rightarrow$ bool and an argument (x) of type α list. For such arguments, the function filter returns the sublist of those items in x which satisfy predicate p; the function exists returns a boolean indicating whether or not any item in x satisfies predicate p and the function all returns a boolean indicating whether or not all the items in x satisfy p. For example, using predicates positive (>0) and even we have:

```
filter positive [1, 2, ~3, 0, 4, 5, 0] = [1, 2, 4, 5]
filter even [1, 2, ~3, 0, 4, 5, 0] = [2, 0, 4, 0]

all positive [1, 2, ~3, 0, 4, 5, 0] = false
all even [1, 2, ~3, 0, 4, 5, 0] = false

exists positive [1, 2, ~3, 0, 4, 5, 0] = true
exists even [1, 2, ~3, 0, 4, 5, 0] = true
```

Figure 3.1(b) shows how filter, exists and all may be thought of diagrammatically, rather than showing their actual construction according to the following recursive definitions:

```
fun filter p (a :: x) = if p a then a :: filter p x else filter p x
  | filter p [ ]      = [ ]

fun exists p (a :: x) = if p a then true else exists p x
  | exists p [ ]      = false

fun all p (a :: x) = if p a then all p x else false
  | all p [ ]      = true
```

The base cases are the ones which need careful thought here. The types of the functions are:

$$\text{filter} : (\alpha \rightarrow \text{bool}) \rightarrow \alpha\ \text{list} \rightarrow \alpha\ \text{list}$$
$$\text{exists} : (\alpha \rightarrow \text{bool}) \rightarrow \alpha\ \text{list} \rightarrow \text{bool}$$
$$\text{all} : (\alpha \rightarrow \text{bool}) \rightarrow \alpha\ \text{list} \rightarrow \text{bool}$$

An alternative definition of all could be given in terms of exists and negations which shows the close relationship between the two functions. We introduce non as an operation which negates predicates to express this:

```
fun non p = not ∘ p      (i.e. non p x = not (p x))
val all = non ∘ exists ∘ non
```

For example, if nonpos = non positive, then:

```
all positive [1, 2 ~3, 0, 4, 5, 0]
   = (non ∘ exists ∘ non) positive [1, 2, ~3, 0, 4, 5, 0]
   = non (exists nonpos) [1, 2, ~3, 0, 4, 5, 0]
   = not (exists nonpos [1, 2, ~3, 0, 4, 5, 0])
   = not true
   = false
```

Some other equivalences are:

```
all p (filter p x) = true
exists p = (non null) ∘ (filter p)
(map f) ∘ (filter (p ∘ f)) = (filter p) ∘ (map f)
```

3.4.3 Zip

Another useful process which can be performed on lists is that of 'zipping' two lists together using a binary function on pairs of corresponding items in the two lists. We define the higher order function zip to take a binary function and two lists as arguments, but we assume the binary function is curried (i.e. with type $\alpha \to \beta \to \gamma$ rather than $\alpha \times \beta \to \gamma$):

$$\text{zip} : (\alpha \to \beta \to \gamma) \to \alpha \text{ list} \to \beta \text{ list} \to \gamma \text{ list}$$

(Note how the type of the binary function determines the types of the list arguments and result.) Assuming that the argument lists have the same length, zip works by applying the binary function to the two list heads and recursively repeating this operation on the tails of the lists to form a single list (acting rather like the zip-fastener depicted in Figure 3.1(c)). In general:

$$\text{zip f } [a_1, a_2, \ldots, a_n] \; [b_1, b_2, \ldots, b_n] = [\text{f } a_1 \; b_1, \text{f } a_2 \; b_2, \ldots, \text{f } a_n \; b_n]$$

and zip f x y is undefined when x and y have different lengths. The requirement of equal length lists turns out to be useful as an error check. If we want to allow results for lists with unequal lengths, we will define a different function (e.g. splice is used later). The definition of zip is:

```
fun zip f (a :: x) (b :: y) = f a b :: zip f x y
  | zip f [ ]     [ ]     = [ ]
  | zip f x y = error "zip with unequal length lists"
```

We can now define:

```
val addlists = zip plus
val mullists = zip times
val pairlists = zip pair
```

and then, for example:

```
addlists [1, 2, 3, 4] [5, 6, 7, 8] = [6, 8, 10, 12]
mullists [1, 2, 3, 4] [5, 6, 7, 8] = [5, 12, 21, 32]
pairlists [1, 2, 3, 4] [5, 6, 7, 8]
      = [pair 1 5, pair 2 6, pair 3 7, pair 4 8]
      = [(1, 5), (2, 6), (3, 7), (4, 8)]
```

Both mullists and addlists have type int list → int list → int list and pairlists has type α list → β list → ($\alpha \times \beta$) list.

3.4.4 Accumulate (foldleft) and reduce (foldright)

Another general purpose operation on lists involves iterating along a list applying a binary function f and accumulating a single result rather than a list. At each stage the arguments for f are the result accumulated so far and the next item in the list. (To begin with, some default basic value for the accumulated result must be supplied.) For example, summing the elements of a list can be done by iterating addition in this way using 0 as the initial value for the accumulated result. Multiplying the integers in a list is just an accumulation with the operation times and base case value 1. Figure 3.1(d) should clarify what the higher order function (which we call accumulate) does. The definition of accumulate is:

```
fun accumulate f a (b :: x) = accumulate f (f a b) x
|   accumulate f a [ ]     = a
(accumulate : (α → β → α) → α → β list → α)
```

which gives accumulate the indicated principal type. Note that f is applied to the accumulated result and successive items in the list so that the final application of f has the last item in the list as an argument. For example:

$$\text{accumulate f a } [a_1, a_2, \ldots, a_n] = \text{f } (\cdots (\text{f } (\text{f a } a_1)\ a_2) \cdots)\ a_n$$

The function accumulate bears a close resemblance to procedural loops even though it is defined as a recursive function. One might suspect that an evaluation of an expression of the form accumulate f a x would be less efficient than code performing a loop, but in fact in many optimizing implementations of functional languages such an expression would be compiled into code as a loop. (We return to this point in Chapter 9.)

We illustrate accumulate in the definition of the following functions which respectively add up the integers in a list, multiply the integers in a list, link (or concatenate) a list of lists into a single list, join a list of strings into a single string, reverse one list onto another list and find the maximum and minimum of a nonempty integer list. We make use of max and min which are curried versions of maxpair and minpair to define maxlist and minlist. Superfluous parameters have been dropped from some of the definitions so accumulate appears with only one or two of its arguments in such cases.

```
val sumlist  = accumulate plus 0
val prodlist = accumulate times 1
val link     = accumulate append [ ]
val implode  = accumulate concat ""
val revonto  = accumulate consonto

(fun max a b = if a < b then b else a)
fun maxlist (a :: x) = accumulate max a x
|   maxlist [ ]      = error "maxlist of [ ]"

(fun min a b = if a > b then b else a)
fun minlist (a :: x) = accumulate min a x
|   minlist [ ]      = error "minlist of [ ]"
```

Their types are as follows:

```
sumlist  : int list → int
prodlist : int list → int
link     : (α list) list → α list
implode  : string list → string
revonto  : α list → α list → α list
maxlist  : int list → int       (max : int → int → int)
minlist  : int list → int       (min : int → int → int)
```

The functions maxlist and minlist are undefined for empty lists of integers since there is no obvious default value in such cases. (Later on we define a variant maxposlist which gives the maximum nonnegative integer in a list and returns 0 if there are none.) The expression revonto x y denotes the list formed by reversing y onto x. Thus:

$$\text{revonto}\,[x_1, x_2, \ldots, x_n]\,[y_1, y_2, \ldots, y_m] = [y_m, y_{m-1}, \ldots, y_l, x_1, x_2, \ldots, x_n]$$

In particular, when x is [ ], then revonto [ ] y is the reverse of y. So we can define:

```
val rev = revonto [ ]
```

Let us illustrate this by going through the steps in a calculation of rev [1, 2, 3, 4]:

```
rev [1, 2, 3, 4]
  = revonto [ ] [1, 2, 3, 4]
  = accumulate consonto [ ] [1, 2, 3, 4]
  = accumulate consonto (consonto [ ] 1) [2, 3, 4]
  = accumulate consonto [l] [2, 3, 4]
  = accumulate consonto (consonto [1] 2) [3, 4]
  = accumulate consonto [2, 1] [3, 4]
  = accumulate consonto (consonto [2, 1] 3) [4]
  = accumulate consonto [3, 2, 1] [4]
  = accumulate consonto (consonto [3, 2, 1] 4) [ ]
  = accumulate consonto [4, 3, 2, 1] [ ]
  = [4, 3, 2, 1]
```

This version of reverse turns out to be much more efficient in the use of space than the naive version which repeatedly appends singleton lists on the right of a list. The function revonto is also known as shunt because of its similarity to the way railway carriages are shunted.

Sometimes we want to associate arguments of a binary function f to the right instead of to the left to get

$$f\ a_1\ (f\ a_2\ (\cdots (f\ a_n\ a) \cdots))$$

rather than $f\ (\cdots (f\ (f\ a\ a_1)\ a_2) \cdots)\ a_n$. Accordingly, we define a function similar to accumulate which we call reduce:

```
fun reduce f a (al :: rest) = f al (reduce f a rest)
 |  reduce f a [ ]          = a
(reduce: (α → β → β) → β → α list → β)
```

(accumulate is sometimes called reduceleft or foldleft or just fold, and reduce is sometimes called reduceright or foldright). The two functions reduce and accumulate are duals of each other as can be seen in Figure 3.1(d). In fact, it is possible to define one in terms of the other by reversing the list and swapping the arguments to the binary function (using C). We will show later that this can give a more space efficient version of reduce in ML, but restricts the function unnecessarily in a lazy language. Note that if a binary function f is associative and if f is commutative with respect to a particular value a (i.e. f a b = f b a for any b), then reduce f a x = accumulate f a x for all (finite) lists x. In particular, we could just replace accumulate by reduce in the definitions of sumlist, prodlist, link, implode, maxlist and minlist.

This is because all the following are associative and commute with the indicated values:

plus	(commutes with respect to all arguments)
times	(commutes with respect to all arguments)
append	(commutes with respect to [ ])
concat	(commutes with respect to " ")
max	(commutes with respect to all arguments)
min	(commutes with respect to all arguments)

On the other hand, replacing accumulate by reduce in the definition of revonto also requires us to replace consonto by cons (otherwise it is not type correct). The resulting function no longer reverses but simply appends, that is reduce cons x y = y @ x.

There are other variations for reduce and accumulate to allow for argument f to be uncurried, and to allow for the default value a to be used on the opposite end of the list. Their definitions are left as an exercise.

3.5 List comprehensions (ZF notation)

3.5.1 List comprehensions and generators

There are many situations where we need to perform operations involving nested uses of map, link and filter several times. The resulting expressions can be quite difficult to read despite their brevity, so we will introduce some special notation similar to that used in Miranda and first introduced in KRC (Turner, 1982). Although this notation is not part of the Standard ML syntax, it is a useful aid to thought in the early stages of program design. We illustrate an algorithm for converting the notation into Standard ML expressions after introducing it.

We will write:

$$[E \mid V_1 \in E_1]$$

where E is an expression which may involve free occurrences of the name V_1 and expression E_1 denotes a list. This is read as 'the list of values of E as the value of V_1 ranges over items of the list denoted by E_1'. For example:

$$[2 * x \mid x \in 1 \text{ upto } 20]$$

(read as 'the list of values 2 * x where x comes from 1 upto 20') describes the list of the first 20 positive even integers. The component of the form $V_1 \in E_1$ is called a **generator** since it is used to generate a list of values for

V_1 from the list denoted by E_1 and introduces the name V_1. The whole expression is called a **list comprehension** but the notation is also known as ZF notation (cf Turner, 1982) after the Zermelo-Fraenkel notation for sets. (The notation $\{E\,(x) \mid x \in S \text{ and } p\,(x)\}$ in Zermelo-Fraenkel set theory is used to mean 'the set of elements of the form E (x) such that x is an element of S and p (x) is true'.) As further examples, consider the function sum defined in 2.2.4 (this was defined in terms of given arguments g and x to produce the sum of the values g (y) for y between 0 and x). We can now express this quite succinctly with lists:

```
fun sum g x = sumlist [g y | y ∈ 0 upto x]
```

(Recall that 0 upto x produces [0, 1, . . . , x] when x is not negative. See Appendix 2 for a definition of upto.) Similarly take:

```
minval: (α × int → int) → (α → int) → α → int
```

which we wish to define so that minval g h x computes the minimum value of g (x, y) for y between 0 and h (x). (This function was mentioned in Exercise 2.10 as a generalization of minvalgh described in Exercise 1.14.) We can now define:

```
fun minval g h x = minlist [g (x, y) | y ∈ 0 upto h (x)]
```

Although the new notation is based on set notation, lists rather than sets are intended here because the items are assumed to be generated in a fixed order and repetitions are not excluded. The lists denoted by list comprehensions can be expressed with ordinary expressions as we will show in a moment, but the real power of the notation can best be seen when several generators are used as in:

$$[E \mid V_1 \in E_1;\ V_2 \in E_2;\ \cdots;\ V_n \in E_n]$$

Here, each of the local variables V_i ranges over the values of the corresponding lists E_i and E may involve free occurrences of all the V_is (which should be distinct of course). Furthermore each E_i may involve free occurrences of the preceding V_js $(1 \le j < i)$ so the intended meaning is that E_i may depend on the values taken by $V_1, V_2, \ldots, V_{i-1}$. For example:

```
[x * y div 2 | x ∈ 2 upto 20; y ∈ 1 upto x]
```

denotes the list:

```
[(2 * 1 div 2), (2 * 2 div 2), (3 * 1 div 2), (3 * 2 div 2),
(3 * 3 div 2), (4 * 1 div 2), . . . , (20 * 20 div 2)]
```

which is equal to [1, 2, 1, 3, 4, 2, . . . , 200]. These values are generated by taking the first value of x (i.e. 2) and letting y take the respective values in 1 upto x (which is [1, 2] in this case with x = 2). After this, the next value of x is taken (x = 3) and y ranges over 1 upto x again (i.e. over [1, 2, 3]) and so on until the last value of x (20) and the last value of y (20) are reached.

The generators may still be independent, of course, as in the following example which defines a function of two lists (x and y) producing all possible pairs of items from the first list with items from the second list (i.e. the *cartesian* product of the lists):

```
fun cart x y = [(a, b) | a ∈ x; b ∈ y]
```

So cart [1, 2, 3] [true, false] will evaluate to:

```
[(1, true), (1, false), (2, true), (2, false), (3, true), (3, false)]
```

Here is an example which is quite hard to express without ZF notation. The function perms calculates all the permutations of the items in a list, returning a list of lists:

```
infix --
fun perms [ ]  = [[ ]]
|   perms x    = [a :: y | a ∈ x; y ∈ perms (x--a)]
and    [ ]--a = [ ]
|   (b :: x)--a = if a = b then x else b :: (x--a)
```

The function (--) removes the first occurrence of an item in a list and has type $\alpha^=$ list $\times$ $\alpha^=$ $\rightarrow$ $\alpha^=$ list (because = is used as a comparison on items). The main function perms has type $\alpha^=$ list $\rightarrow$ $\alpha^=$ list list and works as follows. The list of permutations of [ ] is [[ ]] (and not [ ], because [ ] is a permutation of [ ]). For a non-empty list x, the permutations are calculated as all lists of the form a :: y where a is some item in x and y is a permutation of x with a removed.

3.5.2 Translation of list comprehensions

A formal description of the new notation will now be given by showing how any list comprehension can be replaced by an equivalent expression involving just function applications. We give some equivalences which can be used to convert an expression involving generators into one with fewer generators and ultimately no generators. After giving this relatively simple translation scheme, we give a slightly less obvious alternative which is more efficient. We make use of abstractions in the translation to save having to name the extra functions introduced as part of the conversion result. First:

$$[E \mid V_1 \in E_1] \equiv \text{map } (\textbf{fn } V_1 \Rightarrow E)\ E_1$$

because the application of **fn** $V_1 \Rightarrow E$ to each value in the list denoted by E_1 produces the list of values of E as the argument V_1 ranges over E_1 (which is exactly the same as the list denoted by $[E \mid V_1 \in E_1]$). When $n > 1$:

$$[E \mid V_1 \in E_1;\ V_2 \in E_2;\ \ldots;\ V_n \in E_n]$$
$$\equiv$$
$$\text{link (map } (\textbf{fn } V_1 \Rightarrow [E \mid V_2 \in E_2;\ \cdots\ V_n \in E_n])\ E_1)$$

because map (**fn** $V_1 \Rightarrow [E \mid \cdots]$) E_1 produces the list of values of $[E \mid \cdots]$ as V_1 ranges over E_1. Since this results in a list of lists as the generators V_2 to V_n vary, link is used to form a single list. The generators can thus be removed, one at a time from the right, using these equivalences. Removing more than one generator usually results in expressions which are difficult to read and this shows why the notation is so useful in designing a function. For example:

```
[a :: y | a ∈ x; y ∈ perms (x− −a)]
```

is expanded to:

```
link (map (fn a ⇒ map (fn y ⇒ a :: y) (perms (x− −a))) x)
```

This latter expression is quite difficult to follow even when rewritten as (for example):

```
let fun permswithhd a = map (cons a) (perms (x− −a))
in link (map permswithhd x) end
```

In fact, much more efficiently executable expressions can he derived for list comprehensions, but they are less obviously equivalent. A list comprehension with the general form:

$$[E \mid V_1 \in E_1;\ V_2 \in E_2;\ \cdots;\ V_n \in E_n]$$

is equivalent to the following expression:

```
reduce (fn V₁ ⇒ fn Z ⇒
   reduce (fn V₂ ⇒ fn Z ⇒
      . . .
```

```
reduce (fn Vn ⇒ fn Z ⇒
            E :: Z
        ) Z En
  . . .
    ) Z E2
        ) [ ] E1
```

where Z is a newly introduced variable not occurring elsewhere in the expression. This is in fact equivalent to the optimal form described by Wadler (in Peyton-Jones, 1987) where a formal derivation is given. It is optimal in the sense that the number of (::) operations performed is minimal and equal to the length of the final list. This should be compared to the earlier version which builds several lists and then uses link (and hence @) to rebuild new lists. (Each @ operation requires as many (::) operations as the length of the first of the pair of lists being appended.)

For a strict language like ML, however, there is a another form which sacrifices the cost of some (::) operations in order to minimize the space used during computation. For reasons which we discuss in Chapter 8, accumulate uses much less space than reduce but performs a similar task. If we replace each reduce by an accumulate (swapping the arguments to the abstractions), we get minimal use of space and (::) operations. However, the final list needs to be reversed to give the same order as the original, which doubles the number of (::) operations performed. A possible translation for strict languages is thus:

```
rev (
    accumulate (fn Z ⇒ fn V1 ⇒
        accumulate (fn Z ⇒ fn V2 ⇒
          . . .
              accumulate (fn Z ⇒ fn Vn ⇒
                              E :: Z
                          ) Z En
              . . .
                      ) Z E2
                  ) [ ] E1
    )
```

and the rev can of course be omitted whenever the order of the items in the resulting list does not matter.

We feel that it is important to give these details because we recommend the use of highly readable ZF notation whenever possible in writing programs. When the language does not support the notation, such expressions can be left as comments with an efficient alternative but less readable form inserted for execution. The efficient form is an incantation not intended for human consumption just as machine code generated by compilers is rarely read by humans. In subsequent examples we will use ZF notation and leave the translation as an exercise, but the examples in the ML appendix have been fully expanded to Standard ML.

3.5.3 Qualified generators

Another useful extension of the notation is to allow **conditions** (or **guards**) to qualify a generator so that items in the generated list not satisfying the condition are filtered out. Thus a generator could have the form:

$V_i \in E_i;\ B_i$

where condition B_i will be an expression of type bool, usually involving some of the variables from preceding generators ($V_1 \cdots V_i$). For example:

```
fun ordcart x y = [(a, b) | a ∈ x; b ∈ y; a < b]
```

defines ordcart x y to be the list of pairs of the form (a, b) such that a comes from x, b comes from y and a < b. So ordcart : int list → int list → (int × int) list produces pairs similarly to cart but excludes pairs which do not have a smaller integer in the first position, e.g.

```
ordcart [1, 2, 4] [1, 2, 3] = [(1, 2), (1, 3) (2, 3)]
```

Again, we can give equivalent non-ZF forms for such expressions by using filter (for example). Alternatively, the translation given in the previous subsection can be modified to deal with this case as follows. For each qualified generator of the form $V_i \in E_i;\ B_i$ the corresponding subexpression of the translated form:

```
accumulate (fn Z ⇒ fn Vi ⇒
        Expression
        ) · · ·
```

should be replaced by:

```
accumulate (fn Z ⇒ fn Vi ⇒
              if Bi then Expression else Z
        ) · · ·
```

3.6 Some simple applications of lists

We illustrate some applications of lists and higher order functions to solve some simple problems. More extensive applications are given in the next chapter.

3.6.1 A display tool

Table 3.3 describes a function called stringwith. It has a rather complicated type, but it is really just a simple generalization of implode (which concatenates a list of strings). The first argument for stringwith is a triple of strings which we use as a FRONT, SEP (separator) and BACK when concatenating the string list. FRONT and BACK are always part of the resulting string, but SEP only appears when the string list contains two or more items, in which case it is placed between adjacent items before concatenation.

Such a function can be extremely useful when we want to display lists of values. For example, suppose we have an integer list thelist = [20, 9, 8, 19], and suppose we want to display it as a set (using braces and commas):

{20, 9, 8, 19}

Table 3.3 The function stringwith.

A display tool:

stringwith : (string × string × string) → string list → string

Properties:

stringwith (FRONT, SEP, BACK) $[s_1, s_2, \ldots, s_n]$

$= \text{FRONT} \wedge s_1 \wedge \text{SEP} \wedge s_2 \wedge \text{SEP} \wedge \cdots \wedge s_n \wedge \text{BACK}$ $(n > 1)$

stringwith (FRONT, SEP, BACK) $[s_1] = \text{FRONT} \wedge s_1 \wedge \text{BACK}$

stringwith (FRONT, SEP, BACK) [ ] = FRONT ^ BACK

Definition:

```
fun stringwith (front, sep, back) list
      = let fun sepback  [ ]    = back
              | sepback  [a]    = a ^ back
              | sepback  (a :: x) = a ^ sep ^ sepback x
        in front ^ sepback list end
```

or as a stack like this:

```
TOP = 20
      9
      8
      19
```

We can simply combine stringwith, stringofint and map to produce these outputs from (respectively):

```
stringwith ("{ ", ",", " } ") (map stringofint thelist)
stringwith ("TOP = ", "\n        ", "\n") (map stringofint thelist)
```

In the first expression, we choose the front, separator and back to be, respectively, open brace, comma, and close brace. In the second expression we have "TOP = " at the front, a newline and six spaces separating items and a newline at the end. By using the empty string " ", it is possible to leave any or all of the three strings (FRONT, SEP, BACK) blank. In particular, stringwith (" ", " ", " ") has the same effect as implode. (SML users should note the comments in the SML appendix concerning the displaying of strings at a terminal.)

The definition of stringwith is not particularly complicated once the required behaviour is understood. The auxiliary function sepback distributes the separator between items in a list while concatenating and puts the back string at the end. This just leaves the front to be put on to the result of applying sepback. Unfortunately, the definition requires special consideration for lists with one item, so we cannot easily use our higher order functions which have more regular behaviour. (A variant where the separator and back are the same, making an item terminator, can be defined directly with accumulate or reduce.) Note that the third case in the definition of sepback is only applicable when the list contains at least two items (since we assume the second case overrides the third case when the argument has the form a :: [ ]).

We will develop a more sophisticated collection of display tools in the next chapter (character pictures). We leave it as an exercise to define:

linkwith : (α list $\times$ α list $\times$ α list) $\rightarrow$ α list list $\rightarrow$ α list

which generalizes link in the same way that stringwith generalizes implode.

3.6.2 Sorting lists

The following examples show how the operation of sorting a list of items into ascending order may be expressed in several different ways to give possibly different efficiency but the same overall result. That is to say the different definitions correspond to different algorithms computing the same function.

Instead of restricting ourselves to integer lists and assuming < (or the curried version lessthan) is to be used to order the items, we parameterize on the comparison operator to obtain a higher order sorting function. If we call this parameterized function sortwrt ('sort with respect to'), we can change the ordering and the types of lists to be sorted by simply changing the first argument for sortwrt. For example:

```
sortwrt lessthan [33, 2, 45, 78, 12, 1, 90] = [1, 2, 12, 33, 45, 78, 90]
sortwrt greater [33, 2, 45, 78, 12, 1, 90] = [90, 78, 45, 33, 12, 2, 1]
sortwrt dictless ["rat", "cat", "rabbit", "dog"]
                 = ["cat", "dog", "rabbit", "rat"]
```

where dictless s1 s2 = true if and only if s2 comes before s1 in dictionary order (also called lexical order).

Insert sort

The simplest **sorting algorithm** is based on insertions of items into an ordered list in a way which preserves the order. An item is inserted into the appropriate place in an ordered list by the function:

```
insertwrt : (α → α → bool) → α → α list → α list

fun insertwrt before item   [ ]      = [item]
|   insertwrt before item   (a :: x) = if before a item
                                       then item :: a :: x
                                       else a :: insertwrt before item x
```

The parameter before can be any (curried) comparison function and we have assumed our earlier convention that before a b means that b comes before a in the required ordering. Note that in order to represent a total ordering, before should be transitive, antisymmetric and either before a b = true or before b a = true for each a and b of the appropriate type. The definition of insertwrt and insert_sortwrt does not prevent inappropriate functions (with the correct type) being used, but the behaviour of the resulting applications will not be so predictable for such functions.

To sort an entire list, we insert each item in turn into a newly created ordered list, which is initially [ ]. As we scan the old list, the new list is gradually accumulated via insertions. This leads to the definition:

```
insert_sortwrt : (α → α → bool) → α list → α list
fun insert_sortwrt before = let fun insertin x a = insertwrt before a x
                            in accumulate insertin [ ] end
```

Insert sort is an inefficient algorithm because each insertion can (in the worst case) require a comparison of the new item with all the items in the list into which it is inserted. This worst case arises on every insertion if the original list is ordered already and on average, for lists of length n, the number of comparisons is of order n^2. Another well known algorithm is **quicksort** which is of order $n * \log n$ on average (but still of order n^2 in the worst case).

Quicksort

This method for sorting a list involves splitting the tail of the original list into two lists containing, respectively, the items less than the head of the list and the items greater than or equal to the head of the list. These resulting lists can be recursively sorted in the same way and then linked up (appended) with the head in the middle to form the final ordered list.

Let us begin with a non-parameterized version which only sorts integers:

```
sort : int list → int list

fun sort [ ]       = [ ]
|   sort (a :: x) = let val low = filter (lessthan a) x
                        and high = filter (non (lessthan a) ) x
                    in sort low @ [a] @ sort high
                    end
```

Now to generalize, we make this whole definition auxiliary to a main function which introduces the comparator as a parameter. We replace lessthan by before in the definition to make it clearer that this parameter need not be related to the function lessthan which we have previously defined. We will call the general function sortwrt:

```
sortwrt : (α → α → bool) → α list → α list

fun sortwrt before
    = let fun sort [ ]       = [ ]
          |   sort (a :: x) = let val low = filter (before a) x
                                  and high = filter (non (before a) ) x
                              in sort low @ [a] @ sort high
                              end
      in sort end
```

In Chapter 5 we will introduce a data type tree which enables us to express another sorting algorithm (treesort).

The final example in this section makes use of ZF notation rather than direct use of higher order functions. It is also another illustration of a program derived through reasoning about the particular problem.

3.6.3 Summands

Consider the following problem. We wish to produce for given integers s and n all the lists consisting of exactly n positive integers which add up to s. The numbers adding up to s are called **summands** of s, and we are to produce all the possible lists of summands (rather than just one). However, we only want ordered lists produced, so that similar lists like [1, 2, 2] and [2, 2, 1] and [2, 1, 2] are represented once only by the ordered version [1, 2, 2].

We will define a function summands : int → int → int list list so that for n > 0 and s > 0, summands s n returns the list of all the integer lists we want (e.g. summands 5 3 = [[1, 1, 3], [1, 2, 2]]). We begin by considering how the problem can be broken down into smaller problems, perhaps with a view to using recursion or basic list operations to solve the subproblems. In fact we will use recursion on the number of summands to be found. We note that when n > 1, each of the solutions we produce should have the form a :: y where y is a list of length n − 1. Furthermore, if a :: y adds up to s then y should add up to s − a. This means that y should be one of the lists of length n − 1 and sum s − a produced by summands (s − a) (n − 1) which should be a list of such lists. With care, we should be able to put finite bounds on sensible choices for the first item so that a recursive application of summands can be used. In forming the final list of solutions, we could either generate all lists of summands and then filter out the ordered ones, or better still generate only ordered lists in the first place (if this can be done simply). One way to ensure that only ordered lists are produced is to use an extra parameter to keep track of the minimum integer that can be chosen to begin a summand list. An auxiliary recursive function summandsover is defined with an extra integer argument m which is to be the minimum integer that can be placed in a solution list. This value is initially 1, but as a possible solution list is grown from the front, m records the latest integer chosen in order to ensure that the list remains ordered. Thus a :: y is a member of summandsover m s n if a ≥ m and y is a member of summandsover a (s − a) (n − 1) provided that n > 1 and s ≥ a. This gives us a recurrence of the form:

```
summandsover m s n = [a :: x | a ∈ m upto E;
                              x ∈ summandsover a (s − a) (n − 1) ]
```

for n > 1 where E is an expression which must be chosen to give an upper bound for possible choices of a(≥ m). One possible upper bound is s. A much better choice is s div n since if a is larger than this value, it is impossible to find n − 1 subsequent integers larger or equal to a and adding up to s.

In the case where the n = 1 we have the single solution [s] provided s is not too small (i.e. provided s ≥ m) and no solutions when s < m, that is:

```
summandsover m s 1 = if s < m then [ ] else [[s]]
```

In the final definition, however, we drop this test for s < m because we will ensure that summandsover is only ever applied to integers m, s, n > 0 with s ≥ m. The final definition is thus:

```
local
  fun summandsover m s 1  = [[s]]
  |   summandsover m s n  = [a :: x | a ∈ m upto (s div n);
                                  x ∈ summandsover a (s − a) (n − 1)]
in
  fun summands s n = if n < 1 or s < n
                     then [ ]
                     else summandsover 1 s n
end
```

To justify this definition, we need to show that summands s n is defined and correct for all integers s and n. This follows from a proof that summandsover m s n is defined and correct for all integers m, s, n > 0 such that s ≥ m ∗ n. This latter fact can be established by a straightforward proof involving induction on n ≥ 1 which we leave as an exercise. The key to the proof is really the observation that s ≥ m ∗ n whenever summandsover is called with arguments s, m, n.

In the final section of this chapter, we return to proofs of properties of programs to see how to use induction with lists. Before doing that, we just tidy up this example by combining summands and stringwith to produce pretty layouts of solutions to the summands problem. Each item in the list of solutions produced by summands s n is a list of integers which could be presented using:

```
val displaysol = stringwith ("solution : ", ",", "") ∘ (map (windowint' 4))
```

where windowint′ is a curried version of windowint defined in Chapter 1 to produce the string representation of an integer in a given space (**fun** windowint′ n m = windowint (n, m)). The entire list of solutions can then be presented with each one on a separate line by applying this function to each solution and then connecting the resulting strings with (say):

```
stringwith (
        "LISTS OF LENGTH" ^ nrep ^ " WITH SUM " ^ srep ^ " \n ",
        "\n"
        "\nTOTAL = " ^ total
          )
```

where nrep, srep and total are the string representations of n, s and the number of solutions, respectively. Collecting this together, we define:

```
fun display_summands s n
     = let val solutions = summands s n
           val total = stringofint (length solutions)
           val srep = stringofint s
           val nrep = stringofint n
       in stringwith (
           "LISTS OF LENGTH" ^ nrep " WITH SUM " ^ srep "\n",
           "\n",
           "\nTOTAL = " ^ total
                          ) (map displaysol solutions)
       end
```

The string produced by, for example, display_summands 6 3 would then look like this when printed out:

```
LISTS OF LENGTH 3 WITH SUM 6
solution:     1,     1,     4
solution:     1,     2,     3
solution:     2,     2,     2
TOTAL = 3
```

3.7 Inductive proofs and lists

3.7.1 Structural induction for lists

We will frequently need to establish that some property holds for all lists (for example, f x = g x for all x : α list). A natural way to do this is often to use some form of induction over lists, and a particularly natural form of induction for lists is **structural induction**. Structural induction makes direct use of the recursively described structure of data objects (in this case, lists) and has cases corresponding to the cases in the description of the type. So, if we take some arbitrary type T and consider lists of type T list, structural induction over these lists is expressed by the following:

Principle of structural induction for lists:

In order to prove that:

P (x) holds for all (well-defined, finite) lists x : T list

it is sufficient to prove that:

(1) (base case) P ([ ]) is true
(2) (step case) P (a :: y) follows from the assumption P (y) for all (well-defined) a : T and all (well-defined, finite) y : T list.

As usual, the assumption in (2) is referred to as the **induction hypothesis** (abbreviated as IH). The validity of this form of induction can be established using the more general well-founded induction discussed in Section 1.5.5. We need to restrict lists to being well-defined and finite so that we know that they are constructed from [ ] by a finite number of :: operations with elements of T. This induction rule is therefore a natural one for a strict interpretation of functions where all well-defined lists are finite. In Chapter 8, we show that a non-strict interpretation does not guarantee the finiteness of lists and this induction rule is no longer appropriate for establishing properties of values of type T list for some T. Until then, however, we will take well-definedness and finiteness as assumed in inductive proofs (i.e. *for all* should be read as *for all well-defined, finite*).

3.7.2 Example of structural induction

As an example, we prove that for all x : α list:

map f (map g x) = map (f ∘ g) x

for any (appropriately typed) functions f and g. First, for the base case, we calculate that:

(1) map f (map g [ ]) = map f [ ] = [ ] = map (f ∘ g) [ ]

using the definition of map. For the step case, we must show that:

(2) for any a : α and y : α list,
if map f (map g y) = map (f ∘ g) y is assumed (IH)
then map f (map g (a :: y)) = map (f ∘ g) (a :: y) follows.

Again, using the definition of map, we calculate that:

```
map f (map g (a :: y)) = map f (g a :: map g y)
                       = f (g a) :: map f (map g y)
                       = f (g a) :: map (f ∘ g) y          (by IH)
                       = (f ∘ g) a :: map (f ∘ g) y        (by definition of ∘)
                       = map (f ∘ g) (a :: y)              (by definition of map)
```

So, by structural induction the result is proved.

3.7.3 Generalizing the goal

It is quite common for an attempt to use structural induction to fail because the induction hypothesis is too weak to establish the required consequence. The usual remedy is to go back to the initial goal statement and to try to generalize it (making a stronger statement). A simple example of this follows.

We would like to prove that for all x, y : α list:

```
revonto y (rev x) = x @ y                                  (3.1)
```

where we assume the definitions:

```
fun [ ] @ y       = y
|   (a :: x) @ y = a :: (x @ y)
fun revonto x [ ]     = x
|   revonto x (a :: y) = revonto (a :: x) y
fun rev x = revonto [ ] x
```

A direct attempt to prove the goal (3.1) by structural induction on the list x begins to look feasible, until one gets to the step case and needs to show that (after some calculation):

```
revonto y (revonto [a] x) = a :: (x @ y)
```

using only the assumption (derived from the induction hypothesis) that:

```
revonto y (revonto [ ] x) = x @ y
```

at which point we are stuck. The problem is that revonto [ ] x or equivalently rev x needs to be generalized to revonto r x for any r : α list in the induction hypothesis. Going back to the goal (3.1), we see that we should generalize the left-hand side to revonto y (revonto r x) and, after a little thought, we see that the appropriate generalization of the goal is:

```
revonto y (revonto r x) = revonto (x @ y) r                (3.2)
```

Clearly, the original goal (3.1) follows from (3.2) by choosing r = [ ] in (3.2). That is:

```
revonto y (rev x) = revonto y (revonto [ ] x)
                  = revonto (x @ y) [ ]       (assuming (3.2) with r = [ ])
                  = x @ y
```

which proves (3.1). The problem of proving the more general goal (3.2) by structural induction on x now goes through easily and mechanically. We give the details for completeness:

(1) (base case) (x = [ ])
```
revonto y (revonto r [ ])
     = revonto y r                        (by definition of revonto)
     = revonto  ([ ] @ y)  r              (by definition of @)
```

(2) (step case) (x = a :: z)
```
revonto y (revonto r (a :: z))
     = revonto y (revonto (a :: r) z)
     = revonto  (z @ y)  (a :: r)         (by IH)
     = revonto  (a :: (z @ y))  r         (by definition of revonto)
     = revonto  ((a :: z) @ y)  r         (by definition of @)
```

By structural induction, the goal (3.2) is proved. Note that the inductive hypothesis is actually:

for all r : α list, revonto y (revonto r z) = revonto (z @ y) r

which justifies our use of a particular a :: r in place of r. If the reader finds this confusing, he/she can always rewrite the hypothesis in another equivalent form:

for all s : α list, revonto y (revonto s z) = revonto (z @ y) s

before substituting a :: r for s as the required special case.

The problem of finding the appropriate generalization of a goal which allows a smooth proof by induction is often the only imaginative step needed in simple proofs. The details can often be completed quite mechanically after the discovery of an appropriate generalization. Sometimes this discovery is not easy. For example, in attempting to prove (by structural induction) that:

```
rev (rev x) = x
```

for all x : α list, it is not, at first, easy to see that the appropriate generalization is (3.2) (as given in the previous example). By specializing (3.2) with y = r = [ ] we have that:

```
revonto [ ] (revonto [ ] x) = revonto ( [ ] @ x) [ ]
```

from which rev (rev x) = x follows easily.

In Chapter 5 we will show how to generalize structural induction for use with many other types (in addition to lists). Meanwhile, Chapter 4 provides some longer examples of programs which make use of the many operations on lists which we have introduced in this chapter.

EXERCISES

3.1 What types can be given (if any) to the following 'expressions':

```
[5, 8]          5 :: 8          [(5, 8)]
[[5], [8]]      ([5], [8])      5 :: [8]
(5, [8])        [5, [8]]        [5 :: [8]]
```

3.2 Give a definition of copy : int → α → α list (see Table 3.1 for a description of copy). Can you also define copy using ZF notation?

3.3 What are the principal types of f, g and h in the following definitions?

```
fun f a b c = if b c then a else a & c
and g a (b, c) = (a :: h b, h c)
and h x = copy x x
```

3.4 Describe some relationships between length and upto, explode and implode.

3.5 Define downto by analogy with upto for counting down from a higher to a lower number. Define fromto which unifies upto and downto (and is totally defined).

3.6 What do drop n x and front n x denote when n > length x and when n ≤ 0?

3.7 If we define:

```
fun select n = hd ∘ (drop (n − 1))
fun sublist n m = (front m) ∘ (drop (n − 1))
```

Describe the types and behaviour of select and sublist for all possible arguments.

3.8 Define a function back so that back n x produces the last n items of list x when $n \geq 0$ and length $x \geq n$. Look at alternative ways in which you might define back and discuss their relative merits (particularly with regard to arguments not satisfying the given constraints).

3.9 Use higher order list operations to define innerproduct so that:

$$\text{innerproduct } [x_1, x_2, \ldots, x_n] \, [y_1, y_2, \ldots, y_n] = x_1 * y_1 + x_2 * y_2 + \ldots + x_n * y_n$$

3.10 Define a variant of zip called splice which works with lists of different lengths and which simply appends the remaining tail of one argument list to the result when the other argument list runs out (i.e. when one list is [ ]). Similarly, define zip′ which simply throws away the remaining tail when one list runs out. What are the types of these variants?

3.11 Define functions similar to accumulate and reduce to operate on a function instead of a list of values so that it can be used to sum the values of the function and to find the minimum value of the function over a given range.

3.12 Given the following equivalence involving an operator et:

```
filter q ∘ filter p = filter (p et q)
```

deduce the type and an appropriate definition for et.

3.13 Use accumulate to define length and majority where majority counts the difference between the votes 'for' (true, say) and 'against' (false) from a bool list, e.g. majority [true, false, false] = ~1.

3.14 Redefine filter and map in terms of reduce (Figure 3.1 may help you).

3.15 When a map is followed by a reduce, two scans of lists are done, e.g. reduce g a (map f x) involves a scan of x to calculate map f x and a scan of this intermediate list with reduce to produce the final result.

Define a combined reducemap which does the map and reduce at the same time with one list scan.

3.16 Convert the following definition of sumprod, which calculates the sum and product of a list of integers at the same time, into a definition using accumulate (once):

```
fun sumprod [ ] = (0, 1)
|   sumprod (x :: y) = let val (a, b) = sumprod y
                       in (x + a, x * b) end
```

3.17 Looking at Figure 3.1, one might conclude that:

```
all p    = reduce (p_and) true (= accumulate (p_and) true)
exists p = reduce (p_or) false (= accumulate (p_or) false)
```

where p_and a b = p a & b, p_or a b = p a or b. Why might definitions based on these equivalences give less efficient programs?

3.18 Define linkwith by analogy with stringwith but where:

linkwith: (α list $\times$ α list $\times$ α list) $\rightarrow$ α list list $\rightarrow$ α list

3.19 Define transpose: α list list $\rightarrow$ α list list which when given a list of lists representing the rows of a matrix, returns a list of lists representing the rows of the transposed matrix (= columns of the argument matrix). What does your function do when the argument list contains lists of different lengths?

3.20 Redefine the quicksort algorithm so that low and high are collected together with one scan of the tail of the list.

3.21 Define a specialised version of sortwrt, setsortwrt which removes duplications while sorting. What is the type of setsortwrt?

3.22 Define a merge sort which is based on merging two sorted lists. (Hint: Convert the original list to a list of lists of length one. At each recursive step convert the current lists of sorted lists to a shorter list of sorted lists by merging them in pairs.)

3.23 Give simple equivalences for ZF expressions with guards using the function filter.

3.24 What does sum g x denote when x $<$ 0 assuming the definition in Section 3.5?

3.25 Modify the function summands (Section 3.6.3) so that 0 may appear in the resulting lists.

3.26 Prove the correctness of summands in the way suggested in Section 3.6.3. Prove also that when n * m = s (m ≥ 0 and n ≥ 1):

```
summandsover m s n = [copy n m]
```

using your definition of copy from Exercise 3.2.

3.27 Generalize the function summands to deal with all the combinations of coins and notes adding up to a fixed sum in some currency.

3.28 Define a predicate lexicalord on pairs of strings which asks whether or not they are in the correct dictionary (or lexical) order. Generalize this predicate to a function lex so that lex p defines an ordering on pairs of lists using p as the ordering for individual items in the lists. (lex should have type (α → α → bool) → (α list → α list → bool).)

3.29 Part of Pascal's triangle is depicted below. Each row is obtained in a very simple way from the previous row (involving additions of neighbouring pairs):

```
              1
             1 1
            1 2 1
           1 3 3 1
          1 4 6 4 1
        1 5 10 10 5 1
      1 6 15 20 15 6 1
    1 7 21 35 35 21 7 1
```

Define a function pascal : int → (int list) list so that pascal n forms the first n rows of such a triangle. Separately define a function of type (int list) list → string for displaying the triangle.

3.30 Prove the following using structural induction and/or other equivalences that have already been shown:

(a) revonto (as defined in Section 3.7.3) = accumulate consonto

(b) all p (filter p x) = true for all (well-defined, finite) lists x and predicate p

(c) reducemap (see Exercise 3.15) does the same as a reduce and a map

(d) x @ [ ] = x for all lists x

(e) @ is associative (i.e. (x @ y) @ z = x @ (y @ z))

(f) rev (x @ y) = rev y @ rev x for all lists x, y

(g) reduce f a x = accumulate (C f) a (rev x)

A proof of (g) is not so obvious so here is a hint you may wish to use. If you assume, from the definition of rev that rev (a :: z) = rev z @ [a] then a straightforward structural induction on x goes through but it requires an auxiliary result concerning accumulate with an argument list of the form x1 @ x2. This auxiliary result can be proved separately (by induction).

Chapter 4
Extended Examples: Pictures and Life

The following examples bring together some of the functions introduced in previous chapters to build some useful programs. The first example concerns *character pictures* which are a kind of poor-man's graphics. The second example is concerned with the calculation of generations for what J. H. Conway calls the *game of life*.

There are two particular aspects of these examples which we would like to draw attention to. First, we refrain from constructing a single monolithic function which we call a final program in both cases. Instead, we build a collection of tools (functions) which can be put together in various ways with ease. This style is encouraged by interactive programming languages which allow us to experiment with the tools which we have built in a simple and quick way. It would be relatively easy, if we were so inclined, to choose one particular composition of the tools (described by a single expression) and name this as the final program. However, this does not seem particularly useful when we wish to continue experimenting with the functions we have built.

A second aspect of these examples is that they indicate the need for a disciplined way of separating concerns so that larger problems can be conveniently broken into subproblems. In fact we will find that we are implicitly describing new types to solve the problem of modularity of design. This implicit construction of new types will be made explicit in Chapters 5 and 7.

4.1 Character pictures

With a functional language it is particularly easy to separate the main computation in a program from the processing of results for display at a terminal (or listing in a file or at a printer). We do not have the problem of having to mix print statements in with the main computation because we only have expressions not statements as program components. Instead of such a mix, we can usually define separately a main function which produces the results, and another pretty-printing function which formats the results and produces a final string (to be shown at a terminal, written to a file or printed out). The functions can simply be composed to produce the results in the required format. This has the particular advantage that some standard formatting operations can be defined for general purpose use in all programs so that output does not have to be designed from scratch for each new program.

In this example, we put together some string processing functions and list operations (particularly the higher order list operations) to build functions which are useful for displaying or tabulating results as **character pictures**. To help understand our notion of a character picture, the reader is encouraged to look at the examples in Figure 4.1 and to try to describe (informally) the arrangement of the text in each example.

The natural tendency is probably not to describe the text line by line as lists of characters, but rather to give a more hierarchical description of how the text might be constructed. In fact, in the implementation of pictures, we will use lists of strings of printable characters to represent the lines of a (character) picture. The operations for building pictures, on the other hand, should correspond to the hierarchical constructions one would naturally use to describe such pictures. Note that the list of strings can eventually be formed into a single string with newline characters to display the picture, but we will see that it is useful to delay doing this until a final picture is constructed so that the picture building operations are easy to define and use.

We have two tasks to perform in implementing pictures. One is to decide on a suitable basic collection of operations which allow us to construct pictures relatively easily. The other is to decide upon a convenient representation for pictures using the types of values we have introduced so far (integers, booleans, strings, tuples, lists, functions) which will allow us to implement the required operations. Usually, the former task should precede the latter since we can only make a good choice of representation when we know what is to be implemented. However, we cannot easily judge what we want implemented until we have had a chance to experiment and find which operations are more useful. Such experimenting requires an implementation. This chicken and egg situation can be resolved by building **prototypes** with the expectation that we may well change our minds about the collection of operations and

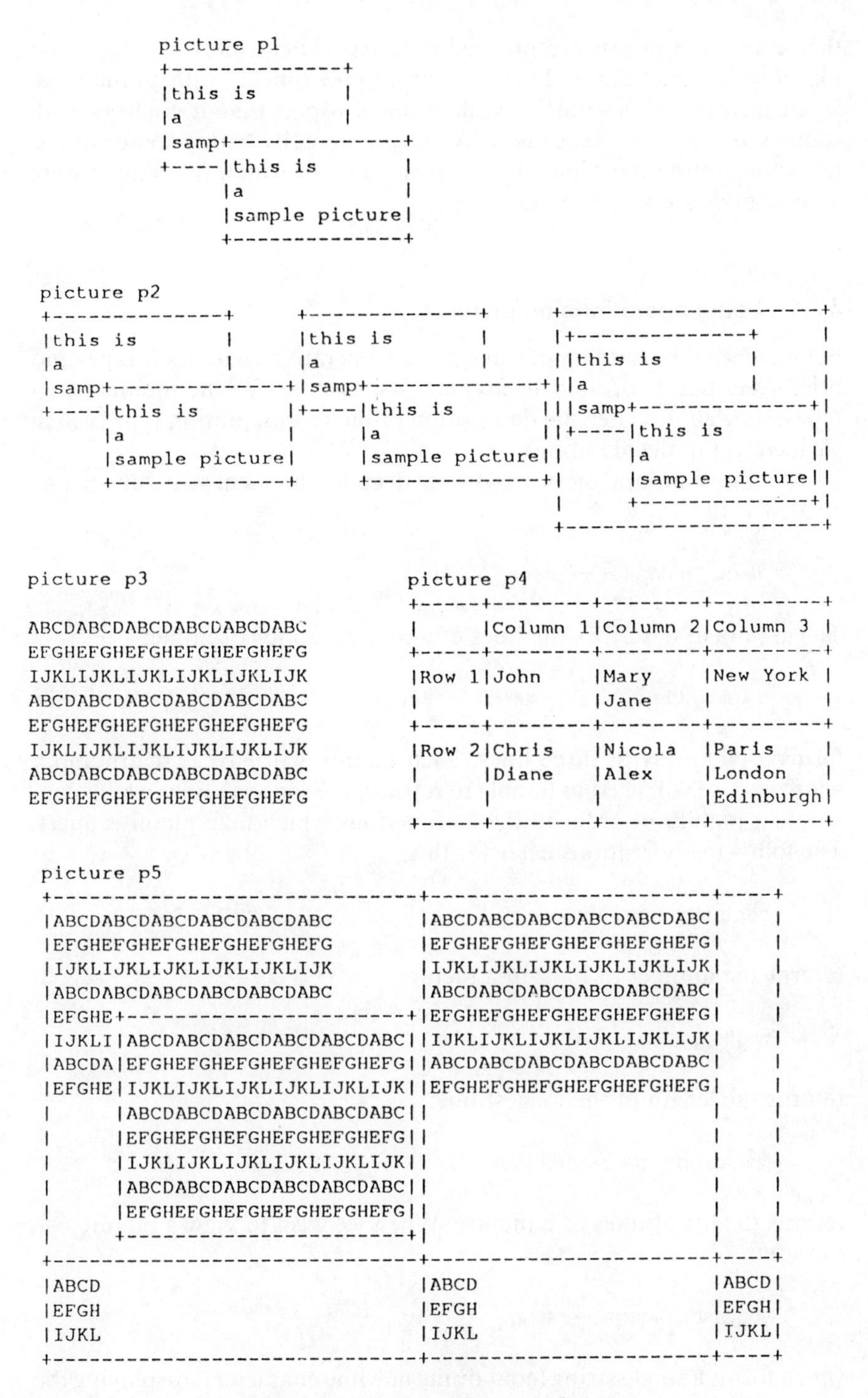

Figure 4.1 Some (character) pictures.

the representations as we proceed and experiment. Our ability to use higher order functions and to create prototypes quickly with a functional language makes this a much less daunting prospect than it might be with some, more verbose, languages. We begin, here, by listing some suggestions for useful operations on pictures, some of which operations were arrived at as a result of experiments.

4.1.1 Some operations on pictures

Below we give a summary of some picture operations with their types and brief descriptions of their behaviour. We assume, for the moment that type picture abbreviates the description of the representation type (which we have yet to decide upon).

Simple atomic pictures with no deep hierarchical structure can be created with:

```
mkpic : string list → picture
```

The argument describes the lines of a picture, so for example:

```
mkpic ["this is", "a", "sample picture"]
```

forms a picture with three lines. Each picture will have a depth and a width and we will need to be able to retrieve the separate lines which constitute a picture in order to define functions which take pictures apart. The following operations cater for this:

```
depth : picture → int
```

returns the number of lines in a picture;

```
width : picture → int
```

returns the length of the longest line;

```
linesof : picture → string list
```

returns the list of lines of a picture. When we wish to view a picture, we can use:

```
showpic : picture → string
```

which forms a single string (containing newline characters) displaying the lines of a picture. The other operations all produce a picture as result;

they allow us to create new pictures from existing ones:

```
frame : picture → picture
```

produces a picture by surrounding the argument picture with a box drawn using "−" and "|" (and "+" at the corners);

```
row : picture list → picture
```

forms a single picture by putting the pictures in the argument list side by side;

```
column : picture list → picture
```

forms a single picture by lining up the pictures in the argument list as a column;

```
rowwith : (string * string * string) → picture list → picture
```

is a generalization of row. An expression such as rowwith (frnt, sep, bck) piclist forms a picture similarly to row, but the pictures are separated by (a column of copies of) the string sep. Copies of frnt are also added to the left-hand edge and copies of bck to the right-hand edge. This is similar in structure to the function stringwith described in the previous chapter (see Table 3.3). Any of the strings can of course be "" – the null string.

```
colwith : (string * string * string) → picture list → picture
```

is similar to rowwith but forms a column. The three strings are used for the top, separator and bottom respectively, and if any of them consists of more than one character, a line for each character is formed (i.e. the strings are written downwards and duplicated along a row to the width of the final picture).

```
indent : int → picture → picture
```

when applied to n ≥ 0 and a picture pic, forms a picture with n leading spaces before each line of pic.

```
lower : int → picture → picture
```

when applied to n ≥ 0 and a picture pic, forms a picture with n blank lines followed by the lines of pic.

```
header : string → picture → picture
```

forms a picture from a string (the heading) and another picture by placing the heading above the picture with a line of "~" underneath.

```
padside : int → picture → picture
```

produces a picture from integer (n) and picture (pic) by extending the lines of pic if they are shorter than n with an appropriate number of spaces.

```
padbottom : int → picture → picture
```

similarly extends the number of lines in a picture pic to a given integer using blank lines at the bottom.

```
nullpic : picture
```

denotes the simplest picture of all (with no lines).

The final four operations (table, paste, cutfrom and tilepic) are probably the most interesting and perform more sophisticated tasks. They can be built from the above operations:

```
table : (picture list list) → picture
```

This forms a table when supplied with a list of the rows of the table. Each row should be a list of pictures. The pictures p4 and p5 in Figure 4.1 are built with this operation.

```
paste : int → int → picture → picture → picture
```

paste n m pic1 pic2 places pic2 on top of pic1 at the point after n characters down and m characters along. It is robust in that it works for negative n and m and when pic1 is too small.

```
cutfrom : picture → int → int → int → int → picture
```

cutfrom pic n m d w produces a picture of depth d and width w cut from pic starting at the point after n characters down and m characters along. None of the integers are required to be positive.

```
tilepic : int → int → picture → picture
```

tilepic d w pic produces a picture with depth d and width w which is made up of copies of pic (the *tile* picture). For example, picture p3 in Figure 4.1 is constructed with tilepic.

To illustrate some of these operations, consider the pictures in Figure 4.1. If we first define:

```
val p0 = frame (mkpic ["this is", "a", "sample picture"])
```

then p1 and p2 are constructed as follows:

```
val p1 = paste 3 5 p0 p0
val p2 = row [p1, p1, frame p1]
```

The third picture is constructed from a tile picture called alpha:

```
val alpha = mkpic ["ABCD", "EFGH", "IJKL"]
val p3 = tilepic 8 23 alpha
```

The fourth picture is a table made from 12 basic pictures arranged in 3 rows. We leave it to the reader to complete the details of the basic pictures. The final definition of p4 has the form:

```
val p4 = table [[nullpic, bp1, bp2, bp3],
                [bp4, bp5, bp6, bp7],
                [bp8, bp9, bp10, bp11]]
```

where bp1, . . . , bp11 are basic pictures constructed with mkpic.

The final picture is also a table defined as follows:

```
val p5 = table [[paste 4 5 p3 (frame p3), p3],
                [alpha, alpha, alpha]]
```

Note that the first row only has two pictures specified, so a blank picture appears in the final table to keep it rectangular.

Most of the basic operations are only really useful in defining the more sophisticated ones such as table. One we have not illustrated, however, is header. An expression such as header "HEADING" p3 would produce:

```
HEADING
~~~~~~~~~~~~~~~~~~~~~~~
ABCDABCDABCDABCDABCDABC
EFGHEFGHEFGHEFGHEFGHEFG
IJKLIJKLIJKLIJKLIJKLIJK
ABCDABCDABCDABCDABCDABC
EFGHEFGHEFGHEFGHEFGHEFG
IJKLIJKLIJKLIJKLIJKLIJK
ABCDABCDABCDABCDABCDABC
EFGHEFGHEFGHEFGHEFGHEFG
```

The same effect could be achieved by:

```
colwith (" ", "~", " ") [mkpic ["HEADING"], p3]
```

which makes a picture with the heading and then arranges the heading and p3 in a column using "~" as a separator. In fact we define:

```
fun header h p = colwith (" ", "~", " ") [mkpic [h], p]
```

4.1.2 Implementing pictures

We will actually represent a picture with a triple of type int × int × string list so that (d, w, x) contains the depth (d), width (w) and list of lines of the picture (x). We will also pad out the lines with spaces to the width of the longest line when we make a picture (so pictures are rectangular rather than ragged). Some alternatives we might have used in the representation are: (1) ragged rather than rectangular lists of strings (i.e. of differing lengths) for the lines, (2) exclusion of the width and depth (which could be calculated when needed rather than precalculated) and (3) a single string with newline characters (from which the lines, width and depth could be calculated if required). Most of the operations mentioned above turn out to be more efficient with the chosen representation (but even better representations may be possible with the richer collection of types introduced in subsequent chapters).

Table 4.1 gives the implementation of the basic picture operations using the chosen representation. Note that we have written:

```
type picture = (int × int × string list)
```

which is a Standard ML declaration of a type abbreviation. In general, a declaration of the form:

```
type Tname = Texp
```

introduces Tname as an abbreviation for the type described by Texp. It is important to realize that we are not introducing new types with such declarations. We are merely abbreviating descriptions of types we have already seen.

There are a small number of auxiliary functions used which have not yet been defined. For example:

```
linkwith : (α list × α list × α list) → α list list → α list
```

was described in Exercise 3.18 as being similar to stringwith. The expression:

```
linkwith (front, sep, back) llist
```

denotes the list formed by linking together the lists in llist (a list of lists) but with a copy of the list sep between each one and with front and back adjoined to the ends of the final list. The function maxposlist : int list → int is similar to maxlist but returns 0 for any list not containing positive integers, including [ ]. The function dashes : int → string returns a string of "-" 's of the given size. These latter two functions are simply defined by:

```
val maxposlist = accumulate max 0
fun dashes n = implode (copy n "-")
```

We explain the construction of some of the more complicated definitions appearing in Table 4.1.

The function mkpic pads the lines and calculates the depth and width. The size of each line need not be the same, so the list of sizes is recorded as the shape. The final width (finalw) is the size of the longest line (i.e. maxposlist shape). The lines are processed to extend them to this size as necessary by 'zipping' an extend function along the list of lines and the list of their sizes (shape).

In the definitions for padside and padbottom, spaces and (respectively) blank lines are added to make the width/depth up to the required size. However, the picture is returned unaltered if the integer argument is too small. These functions are used in the definitions of rowwith and colwith to extend pictures before forming a row or column so that the resulting list of lines is again rectangular rather than ragged.

The function colwith works as follows. Given arguments (f, s, b) and piclist, first the width of the widest picture in piclist is calculated as w′. Each character in the strings f, s, b needs to be duplicated to form a line of width w′. Thus flines is the list of lines formed by duplicating each of the characters in f, slines is the list of lines formed by duplicating each of the characters in s and blines is the list of lines formed by duplicating each of the characters in b. The final list of lines (sl′) is formed by linking these in with the lines of each picture (padded to width w′).

The function rowwith is very similar to colwith. In both functions we need to take care of the case when all pictures are nullpic or the list of pictures is [ ]. With all the operations we are careful to ensure that any picture formed as a triple (d, w, sl) satisfies the constraints of the representation, namely that:

```
d = length sl
member sl s   implies   size s = w
```

The definitions of the more sophisticated picture operations are discussed next.

Table 4.1 Definitions of basic picture operations.

```
type picture = (int × int × string list)

fun mkpic linelist
    = let val d = length linelist
          val shape = map size linelist
          val finalw = maxposlist shape
          fun extend line len = if len < finalw
                                then line ^ spaces (finalw − len)
                                else line
          val extendedlines = zip extend linelist shape
      in (d, finalw, extendedlines) end

fun depth (d, w, sl) = d
fun width (d, w, sl) = w
fun linesof (d, w, sl) = sl
val nullpic = (0, 0, [ ])

fun padside n (d, w, sl)
    = if n ≤ w then (d, w, sl)
               else (d, n [s ^ spaces (n − w) | s ∈ sl])
fun padbottom n (d, w, sl)
    = if n ≤ d then (d, w, sl)
               else (n, w, sl @ copy (n − d) (spaces w))

fun rowwith fsb piclist
    = let val d' = maxposlist (map depth piclist)
      in if d' = 0
         then nullpic
         else let val blocks = map (linesof ∘ padbottom d') piclist
                  fun mkline n = stringwith fsb (map (select n) blocks)
                  val sl' = map mkline (1 upto d')
                  val w' = size (hd sl')
              in (d', w', sl') end
      end
val row = rowwith ("", "", "")

fun colwith (f, s, b) piclist
    = let val w' = maxposlist (map width piclist)
          val flines = map (implode ∘ (copy w')) (explode f)
          val slines = map (implode ∘ (copy w')) (explode s)
          val blines = map (implode ∘ (copy w')) (explode b)
          val sl' = linkwith (flines, slines, blines)
                             (map (linesof ∘ padside w') piclist)
          val d' = length sl'
      in (d', w', sl') end
val column = colwith ("", "", "")
```

Table 4.1 *(Cont.)*

```
fun indent n (d, w, sl)
   = if n < 1 then (d, w, sl)
              else (d, w + n, map (concat (spaces n)) sl)
fun lower n (d, w, sl)
   = if n < 1 then (d, w, sl)
              else (d + n, w, copy n (spaces w) @ sl)

fun frame pic
   = let val pic' = rowwith ("|", " ", "|") [pic]
         val edge = mkpic [ "+" ^ dashes (width pic) ^ "+" ]
     in column [edge, pic', edge] end

fun showpic (d, w, sl) = stringwith (" ", "\n", "\n") sl
```

4.1.3 Tables of pictures

The operation table produces rectangular tables which may be used for tabulating results for display and takes a list of picture lists as argument. Each picture list constitutes a row of the table, and the result is a single picture with the rows and columns aligned and separated by −, | and + at intersection points.

There are two subproblems which need to be tackled before such a table can be produced. First, the picture lists may have different lengths, in which case we should add an appropriate number of blank pictures to ensure that the table keeps its rectangular shape. Secondly, the individual pictures may have different sizes so we need to pad them out appropriately. We do not need all pictures to have the same size but, for any row, all the pictures should be padded to the depth of the deepest picture in that row and for any column, all the pictures should be padded to the width of the widest picture in that column. This will ensure proper alignment, and the resulting widths of the columns can be used to calculate the **spacer** (which is built from − and +) and put between each picture row. The spacer and pictures are then easily put together using colwith and rowwith. The definition is given in Table 4.2 with the definitions of paste and cutfrom (see below). The list of lists of pictures is made rectangular with a function:

mkrect : α list list → α → α list list

The second argument (in this case nullpic) is used to fill in the short lists. This same function could also be used in the definition of mkpic with spaces to fill in the lines. However, we preferred to write a special version there which avoids exploding and imploding strings unnecessarily. (It is

Table 4.2 Definitions of table, paste, cutfrom and tilepic.

```
fun table [ ] = nullpic
  | table piclistlist
        = let val newpics = mkrect piclistlist nullpic
              val picwidths = map (map width) newpics
              val colwidths = map maxposlist (transpose picwidths)
              val picrowlists = map (zip padside colwidths) newpics
              val tablerows = map (rowwith ("|", "|", "|")) picrowlists
              val sep = stringwith ("+", "+", "+") (map dashes colwidths)
              val sl' = linkwith ([sep], [sep], [sep]) (map linesof tablerows)
              val d' = length sl'
              val w' = size (hd sl')
          in (d', w', sl') end

fun paste n m pic1 pic2
   = if n < 0  then paste 0 m (lower (~n) pic1) pic2 else
     if m < 0 then paste n 0 (indent (~m) pic1) pic2 else
                   paste0 n m pic1 pic2
and paste0 n m pic1 pic2
   = let val pic1' = padbottom (n + depth pic2) (padside (m + width pic2) pic1)
         fun stringop line line' = implode (spliceat m overlay
                                                        (explode line)
                                                        (explode line'))
         val sl' = spliceat n stringop (linesof pic1') (linesof pic2)
         val w' = if null sl then 0 else size (hd sl')
         val d' = length sl'
     in (d', w', sl') end
and spliceat n f x y = if n < 1 then splice f x y
                                else hd x :: spliceat (n - 1) f (tl x) y
and overlay a b = b
fun cutfrom pic n m a b
   = if n < 0  then cutfrom (lower (~n) pic) 0 m a b  else
     if m < 0 then cutfrom (indent (~m) pic) n 0 a b  else
     if a < 0  then cutfrom pic (n + a) m (~a) b       else
     if b < 0  then cutfrom pic n (m + b) a (~b)       else
                   cut0 pic n m a b
and cut0 pic n m a b
   = let val pic' = padbottom (n + a) (padside (m + b) pic)
         fun edit str = substring (m + 1) b str
         val newsl = map edit (sublist (n + 1) a (linesof pic'))
     in  (a, b, newsl) end

fun tilepic d w tile
   = let val dt = depth tile
         val wt = width tile
         val ndeep = (d + dt - 1) div dt
         val nacross = (w + wt - 1) div wt
         val col = column (copy ndeep tile)
         val excess = row (copy nacross col)
     in cutfrom excess 0 0 d w end
```

better to use mkrect when string is equivalent to char list.) The definition of mkrect is:

```
fun mkrect listlist default
  = let val shape = map length listlist
        val maxrow = maxposlist shape
        fun extend len list
          = if len < maxrow
              then list @ (copy (maxrow − len) default)
              else list
    in zip extend shape listlist end
```

Another auxiliary operation:

```
transpose : α listlist → α listlist
```

is used to convert a list of rows into a list of columns which we define here:

```
fun transpose [ ]        = [ ]
|   transpose listlist  = if exists null listlist
                          then [ ]
                          else (map hd listlist)
                                 :: transpose (map tl listlist)
```

Incidentally, the operation frame could now be redefined in terms of table as:

```
fun frame picture = table [[picture]]
```

4.1.4 Picture pasting and cutting

The picture operation paste allows us to paste one picture in front of another at chosen coordinates, thus possibly obscuring part of the underlying picture, and cutfrom can be used to cut out a part of a picture. In defining paste : int → int → picture → picture → picture we begin by defining paste0 (with the same type) which assumes that the integer coordinates (m and n respectively) are both non-negative, so that the front picture (the last argument) is placed with its top left corner just below the mth line starting just after the nth character from the top left corner of the back picture. We must take care to ensure that the back picture is padded appropriately in case the coordinates take the front picture beyond the bounds of the back picture. First, however, we need to decide how the overlaying can be done. Roughly speaking, it will involve taking an appropriate row from each picture and splicing the characters of one row into an appropriate place in the other row, displacing any characters already there. There are two cases to consider depending on the lengths of the lines (see Figure 4.2). Abstracting away from the details, we solve this problem by introducing a higher order operation which can be re-used on the lists of lines of two pictures as well as just the lists of characters in the individual lines.

The operation splice is very similar to zip and takes a (curried) binary function along with two lists to be *joined* element by element using the binary function. The difference is that if one list is shorter than the other, the remainder of the longer list is kept at the end of the result using splice (whereas zip would be undefined). The type of splice is not as general as zip, it is:

$$\text{splice} : (\alpha \rightarrow \alpha \rightarrow \alpha) \rightarrow \alpha \text{ list} \rightarrow \alpha \text{ list} \rightarrow \alpha \text{ list}$$

Once this is defined, we use it to define spliceat, which takes an integer argument (n) as well as a function and two lists, and counts n elements along the first list before performing the splice (n should not be negative). The definitions of splice and spliceat are:

```
fun splice f [ ] y = y
  | splice f x [ ] = x
  | splice f (a :: x) (b :: y) = f a b :: splice f x y

fun spliceat 0 f x        y = splice f x y
  | spliceat n f (a :: x) y = a :: spliceat (n − 1) f x y
  | spliceat n f [ ]      y = error "spliceat n f [ ]"
```

The overlaying of one string on another can then be done using spliceat with an appropriate integer, the splice function overlay and the two lines (exploded into lists of characters). overlay is defined by:

```
fun overlay a b = b
```

and just covers a character (a) coming from the first line by a character (b) coming from the second line. For a given n, if the operation on two lines is called stringop, say, then the pasting of one picture on another can be performed by spliceat again but using stringop as the binary function on lines of the pictures (see Figure 4.2).

Finally we extend the previous description for pasting one picture (p1, say) on another picture (p2, say) at coordinates (m, n) to allow for the cases when m and n are negative. It is reasonable to allow negative coordinates so that the front picture can overlap to the left and above the back picture as in Figure 4.3. This is easily accommodated in the final function paste which checks to see if m or n are negative, and if so, lowers

(a)

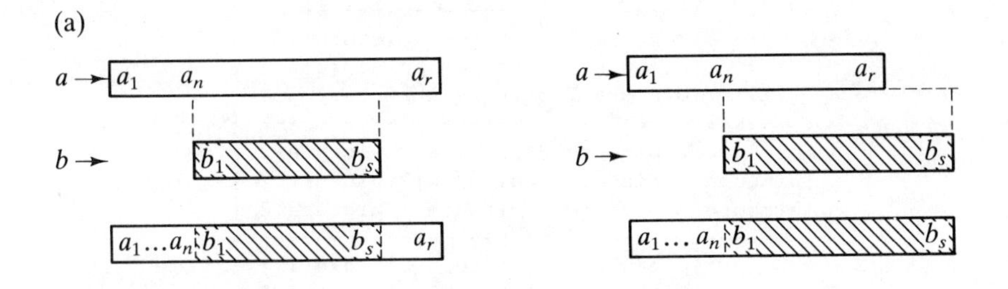

(b)

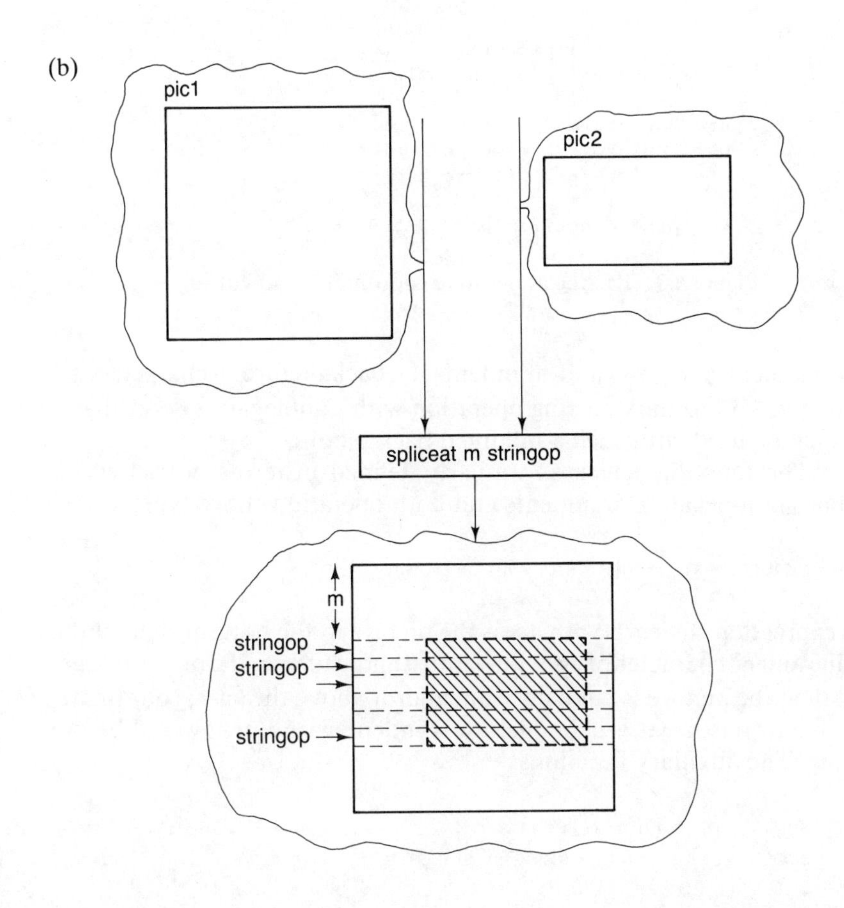

Figure 4.2 (a) Splicing line $b = [b_1, \ldots, b_s]$ onto line $a = [a_1, \ldots, a_r]$ at n when $n + s \leqslant r$ and when $n + s > r$ (using function stringop = spliceat n overlay). (b) Splicing two pictures together using stringop on the lines.

```
        +--------------------------------+
        |picture 1 picture 1 picture 1 |
        |picture 1 picture 1 picture 1 |
        |picture 1 picture 1 picture 1 |
+----------------------------------------+
|picture 2 picture 2 picture 2 picture 2 |
|picture 2 picture 2 picture 2 picture 2 |
|picture 2 picture 2 picture 2 picture 2 |
+----------------------------------------+
        |picture 1 picture 1 picture 1 |
        |picture 1 picture 1 picture 1 |
        +--------------------------------+

val pic3 = paste 4 ~8 pic1 pic2


   |picture 1 picture 1 pictur
   |picture 1 picture 1 pictur
------------------------------
ure 2 picture 2 picture 2 pict
ure 2 picture 2 picture 2 pict
ure 2 picture 2 picture 2 pict

val pic4 = cutfrom pic3 2 5 6 30
```

Figure 4.3 Pasting at negative coordinates and cutting.

the back picture ~m rows and/or indents the back picture ~n characters accordingly. An ordinary pasting operation with non-negative coordinates can then be used with such a modified back picture.

The function cutfrom is similarly defined in terms of cut0 which assumes non-negative arguments and both operations have type:

picture → int → int → int → int → picture

The expression cutfrom pic m n d w is the picture to the bottom right of the mth line and n^th^ character of pic with depth d and width w. If d or w are negative, then the picture is cut back from and/or above the (m, n) coordinate, and if m or n is negative, the picture is indented and/or lowered before cutting. The auxiliary functions:

sublist : int → int → α list → α list
substring : int → int → string → string

are defined when the integer arguments (n, m say) are respectively positive and non-negative and the sublist (respectively substring) beginning at the nth item with length (size) m exists. They are defined as follows:

fun sublist n m x = front m (drop (n − 1) x)
fun substring n m s = implode (sublist n m (explode s))

Note the convention here is that items in strings and lists are numbered from 1. (Some people use the convention that the frontmost item is the 0th item.)

4.1.5 Tiling a picture

The function tilepic : int → int → picture → picture which makes a tiled picture of a given size from a basic tile is easily constructed using row and column. If the given tile has depth dt and width wt and the required depth and width of the resulting picture are d and w, then we first calculate how many tiles we need down and across:

down we need ndeep = (d + dt − 1) div dt
across we need nacross = (w + wt − 1) div wt

These round up to the nearest whole number above or equal d/dt and w/wt respectively. The ndeep is used to make a column with copies of the tile and the nacross is used to make a row of copies of the column. Finally the resulting picture is trimmed down to the required shape (see the definition in Table 4.2).

The implementations of picture operations should be regarded as prototypes. Many optimizations could be introduced. Furthermore, the operations could be made more robust. For example, pictures containing control characters are not catered for. Rather than 'hack out' repairs for special cases, the prototypes should be used to study the deficiencies, optimizations and, possible generalizations before going on to design a final version with a special *abstract type* for pictures. (Abstract types are described in Chapter 7.)

We hope that these pictures also provide a stepping stone for designing and constructing more general graphical output at a graphics terminal. The reader is referred to Henderson (1982a) for more information about functionally described graphics pictures.

4.2 Game of life

The next example concerns implementing the *game of life* which was originally invented by J.H. Conway around 1969. Although this is referred to as a game, it is really the study of phenomena which can be observed in evolving configurations of **populations**. (It can also be regarded as a special case of **cellular automata** with two states.)

We begin with a board divided into squares (*cells*). Cells are regarded as having eight neighbours which are the immediate adjacent

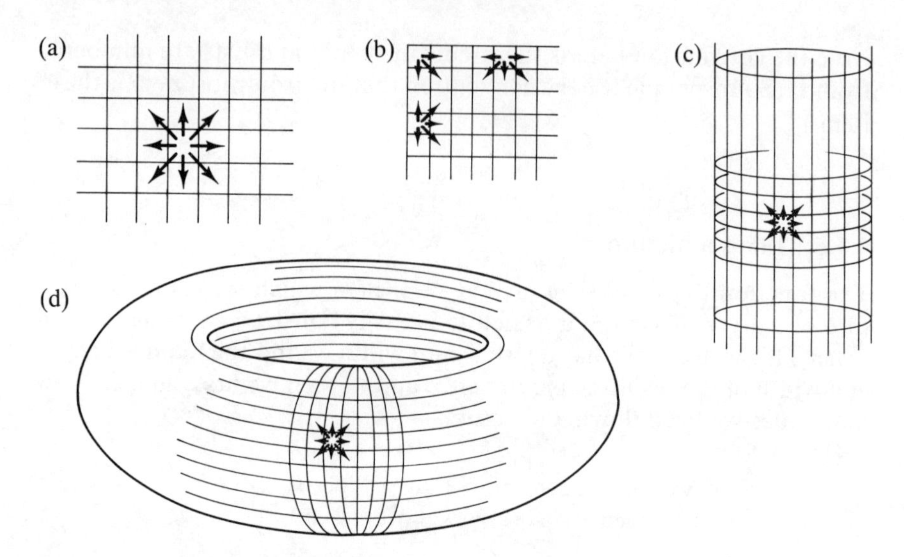

Figure 4.4 Boards, cells and neighbours. (a) All cells have eight neighbours (infinite board). (b) Edge cells may have fewer neighbours on a bounded board. (c) Wraparound in one direction forms a cylindrical board. (d) Wrap-around in two directions forms a toroidal board with a finite number of cells.

cells including those on the diagonals (see Figure 4.4). The board may be infinite or it may be a finite rectangle (in which case the neighbours of cells at the edge are fewer) or it may be cyclic (see Figure 4.4). Cyclic boards can be thought of as rectangles where the neighbours of cells at the edge include corresponding cells from the opposite edge.

In a particular configuration or **generation**, each cell is either **alive** or **dead**. From any such generation, a next generation can be calculated according to some preset rules which are described in Table 4.3. This means that from any initial configuration, we can calculate subsequent generations and observe how the patterns evolve. An example evolution is shown in Figure 4.5. We will again provide tools for exploring rather than a single function or program. In particular we will provide: a function to calculate the next generation from a given generation; a means of displaying generations; and a means of describing initial generations.

4.2.1 Representing a generation

In any particular generation, we just need to record which are the live cells and which are dead cells. We will assume that the number of live cells of a generation is finite, but we do not restrict ourselves to any particular upper bound for the size of a population (except when the board is finite). This leads us to a particularly convenient representation of

Table 4.3 Rules for calculating the next generation

(1) The next generation is the union of the survivors and the newborn, calculated simultaneously from the live cells (squares) of the current generation.

(2) A live cell is a *survivor* in the next generation if it has *either two or three* live neighbours in the current generation. (It dies from loneliness or overcrowding otherwise.)

(3) A dead cell becomes a *newborn*, live cell in the next generation if it has *exactly three* live neighbours in the current generation.

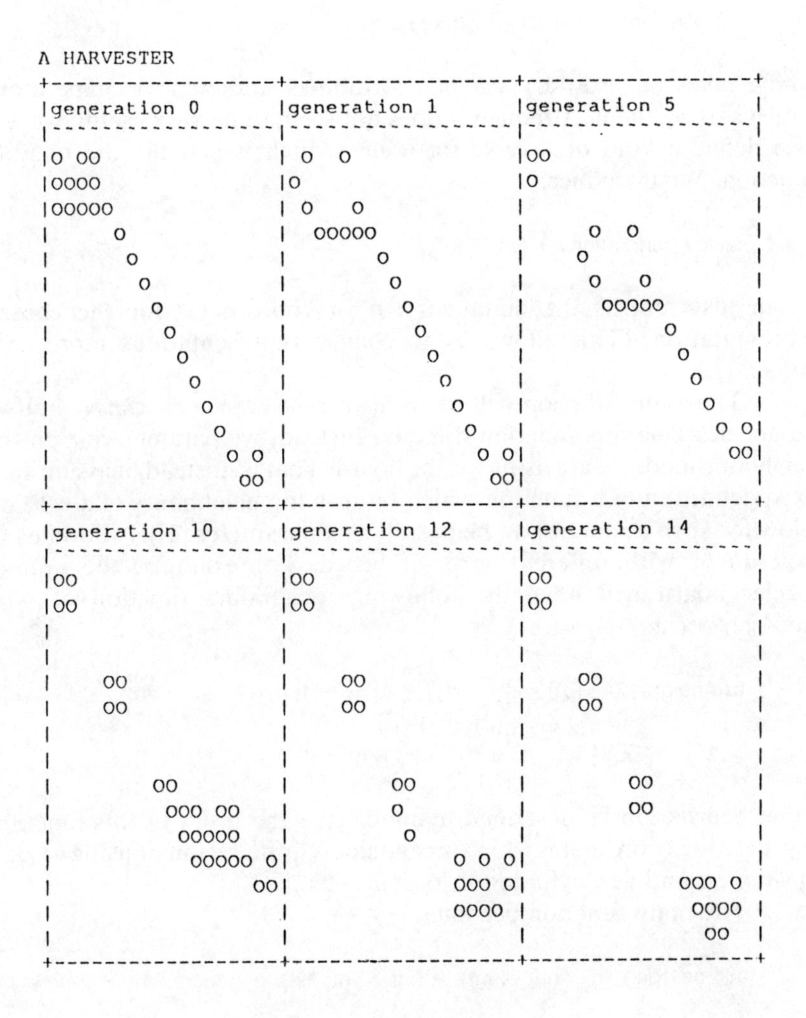

Figure 4.5 Example generations.

a generation as a list of coordinates of the live cells. However, for convenience of calculation, we will assume the additional constraint that the list is sorted and that duplicated coordinates are not present. The sorting order will be lexical order for pairs of integers; that is, (x1, y1) is less than (x2, y2) if either $x1 < x2$ or $x1 = x2$ and $y1 < y2$. We introduce the abbreviation:

```
type generation = (int × int) list
```

for convenience. We will also define a function:

```
mkgen : (int × int) list → generation
```

which takes an arbitrary list of coordinates and removes repetitions whilst sorting them. Although it does not seem to be very useful, we will also define a kind of inverse for mkgen which is actually the identity function. We introduce:

```
alive : generation → (int × int) list
```

which just returns the argument list of coordinates for the chosen representation. (This allows us to change representations more conveniently.)

The main function will be nextgen : generation → generation, but we do not describe this function directly. Instead, we parameterize on the neighbourhoods we are using for the board. That is, instead of assuming a fixed definition of a function which returns the neighbours of a cell, we allow for such a function to be passed as a parameter. This allows us to experiment with different sorts of board. For example, the infinite regular board will have the following neighbours function of type (int × int) → (int × int) list:

```
fun neighbours (i, j) = [(i - 1, j - 1), (i - 1, j), (i - 1, j + 1),
                         (i, j - 1), (i, j + 1),
                         (i + 1, j - 1), (i + 1, j), (i + 1, j + 1)]
```

Other boards can be described by modifying the result of this function (e.g. deleting coordinates which are outside a finite region or using n mod k to wrap around as a cylinder or torus).

The main function becomes:

```
mk_nextgen_fn : ( (int × int) → (int × int) list) → generation → generation
```

which when supplied with a suitable neighbourhood function produces a next generation function. For example, we might define:

```
val nextgen = mk_nextgen_fn neighbours
```

and then use nextgen to calculate the generations for an infinite board.

The definitions of mk_nextgen_fn, mkgen and alive are given in Table 4.4, along with definitions of lexordset : (int × int) list → (int × int) list which simultaneously sorts and removes repetitions by a slight adaptation of the quicksort algorithm, and lexless and lexgreater both of type (int × int) → (int × int) → bool which compare integer pairs with the lexical ordering.

The missing function occurs3 : (int × int) list → (int × int) list searches a list of coordinates (not necessarily ordered) for any coordinates which occur *exactly* three times. Its definition is left as an exercise, but a solution is given in the Standard ML appendix.

4.2.2 Displaying a generation

It is very difficult to visualize the patterns in a generation from a list of coordinates of the live cells. We would like to have some way of displaying a generation as a two dimensional figure, by constructing

Table 4.4 Definitions of main 'life' functions.

```
local
  fun lexordset [ ] = [ ]
  | lexordset (a :: x) = lexordset (filter (lexless a) x) @ [a] @
                         lexordset (filter (lexgreater a) x)
  and lexless (a1, b1) (a2, b2)
      = if a2 < a1 then true else
        if a2 = a1 then b2 < b1 else false
  and lexgreater pr1 pr2 = lexless pr2 pr1
  fun occurs3 x = . . . EXERCISE . . .
  fun twoorthree n = n = 2 or n = 3
in
  fun alive livecoords = livecoords
  fun mkgen coordlist = lexordset coordlist
  fun mk_nextgen_fn neighbours gen
    = let val living = alive gen
          val isalive = member living
          val liveneighbours = length ∘ filter isalive ∘ neighbours
          val survivors = filter (twoorthree ∘ liveneighbours) living
          val newnbrlist = [nbr | crd ∈ living;
                                  nbr ∈ neighbours crd ; not (isalive nbr) ]
          val newborn = occurs3 newnbrlist
      in mkgen(survivors @ newborn) end
end
```

strings from the sorted list of coordinates. The string(s) could contain, for example, 'X' or 'O' to indicate live cells and spaces for dead cells. Thus we need to define a function:

```
plot : (int × int) list → string list
```

The picture building operations (such as mkpic) from the previous example (Section 4.1) could be used to create pleasing displays from the resulting strings. We leave the definition and details of the display function as an exercise. (A hint is given in the exercises at the end of the chapter and a solution is given in the appendix on Standard ML.)

4.2.3 Describing initial generations

The functions defined so far are adequate for experimenting with the game of life. However, it is a tedious task to write down a long list of co-ordinates for an initial generation. This problem is simply overcome by naming parts of configurations which can be put together with simple list operations like @. For example, a glider (see Figure 4.6) at the origin could be defined as the following list of coordinates:

```
val glider = [(0, 0), (0, 2), (1, 1), (1, 2), (2, 1)]
```

(The glider moves diagonally across the board at the rate of one cell in four generations unless it comes into contact with something else.) We have displayed this with the first (*x*-coordinate) counting down from the top of the picture and the second (*y*-coordinate) counting in from the left. The convention used is entirely local to the definition of the display function and can easily be changed. Similarly, a bale (also at the origin) is:

```
val bale = [(0, 0), (0, 1), (1, 0), (1, 1)]
```

which is a stable configuration of four live cells. A barberpole is another configuration (of varying size) and shown in Figure 4.6. This could be described by a function:

```
barberpole : int → (int × int) list
```

which returns the coordinates for a given size pole.

Before we can put such configurations together, we need to be able to move them to different positions (other than the origin). We suggest an infix operator for this purpose:

```
+-----------------------------------------------+
|a glider    a bale    a blinker     a spaceship|
|-----------------------------------------------|
|O O         OO          O              O       |   ( "O" = live )
| OO         OO          O               O      |   ( " " = dead )
| O                      O           O   O      |
|                                     OOOO      |
+-----------------------------------------------+
```

```
+--------------+---------------------+------------+
|barberpole    |genB (see text)      |an eater    |
|of size 6     |                     |and a glider|
|--------------|---------------------|------------|
|OO            |                     |            |
|O O           |                     |            |
|              |  O O       OO       |  O O       |
|  O O         |   OO       OO       |   OO       |
|              |   O                 |   O        |
|    O O       |                   OO|      OO    |
|              |                    O|      O O   |
|      O O     |                 O O |        O   |
|              |                     |        OO  |
|        O O   |               O O   |            |
|              |                     |            |
|          O O |             O O     |            |
|           OO |            O        |            |
|              |            OO       |            |
+--------------+---------------------+------------+
```

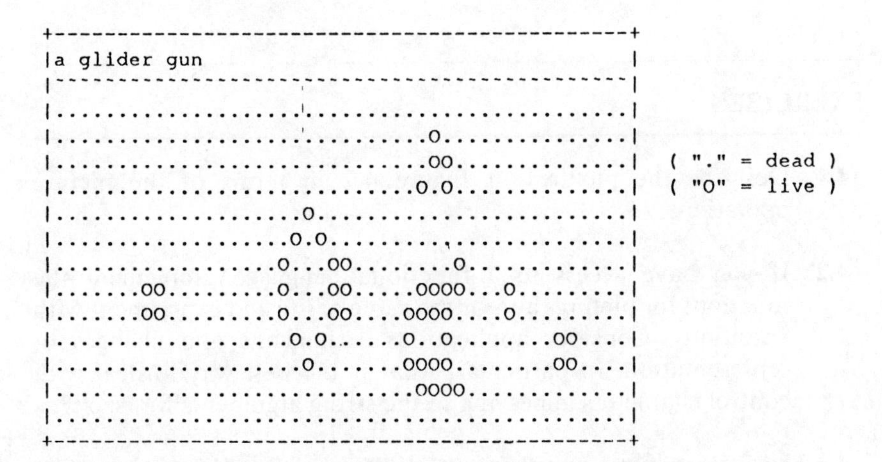

Figure 4.6 Example configurations.

```
at : ((int × int) list × (int × int)) → (int × int) list

infix 6 at      (infix with priority 6)
fun coordlist at (x, y) = let fun move (a, b) = (a + x, b + y)
                          in map move coordlist    end
```

It is now easy to combine components and form an initial generation, as in:

```
val genA = mkgen (glider at (3, 4) @ bale at (30, 40))
val genB = mkgen (glider at (2, 2)
                 @ bale at (2, 12)
                 @ rotate (barberpole 4) at (5, 20) )
```

The function rotate in the latter example simply rotates the coordinates in a list through a quarter turn about the origin and its definition is left as an exercise.

The generation genB is depicted in Figure 4.6 along with some other configurations and the reader is referred to the following for more information about the game of life. Conway's game was first reported in *Scientific American* (October 1970) in Martin Gardner's 'Mathematical Games' column. It is also mentioned in the January 1972, October 1983 and May 1985 issues of *Scientific American.* There is also a book (Berlekampe *et al*, 1982) which includes descriptions of how a board can be set up to act as a universal computer.

In the next three chapters we turn our attention to the possibilities for defining and using new, special purpose types in functional programs.

EXERCISES

4.1 Describe the pictures in Figure 4.7 in terms of the picture operations.

4.2 If you have access to a functional language, implement the functions for pictures and/or the game of life and experiment with variations. Consider applications, extensions and changes of representation. In particular, what is the best way to deal with control characters appearing in the string arguments for mkpic?

4.3 Use the pictures to give pretty displays of Pascal's triangles (see Exercise 3.29).

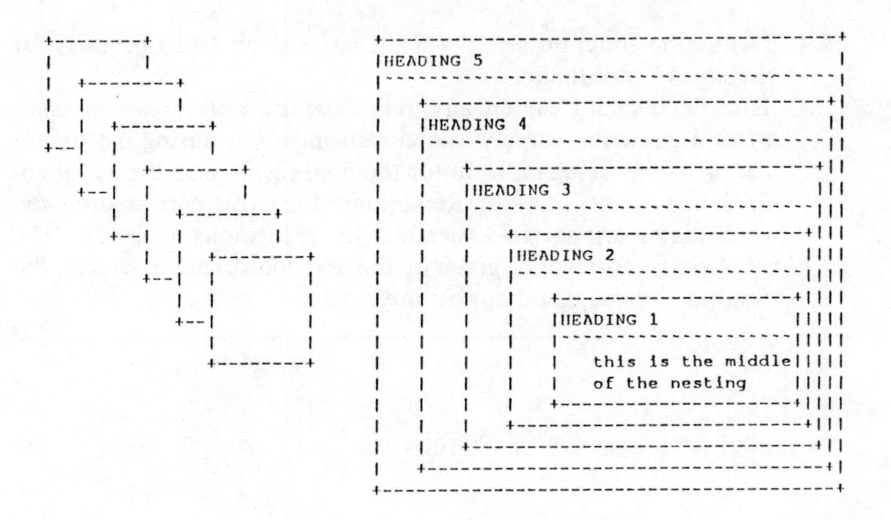

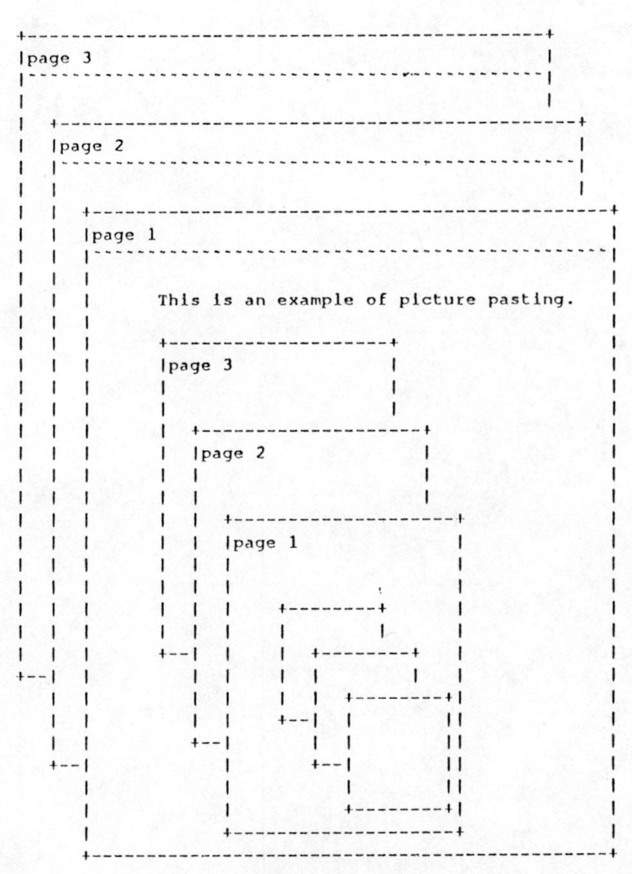

Figure 4.7 See Exercise 4.1.

4.4 Define the function plot : (int × int) list → string list to be used for displaying coordinates.
Hint: You could use an auxiliary function plotfrom which takes three arguments, namely: the current position during plotting; a list of strings being built up for the final result; and the list of coordinates to be plotted. Remember that you can assume the coordinates are sorted lexically with repetitions removed. The smallest x value will be given by the first coordinate; however, the smallest y value could appear anywhere.

Chapter 5
New Types (Concrete Types)

So far, we have worked with a particular collection of types formed from a particular collection of type operators:

int, bool, string, unit, →, list, (_×_), (_×_×_), · · ·

Any values we have considered in programs are automatically associated with these types. Suppose we now want to write programs dealing with things like playing cards, books, votes, money, dates, trees of integers, etc.; how will we introduce such objects or values? One possibility is to find convenient types formed with the above type operators which can be used to represent (or simulate) such values. We did this in the previous chapter when we introduced the abbreviations:

type picture = int × int × string list
type generation = (int × int) list

The drawback is that the type system is not directly supporting the abstractions which we wish to use, and programs are therefore more susceptible to errors being introduced through accidental misuse of representations which cannot he detected by type checking. In many programming languages, this is our only option. However, modern languages like Standard ML, Hope, Miranda, Lazy ML and Ponder have extensible type systems. They allow us to introduce arbitrary new type operators and corresponding new data values into programs without having to simulate or encode the values using a fixed collection of types. A single, simple mechanism allows us to extend the type system to form very rich collections of types and the mechanism is almost the same in each of these languages. The mechanism is based on the mathematical concept of free algebras which we will discuss later after giving some examples.

5.1 Defining new types

When we introduce a new type, there are some associated administrative concerns which need to be dealt with. We will need to specify a name for the new type; we will need a means for constructing values of the new type (and inspecting the values); and we will need some canonical way of describing the values of the new type (e.g. for displaying values of the new type). We will see that the latter two problems of constructing and describing values can be simultaneously solved with the single concept of **constructors**.

We introduce new constructors which are either constants of the new type or functions which produce results of the new type. These will serve the dual purpose of creating values and being part of the description of the values created.

The question is, how should constructors be introduced? Defining the constructors as we do other values is not the answer because if we were to give definitions what would we define the new constructors in terms of? For the purposes of applicative programming, it is sufficient just to name the new constructors. This is a much simpler approach than that found in many current imperative languages. In Pascal we would have to describe a storage structure such as a record with pointers or an array to store values of the new type and then implement constructors in terms of memory allocation and initialisation of the storage structure. Here, we just name the constructors and then the storage representation along with the actual mechanism for constructing and storing values can be handled automatically. This is not only convenient but necessary if we are to exclude storage details from applicative languages. Cardelli (1984) describes how efficient the representations can be if type information is used carefully in compiling so that the compiler-created storage details can be as efficient as programmer-created storage details, and will often be more regular and reliable.

Furthermore, we need not introduce selectors and predicates for inspecting values of a new type if the new constructors can be used in patterns. This means that all the information needed to introduce the type is its name, the names of the constructors and the argument type of each constructor (when it is not a constant). Such new types will be called **concrete** or **freely generated** types to distinguish them from the abstract types which we consider in Chapter 7.

In the simplest case, we just introduce constants, as in the following section.

5.1.1 Types with constants only

Such types are equivalent to the finite enumeration types found in other languages such as Pascal, and we introduce them by enumerating the constants as in the following examples:

```
datatype direction = Up | Right | Down | Left
datatype vote = For | Against | Abstain
datatype month = Jan | Feb | Mar | Apr | May | Jun
                | Jul | Aug | Sep | Oct | Nov | Dec
datatype colour = Red | Orange | Yellow | Green | Blue | Indigo | Violet
datatype suit = Clubs | Diamonds | Hearts | Spades
datatype cardvalue = Two | Three | Four | Five | Six | Seven
                   | Eight | Nine | Ten | Jack | Queen | King | Ace
```

In all, these type definitions introduce six new types (direction, vote, month, colour, suit and cardvalue) and 43 new values, described by the constants appearing to the right of the = signs. (The keyword **datatype** is used in ML to introduce new type names which are not just abbreviations for existing types.) The first type definition introduces four new, distinct values with type direction:

```
Up : direction    Right : direction    Down : direction    Left : direction
```

and indeed they are the only values defined for this type. Similarly, For, Against and Abstain are introduced as the only three values of type vote and so on (with 12 new values of type month, 7 new values of type colour, 4 new values of type suit and 13 new values of type cardvalue).

The new types can be combined with existing types (in appropriate ways) so we can write expressions like:

```
[Up, Up, Right, Down, Left, Down, Left]
```

which is a value of type direction list. Conversely, if we tried to write something like [Up, Orange] it would be a type error because items in a list have to have the same type but we have Orange : colour and Up : direction.

We will keep to the convention (not enforced by ML but enforced in Miranda) that constructor (constant) identifiers begin with an upper-case letter so that they can be distinguished more easily in expressions. An exception here will be the constants true and false which we have already been using, but which could have been introduced by:

```
datatype bool = true | false
```

We also regard the empty tuple ( ) as the only constant of type unit which is predefined in ML by a type definition with one constant:

```
datatype unit = ( )
```

Note that any enumeration type will automatically be an equality type allowing values of the same type to be compared with =. So, for example, Up = Down is a valid expression of type bool with value false and member [Up, Left] Left = true. (Recall that member : $\alpha^{=}$ list → $\alpha^{=}$ → bool, so it should only be used with instance types for $\alpha^{=}$ which are equality types. In the example, the instance type for $\alpha^{=}$ is direction.)

New constants introduced in type definitions can naturally be used in patterns. This allows us to define functions with arguments of the new type by case analysis as in:

```
fun turn Up    = Right
  | turn Right = Down
  | turn Down  = Left
  | turn Left  = Up
```

which makes turn : direction → direction.

Generalizing slightly, we introduce new types with constructors which are not constants.

5.1.2 Introducing constructors with arguments

A constructor with an argument will act as a function which produces a value of the new type when given an argument of the appropriate type. The type of the argument is specified when the constructor is introduced in the new type definition (using a keyword **of** in ML). For example, if we introduce:

```
datatype card = Card of (cardvalue × suit)
```

then card is a new type name and Card is a constructor of values of type card. The type of the constructor is a functional type:

```
Card : (cardvalue × suit) → card
```

and so can be applied to a value of type cardvalue × suit to produce a value of type card. This means that the following are meaningful expressions:

```
Card (Two, Diamonds)
Card (King, Clubs)
let val pr = (Queen, Spades) in Card pr end
map Card [(Six, Hearts), (Ten, Hearts), (Five, Diamonds)]
```

The first two of these expressions are also canonical descriptions of the values of type card which they represent (i.e. they are fully evaluated expressions). The third expression simplifies to (evaluates to):

```
Card (Queen, Spades)
```

and the last expression evaluates to:

```
[Card (Six, Hearts), Card (Ten, Hearts), Card (Five, Diamonds)]
```

(a value of type card list). This clearly shows the dual use of the constructor as both standing for an operation and also as part of the description of the constructed data value. In general if $C : T \rightarrow T'$ is a constructor and E is an expression of type T which evaluates to (canonical form) a, then $C\ E$ evaluates to the canonical form C a.

Note that use of the constructor Card is the *only* way values of type card can be produced and a value of type cardvalue × suit is not itself a card. This means that all the defined values of type card *must* have the form Card (cv, s) for some cv : cardvalue and s : suit. The importance of this becomes more apparent when we consider the use of new constructors in pattern matching. It seems quite natural to allow definitions of functions with card argument patterns taking this form. Thus we might write:

```
fun suitof (Card (cv, s)) = s
fun valueof (Card (cv, s)) = cv
fun isheart (Card (cv, Heart)) = true
  | isheart (Card (cv, s))       = false   (otherwise)
```

giving us two selectors and a predicate:

```
suitof : card → suit
valueof : card → cardvalue
isheart : card → bool
```

These and other functions can be introduced by the programmer when needed using pattern matching so that there is no need to make them a part of the type definition.

It is generally good programming practice to use new types even when there is a convenient built in type which can be used to represent values, because this gives us more protection through type checking. For example, if we want to do computations with people's heights and ages represented as integers, we should define:

```
datatype height = Ht of int
datatype age = Age of int
```

Then heights have the form Ht (n) and ages have the form Age (n) for some n : int. The constructors Ht : int → height and Age : int → age do the appropriate conversions between integers and the new types. This is desirable, because integers can always be added (perhaps by mistake) whereas it is not natural to add an age to a height and indeed Ht (190) + Age (30) will be caught as a type error. A special operation can still be introduced if one really does want to add ages and heights (producing an integer) as follows:

```
fun funnyop (Ht n, Age m) = n + m
```

so funnyop : height × age → int and it must be explicitly used instead of + with heights and ages.

When there is a single constructor, as in these examples, it is possible (in a strict language implementation) to ensure that no runtime penalty is paid by introducing the new types. Type information should be used during type checking only and after type checking, the function funnyop can be compiled to the addition operation and Ht and Age treated as identity operations so that they can be removed by peephole optimization of the runtime code (see Cardelli, 1984).

Returning to our examples from the previous chapter, we see that we would do better to define, for example:

```
datatype picture = Pic of (int × int × stringlist)
datatype generation = Gen of (int × int) list
```

and modify definitions accordingly. For example, we want:

```
fun alive (Gen coordlist) = coordlist
fun mkgen coordlist = Gen (lexsortset coordlist)
```

which explains our earlier description of the types of these functions as:

```
alive : generation → (int × int) list
mkgen : (int × int) list → generation
```

We leave it as an exercise to go through the other definitions of that chapter using this modification.

In general, a type definition can introduce many constructors which give alternative (or **variant**) constructions for values. In the earlier examples of enumeration types, we had several constructors but these were special cases since the constructors were all constants.

5.1.3 Types with alternative constructors

Suppose we want to introduce a type author and a type book. Authors are usually just given by strings, but we want a special case for 'anon' (anonymous). Similarly, books are to be described by their title (a string) and a list of authors, but we want to distinguish paperbacks and hardbacks. One way to do this is to define:

```
datatype author = Author of string
                | Anon
datatype book = Paperback of (string × author list)
              | Hardback of (string × author list)
```

This introduces the types author and book along with the four constructors:

```
Author : string → author
Anon : author
Paperback : (string × author list) → book
Hardback : (string × author list) → book
```

So we can create objects of type book and author in different ways. For example:

```
val thisbook = Paperback (''Elements of Functional Programming''
                          [Author ''C.M.P. Reade''])
val thatbook = Hardback (''The Unknown'', [Anon])
```

Correspondingly, functions which we define by pattern matching against values of type book (or author) must have more than one case:

```
fun title (Paperback (s, al)) = s
|   title (Hardback (s, al))  = s
fun authorlist (Paperback (s, al)) = al
|   authorlist (Hardback (s, al))  = al
fun soft (Paperback (s, al)) = true
|   soft (Hardback (s, al))  = false
```

These functions are well defined because they provide a defined result for each possible defined argument of type book and the different cases are quite disjoint. That is, we assume that:

(a) Every value of a new type is constructed via one of the specified constructors for that type, and

(b) Values constructed via different constructors are distinct.

Then, when title (for example) is applied to some expression (E, say) we know that the value of E must be of type book (otherwise the expression cannot be type correct) and so it should have one of the two forms appearing as patterns in the definition of title. The appropriate case is found by matching the value of E against each of the patterns.

We also assume an obvious test for equality for new types provided that it is possible to test all the component (argument) types for equality. In the example of type book, the component types are string and author list and for type author the only component type is string. Since = is defined for strings, it is also defined for type author and hence for type author list and hence for type book. From (a) and (b) above, we draw the obvious conclusion that = for type book is given completely by:

```
(Hardback (s1, x1) = Hardback (s2, x2)) = (s1 = s2 & x1 = x2)
(Paperback (s1, x1) = Paperback(s2, x2)) = (s1 = s2 & x1 = x2)
(Hardback (s1, x1) = Paperback (s2, x2)) = false
(Paperback (s1, x1) = Hardback (s2, x2)) = false
```

where s1, s2 stand for arbitrary (well-defined) strings and x1, x2 stand for arbitrary (well-defined) author lists. We take such definitions of equality for granted from now on (for the types which allow it).

Note that new types are essentially disjoint unions of the component types appearing as arguments of the constructors and we can think of the constructors as just labelling functions which mark values of the union so that the component type (which they have been constructed from) can be discerned. To illustrate this further, we will construct a type mix which is the (disjoint) union of the types int and string:

```
datatype mix = Int of int
             | Str of string
```

We can think of the constructors Int : int → mix and Str : string → mix as labelling integers/strings to make mix values. A mixed list of integers and strings can now be constructed within the type system as a mix list and we can retrieve the integers (say) from a mix list without the possibility of confusing integer and string values. If we define:

```
val mix1 = [Int 5, Str "aa", Str "xyz", Int 7]
fun getints [ ]         = [ ]
 |  getints (Int n :: x) = n :: getints x
 |  getints (Str s :: x)= getints x
```

then mix1 : mix list, getints : mix list → int list and getints mix1 = [5, 7].

5.1.4 Recursive types

Type definitions are assumed to be recursive by default so that the new type name can appear as part of an argument type for a constructor. This means that a constructor can build values of the new type out of other values of the new type. As a simple example, take the following definition of a type representing (grossly simplified) file systems:

```
datatype file = Text of string list
              | Directory of file list
```

This says that a file is either a text file in which case it is composed of a string list (the text) or it is a directory in which case it is composed of a list of (sub) files. The constructors have types Text : string list → file and Directory : file list → file and so, assuming s1, . . . , s4 are string lists, we could define the following value of type file:

```
val file1 = Directory [Text s1,
                       Text s2,
                       Directory [Text s3, Directory [ ]]
                       Text s4
                       ]
```

The value file1 : file is a directory with a list of four subfiles. The third subfile is also a directory with two subfiles, one of which is an empty directory.

Types with an unbounded collection of values can be constructed with recursively defined types. We could even use a recursive type definition to introduce a numeric type as follows:

```
datatype number = Zero | Succ of number
```

This introduces constructors Zero : number (a constant) and Succ : number → number which constructs a new value of type number when applied to a given value of type number. Later, we will introduce several other recursive types, but we will not make much use of this particular one even though it is rather an elegant definition of the natural numbers. Although we could write very natural definitions of primitive recursive functions by pattern matching with the two cases, it is impractical to have to write, for example, Succ (Succ (Succ (Succ (Zero)))) for 4. It is also expecting a bit too much of a compiler to spot that it can use direct hardware implementations of addition and multiplication from primitive recursive definitions such as:

```
fun numbplus (Zero, m) = m
|   numbplus (Succ n, m) = Succ (numbplus (n, m))

fun numbmult (Zero, m) = Zero
|   numbmult (Succ n, m) = numbplus (m, numbmult (n, m))
```

Once again, equality should be defined on recursively defined types provided it is defined for all the (other) types appearing as components. The type number has no component types (other than number itself) and file has just string list, so an equality operation is defined for each of these types.

There, is a rather subtle question we could ask about recursive types and that is whether or not they allow the construction of infinite objects. For example, could we have infinity : number satisfying infinity = Succ infinity or a directory containing itself as a subfile? For the moment, we will assume a strict interpretation for constructors which effectively bans such infinite objects. All values will be describable by a finite nesting of constructors (and function values). We discuss why this follows from a strict interpretation and look at the alternative possibility of programming with infinite objects in Chapter 8.

5.1.5 Mutually recursive types

The new type definitions above all have the same general form. A new type name is introduced along with a finite number of new constructor names, each one being either a constant or having a specified argument type. The argument types can involve recursive references to the new type. In general, we may want to introduce several new types simultaneously where arguments to constructors can involve any of the new types. This allows for mutual recursion between the types as in the following example:

```
datatype part = Basicpart of int
              | Compoundpart of (int × components list)
    and components = Quantity of (part × int)
```

Here, the constructors have types:

```
Basicpart : int → part
Compoundpart : (int × components list) → part
Quantity : (part × int) → components
```

so a part may be basic with an integer (indicating the part number) or compound and built from an integer (the part number) and a components list. Conversely, components can be built from a part and an integer (indicating the quantity). This allows us to build parts such as:

```
val p4 = Basicpart 34
val p3 = Basicpart 33
```

```
val p2 = Compoundpart (32,
                       [Quantity (p4, 1), Quantity (p3, 2)]
                      )
val p1 = Compoundpart (31,
                       [Quantity (p2, 4), Quantity (p3, 1)]
                      )
```

which show the nesting of parts within components within parts. We leave it as an exercise for the reader to write out the value of p1 in its canonical form (involving just the constructors Compoundpart, Basicpart, Quantity, ::, [ ] and integer constants).

Note how tree-like (i.e. nested) data structures can be modelled very easily with this simple type definition mechanism. Note also that the problems of pointer (reference) handling for data structures with recursive types are avoided completely by being handled automatically. These are a source of many programmer errors in imperative languages where decisions about pointers or direct reference to component structures must be made explicitly by the programmer.

5.1.6 New type operators

It was noted in Chapter 2 that basic types like int and bool may be regarded as degenerate cases of type operators which happen to have no arguments. Thus list is a type operator which takes one type argument, → is an (infix) type operator which takes two type arguments, and bool, int, string, unit and all the new types introduced so far in this chapter are type operators with no argument types. The definition of a new type operator with arguments will be exactly the same as the definition of a type except that the type name will be preceded by a tuple of type variables. That is, type operator definitions are parameterized type definitions and we sometimes refer to a type operator as a parameterized type. The parameters may be used in the argument types of the constructors thus making the constructors polymorphic.

For example, suppose we want to generalize the following basic type which defines a type of integer matrices:

```
datatype int_matrix = Matrix of (int list list)
```

with the constructor Matrix : (int list list) → int_matrix. We want to have matrices with other types as well as integers for elements, but prefer to use just one polymorphic constructor Matrix for all matrices. By parameterizing the above definition, we can introduce a type operator instead of a fixed type:

```
datatype α matrix = Matrix of (α list list)
```

Now, for any type T, we also have the type T matrix and the constructor is polymorphic with type:

```
Matrix : (α list list) → α matrix
```

For example, we may write:

```
Matrix [[1, 2], [3, 4], [5, 6]] : int matrix
Matrix [[pic1], [pic2]] : picture matrix
Matrix [[Matrix [[true, false], [false, false]]]] : (bool matrix) matrix
Matrix [[I, I], [I, I]] : (α → α) matrix
```

With the facility to define type operators, we do not have to treat lists as a special predefined type operator. We can simply define:

```
datatype α list = :: of (α × α list)
                | [ ]
```

which introduces the polymorphic constructors:

```
:: : (α × α list) → α list
[ ] : α list
```

This really shows the full power of the type definition mechanism. All types and type operators except for the tuple and function type operators (× and →) could be introduced by the programmer. Predefined types are only included for efficiency purposes. In particular, the predefined types of int and string could be modelled as new types, but this would not be very convenient.

Another example of a type operator which we shall make use of in later examples is possible. If part of a computation involves searching for a value in a data structure (such as looking to see if the first part of an input string is a sequence of digits) then we need to be able to handle both a successful search and an unsuccessful search. A function which performs the search must report whether or not the search was successful and return an appropriate result in the successful case. However, strong typing requires that the value returned in both cases is of the same type. A common solution to this problem is to have the function return a pair which consists of a boolean value (indicating success or failure) and a normal result value (which is some arbitrarily chosen default value in the case of failure). A better solution would be to make use of the following type operator:

```
datatype α possible = Ok of α
                    | Fail
```

A function searching for a value of type α would then return a result of type α possible which will be either the constant Fail : α possible or the constructor Ok : $\alpha \rightarrow \alpha$ possible applied to a value of type α which is the result in the successful case. This eliminates the need for an arbitrary result value in the unsuccessful case. Another function which is to continue processing the result can then be defined for the two cases. For example, suppose the function findpos is to search an integer list and return the first positive value it finds if there is one. This function could be defined to return an int possible, and another function (report : int possible → string, say), can be defined separately:

```
fun findpos [ ] = Fail
  | findpos (n :: x) = if n > 0 then Ok (n) else findpos x
fun report Fail = "Failed to find a positive value"
  | report (Ok n) = "The value found is:- " ^ stringofint n
```

Types of the form α possible are particularly useful when writing functions to parse an input string or token list. In particular, operations for lexical and syntactic analysis for a compiler can be expressed succinctly with types such as:

```
parser : token list → (syntax_tree × token list) possible
```

where the type token would represent the lexical items such as identifiers, keywords and symbols, and the type syntax_tree would be designed to represent the syntactic structure of a program which has been parsed from a token list. Such parsers return a token list as well as a syntax_tree if they are successful. The returned token list contains the remaining unanalysed input in case it is required for subsequent processing.

We give an example of this in the next chapter. In the next two sections, we look at some more specific type operators for creating tree and graph types.

5.2 Trees and graphs

Trees and graphs crop up frequently in computer science and there are many ways of describing them. We will first take a look at trees, but rather than pick on one sort of tree, we will look at several variations.

5.2.1 Bintree (binary trees with leaf values)

We will call the objects depicted in Figure 5.1 **bintrees**. These are binary trees (because there are pairs of branches to subtrees) with leaves labelled by values of a specific type. More precisely, we will call a bintree with leaf values of type α, an α bintree, so Figure 5.1 depicts three values of type int bintree : a bool bintree, a string bintree and a mix bintree.

In order to design a suitable type (operator) definition for these objects, we consider how they might be constructed. We see that there is a degenerate case of a single leaf containing (constructed from) a value of type α (where α is the leaf value type), and a general case of compound bintrees. Each compound bintree could be constructed by joining the two smaller bintrees immediately below the top point as depicted in Figure 5.2. This suggests that we need only two constructors which we will call

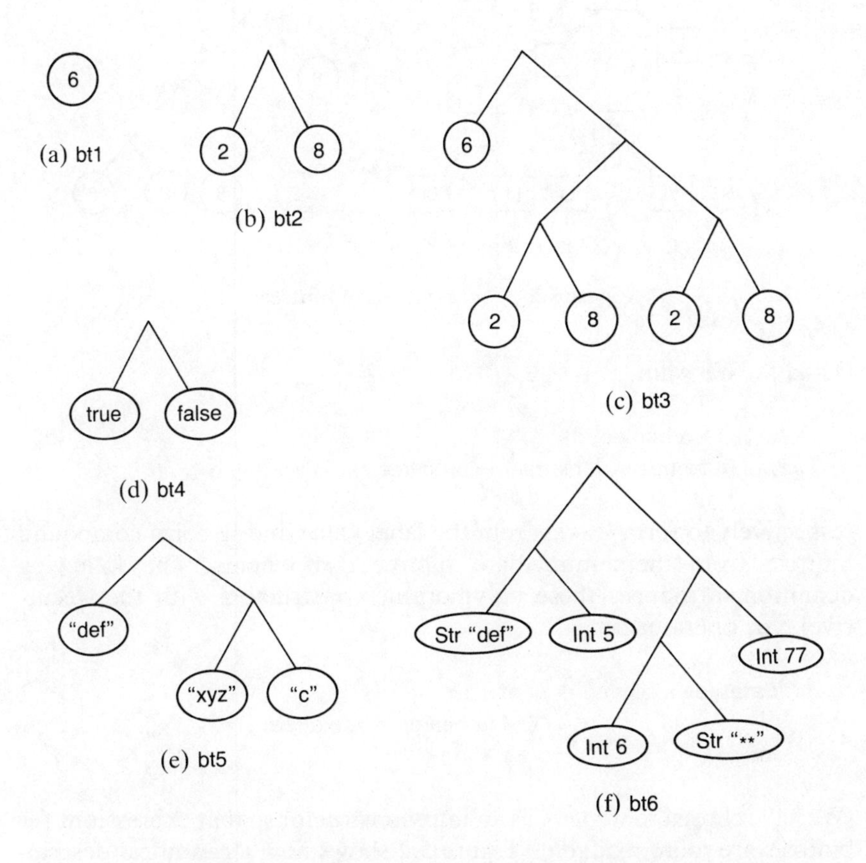

Figure 5.1 Bintrees (binary leaf labelled trees).

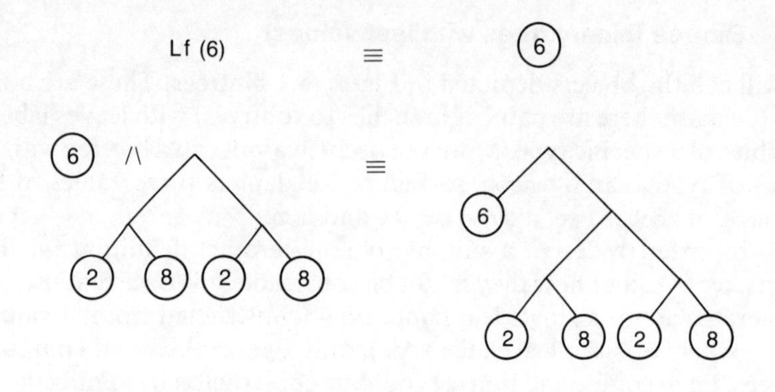

Lf 6 /\ ((Lf 2 /\ Lf 8) /\ (Lf 2 /\ Lf 8))

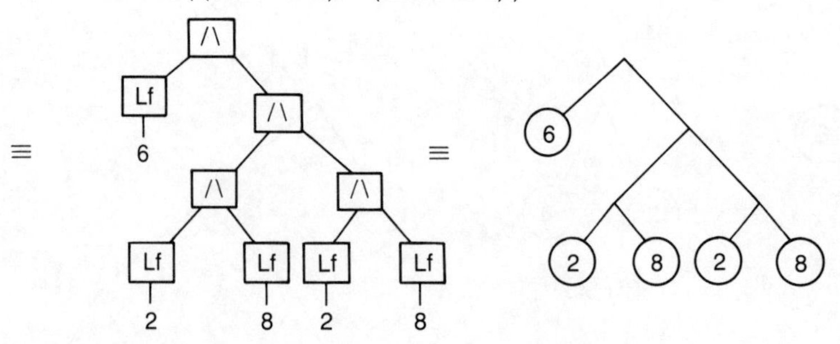

Figure 5.2 Construction of bintrees.

Lf and /\. We want:

Lf : $\alpha \rightarrow \alpha$ bintree
/\ : (α bintree $\times$ α bintree) $\rightarrow$ α bintree

respectively to form leaves from the label value and to form compound bintrees from their immediate subtree components. The following definition introduces these polymorphic constructors with the (recursive) type operator bintree:

datatype α bintree = Lf **of** α
| /\ **of** (α bintree $\times$ α bintree)
infix /\

(We have chosen to write /\ as an infix constructor so that expressions for bintrees are more readable.) Figure 5.2 shows how a canonical description of a bintree in terms of the constructors corresponds to the diagrams. We also give definitions of the particular bintrees depicted in Figure 5.1 with their types:

```
val bt1 = Lf 6
val bt2 = Lf 2 /\ Lf 8
val bt3 = bt1 /\ (bt2 /\ bt2)
val bt4 = Lf true /\ Lf false
val bt5 = Lf "def" /\ (Lf "xyz" /\ Lf "c")
val bt6 = (Lf (Str "def") /\ Lf (Int 5))
          /\
          (((Lf (Int 6) /\ Lf (Str "**")) /\ Lf (Int 77))

bt1 : int bintree
bt2 : int bintree
bt3 : int bintree
bt4 : bool bintree
bt5 : string bintree
bt6 : mix bintree
```

Having introduced bintrees with constructors we next define some operations on bintrees. Some simple bintree operations are left and right (both of type α bintree → α bintree) which select the left and right (immediate) subtrees of a bintree but are undefined for bintrees which are simple leaves. The predicate isleaf : α bintree → bool asks whether a binary tree is a simple leaf or not, and two functions leftmostleaf : α bintree → alpha and sumofleaves : int bintree → int return the (value at the) leftmost leaf and the sum of the (integer values at the) leaves of a bintree respectively. These functions are defined as follows:

```
fun left (t1 /\ t2) = t1
 |  left (Lf a)     = error "left of Lf is undefined"

fun right (t1 /\ t2) = t2
 |  right (Lf a)     = error "right of Lf is undefined"

fun isleaf (t1 /\ t2) = false
 |  isleaf (Lf a)     = true

fun leftmostleaf (t1 /\ t2) = leftmostleaf t1
 |  leftmostleaf (Lf a)     = a

fun sumofleaves (t1 /\ t2) = sumofleaves t1 + sumofleaves t2
 |  sumofleaves (Lf a)     = a
```

Then, for example:

```
leftmostleaf bt3 = leftmostleaf (bt1 /\ (bt2 /\ bt2))
                 = leftmostleaf (bt1)
                 = leftmostleaf (Lf 6) = 6
```

and:

```
sumofleaves bt3 = sumofleaves bt1 + sumofleaves (bt2 /\ bt2)
                = sumofleaves (Lf 6) + sumofleaves bt2 + sumofleaves bt2
                = 6 + (2 + 8) + (2 + 8) = 26
```

5.2.2 Higher order bintree operations

There are many other operations which may be of use, but we will not try to define them directly. Instead, we want to define higher order tree operations analogously to the list operations map, accumulate, etc., defined in Chapter 3.

Many operations on binary trees will involve scanning the tree along with the application of some function (f) to the values at leaves of the tree and the use of some binary function (g) to combine results returned from scans of the left and right subtrees (when the tree is not a simple leaf). Accordingly we define a general purpose bintree function which we will call btreeop:

```
fun btreeop f g (Lf a)      = f a
  | btreeop f g (t1 /\ t2) = g (btreeop f g t1) (btreeop f g t2)
```

The most general type we can infer for the general purpose function is:

btreeop : $(\alpha \rightarrow \beta) \rightarrow (\beta \rightarrow \beta \rightarrow \beta) \rightarrow (\alpha \text{ bintree} \rightarrow \beta)$

(Note that we have assumed a curried binary function for the second argument.) Operations such as leftmostleaf and sumofleaves can easily be defined in terms of btreeop. For example:

```
val sumofleaves = btreeop I plus
```

As a tree is scanned with btreeop I plus, the identity function I is applied to the values encountered at the leaves (thus returning the value unchanged) and plus is applied to the results returned from scanning left and right subtrees thus summing all the values at the leaves. This is analogous to the use of reduce plus 0 for summing lists. Other generalized tree operations such as btreemap which simply maps a function over the leaves of a tree (analogously to map in the case of lists) can be defined as special cases of btreeop:

```
fun btreemap f = btreeop (Lf ∘ f) join
and join t1 t2 = t1 /\ t2
```

The function join : α bintree $\rightarrow \alpha$ bintree $\rightarrow \alpha$ bintree is just a curried version of the constructor and btreemap : $(\alpha \rightarrow \beta) \rightarrow \alpha$ bintree $\rightarrow \beta$ bintree, when applied to a function f and bintree t, performs a btreeop scan of the tree. At

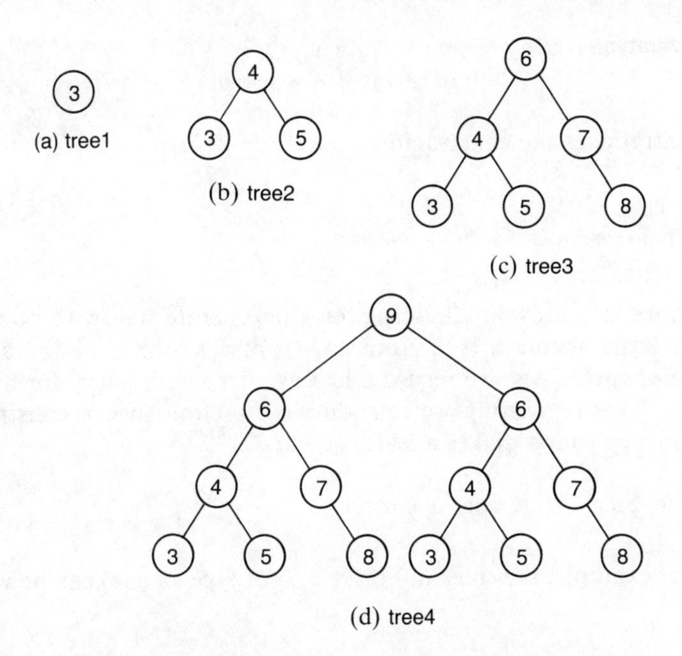

Figure 5.3 Trees (with internally labelled nodes).

each leaf of t, f is applied to the value and a leaf is made with the result (since (Lf ∘ f) a = Lf (f a)). The bintrees formed from the scans of left and right subtrees are combined by /\ to form a resulting bintree and the shape of the argument tree is preserved in the result. For example:

```
btreemap (plus 1) (Lf 5 /\ (Lf 2 /\ Lf 8))
                 = (Lf 6 /\ (Lf 3 /\ Lf 9))
```

There are other sorts of tree used in computing which usually give rise to different type definitions. The S-expressions used in LISP (McCarthy *et al.*, 1962) are essentially the same as the values of type atom bintree where atom is a type rather like mix for all the atomic values like integers, characters and other constants (including the special constant NIL). Since LISP is not a strongly typed language, atoms and S-expressions are not type checked and distinctions between the different sorts of atom and S-expressions must therefore be made by runtime tests.

Another common form of tree is one where values can appear at the internal nodes rather than at the leaves.

5.2.3 Trees with internal node values

Trees with internal node values as depicted in Figure 5.3 will be referred to just as trees. An appropriate type (operator) definition would be:

```
datatype α tree = Empty
                | Tr of (α tree × α × α tree)
```

which introduces the constructors:

```
Empty : α tree
Tr : (α tree × α × α tree) → α tree
```

The former is a constant standing for a degenerate tree with no nodes, and the latter forms a tree from two subtrees and a node value of type α. For such trees, we regard a leaf as a tree with Empty for both its subtrees. To save writing we introduce a function (not a constructor) leaf : $\alpha \rightarrow \alpha$ tree which makes a leaf:

```
fun leaf a = Tr (Empty, a, Empty)
```

Then, for example, the trees in Figure 5.3 (of type int tree) can be written as:

```
val tree1 = leaf 3
val tree2 = Tr (leaf 3, 4, leaf 5)
val tree3 = Tr (tree2, 6, Tr (Empty, 7, leaf 8))
val tree4 = Tr (tree3, 9, tree3)
```

and the value of tree4 (i.e. the canonical form when written out) is:

```
Tr (Tr (Tr (Tr (Empty, 3, Empty),
            4,
            Tr (Empty, 5, Empty))
        6,
        Tr (Empty,
            7,
            Tr (Empty, 8, Empty))),
    9,
    Tr (Tr (Tr (Empty, 3, Empty),
            4,
            Tr (Empty, 5, Empty)),
        6,
        Tr (Empty,
            7,
            Tr (Empty, 8, Empty))))
```

The selectors and predicates for such trees will not be defined, since we will use patterns as in the following definitions of some useful tree operations:

```
fun flatten Empty = [ ]
|   flatten (Tr (t1, a, t2)) = flatten t1 @ [a] @ flatten t2

fun treemap f Empty = Empty
|   treemap f (Tr (t1, a, t2))
                    = Tr(treemap f t1, f a, treemap f t2)
```

The higher order operation treemap: $(\alpha \rightarrow \beta) \rightarrow (\alpha$ tree $\rightarrow \beta$ tree) applies a function to each node value in a tree to produce a new tree with the same shape as the original (it is the tree counterpart of the list operation map and the bintree operation btreemap). The function flatten : α tree $\rightarrow \alpha$ list produces a list of the node values in a tree in what is usually called inorder. That is, the top node value is placed in between lists of the left and right subtree node values which are similarly ordered. Corresponding definitions of preorder and postorder listings of the values are quite simple to express and compare:

```
fun preorder Empty = [ ]
|   preorder (Tr (t1, a, t2))
                = [a] @ preorder t1 @ preorder t2

fun postorder Empty = [ ]
|   postorder (Tr (t1, a, t2))
                = postorder t1 @ postorder t2 @ [a]

(val inorder = flatten)
```

Hence, referring to tree3 defined above and depicted in Figure 5.3 (c), we have:

```
inorder tree3 = [3, 4, 5, 6, 7, 8]
preorder tree3 = [6, 4, 3, 5, 7, 8]
postorder tree3 = [3, 5, 4, 8, 7, 6]
```

As an example, we show the steps in a calculation of the first of these. First, we note that for any n:

```
flatten (leaf n) = flatten (Tr (Empty, n, Empty))
                 = flatten Empty @ [n] @ flatten Empty
                 = [ ] @ [n] @ [ ]
                 = [n]
```

Now we can compute:

```
inorder tree3 = flatten tree3 = flatten (Tr (tree2, 6, Tr (Empty, 7, leaf 8)))
              = flatten tree2 @ [6] @ flatten (Tr (Empty, 7, leaf 8))
              = (flatten (leaf 3) @ [4] @ flatten (leaf 5)) @ [6] · · ·
              = [3] @ [4] @ [5] @ [6] @ (flatten Empty @ [7] @
                                              flatten (leaf 8))
              = [3, 4, 5, 6, 7, 8]
```

The excessive number of applications of @ suggest that we could flatten a tree more efficiently. In fact, we can avoid any applications of @ by using an extra parameter as shown in Exercise 5.29.

We should also introduce a generalized tree operation (analogous to btreeop). This function will take as arguments a constant value (c), a function (g) and a tree (t). The value c is to be returned in the case when t is Empty and, otherwise, g is used to combine the results from recursive processing of the left and right subtrees of t along with the value at the top node itself. Thus we define:

```
fun treeop c g Empty = c
|   treeop c g (Tr (t1, a, t2))
                    = g (treeop c g t1, a, treeop c g t2)
```

We have chosen to make the argument g uncurried so that it takes a triple of arguments rather like Tr. The action of treeop c g can then be regarded as a replacement of each Tr and Empty in a tree by g and c respectively:

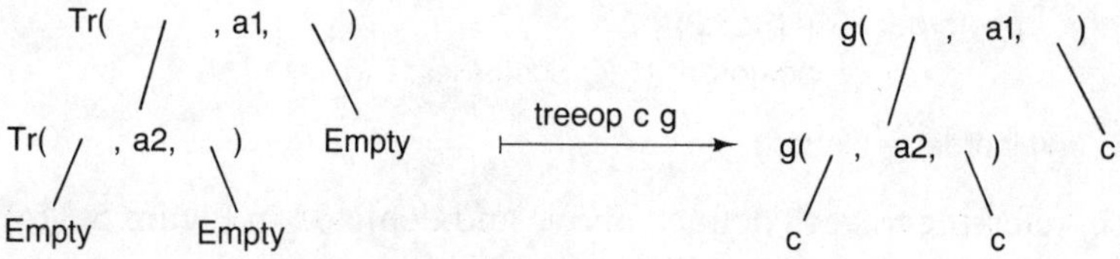

```
        Tr(  /  , a1,  \  )                               g(  /  , a1,  \  )
            /           \                                    /           \
 Tr(  / , a2,  \ )     Empty      treeop c g          g( / , a2, \ )      c
     /          \                 ---------->           /         \
  Empty        Empty                                   c           c
```

Often, this type of tree is used to keep a collection of items in order where use of a list makes insertions too costly. We will illustrate this by giving an implementation of a tree-sort algorithm which is used to sort lists. This algorithm is very similar to both the quicksort and the insertsort algorithms of Chapter 3, but a tree is used to organize the positioning of items rather than a list (as in insertsort) or the tree-like nesting of recursive calls in quicksort. As a list is scanned, items are inserted into a tree in the correct position so that when the tree is finally flattened, the resulting list is ordered. We call a tree **ordered** if it produces an ordered list when flattened. This is equivalent to saying that Empty is ordered and Tr (t1, a, t2) is ordered if every node value in t1 is less than or equal to a and every node value in t2 is greater than or equal to a and t1 and t2 are also ordered. (Usually, if an ordered tree is used to hold repeated items, some convention is adopted for placing multiple occurrence to the left (or right) in a consistent way, e.g. we assume values in the right subtree are strictly greater, or those in the left subtree are strictly smaller than the value at the top.) Of course, all this is relative to some total ordering of the type of values appearing as node items. For simplicity, we will restrict our attention to int tree with the usual ordering of integers.

The insertion of an item into an ordered tree in such a way as to produce an ordered tree again requires inspection of the node values. We begin by looking at the top node value (for a non-empty tree) and use this to decide whether we need to proceed with the insertion in the left or right subtree by a simple comparison of the value to be inserted with the node value. Suppose the value to be inserted is the smaller of the two. This means that the insertion has to take place in the left subtree and the final tree will be formed by combining the result of the left insertion with the original right subtree and topmost node value. As the insertion recurses down subtrees, the number of comparisons made will be equal to the depth of the tree along the particular path and usually this is much smaller than the total number of nodes. In fact the average number of comparisons needed to insert an item in a tree (of size n say) is of order log(n) rather than order n/2 as in the case of list insertion. The definitions of:

```
treeinsert : int → int tree → int tree and
treesort : int list → int list
```

are as follows:

```
fun treeinsert Empty m = leaf m
|   treeinsert (Tr (t1, n, t2)) m
                   = if (lessthan n) m        (i.e. m < n)
                     then Tr (treeinsert t1 m, n, t2)
                     else Tr (t1, n, treeinsert t2 m)
fun treesort x = flatten (accumulate treeinsert Empty x)
```

The sort works by beginning with an empty tree and accumulating items in the tree using treeinsert with each item of the argument list in turn. (The tree at any stage will be ordered because it is formed from Empty using only treeinsert which preserves the order.) The final list is just formed by flattening the final tree. Figure 5.4 shows the intermediate trees formed during a treesort.

5.2.4 More general trees

The types α bintree and β tree can be considered as special cases of the following type of binary tree:

```
datatype (α, β) abtree = Leaf of α
                       | Node of ((α, β) abtree × β × (α, β) abtree)
```

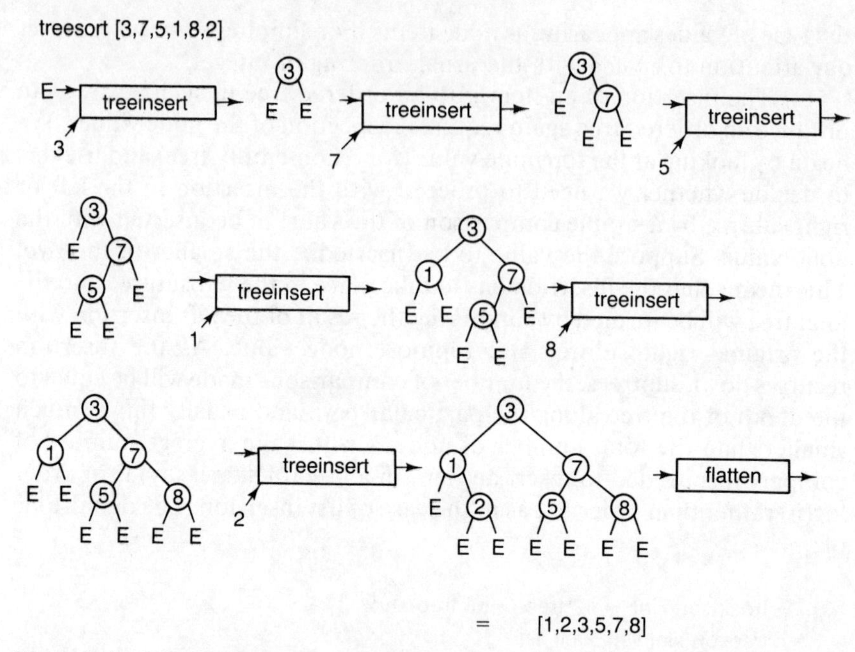

Figure 5.4 Intermediate trees formed during a treesort (E is written explicitly where Empty subtrees appear).

This type operator has two parameters (α and β) which represent the types labelling the leaves and internal nodes respectively. The constructors are:

Leaf : $\alpha \rightarrow (\alpha, \beta)$ abtree
Node : $((\alpha, \beta)$ abtree $\times \beta \times (\alpha, \beta)$ abtree$) \rightarrow (\alpha, \beta)$ abtree

When β is unit (the type whose only proper value is ( )), there is effectively no information at the internal nodes of such a tree and Leaf and Node play the roles of Lf and /\, that is (α, unit) abtree is isomorphic to α bintree. Conversely, if α is restricted to be unit, then there is effectively no information at the leaves which become just empty subtrees. In this case, Node plays the role of Tr and Leaf ( ) plays the role of Empty and (unit, β) abtree is isomorphic to β tree.

Another generalization is to allow arbitrary numbers of subtrees for a tree. We could do this by letting a component of a tree be a list of immediate subtrees. In this case a leaf would just be a tree with an empty list of subtrees. Let us call these 'vtrees' (for **variable offspring trees**), then we can define the type operator vtree by:

datatype α vtree = Vtree **of** $\alpha \times (\alpha$ vtree) list which introduces the constructor:

Vtree : ($\alpha \times$ (α vtree) list) $\rightarrow$ α vtree

We could also use the abbreviation α forest as follows:

type α forest = (α vtree) list

We leave it as an exercise to define appropriate functions for use with the (parameterized) types abtree and vtree. In the next subsection we look at graphs (which can be regarded as another generalization of trees).

5.2.5 Graphs

Mathematically, a **(directed) graph** consists of nodes and arrows (arcs) linking some pairs of nodes as depicted in Figure 5.5. They can also be thought of as just binary relations on a set of nodes (node1 is related by the binary relation to node2 if and only if there is an arc from node1 to node2 in the graph). There are many variations on this theme, such as graphs allowing labelling of arrows (arcs) and/or undirected arcs (which can be modelled as pairs of arcs going in opposite directions) and **multigraphs** where more than one arc is possible (in the same direction) between two nodes. The number of nodes in a graph and the number of arcs is usually taken to be finite, but infinite graphs are sometimes considered.

Because of the large number of variations and different applications of graphs it seems inappropriate to look for a universal definition which can cover all cases and still be simple enough to use. Instead, we will take a particular application of graphs involving searching in order to illustrate a rather unusual representation technique. We will illustrate how types with functional components may be used to represent a

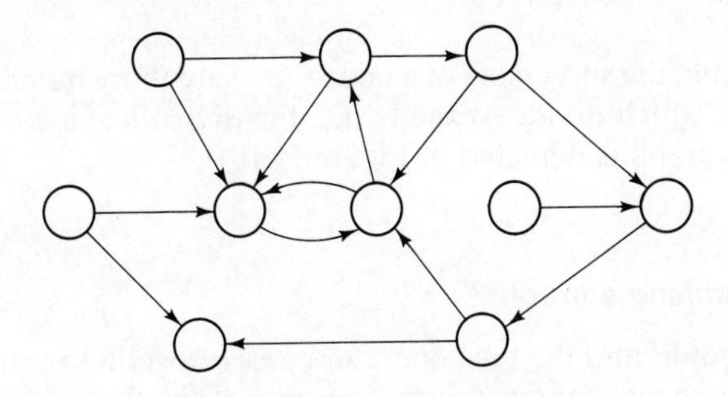

Figure 5.5 A graph.

particular abstract feature of such graphs without commitment to other details. The possibility of using functions as components of data structures allows us to do this.

Our intention is to capture the aspect of graphs which allows us to discover all the nodes which are immediately accessible from a given node (following some arc from tail to head). If we call the list of immediately accessible nodes from a given node n the successors of n, then we can focus our attention on a function (succ) which returns the successors of any node. Actually, each graph will have its own successor function, and we are only interested in the successor function aspect of any graph. This suggests the following type definition:

```
datatype α graph = Graph of (α → α list)
```

The parameter α is the type of the nodes, and each α graph is constructed from a successor function of type $\alpha \to \alpha$ list by the constructor:

```
Graph : (α → α list) → α graph
```

In the literature, many other representations for graphs are considered to optimize certain graph operations. These other representations can still be used in the description of the function for finding successors which constitutes this more abstract functional representation (see Exercise 5.10). Figure 5.6(a) depicts a very small graph with nodes of type bool which is defined by:

```
fun succ1 b = [not b]
val g1 = Graph (succ1)
```

In contrast, the following graph is infinite with nodes of type int:

```
fun succ2 n = if n < 2 then [ ]
              else [m | m ∈ 2 upto (n div 2); n mod m = 0]
val g2 = Graph (succ2)
```

For this graph, the successors of a node n (> 1) are those numbers between 2 and n div 2 which divide n exactly (i.e. the divisors of n greater than 1). Part of this graph is depicted in Figure 5.6(b).

5.2.6 Searching a graph

We bring graphs and the type operator possible together in the definition of some search algorithms. Given a graph g of the form Graph (succ) and any starting node (say a), we can explore the graph from a by applying

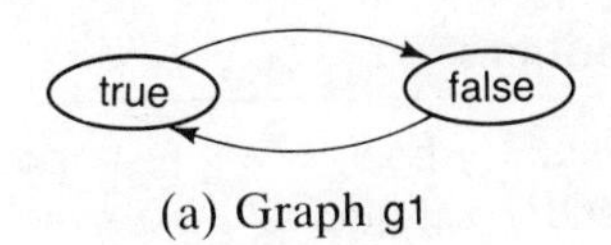

(a) Graph g1

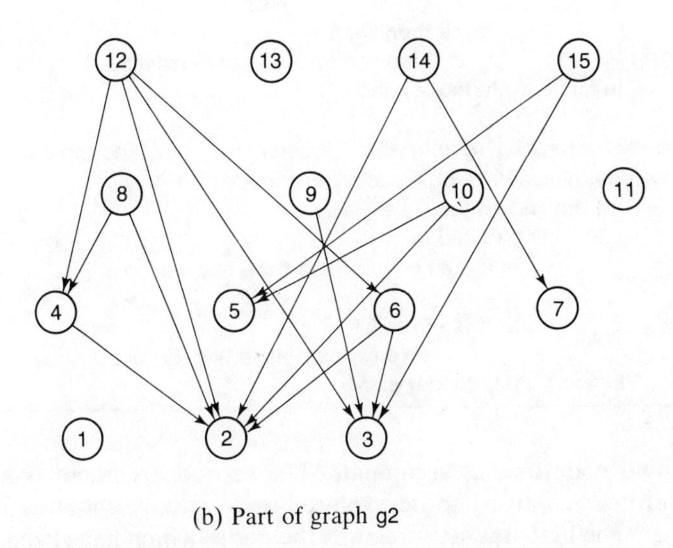

(b) Part of graph g2

Figure 5.6 The graphs g1 and g2.

succ to a to obtain the list of immediate successors. Each of the values in this list gives us further nodes from which we can continue the exploration. By keeping a record of the nodes we have visited (e.g. as a list) we can avoid repeating searches by comparing new successors with nodes that have been visited. We continue searching until a node is found which satisfies a given predicate (p).

We will describe a **depth-first search** and also a **breadth-first search** of the nodes which are reachable from some given starting node by following chains of successors. For depth-first search we want to look at a node and then at its first successor. The descendants of the first successor are all inspected before the second successor, and similarly the second successor and its descendants are inspected before the third successor (and so on). Breadth-first search requires that we look at all the immediate successors before their descendants. Furthermore, the immediate successors of each of the immediate successors must all be inspected before going down to the next level (and so on).

The definitions in Table 5.1 show how similar breadth-first and depth-first searches are. In both cases, the search function find is defined

Table 5.1 Graph searching algorithms.

```
(depthsearch: α⁼ graph → (α⁼ → bool) → α⁼ → α⁼ possible)
fun depthsearch (Graph succ) p startnode
  = let fun find visited [ ] = Fail
          | find visited (a :: x)
              = if member visited a then find visited x
                                     else
                 if p a then Ok a
                        else find (a :: visited) (succ a @ x)
     in find [ ] [startnode] end

(breadthsearch: α⁼ graph → (α⁼ → bool) → α⁼ → α⁼ possible)
fun breadthsearch (Graph succ) p startnode
  = let fun find visited [ ] = Fail
          | find visited (a :: x)
              = if member visited a then find visited x
                                     else
                 if p a then Ok a
                        else find (a :: visited) (x @ succ a)
     in find [ ] [startnode] end
```

to take two node lists as arguments. The second argument is a list of (pending) nodes waiting to be explored and initially contains just the start node. The first argument records the nodes which have been visited and is initially [ ]. The visited nodes have been tested (with the predicate p) and have failed (produced false). At each stage, the first node in the pending list is checked against the visited list to see if it has already been tried and just dropped if it has. Otherwise, the node is tested and if this is the required node it is returned as the result (with Ok). If the node fails the test, then its successors are found and these new nodes are added to the pending list before the search continues. For depth-first search, the new nodes are added to the front of the pending list. Breadth-first search differs only in that the successors are placed at the end of the list rather than at the front so the unvisited descendants are 'queued' instead of being 'stacked up'.

Some applications of graphs and the searching algorithms are suggested in the exercises. In the next section, we explore further the possibilities of using functions in data structures. This is a more advanced topic and can be omitted on a first reading.

5.3 Structures containing functions

We have already made use of a data structure with functional components in the previous example of graphs. In this section we will discuss further examples where direct use of functions provides an alternative means of representation and leads to an **object oriented** programming style. The power gained by allowing functions to be items of data and components of data structures should not be underestimated. Frequently, complex data structures used in programming languages without a higher order facility are just substitutes for a more natural representation involving functions. The first example begins with direct use of a function to model some data object.

5.3.1 Associations

A very useful concept for functional programming is that of a collection of **bindings** or **associations** which are used to associate or pair values of one type with values of another type. LISP programmers usually refer to such objects as association lists but they can also be thought of as partial mappings (functions). As a simple example, suppose we have a list of person names with corresponding ages for each name (i.e. a list of pairs) then we would like to be able to look up the age of a given person using the list. Thus we would be using the list to obtain a mapping from names to ages. Later, we may wish to add more names with corresponding ages or provide a new age to be associated with a name we already have an age for.

With imperative languages, it would be natural to use an in-place update to make the last kind of change (provided the previous association is no longer needed in the computation). With applicative languages we have no corresponding concept of something being no longer needed in a computation, but we can still define an operation which forms a new collection of associations as the result of adding new associations to a previous collection. Associations are often used as a functional counterpart for the state of an imperative program to keep the latest associations, so a criterion for designing an implementation should be that the operation of adding new associations to override old ones is efficient. Rebuilding an entire collection of associations from scratch to accommodate new associations would clearly not be efficient.

We will define a function assoc which takes a list of pairs (some new associations) together with the old associations to form resulting associations. Thus we might write:

```
assoc [("George", 17), ("Mary", 20)] oldassocs
```

to associate 17 with "George", 20 with "Mary" and other associations (apart from those for "George" and "Mary") as indicated by oldassocs. The only other operation we want for associations involves looking up the value associated (in a pair) with a given value. A traditional solution to this is to keep the associations as a list and to search down the list for the most recent association for a given value. This suggests something like:

```
datatype (α, β) associations = Assoc of ((α × β) list × (α, β) associations)
                                | Emptyassoc

fun assoc list oldassocs = Assoc (list, oldassocs)
fun lookup (Assoc (x, old)) a = ···
```

In the following implementation, however, we do not introduce new types (α, β) associations, but instead identify them with existing functional types:

```
type (α, β) associations = α → β
```

Since associations are used to look up associated values, we identify the association with the look-up function itself. Thus assoc pairlist oldassoc will be a function which when given a value to look up, will return the associated value in pairlist (or oldassocs):

```
fun assoc [ ] oldassocs a = oldassocs a
  | assoc ((a1, b1) :: rest) oldassocs a
                         = if a = a1
                           then b1
                           else assoc rest oldassocs a
```

Note that oldassocs will be a similar function which is used as the default if no association is found in the pairlist argument. We don't need to define lookup which degenerates to the identity function (i.e. lookup assocfn a = assocfn a). The type of assoc is:

```
assoc : (α⁼ × β) list → (α⁼ → β) → α⁼ → β
```

If multiple associations are given for a value a, the first one found (leftmost in the list) is used to return an answer. To start with, we might define an empty association as a function which is undefined for all arguments, and then finite associations can be built from that using assoc:

```
fun emptyassoc a = error "no association found"
val example1 = assoc [(1, "a"), (2, "b"), (3, "c")] emptyassoc
val example2 = assoc [(2, "e"), (4, "xxx")] example1
```

Then, example2 (3) = example1 (3) = "c", example2 (2) = "e", example1 (2) = "b", and example2 (5) is undefined. We could also begin with a fully defined default function if we prefer. For example, we might define atlocation as an association of integers with integers which is the identity in all but a finite number of cases:

```
val atlocation = assoc [(1, 100), (6, 50), (7, 200)] I
```

which makes atlocation : int → int and:

```
atlocation 1 = 100
atlocation 6 = 50
atlocation 7 = 200
atlocation n = I (n) = n   in all other cases
```

This last example is intended to suggest how associations (and hence functions) play a similar role to that played by arrays in imperative languages. There are many applications of associations and alternative representations, some of which are discussed in the exercises.

5.3.2 Priority structures

In this example we show how a general concept (that of a priority structure) can unify several different concepts (e.g. stacks, queues, priority lists) by means of a data structure with functional components.†

Consider the following **mechanisms** which are frequently used in computing: (1) a stack which contains a collection of items that can be added to (by pushing) and retrieved (by popping) in such a way that the last item added is the first retrieved (i.e. last in – first out or LIFO); (2) a queue which also contains a collection of items that can be added to or retrieved, but items are added to the back of the queue and retrieved from the front to achieve a last in last out regime (LILO); and (3) a priority list which generalizes the notion of stack and queue by allowing items to be added at different places depending on some priority ordering.

Each of these mechanisms can be implemented with different types. However, we will show their commonality as objects which (1) can have items added to produce a new object with similar properties, (2) can be used to produce a next item and similar object with this item removed (when the object is not empty) and (3) can be made to report the number of items currently stored. We will define:

```
datatype α priority
           = Prio of (α → α priority,
                      unit → (α × α priority),
                      int)
```

†These examples were based on suggestions by Mike Fourman.

Thus a priority structure is an object of the form Prio (f, g, n) with three components, two of which are functions and one is an integer. The functional components are used for adding and retrieving items and return new priority structure objects with similar components. The integer just records the number of stored items.

Since the type unit has only the empty tuple ( ) as a value it provides a dummy argument for the second function which appears to serve no purpose. It would be reasonable to ask why a function with argument type unit is used as a component instead of directly incorporating a value of the result type ($\alpha \times \alpha$ priority) as a component. The reason is that a function gives us a means of delaying evaluation of the component and also allows us to create recursively defined objects. In fact the use of a function to delay evaluation is only necessary in a non-lazy language, and we could simply use the components directly in a lazy language. Chapters 8 and 9 go into this problem in more detail. We could also have had a function of type unit → int for the third component which could be used to report the number of stored items, but delaying evaluation of a simple integer is not necessary here.

The conventional approach to implementing stacks and queues etc. is to define a type (without functional components) which can be used to represent the items stored in a stack or queue, and then to define (globally) appropriate functions for retrieving and adding items to any such object. In contrast, here, we are regarding the adding and retrieving functions as *local* components of each object of type α priority. This is usually what is meant by an **object oriented style**, where each object contains the relevant functions for using the object. Global operations applicable to any object of the type can easily be derived from this representation by selecting the appropriate component function of each object. For example, the definitions:

```
fun additem (Prio (f, g, n)) a = f a
fun getitem (Prio (f, g, n)) = g ( )
fun sizestruct (Prio (f, g, n)) = n
```

introduce:

```
additem: α priority → α → α priority
getitem: α priority → α priority
sizestruct: α priority → int
```

and explain that (1) an item can be added to any priority structure by the use of its first functional component; (2) an item and new priority structure can be retrieved from a given priority structure by the use of its second functional component, and (3) the size of a priority structure is given by its third component.

This also illustrates the use of data objects containing component functions which create further data objects of a similar nature. This is an important aspect of an object oriented programming style.

Having presented the type definition, we next need to construct objects (values) of such a type and this is not quite so easy. For example, if we try to define an empty stack, we will form an object of the form Prio (f, g, n) but we first need to describe the functions f and g. These functions return other (larger) objects of the same type which must also be described. (Try it.) What we need to do is present a uniform way of constructing any value of the type from values of another type which carry sufficient information for this purpose. We will refer to these other values as our **inner representations**. Priority structures like stacks and queues with different inner representations can be used alongside each other but an inner representation must be decided upon when an initial priority structure is constructed and its functional components described. The inner representation does not need to be referred to again when we use the functional components of the initial structure to create further priority structures.

For example, for stacks, we will choose as our inner representation a pair consisting of an integer and a list. The list contains the items in the stack with the latest item at the front of the list. The integer will give the size of the stack and will be equal to the length of the list. We will define a function mkstack which converts any such pair into a priority structure:

```
fun mkstack (list, n) = let fun f a = mkstack (a :: list, n + 1)
                            fun g ( ) = if n < 1
                                        then error "emptystack underflow"
                                        else (hd list, mkstack (tl list, n - 1))
                        in Prio (f, g, n) end
```

Note how the same function mkstack : (α list × int) → α priority is used recursively to describe the results of the component functions f and g. When f is supplied with an item to be added (to the object of which f is the additem component) it returns a priority structure constructed with mkstack. The inner representation (list, n) of the current object is used to make (a :: list, n + 1) which will be the inner representation of the new object. Similarly, g obtains the head and tail of the current inner representation and uses the tail to form a new object with mkstack. Now to define an empty stack, we could merely write:

```
val emptystack = mkstack ([ ], 0)
```

However, we really want to restrict this application to be our only use of the function mkstack in order to ensure that subsequent stacks are created from the components of emptystack rather than from scratch. To achieve this, we can embed the definition of mkstack inside the definition of emptystack so that it is not available globally. We should therefore replace the previous two definitions with the following:

```
local
  fun mkstack (list, n)
      = let fun f a = mkstack (a :: list, n + 1)
              fun g ( ) = if n < 1
                          then error "emptystack underflow"
                          else (hd list, mkstack (tl list, n − 1))
        in Prio (f, g, n) end
in
  val emptystack = mkstack ([ ], 0)
end
```

Now we can create new stacks by accessing the components of emptystack via the functions additem and getitem.

For a comparison, here is a definition of the empty queue. Again we choose a pair consisting of a list and an integer as a representation. The back of the queue is the head of the list, and the size of the queue is given by the integer. This time, however, we do not assume that the integer (n, say) gives the exact length of the list, but that it is at most the length of the list. The items of the queue are thus the front n items of the list. The function select : int → α list → α retrieves the nth item of a list (see Exercise 3.7 for a definition) and is used to obtain the first item in the queue:

```
local
  fun mkqueue (list, n)
      = let fun f a = mkqueue (a :: list, n + 1)
              fun g ( ) = if n < 1
                          then error "emptyqueue underflow"
                          else (select n list, mkqueue (list, n − 1))
        in Prio (f, g, n) end
in
  val emptyqueue = mkqueue ([ ], 0)
end
```

This gives a rather unusual representation of queues as ever-growing lists. New items are added to the front of the list (which is the back of the queue) but items are not removed from the list when items are dropped from the queue. Instead, the integer determining the accessible part of the list representing the queue is decremented. (This may not be a good representation for fast changing queues because reclamation of unused parts of the list beyond the current queue size is prevented.)

The more general mechanism of priority lists with a priority ordering can be handled in the same way by providing details of the priority ordering when the initial list is created. If we assume before : $\alpha \rightarrow \alpha \rightarrow$ bool represents a total ordering of values of type α (i e. before a b = true means b is before a in the ordering), then we can define emptyprio with such a before as a parameter:

```
fun emptyprio (before)
     = let fun mkprio (list, n)
                = let fun f a    = mkprio (insertwrt before a list, n + 1)
                          fun g ( ) = if n < 1
                                         then error "emptyprio underflow"
                                         else (hd list, mkprio (tl list, n - 1))
                   in Prio (f, g, n) end
        in mkprio ([ ], 0) end
```

The auxiliary function insertwrt uses the parameter before to decide where an item is to be placed in a list and its type and definition are:

```
insertwrt : (α → α → bool) → α → α list → α list

fun insertwrt before a [ ] = [a]
|    insertwrt before a (b :: x) = if (before b) a
                                    then a :: b :: x
                                    else b :: (insertwrt before a x)
```

It should be noted that if before b a = true for all a and b, then the priority lists constructed should behave like stacks (even though before is not a proper total ordering of values). Conversely, if before b a is always false, queues are constructed.

One of the drawbacks of this object oriented style of programming is that specifying properties becomes much more complex and ensuring that all objects constructed have the specified properties requires analysis of the initial objects as and when they are introduced. Note that hiding the functions mkstack, mkqueue and mkprio does not prevent them being redefined at top level and used with erroneous arguments to create badly behaved priority objects. This may be a convenience when such objects are wanted, but it is a serious problem if they are not wanted. In Chapter 7 we introduce abstract types which show how the type operator priority could be made safer by incorporating the definitions of additem, getitem, sizestruct and the initial objects emptystack, emptyqueue and function emptyprio as operations of the type. This would localize the decisions about representation but it would also prevent a programmer from subsequently introducing new initial priority structures or similar ones with different inner representations. The choice seems to be between the ability to ensure correctness locally and the flexibility allowed by delaying the time at which representation is fixed.

5.4 Algebras and inductive proofs

In this section, we briefly note the relationship between types and algebras and show how to use structural induction on arbitrary new types.

5.4.1 Algebras

The mathematical notion of an **algebra** is simply a set of values with a particular collection of functions operating on those values. Clearly, the idea of a type in programming is closely related to this general notion of algebra. We can (and should) think of a type as the combination of the values of the type and the operations defined on these values. This helps us to use values in appropriate ways (via the associated functions) so that we are less likely to make mistakes.

As we have seen in this chapter, the values of concrete types are intimately related to the constructors of the type. In fact, there is a standard mathematical construction which reflects this relationship exactly, and that is the **free algebra** or **free word algebra** construction.

5.4.2 Free algebras

Roughly speaking, the free algebra construction is a way of constructing an algebra from nothing more than a collection of constructors with associated information about their types. Given a collection of constructors associated with a new type we construct an algebra as follows. The values of the algebra will be the set of expressions in canonical form that can be formed with the constructors. (These are the values we associate with the new type.) The functions of the algebra are defined as follows. For each constructor we define a corresponding function which operates on expressions to return an expression in the set. The function forms the result expression which describes the application of the constructor to the argument expressions. That is, if (E_1, E_2) is an argument pair of expressions (in canonical form) for the function associated with constructor C then the result will be the expression $C\ (E_1, E_2)$ which is also in canonical form.

Let us illustrate this with a complete example. We consider the constructors introduced by the following new type definition:

```
datatype t = C0
           | C1 of t
           | C2 of t × t
```

Thus t is the name of the new type, C0 is a constructor (constant name) of type t, C1 is a constructor (function name) with type t → t and C2 is a function name with type t × t → t. Now consider the set of all expressions that can be formed from these constructors. We classify these according to how complex (deep) they are. The simplest expressions (with depth 1) are those that can be formed with just a constant constructor. In this case we just have:

```
C0
```

The next level are those expressions that can be formed from the simplest expressions by a single application of a constructor. In this case we have:

```
C1 (C0)
C2 (C0, C0)
```

The next level consists of the expressions (of depth 3) which can be formed from the previous levels by a single application of a constructor. (We do not include in this level any expressions which already appear in previous levels.) This gives us:

```
C1 (C1 (C0))
C1 (C2 (C0, C0))
C2 (C0, C1 (C0))
C2 (C0, C2 (C0, C0))
C2 (C1 (C0), C0)
C2 (C1 (C0), C1 (C0))
C2 (C1 (C0), C2 (C0, C0))
C2 (C2 (C0, C0), C0)
C2 (C2 (C0, C0), C1 (C0))
C2 (C2 (C0, C0), C2 (C0, C0))
```

Similarly, expressions at level n (with depth n) are those new expressions that can be formed by applying a constructor to expressions in the previous levels (1 · · · n − 1). The union of all these levels (n = 1, · · ·) gives the complete set of finite expressions which are the values of the algebra (and the values of the new type).

In addition to the set of values, the algebra provides a function for each constructor. In the case of a constant constructor, this degenerates to just a particular value in the set. For our example, corresponding to the constant name C0, there is the constant which is an element of the set (at level 1), namely the expression C0. Corresponding to the constructor C1, there is a function which takes as argument any expression in the above set (say *E*) and forms as result the expression C1 (*E*). Similarly, the function corresponding to the constructor C2 takes as argument a pair of expressions from the set (say (E_1, E_2)) and forms as result the expression C2 (E_1, E_2).

The combination of the set of values and the constant and two functions constitute an algebra which is known as the *free algebra generated by* C0 : t, C1 : t → t and C2 : (t × t) → t. Not surprisingly, this algebra is precisely what we want to associate with the type t introduced by the above definition.

If a constructor has arguments of some other type, say C3 : T → t where T does not involve the new type name t, then we include values of the form C3 (E) in the set for all values E of type T. The function corresponding to C3 will map each element E in the set of values of type T to the element C3 (E). The algebra is said to be generated from the constructors and the sets of values of type T as well. If the type t is parameterized (i.e. t is a type operator) then the whole construction is just parameterized as well. We can think of t as generating an algebra from any given set of values X (representing the values of a parameter type).

Sometimes, the values generated with this 'free' construction do not coincide with the values we want in our type, but are close to what we want. In such cases, the mechanism for defining abstract types which we introduce in Chapter 7 can be used.

We will not go into a rigorous mathematical treatment of algebras here, but refer the interested reader to ADJ (1978a). We will, however, use results from this theory to justify the use of structural induction for new types.

5.4.3 Structural induction

According to our discussion about the values of a new type, each value is constructed from either no values of the type (at level 1) or from strictly simpler values (which are subexpressions of the given value). The values thus carry all the information about their construction. This fact, along with the fact that expressions are finite, allows us to justify an extension of the structural induction we used with lists for use with any new type, based on the complexity (depth) of the expressions. For our particular example of type t with constructors C0, C1, C2, structural induction allows us to prove that a property P holds for all (proper) values of type t by establishing that:

(1) P (C0) holds;

(2) P (C1 (x)) follows from the assumption that P (x) holds;

(3) P (C2 (x_1, x_2)) follows from the assumptions that P (x_1) and P (x_2) hold.

More generally, given a definition of a new type t introducing constructors $C_0, \ldots, C_n$, we have the following principle:

Principle of structural induction for new type t

In order to prove that:

P (x) holds for all values x : t

it is sufficient to prove that for each constructor C_i:

(1) if C_i is a constant constructor then $P(C_i)$ is true;

(2) if C_i is a constructor with argument type:

$$T_1 \times T_2 \cdots T_j \ (j > 0)$$

then $P(C_i(x_1, \ldots, x_j))$ follows from the assumptions $P(y_1)$, $P(y_2), \ldots, P(y_k)$, where $y_1 \cdots y_k$ are those members of $x_1 \cdots x_j$ with type t. [We assume that each T_k $(1 \leq k \leq j)$ is either t itself or does not involve t. More complex cases are not covered here.]

Once again this principle implicitly assumes that we are only considering well-defined values of type T when we say 'for all . . . : T. . .' and that t only has finitely constructed values as we specified in the description of the algebra. The principle can be established as a special case of general induction for well founded orders using the subexpression ordering of values of type t (see Section 1.5.5). If t is parameterized, then the principle holds for each instance type (e.g. for any monotype T, we can use the principle to prove things about T t).

We illustrate the use of this principle with some simple examples below.

5.4.4 Example: bintrees

Bintrees were introduced with:

```
datatype α bintree = Lf of α
                   | /\ of (α bintree × α bintree)
```

In this case, the use of structural induction boils down to the following (where T represents any type).

In order to prove P (x) for all x : T bintree, we must show that:

(1) P (Lf (a)) holds for all a : T;

(2) P (t1 /\ t2) holds assuming P (t1) and P (t2) hold.

As an example, we prove that reflect (reflect x) = x for all x : *T* bintree (for any type *T*) where reflect : α bintree → α bintree is defined by:

```
fun reflect (Lf a) = Lf a
|   reflect (t1 /\ t2) = (reflect t2) /\ (reflect t1)
```

First:

```
reflect (reflect (Lf a)) = reflect (Lf a) = Lf a
```

for all a : *T*, which establishes the base case. Secondly, assuming the induction hypotheses that:

```
reflect (reflect t1) = t1
reflect (reflect t2) = t2
```

it is easy to show that:

```
reflect (reflect (t1 /\ t2)) = reflect ((reflect t2) /\ (reflect t1))
                             = (reflect (reflect t1)) /\ (reflect (reflect t2))
                             = t1 /\ t2
```

This establishes the step case, and the result follows by structural induction.

5.4.5 Example: trees

For a slightly harder example, we will prove that the treeinsert operation which we used to place integers into integer trees really does preserve the order when the argument tree is ordered. Recall that we defined:

```
datatype α tree = Tr of (α tree × α × α tree)
                | Empty
```

So to prove *P* (t) for all t : *T* tree (for any type *T*) by structural induction, we must show that:

(1) *P* (Empty) holds;

(2) *P* (Tr (t1, a, t2)) follows from *P* (t1) and *P* (t2) for all a : *T* and t1, t2 : *T* tree.

First, we give a more formal description of ordered trees. For this example we are only interested in int tree, and we will define a predicate orderedtree : int tree → bool which expresses the idea of an ordered tree as directly as possible (without concern for efficiency of computation):

```
fun orderedtree (Empty) = true
|   orderedtree (Tr (t1, a, t2)) = alltree (lessthan a) t1 &
                                   alltree (greatereq a) t2 &
                                   orderedtree t1 &
                                   orderedtree t2
and alltree p (Empty) = true
|   alltree p (Tr (t1, b, t2)) = alltree p t1 & p b & alltree p t2
and greatereq a b = not (lessthan a b)
```

The function alltree : $(\alpha \rightarrow$ bool$) \rightarrow \alpha$ tree $\rightarrow$ bool just asks if a given predicate holds for all the items in a given tree. We leave it as an exercise for the reader to prove that orderedtree t implies ordered (flatten t) for any t : int tree and a suitable definition of ordered : int list → bool.

The treeinsert operation was given earlier by:

```
fun treeinsert Empty m = leaf m
|   treeinsert (Tr (t1, n, t2)) m
                          = if (lessthan n) m
                            then Tr (treeinsert t1 m, n, t2)
                            else Tr (t1, n, treeinsert t2 m)
```

where leaf m = Tr (Empty, m, Empty). We will prove that for all t : int tree and n : int, if orderedtree t = true then orderedtree (treeinsert t n) = true. The base case is proved by showing that:

```
orderedtree (treeinsert Empty n)
    = orderedtree (Tr (Empty, n, Empty)) = true
```

This is straightforward from the definitions and we leave the details as an exercise. The step case is proved by assuming that:

(1) orderedtree (t1) = true implies orderedtree (treeinsert t1 n) = true and

(2) orderedtree (t2) = true implies orderedtree (treeinsert t2 n) = true

and then proving that:

(3) orderedtree (Tr (t1, a, t2)) = true

implies

(4) orderedtree (treeinsert (Tr (t1, a, t2)) n) = true

We assume (3) and establish that (4) is true by considering the cases $n < a$ and $n \geq a$ separately. For the first case, (4) simplifies to orderedtree

(Tr (treeinsert t1 n, a, t2)) = true which is equivalent to the conjunction of the following four statements:

(5) orderedtree (treeinsert t1 n) = true

(6) orderedtree (t2) = true

(7) alltree (greatereq a) t2

(8) alltree (lessthan a) (treeinsert t1 n)

The first three of these follow easily from (3) along with (1). The need to prove (8) from the fact that alltree (lessthan a) t1 and lessthan a n suggests that we should establish the following auxiliary result (lemma) from which (8) follows easily:

alltree p t = true and p n = true implies alltree p (treeinsert t n) = true

The proof of (4) for the case n ≥ a is analogous to the case n < a but using (2) instead of (1) and this same lemma is needed again.

We leave the remaining details of the proof and the proof of the lemma as further exercises. We conclude this chapter with some general observations about the use of new types.

5.5 New type definitions in general

5.5.1 General form and scope of parameters

The general form for a type definition introducing one or more type operators (simultaneously) is:

datatype $TVars_1\ Top_1 = C_{11}$ **of** $T_{11} \mid C_{12}$ **of** $T_{12} \cdots \mid C_{1n_1}$ **of** T_{1n_1}
and $TVars_2\ Top_2 = C_{21}$ **of** $T_{21} \mid C_{22}$ **of** $T_{22} \cdots \mid C_{2n_2}$ **of** T_{2n_2}
...
and $TVars_m\ Top_m = C_{m1}$ **of** $T_{m1} \mid C_{m2}$ **of** $T_{m2} \cdots \mid C_{mn_m}$ **of** T_{mn_m}

where Top_i (i = 1, . . . , m) are the new type operator names, and $TVars_i$ (i = 1, . . . , m) are sequences of distinct type variables such as (α, β, γ). The sequence may be just a single type variable or the empty sequence when a type constant is being introduced. For each i (i = 1, . . . , m) and j (j = 1, . . . , n_i), T_{ij} is a type expression and C_{ij} is a newly introduced constructor of type $T_{ij} \rightarrow (TVars_i\ Top_i)$. Any '**of** T_{ij}' can be omitted in which case C_{ij} is a constant of type $(TVars_i\ Top_i)$. All the constructors in the definition must be distinct. The type expressions (T_{ij}) are composed of previously defined type operators but they may also include recursive references to

$Top_1, \ldots, Top_m$ and references to the variables in $TVars_i$. A type variable introduced as a parameter on the left-hand side of a type operator definition (e.g. in $TVars_i$) has a scope which is the right-hand side of the definition of Top_i including $T_{i1}, T_{i2}, \ldots, T_{in_i}$. Thus occurrences of the type variable in say T_{ij} (the argument type of the constructor C_{ij}) are bound by the left-hand occurrence in $TVars_i$ which is analogous to the use of (value) variables as parameters in function definitions. This means that variables can be safely repeated in the definitions of two or more type operators and they remain independent. In particular:

```
datatype α point = Point of α
     and α line  = Line of (α point × α point)
```

is equivalent to:

```
datatype α point = Point of α
     and β line  = Line of (β point × β point)
```

5.5.2 Equality for new types

We gave some examples of new types earlier in this chapter for which a natural equality operation existed (and could be automatically inferred). In general, an equality operation can be inferred for a new type such as $T\ Top_i$ (for Top_i introduced as above), provided that equality is defined for the parameter type(s) T and for all the types T_{ij} ($j = 1, \ldots, n_i$) appearing as argument types for the constructors. (Since some of these argument types may involve the newly introduced type operators, we have to calculate the admissibility of equality in a mutually recursive way.)

So far, the only types which do not admit an equality operation are those involving function types. The following table gives some examples:

Types with equality	*Types without equality*
int list	(int → int) list
int tree	(int → int) tree
(int tree) list	int graph
(int bintree) possible	(int → int) graph
bool bintree × string possible	int priority

Graphs and priority structures both involve functional components regardless of the parameter type, so equality cannot be automatically defined for any type formed with these.

5.5.3 Type definitions are generative

In the examples given so far, we have been regarding type definitions as global. If we use type definitions locally in expressions and have nested scopes for type definitions, we need to specify how the definitions interact. (Type definitions must be global in Miranda so these problems do not arise.)

If a type name or constructor is redefined locally, the local definition overrides any previous definition throughout the local scope. For example, in the context of the standard definition of type bool and the definition of & : (bool × bool) → bool, we might introduce a more local definition:

```
let datatype bool = true | false
in true & false end
```

But this will be a type error because & : (bool × bool) → bool was defined in the context of the global definition of bool not this local one. Thus even though the local definition of bool has exactly the same form as the global one (assumed to be predefined), it is introducing a new type and new constructors which are distinguished from any more globally introduced types and constructors. Type definitions are said to be **generative** because they always introduce new types whenever they are evaluated. An alternative approach (not adopted here or in ML) is to allow non generative definitions where types are taken to be compatible if they are introduced by equivalent definitions. This approach is rejected because it leads to more accidental misuse of types being accepted as correct.

One manifestation of the generative nature of types which can occur in developing definitions interactively in ML is worth mentioning because it can cause problems if one is unaware of the effects. It is quite common to have a type definition along with definitions of related functions in a file. These can then be evaluated by loading the file in an interactive session. If the file is subsequently edited (say, by changing a function name and correcting some of the definitions) and then reloaded for re-evaluation, this has the effect of introducing another new type which is more local (more recent) than the one introduced the first time the file was loaded. Confusion can arise if one tries to use objects and functions defined in the context of the first occurrence of the definition within the context of the second occurrence of the definition. The type checker will not confuse the two types and will report type mismatches.

Another problem of local type definitions is that they allow expressions to be written which have a canonical form and type involving identifiers which are out of scope. For example, if a type definition is local to an expression E we should expect the scope of the constructors of that type and the new type name itself to be E. (When the type definition is recursive, the scope of the type name will include the right-hand side of the definition as well.) But then what is the value and indeed the type of the following expression?

```
let datatype T1 = Localval1 | Localval2
in Localval2 end
```

The obvious answer is Localval2 : T1, but both Localval2 and T1 are out of scope at the top level (being local names). Hence, this should be reported as an error. (In Chapter 7 we discuss the use of *modules* as another mechanism for sharing/exporting/controlling the scope of types in large-scale programming.)

5.5.4 Comparing the procedural approach

In Table 5.2 we compare the definition of the type operator bintree with an analogous definition of binary tree storage structures in Pascal (specialized to integer trees since Pascal is not polymorphic). Although the Pascal type and function definitions are more complex than the corresponding ML definitions, the associated storage structures may be updated in place and used in very non-functional ways.

Table 5.2 Pascal definitions for bintrees (with integer labels) including definitions of constructors Lf and Pr, predicate isleaf, selectors left and right and leaflabel (the procedure 'error' is assumed).

```
TYPE alpha          = integer;
     bintreeVariant = (leaf, pair);
     bintreePointer = ↑ bintree;
     bintree        = RECORD
                      CASE variant : bintreeVariant of
                        leaf : (leafval : alpha);
                        pair : (leftptr, rightptr : bintreePointer)
                      END;
FUNCTION Lf (n : alpha) : bintreePointer;
    var temp : bintreePointer;
  BEGIN
    new (temp, leaf);
    temp ↑ .leafval := n;
    Lf := temp
  END;
FUNCTION Pr (t1, t2 : bintreePointer) : bintreePointer;
    var temp : bintreePointer;
```

Table 5.2 *(Cont.)*

```
    BEGIN
      new (temp, pair);
      temp ↑ .leftptr := t1;
      temp ↑ .rightptr := t2;
      Dot := temp
    END;
  FUNCTION left (t : bintreePointer) : bintreePointer;
    BEGIN
      CASE t ↑ .variant of
        pair : left := t ↑ .leftptr;
        leaf : error ("left of leaf")
      END
    END;
  FUNCTION right (t : bintreePointer) : bintreePointer;
    BEGIN
      CASE t ↑ .variant of
        pair : right := t ↑ .rightptr;
        leaf : error ("right of leaf")
      END
    END;
  FUNCTION isleaf (t : bintreePointer) : boolean;
    BEGIN
      CASE t ↑ .variant of
        pair : isleaf := false;
        leaf : isleaf := true
      END
    END;
  FUNCTION leaflabel (t : bintreePointer) : alpha;
    BEGIN
      CASE t ↑ .variant of
        pair : error ("leaflabel of non-leaf");
        leaf : leaflabel := t ↑ .leafval
      END
    END;
```

Here, the gap between the functional and procedural approaches to programming seems to widen. In procedural programming, efficiency is often gained by judicious use of structures which are frequently in-place updated to minimize the use of space needed in a computation. To gain efficiency in functional programming, one must consider the possibilities for performing larger steps in one go without building on many piecemeal and costly constructions of intermediate data structures. The comparison is more complicated by the fact that the absence of in-place updating enhances the possibilities for sharing data structures. For example, let us consider the replacement of the leftmost leaf of an integer binary tree by an arbitrary value (such as one more than its original value). With the Pascal storage structure, we may literally replace the value by an in-place update provided the old tree is no longer needed for subsequent computations. In functional programming, such an operation on a tree requires the construction of a new tree which differs in the value of one of its leaves from some given tree. However, the newly constructed tree may have much in common with the original tree and could share many of its subtrees as depicted in Figure 5.7.

Another important point is that the use of very generalized functions (such as btreeop) in programming allows one to discern and focus on the basic structure of an algorithm more easily and also allows one to avoid the many programming errors which can arise from incomplete case analysis and contorted flows of control which do not match the data structures used in an algorithm. The higher level

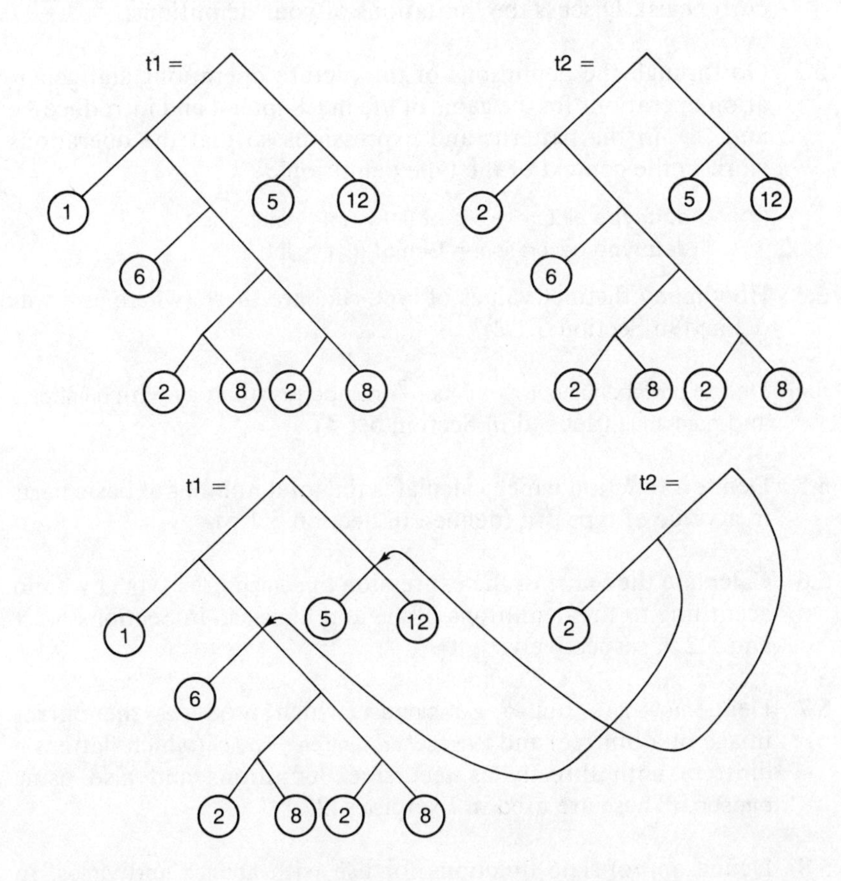

Figure 5.7 Bintrees t and t′ differ in one leaf and may share other subtrees.

operations also allow one to escape from the piecemeal patching and rearrrangements of data structures (which is often a source of errors) and to describe larger transformations more succinctly.

The simplicity of definition and use of new types should also encourage clearer and safer programming habits. However, even though the types that can be described in the way we have indicated in this chapter are very rich, they are not quite enough for modern programming methods. We need to go still further and introduce abstract types as well as concrete types for programming. We do this in Chapter 7 after giving an extended example of the use of concrete types in the next chapter.

EXERCISES

5.1 Define concrete types for dates and money values (in alternative currencies). Discuss the limitations of your definitions.

5.2 Go through the definitions of the picture operations and generation operations for the game of life in Chapter 4 and introduce Pic and Gen in the patterns and expressions so that the operations work in the context of the type definitions:

```
datatype picture = Pic of (int × int × string list)
datatype generation = Gen of ((int × int) list)
```

5.3 How many distinct values of type card are there (where card was defined in Section 5.1.2)?

5.4 Define power : number × number → number by analogy with numbplus and numbmult (defined in Section 5.1.4).

5.5 Define a function which calculates the total number of basic parts in a value of type part (defined in Section 5.1.5).

5.6 Calculate the value of the expression btreemap (plus 1) bt3 by hand according to the definitions of bt3 and btreemap in Sections 5.2.1 and 5.2.2, respectively.

5.7 Define reflect : α bintree → α bintree (which produces the mirror image of a bintree) and leavesof : α bintree → α list (which flattens a bintree) both directly as recursive definitions and also using btreeop. (These are used in Exercise 5.27.)

5.8 Define appropriate functions for use with abtrees and vtrees. In particular, give some most general higher order functions and

```
val pretty1 = ((((Lf 3 /\ Lf 4) /\ (Lf 5 /\ (Lf 6 /\ Lf 7))) /\ Lf 8) /\ Lf 9)
val pretty2 = pretty1 /\ pretty1
```

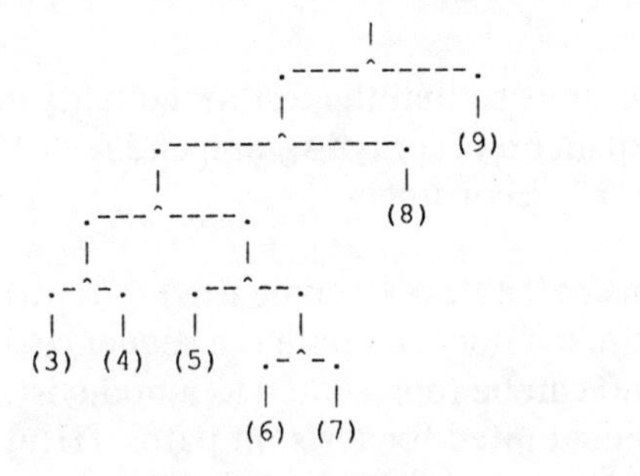

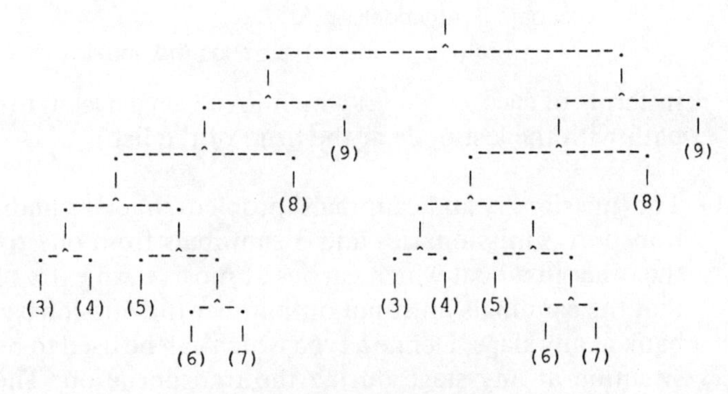

Figure 5.8 See Exercise 5.9.

show how they can be used to define some particular operations on the trees.

5.9 Since the standard display of trees (and also bintrees, abtrees and vtrees) can be rather unreadable it would be useful to have character picture displays of trees. Define operations which produce pictures of trees. Note that these should be parameterized by functions which can be supplied to draw pictures of leaf or node values. Do this for all the different kinds of tree mentioned. Figure 5.8 is an example for the binary trees.

5.10 A common representation of graphs with nodes of type α uses values of type $(\alpha \times \alpha)$ list which defines the pairs of nodes connected by an arrow. Define a function which converts values of type $(\alpha \times \alpha)$ list into graphs using the representation:

datatype α graph = Graph **of** ($\alpha \rightarrow \alpha$ list)

5.11 Simplify the graph search functions of Table 5.1 for use when graphs are to be regarded as trees (i.e. no check is made for repeated visits to nodes).

5.12 Extend the representation of graphs so that the test for equality of nodes is incorporated as part of an object of type graph and rewrite the search functions of Table 5.1 accordingly.

5.13 Show how the search functions of Table 5.1 can be used to return the path to a node rather than just a node. (A path is a sequence of nodes connected by arrows and can be represented as a node list.) The predicate p should also be adapted for tests on paths. (Hint: Construct a new graph before the search begins; define:

```
succpath (Path nodelist)
      = [Path (a :: nodelist) | a ∈ succ (hd nodelist)]
```

in terms of succ : $\alpha \rightarrow \alpha$ list which uses Path (nodelist) to represent a path with the last node at the head of the list.)

5.14 The 'missionary and cannibals' problem involves finding a way to transport 3 missionaries and 3 cannibals from one river bank to the other in a boat which carries at most 2. An extra constraint is that the cannibals must not outnumber the missionaries on either bank at any stage. Define a type which can be used to represent the situation at any stage during the transportation. Then define a graph which represents the legal nodes (situations) which can be reached from a legal node. Use the graph searching algorithms to find the solution from your graph.

5.15 In the definition of assoc (Section 5.3.1) it seems that associations will not allow enquiries to find out if a value has an associated value at all. Show that by taking an instance type of β possible for the result type and default function returning Fail, a predicate for making such an enquiry can be defined using the same implementation.

5.16 Define an alternative to the function:

$$\text{assoc} : (\alpha^{=} \times \beta) \text{ list} \rightarrow (\alpha^{=} \rightarrow \beta) \rightarrow \alpha^{=} \rightarrow \beta$$

namely:

$$\text{assocall} : (\alpha^{=} \times \beta) \text{ list} \rightarrow \alpha^{=} \rightarrow \beta \text{ list}$$

which returns a list of values associated with a given value in the order they appear in the pair list, e.g.

```
assocall [(1, "a"), (2, "b"), (2, "cc"), (1, "ab")] 1
        = ["a", "ab"].
```

(Note that [ ] is returned for absent associations so a default is not required.) Suggest a suitable function (combine) for combining list association functions so that:

combine (assocall l1) (assocall l2) : $\alpha^{=} \rightarrow \beta$ list

and the result applied to a gives the associations of a in l2 if there are none in l1 and gives the associations of a in l1 followed by those in l2, otherwise. The use of such functions for backtracking computations is discussed in Wadler (1985).

5.17 Define a type which represents associations as lists of lists of pairs (the top list being the latest associations). Define appropriate assoc and lookup functions for this type.

5.18 Define associations as objects with assoc and lookup components (i.e. functional components). Define an initial association generator newassoc for use with this type.

5.19 Consider three priority levels High, Low, Medium to be used in priority lists so that new High-priority items go in front of Low- and Medium-priority items but after other High-priority items. Similarly Medium-priority items are added before the Low-priority ones but after all others and Low-priority items go to the back. Show that the function emptyprio defined in Section 5.3.2 can be used to implement such a priority list by labelling items with their priority and choosing an appropriate ordering predicate as argument for emptyprio.

5.20 A 'deque' is a double-ended queue which can have items added in the normal way for a queue or pushed onto the front like a stack. Suggest several different ways to implement deques using priority.

5.21 Define another empty queue of type α priority with a different inner representation (for frequently changing queues).

5.22 Redefine emptystack and emptyqueue from Section 5.3.2 avoiding the use of **local** (but still keeping the functions mkstack and mkqueue local to the corresponding definitions).

5.23 Give a formal definition of all the values of type t where t is defined as in Section 5.4.2 with constructors C0, C1, C2.

5.24 Define a predicate ordered : int list → bool and prove that orderedtree (x) implies ordered (flatten x).

5.25 There is a natural correspondence between values of type α tree and α forest (= α vtree list). Define functions which convert from one type to the other and show formally (by structural induction) that converting from either type and back again gives the original value.

5.26 If you are familiar with a structured procedural programming language such as Pascal or C or ALGOL68, define suitable representations for values of type α tree and (α, β) abtree in the language (for some fixed α and β). Define appropriate selectors, predicates and constructors for your representation.

5.27 Using the definitions from Exercise 5.7, prove by structural induction that:

```
reflect (reflect t) = t
leavesof (reflect t) = rev (leavesof t)
```

for all (finite, well defined) bintrees t. (Hint: Use the result that rev (x @ y) = rev y @ rev x from Exercise 3.30.)

5.28 Generalise the statement of the principle of structural induction for use with simultaneous, mutually recursive definitions of several types $(t_1, \ldots, t_n)$ to establish properties P_i for values of type t_i $(i = 1, \ldots, n)$.

5.29 Consider the following definition of a function flattenwith which operates in a similar way to flatten but has an extra argument list to be appended to the result:

```
flattenwith : α tree → α list → α list
fun flattenwith Empty x = x
 |  flattenwith (Tr (l, a, r)) x
                        = flattenwith l (a :: flattenwith r x)
```

Prove (using structural induction) that for all trees t and lists x of appropriate types:

```
flattenwith t x = (flatten t) @ x
```

and hence that

```
flatten t = flattenwith t [ ]
```

Note that if flattenwith is used to flatten a tree then no @ operations are necessary and the number of :: operations is equal to the number of items in the tree. Estimate the average number of :: operations used in an application of flatten.

5.30 This exercise illustrates how tuples (in particular pairs) may be replaced by functions. First, recall that K is a curried version of fst which returns the first of two arguments:

```
fun K a b = a
```

Similarly, we define its counterpart which (for reasons which will become clear in later chapters) we call KI:

```
fun KI a b = b
```

Now consider the following definitions:

```
fun mkpair a b f = f a b
and first pr = pr K
and second pr = pr KI
```

The result of applying mkpair to items a and b is a function (representing the pair). This function expects to be applied to a selector f (which is also function) to retrieve the components. first and second retrieve components by supplying the selectors K and KI to a pair. What are the principal types of mkpair, first and second? Show that the following equations hold:

```
first (mkpair a b) = a
second (mkpair a b) = b
```

Now define eqpair so that:

```
eqpair (mkpair a1 b1) (mkpair a2 b2)
```

is true if both a1 = a2 and b1 = b2 are true. What is the type of this eqpair?

Chapter 6
Extended Example: Command Interpreter

In this chapter, we will illustrate the use of new types in the design and implementation of an interpreter for a language of commands. The abstract syntax of the command language is conveniently expressed as a new data type and the interpreter is defined as a function over the new type. (The interpreter provides a functional description of the behaviour associated with the imperative constructs of the language.)

The chapter also includes the development of a parser for the command language (i.e. a function processing strings to recognize commands) and illustrates some general techniques and re-usable parser building operations.

6.1 Syntax trees for a language of commands

We start by introducing a very small imperative programming language consisting of commands and show how a type for values representing programs in this language may be defined. The (abstract) syntax of the commands is described as follows:

A Command is
either
  An Assignment, in which case it has two components:
    A variable (which is assigned to)
    An expression (whose value is assigned)
or
  A Sequence, in which case it has two components:
    A command (which is to be done first)
    A command (which is to be done second)
or
  A Conditional, in which case it has three components:
    An expression (which is the test)
    A command (which is the true branch)
    A command (which is the false branch)
or
  A While loop, in which case it has two components:
    An expression (which is the loop test)
    A command (which is the body of the loop)

We refer to this as the **abstract syntax** because it just describes the syntactic structure of commands in terms (ultimately) of expressions and variables, but it is not committed to any particular choices of symbols for writing out such commands. A more detailed description which includes such lexical information is usually referred to as a **concrete syntax**. For example, assignments might be written with the infix symbol :=, sequences with ; between commands, while-loops with the keywords WHILE, DO and END etc. For such a concrete syntax, Figure 6.1 shows an example command and its abstract syntactic structure as a syntax tree.

We define a type command which describes the possible forms of syntax trees for this particular language. Values of this type may then be used to represent programs of the language and the values might be generated from strings by a parser. That is, a parser might be given a string representing a command, and would produce (when the string contained no errors) a program in its abstract form as a value of type command.

For the moment, we assume we have a type expression which represents the possible forms an expression may have, and a type variable. The (recursive) definition of type command can then be written down directly from the above description of commands:

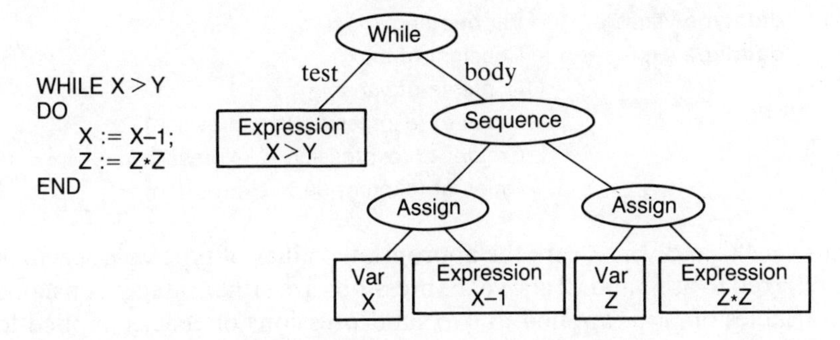

Figure 6.1 Syntactic structure of a command.

```
datatype variable   = (see later)
datatype expression = (see later)

datatype command   = Assign of (variable × expression)
                   | Sequence of (command × command)
                   | Conditional of (expression × command ×
                                       command)
                   | While of (expression × command)
```

This definition introduces the constructors:

```
Assign      : variable × expression → command
Sequence    : command × command → command
Conditional : expression × command × command → command
While       : expression × command → command
```

which correspond to the four possible ways of constructing commands. The example in Figure 6.1 can be expressed in the form:

```
While (e, Sequence (Assign (v1, e1), Assign (v2, e2)))
```

where e, e1 and e2 denote (the abstract structure of) the expressions X > Y, X − 1 and Z ∗ Z respectively, and v1 and v2 stand for the variables X and Z. In order to complete the example, let us give a description of the abstract syntax of expressions and define the types expression and variable for this language. To keep the example simple, we will assume expressions are built by applications of a small number of binary operators to variables and integer constants. We will also assume that all expressions are integer expressions and interpret 0 and 1 as false and true, respectively, in tests. This leads to type definitions:

```
datatype variable    = Var of string
datatype expression = Constant of int
                     | Contents of variable
                     | Minus of (expression × expression)
                     | Greater of (expression × expression)
                     | Times of (expression × expression)
```

Thus Var "X" and Var "Z" are the appropriate values of type variable which we referred to as v1 and v2 above. Expressions are either integer constants or variables or Minus applied to two subexpressions or Greater applied to two subexpressions or Times applied to two subexpressions. Other variants could easily be added (see Exercise 6.1). Note that if a variable occurs in an expression, it is its contents (relative to some store) that is used in calculating the expression value. For this reason we use the constructor Contents to turn a variable into an expression. With these definitions, the example in Figure 6.1 can now be written out completely as:

```
While (Greater (Contents (Var "X"),
                Contents (Var "Y")),
       Sequence (Assign (Var "X",
                         Minus (Contents (Var "X"),
                                Constant 1)),
                 Assign(Var "Z",
                        Times (Contents (Var "Z"),
                               Contents (Var "Z")))
                )
      )
```

The type definitions of expression, variable and command show how we can tailor a type to suit the structure of the objects we are interested in. Furthermore, operations on the objects can be defined by pattern matching so that the various cases can be considered separately. To illustrate this, we will develop an interpreter for the simple language of commands we have introduced as a function defined for values of type command.

6.2 Stores and (integer expression) values

In order to interpret commands, we will need to be able to evaluate expressions of the language such as X − 1. We introduce a special type for the integer values denoted by these expressions rather than just use int:

```
datatype intvalue = Intval of int
```

Since expressions involve assignable variables (like X), evaluation of expressions depends on the store which determines the contents of such variables. Accordingly, we will introduce a type store with two primitive operations and a constant (initial) store:

fetch : variable × store → intvalue
update : store × variable × intvalue → store
store0 : store

The function fetch returns the intvalue associated with a variable by a store (i.e. its contents in that store) and update, given a store (s), a variable (v) and an intvalue (a) produces a store which is the same as s except that it associates the intvalue contents a with v instead of whatever s associated with v. The constant store0 has contents Intval 0 for each variable. We postpone a definition of type store and implementations of these functions and constant until later. Meanwhile here is a more formal specification of the required behaviour of fetch, update and store0:

For any variables v and v′, store s and intvalue a, we assume
fetch (v, update (s, v, a)) = a
v ≠ v′ implies fetch (v, update (s, v′, a)) = fetch (v, s)
fetch (v, store0) = Intval 0

(We choose an initial store with zero as the contents of each cell for simplicity. Alternatives are considered in Section 6.5 and the exercises.)

6.3 Evaluation of expressions

The evaluation of an expression can be described by a curried function:

evalexp : expression → store → intvalue

so that for expression e and store s, evalexp e s produces the intvalue of the expression e relative to store s. The definition of evalexp is:

```
fun evalexp (Constant n) s      = Intval n
  | evalexp (Contents v) s      = fetch (v, s)
  | evalexp (Minus (e1, e2)) s  = let val Intval n1 = evalexp e1 s
                                      and Intval n2 = evalexp e2 s
                                  in Intval (n1 - n2) end
  | evalexp (Times (e1, e2)) s  = let val Intval n1 = evalexp e1 s
                                      and Intval n2 = evalexp e2 s
                                  in Intval (n1 * n2) end
  | evalexp (Greater (e1, e2)) s = let val Intval n1 = evalexp e1 s
                                      and Intval n2 = evalexp e2 s
                                  in if n1 > n2 then Intval (1)
                                                else Intval (0) end
```

The intvalue of a constant is independent of the store s, but the intvalue of a variable in an expression is determined by the store so fetch is used. In the other cases for an expression, the arguments to a binary operator are both evaluated in the same store and the appropriate binary operation performed on the results. When an operation returns a boolean result, this is encoded as Intval (0) for false and Intval (1) for true.

6.4 Interpretation of commands

The interpretation of a command will be a function transforming stores to stores. We will define:

```
interpret : command → store → store
```

so that for command c and store s, interpret c s will be the store produced when command c is obeyed starting with store s. Equivalently, one can think of interpret c as an action (function) on stores such that applied to some store s, a store is produced which is the result of obeying command c starting in store s.

The basic command is the assignment and the interpretation of an assignment should be a function which makes a small modification to a store s to produce a store s′. If the assignment is Assign (v, e), then the modification will be an update to the variable v, and s′ will be update (s, v, a) for some intvalue a. The value a will be the result of evaluating the expression e given in the assignment, and the evaluation should be done using the store s. That is, we want a = evalexp e s. The case for the assignment is thus:

```
interpret (Assign (v, e)) s = let val a = evalexp e s
                              in update (s, v, a) end
```

The interpretation of a sequence of commands is simply the composition of the separate interpretations of the two commands (as store transformations). That is:

```
interpret (Sequence (c1, c2)) s = interpret c2 (interpret c1 s)
```

or, equivalently:

```
interpret (Sequence (c1, c2)) = (interpret c2) ∘ (interpret c1)
```

To interpret a while-loop or a conditional in a given store, the test expression is evaluated in the store (evalexp e s) and appropriate action is taken depending on the (encoded) boolean result. We use a function:

```
switch : intvalue → (store → store) → (store → store) → store → store
```

in defining the Conditional and While cases. The function switch is passed the value of a test and the choice of actions (i.e. two functions from stores to stores) along with the store. It applies the appropriate action to the store, where the choice is determined by the value of the test. If the value of the test is Intval 1 then the first action is chosen (applied to the store), and if the test gives Intval 0 then the second action is chosen. Values other than Intval 0 and Intval 1 are not dealt with so they cause a runtime error if they arise:

```
fun switch (Intval 1) f g s = f s
|   switch (Intval 0) f g s = g s
|   switch (Intval n) f g s = error "non boolean valued test"
```

For conditionals, the possible actions are just the two branches, so:

```
interpret (Conditional (e, c1, c2)) s
   = switch (evalexp e s) c1 c2 s
```

For a while-loop with body c, the possible actions are nothing (represented by the identity function) in the false case and the composition of the body with the action of the whole loop again in the true case. Thus the loop body is done once, and the whole loop repeated with the resulting store. This gives:

```
interpret (While (e, c)) s
   = switch (evalexp e s) (interpret (While (e, c)) ∘ interpret c) I s
```

which could also be written as:

```
interpret (While (e, c))
   = let fun body s = interpret c s
         fun loop s = switch (evalexp e s) (loop ∘ body) I s
     in loop end
```

The complete definition of interpret is:

```
fun interpret (Assign (v, e)) s
      = let val a = evalexp e s
        in update (s, v, a) end
|   interpret (Sequence (c1, c2)) s
      = interpret c2 (interpret c1 s)
|   interpret (Conditional (e, c1, c2)) s
      = switch (evalexp e s) c1 c2 s
|   interpret (While (e, c)) s
      = switch (evalexp e s) (interpret (While (e, c)) ∘ interpret c) I s
```

It is left as an exercise to rewrite the last case of the interpreter definition in terms of the higher order function loopwhile defined in Section 2.2.5.

As an example, we will calculate interpret c store0 where c is the command represented by X := 1 − Y; X := X * X. Written out as a value of type command, we have:

```
val c = Sequence (Assign (Var "X", Minus (Constant 1,
                                          Contents (Var "Y"))),
                  Assign ("Var "X", Times (Contents (Var "X"),
                                           Contents (Var "X"))))
```

However, we will use the abbreviated (concrete syntax) notation in the example to save space and rely on the context to avoid ambiguity.

The definition of interpret first gives us:

```
interpret (X := 1 − Y, X := X * X) store0
    = interpret (X := X * X) (interpret (X := 1 − Y) store0)
```

and then:

```
= interpret (X := X * X) (update (store0, Var "X", a))
```

where a = evalexp (1 − Y) store0. Using the definition of evalexp this gives:

```
a = Intval (1 − 0) = Intval 1
```

since:

```
evalexp (Constant 1) store0 = Intval 1
```

and

```
evalexp (Contents (Var "Y")) store0 = fetch (Var "Y", store0) = Intval 0
```

Now we can calculate the final store as:

```
interpret (X := X * X) store1 = update (store1, Var "X", b)
```

where:

```
store1 = update (store0, Var "X", Intval 1)
```

and

```
b = evalexp (X * X) store1
  = Intval (n * n)   where   Intval n = fetch (Var "X", store1)
  = Intval (n * n)   where   Intval n = Intval 1
  = Intval (n * n)   where   n = 1
  = Intval 1
```

The final state can be simplified to:

```
update (update (store0, Var "X", Intval 1), Var "X", Intval 1)
```

We cannot simplify this any further without some knowledge of the way stores are represented.

6.5 Representation of stores

Returning to the problem of defining type store, we note that the information contained in a store (namely, the association of an intvalue with each variable – giving its contents) can be represented by a function of type variable → intvalue. Other data structures are possible (see Exercise 6.5), but a simple function introduces no unnecessary detail. We define:

```
datatype store = Store of (variable → intvalue)
```

Values of type store will have the form Store f where f is a function of type variable → intvalue. The initial store can be defined as:

```
val store0 = let fun f v = Intval 0
             in Store f end
```

(or more directly as **val** store0 = Store (K(Intval 0)), using the constant function former K). This represents the store where all variables are initialized with Intval 0 for their contents. An alternative which we might also find useful is:

```
val nullstore = let fun f (Var str) = error "uninitialized variable: " @ str
                in Store f end
```

This is a totally undefined store and would produce an error report if we try to find the contents of any variable. Once a store has been formed from this by update operations, the updated values can safely be fetched.

In general, if v is a variable and s is a store of the form Store f, the contents of v in s can be obtained by applying f to v which will produce an intvalue (of the form Intval n). Thus we can define:

```
fun fetch (v, Store f) = f v
fun update (Store f, v, a) = Store (assoc [(v, a)] f)
```

The function assoc, used in the last definition, was defined in the previous chapter. The expression assoc [(v, a)] f returns a modified contents function which is equivalent to:

```
fun newf v' = if v = v' then a else f v'
```

We leave it as an exercise for the reader to establish that the required behaviour of stores is satisfied by this representation and these definitions.

6.6 Parsing

Having described an interpreter for our simple language of commands it would be useful to have a convenient notation for writing commands succinctly as strings. We can then define a parser which converts such strings to values of type command.

The method we use for describing a parser is based on one of the techniques described in Burge (1975) and uses some notation suggested in Fairbairn (1986). This provides a good demonstration of the use of higher order programming techniques and the tools we introduce can easily be re-used and modified for creating other parsers.

6.6.1 Tokens and parsers

Although we ultimately want a function which converts strings to syntax trees (elements of type command), we split the task into two phases. This is a customary technique used by compiler writers which increases efficiency and separates out two subproblems. The string is first chopped up into separate lexical items or **tokens** by a lexical analyser. The parser proper then tries to construct the syntax tree from a token list.

Let us define a type for simple tokens as follows:

```
datatype token = Ident of string
               | Symbol of string
               | Number of int
```

This allows us to classify lexical items into identifiers, numbers and other symbols. Given a string such as:

```
"WHILE X > Y DO X := X - 1; Z := Z * Z END"
```

the lexical analyser should break this up into the following token list:

```
[Symbol "WHILE", Ident "X", Symbol ">", Ident "Y", Symbol "DO",
 Ident "X", Symbol ":=", Ident "X", Symbol "-", Number 1, Symbol ";",
 Ident "Z", Symbol ":=", Ident "Z", Symbol "*", Ident "Z",
 Symbol "END"]
```

We will return to the definition of the lexical analyser later. Assuming we can create such token lists, we can proceed with the definition of a parser which should produce the value of type command that the token list represents. The example above should produce:

```
While (Greater (Contents (Var "X"), Contents (Var "Y")),
       Sequence (Assign (Var "X", Minus (Contents (Var "X"),
                                         Constant 1)),
                 Assign (Var "Z", Times (Contents (Var "Z"),
                                         Contents (Var "Z")))))
```

We will also need to describe parsers for constituent components of commands such as expressions, assignments, conditionals, etc.

As we noted in the previous chapter, a parser should be capable of returning only a possible result so that a failure can be reported. Furthermore, in the general case, the result of a successful parse should contain not only the syntax tree but also a list of remaining tokens which were unconsumed by the parser. For example, given the token list:

```
[Ident "X", Symbol ":=", Ident "Y", Symbol ";",
  Ident "X", Symbol ":=", Ident "X", Symbol "-", Number 1]
```

produced from the string "X := Y; X := X − 1", then a parser looking for an assignment should succeed, returning a pair consisting of the command value:

```
Assign (Var "X", Contents (Var "Y"))
```

along with the remaining token list:

```
[Symbol ";", Ident "X", Symbol ":=", Ident "X", Symbol "-", Number 1]
```

which represents the string "; X := X − 1" following on from the first assignment statement.

We use the type operator possible which we defined in the previous chapter as:

```
datatype α possible = Ok of α
                    | Fail
```

This allows a parser to return results of the form Ok (tree, toklist) or Fail. Thus the type of a parser for commands should be:

token list → (command × token list) possible

We will also have parsers for type expression, variable, etc., so we introduce the following abbreviation to save writing large type expressions:

type α parser = token list → (α × token list) possible

6.6.2 A grammar for the concrete syntax

We need to specify the concrete syntax of items to be parsed, that is we should formally describe the string representations of syntactic items of our language, and this is most easily done with a (BNF) **grammar**.

Usually a grammar is presented as a set of rules explaining how each class of syntactic items is composed of items from other syntactic classes. For example, a grammar rule such as:

assign ::= *variable* ":=" *exp*

says that an assignment is a variable followed by the (terminal) symbol ":=" followed by an expression. When there are alternative forms for items in a class, several rules are usually combined using '|' as in:

cexp ::= "(" *exp* ")"
  | *variable*
  | *number*

This says that a *cexp* is either a "(" followed by an expression followed by a ")" or a variable or a number. The convention used here is that unquoted words like *cexp* and *exp* are non-terminal symbols standing for syntactic classes. Terminal symbols like "WHILE" and ":=" are quoted. Other symbols like the vertical bar are part of the notation for rules. We will also use square brackets to enclose optional items as in:

command ::= *unitcom* [";" *command*]

This says that a *command* is a *unitcom* followed (optionally) by a semicolon and another *command*.

Table 6.1 contains the grammar rules for expressions (*exp*) and commands along with some auxiliary syntactic classes. In addition to explaining the actual terminal symbols used to write commands and

Table 6.1 Grammar rules for expressions and commands.

exp	::=	*aexp* [">" *aexp*]
aexp	::=	*bexp* ["−" *aexp*]
bexp	::=	*cexp* ["*" *bexp*]
cexp	::=	"(" *exp* ")"
	|	*number*
	|	*variable*
command	::=	*unitcom* [";" *command*]
unitcom	::=	*whilecom*
	|	*ifcom*
	|	*assign*
whilecom	::=	"WHILE" *exp* "DO" *command* "END"
ifcom	::=	"IF" *exp* "THEN" *command* "ELSE" *command* "ENDIF"
assign	::=	*variable* ":=" *exp*

expressions, the rules also specify precedences. For example, an expression is an *aexp* with an optional ">" and another *aexp*. Similarly an *aexp* is constructed from a *bexp* which in turn is constructed from a *cexp*. This means that subexpressions involving multiplications must be constructed before subexpressions involving subtractions which must in turn be constructed before subexpressions involving a comparison (with ">"). However, parenthesized subexpressions override this precedence ordering as can be seen from the rule for a *cexp* which can contain an *exp* in parentheses.

6.6.3 Parser builders

We now come to the main problem of constructing particular parsers. In order to do this, however, we move to a higher level and consider how we might construct parsers from other parsers rather than from scratch. Ultimately, we will need to build some trivial basic parsers from scratch, but all the complex parsers can be built from other parsers which parse components. For example, a parser for an assignment will need to find a variable followed by the symbol ":=" followed by an expression. Thus it should be built from a parser for variables, a parser for the symbol ":=" and a parser for expressions.

If we define a parser operator ⟨&⟩ (to be read as "followed by") which combines two parsers to form a single parser, then the description of the parser for assignments could be very simple indeed:

```
variable ⟨&⟩ literal ":=" ⟨&⟩ exp
```

Here we assume:

```
variable : variable parser
exp : expression parser
literal : string → string parser
⟨&⟩ : (α parser × β parser) → (α × β) parser
```

We will define each of these properly in a moment.

Corresponding to the use of '|' in grammar rules, we will also define an infix parser builder ⟨|⟩. This combines a pair of parsers to form a single parser which uses the component parsers as alternatives. Thus, for example, we might write:

```
assign ⟨|⟩ whilecom
```

for a parser which succeeds if it finds either an assignment (*assign*) or a while command (*whilecom*). The type of this parser builder is:

```
⟨|⟩ : (α parser × α parser) → α parser
```

There is another important parser builder which we need and that allows us to modify the result returned by a parser. Note that the result returned by a parser built with ⟨&⟩ contains a component which is a pair of values returned by the individual parsers (of type $\alpha \times \beta$). Frequently, we want to convert such a parser into one which returns a single result (of type γ say). To do this we must supply a modifier function of type $(\alpha \times \beta) \rightarrow \gamma$. Given a parser and modifying function, we build a modified parser with the infix operator modify. For example, the parser described by:

```
variable ⟨&⟩ literal ":=" ⟨&⟩ exp
```

actually has type:

```
(variable × (string × expression)) parser
```

but we want to convert it into a command parser to recognize assignments. If we define:

```
mk_assign_node : variable × (string × expression) → command
```

then the parser for assignments can be described by:

```
val assign = (variable ⟨&⟩ literal ":=" ⟨&⟩ exp) modify mk_assign_node
```

which has type command parser. The definition of the function which converts the tuple into a command is simply defined as:

```
fun mk_assign_node (v, (s, e)) = Assign (v, e)
```

We have deliberately chosen to use infix symbols to represent the parser builders so that the description of parsers can look very much like the grammar rules from which they are derived. The modifiers explain what is to be built with the results of a parse and it is convenient to separate out this information (see Fairbairn, 1986a).

The definitions of the parser builders are given in Table 6.2 along with some additional ones which are convenient to use in parsing options and sequences.

The parser builders ⟨&⟩ and ⟨|⟩ are right associative infix operators and modify is left associative. We also specify that ⟨&⟩ has higher precedence than ⟨|⟩ which has higher precedence than modify. The parser formed by parser1 ⟨|⟩ parser2 is defined to try parser1 on the argument. The result is passed to the locally defined function parser2_if_fail which simply returns the same result if it was successful. If the first result was Fail, then parser2 is tried on the original argument. The result of this is then the overall result, so if both parsers fail we just get the result Fail.

The parser formed by parser modify f is defined to try the parser on the argument and then apply the locally defined modresult to the result. If the intermediate result is Fail then this is left unchanged, but if the result was successful then the first component of the result pair is changed using f. (The second component is the unconsumed token list and this is not modified.)

The parser formed by parser1 ⟨&⟩ parser2 similarly starts by applying parser1 to the argument and uses the locally defined function parser2_after on the result. This local function is defined to leave failures as failures, but to pick up the unconsumed token list in the successful case. The second parser (parser2) is used on this token list to produce a second result. However, it is modified to pair up the first result with the second result when it is successful. Recall that when pair x1 is applied x2 say, it produces (x1, x2). So, if parser1 s returns Ok (x1, s1) and parser2 s1 returns Ok (x2, s2) then the final result is Ok (pair x1 x2, s2) which is equal to Ok ((x1, x2), s2).

emptyseq: (α list) parser is a parser which always succeeds because it is looking for an empty sequence of items and it does not consume any tokens. It returns the empty list [ ].

optional pr is a parser which always succeeds. It is essentially just pr ⟨|⟩ emptyseq which tries the parser pr and if this fails, it tries emptyseq which succeeds. However, the result of pr must be modified to form a list so that a list is returned in both cases. If pr succeeds its result item a is

Table 6.2 Parser builders.

```
infixr 4 ⟨&⟩
infixr 3 ⟨|⟩
infix  0 modify

fun (parser1 ⟨|⟩ parser2) s
  = let fun parser2_if_fail Fail = parser2 s
          | parser2_if_fail x    = x
    in parser2_if_fail (parser1 s) end

fun (parser modify f) s
  = let fun modresult Fail          = Fail
          | modresult (Ok (x, y))= Ok (f x, y)
    in modresult (parser s) end

fun (parser1 ⟨&⟩ parser2) s
  = let fun parser2_after Fail            = Fail
          | parser2_after (Ok (x1, s1)) = (parser2 modify (pair x1)) s1
    in parser2_after (parser1 s) end

fun emptyseq s = Ok ([ ], s)

fun optional pr = (pr modify (consonto [ ]))
                  ⟨|⟩ emptyseq

fun sequence pr
  = let fun seqpr s = ((pr ⟨&⟩ seqpr modify (op ::))
                       ⟨|⟩ emptyseq) s
    in seqpr end

fun seqwith (front, sep, back) pr
  = let val sep_pr = sep ⟨&⟩ pr              modify snd
        val items  = pr  ⟨&⟩ sequence sep_pr modify (op ::)
    in front ⟨&⟩ optional items ⟨&⟩ back modify (link ∘ fst ∘ snd) end

fun parserList [ ]          = emptyseq
  | parserList (pr :: rest) = pr ⟨&⟩ (parserList rest) modify (op ::)

fun alternatives [ ]          = K Fail
  | alternatives (pr :: rest) = pr ⟨|⟩ alternatives rest
```

modified with consonto [ ] thus returning a singleton list [a], otherwise [ ] is returned. The operator optional thus has type

α parser → (α list) parser

We do not use the other operators for our particular problem, but they are included for completeness. A parser of the form sequence pr always succeeds and repeatedly uses pr until it fails collecting a list of the items found. The operator sequence has the same type as optional. The parser seqwith (front, sep, back) pr, where front, sep, back and pr are all parsers, looks for a 'front' followed by a list of 'pr's separated by 'sep's and ending with a 'back'. Only the items returned by pr are kept in the result. The operator seqwith has type:

$$(\alpha \text{ parser} \times \beta \text{ parser} \times \gamma \text{ parser}) \to \delta \text{ parser} \to (\delta \text{ list}) \text{ parser}$$

The operator parserList takes a list of parsers for an argument and uses each one in turn (combined with ⟨&⟩) to parse a list of items. It thus generalizes ⟨&⟩ for use with more than 2 parsers (of the same type). The type of the operator is:

$$\text{parserList} : (\alpha \text{ parser}) \text{ list} \to (\alpha \text{ list}) \text{ parser}$$

Finally, alternatives generalizes ⟨|⟩ for use with a list of parsers to be tried in turn as alternatives. It succeeds when any of the argument list of parsers succeeds and fails if they all fail. This operator has type:

$$\text{alternatives} : (\alpha \text{ parser}) \text{ list} \to \alpha \text{ parser}$$

6.6.4 Basic parsers

The only basic parsers we need are:

```
number : int parser
variable : variable parser
```

along with those of the form literal a for some string a. Actually, literal is really a parser builder, but we include it in this section because it is defined in terms of the particular choice of type token. The other parser builders are quite independent of type token and really have more general types than we have indicated. The definitions of the basic parsers are as follows:

```
fun number (Number n :: s) = Ok (n, s)
  | number other           = Fail
fun variable (Ident x :: s) = Ok (Var x, s)
  | variable other          = Fail
fun literal a (Symbol x :: s) = if a = x then Ok (x, s) else Fail
  | literal a other           = Fail
```

This makes literal : string → string parser.

6.6.5 Parsers for commands and expressions

We are now in a position to put the parser builders together with the basic parsers to form the main command parser and expression parser. We present the parser definitions in Table 6.3 and we draw particular attention to the similarity between these definitions and the grammars presented in Table 6.1.

Table 6.3 Parsers for commands and expressions.

```
(************* THE EXPRESSION PARSERS (compare with the grammar) ***************)

fun exp s  = (aexp (&) optional (literal ">" (&) aexp) modify opt_compare ) s
and aexp s = (bexp (&) optional (literal "-" (&) aexp) modify opt_sub     ) s
and bexp s = (cexp (&) optional (literal "*" (&) bexp) modify opt_mul     ) s
and cexp s = ( (literal "(" (&) exp (&) literal ")"    modify unparenth  )
             (|) (number                               modify Constant   )
             (|) (variable                             modify Contents   ) ) s

(******************************** AUXILIARY OPS *********************************)

and unparenth (bra, (e, ket))       = e
and opt_compare (e1, [ ])           = e1
  | opt_compare (e1, [(oper, e2)])  = Greater (e1, e2)
  | opt_compare other               = error "impossible"
and opt_sub (e1, [ ])               = e1
  | opt_sub (e1, [(oper, e2)])      = Minus (e1, e2)
  | opt_sub other                   = error "impossible"
and opt_mul (e1, [ ])               = e1
  | opt_mul (e1, [(oper, e2)])      = Times (e1, e2)
  | opt_mul other                   = error "impossible";

(*************** THE COMMAND PARSERS (compare with the grammar) ****************)

fun command s  = (unitcom (&) optional (literal ";" (&) command) modify opt_seq     ) s
and unitcom s  = (whilecom
                 (|) ifcom
                 (|) assign  ) s
and whilecom s = (literal "WHILE" (&) exp     (&)
                  literal "DO"    (&) command (&)
                  literal "END"                         modify mk_while_node  ) s
and ifcom s    = (literal "IF"    (&) exp     (&)
                  literal "THEN"  (&) command (&)
                  literal "ELSE"  (&) command (&)
                  literal "ENDIF"                       modify mk_if_node     ) s
and assign s   = (variable (&) literal ":=" (&) exp     modify mk_assign_node) s

(******************************** AUXILIARY OPS *********************************)

and opt_seq (c1, [ ])                 = c1
  | opt_seq (c1, [(semicol, c2)])     = Sequence (c1, c2)
  | opt_seq other                     = error "impossible"
and mk_while_node (w, (ex, (d, (com, e)))) = While (ex, com)
and mk_if_node (i, (ex, (t, (c1, (e, (c2, f)))))) = Conditional (ex, c1, c2)
and mk_assign_node (v, (coleq, e))    = Assign (v, e);
```

Each occurrence of a terminal string has been replaced by the corresponding parser created by literal and each syntactic class is replaced by the parser for that class (which we have given the same name). A sequence of parsers is connected with the 'followed by' operator ⟨&⟩, alternatives are connected by ⟨|⟩, and the function optional is used to replace the bracketed items. The only other differences are the use of modifiers to describe what is to be built and the presence of parameters in the definitions. (These parameters are really redundant, but ML requires them for mutually recursive definitions.) Note that parsers have to be defined together when there is mutual recursion between them as can be seen in these examples. The auxiliary, result-modifying functions such as opt_compare could have been defined in advance, but we prefer to see their definitions after seeing where they are used. The modifiers of the form opt_... deal with the results of parsing for optional items. These results will contain either an empty list (when the item is absent) or a singleton list (when the item is present).

We have not described parsers with sophisticated error reporting since we wished to demonstrate the basic principle underlying their construction. Operators like literal, ⟨|⟩, ⟨&⟩ can be extended to allow for error reporting, but we leave such problems as exercises. At the top level, we should provide a check to make sure all the argument list of tokens is used up and abort with a suitable error report if it is not. The following function:

```
report : (α × token list) possible → α
```

does this by the simple use of error along with a string retrieved from the token list, using lit : token → string:

```
fun lit (Symbol  s) = s
  | lit (Number n) = stringofint n
  | lit (Ident    s) = s

fun report Fail            = error "Parse Error"
  | report (Ok (c, [ ])) = c
  | report (Ok (c, x))   = error (stringwith (
                                   "Syntax Error\nUnparsed:-\n",
                                   " ",
                                   "\n")
                                   (map lit x))
```

We define the main parser as the composition of report and command:

```
val main_parser = report ∘ command
```

which is then a partial function with type token list → command.

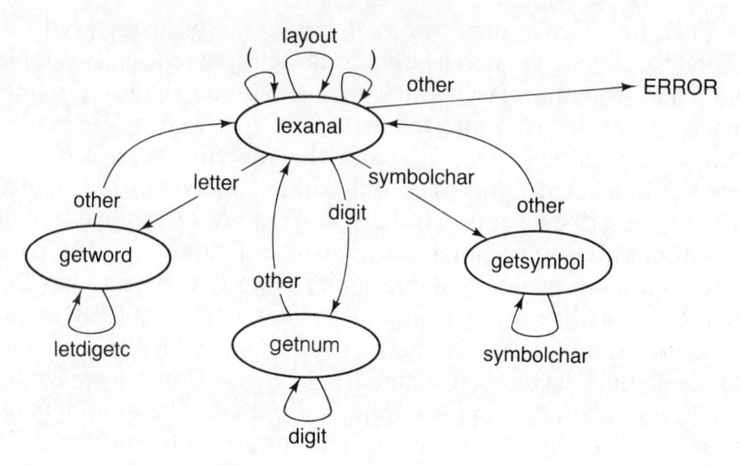

Figure 6.2 Graph showing states in lexical analysis.

6.6.6 A lexical analyser

The final problem is the definition of a **lexical analyser**. Similar techniques can be used here, since lexical analysis is a simple form of parsing for tokens from lists of characters. Thus we could just alter our basic parsers to work on character lists and re-use the parser builders.

For our particular example, this is a bit of a sledgehammer, so we will construct an analyser directly from a simple description of the structure of tokens. The structure is expressed as a graph in Figure 6.2 which can be thought of as part of the representation of a finite state automaton (see, for example, Wood (1987) for a definition of *finite state automaton*). The node labelled lexanal is the initial state and the next state (or node) is determined by the next input symbol. Layout characters such as spaces are skipped over and the state is left as lexanal. Similarly parentheses cause no change of state (although they generate a token unlike layout characters). If an alphabetic letter is encountered then there is a change of state to getword. This latter state is maintained while letters or digits or primes or underscores are encountered. (These are the characters we allow in identifiers after an initial letter.) Other characters return the state to lexanal. If a digit is encountered while in the lexanal state, then the state is changed to getnum which deals with subsequent digits and returns the state to lexanal when a non-digit is encountered. Finally, a symbolic character such as a colon or operator symbol causes a change of state from lexanal to getsymbol which allows subsequent symbolic characters to be collected. Other characters are not recognized by the analyser.

One might have expected getword to be replaced by getident, but the word collected from this state is only classified as an identifier if it is not listed as a keyword. The following definitions of keyword : string → bool and keycheck : string → token allow us to form the appropriate token when a word has been collected:

```
val keyword = member ["IF", "THEN", "ELSE", "ENDIF", "WHILE",
                      "DO", "END"]
fun keycheck s = if keyword s then Symbol s else Ident s
```

We assume that the string of characters which we are to analyse has been exploded to an object of type string list and we will make use of several predicates for inspecting characters and a function to form integers from digits. In addition to the following, which were defined in Chapter 1:

```
digit : string → bool
letter : string → bool
```

we also define:

```
letdigetc : string → bool
layout : string → bool
symbolchar : string → bool
intofdigit : string → int
```

as follows:

```
fun letdigetc a = if letter a then true else
                  if digit a  then true else
                  member ["'", "_"] a
val layout = member [" ", "\n", "\t"]
val symbolchar = member ["*", "+", "/", "-", ">", ":", "=", ";"]
fun intofdigit d = ord d - ord "0"
```

The function intofdigit : string → int is intended for use on the digits "0", . . . , "9" to obtain the corresponding integer.

The definition of the lexical analyser lexanal is given in Table 6.4 together with some mutually recursively defined functions.

Their types are:

```
lexanal : string list → token list
getword : string list → string list → token list
getsymbol : string list → string list → token list
getnum : int → string list → token list
```

Table 6.4 A lexical analyser.

```
fun  lexanal [ ]    = [ ]
  |  lexanal (a::x) = if layout a then lexanal x else
                      if a =  "(" then Symbol "(" :: lexanal x else
                      if a =  ")" then Symbol ")" :: lexanal x else
                      if letter a then getword [a] x else
                      if digit a then getnum (intofdigit a) x else
                      if symbolchar a then getsymbol [a] x else
                      error ("Lexical Error : unrecognized token "
                                ^ implode (a :: x))
and  getword l [ ]      = [keycheck (implode (rev l))]
  |  getword l (a :: x) = if letdigetc a
                          then getword (a :: l) x
                          else keycheck (implode (rev l)) :: lexanal (a :: x)
and  getsymbol l [ ]      = [Symbol (implode (rev l))]
  |  getsymbol l (a :: x) = if symbolchar a
                            then getsymbol (a :: l) x
                            else Symbol (implode (rev l)) :: lexanal (a :: x)

and  getnum n [ ]      = [Number n]
  |  getnum n (a :: x) = if digit a
                         then getnum (n * 10 + intofdigit a) x
                         else Number n :: lexanal (a :: x)
```

These functions clearly correspond to the nodes of the graph depicted in Figure 6.2. The last three have additional parameters which are used to accumulate values. In the case of getword, letters, digits, primes and underscores are collected (in reverse order) and converted into a single string when a different sort of character is encountered or the input finishes. This is where keycheck is used. Similarly, getsymbol accumulates symbolic characters (in reverse order) and getnum accumulates a number (calculating an integer as digits are encountered).

Note that arrows in the graph (state transitions) correspond to the calling patterns of the functions. For example, lexanal calls getword when a letter is encountered, calls getnum when a digit is encountered and calls getsymbol when a symbolic character is encountered.

Note that the theory underlying parser construction is well developed and there are many more advanced techniques for producing highly efficient parsers. The reader is referred to Burge (1975) for further methods of parser construction with functional programs. See also Wadler (1985) for a particularly elegant way of allowing backtracking using (lazy) lists instead of 'possible' results.

EXERCISES

6.1 Extend the type expression to allow more operations (e.g. by using a type operator).

6.2 Draw a complete tree for the example in Figure 6.1 incorporating the syntactic structure of the expressions and variables.

6.3 Redefine the interpreter in terms of loopwhile (defined in Chapter 2).

6.4 Write the following commands (c) out as values of type command, then calculate the steps in an evaluation of interpret c store0 and an evaluation of interpret c nullstore:

(a) X := 3; Y := X * X

(b) X := 3; WHILE X > 1 DO X := X − 1 END

(c) X := Y + 1; IF X > Y THEN WHILE X > 1 DO X := X − 1 END ELSE X := X * X

6.5 Re-implement stores using a new type with Store0 and Update as constructors. Define fetch for this implementation.

6.6 Extend the type intvalue to include an explicit 'error' value which can be used in unitialized stores. Discuss differences of behaviour of the interpreter adapted for use with the new intvalue type and the original version using nullstore (described in Section 6.5).

6.7 Give an object-oriented representation of stores with functional update and fetch components. Define store0 for this representation along with the global update and fetch operations.

6.8 Design a type to represent simple assembler instruction codes and a simple assembler language (e.g. lists of numbered instructions). Write an interpreter for your assembler language. Write a compiler which converts values of type command to assembler code. What relationship should hold between the assembler language interpreter, the command interpreter and the compiler?

6.9 Design an abstract syntax, concrete syntax and interpreter for a richer command language than the one presented here.

6.10 Modify the parser builders to allow for error reporting. For example, after ifcom has found an IF but failed to find an ELSE, there is little point in trying alternatives and the absence of the ELSE should be reported with an indication of where it was expected. A modified version of literal called mustfind which takes an additional string as a parameter (for error messages) might be useful for this purpose.

6.11 Consider a grammar with a rule of the form:

$$A ::= A\ B \mid C$$

(this is called **left recursive**). What would happen if a parser was built to follow the structure of this rule with ⟨&⟩ and ⟨|⟩? Can you solve the problem by defining a special parser operator for just such situations and which behaves well:

```
fun A x = leftrecseq C B x
```

You may prefer to incorporate an extra parameter f which is used to build a result of the form:

```
f (. . . f (f (f (c, b1), b2), b3), . . . bn)
```

Chapter 7
Abstract Data Types and Modules

In the previous two chapters, emphasis was given to the role of data types in designing and organizing abstractions with which to do computations. In this chapter we introduce abstract data types which allow types to play an even more prominent role in program design.

As well as just being an extension of our notion of type, abstract data types provide another powerful abstraction mechanism which blends particularly well with the functional abstraction mechanism we have been using. Abstract data types are particularly useful in the design of large-scale programs and for the modular construction of programs. For modern programming methods, abstract data types have become a major tool for the design of programs (imperative and applicative). This is because they provide a convenient way of separating concerns in building components of programs.

7.1 Abstract data types

Functional programming emphasizes the use of functions as a major abstraction mechanism, allowing us to separate details of the implementation of components (function definitions) from their use. Similarly, abstract data types allow the use of a type to be separated from and made independent of decisions about implementation of the type. These two forms of abstraction (function and type) are closely linked because, as we will see, abstract data types are essentially collections of functions defined together.

Concrete types emphasize the form (structure) of values as composite objects built with constructors. In contrast, abstract types emphasize the logical behaviour of values. Values of an abstract data type are considered *abstract* in the sense that their structure is considered irrelevant and suppressed. The logical properties of the values are determined by their behaviour with respect to a collection of primitive functions that can be applied to them. We can often characterize the behaviour of a collection of primitive functions of a type in a precise way, by specifying certain relationships that hold between them independently of any particular representation of the values of the type. This means that the values can be indirectly described through the relationships between the primitive functions and this allows us to separate the specification of the relationships from the details of the implementation.

In fact, we have already been using the idea of abstract types informally in some earlier examples. A good example was our use of the type store in Chapter 6. When we introduced this type, we postponed a discussion of its definition, but specified some operations that we needed and some properties we required the operations to have. This allowed us to use the operations in designing the interpreter without full knowledge of their implementation. We were then able to return to the problem of defining the operations at a later stage, and we were free to consider various alternative implementations (see Exercises 6.5 and 6.7). The only constraint we had in defining the type and implementing the operations was that the specified properties had to be satisfied. More precisely, the task was to provide a type store with functions/constants of the following types:

```
fetch : variable × store → intvalue
update : store × variable × intvalue → store
store0 : store
```

These had to satisfy the constraints:

For any variables v and v′, store s and intvalue a,

```
fetch (v, update (s, v, a)) = a
v ≠ v′ implies fetch (v, update (s, v′, a)) = fetch (v, s)
fetch (v, store0) = Intval 0
```

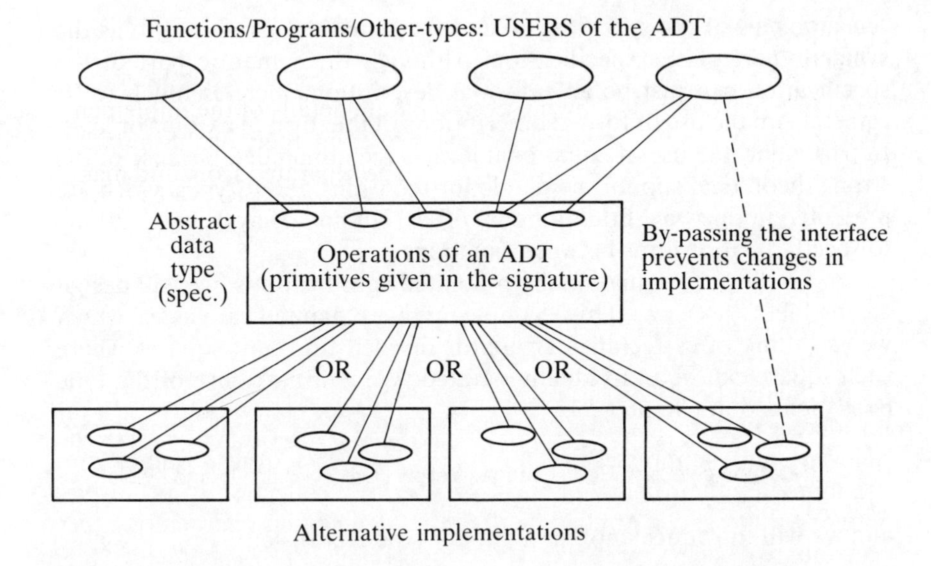

Figure 7.1 Abstract data type specifications as interfaces.

When we made use of the operations, assuming only these properties, we were treating stores as an abstract type. When we came to define the operations, we considered possible concrete types which could be used to represent or implement the abstract type.

The specification of an abstract type provides an interface between users of the type and the implementation of the type. Only the specification is needed in order to use the type (i.e. no details of the implementation should influence our use of the type). Furthermore, only the specification should be referred to when an implementation is designed (i.e. none of the programs/functions using the type need to be considered when the implementation is decided upon). A change in the chosen representation for values of an abstract type can be made safely without the need to redefine any functions which make use of the type, provided the new implementation satisfies the same specified behaviour (see Figure 7.1).

7.1.1 Specification of abstract data types

When we design a new abstract type for use in programming, we need to specify two things. The first is a list of names of the functions that we regard as the basic operations of the abstract type (with the details of the types of each function). This is called the **signature** of the abstract type. The second thing we need is an interpretation-independent description of the behaviour of the functions. Sometimes this is referred to as the

semantic part of the specification and the signature is referred to as the **syntactic part** of the specification. Although the semantic part of the specification can just be an informal description, there is much to be gained from the use of formal descriptions in the form of axioms or laws. In particular, the use of equational laws is recommended because of the strong theoretical support available for reasoning about types which are presented in this way. Equations are often (but not always) a natural way to specify relationships between functions.

To illustrate equationally presented specifications, we will design an abstract type canvas. This example involves 'painted canvasses' which we can think of as rectangular boards divided into unit squares where each square can be individually painted. We will make use of the type colour defined in Chapter 5 by:

```
datatype colour = Red | Orange | Yellow | Green | Blue | Indigo | Violet
```

and we will introduce another auxiliary type coordinate:

```
datatype coordinate = Coord of int × int
```

Coordinates are just pairs of integers which may be used to indicate particular squares on canvasses. The signature of the abstract type canvas will be:

```
type canvas
newcanvas : colour → int → int → canvas
sizecanvas : canvas → (int * int)
colourof   : canvas → coordinate → colour
paint      : colour → coordinate → canvas → canvas
```

The first operation is intended for the initial creation of a canvas with a particular colour and size. We should think of newcanvas c m n as a canvas where all squares have colour c and the size of the canvas is m by n. That is, the canvas is divided into m by n squares. (It does not matter which of these integers is regarded as the depth and which is regarded as the width as long as we are consistent.) Given any canvas, sizecanvas reports its size as a pair of integers and colourof reports the colours of individual squares given by coordinates. That is, if c is a canvas and crd is a coordinate of a square on the canvas, then colourof c crd tells us the colour of that square. Finally paint allows us to construct a new canvas from a given canvas by giving a new colour to a square at a specified coordinate. That is, paint clr crd c is the canvas constructed from c by painting the square at coordinate crd with the colour clr. A more formal description of the behaviour of the functions listed in the signature is provided by the following laws:

```
For all coord, coord' : coordinate
For all clr           : colour
For all m, n          : int
For all canvas        : canvas

colourof (newcanvas clr m n) coord = clr
        provided coord is on the canvas newcanvas clr m n

colourof (paint clr coord canvas) coord = clr
        provided coord is on the canvas paint clr coord canvas

colourof (paint clr coord canvas) coord' = colourof canvas coord'
        provided coord is not equal to coord'

sizecanvas (newcanvas clr m n) = (m, n)

sizecanvas (paint clr coord canvas) = sizecanvas canvas
```

However, these laws are not completely precise. For example, they do not describe exactly when a coordinate is on a canvas and what the colour of a square is if it is not on a given canvas. The laws can be made more precise by introducing an auxiliary operation (predicate):

```
is_on : coordinate → canvas → bool
```

Using this predicate, we give a more detailed equational specification:

```
For all coord, coord' : coordinate
For all clr           : colour
For all m, n, m1, n1  : int
For all canvas        : canvas

1) colourof (newcanvas clr m n) coord' = clr
2) colourof (paint clr coord canvas) coord'
       = if coord = coord' & is_on (coord, canvas)
         then clr
         else colourof canvas coord'

3) sizecanvas (newcanvas clr m n) = (m, n)
4) sizecanvas (paint clr coord canvas) = sizecanvas canvas

5) is_on (Coord (n1, m1), newcanvas clr m n)
       = m1 > 0 & m1 ≤ m & n1 > 0 & n1 ≤ n
6) is_on (coord', paint clr coord canvas) = is_on (coord', canvas)
```

These more formal descriptions of the properties allow us to deduce information about subtle cases. For example, it is possible to create a canvas with negative or zero depth (or width), but we could not change it by painting on it. We know this because, firstly, equation (3) holds for all integers m and n including negative values so the size of a canvas created with negative integers is well defined. Secondly, we can deduce from (5) that (for all coord, clr, m and n):

```
m ≤ 0 or n ≤ 0
   IMPLIES
is_on (coord, newcanvas clr m n) = false
```

Thirdly, we can deduce from (2) that (for all coord, canvas, clr, m and n):

```
is_on (coord, canvas) = false
   IMPLIES
colourof (paint clr coord canvas) coord = colourof canvas coord
```

These implications express the facts that no coordinate is on a canvas created with a negative depth or width, and the colour of a painted coordinate remains the same when the coordinate is not on the canvas. The latter implication together with (1) also shows that if we were to ask for the colour of a coordinate which is not on the canvas, we get the background colour (rather than an undefined result).

The equations should not be regarded as functional program definitions because the left-hand sides can be more general than those we have allowed in pattern matching definitions. They are specifications rather than programs and many different functions may satisfy the specification. No details have yet been given as to the exact structure of values of type canvas and how the functions access and manipulate components of the values.

Such specifications do not form an executable part of Standard ML programs. In the next section, we look at ways in which we might implement the specified type.

7.1.2 Implementing abstract data types

Ideally, we would like a programming language which accepts formal specifications of types and produces implementations automatically so that the programmer is left with the task of specification only. Much research has been done in this area, particularly with the use of equational laws as a means of specification and the possibilities for automatic implementation from such specifications are very interesting. Often, the laws can be written in such a way as to be directly runnable as a form of rewriting system. However, there are some attendant problems with this approach. In particular, automatic derivation of an implementation from arbitrary laws is not theoretically possible, so restricted forms of laws have to be used or additional guidance supplied by the programmer. There is also the problem of ensuring completeness and consistency of the laws and of achieving reasonable efficiency in the implementation. Tools for dealing with formal specifications are currently considered to be part of specification languages rather than programming languages but the gap is being slowly bridged between specification and programming languages.

Even when there is no direct support for the use of abstract types in a programming language, they can still be used as a design tool. Abstract types can be designed and specified on paper, and then implemented using whatever types are available in a given language. The programmer then has the problem of deciding upon implementations and also ensuring adherence to consistent use of the implementations.

Here we adopt the compromise used in the abstract type mechanisms of SML, Hope and Miranda, which is for the programmer to provide a particular representation for values of the abstract type using values of another type (i.e. to describe a particular implementation with a concrete type or previously defined abstract type). The operators listed in the signature of the abstract type can then be defined in terms of operations on the representation type, so that the abstract type can be simulated. These languages do, however, provide some additional support for the use of abstract types. They allow a clear distinction to be made between values of the simulating type and those of the abstract type when type checking. This is done by enforcing the restriction that only the operations which are given in the signature of an abstract type (and operations subsequently defined in terms of these) may be used to manipulate values of the abstract type.

To explain this further, let us consider a possible implementation of canvasses. We could represent a canvas as a value with three components to record the height and width and the colours of squares. The colours of squares could be recorded in the form of a function (association) mapping coordinates to colours. A suitable (concrete) type definition for such an implementation would be:

```
datatype canvas = Cnvs of int × int × (coordinate → colour)
```

The basic canvas functions could then be implemented as:

```
fun newcanvas clr m n = Cnvs (m, n, K clr)
fun sizecanvas (Cnvs (m, n, f)) = (m, n)
fun colourof (Cnvs (m, n, f)) coord = f coord
fun paint clr (Coord (m1, n1)) (Cnvs (m, n, f))
    = if m1 > 0 & m1 ≤ m & n1 > 0 & n1 ≤ n
      then Cnvs (m, n, assoc [(Coord (n1, m1), clr)] f)
      else Cnvs (m, n, f)
```

These definitions are relatively straightforward. We have used K clr to form the function which always returns clr when applied to a coordinate (i.e. K clr coord = clr) in the description of the canvas formed by newcanvas. The function paint modifies this colour-of-squares function (using assoc) only when the coordinate is on the canvas. The expression assoc [(Coord (m1, n1) , clr)] f describes a function which maps Coord (m1, n1) to clr but has the same effect as f on all other arguments.

One can check by hand (although it is clearly advantageous to have an automatic proof checker) that this implementation does indeed satisfy the equations of the specification. For example:

```
colourof (newcanvas clr m n) coord = colourof (Cnvs (m, n, K clr)) coord
                                   = K clr coord
                                   = clr
```

The other equations are a little messier to check but follow from straightforward substitutions and reasoning about conditionals. We also need a definition of the auxiliary function is_on in order to check all the equations. For example:

```
fun is_on (Coord (m1, n1), Cnvs (m, n, f))
      = m1 > 0 & m1 ≤ m & n1 > 0 & n1 ≤ n
```

We leave the other equations for the reader to check as an exercise.

Having chosen a representation, SML allows us to go a step further by providing a way of enforcing the abstraction so as to protect the integrity of the representation. In order to ensure proper use of canvasses as an abstract type, we require that:

(1) Any value of type canvas is formed only via operations listed in the signature (i.e. constructed with either newcanvas or paint).

(2) Only the functions listed in the signature can be used on values of type canvas.

Morris (1973) called these requirements (1) **authentication** and (2) **secrecy**. The authentication requirement prevents the formation of erroneous values which bypass the use of functions in the signature. For example if we define:

```
local
  fun f (Coord (m1, n1)) = if m1 < n1 then Red else Blue
in
  val funnycanvas = Cnvs (10, 10, f)
end
```

then funnycanvas is not an authentic value of type canvas (it is created by neither newcanvas nor paint) and we should regard this as a type error.

The secrecy requirement prevents us from defining additional functions in terms of the representation instead of in terms of the primitives of the type. Access to the details of values of type canvas is restricted to the access provided by the functions listed in the signature. For example, we should not allow:

```
fun get_paint_fn (Cnvs (m, n, f)) = f
```

which directly accesses the third component of our representation. Although this access might seem harmless, it bypasses the interface. Subsequent changes in the choice of representation may then require changes to functions other than those listed in the signature which defeats one of the main purposes of using an abstract type.

Standard ML and Miranda provide a simple mechanism for enforcing the above requirements. In SML, we can introduce an abstract type using **abstype** instead of **datatype** when we describe the implementation and delineate the definitions of functions (and constants) which are to form the signature using **with** and **end**. The complete ML definition of an abstract type canvas should look like this:

```
abstype canvas = Cnvs of int × int × (coordinate → colour)
with
   fun newcanvas clr m n = Cnvs (m, n, K clr)
   fun sizecanvas (Cnvs (m, n, f)) = (m, n)
   fun colourof (Cnvs (m, n, f)) coord = f coord
   fun paint clr (Coord (m1, n1)) (Cnvs (m, n, f))
      = if m1 > 0 & m1 ≤ m & n1 > 0 & n1 ≤ n
         then Cnvs (m, n, assoc [(Coord (n1, m1), clr)] f)
         else Cnvs (m, n, f)
end
```

Only the representation is described since the specification is not part of an SML program. The signature can easily be inferred from this description, and the type checker ensures that only those values introduced between **with** and **end** are subsequently available for operating on and creating values of type canvas. The mechanism works simply by restricting the scope of the constructor Cnvs to the block of definitions enclosed by **with** and **end**. It is a type error to use Cnvs either in expressions or patterns beyond this scope. Since Cnvs must be used to access the representation of values of type canvas directly, this scope rule enforces the requirements that such access is limited to the functions given in the signature.

There is one other aspect of the mechanism which is important for hiding the representation information, and that concerns the reporting of values of type canvas. A value of type canvas is represented by a value which will have the form Cnvs (m, n, f). However, we should regard this canonical form as a description of the representation only and not of the abstract value. Abstract values do not have canonical representations and therefore cannot be displayed. (This also means that the scope rule for the constructor does not have to be overruled for the purpose of displaying abstract values.)

Furthermore, abstract types are never types with (automatic) equality. That is, an equality operation cannot be automatically inferred for values of an abstract type. It would be dangerous to assume that an equality operation for the representation type is appropriate for the abstract type because we may well allow several alternative representations for the same abstract value. If an equality test is deemed appropriate for an abstract type, it should be defined in terms of the representation and included in the signature of the abstract type.

7.1.3 Alternative implementations

We only need one implementation of an abstract type in order to use it. However, we will describe a different implementation of type canvas in order to demonstrate the use of abstract types as interfaces. If we have written a large program using the above definition of type canvas, we could, if we so wished, replace the definition of the type by another definition (which satisfies the same specification) without having to consider any applications of the type in the rest of the program. The changes are thus confined to one place (the body of the type definition).

The alternative definition uses two constructors:

```
Paint : (colour × coordinate × canvas) → canvas
```

and:

```
Newcanvas : (colour × int × int) → canvas
```

These both have as their scope the definitions enclosed by **with** and **end** in the type definition. This time, we prefer to define the auxiliary function is_on explicitly for use in the other definitions. We use the **local** construct to allow is_on to be defined along with the other functions (and having access to the representation in its definition) but it is excluded from the final collection of functions which are exported as primitives of the type. The function is_on is not part of the signature of the type.

```
abstype canvas = Paint of colour × coordinate × canvas
               | Newcanvas of colour × int × int
with
  local
    fun is_on (Coord (m1, n1), Newcanvas (clr, m, n))
          = m1 > 0 & m1 ≤ m & n1 > 0 & n1 ≤ n
    | is_on (coord', Paint (clr, coord, cnvs))
          = is_on (coord', cnvs)
  in
    fun newcanvas clr m n = Newcanvas (clr, m, n)
    fun paint clr coord cnvs = Paint (clr, coord, cnvs)
    fun sizecanvas (Newcanvas (clr, m, n)) = (m, n)
    |   sizecanvas (Paint (clr, coord, cnvs)) = sizecanvas cnvs
    fun colourof (Newcanvas (clr, m, n)) coord = clr
    |   colourof (Paint (clr, coord, cnvs)) coord'
          = if coord = coord' & is_on (coord', cnvs)
            then clr
            else colourof cnvs coord'
  end
end
```

It is even easier to see that this implementation satisfies the specification because it closely follows the form of the equations in the specification. With this implementation, the representing values reflect the history of paint operations in their structure. This history is hidden by the abstraction which is exactly as it should be. For example, when coord1 = coord2 is false then:

```
Paint (clr1, coord1, Paint (clr2, coord2, cnvs))
Paint (clr2, coord2, Paint (clr1, coord1, cnvs))
```

are two different representations of the same abstract value. Two different squares on cnvs have been painted in both cases, but the representations show the order in which the squares were painted. This order is irrelevant to the logical behaviour of the resulting canvas and cannot be uncovered by the primitives of the type.

7.2 Further examples

7.2.1 Ordered integer lists

As another example, we illustrate how the abstraction mechanism can be used to form a **subtype** of a type. We select all the values of a type satisfying a certain property and form a new type from this subset of values.

Suppose we intend to make extensive use of ordered sequences (lists) of integers in a program. We could use values of the type int list to represent the sequences and manipulate them with list operations such as sort, insert, hd and tl. Provided we take care to distinguish the use of integer lists to represent ordered sequences and the use of arbitrary integer lists for other purposes, there seems to be no harm in this approach. However, in a large program, it is easy to make mistakes with such an informal simulation of the values we really want to work with by values of a type we happen to have already defined. In order to obtain assistance in avoiding such mistakes, we will introduce a new abstract type ordintlist. The values of the new type will represent our ordered lists of integers (i.e. the subset of values of type int list which are ordered. The type checker will be able to warn us if we confuse an ordinary integer list with a value of the new type. Corresponding to the primitive list operations ::, null, hd, tl we will have new operations which are defined for the new type. The signature of the new type will be:

```
type ordintlist
null_oil   : ordintlist → bool
nil_oil    : ordintlist
hd_oil     : ordintlist → int
tl_oil     : ordintlist → ordintlist
insert_oil : int → ordintlist → ordintlist
order      : int list → ordintlist
```

Informally, we want null_oil, nil_oil, hd_oil, tl_oil, to be the counterparts of the list operations null, [ ], hd, tl respectively, while insert_oil adds an integer to an ordintlist rather like :: and order forms an ordered list of integers from an arbitrary int list (by sorting).

At first glance, one might think that a concrete type with constructors nil_oil and insert_oil could be defined so that the other functions can be introduced by pattern matching. The problem with this approach is that the associated values will be freely generated by these two constructors and this is not desirable. For example, we would like to think of the values:

```
insert_oil 5 (insert_oil 3 nil_oil)
```

and:

```
insert_oil 3 (insert_oil 5 nil_oil)
```

as the same even though they were constructed in different ways so that when hd_oil is applied to them we get 3 in both cases. This means that insert_oil is not a constructor that we should allow to be used in pattern matching and the selectors hd_oil and tl_oil are not inverses for insert_oil.

The relationships between the functions listed in the signature are too complex to be described by pattern matching alone. The function hd_oil should return the smallest integer that has been inserted into a nonempty ordintlist and tl_oil should return the ordintlist containing all the integers except the smallest. We leave it as an exercise for the reader to express the expected behaviour of the ordintlist functions more formally (e.g. with equations).

Below, we give an implementation which uses integer lists. We make use of auxiliary functions insert : int → int list → int list and sort : int list → int list which were defined in previous chapters but we repeat the definitions for easy reference:

```
abstype ordintlist = Ordered of int list
with
  local
    fun insert n [ ] = [n]
    |   insert n (a :: x) = if (lessthan a) n then n :: a :: x
                                             else a :: insert n x
    fun sort [ ] = [ ]
    |   sort (a :: x) = let val low = filter (lessthan a) x
                            and high = filter (non (lessthan a)) x
                        in sort low @ [a] @ sort high end
  in
    fun null_oil (Ordered [ ])     = true
    |   null_oil (Ordered (a :: x)) = false
    val nil_oil = Ordered [ ]
    fun hd_oil (Ordered (a :: x)) = a
    |   hd_oil (Ordered [ ])      = error "hd_oil of nil_oil"
    fun tl_oil (Ordered (a :: x)) = Ordered x
    |   tl_oil (Ordered [ ])      = error "tl_oil of nil_oil"
    fun insert_oil n (Ordered x) = Ordered (insert n x)
    fun order x                  = Ordered (sort x)
  end
end
```

It is important to realize that the 'sealing off' of the representation and choice of a particular signature does not prevent further functions being defined for the abstract type in terms of the basic functions named in the signature. For example, we might introduce an ordintlist version of accumulate as follows:

```
fun acc_oil f a oil = if null_oil oil
                      then a
                      else acc_oil f (f a (hd_oil oil)) (tl_oil oil)
```

which has type $(\alpha \to \text{int} \to \alpha) \to \alpha \to \text{ordintlist} \to \alpha$. However, the use of an abstract type definition prevents us from writing Ordered [1, 5, 3] which is not an authentic value of type ordintlist. In order to create an object of type ordintlist containing the integers 1, 5 and 3, we could use any of the following:

```
insert_oil 1 (insert_oil 3 (insert_oil 5 nil_oil))
insert_oil 1 (insert_oil 5 (insert_oil 3 nil_oil))
insert_oil 3 (insert_oil 1 (insert_oil 5 nil_oil))
insert_oil 3 (insert_oil 5 (insert_oil 1 nil_oil))
insert_oil 5 (insert_oil 1 (insert_oil 3 nil_oil))
insert_oil 5 (insert_oil 3 (insert_oil 1 nil_oil))
```

as well as applying order to any of the lists:

```
[1, 3, 5]  [1, 5, 3]  [3, 1, 5]  [3, 5, 1]  [5, 1, 3]  [5, 3, 1]
```

all of which produce an ordintlist represented by Ordered [1, 3, 5]. In fact, we know that any value of type ordintlist (which must be formed from either order or insert_oil or nil_oil) will be represented by a value with the form Ordered x where x is an ordered list. This follows from the definitions of these functions and the fact that insert preserves the ordered property. (To show this formally, we need to use induction on the set of expressions of type ordintlist formed by insert_oil, nil_oil and order.)

When an implementation for an abstract type is chosen so that there is exactly one representation for each abstract value, then the abstract type is isomorphic to a subtype of the implementation type. Here, each ordered integer list x corresponds to a unique element Ordered x of type ordintlist, and each element of ordintlist is represented by a unique ordered integer list.

As another example of a subtype, consider the type picture introduced in Chapter 4 where we described some operations we wanted to use with the type. When we chose a representation, we used the type:

```
int × int × string list
```

However, not all values of this latter type were considered to be representations of pictures. We required that if (d, w, sl) was to represent a picture, then the depth d should be equal to the length of the string list sl and that each string in the string list should have size w. We suggested in Chapter 5 that defining a new type:

```
datatype picture = Pic of int × int × string list
```

would help us to distinguish arbitrary triples from pictures formed with the constructor Pic. However, it would be better to use an abstract type definition in order to guarantee that the properties hold for any representing value. We leave it as a simple exercise for the reader to select appropriate primitives to form an abstract type picture.

7.2.2 Polynomials

We will illustrate how a representation may be chosen to optimize certain operations of an abstract type using, as an example, a type for polynomials of one variable.

Polynomials of one variable are often written down as expressions of the form:

$$a_0 + a_1x + a_2x^2 + a_3x^3 + \cdots + a_nx^n$$

where x is the variable and the a_i are coefficients which might be integers, real numbers or possibly complex numbers. (We will assume coefficients are integers here for the sake of simplicity.) Terms (a_ix^i) are usually omitted when $a_i = 0$ and the largest power of x with a non-zero coefficient is called the degree of the polynomial. Such polynomials have many uses in mathematics, but we need not concern ourselves with applications here except to note that the principal operations on polynomials which we intend to implement are addition, multiplication and evaluation (for a given value of x). These operations are explained informally in Table 7.1.

The significant information captured by a polynomial is the association of a unique coefficient with each power of x and this is all we need to know to implement the operations. In the polynomial:

$$2 - x^2 + 4x^5 \quad \text{i.e.} \quad 2x^0 + (\tilde{}1)\, x^2 + 4x^5$$

coefficient 4 is paired with the fifth power of x, ~1 with the second power of x, 2 with the zeroth power of x, and all other powers of x have 0 paired with them. We will assume that we are dealing with sparse polynomials which have a relatively small number of non-zero coefficients compared with the degree, so a good representation for such polynomials would be a list of the pairings of non-zero coefficients with the associated power of x. This suggests that we might define something like:

```
abstype polynomial = Poly of (int × int) list
with
    ...
end
```

Table 7.1 Some basic polynomial operations.

Adding polynomials

To add say $2 - x^2 + 4x^8$ and $6 - 3x^2$, we just sum the corresponding coefficients which have the same powers of x in the two polynomials. Thus we get:

$$\begin{array}{l} 2 - \ x^2 + 4x^8 \\ \underline{6 - 3x^2 \qquad\quad} + \\ 8 - 4x^2 + 4x^8 \end{array}$$

Note that $6 - 3x^2$ implicitly gives us a zero coefficient for x^8.

Multiplying polynomials

We take all possible pairs of terms (one from each polynomial) and multiply them together by multiplying the coefficients and multiplying the xs (which amounts to adding the powers of x together). After doing this, we collect up all the resulting terms and combine those with the same powers of x by adding their coefficients. For example, $2 - x^2 + 4x^8$ multiplied by $6 - 3x^2$ first gives us:

$$\begin{array}{ll} 2 * 6 & = 12 \\ 2 * \tilde{}3x^2 & = \tilde{}6x^2 \\ \tilde{}x^2 * 6 & = \tilde{}6x^2 \\ \tilde{}x^2 * \tilde{}3x^2 & = 3x^4 \\ 4x^8 * 6 & = 24x^8 \\ 4x^8 * \tilde{}3x^2 & = \tilde{}12x^{10} \end{array}$$

Now collecting up $(12) + (\tilde{}6x^2) + (\tilde{}6x^2) + (3x^4) + (24x^8) + (\tilde{}12x^{10})$ we get $12 - 12x^2 + 3x^4 + 24x^8 - 12x^{10}$.

Evaluating polynomials

Given a value for the variable x (assume an integer value for simplicity), the appropriate powers of x can be computed, multiplied by the corresponding coefficient and then the terms added. Actually, the simple-minded way of evaluating each term separately can be very inefficient, so instead we use a well known method for cutting down on re-evaluations of powers of x by regrouping the terms. For example:

$$ax^2 + bx^5 + cx^{11}$$

can be regrouped as:

$$x^2 * (a + x^3 * (b + x^6 * c))$$

With such a representation the above example would be represented as:

```
Poly [(4, 5), (~1, 2), (2, 0)]
```

where the pair (a, i) represents the term ax^i.

In fact, we will arrange the implementation so that we always have the pairs representing terms in decreasing order of powers of x and there will be no pair with a zero coefficient. The implementation of the type is given in Table 7.2 where the basic operations polyadd, polymul and evalpoly are supplemented with some further polynomial operations.

When two polynomials are added with addpoly, the pair list representing the result will be correctly ordered and have no terms with zero coefficients (since we assume the same properties for the argument representations).

To multiply polynomials, we first consider the simple case of multiplying two terms (a, n) and (b, m) giving the result ((a * b), (n + m)). The complete polynomials are multiplied by expanding out the multiplication of each term in one polynomial by each term in the other. This can be done in several ways, but we choose to do it by first taking a fixed term from the first polynomial and multiplying it by each term in the second polynomial. We obtain a polynomial (with the pairs still in the correct order) when we do this, so that we will end up with a list of polynomials, one for each term in the first polynomial. Since the pairlist representing each polynomial is correctly ordered, we may add up the list of polynomials by accumulating with polyadd, and this takes care of collecting together the terms with the same coefficients.

Table 7.2 Implementation of abstract type polynomial.

```
abstype polynomial = Poly of (int X int) list
with
  local (**** auxiliary definitions ***********)

    fun combine termlist1 [ ] = termlist1
    |   combine [ ] termlist2 = termlist2
    |   combine ((a, m) :: tl1))    ((b, n) :: tl2))
        = if m > n then (a, m) :: combine tl1 ((b, n) :: tl2) else
          if m < n then (b, n) :: combine ((a, m) :: tl1) tl2 else
          if a + b = 0 then combine tl1 tl2
                       else (a + b, m) :: combine tl1 tl2

    fun termmul (a, m) (b, n) = ((a * b), (m + n))

    fun fast (sofar, n) [ ] = sofar *  power x n
    |   fast (sofar, n) ((a, m) :: rest)
        = let val sofar' = sofar * power x (n - m) + a
          in fast (sofar', m) rest end

    fun power x 0 = 1
    |   power x 1 = x
    |   power x 2 = x * x
    |   power x n = if even x
                    then power (power x (n div 2)) 2
                    else power (power x (n div 2)) 2 * x

  in (**** main definitions ****************)
```

Table 7.2 *(Cont.)*

```
        fun polyadd (Poly p1) (Poly p2) = Poly (combine p1 p2)

        fun polymul (Poly p1) (Poly p2)
            = let val termlists = [map (termmul t1) p2 | t1 ∈ p1]
              in Poly (accumulate combine [ ] termlists) end

        fun evalpoly xval (Poly [ ]) = 0
        |   evalpoly xval (Poly ((a, n) :: tl)) = fast (a, n) tl

        fun mkpoly pairlist
            = let val termlists = [[(a, n)] | (a, n) ∈ pairlist;
                                              not (a = 0 or n < 0)]
              in Poly (accumulate combine [ ] termlists) end

        fun scalarmul (Poly termlist) s
            = if s = 0 then Poly [ ]
                       else Poly [(a * s, n) | (a, n) ∈ termlist]

        fun degree (Poly [ ]) = 0
        |   degree (Poly ((a, n) :: tl)) = n

        fun coeff (Poly [ ]) n = 0
        |   coeff (Poly ((a, m) :: tl)) n
            = if n > m then 0 else
              if n = m then a else coeff (Poly tl) n

        fun listterms (Poly termlist) = termlist
    end
end
```

The evaluation of a polynomial by evalpoly uses an auxiliary function fast applied to the first pair and the rest of the list (for non-zero polynomials). At each step, fast notes the next pair and calculates the difference in the powers of x to be computed. A current value sofar and remaining power of x still to be calculated are passed as an argument pair to the function fast. The powers of x are calculated by a binary chop so that, for example, x^{11} is calculated as $(x^5)^2 * x$ rather than $x * x^{10}$.

The important computational savings made by the rebracketing and binary chop are perhaps best illustrated with an example. Consider the evaluation of $3x^{10} + x^5 - 2x^2 + 3x$ which is represented as Poly [(3, 10), (1, 5), (~2, 2), (3, 1)]. During the evaluation, the function fast is applied to successive arguments as follows (where x^i abbreviates power x i):

$$\text{fast } (3, 10)\ [(1, 5), (-2, 2), (3, 1)]$$
$$= \text{fast } ((3 * x^{10-5} + 1, 5)\ [(-2, 2), (3, 1)]$$
$$= \text{fast } ((3 * x^{10-5} + 1) * x^{5-2} - 2, 2)\ [(3, 1)]$$

$$= \text{fast } (((3 * x^{10-5} + 1) * x^{5-2} - 2) * x^{2-1} + 3, 1)\ [\ ]$$
$$= ((((3 * x^{10-5} + 1) * x^{5-2} - 2) * x^{2-1} + 3) * x^1)$$
$$= (((3 * x^5 + 1) * x^3 - 2) * x + 3) * x$$

This final expression calls for an evaluation of power x 5, power x 3 and power x 1. However, power x 5 calls for an evaluation of power (power x 2) 2 * x and power x 2 is given by x * x. Similarly power x 3 is just power (power x 1) 2 * x or power x 2 * x. This means that the total number of multiplications performed is 3 (for x^5) + 2 (for x^3) + 4 (for coefficients) = 9. A completely naïve calculation with the original polynomial would give $9 + 4 + 1 + 4 = 18$.

Two important points should be noted for the definitions:

(1) Each of the main operations (evalpoly, polymul and polyadd) assume that the argument polynomials are represented by lists satisfying certain constraints (namely, that the terms were ordered and had non-zero coefficients and non-negative powers).

(2) Both the addition and multiplication operations produce polynomials represented by lists satisfying these same conditions.

By using an abstract type definition, we can ensure that the integrity of the representation is preserved and only operations which create lists in the correct form are available. Among the other operations we define mkpoly which creates a polynomial from an arbitrary list of integer pairs and ensures that the representation has the appropriate form. There is also scalarmul (which multiplies all the coefficients of a polynomial by a given integer); degree (which finds the degree of a polynomial); coeff (which returns the coefficient for a given polynomial and power of x); and listterms (which lists out the terms of a polynomial as integer pairs). The signature of the type will thus be:

```
type polynomial
mkpoly    : (int × int) list → polynomial
polyadd   : polynomial → polynomial → polynomial
polymul   : polynomial → polynomial → polynomial
scalarmul : polynomial → int → polynomial
polysub   : polynomial → polynomial → polynomial
degree    : polynomial → int
coeff     : polynomial → int → int
listterms : polynomial → (int × int) list
```

Other basic operations which might usefully be included in the abstract type definition such as polydivide (which could return a polynomial possible) and polyderiv (producing the derivative of a polynomial) are left as exercises.

7.2.3 Integer sets

The next example is intset, an abstract type for **finite sets of integers**. Finite sets of integers are quite similar to lists of integers in the way they are used, but they abstract away from certain details extant in lists, namely: the ordering of the items in a list and the number of repetitions of an item in a list. Often, finite sets are useful just to collect items and to check to see if an item has been collected. We may also want to remove an item from a set. This limited use of sets requires a signature of the following nature:

```
type intset
emptyset  : intset
insertset : intset → int → intset
removeset : intset → int → intset
memberset : intset → int → bool
```

The informal description of the primitives is:

> emptyset is a constant denoting the empty set.
> insertset s n produces the set with the same members as s but including n as well.
> removeset s n is a set with the same members as s except that n is not a member.
> memberset s n asks if n is a member of s.

A more formal (equational) specification is the following:

```
For all m, n : int; s : intset
memberset emptyset n = false
memberset (insertset s n) m = if n = m then true else memberset s m
memberset (removeset s n) m = if n = m then false else memberset s m
```

Other equations might have sprung to mind, such as:

```
removeset (insertset s n) n = removeset s n
removeset emptyset n = emptyset
insertset (insertset s m) n = insertset (insertset s n) m
insertset (insertset s n) n = insertset s n
```

However, the three we have chosen are sufficient to capture the required (externally observable) behaviour of the functions. The equations are said to be **sufficiently complete** because they have the following property:

Let E be an expression of some predefined type other than intset which involves a subexpression of type intset. Then the equations can be used to show that $E = E_1$ where E_1 does not involve any operations from intset.

This can sometimes be a hard property to show, but the following method for constructing equations allows us to obtain a sufficiently complete collection more easily. We first distinguish those operations of the abstract type whose result type is some previously given type and not the abstract type. These functions are called the **observers** of the type because they provide the only means we have to inspect or observe the behaviour of abstract values of the new type. The other operations are (potentially if not actually) constructors of values of the new type. (The standard terminology 'constructor' is used here to indicate that the functions create values of the new type. It does not quite coincide with our previous use of the term to indicate functions which *uniquely* create values of a concrete type and which can consequently be used in pattern matching.) In this example, memberset is the only observer.

We next create equations whose left-hand sides are of the form:

observer E_1 E_2 . . . = . . .

where those expressions E_1, E_2 . . . which have the abstract type as their type should account for all possible combinations of the constructing functions and the right-hand sides should only involve strictly simpler subexpressions of the abstract type if any. (The notion of 'simpler' is arbitrary apart from the requirement that it represents a well founded ordering of expressions.) For our example, there are three cases accounting for expressions of the form emptyset, insertset s a and removeset s a, respectively and the right-hand sides involve only strict subexpressions of these arguments.

It is not necessarily wrong to add additional equations like:

```
removeset emptyset n = emptyset
```

but this restricts the possibilities for implementation. We might want to allow an implementation where there were several different representations for the empty set. Each representation will have the same observable properties (namely that they have no members according to memberset), but the representation for emptyset and removeset emptyset n might look different internally.

We will now suggest three different implementations of the type.

The first implementation we define represents sets as lists of integers which are ordered and have no repetitions. These additional properties of the representing lists are implicitly assumed in the definitions and also preserved by each operation which generates a set. The auxiliary functions:

```
member' : int list → int → bool,
insert' : int list → int → int list
remove' : int list → int → int list
```

respectively find whether or not an integer is in an ordered list, place an integer in the correct position in an ordered list if it is not already present and remove an integer from an ordered list if it is present. Note how the auxiliary functions are able to cut short the scanning of a list in some cases because of the assumption about the properties of the list:

```
fun member' [ ] a      = false
  | member' (b :: x) a = if (lessthan b) a then false else
                         if a = b then true else member' x a
fun insert'  [ ] a     = [a]
  | insert'  (b :: x) a = if (lessthan b) a then a :: b :: x else
                         if a = b then b :: x else b :: insert' x a
fun remove' [ ] a      = [ ]
  | remove'  (b :: x) a = if (lessthan b) a then b :: x else
                         if a = b then x else b :: remove x a

abstype intset = Set of int list
with
  val emptyset = Set [ ]
  fun insertset (Set x) a = Set (insert' x a)
  fun memberset (Set x) a = member' x a
  fun removeset (Set x) a = Set (remove' x a)
end
```

The second implementation uses arbitrary integer lists (unordered and with possible repetitions) to represent integer sets. Insertion is now simply a (::) operation and is thus very efficient no matter how big the set is. However, membership must now be tested with a complete search of the list (using member) and removeset is implemented using the auxiliary function:

removeall : $\alpha^{=}$ list → $\alpha^{=}$ → $\alpha^{=}$ list

which has to remove all occurrences of an item in a list. The second implementation is given by:

```
fun removeall [ ] a = [ ]
|   removeall (b :: x) a = if a = b then removeall x a
                                     else b :: removeall x a

abstype intset = Set of int list
with
  val emptyset = Set [ ]
  fun insertset (Set x) a = Set (a :: x)
  fun memberset (Set x) a = member x a
  fun removeset (Set x) a = Set (removeall x a)
end
```

The third implementation of intset uses ordered trees as the representation (see Chapter 5). This makes membership checks much faster for large sets, but insertion is not as fast as in the previous implementation and removal requires the complete rebuilding of a tree in general. We check for membership before doing removals or insertions in order to save rebuilding trees unnecessarily. The auxiliary functions on trees are all included here for completeness. The function membertree : int tree → int bool finds if an integer is in an integer tree assuming the tree is ordered (see Chapter 5):

```
fun membertree Empty a = false
|   membertree (Tr (t1, b, t2) ) a = if a = b then true else
                                     if (lessthan b) a then membertree t1 a
                                                       else membertree t2 a
```

The function treeinsert : int tree → int → int tree was defined in Chapter 5 and inserts an integer into an ordered integer tree, preserving the order:

```
fun treeinsert Empty a = Tr (Empty, a, Empty)
|   treeinsert (Tr (t1, b, t2)) a = if (lessthan b) a
                                    then Tr (treeinsert t1 a, b, t2)
                                    else Tr (t1, b, treeinsert t2 a)
```

Finally, removetree : int tree → int → int tree removes an item from a tree. This is done by first forming a list of the items in the tree, then filtering out those items that are still wanted and then rebuilding a tree. The function buildtree : int list → int tree does this latter task by accumulating with treeinsert and Empty. For rather subtle reasons of efficiency, we prefer to use preorder : int tree → int list to form the list from the tree rather than flatten. This is because the shape of a tree formed by buildtree from an ordered list is completely unbalanced which in turn gives poor performance when it is being searched. The list returned by flatten will always be ordered when its argument tree is ordered, but the list returned by preorder need not be ordered. A much better solution to this problem of unbalanced trees is suggested in Exercise 7.13. We also use a faster version of preorder which avoids append operations. (See Exercise 5.29 for a similar optimization of flatten.) This introduces preordwith : int tree → int list → int list which both preorders a tree and appends a list to the result (without using @). The remaining auxiliary definitions are:

```
fun removetree t a = buildtree (filter (noteq a) (preorder t))
and buildtree list = accumulate treeinsert Empty list
and preorder t = preordwith t [ ]
and preordwith Empty x = x
|     preordwith (Tr (t1, b, t2)) x = b :: preordwith t1 (preordwith t2 x)
```

and the third implementation of intset is given by:

```
abstype intset = Set of int tree
with
   val emptyset = Set Empty
   fun insertset (Set t) a = if membertree t a
                             then Set t
                             else Set (treeinsert t a)
   fun memberset (Set t) a = membertree t a
   fun removeset (Set t) a = if membertree t a
                               then Set (removetree t a)
                               else Set t
end
```

7.2.4 Extending the type intset

If intset were to be used more widely in programming, we would need several other set operations. Unfortunately, many useful set operations would be much less efficient than they could be if we were forced to define them in terms of the restricted number of primitives. Worse still, some common set operations cannot be implemented at all in terms of the primitives of intset. For example, the following cannot be implemented without access to the representation:

```
union        : intset → intset → intset
difference   : intset → intset → intset
intersection : intset → intset → intset
isemptyset   : intset → bool
subset       : intset → intset → bool
eqset        : intset → intset → bool
elements     : intset → int list
image        : (int → int) → intset → intset
```

where:

union s1 s2 denotes the set whose members are members of either s1 or of s2 (or of both).

difference s1 s2 denotes the set whose members are in s1 but not in s2.

intersection s1 s2 is the set whose members are members of both s1 and s2.

isemptyset s is true if s has no members.

subset s1 s2 is true if the members of s1 are also members of s2.

eqset s1 s2 is true if s1 and s2 have the same members.

elements s produces a list of the distinct members of s in increasing order.

image f s produces the set of integers obtained as the result of applying f to each member of s.

We could solve this problem by considering an alternative abstract type which included all these in addition to the primitives of intset (possibly renamed in case both types are used in a program). We leave it as an exercise for the reader to specify the expected behaviour of the functions in such an extension and to modify each of the three implementations to incorporate the additional functions.

We will, however, look at another variation on the type of integer sets. The definition of integer sets can be modified to accommodate **infinite sets** in a functional language. In order to create an infinite set, we would need an alternative to emptyset and insertset since these only allow finite sets to be described. One method might be to specify those elements which are in the set by an integer predicate p such that p n = true if n is in the set and false if n is not in the set. Let us call the operation which creates a set from such a predicate setof, then the set of positive integers may be given as:

```
setof (greater 0)
```

The function setof gives us a clue as to how an infinite set might be represented. We could simply use a predicate as the representation for an infinite set and the abstract type could be implemented as:

```
abstype intset' = Set of (int → bool)
with
  fun setof p = Set p
  val emptyset' = Set (K false)
  fun insertset' (Set f) a = (Set (assoc [(a, true)] f))
  fun memberset' (Set f) a = f a
  fun removeset' (Set f) a = (Set (assoc [(a, false)] f))
end
```

which has as a signature:

```
type intset'
setof       : (int → bool) → intset'
emptyset'   : intset'
insertset'  : intset' → int → intset'
removeset'  : intset' → int → intset'
memberset'  : intset' → int → bool
```

and can be specified by:

```
For all m, n : int ; s : intset' ; f : int → bool
memberset' (setof f) n = f n
memberset' emptyset' n = false
memberset' (insertset' s n) m = if n = m then true else memberset' s m
memberset' (removeset' s n) m = if n = m then false else memberset' s m
```

An obvious next step would be to parameterize intset and adapt the definition to one of an abstract type constructor set so that intset is equivalent to int set.

7.3 Parameterized abstract types

In the same way that concrete types (introduced with **datatype**) could be regarded as a special case of type operators, we can introduce **abstract type operators** as parameterized abstract types. For example, intset could be modified to a definition of a parameterized abstract type $\alpha^{=}$ set with signature:

```
type α⁼ set
emptyset    : α⁼ set
insertset   : α⁼ set → α⁼ → α⁼ set
removeset   : α⁼ set → α⁼ → α⁼ set
memberset   : α⁼ set → α⁼ → bool
```

The parameterized version has the same equational specification as before. The membership test forces us to only allow parameter types for which equality is defined (hence the use of $\alpha^{=}$ rather than α). Unfortunately, only one of the three implementations we suggested for intset can be generalized because the other two made direct use of lessthan which is only defined for integers. The second implementation (which used removeall) can simply be generalized by rewriting the first line as:

```
abstype α⁼ set = Set of α⁼ list
```

Similarly, we might consider generalizing our first example of an abstract type canvas by parameterizing with respect to the auxiliary type colour. The resulting type operator would generate a type (from an arbitrary argument type) which had functions for creating and filling in squares of a two-dimensional board as well as returning the values found at a square. A more appropriate name for such a type operator might be twoDarray (two-dimensional arrays). We give a definition below where we have changed the names of the functions as well as the type and modified the specification so that it is an error to access or update squares (locations) which are not in an array or to create an array with a non-positive dimension:

```
abstype α twoDarray = Array of int × int × coordinate → α
with
  fun newarray a m n = if m > 0 & n > 0
                       then Array (m, n, K a)
                       else error ''newarray with dimension <1''
  fun sizearray (Array (m, n, f)) = (m, n)
  fun contentsarray (Array (m, n, f)) (Coord (m1, n1))
                    = if m1 > 0 & m1 ≤ m & n1 > 0 & n1 ≤ n
                      then f (Coord (m1, n1))
                      else error ''contentsarray out of bounds''
  fun updatearray (Array (m, n, f)) (Coord (m1, n1)) a
                 = if m1 > 0 & m1 ≤ m & n1 > 0 & n1 ≤ n
                   then Array (m, n, assoc [(Coord (n1, m1), a)] f)
                   else error ''updatearray out of bounds''
end
```

This implementation has the following signature:

```
type : α twoDarray
newarray : α → int → int → α twoDarray
sizearray : α twoDarray → (int × int)
contentsarray : α twoDarray → coordinate → α
updatearray : α twoDarray → coordinate → α → α twoDarray
```

and satisfies the following specification. We have separately specified when the array operations are defined, and the equations are required to hold only for defined expressions (*iff* abbreviates *if and only if*):

DEFINED (newarray a m n) *iff DEFINED* (a), *DEFINED* (m),
DEFINED (n),
and m > 0 & n > 0
DEFINED (updatearray x c a) *iff DEFINED* (x), *DEFINED* (c),
DEFINED (a),
and is_in (c, x) = true

DEFINED (sizearray x) *iff DEFINED* (x)
DEFINED (contentsarray x c) *iff DEFINED* (x), *DEFINED* (c) *and* is_in (c, x) = true

where

is_in (coord (m1, n1), newarray a m n) = m1 > 0 & m1 ≤ m & n1 > 0 & n1 ≤ n
is_in (coord, updatearray x c a) = is_in (coord, x)

EQUATIONS (for all DEFINED expressions):

```
sizearray (newarray a m n) = (m, n)
sizearray (updatearray x c a) = sizearray x
contentsarray (newarray a m n) coord = a
contentsarray (updatearray x c a) coord = if c = coord then a else
                                              contentsarray x coord
```

We have discussed the parameterization of an abstract type with respect to an arbitrary argument type (or an arbitrary type with equality in the case of sets). However, we regard an abstract type as a combined collection of functions satisfying certain properties as well as just the values of the type. Something we may well find useful is a way of parameterizing with respect to such a collection rather than just a type name and we show a mechanism for doing this in the next section.

7.4 Environments and modules

Many modern programming languages provide constructs which allow large-scale programs to be put together from components which can be compiled and tested separately. These program units go under various names like *packages*, *modules*, *clusters*. For a functional language, the concept of *environment* is useful for dealing with separate units and a sophisticated module mechanism is provided for the creation and manipulation of environments in SML. We give a brief discussion of this mechanism below.

7.4.1 Environments

In Chapter 1 it was stated that from a theoretical point of view, it was possible to ignore the separate construct of definition and concentrate on expressions only. That is, we can always regard definitions as auxiliary to some final main expression in which case they are syntactic sugar for an applied abstraction. From a practical programming point of view, the separate construct of definitions is highly desirable. The result of evaluating a collection of definitions is an **environment** which associates values with value names and types with type names introduced in the definitions. By making the concept of environment explicit, we can consider separately (1) the creation of environments by definitions and (2) the evaluation of expressions in the context of some environment. When expressions and indeed other definitions are evaluated, they are evaluated with respect to some existing environment. The evaluation of an expression in an environment appropriate for the names used in the expression produces a value. The evaluation of a definition in an environment (appropriate for the names not defined in the definitions) is an environment.

For programming on a larger scale, there is a need for creating re-usable, shareable environments. For example, we might want to have some definitions evaluated immediately to form an environment in which we want to work. Instead of entering the environment created (for immediate interactive work), we might prefer to keep it separately. On another occasion we might have an expression evaluated in this environment, and re-use the environment on several different occasions either interactively or otherwise. We might want to extend a kept environment with further definitions either temporarily or to form yet another environment to be kept for later use. We might even want to write definitions which can be used to extend any environment (or a certain restricted class of environments) rather than just a particular one. Such environments and environment extensions could be shared by several programmers working as a group on a large program.

There are many different ways in which to control the use of environments. With a functional programming language it seems appropriate to allow environments or **environment structures** to be manipulated as a kind of data object (at a higher level) by functional objects (of a higher sort). This would enable us to do functional programming at a higher level to give structure and coherence to large programs. In combination with a persistence mechanism to preserve the environments (between interactive sessions or for permanent retention in a file system), this approach leads to a powerful means for program structuring.

An important question which seems worth asking is why do we not allow environments to be just ordinary data objects so that we can use ordinary expressions to describe manipulations on them. The answer is that environments will in general contain type information and we cannot allow such information to be manipulated in expressions without sacrificing strong typing (with static checking of types) and safe separate compilation. Environments without type bindings can in fact be replaced by simple data structures carrying the collection of values defined in the environment. When we wish to manipulate type information (assuming that we want to keep static type checking), we must regard these manipulations as outside the main programming language and at a new level of abstraction where only a limited form of manipulation (which can be statically determined) is allowed.

Such a new level is provided by a *module* mechanism for SML proposed by MacQueen (1984) which is an extension of the concept of module used in Hope.

7.4.2 Modules

Modules are essentially environments (**structures**) and operations on environments (**functors**). We adopt the terminology of MacQueen here and just outline the main concepts and their application. Preliminary implementations of the design are currently available but (at the time of writing) the design has not been completely fixed. The reader is referred to MacQueen (1984, 1986) for more detailed information.

To begin with, we will consider simple modules without parameters (structures), and then introduce the more sophisticated notion of parameterized module (functor) afterwards.

Structures

Given a self-contained collection of definitions of either types or values, it is useful to think of the environment they create as an object which we will call a **structure**. A structure is denoted by enclosing the definitions as follows:

struct *DEFS* **end**

where DEFS is the collection of definitions. Such a structure can be named in a definition:

structure A = **struct** *DEFS* **end**

but only the value components of structures and not the structures themselves may be manipulated as values. If x is a component of structure A, it can be referred to as A.x. Large programs can be built from such units which are kept modular by the following *closure* restriction: global names in a structure (i.e. names not defined within the structure but assumed to be defined elsewhere) should be limited to components of other structures. (An exception is made for the pervasive, built-in primitives of the programming language like 5 and true.) This ensures that the contextual dependency of a structure is limited to other, named structures rather than arbitrary values. (The restriction is enforced to allow for separate compilation and may be made more flexible in the future according to Harper *et al.* (1987).)

Libraries would naturally be built as a collection of structures. For example, we might define:

```
structure ListOps = struct
                        fun accumulate . . .
                        fun reduce . . .
                        fun member . . .
                        . . .
                    end
```

If such a structure has been defined, we can think of it as a box containing all the general purpose list operations we might want to have access to. The names contained in the structure are not directly visible and do not clutter up our working environment. When we want to use accumulate, we simply refer to it as Listops.accumulate which we can rename locally if we wish:

```
let val acc = Listops.accumulate
in acc times 1 end
```

There is also a construct **open** in SML for opening up a box (structure) and spilling out the contents so that the names are directly visible in the context where the box is opened. For example, if *DEFS* are some definitions which refer directly to the list operations, we can write:

```
local
  open Listops
in
  DEFS
end
```

to make the list operations available (locally and temporarily) for the purpose of introducing the *DEFS*.

Signatures

Each structure has a **signature** which is the collection of type and value names (along with their types) which are defined by the structure. For example, if we define:

```
structure B = struct
                  datatype counter = C of int
                  val bottom = C(0)
                  val top = C(99)
                  fun next (C x) = if C x = top then bottom
                                                 else C (x + 1)
                  fun above (C x) (C y) = y > x
              end
```

then the signature of B is SIGB where:

```
signature SIGB = sig
                     datatype counter = C of int
                     val bottom : counter
                     val top    : counter
                     val next   : counter → counter
                     val above  : counter → counter → counter
                 end
```

(It is convenient – in particular for parameterization which we discuss in a moment – to be able to name signatures as well as structures.) Signatures play an analogous role in the level of structures and structure manipulations that types play in the ordinary programming level of value manipulation. The analogy is not exact, but it is useful to think of the two programming levels in this way:

(1) Program level (value manipulation):
    values   types   functions
(2) Module level (environment structure manipulation):
    structures   signatures   functors (see later)

In the above example of SIGB, we see that the signature contains the names of values with associated types and also the name of a new type counter. However, the full definition of the concrete type is part of the signature rather than just the name of the type and the names of the constructors. All the information carried by a concrete type definition is needed to check correct use of the constructors in patterns as well as expressions and this information is given in a precise form by the type definition. For an abstract type or type abbreviation, the signature would just contain:

type t = *Texp*

where *Texp* is a type expression describing the type t.

Restrictions on the use of global names in structures ensures that signature descriptions are context independent. The signature can also be left implicit in (and derived automatically from) a structure definition. Now suppose we want to define another structure C and we wish to make use of the function above from the structure B within C. The closure restriction means that we first have to name B as a component of C and then we can refer to above as a component of this component:

```
structure C = struct
                 ...
                 structure X  = B
                 ...
                 ... X.above ...
                 ...
              end
```

We have chosen to use the local name X for the structure component here. Thus X is just another name for B and will have the same components.

Functors

For a fully generalized modular construct, some form of parameterization of the structures is needed, so that a structure can be re-used in different contexts with some of the interdependencies abstracted away from. Instead of just having a **struct** expression or named structure providing an environment when it is evaluated, we can have **functors** (structure operators) applied to structures to form new environment structures.

In parameterization, we distinguish between formal and actual parameters for modules. A formal parameter should just specify the signature of (and give a formal name for) possible argument structures for a functor. When the functor is applied to actual parameters, the argument structure should contain components matching the signature of the formal parameter. Usually the structure will contain more defined identifiers then the specifying signature demands, so by 'match' we mean that actual values and types are defined for those identifiers named in the signature (with matching types). For example, the structure B could be passed as an argument to functors with any of the formal parameter signatures SIGB or SIG1 or SIG2 where:

```
signature SIG1 = sig
                    type counter
                    bottom : counter
                    top    : counter
                    next   : counter → counter
                    above  : counter → counter → counter
                 end
```

```
signature SIG2 = sig
                     type counter
                     bottom : counter
                     next   : counter → counter
                     above  : counter → counter → counter
                 end
```

The signature SIGB matches all the components of structure B exactly, whereas SIG1 omits details of the constructor (requiring just the type name to match) and SIG2 specifies a subset of the actual components of B.

This parameter mechanism generalizes the idea of abstract types (which can be regarded as special cases). The omission of constructor details of a type in a parameter signature provides an abstraction mechanism. For example, we could regard structure B with signature SIGB as an implementation of an abstract type whose signature is SIG1.

The abstract types described in previous sections could only be parameterized with respect to type variables (to make type operators). This module parameter mechanism generalizes this to the abstraction of a structure (abstract type) with respect to structure parameters.

To illustrate this, let us consider a structure which is a generalization of association lists. We call this a **dictionary.** Dictionaries have a function which allows values to be associated with a key and then entered into a dictionary, a function which uses a key to 'lookup' a value in a dictionary and function to create a new dictionary. The difference between dictionaries and association lists is that we assume that the type of the keys is not arbitrary in a dictionary. In fact we require keys to have an ordering predicate so that we can use ordered trees to speed up lookup operation if we wish. (A similar generalization could be done for set so that the ordered tree implementation of intset could be retained but with lessthan treated as a parameter.)

To make this more precise, we define two signatures. The first signature specifies exactly what we need to assume is available for the type of key.

```
signature KEY = sig
                    type key
                    val before  : key → key → bool
                    val matches : key → key → bool
                end
```

This signature will be used to specify the parameter of a functor which will create a structure containing dictionary operations. The signature can be thought of as the signature of an abstract data type, so we are effectively specifying an abstract data type as a parameter. There is, however, no mechanism for enforcing further (e.g. equational) constraints on the parameter as well. We cannot, for example, enforce the additional constraint that before describes a total ordering on values of type key and that matches describes an equivalence relation on values of type key. This sort of thing can be done in specification languages such as CLEAR (Burstall and Goguen, 1981), however.

The signature of dictionary structures will be:

```
signature DICTIONARY
          = sig
              structure K : KEY
              type α dict
              val newdict : α dict
              val lookup : α dict → K.key → α
              val enter : α dict → K.key → α → α dict
            end
```

This contains a type operator dict which is parameterized with respect to the type of the items stored in the dictionary (with an ordinary type parameter). The function newdict is available for creating a new dictionary and lookup and enter can be used to find items and enter new items in a dictionary. Since the types of these latter two functions involve the type key, we include a structure K as a component of the dictionary structure and K.key refers to the type component key of structure K.

The next step is to define the functor (MkDict) itself which will define a structure with signature DICTIONARY in terms of a parameter with signature KEY:

```
functor MkDict (Keystruct : KEY): DICTIONARY
   = struct
       structure K = Keystruct
       abstype α dict = Emp
                      | Item of K.key × α × α dict × α dict
       with
         val newdict = Emp
         fun lookup Emp k′ = error "not found in dictionary"
         |   lookup (Item (k, a, d1, d2)) k′
             = if K.matches k k′ then a else
               if K.before k k′  then lookup d1 k′
                                 else lookup d2 k′
         fun enter Emp k′ b = Item (k′, b, Emp, Emp)
         |   enter (Item (k, a, d1, d2)) k′ b
           = if K.matches k k′ then Item (k′, b, d1, d2) else
             if K.before k k′ then Item (k, a, enter d1 k′ b, d2)
                              else Item (k, a, d1, enter d2 k′ b)
       end
     end
```

Actually, this does not quite conform to the closure restriction because our function error is not a pervasive value and must be defined locally (see the appendix on SML for how this is done). We have neither imported nor redefined the type tree in order to define the type dict, but the definition of type dict is essentially the same as that of tree. There is an empty case Emp and a node case Item which contains a key and a value associated with the key as well as two subdictionaries. The ordering is maintained as for ordered trees with the first subdictionary containing keys which come before the top level key and the second subdictionary containing keys which do not come before or match the top level key. Note that K.matches can be an equality test, or something more general which allows close matches which are not exact. If a second item is entered with a key which already matches a key in the dictionary, we have chosen to replace the old key and item with the new key and item. This can easily be altered to produce an error or to leave the old key and item untouched. Finally, let us create a dictionary structure by using this functor with integers as the keys. We must specify not only the type of the keys but also the operations before and matches we wish to use. This is done by describing a structure with signature KEY which is to be used as an argument for the functor:

```
structure IntKey = struct
                       type key = int
                       fun before (x : key) (y : key) = y < x
                       fun matches (x : key) (y : key) = x = y
                   end

structure IntDict = MkDict(IntKey)
```

In the context of these definitions, we can access components of IntDict such as IntDict.enter or simply open up the structure by writing **open** IntDict which would make the following available in the current environment:

```
structure K : KEY
type α dict
val newdict : α dict
val lookup : α dict → K.key → α
val enter : α dict → K.key → α → α dict
```

where K = IntKey and so K.key = int.

7.5 Bibliographic remarks

An early paper suggesting the abstract approach to types is Morris (1973). The algebraic approach to abstract data types and specifications was pioneered by Zilles (1974), Guttag (1975), and Goguen *et al.* (ADJ,

1978a, b). Much work has been done since then and it is not possible to give a comprehensive survey of the literature here. A selection of some subsequent work is Guttag and Horning (1978), Guttag (1982), Goguen and Meseguer (1983), Ehrig and Mahr (1985), Kreowski (1985). For work on algebraic specification languages such as CLEAR, OBJ and LARCH see, for example, Goguen and Tardo (1979), Burstall and Goguen (1981), Sannella and Wirsing (1983), Guttag, Horning and Wing (1985). Equations as a basis for programming are discussed in O'Donnell (1985).

The details of the module system of Standard ML are given in Harper *et al.* (1986) and MacQueen discusses the use of *dependent types* to express module systems in MacQueen (1986). A more formal description of the module system can be found in Harper *et al.* (1987). The module mechanism is quite advanced and goes beyond the mechanisms available in other languages (such as Ada and Modula 2) in many respects. A simpler 'library mechanism' is implemented in Miranda and uses 'include' and 'export' directives in programs ('scripts') but does not allow for parameterization of scripts.

EXERCISES

7.1 Use the primitives of type canvas to create a checkered canvas with size 8 by 8 using Red and Blue for alternate squares. Similarly, use the primitives to define a function:

striped : int → int → colour → colour → canvas

which constructs a vertically striped canvas (with stripes of width one square) for a given size and two colours.

7.2 (Cardelli) Define an abstract type for mixing colours. Each colour is internally represented as a triple of numbers between 0 and 15 giving relative proportions of primary colours red, blue and yellow. The abstract operations (where colour is the new type name) are:

mix : colour × int × colour × int → colour

which can be used for mixing two colours in arbitrary proportions. We also have constants:

red : colour
blue : colour
yellow : colour
white : colour

for the three primary colours along with white which is represented with (0, 0, 0).

7.3 Show that the function order : int list → ordintlist defined in Section 7.2.1 is redundant in the sense that it could be defined in terms of the other primitives of the abstract type ordintlist. Why do you think this was not done in the example?

7.4 Define a function list_oil : ordintlist → int list which enumerates items of an ordintlist using acc_oil defined in Section 7.2.1

7.5 Use equations to express the desired properties of the primitives of type ordintlist.

7.6 Give a different implementation of the abstract type ordintlist using ordered trees.

7.7 Prove that the implementations of type ordintlist (the one given in the chapter and the one suggested in the previous exercise) both satisfy the equations you produced in answer to Exercise 7.5.

7.8 Write implementations for types picture and generation (see Chapter 4) as abstract types.

7.9 Define polynomial operations polydivide, polysub and polyderiv either as part of the type definition polynomial (using the representation) or using the other polynomial operations.

7.10 Define mkset : int list → intset both in terms of the primitives of the type and directly as an extension in each of the three implementations.

7.11 Specify and implement (in three different ways) the extended version of intset with the operations suggested in Section 7.2.4. (You might prefer to just suggest some equivalences rather than attempt a complete equational specification which is not easy.)

7.12 Implement an abstract type for queues (with items of type α) using the type (int → α) × int × int in the representation. (The functional component should indicate which items are at which (relative) positions in the queue. The second component is just the position of the front and the third component is the position of the back of the queue.) Add an additional function position to the type which retrieves the value at a given position in the queue (but counting the front as position 1).

7.13 Two-three-trees have two sorts of nodes (as well as empty trees): (a) a two-node with two subtrees and one item, and (b) a three-node with three subtrees and two items. Such a tree with integer items is ordered if (a) the item in any two-node is above all items contained in the left subtree and below all items contained in the right subtree, and (b) in any three-node with items m and n and subtrees t1, t2, t3, m is above all items in t1 and below all items in t2 and n is above all items in t2 and below all items in t3. Two-three-trees can be kept 'balanced' as well as ordered (so that all empty subtrees have the same depth in the tree) by turning two-nodes into three-nodes and vice versa. First of all, implement integer two-three-trees as a concrete type and define an insert operation which preserves order and balance. Then use this type for another implementation of intset. (Some suggestions are given in the solutions, but see Reade (1989) for a detailed solution.)

7.14 In some preliminary versions of Miranda, a concrete type definition analogous to:

```
datatype ordintlist = Nil_oil
                    | Cons_oil of int × ordintlist
```

could be qualified with some laws (rewrite rules) such as:

```
Cons_oil (n, Cons_oil (m, x))  ⟹  Cons_oil (m, Cons_oil (n, x))
                                   IF n > m
```

which would be repeatedly applied to put data values into a normal form where no rules apply. Show that by using two versions of the constructor Cons_oil (Cons_oil as a proper constructor and cons_oil as an ordinary function), such a law can be expressed by an ordinary definition. What changes would have to be made to subsequent uses of Cons_oil in expressions and patterns to achieve the same effect that the law achieves?

7.15 Define an abstract data type operator relation so that $(\alpha^=, \beta^=)$ relation represents binary finite relations between values of type $\alpha^=$ and $\beta^=$. The signature should contain:

```
makerel : (α⁼ × β⁼) list → α⁼ list → β⁼ list → (α⁼, β⁼) relation
dom     : (α⁼, β⁼) relation → α⁼ list
range   : (α⁼, β⁼) relation → β⁼ list
relates : (α⁼, β⁼) relation → α⁼ → β⁼ list
invert  : (α⁼, β⁼) relation → (β⁼, α⁼) relation
eqrel   : (α⁼, β⁼) relation → (α⁼, β⁼) relation → bool
```

where makerel forms a relation from a list of pairs and lists of additional elements in the domain and range (not mentioned in the list of pairs). dom (respectively range) returns the unique values in the domain (range) in arbitrary order. relates forms a function from a relation returning the list of values related to a given value. invert reverses a relation and eqrel asks if two relations are the same (ignoring ordering of the domain and range lists and pair list). Discuss variations and choices made in the implementation as well as any ambiguities in the specification which you resolve. Define further functions in terms of the above primitives:

image : $(\alpha^{=}, \beta^{=})$ relation → $\alpha^{=}$ list → $\beta^{=}$ list
preimage : $(\alpha^{=}, \beta^{=})$ relation → $\beta^{=}$ list → $\alpha^{=}$ list
closure : $(\alpha^{=}, \beta^{=})$ relation → $(\alpha^{=}, \beta^{=})$ relation
isPartialOrder : $(\alpha^{=}, \beta^{=})$ relation → bool
isPartialFunction : $(\alpha^{=}, \beta^{=})$ relation → bool
compose : $(\alpha^{=}, \beta^{=})$ relation → $(\beta^{=}, \gamma^{=})$ relation → $(\alpha^{=}, \gamma^{=})$ relation
is1_1 : $(\alpha^{=}, \beta^{=})$ relation → bool

using the standard meanings for such terms (closure means transitive, reflexive closure).

7.16 Define a functor which generalizes twoDarray to array where the coordinates (indices) and dimensions are not assumed to be pairs of integers but given by a structure parameter.

Chapter 8
Lazy Evaluation

In this chapter we turn attention to an important aspect of functional languages concerning the assumed method of evaluation. In particular, we will discuss the use of **lazy** functional languages. The term *lazy* derives from the mechanism of **lazy evaluation** (see Henderson and Morris (1976), Friedman and Wise (1976)), which ensures that expressions or components of structures are expanded in a demand driven way and are not evaluated more than is necessary to provide a value at the top level. This chapter emphasizes the practical consequences of using a lazy functional language. A more theoretical treatment of the concept and technical details of language implementation techniques are given in later chapters.

Laziness can have quite far reaching effects on programming because it provides a further separation of control and calculation in programs and so can be used as an additional abstraction mechanism. We will show how laziness ensures that definitions are **fully substitutive**, how laziness allows us to use **infinite data structures** in computations and how laziness affects our understanding of efficiency of computation. Furthermore, we will see that laziness is important if we are to describe interactive programs functionally. We also look at how functions can be viewed as communicating processes which compute in a demand driven way under lazy evaluation and how systems of communicating processes can be used in solving problems.

8.1 Evaluation order and strictness

When we write down function definitions, we can view them as laws. Thus in the context of a definition such as:

```
fun f x = g (h x x)
```

(assuming g and h have been defined) we know that for any argument x, the value denoted by f x is equal to the value denoted by g (h x x). We can also view definitions as prescriptions (procedures) for evaluating expressions, so that the above definition can be read as:

> For any expression x, the expression f x can be replaced by (rewritten as) g (h x x) in order to evaluate it.

These views are compatible in the sense that the result of a terminating evaluation of an expression by substitutions (rewriting) gives us a fully simplified expression denoting the same value as the original expression (i.e. the *canonical form* of the original expression). Evaluation is thus a process by which a canonical form of an expression is deduced from the laws.

8.1.1 Evaluation order

We pointed out in Chapter 2 that during evaluation of an expression, different subexpressions could be selected for simplification (reduction) at each stage, but that different canonical forms could not be produced by choosing different strategies for evaluation. (This is a fundamental property of functional languages where there are no 'side-effects' which might affect the value produced by an expression evaluation.) However, this is not the whole story. We also intimated that some reduction strategies might not lead to a canonical form for some expressions while other strategies could lead to a canonical form. For example, consider the expression f 3 in the context of the following definitions:

```
fun g x = 5
fun h x y = h y x
fun f x = g (h x x)
```

Treating the definitions as rules, we can evaluate f 3 as follows:

```
f 3 = g (h 3 3)    by the definition of f (with x = 3)
    = 5            by the definition of g (with x = h 3 3)
```

However, a naïve approach to evaluation may not succeed in deriving the result, because it gets caught in a loop:

```
f 3 = g (h 3 3)    by the definition of f (with x = 3)
    = g (h 3 3)    by the definition of h (with x = y = 3)
    = g (h 3 3)    by the definition of h (with x = y = 3)
    = g (h 3 3)    by the definition of h (with x = y = 3)
      . . .
```

Here, we are attempting to fully evaluate the argument (h 3 3) by using the definition of h before using the definition of g. This corresponds to a very common **call by value** computation rule of programming languages where arguments are fully evaluated before outer function applications are evaluated. In the context of functional languages, this also goes under the names of **eager** evaluation (because arguments are evaluated eagerly whether or not they are needed) and **applicative order** evaluation.

The more successful evaluation of f 3 resulting in the value 5 corresponds to another computation rule termed **call by name**. This has other names in a functional context: **normal order** evaluation and **outermost reduction order**, and is closely linked with **lazy evaluation** and **call by need**. (These latter two terms are sometimes reserved to mean something more than normal order evaluation as we discuss in a moment.) Normal order evaluation delays evaluation of arguments to functions until they are actually needed by simplifying expressions at the outermost level possible at each step. For example, in evaluating $E_1\ E_2$, we first evaluate E_1 until we obtain a function (a primitive or an abstraction described in terms of parameters and a body). The application of the function to argument E_2 is then evaluated in such a way that E_2 is simplified only when it needs to be (and as little as possible) to determine a final answer. With this strategy, an expression like:

```
snd (error "undefined", 5)
```

would evaluate to 5 whereas eager evaluation would fail to terminate with a defined result. (Recall that error s is regarded as being totally undefined and an attempt to evaluate it should cause computation to be aborted with no proper result even though s may be printed as part of an error message.)

Normal order evaluation is said to be **safe** in that it produces a unique canonical form whenever it exists whereas eager evaluation is clearly **unsafe**.

Unfortunately, simple-minded normal order evaluation can be extremely inefficient because it requires a new evaluation of the expression appearing as the actual argument of a function to be started from scratch whenever the argument is needed in the body of the function. For example, assuming double is defined by:

```
fun double x = plus x x
```

the evaluation of double (fact 5) begins with:

```
double (fact 5) = plus (fact 5) (fact 5)
```

with call by name, which would then require (fact 5) to be evaluated twice. We use the term *lazy evaluation* (or *call by need*) for a more sophisticated reduction mechanism than this simple-minded normal order evaluation which ensures that arguments are evaluated once at most. This can be implemented by the substitution of pointers to an argument expression rather than the substitution of a copy of the expression so that the result of any subsequent evaluation can be shared by each reference to it. (More details of this implementation technique which uses a graph to represent expressions with shared subexpressions are given in Chapter 13.)

Lazy evaluation gives the same result as normal order evaluation, because the use of data sharing to avoid duplicating evaluations only affects the efficiency not the result. A pictorial notation could be used to follow such an evaluation, and we might express the previous evaluation step with lazy evaluation as:

```
double (fact 5) = plus
                        ||
                        ||____> fact 5
```

We have used arrows to point to a subexpression in order to indicate sharing.

The reason that this evaluation technique is relatively new and was never considered for procedural languages is that it is incompatible with languages where side-effects can change the outcome of an expression evaluation. For example, if the evaluation of E were to have a side-effect such as the printing of a string at the terminal before producing an integer result, then double E and plus E E would produce different side-effects under lazy evaluation. Most of the programming problems associated with different evaluation orders in procedural languages arise from the presence of side-effects. With a purely functional language, we only need to consider the problem of termination.

Because different evaluation orders give different termination behaviour, we should ask which behaviour is correct. This depends on what we think a function definition means. If we regard function definitions as laws which must hold even for expressions with no canonical form, then we must regard eager evaluation as only an approximation of correct behaviour (its inability to return a result does not imply there is no canonical form). Hence we would regard g (h 3 3) as the same as 5 in the context of the above definitions even though evaluation of h 3 3 would not terminate (h 3 3 is undefined).

Conversely, if we think eager evaluation is in some sense the *correct* method, then we must modify our reading of definitions as equations and our way of reasoning with definitions. We would have to regard a definition of the form:

fun f x = E

as meaning that for all *defined* x, f x is equivalent to E. In reasoning about equivalences, therefore, we should only replace an occurrence of f (E_1) by E [E_1/x] (substituting E_1 for x in E) when we have first established that E_1 is defined. This greatly reduces the **substitutivity of equality** property of the language (also called the **referential transparency** of the language).

8.1.2 Strictness of functions

If we want to continue to think of functional programs as having an independent meaning (as mathematical functions and values) and evaluation techniques as being either correct or incorrect according to whether or not they calculate these given meanings accurately, we need to specify when expressions should be defined. We want our intended meanings to dictate how evaluation should be done and not vice versa.

Instead of talking in terms of evaluations, we should really speak about functions being strict or non-strict where:

> A function is said to be **strict** if the result is undefined when it is applied to an undefined argument, and is said to be **non-strict** otherwise.

In Chapter 10, we will be more explicit about the notions of defined and undefined. For the time being, we just assert that lazy evaluation is compatible with a non-strict interpretation of function definitions and supports full substitutivity. With lazy evaluation, constructors are assumed to be non-strict and other newly defined functions are only strict if this is required by the definition (i.e. if they inspect the argument by pattern matching or use other strict functions on the argument). Arithmetic primitives such as +, * are strict.

In contrast, eager evaluation is compatible with a strict interpretation of function definitions where all newly defined functions and constructors (and primitives) are assumed to be strict.

8.1.3 Reasoning about termination

It is useful to introduce an abbreviation Ω to stand for an expression which is totally undefined and whose evaluation never terminates (under any strategy). We could define Ω as being either error "undefined" or as:

```
let fun f x = f x in f ( ) end
```

and it has type α (that is to say it is a polymorphic expression that has an instance in every type). This expression will help us in establishing some properties about functions and expressions. For example, with a non-strict interpretation of our language, we have that:

$$\Omega :: E \neq \Omega$$

and that:

$$E :: \Omega \neq \Omega$$

and even that:

$$\Omega :: \Omega \neq \Omega$$

which expresses the non-strictness of ::. Now, consider the definition:

```
fun tl (a :: x) = x
|   tl [ ]      = error "tl of [ ] is undefined"
```

then tl $(\Omega :: E) = E$ because the actual argument $\Omega :: E$ matches the first pattern (without any need to evaluate Ω) and the component E can be selected as the result. Another way of expressing this is to say that the first line of the definition should be read as 'for all argument expressions of the form a :: x, tl produces x'. Then since $\Omega :: E$ has the form a :: x, we must be able to substitute Ω for a and E for x to obtain E as result.

Now, what happens when we evaluate tl (Ω)? According to our informal description for pattern matching definitions given in Chapter 1, we should try to match the (value denoted by the) actual argument with each of the patterns in turn until one matches. However, as in the previous example, we do not need to evaluate the argument expression fully to perform the match. We just need to evaluate it until it has a form which produces a successful match or until it is clear that a match is not possible with a particular pattern. In this example, some evaluation of the argument is necessary to determine whether or not it has the form $E_1 :: E_2$, but any attempt to evaluate Ω will fail so tl (Ω) is undefined. We could also express this as tl $(\Omega) = \Omega$ which shows that the function tl has to be strict (even for a non-strict interpretation of the language).

As another example, consider the definition:

```
fun K5 x = 5
```

Then K5 $(\Omega) = 5$ under lazy evaluation, since Ω matches x without any need for evaluation. The function K5 is thus non-strict.

As an even more subtle example, consider the definition:

```
fun K5pr (x, y) = 5
```

Clearly, with lazy evaluation, we expect K5pr $(\Omega, \Omega) = 5$, but what about the evaluation of K5pr Ω? Recall that Ω has type α, and therefore it has an instance type $\beta \times \gamma$, so the expression does make sense as far as types are concerned. The question is, does Ω need to be evaluated in order to match (x, y) or not? If we answer 'yes' to this question, we are suggesting that (Ω, Ω) of type $\beta \times \gamma$ denotes a value which can be distinguished from the completely undefined Ω (of type $\beta \times \gamma$) whereas answering 'no' suggests that these expressions are completely equivalent. The choice is a subtle matter of language design, and there is no right answer. Some of the mathematical tools necessary to analyse and explore the consequences of this and similar choices is introduced in Chapter 10. Here, we follow the second choice which says that if an expression has type $\beta \times \gamma$ then it can be assumed that any value it may denote has a form which matches (x, y). This choice means that whenever it makes sense as far as types are concerned, we can interchange Ω and (Ω, Ω). A similar argument can be given for other tuples and nested tuples. Patterns composed of tuples are called **irrefutable** by Wadler in Peyton-Jones (1987) when they are considered to be the only possible forms a value of the indicated type can have. Conversely, patterns involving other constructors are said to be **refutable** when arguments need to be evaluated to match the pattern (but see Exercise 8.1). With these assumptions about the language, we can deduce that:

K5pr (Ω) = K5pr $(\Omega, \Omega) = 5$

We will see more examples of the consequences of lazy evaluation below where we discuss its practical programming advantages. We should point out here that Standard ML is *not* a lazy language. It has strict semantics and uses eager evaluation. We will continue to use Standard ML notation for examples (extended where necessary), but warn the reader that many of the expressions we write assuming lazy evaluation will be undefined in Standard ML. It is, however, relatively easy to translate the examples into Miranda, Lazy ML and Ponder which are lazy languages. The Miranda appendix contains most of the translated examples. Chapter 9 deals with some alternative techniques for delaying evaluation in a strict language like SML.

8.2 Programming with lazy evaluation

8.2.1 Delay of unnecessary computation

We will show via some examples that the assumption of lazy evaluation can lead to a less constrained programming style. This is because some natural definitions which would be classified as highly inefficient under an eager evaluation turn out to be much more efficient under lazy evaluation. Lazy evaluation automatically delays computations until they are needed to produce a result. Sometimes the expensive evaluation of a subexpression can be completely avoided. Consider our definitions of & and or from Chapter 1:

```
fun true & b = b
  | false & b = false
fun true or b = true
  | false or b = b
```

If we evaluate an expression of the form E_1 & E_2, then we clearly have to evaluate E_1 to match the correct pattern in the definition of &. However, the evaluation of E_2 might not be necessary – it depends upon the value of E_1. If E_1 evaluates to true then we must go ahead and evaluate E_2 to get the value of the whole conjunction. On the other hand, if the value of E_1 is false, then there is no need to evaluate E_2 because the final result must be false in any case. Similarly, when E_1 or E_2 is evaluated, then E_1 has to be evaluated but E_2 only needs to be evaluated when E_1 = false. In a non-lazy language, the pair of arguments for these boolean functions would be completely evaluated before the match, thus potentially wasting computations.

It is essential in a non-lazy language that the conditional expression is considered as a special form whose evaluation does not require full evaluation of the two subexpressions forming the branches of the conditional. So, for example:

if true **then** E_1 **else** $\Omega = E_1$
if false **then** Ω **else** $E_2 = E_2$
if Ω **then** E_1 **else** $E_2 = \Omega$

Without such an exception, conditional bodies of recursively defined functions would be useless because they would never produce results when applied. (The branch containing the recursive application would always need to be evaluated regardless of the test.)

In a lazy functional language, conditionals can be treated as ordinary functions and need not be classed as special forms. If we define:

```
fun cond true x y = x
  |   cond false x y = y
```

then cond E_1 E_2 E_3 has exactly the same behaviour as **if** E_1 **then** E_2 **else** E_3 under lazy evaluation:

$$\text{cond true } E_1\ \Omega = E_1$$
$$\text{cond false } \Omega\ E_2 = E_2$$
$$\text{cond } \Omega\ E_1\ E_2 = \Omega$$

As another example of how lazy evaluation can lead to the avoidance of unnecessary computation, we consider the test for equality of lists. We assumed that such a test can be inferred automatically from a test for equality of items in a list, although we could define it for ourselves. We will assume that such a test behaves as though it is defined by:

```
fun ([ ] = [ ]) = true
  |   ((a :: x) = (b :: y)) = (a = b) & (x = y)
  |   ((a :: x) = [ ]) = false
  |   ([ ] = (b :: y)) = false
```

Now if we compute the equality of two long lists with different first items (say, 1 :: E_1 = 2 :: E_2) we get:

$$1 :: E_1 = 2 :: E_2 = (1 = 2)\ \&\ (E_1 = E_2)$$
$$= \text{false}\ \&\ (E_1 = E_2)$$
$$= \text{false}$$

and the evaluation of the tails (denoted by subexpressions E_1 and E_2) has proved to be unnecessary.

With this sort of computational saving in mind, a freer style of programming is encouraged. A classic illustration of this point is provided by the following problem concerning binary trees. Recall that we defined the type bintree in Chapter 5 by:

```
datatype α bintree = Lf of α
                   | /\ of (α bintree × α bintree)
```

We wish to find out if two bintrees contain the same leaf-values in the

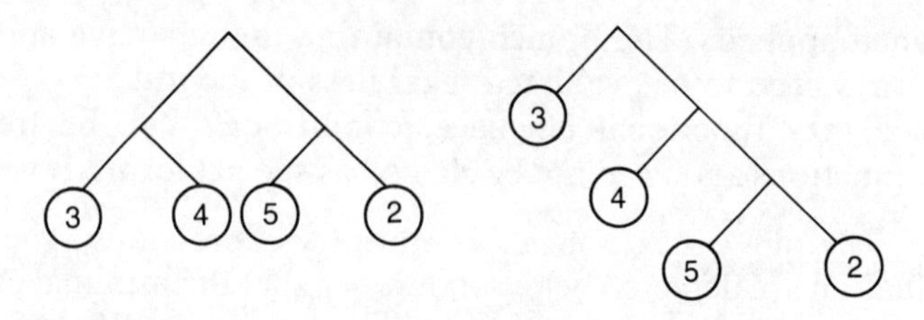

Figure 8.1 Bintrees with the same leaves (in order).

same order even though the trees may be a different shape (see Figure 8.1). We will define the function:

```
eqleaves : α⁼ bintree → α⁼ bintree → bool
```

to test for leaf equality of two bintrees so, paraphrasing the problem, we want eqleaves t1 t2 to be true if and only if the lists of leaves of t1 and t2 (in left to right order) are the same. But this specification of the problem gives us a direct solution because we can simply define:

```
fun eqleaves t1 t2 = leavesof t1 = leavesof t2
and leavesof (Lf x) = [x]
|   leavesof (t1 /\ t2) = leavesof t1 @ leavesof t2
```

Here, leavesof : α bintree → α list removes the structure to return just the list of leaves found in a tree and eqleaves is just defined as an equality test on the lists of leaves of the two trees. Someone who is only familiar with eager evaluation where the arguments to a function are evaluated before the function is applied might well comment on the inefficiency of the algorithm implied by the definition of eqleaves. It seems that the entire lists of leaves of the trees are calculated by leavesof before any comparison is done. If one considers the evaluation of eqleaves t1 t2 for two large trees t1 and t2 which happen to differ in the very first leaf, the two lists leavesof t1 and leavesof t2 would be produced in their entirety before being compared to find a difference in the heads of the lists (under eager evaluation). However, a lazy evaluation strategy would automatically avoid the unnecessary computation of the tails of the two lists, saving both time and storage space. The same improvement in terms of efficiency could be gained for an eager evaluation by careful use of conditionals but this requires more effort from the programmer and produces a less straightforward solution.

In lazy evaluation, control, in the sense of the order in which functions are called in an evaluation, moves back and forth between functions to give a quasi-parallel or coroutine-like behaviour. For example, let us consider the evaluation of:

$$\text{eqleaves (Lf } (3 * 2)) \text{ (Lf } (3 + 3) \text{ /\textbackslash{} (Lf } E_L \text{ /\textbackslash{} } E_T))$$

where E_L : int and E_T : int bintree are arbitrary expressions. The steps in the evaluation are depicted below and we see that the minimal expansion of definitions is used to generate the final answer false. We have:

```
eqleaves (Lf (3 * 2)) (Lf (3 + 3) /\ (Lf E_L /\ E_T))
  = leavesof (Lf (3 * 2)) = leavesof (Lf (3 + 3) /\ (Lf E_L /\ E_T))
  = [3 * 2] = leavesof (Lf (3 + 3) /\ (Lf E_L /\ E_T))
  = [3 * 2] = (leavesof (Lf (3 + 3)) @ leavesof (Lf E_L /\ E_T))
  = [3 * 2] = ([3 + 3] @ leavesof (Lf E_L /\ E_T))
  = (3 * 2 :: [ ]) = ((3 + 3) :: ([ ] @ leavesof (Lf E_L /\ E_T)))
  = (3 * 2 = 3 + 3) & ([ ] = ([ ] @ leavesof (Lf E_L /\ E_T)))
  = (6 = 6) & ([ ] = ([ ] @ leavesof (Lf E_L /\ E_T)))
  = true & ([ ] = ([ ] @ leavesof (Lf E_L /\ E_T)))
  = [ ] = ([ ] @ leavesof (Lf E_L /\ E_T))
  = [ ] = leavesof (Lf E_L /\ E_T)
  = [ ] = (leavesof (Lf E_L) @ leavesof E_T)
  = [ ] = ([E_L] @ leavesof E_T)
  = [ ] = (E_L :: ([ ] @ leavesof E_T))
  = false
```

In this evaluation, we have been completely lazy in avoiding computations of subexpressions (like $3 * 2$) until they are seen to be necessary for the final answer. We have shown each step in the reduction and note that the evaluation of either of the subexpressions E_L and E_T was unnecessary in this example.

The example illustrates that breaking the original problem up into the natural subproblems (of determining the lists of leaves and comparing the lists of leaves) does not carry an efficiency penalty by causing large, unnecessary intermediate objects to be calculated. This gives greater flexibility in designing and combining program components. The reader is encouraged to rewrite the definition of eqleaves so that it gives efficient calculations when used with an eager language. This should help to clarify the point that with eager evaluation, the programmer has to deal with the problem of mediating between the calculation of the leaves and the comparison in order to keep the two in step. (A solution is provided in the next chapter.)

In previous chapters we have not taken advantage of this freer programming style since we wanted to develop programs which would be reasonably efficient in a non-lazy language as well as for a lazy language. For example, consider our definition of exists : $(\alpha \to \text{bool}) \to \alpha$ list $\to$ bool:

```
fun exists p [ ] = false
 |  exists p (a :: x) = if p a then true else exists p x
```

If we were assuming lazy evaluation, we might have preferred to decompose the problem of finding out if a list x contained an item satisfying a predicate p into two subproblems: (1) forming a sublist of those items in x satisfying p (a problem which we already have a function to solve), and (2) determining whether or not the resulting list is empty, that is:

```
fun exists p x = not (null (filter p x))
```

This definition is efficient for lazy evaluation and processing of the list stops when a first item satisfying p is found. It is not very good for eager evaluation because the filtering is completed before the test for an empty resulting list can begin.

There are other differences which can cause problems in writing general purpose programs for lazy and non-lazy languages. For example, accumulate was defined to accumulate a result whilst scanning a list:

```
fun accumulate f a [ ] = a
 |  accumulate f a (b :: x) = accumulate f (f a b) x
```

This means that the result is not available until the full scan has been completed. In particular, we can calculate for any f, a and b that:

$$\begin{aligned} \text{accumulate f a (b :: } \Omega) &= \text{accumulate f (f a b) } \Omega \\ &= \Omega \end{aligned}$$

Conversely, the related function reduce defined by:

```
fun reduce f a [ ] = a
 |  reduce f a (b :: x) = f b (reduce f a x)
```

might produce some of the result without a full scan of the list. This depends on the strictness of the argument f. If f is non-strict in its second argument, then:

$$\begin{aligned} \text{reduce f a (b :: } \Omega) &= \text{f b (reduce f a } \Omega) = \text{f b } \Omega \\ &\neq \Omega \text{ (for non-strict f)} \end{aligned}$$

In particular, if we were to define the append operation as:

```
fun (x @ y) = reduce cons y x
```

then items from the first list x in an appended list x @ y can be retrieved without evaluation of y. We can show that:

$$[x_1, x_2, \ldots, x_n] @ \Omega = x_1 :: x_2 :: \ldots x_n :: \Omega$$

If, instead, we had defined @ in terms of rev and revonto as suggested in Chapter 3:

```
fun (x @ y) = revonto y (rev x)
and rev x = revonto [ ] x
and revonto y x = accumulate consonto y x
and consonto y a = a :: y
```

we would find that $x @ \Omega = \Omega$ for all x.

For this chapter, we assume a version of @ with the more pleasant properties exhibited by the definition with reduce. Other operations which scan constructed data objects should also be defined to take laziness into account wherever possible. They should be defined so that no unnecessary scanning of argument data is forced by the definition.

It seems unfortunate that a common style of programming is not possible for both lazy and non-lazy evaluation. The subtle differences that appear really make the case for further separation of specification and optimisation concerns in programming. It is often the case that the most natural specification of a function is closer to being an efficient program for lazy evaluation than it is for non-lazy evaluation. Knowledge of equivalences and performance of function definitions becomes more important for gaining efficiency in non-lazy implementations. Some commonality can be regained by turning to a more transformational approach to program construction.

Another important advantage of lazy evaluation is the possibility of introducing infinite data structures which we discuss next.

8.2.2 Infinite data structures

Up to now we have precluded objects other than functions from being defined recursively and assumed that lists and other data structures were finite. In this section we will argue that it is not only meaningful but very useful to allow other objects (such as lists) to be defined recursively. This leads to the possibility of using infinite data structures in programs which often means considerably simpler solutions to programming problems. (Recursively described data objects can be thought of as an applicative counterpart to the cyclic/re-entrant data structures often used in procedural programming, e.g. doubly-linked lists, threaded trees, etc.)

The following recursive definitions may be understood as descriptions of the infinite bintrees depicted in Figure 8.2 (which also have representations as finite graphs):

```
val rec infbt1 = (Lf 6 /\ infbt1)
val rec infbt2 = (infbt2 /\ Lf 2) /\ (Lf 3 /\ infbt1)
```

We use the notation **val rec** to introduce recursive definitions of values which need not be functions. In Standard ML, this notation can only be

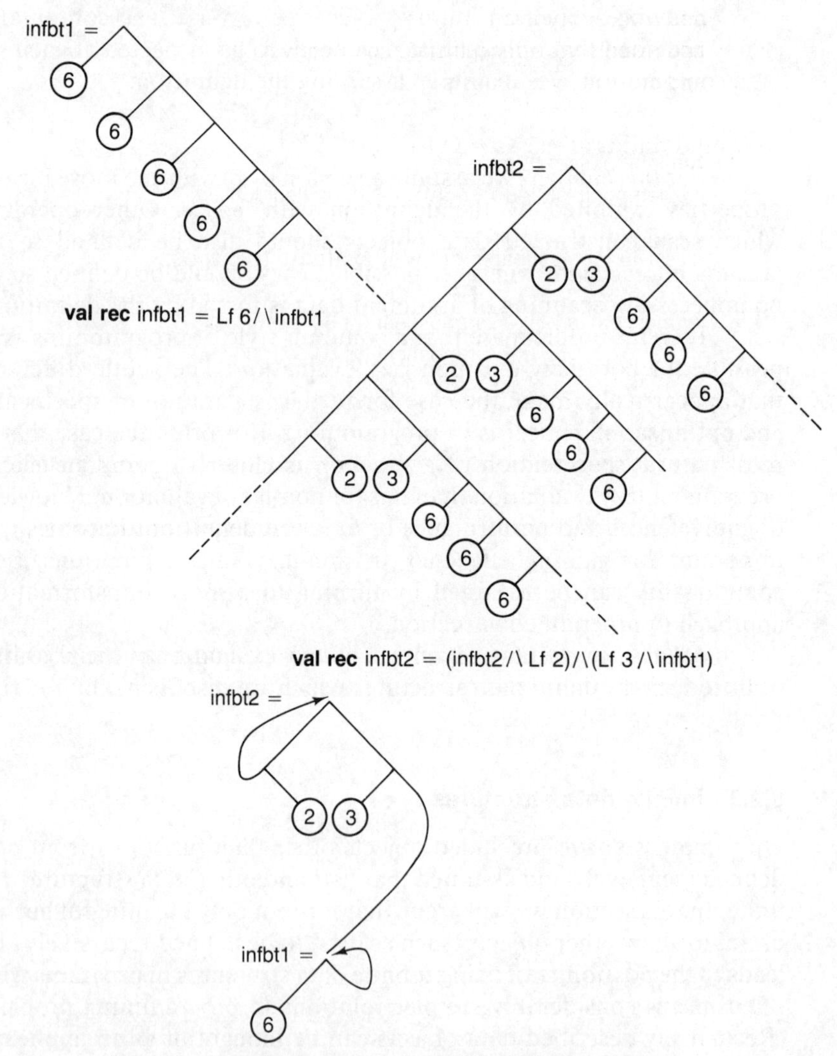

A minimal graph representation of the infinite trees.

Figure 8.2 Some recursively defined, infinite bintrees.

used when the right-hand sides are functional abstractions (e.g. with the form **fn** V ⇒ E), so the above example could not be expressed. In other languages (e.g. most implementations of LISP) such a recursive definition can cause the system to become catatonic while it attempts to evaluate the full infinite object.

The (infinite) bintree infbt1 has Lf 6 as its left subtree, and its right subtree is the same tree as infbt1 itself. Similarly, infbt2 contains itself as the left subtree of its left subtree, and contains infbt1 as the right subtree of its right subtree.

Having defined an infinite object, we can use it in computations safely provided that only a finite part needs to be inspected at each stage in a computation. For example, assuming the definition:

```
fun leftmostleaf (Lf x) = x
  | leftmostleaf (left /\ right) = leftmostleaf left
```

the expression leftmostleaf infbt1 will evaluate to 6 thus:

```
leftmostleaf infbt1 = leftmostleaf (Lf 6 /\ infbt1)
                    = leftmostleaf (Lf 6)
                    = 6
```

In a strict interpretation, infbt1 would be undefined, as would leftmostleaf infbt1.

As another example, consider the recursive definition:

```
val rec ones = 1 :: ones
```

which defines ones to be a list with 1 as its head and a tail equal to itself. Substituting the definition of ones for the occurrence of ones on the right-hand side, we can see that:

```
ones = 1 :: ones
     = 1 :: 1 :: ones
     = 1 :: 1 :: 1 :: ones
     =      . . .
     = 1 :: 1 :: 1 :: 1 :: . . .
```

Thus the head of the tail of ones is also 1, and so on (i.e. ones is an infinite list of 1s).

If we wish to use ones or infbt1 in defining other objects, we need the system to behave by not falling into 'black holes' through expanding the infinite object when only a finite part needs to be evaluated. Now consider the expression:

```
front 5 (map double (leavesof infbt1))
```

Under lazy evaluation, leavesof will still work on some infinite trees to produce an infinite list. Similarly map can be used to apply a function to every item in an infinite list to produce an infinite list, and front 5 returns the first 5 items of any list with 5 or more items even if the list is infinite. Lazy evaluation will thus produce the result:

```
[12, 12, 12, 12, 12]
```

having evaluated only those finite parts of the infinite intermediate objects necessary to compute the result.

Of course, if we asked for ones or leavesof infbt1 to be printed in full we should expect an infinite computation to be started but the list could be produced at the terminal while the computation runs. Later, we will see how this enables us to write interactive programs functionally (with output to and input from the user at a terminal.

Lazily evaluated lists, which may be infinite, are often called *streams* and they can be extremely useful in describing computations which might be quite awkward to express without them. We illustrate how streams may be used to simplify problem-solving in the following examples.

We first define the infinite list of natural numbers recursively as follows:

```
fun from n = n :: from (n + 1)
val nat    = from 1
```

(As an exercise, what would you expect Standard ML to do with these definitions?) Expanding the definition we see that:

```
nat = from 1
    = 1 :: from 2
    = 1 :: 2 :: from 3
    = 1 :: 2 :: 3 :: from 4
      . . .
    = 1 :: 2 :: 3 :: 4 :: 5 :: . . .
```

The list nat could equally well (but more obscurely) be defined as:

```
val rec nat = zip plus ones (0 :: nat)
```

To see why, recall that zip applies a binary function to corresponding elements along two lists, so the elements of ones (namely 1) are added to the elements of nat preceded by 0. Expanding this second definition we get:

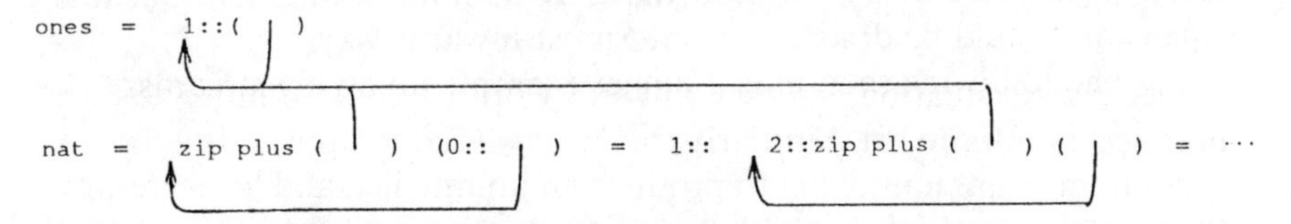

Figure 8.3 Unwinding the definition of nat.

$$
\begin{aligned}
\text{nat} &= \text{zip plus ones } (0 :: \text{nat}) \\
&= \text{zip plus } (1 :: \text{ones})\ (0 :: \text{nat}) \\
&= (1 + 0) :: \text{zip plus ones nat} \\
&= 1 :: \text{zip plus ones nat}
\end{aligned}
$$

At this point we can see that the head of nat is 1. We can use this information to get the next element of nat by further substitutions, denoting the tail of nat by nat′:

$$
\begin{aligned}
\text{nat}' &= \text{zip plus ones nat} \\
&= \text{zip plus } (1 :: \text{ones})\ (1 :: \text{nat}') \\
&= (1 + 1) :: \text{zip plus ones nat}' \\
&= 2 :: \text{zip plus ones nat}'
\end{aligned}
$$

and nat $= 1 :: \text{nat}' = 1 :: 2 :: \text{nat}''$ where $\text{nat}'' = \text{zip plus ones nat}'$. More graphically, we can depict the expression unwinding with pointers as in Figure 8.3, which shows the sharing of expressions (like the one for nat′) by a pointer (in this case to the tail of the already partly evaluated expression for nat).

As another subtle example we define factorials. See if you can convince yourself that the following defines factorials to be the list of factorials of the non-negative integers $1 :: 1 :: 2 :: 6 :: 24 :: 120 :: \ldots$:

```
val rec factorials = 1 :: zip times nat factorials
```

One way to see this is to write out an initial segment of the infinite list nat in a row. Underneath, begin to write down the elements of the list factorials starting with 1 (written below the first element of nat). At each step, multiply the last known factorial by the integer above it to get the next factorial as in Figure 8.4. In general, we can expand the definitions

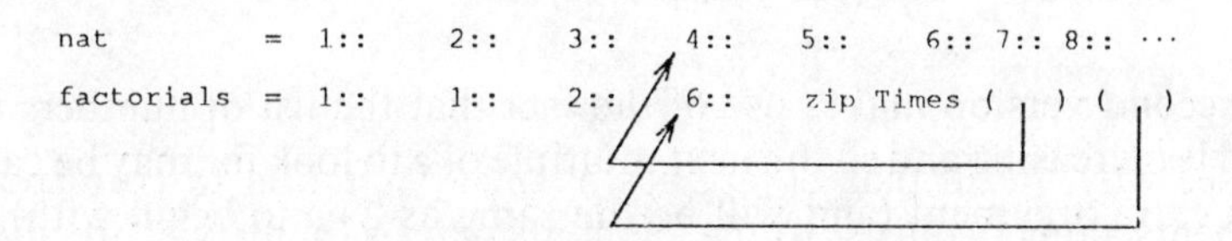

Figure 8.4 Unwinding the definition of factorials.

to try to get more and more information about an infinite list, but this expansion should be done in an outermost-inwards way.

The following section is a longer example involving streams.

8.2.3 Example: prime numbers (Eratosthenes sieve)

Eratosthenes sieve is a method for finding prime numbers by filtering out (sieving) the non-primes from the integers from 2 onwards. The sieving process is given by the following steps:

> Given a list (initially 2, 3, 4, . . .) take the first item as the next prime and remove all multiples of it in the list; repeat this process using the resulting list each time.

Since each number in the list 2, 3, 4, . . . is either a prime or the multiple of some previous prime in the list, only the primes survive the sieving process. By using an infinite list to begin with, we can postpone decisions on how far we want to go and get a clearer description of the numbers wanted. We temporarily assume we have already defined sift, where sift a x removes all multiples of the integer a from the list x. The main function sieve : int list → int list is then defined to produce the head of an argument list followed by the result of sifting out multiples of the head from the tail and then recursively applying sieve to the sifted tail:

```
fun sieve (a :: x) = a :: sieve (sift a x)
```

The primes are then given by:

```
val primes = sieve (from 2)
```

It remains to define sift : int → int list → int list. We begin with a simple definition of sift, and then improve it with a version which does not use division or multiplication. The first version uses the function multipleof : int → int → bool where multipleof a b asks if there is zero remainder on division of b by a:

```
fun multipleof a b = (b mod a = 0)
fun sift a x = filter (non (multipleof a)) x
```

The second version makes use of the fact that the list of numbers to be sifted is increasing and so the next multiple of a to look for may be carried as an extra argument (and will be the same as 2 * a to begin with). The operation:

```
nextfind : int → int → int list → int list
```

is defined so that nextfind a b x will test the next item in the list x and compare it with b (the current multiple of a to look for). If the item is less than b it is kept, if it is equal to b it is dropped, and if it is greater than b then the next multiple of a (= a + b) must be used for comparisons:

```
fun nextfind a b (c :: x)
    = if c < b then c :: nextfind a b x else
      if c = b then nextfind a (a + b) x else
                    nextfind a (a + b) (c :: x)
fun sift a x = nextfind a (2 * a) x
```

Having given these definitions we may now ask for the 10th element or the first 100 elements of primes or all of primes (in which case the computation should proceed until space ran out on the machine but producing primes at the terminal as they are uncovered).

At this point, it seems useful to consider how infinite values might be represented during computation and how they might be printed.

8.2.4 Weak head normal form

We have been using the term **canonical form** to mean some standard representation of values. However, this glosses over some technical details concerning the distinction between values and their representation, which we need to address, especially if we are to allow computations with infinite values.

The term **normal form** is usually used to mean an expression which cannot be reduced to a simpler expression. However, the concept of **weak normal form** turns out to be more important for functional program evaluation. A weak normal form is an expression which is in normal form apart from possibly any subexpression which forms the body of an unapplied function. During evaluation, any expression denoting the body of a function is usually only evaluated when the function is applied. Although we might well regard simplification of a function body as a useful technique for reasoning about and transforming programs, we do not usually regard it as a part of program evaluation. Also, since function values are not usually displayed at the top level and have no canonical representation, we do not need to inspect the bodies of unapplied functions when results of evaluations are displayed. This means that evaluation should at most need to produce a weak normal form.

Now, when we come to consider lazy evaluation and the prospect of infinite values, we need to explain further how they can be represented and how the result printed is related to the process of evaluation. Another useful concept, here, is that of **weak head normal form** which is an expression which is either an abstraction or primitive function (i.e. an unapplied function) or a constructor with arbitrary argument expressions (unevaluated). For example:

```
3 + 2 :: tl ones
```

is in weak head normal form. It is equivalent to (op ::) (3 + 2, tl ones) which shows that it is a constructor with unevaluated argument expressions. Subsequent reduction of an expression in weak head normal form will never change the form of the head part of the expression (the outermost constructor in this case) since further reductions only affect the subexpressions. Reducing an expression to a weak head normal form can be seen as a first step in finding a weak normal form.

It is useful to separate out this first step for the following reasons. When a value such as an infinite list or infinite bintree is to be calculated, we would like the result to be produced in stages as the calculation proceeds rather than waiting until the value has been completely determined since this will not be possible in a finite time. When a weak head normal form has been produced, the head or top level of the final expression will be known. If it is an abstraction or primitive function or a constant (constructor with no arguments) then evaluation is complete for we have a weak normal form. The only other case is a constructor with unevaluated arguments. If the result is to be printed, then printing this value will require a mixture of printing symbols for the constructor and evaluation of the arguments in the appropriate order. Clearly, as each argument is evaluated, it should be reduced to a weak head normal form first to see if any printing can be done before proceeding further. Thus at each stage, weak head normal forms should be produced, and only the demand for further printing should force further reduction.

Similarly, when an argument expression is to be reduced to match it against a pattern with a constructor in a definition, the evaluator should suspend the reduction after a weak head normal has been found and proceed with the match. The match may of course generate further demand for information about the arguments of a constructor causing them to be evaluated, but these should again be demands for reduction to weak head normal form.

Such demand driven evaluation with suspensions can be regarded as a special case of several components of a program working independently and communicating via demands. In the example of eqleaves, we used two processes which respectively flattened trees and compared lists. These processes automatically communicated (under lazy evaluation) in such a way as to do only work which was demanded and necessary to produce the result. In the next section, we explore the idea of functions as communicating processes a little further.

8.2.5 Functions as communicating processes

Many algorithms are naturally organized as systems of independent processes passing data to each other. A classic example of a program which is naturally separated into processes passing data is a compiler. The compiler can be seen as consisting of a lexical analyser which is a process accepting a stream of characters and producing a stream of tokens for the syntax analyser. This latter produces a tree representing the syntactic structure of the program (if there are no errors) to be used by a code generator or an optimizer. It seems far simpler to describe a compiler as separate processes in this way and assume the implementation will handle the interaction and timing (or interweaving) of processes to ensure that data is not produced too fast for the consumer. The alternative is for the programmer to interweave the separate processes into one program obscuring the logical structure.

The diagrams of interconnected black boxes introduced in Chapter 1 to depict functions bear an important resemblance to data flow diagrams which are used to depict networks of processes passing data to each other. We can think of processes as functions consuming data and producing data for other functions in the usual way as subexpressions and thus describe systems of processes as expressions in a functional language. The networks corresponding to expressions in Figure 8.5 represent separate processes (functions) as boxes and the wires indicate communication channels between the processes. Lazy evaluation corresponds to a particular **coroutine** control of the processes, whereby each process is driven by demand for some output from another process

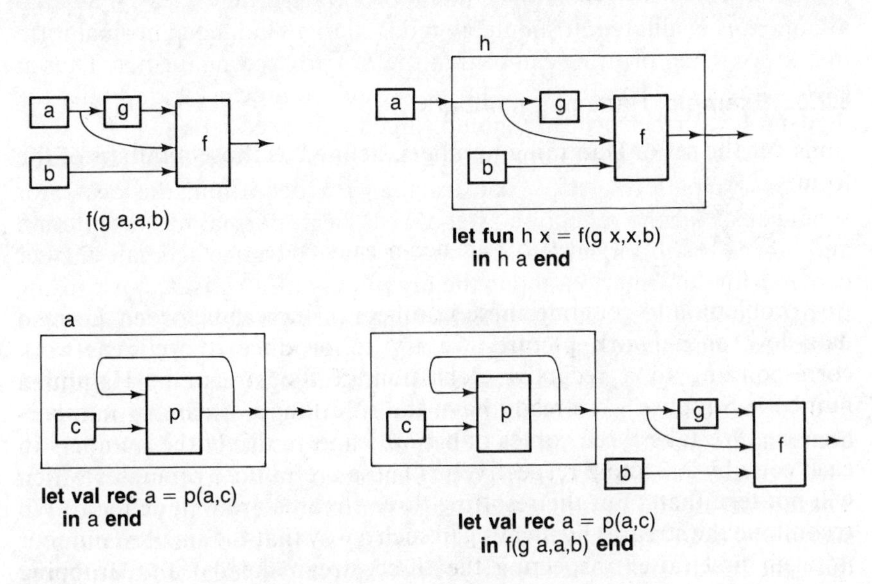

Figure 8.5 Functions as processes.

requiring some input. Processes are suspended as soon as the demand is satisfied (a weak head normal form is produced), but may be resumed when further demands are placed on them.

In general processes could be controlled in several ways including being run in parallel (stopping temporarily if arguments are not ready or storage space for results is not available). The separate processes can run at different speeds quite independently except for the constraints imposed by the availability of data which one process may require from another. However, to ensure the same results are produced as when lazy evaluation is used, other restrictions are needed which prevent more eager evaluations running away with unnecessary computations. By the use of **strictness analysis** (Mycroft, 1981; Mycroft and Nielson, 1983; Burn *et al.*, 1985) it is possible to determine syntactically which arguments to a function may be safely evaluated eagerly (non-lazily) without danger of falling into avoidable 'black holes' and thus preserving the non-strict semantics. This is particularly useful for parallel implementations where many processes are available to evaluate expressions eagerly. Because strictness analysis is static (syntactic) it is necessarily conservative, and more sophisticated transformations and analysis may produce more efficient versions at the cost of greater programming effort.

Some examples of the use of process networks where the data passing between processes is in the form of streams of values were described by Kahn (1974) and Kahn and MacQueen (1977). It is often useful to use such a network for solving a problem and then to describe the network with recursive definitions in a lazy functional language. We illustrate this in the following example.

8.2.6 Example: Hamming numbers

Consider the set of Hamming numbers, defined as those numbers of the form:

$2^p * 3^q * 5^r$ where p, q, r are non-negative integers

The problem is to generate these numbers in increasing order. Using a data-flow or network picture, we try to produce a cyclic network corresponding to a recursive definition of the stream of Hamming numbers. Suppose we already have the solution: a stream of numbers hamming. We take three copies of hamming and multiply the numbers in each copy by 2, 3 and 5 respectively. (These are infinite processes which will not terminate, but the resulting three streams are well defined.) We recombine the streams by merging in such a way that the smallest number is taken first (after inspecting the three stream heads) and dropping repetitions (see Figure 8.6(a)). Now the resulting stream will be increas-

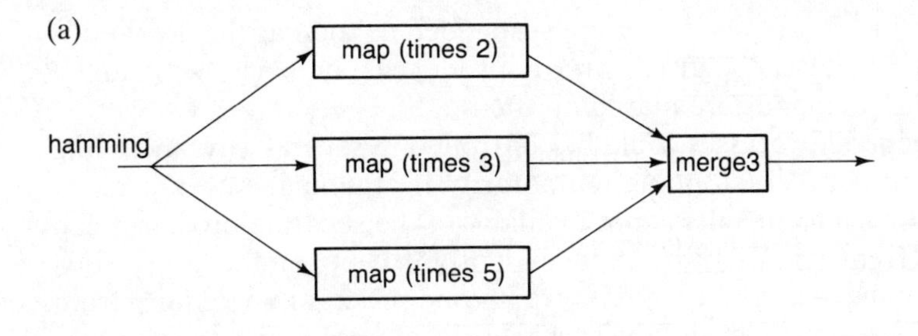

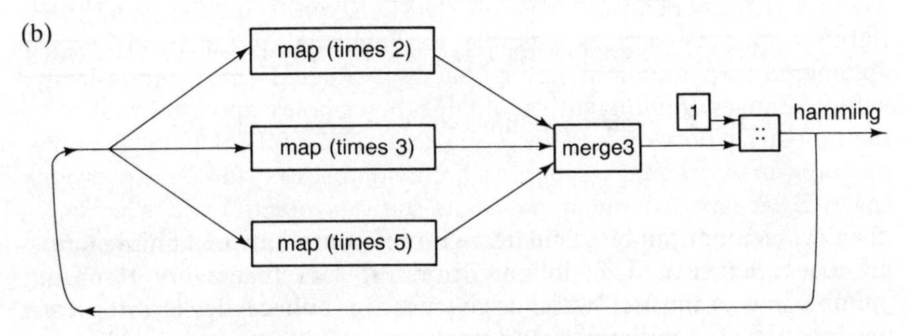

Figure 8.6 Hamming number generation.

ing, and every Hamming number except the first ($1 = 2^0 * 3^0 * 5^0$) will be included. Thus we merely have to put a 1 on the front, and we have reconstructed hamming to be fed back in to the beginning, closing the loop (see Figure 8.6(b)).

The loop in the diagram corresponds to a recursive definition of a stream and writing this as a functional program is now trivial:

```
fun merge2 (a :: x) (b :: y) = if a < b then a :: merge2 x (b :: y)
                               else
                               if a > b then b :: merge2 (a :: x) y
                               else a :: merge2 x y

fun merge3 x y z = merge2 x (merge2 y z)

val rec hamming = 1 :: merge3 (map (times 2) hamming)
                              (map (times 3) hamming)
                              (map (times 5) hamming)
```

Such a recursive definition of a list will not always be well defined and we should check that the recursion is well founded. In this case the first element can be calculated without inspecting the list and at every stage

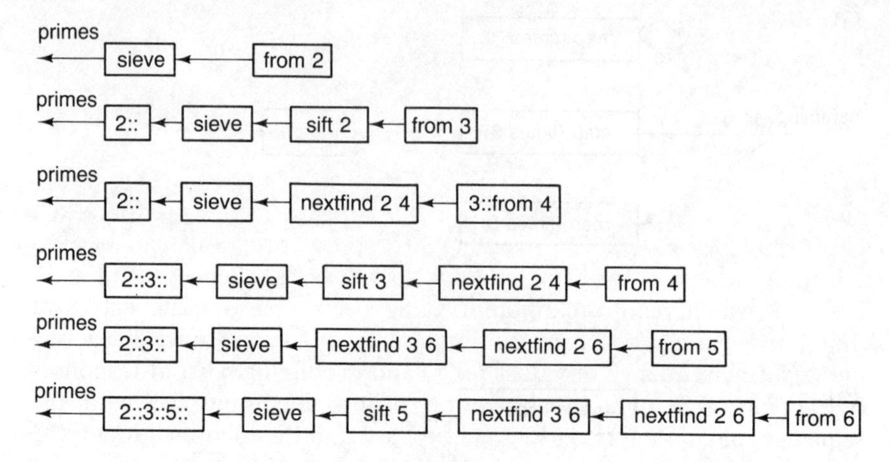

Figure 8.7 Evolution of processes with Eratosthenes sieve.

the next element can be calculated with reference only to a finite number of other elements. This follows from the fact that every Hamming number except the first (which is given as 1) is either twice or three times or five times another strictly smaller Hamming number. Also the merging of the three lists produces a number whenever there are three numbers available at the heads of the incoming lists and this guarantees availability of a further number for each of the three lists (so they cannot run dry and cause the system to deadlock).

The drawback of network diagrams is that they do not allow higher order functions to be represented easily and they do not show how networks corresponding to functional programs can expand dynamically. The evolution of a network during evaluation is not easily seen from the initial connections in all cases. An example of a dynamically expanding network is the sieve of Eratosthenes which evolves as in Figure 8.7.

In the next section, we look at a fundamental use of streams and communicating processes to provide a functional way to describe interactive programs.

8.3 Interactive functional programs

The concept of **sequences of actions** is an aspect of procedural programs which seems fundamental to their design and yet it appears at first sight to be absent from functional programs. Such a lacking might cause problems in the design of functional programs for interactive use since such programs are generally expressed procedurally in the form:

```
...
read something;
do some processing;
write something;
... etc.
```

and one often thinks in terms of the 'current state' of the computation. However, these dynamic aspects of procedural programs can be described in a static way using streams to replace sequences in time. A program which reads in different values of X and outputs values at different stages can be expressed functionally as a single function f acting on a list (the sequence of values for X) and producing a list of responses (see Figure 8.8). The identification of the incoming list with the sequences of characters typed at a keyboard and the identification of the outgoing list with the characters to be displayed on a screen are just special cases of the application of f (which could just as easily be applied to values in a file and produce values in a new file). Lazy evaluation is important if we wish to treat interactive programs in a purely functional way. In the simplest case, an interactive program is a function producing a list of characters (to be displayed at a terminal) and takes an argument list of characters (from a keyboard). We rely on laziness for output to be produced before the entire input list is available and the program only inspects the incoming list as and when it requires information from it in order to produce more output. The programming environment has to be set up so that an interactive program is suspended if input is not ready when it is required, and the program is restarted when characters are entered at the keyboard.

In the Miranda system, any function f of type char list → char list can be run interactively by evaluating f $- where $- denotes the standard input treated as a character list with ⟨control⟩D representing the end of the string. The output character list is automatically directed to the terminal as standard output (unless redirected).

Unfortunately, SML does not have a separate type of characters and strings are not lists. In order to simplify matters, we will assume that the standard input from the keyboard is a list of characters and that the standard output to a screen is a list of characters as well. To make this compatible with our previous use of SML notation, we will also assume

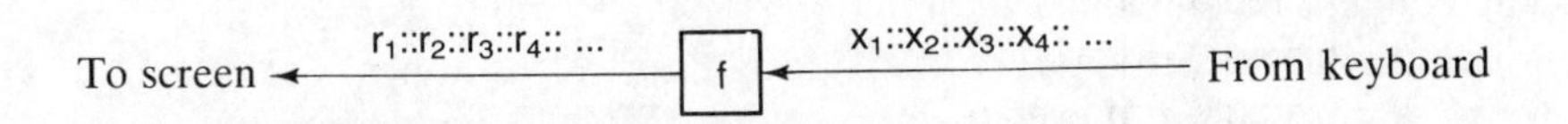

Figure 8.8 Interactive program as a stream function.

characters are strings of length one. We introduce a type abbreviation:

```
type char = string
```

but only use type char for strings of length one. Thus any function of type char list → char list could be used as an interactive program.

8.3.1 The simplistic approach

Let us begin by developing a small example which we call tellbinary : char list → char list. At the centre of the program is a function which converts non-negative integers into their binary representation. This is wrapped up in an interactive program which prompts the user for integers to be entered at the keyboard and then reports their binary representation on the screen. More precisely, we will design the program so that it exhibits the following behaviour:

> The program announces itself and prompts the user to enter some numbers (and also explains how to terminate the program). As a line is entered, the program makes a good attempt to detect numbers (possibly more than one) appearing in the line. The program should report the binary representation of each number it finds in the line and then repeat the prompt. This cycle is repeated until a blank line is entered at which point the program should terminate.

Table 8.1 shows an example interaction with the function tellbinary. Characters typed by the user appear on lines after the prompt >>>. In the example, the user first enters 12 followed by a ⟨return⟩ and gets the binary representation. The user then enters three further numbers separated by spaces and is shown the binary representation of each one. After the third prompt two more numbers are entered, separated by other characters which are ignored. After the fourth prompt, no numbers are found and the prompt is repeated. The user then enters an empty line by just typing ⟨return⟩ which causes the interaction to terminate with a final message.

Before designing the top level of the program, we will discuss some of the component functions we will need. The central function which converts (non-negative) integers to the binary representation as a list of characters is binrep : int → char list which is simply defined as:

```
fun binrep 0 = ["0"]
  | binrep 1 = ["1"]
  | binrep n = if even n
               then binrep (n div 2) @ ["0"]
               else binrep (n div 2) @ ["1"]
```

Table 8.1 An interaction with tellbinary (characters after >>> on a line are typed by the user.

```
+-------------------------+
| PROGRAM  tellbinary     |
| written  by . . .       |
| date . . . . .          |
+-------------------------+

Enter some numbers followed by ⟨return⟩
Just press ⟨return⟩ to terminate the program.

>>>12
Binary representation of 12
is:                 1100

Enter some numbers followed by ⟨return⟩
Just press ⟨return⟩ to terminate the program.

>>>13 5 66
Binary representation of 13
is:                 1101
Binary representation of 5
is:                 101
Binary representation of 66
is:                 1000010

Enter some numbers followed by ⟨return⟩
Just press ⟨return⟩ to terminate the program.

>>>um 3, 56, ,
Binary representation of 3
is:                 11
Binary representation of 56
is:                 111000

Enter some numbers followed by ⟨return⟩
Just press ⟨return⟩ to terminate the program.

>>>er

Enter some numbers followed by ⟨return⟩
Just press ⟨return⟩ to terminate the program.

>>>

+-------------------------+
| tellbinary  FINISHED    |
+-------------------------+
```

Even though the user will be entering input a bit at a time, we write the program as though the entire input is available at the outset as a single data object (a stream). We will use a function which chops up the input character list into a list of lines, where each line is a list of characters containing no newline characters. This function, which we call:

```
choplines : char list → char list list
```

is of general use in interactive programs which process a line at a time. One possible definition is:

```
fun choplines [ ] = [ ]
|   choplines ("\n" :: x) = [ ] :: choplines x
|   choplines [a] = [[a]]
|   choplines (a :: x) = let val line1 :: rest = choplines x
                         in (a :: line1) :: rest end
```

This simply looks for newline characters to finish one line and search for subsequent lines. The third case covers the possibility of the input ending in a character which is not a newline character, and effectively terminates the line as though a newline character had followed.

An (almost) inverse to this function would be one which linked lines up to form a single character list, inserting newline characters between each line. We use a function like this to form the final output, so that the rest of the program can produce a line list for output. However, we feel it is slightly preferable to allow newlines to be inserted as and where they are wanted in the main program, and we just use a simple link to join up the lines. (This allows prompts to be emitted without a newline.) We define linkoutput : α list list → α list which is similar to link except that we do not use accumulate to define it:

```
fun linkoutput x = [a | y ∈ x; a ∈ y]
```

In addition we will use showline : string → char list and showlines : string list → char list list which attach newlines to strings to be output as lines and showstring which just forms a character list from a string to be output without attaching a newline:

```
fun showstring s = explode s
fun showline s = showstring s @ ["\n"]
val showlines = map showline
```

The only other major component is a parsing function which finds the numbers in a list of characters. This is done by a simple lexical scan which looks for sequences of digits and skips over any rubbish between such sequences. A useful, general purpose function for dropping items in a list until some condition is satisfied is:

```
skipuntil : (α → bool) → α list → α list
```

The first argument is a predicate representing the condition and the function is defined by:

```
fun skipuntil p [ ] = [ ]
|   skipuntil p (a :: x) = if p a then a :: x else skipuntil p x
```

For our particular problem, the function findnums : char list → int list begins by using skipuntil digit to find the beginning of a sequence of digits, where digit : char → bool was defined in Chapter 2.

We use checknum : char list → int list which returns [ ] if there are no characters left and otherwise calls getnum to accumulate the digits and repeat the process findnums on the remaining characters:

```
fun findnums x = checknum (skipuntil digit x)
and checknum [ ] = [ ]
|   checknum (a :: x) = getnum (intofdigit a) x
and getnum n [ ] = [n]
|   getnum n (a :: x) = if digit a
                        then getnum (n * 10 + intofdigit a) x
                        else n :: findnums (a :: x)
```

Incidentally, we did define a function getnum in Chapter 6 with a similar definition, but its *continuation* after finding a number was lexanal there, whereas it is findnums here. We leave it as an exercise for the reader to define a parameterized, generic version of getnum which has these two definitions as instances.

The top level program tellbinary is defined in Table 8.2. First, we define three string lists for the banner, the prompt message and the postscript (which is a message to be displayed on exit). In order to understand the main function tellbinary, one must recall that the argument (inchars) is the input character list which will be typed by the user, and the result is a list of characters which will be printed. The body of the main function is simply a composition of choplines, tellbin_io and linkoutput. The function tellbin_io : char list list → char list list is thus the main, line-oriented interactive program (expecting lines of input and producing lines of output).

The lines output by tellbin_io begin with the banner followed by (@) those produced by promptandreport. Similarly, the lines output by promptandreport begin with the prompt followed by the lines produced by report. This latter function report : char list list → char list list is the first function

Table 8.2 Definition of tellbinary.

```
val banner        = ["+---------------------+",
                     "| PROGRAM  tellbinary |",
                     "| written  by ...     |",
                     "| date ...            |",
                     "+---------------------+"]

val promptmessage = [" ",
                     "Enter some numbers followed by ⟨return⟩",
                     "Just press ⟨return⟩ to terminate the program.",
                     " "]

val postscript    = [" ",
                     "+---------------------+",
                     "| tellbinary FINISHED |",
                     "+---------------------+"]

fun tellbinary inchars
    = linkoutput (tellbin_io (choplines inchars))

and tellbin_io lines = showlines banner @ promptandreport lines

and promptandreport lines
    = showlines promptmessage @ showstring ">>>" :: report lines

and report [ ]        = showlines postscript
  | report ([ ] :: x) = showlines postscript
  | report (a :: x)   = showlines (convertline a) @ promptandreport x

and convertline a = [line | n ∈ findnums a; line ∈ answerbin n]

and answerbin n = ["Binary representation of" @ stringofint n,
                   "is:                     " @ binrep n]
```

whose result is described by a case analysis on the argument. If the list of input lines is [ ] then the output ends with the lines of the postscript. Similarly, if the next input line is empty, the output ends with the postscript. In all other cases, the next line a is used by convertline to produce a suitable response. The output is composed of the lines produced by this response followed by the output produced by promptandreport applied to subsequent lines. Finally, convertline : char list → string list first uses findnums to produce the list of numbers found in a line. Each number is converted into a message showing the number and its binary representation by answerbin : int → string list. The lines of these messages are linked into a single list of strings.

Note how lazy evaluation enables part of the output (including the banner and first prompt) to be calculated independently of the input. This allows the banner and prompt to appear on the screen before input is validated (or indeed available). Subsequent output cannot be determined without analysis of the input (argument), but as soon as the next input line is complete the response can be calculated and this together with the repeated prompt can appear. An empty line will allow the full output to be completed regardless of whether or not there were subsequent lines (which would be ignored).

There are several problems with this kind of interactive program. First, it is quite difficult to see how it can be built from general purpose, re-usable components so that designing one interactive program is similar to designing any other. Secondly, it seems a little unnatural to deal with the input as a data object to be passed as an argument to a function as though it were all available in advance. Thirdly, and perhaps most importantly, it is very easy to make sequencing mistakes. To illustrate what we mean by this third point, consider the following modification to the definition of promptandreport. If we had defined:

```
val showprompt = showlines promptmessage @ [showstring ">>>"]

fun promptandreport [ ] = showprompt @ showlines postscript
  | promptandreport ([ ] :: x) = showprompt @ showlines postscript
  | promptandreport (a :: x) = showprompt @ showlines (convertline a)
                                          @ promptandreport x
```

then we would get very different behaviour even though the two versions compute the same result for the same complete input. This latter version requires a pattern match of the input before any of the output is known, so no prompt appears for the user until he/she has already typed in a line. This is obviously undesirable behaviour.

Although the two versions produce the same results for complete arguments, they behave differently for incomplete arguments. We can actually reason about such differences using Ω. We can calculate that with the original version:

```
promptandreport Ω
    = showlines promptmessage @ [showstring ">>>"] @ Ω
```

showing that the prompt message and >>> are produced at the front of the output even when there is no input. With this alternative version, we have:

```
promptandreport Ω = Ω
```

showing that there is no output without input. We need a way to alleviate the problem of this subtle sensitivity in the definitions of interactive programs.

8.3.2 A higher order approach

Most of the difficulties we have with the design of functional interactive programs can be solved or at least alleviated by using a higher order approach. Instead of designing individual interactive programs, we should look for mechanisms which combine interactive programs to produce new ones. We want a rich, easy to use, collection of combining operators (combinators) which can be used to build most interactive programs from a few primitives. We also want *good behaviour* to be preserved by the combinators so that any subtleties of definitions are confined to the operators and primitives. We are then less likely to build something with the combinators which produces unexpected behaviour.

A very general purpose collection of combinators for functional interactive programs has been described by Thompson (1986) and we base the following on this collection. The combinators closely resemble commands which can be found in many procedural languages. These seem to be relatively easy to understand and use.

Before we can describe the combinators, we have to introduce a generalized view of what an interactive program or **interaction** is. Assume first that choplines and linkoutput will be used to interface interactions with character-based input and output. This allows us to concentrate only on interactions which deal with lists of lines as input and produce lists of lines as output. We will abbreviate:

```
type input = char list list
type output = char list list
```

and use the appropriate abbreviation to indicate our intentions. The main generalization is to think of an interaction as some function which possibly consumes input and creates output and at the same time may do some calculation with independent data. (In a conventional, procedural program, the independent data would be stored in variables and an interactive program might alter the store as well as interact with the outside world.) This means that an interaction should be given access to an argument representing input and some other argument (representing other data) and should produce three results. These three results are (1) the unread remainder of the input, (2) the result of any processing of the other data, and (3) the output produced. This idea is encapsulated in the type abbreviation:

```
type (α, β) interaction = (input × α) → (input × β × output)
```

An interaction is parameterized by the type of the independent data supplied as argument (α) and the type of the data returned as result (β). One can think of an interaction of type (α, β) interaction as simply a function from $\alpha \rightarrow \beta$ which also affects input and output. (One might have expected a new type definition here rather than an abbreviation. It turns out to be more useful to keep interactions as functions rather than objects containing functions. The latter causes some problems of non-termination when interactions are defined recursively.)

The key to understanding the definition of an interaction lies in the definition of the main combinator which sequences two interactions. It is similar to the function ⟨&⟩ which we defined in Chapter 6 to sequence two parsers. We will write the sequencer as ⟨@⟩ and pronounce it *then*. This is an infix operator with type:

$$\langle @ \rangle : (\alpha, \beta)\ \text{interaction} \times (\beta, \gamma)\ \text{interaction} \rightarrow (\alpha, \gamma)\ \text{interaction}$$

Given two interactions i1 and i2, the sequenced interaction i1 ⟨@⟩ i2 is a composition of the effects of i1 followed by i2. This will be used in expressions such as the following:

```
write promptmessage ⟨@⟩
readln ⟨@⟩
processinput ⟨@⟩
reportresult
```

where write and readln are primitives described below. Readers familiar with writing procedural programs with input and output will recognize the conventional procedural structure here with ⟨@⟩ playing the role of the statement sequencing operator usually denoted by ';'. We are effectively modelling the state used in procedural programs in order to describe those procedural mechanisms which we find useful as higher order operators. (The notation ';' or at least '⟨;⟩' may be preferred to '⟨@⟩' but ';' cannot be used in Standard ML operator names.)

The definition of ⟨@⟩ is expressed by describing the action of inter1 ⟨@⟩ inter2 on the state in terms of the actions of inter1 and inter2. If (input, a) represents some initial input and independent data, then the first interaction (inter1) should produce from this a triple (in1, b, out1) where in1 is the unread input from input, b is some result data and out1 is the output from the first interaction. The pair (in1, b) is passed on for the second interaction (inter2) to use and this in turn produces a triple (in2, c, out2). The final triple returned by the combined interaction (inter1 ⟨@⟩ inter2) consists of the latter input and data result (in2 and c) along with the appended output out1 @ out2:

```
infix ⟨@⟩
fun (inter1 ⟨@⟩ inter2) (input, a)
   = let val (in1, b, out1) = inter1 (input, a)
         val (in2, c, out2) = inter2 (in1, b)
     in (in2, c, out1 @ out2) end
```

We might have allowed the output of the first interaction to be passed on to the second interaction with an even more general type definition for interaction. However, it seems unwise to allow an interaction to modify output from previous interactions as this might well create the output delay problems we are trying to avoid.

Most interactions we write will consist of a sequence of simpler interactions, and will ultimately be built from very simple primitives such as readln and writeln which we define next. The primitives:

```
write : string → (α, α) interaction
writeln : string → (α, α) interaction
writelns : string list → (α, α) interaction
```

have no effect on the main data and just send, respectively, a string, a string and a newline character, and a list of strings with a newline character each to the output. They are defined by:

```
fun write    s (input, a) = (input, a, [showstring s])
fun writeln  s (input, a) = (input, a, [showline s])
fun writelns x (input, a) = (input, a, showlines x)
```

In addition to the write operations which can be used to write lines which are explicitly passed as an argument, we define:

```
report : (string list, string list) interaction
```

This is used to output the stored data when it is in the form of a list of strings. It is defined as:

```
fun report (input, slist) = (input, slist, showlines slist)
```

Another primitive (readln) is defined to read in a line from the input and transfer the line to the second component of the result for subsequent processing as data. Thus the previous data value is replaced by a char list. To avoid accidentally losing data by overwriting in this way, we can insist that the data is ( ) : unit before a read can be done. We will define an explicit primitive which will allow us to clear the data before a read operation in a moment. The type of the read primitive is:

```
readln : (unit, char list) interaction
```

and it is defined as:

```
fun readln (line1 :: rest, ( )) = (rest, line1, [ ])
|   readln ([ ], ( )) = error "readln at end of input"
```

The data-clearing primitive will be called forget and it has type:

```
forget : (α, unit) interaction
```

It is defined in terms of a more general purpose function which allows us to perform any operation on the stored data. For example, if f : $\alpha \rightarrow \beta$ then we would like to have an interaction editdata f with type (α, β) interaction which has no effect on the input or output. We define:

```
    editdata : (α → β) → (α, β) interaction
fun editdata f (input, a) = (input, f (a), [ ])
```

and then we can implement forget as an edit with a function K ( ) : $\alpha \rightarrow$ unit which just returns the empty tuple ( ):

```
val forget = editdata (K ( ))
```

So far, we have several primitives, but only one combinator (⟨@⟩). Another combinator is a conditional construct which uses a predicate on the stored data to decide which of two alternative interactions to proceed with. The type of the construct is:

```
alt : (α → bool) → (α, β) interaction → (α, β) interaction → (α, β) interaction
```

and it is defined as follows:

```
fun alt p inter1 inter2 (input, a)
    = if p a then inter1 (input, a) else inter2 (input, a)
```

This gives us the ability to sequence interactions and branch on the result of a test. The next combinator is one which allows us to perform a repetition (repeat loop). Suppose we have an interaction which may fail to achieve some goal such as obtaining an integer in a certain range from the user. We would like to repeat the interaction until it is successful. One way to represent success and failure which we used in earlier chapters was to use a type of the form α possible. However, for this combinator, we follow Thompson's technique which assumes a boolean flag is used to indicate success or failure. After an interaction which may fail or succeed, we assume that the stored data will have the form (a, true) in the successful case and (a, false) in the failure case. Thus, given an interaction of type (α, $\alpha \times$ bool) interaction, we want to create an interaction of type (α, α) interaction by repeating the former interaction until it is successful. This suggests a combinator:

```
repeated : (α, α × bool) interaction → (α, α) interaction
```

This is easy to define using the sequence primitive and an interaction modifier which we call checkflag. The function checkflag is passed an interaction of type (α, α) interaction as an argument and modifies it to form an interaction which expects a flagged data component. If the flag is false, it removes the flag and proceeds with the interaction supplied as argument. If the flag is true then it just removes the flag (with no further interaction). The type of this latter function is thus:

checkflag : (α, α) interaction → (α × bool, α) interaction

Here are the definitions of the two combinators:

```
fun checkflag inter (input, (a, true)) = (input, a, [ ])
|   checkflag inter (input, (a, false)) = inter (input, a)

fun repeated inter = inter ⟨@⟩ checkflag (repeated inter)
```

Note that repeated just sequences an interaction with a further repeated interaction which is modified to check the flag first.

The reader is encouraged to try out these combinators and primitives in the construction of some simple interactive programs. Other combinators and primitives can be defined when necessary, but the ones mentioned above are suitable for most cases. We illustrate these by defining another version of tellbinary. The interactive program interbin : (unit, unit) interaction is defined below as the main interaction. The other interaction, promptloop, is a recursively defined auxiliary interaction of the same type:

```
val rec promptloop = writelns promptmessage ⟨@⟩
                     write ">>>" ⟨@⟩
                     readln ⟨@⟩
                     alt null
                       (writelns postscript ⟨@⟩ forget)
                       (editdata convertline ⟨@⟩
                        report ⟨@⟩
                        forget ⟨@⟩
                        promptloop)

val interbin = writelns banner ⟨@⟩
               promptloop
```

The function convertline is defined as before, and we assume the same definitions for the string lists promptmessage, postscript and banner. Note the use of forget to clear the data after reporting or finishing is done. This is necessary for type compatibility.

To use the interaction, we make use of a function:

```
run_io : (unit, unit) interaction → char list → char list
```

which converts an interaction into a function from a character stream to a character stream at the outermost level. The function run_io is a simple version of run which is defined by Thompson (1986) and reports the final data at the end of the interaction. Our version assumes reporting is done by the interaction leaving ( ) as data. It is defined as:

```
fun run_io inter charsin
      = let val (input, ( ), output) = inter (choplines charsin, ( ))
        in linkoutput output end
```

The top-level program to be applied to a character stream from the keyboard in our example is thus:

```
val tellbin2 = run_io interbin
```

and tellbin2 : char list → char list.

When the interaction interbin is run it shows slightly different behaviour to tellbinary. When input is terminated incorrectly (with a ⟨control⟩D before an empty line) the postscript does not appear and the evaluation aborts. We leave it as an exercise to modify the program so that it deals with such cases properly. (The readln has to be changed to allow a test for lack of input lines first.)

8.4 Further lazy programming techniques

Although lazy evaluation tends to encourage the use of more specification-like programs, there are some novel programming tricks that can be done with lazy evaluation to gain efficiency. Because programs written using such tricks can be very subtle, they are best avoided for initial versions of programs. Deriving the more efficient versions from simpler but less efficient versions is likely to be a safer method for obtaining efficient programs. In the following examples, we just illustrate some of the tricks without deriving them from simpler programs.

8.4.1 Example: a lazy dictionary

Consider the problem of scanning some text where identifiers are both defined and used, but the use can precede the definition. We want to associate some value with the identifier which will depend on the definition, and 'lookup' this value at each occurrence where the identifier is used. Because the use may appear before the definition, this might suggest that two passes over the text might be necessary.

Another related problem arises in the description of assemblers and linkers. Identifiers occurring in a program to be assembled have to be translated into an address by the assembler, but the address is determined by the linker which processes the result of the assembler.

With lazy evaluation, it is possible to solve these problems efficiently so that only a single pass over the data is necessary. We will define a lazy dictionary which allows a key to be used to look up an item in the dictionary before the key and item have been inserted into the dictionary. Roughly speaking, it works like this:

> Assume we have a stream of requests for both lookups and insertions for our dictionary. We separate this stream into two different streams, where one contains keys for lookups and the other contains (key, item) pairs for entry into a dictionary. We use the entry stream to build up a dictionary (which may never be completed). We use the final dictionary constructed to answer all the lookup requests to produce a stream of items. Lazy evaluation will ensure that lookups can proceed while the dictionary is still under construction, and will be suspended if the entry is not yet ready. Provided there is exactly one entry for each key requested at the end, the entire output list of items (corresponding to the requests) will be defined.

We begin by defining a type for dictionary requests. We will assume keys are integers for simplicity so that they can be ordered with <:

```
type key = int
datatype α dictrequest = Entry of (key, α)
                       | Lookup of key
```

Now we define two filters which return just the lookup keys and, respectively, just the entry pairs from a dictionary request list:

```
fun getlooks (Lookup k :: rest) = k :: getlooks rest
|   getlooks (Entry (k, a) :: rest) = getlooks rest
fun getentries (Lookup k :: rest) = getentries rest
|   getentries (Entry (k, a) :: rest) = (k, a) :: getentries rest
```

These have types:

```
getlooks : (α dictrequest) list → key list
getentries : (α dictrequest) list → (key × α) list
```

The top level program which processes the requests and returns the list of items which correspond to the keys looked up (in the same order) will be called:

```
dictprocess : (α dictrequest) list → α list
```

and it is defined as:

```
fun dictprocess requests
    = let val finaldict = builddict (getentries requests)
      in map (lookup finaldict) (getlooks requests) end
```

Thus, finaldict is the dictionary built from the entries found in the requests, and the lookups found in the requests are each processed in turn by a lookup in the final dictionary.

We have still to define:

```
lookup : α dict → key → α
builddict : (key × α) list → α dict
```

as well as the type α dict which represents dictionaries with items of type α. We can either use a simple list of (key, item) pairs to represent dictionaries or an ordered tree of pairs. In either case, lookup can be defined in the obvious way to search the list or tree for an appropriate pair. The difficult part is defining builddict so that access is available while the dictionary is being built. We could just use an accumulation of enter operations, but then no information can be returned for a lookup until the dictionary is complete. With the following version, the information becomes available as soon as the appropriate entry is made. We will use an ordered tree to represent the dictionary as we did in Chapter 7:

```
datatype α dict = Emp
                | Item of (key × α × α dict × α dict)
```

Then lookup and builddict are defined as follows:

```
fun lookup Emp k' = error "not found in dictionary"
|   lookup (Item (k, a, d1, d2) k' = if k = k' then a else
                                     if k > k' then lookup d1 k'
                                               else lookup d2 k'

fun builddict [ ] = Emp
|   builddict ((k1, a1) :: rest)
            = let fun smaller (k, a) = k < k1
                  fun larger (k, a)  = k > k1
```

```
                    in Item (k1, a1,
                             builddict (filter smaller rest),
                             builddict (filter larger rest))
                    end
```

The function lookup simply compares keys and searches the left or right subdictionaries (subtrees) if the key is not the same as the one at the top level. The function builddict makes a node from the first entry, and uses the remaining entries to build subdictionaries. The remaining entries are filtered into two lists according to whether keys are larger or smaller than the top level entry and these are then used separately to build the two subdictionaries.

As an illustration of the effect of the dictionary process we calculate that with:

```
requests = [Lookup 3, Entry (1, "x"), Entry (3, "z"), Lookup 1,
            Lookup 2, Entry (2, "y")]
```

we have, first:

```
dictprocess requests
  = map (lookup finaldict) (getlooks requests)
    where finaldict = builddict (getentries requests)
  = map (lookup finaldict) (3 :: getlooks (Entry (1, "x") :: . . .))
    where finaldict = builddict (getentries requests)
  = (lookup finaldict 3) :: (map (lookup finaldict)
                                (getlooks (Entry (1, "x") :: . . .)))
```

Now:

```
getentries requests = (1, "x") :: (3, "z") :: . . .
```

so if we begin evaluating finaldict we get:

```
finaldict = builddict ((1, "x") :: (3, "z") :: . . .))
          = Item (1, "x", builddict . . . , builddict (3,"z") :: . . .)
          = Item (1, "x", builddict . . . , Item (3, "z", . . . , . . .))
```

We need go no further than this in order to calculate:

```
lookup finaldict 3
  = lookup (Item (1, "x", builddict . . . , Item (3, "z", . . . , . . .))) 3
  = lookup (Item (3, "z", . . . , . . .)) 3
  = "z"
```

We can now see the first item of the final result:

```
dictprocess requests = "z" :: map . . .
```

and continuing with the calculation we should eventually get:

```
dictprocess requests = ["z", "x", "y"]
```

We would have had the same result if we had defined builddict by accumulating entries:

```
fun builddict x = accumulate enter Emp x
and enter (k, a) Emp = Item (k, a, Emp, Emp)
|     enter (k, a) (Item (k1, a1, d1, d2))
        = if k < k1 then Item (k1, a1, enter (k, a) d1, d2) else
           if k > k1 then Item (k1, a1, d1, enter (k, a) d2) else
                          Item (k1, a1, d1, d2)
```

but the entire output list would be generated after the argument list had been fully scanned. The difference would be shown in evaluation of a term such as:

```
dictprocess (Lookup 3 :: Entry (1, "x") :: Entry (3, "z") ::
                  Lookup 1 :: Lookup 2 :: Ω)
```

which would give "z" :: "x" :: Ω for our first definition but Ω for the accumulating version. This is because the dictionary (finaldict) can be evaluated as far as:

```
Item (1, "x", builddict . . . , builddict (3, "z") :: . . .)
```

with the first definition (the '. . .'s being Ω in this case), but the second definition will produce a completely undefined dictionary (Ω).

8.4.2 Cyclic programs (example: replacemin)

The following example (from Bird (1984a)) shows another technique which can be used to optimize a program by reducing the number of passes over a data structure. This time, the optimized program looks much more obscure than a straightforward solution, but Bird shows how the optimal program can be derived by systematic means from the original. The task is to define a function:

```
replacemin : int bintree → int bintree
```

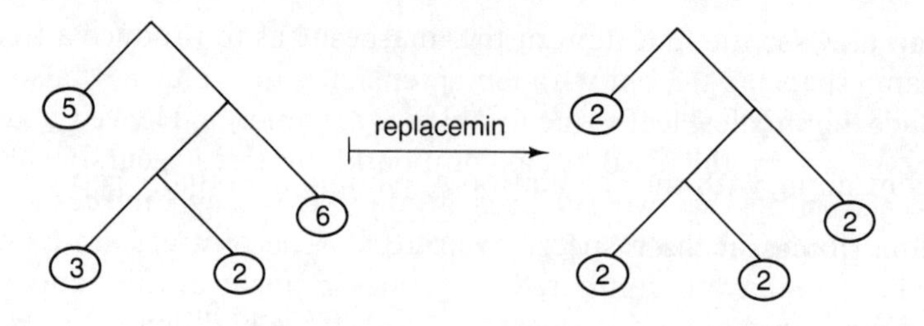

Figure 8.9 The function replacemin.

with the properties that replacemin t is a bintree with the same shape as the (assumed finite) bintree t, but with the value at each leaf equal to the minimum of the values found in the leaves of t. Figure 8.9 illustrates the function.

The straightforward solution would be to scan the tree t to find the minimum leaf value, and then to scan again to construct the new tree, using the minimum value at each leaf construction. It is, however, possible to describe simultaneously and recursively the new tree and the minimum value so that only one scan is required. In order to understand this rather complex definition, we break it down into two steps. We first define an auxiliary function:

```
replaceandmin : (int bintree × int) → (int bintree × int)
```

which, when given a bintree and a replacement value for leaves, simultaneously calculates a bintree and a minimum value. That is:

```
replaceandmin (t, n) = (replace (t, n), mintree t)
```

where replace (t, n) will be a bintree with the same shape as t but with the replacement value n substituted at each leaf. (At this stage, n has nothing to do with the minimum and is some arbitrary replacement number to be supplied as a parameter.) The minimum value in t (= mintree t) is also calculated by replaceandmin as the smallest value found at a leaf of t. These two, quite separate, calculations could be done by defining the two functions replace and mintree, but we define the combined calculation of both results in such a way that only one scan of the argument is made by replaceandmin. The definition is:

```
fun replaceandmin (Lf a, repval) = (Lf repval, a)
|   replaceandmin (t1 /\ t2, repval)
      = let val (newt1, min1) = replaceandmin (t1, repval)
              and (newt2, min2) = replaceandmin (t2, repval)
          in (newt1 /\ newt2, min min1 min2) end
```

In the case of a leaf, replaceandmin (Lf a, repval) has to produce a tree with the same shape as Lf a but with repval replacing the value a. It also has to produce the smallest leaf value found in Lf a, namely a. Hence the result is (Lf repval, a). In the case of a compound bintree, recursive calls of replaceandmin on the two subtrees produce two new bintrees and two minima (found in the respective subtrees). The bintrees are combined and the minima are compared to return a single bintree and overall minimum.

In isolation, this function is very straightforward. What is strange is its application in the definition of replacemin. The function replaceandmin is given the initial tree as argument, but also given the minimum value as an argument. It uses these to produce the final tree as well as the minimum value. That is, one of the arguments of the function is a value which is part of the result of the function:

```
fun replacemin bt
   = let val rec (newbt, minval) = replaceandmin (bt, minval)
     in newbt end
```

Because the actual minimum value does not need to be known until the result is fully known, this cyclic definition will produce the required result.

Another method for achieving the same result without defining such a *cyclic* program is pointed out by Pettorossi and Skowron (1987). This time, we generate a function along with the minimum so that when the function is applied to the minimum it generates the required bintree. For example, if we define:

```
fmin : int bintree → ((int → int bintree) × int)

fun fmin (Lf a) = let fun f m = Lf m
                  in (f, a) end
  | fmin (t1 /\ t2) = let val (f1, min1) = fmin t1
                          and (f2, min2) = fmin t2
                          fun f m = f1 m /\ f2 m
                      in (f, min min1 min2) end
```

Then we can simply define:

```
fun replacemin bt = let val (f, m) = fmin bt
                    in f m end
```

and this definition will work in a strict language as well as a lazy one.

In the last section for this chapter, we discuss another proof technique for use with lazy languages.

8.5 Induction for lazy languages

Let us return to the problem of reasoning about lazily evaluated programs. We have seen that Ω is useful for reasoning about termination behaviour, and we will use it again in an induction rule.

It is important to remember that structural induction cannot be used in general to prove properties of values of a type when the constructors are non-strict. Implicit in the rule for structural induction over a type *T* is the assumption that all values of type *T* are built by a finite number of applications of constructors. Such a rule is invalid when infinite objects can be created by recursive definitions, because infinite objects are effectively built with an infinite number of applications of constructors.

If we want to reason about all the values of a type with non-strict constructors, then we must not only take into account the finite fully defined objects, but also the infinite and partially defined values. For example, under lazy evaluation, the objects of type bool list which can be described include (1) the finite total lists:

```
[ ]
[true]
[false]
[true, true]
[true, false]
...
```

as well as (2) infinite lists such as:

```
[true, true, . . .]
[false, false, . . .]
[true, false, true, false, . . .]
...
```

and (3) partial lists denoted by expressions such as:

```
Ω
true :: Ω
false :: Ω
true :: true :: Ω
true :: false :: Ω
...
```

There are even partial lists with undefined items as well as those with an eventually undefined tail:

Ω :: [ ] = [Ω]
Ω :: Ω
Ω :: Ω :: [ ] = [Ω, Ω]
Ω :: Ω :: Ω
. . .
true :: Ω :: [ ] = [true, Ω]
. . .

Chapter 10 explores these strange objects in more detail. For the moment, we are interested in proof rules which will help us prove that some property P holds for a (possibly infinite or partial) object of type T, assuming lazy evaluation (i.e. non-strict constructors).

The following proof rule is based on **fixed point induction** (Scott) which can be used to prove properties of recursively defined values. Suppose that we have a definition of an object a which can be expressed in the form:

val rec a = E (a)

where E (a) is some expression involving a. (Without loss of generality, we can regard E (a) as a function E applied to a.) To prove that P (a) holds, for *admissible* predicates P (see below), the induction rule states that it is sufficient to establish:

(1) $P(\Omega)$ holds, and
(2) $P(E(x))$ follows from the assumption that $P(x)$ holds.

Unfortunately, this rule does not hold for arbitrary P. Roughly speaking, an admissible predicate is one which holds for limiting infinite cases whenever it holds for all the finite, partial (approximating) cases. The exact definition of admissible predicate is rather involved and we will postpone a proper definition until Chapter 10. Most predicates we want to work with turn out to be admissible, and in particular, if $P(x)$ has the form:

For all $x_1, \ldots, x_n$ $E_1(x) = E_2(x)$

then it is automatically admissible.

We illustrate the rule with some rather simple examples. First, we will prove that:

revonto y ones = Ω

for all y : int list by fixed point induction on the definition of ones. We assume that revonto and ones are defined by:

```
fun revonto y [ ] = y
|   revonto y (a :: x) = revonto (a :: y) x

val rec ones = 1 :: ones
```

Now, P (x) is: For all y: int list, revonto y x = Ω, so the induction rule says that we have to establish:

(1) For all y: int list revonto y Ω = Ω, and
(2) For all y: int list revonto y x = Ω implies revonto y (1 :: x) = Ω.

We establish (1) simply by observing that the definition of revonto requires a pattern match of the second argument so it will be undefined when the argument is completely undefined. For (2) we calculate:

```
revonto y (1 :: x) = revonto (1 :: y) x
```

by the definition of revonto. But now the inductive hypothesis is that for any y: int list

```
revonto y x = Ω
```

The y in this hypothesis is arbitrary, so we can choose to replace it by 1 :: y if we wish. This establishes that revonto (1 :: y) x = Ω and hence that

```
revonto y (1 :: x) = Ω
```

which is what we had to prove for (2). So, by fixed point induction:

```
revonto y ones = Ω
```

for all y: int list.

For another example, consider the following definition of a function:

```
nodups : α⁼ list → α⁼ list
```

which removes repeated items (duplicates) in a list:

```
fun nodups x = finddups [ ] x
and finddups sofar [ ] = [ ]
|   finddups sofar (a :: x) = if member sofar a
                              then finddups sofar x
                              else a :: finddups (a :: sofar) x
```

(finddups carries an extra parameter to record the items found so far.)

What would we expect to happen if we evaluate nodups ones? Informally, we might expect that the resulting list would contain a 1 but nothing else. However, we would not expect the result to be [1] because it would take infinitely long to establish by evaluation that there are no other items in ones apart from 1. A more reasonable result would be 1 :: Ω which indicates that a first item could be produced, but the tail is undefined. (A lazy evaluation of the list could print out the first 1 but would then hang while it scanned the length of ones for a different item.) We first use the fixed point induction rule to establish that:

For all y : int list, (member y 1 = true implies finddups y ones = Ω)

using the recursive definition of ones again. The implication involving only equalities with no occurrence of ones in the antecedent (member y 1 = true) is also guaranteed to be an admissible predicate. We first show that:

For all y, member y 1 = true implies finddups y $\Omega = \Omega$

which follows from the fact that finddups is defined by a pattern match of the second list parameter, so finddups y $\Omega = \Omega$ for all y regardless of whether or not 1 is a member. Next we assume the inductive hypothesis from (2):

For all y, member y 1 = true implies finddups y x = Ω

and try to show that:

For all y, member y 1 = true implies finddups y (1 :: x) = Ω

Assuming for some y that member y 1 = true, we have that:

```
finddups y (1 :: x) = if member y 1 then finddups y x
                                     else 1 :: finddups y x
                    = if true        then finddups y x
                                     else 1 :: finddups (1 :: y) x
                    = finddups y x
                    = Ω                        (by the inductive hypothesis)
```

This establishes the step case (2) and so by fixed point induction we have shown that:

For all y : int list, member y 1 = true implies finddups y ones = Ω

We can now calculate that:

```
nodups ones = finddups [ ] ones
            = finddups [ ] (1 :: ones)          (by the definition of ones)
            = if member [ ] 1 then . . .
                              else 1 :: finddups [1] ones
            = 1 :: finddups [1] ones
            = 1 :: Ω
```

where we have used the previous result in the last step knowing that member [1] 1 = true.

The above proofs involved particular values of a type, but we also want to be able to prove that a property holds for all values of a type including partial values and any infinite values. The usual form of structural induction is only valid for total finite values, but such proofs can often be done using an extended form of structural induction. Here is an example of a structural induction rule which can be used for lazy lists (of type *T* list for some type *T*) which we will call **lazy-list induction**. To prove that *P* (l) holds for all l : *T* list, including partial and infinite lists, where *P* is an *admissible* predicate, it is sufficient to show that:

(1) *P* (Ω) holds;
(2) *P* ([ ]) holds;
(3) *P* (a :: x) follows from the assumption that *P* (x) holds for any x : *T* list and any a : *T*.

As an application, we show that @ is associative for lazy lists. We let *P* (l1) stand for:

For all l2, l3 : *T* list (l1 @ l2) @ l3 = l1 @ (l2 @ l3)

which is admissible, and check that:

(1) *P* (Ω) holds: (Ω @ l2) @ l3 = Ω = Ω @ (l2 @ l3);
(2) *P* ([ ]) holds: ([ ] @ l2) @ l3 = l2 @ l3 [ ] @ (l2 @ l3);
(3) *P* (a :: x) follows from the assumption that *P* (x) holds for any x : *T* list and a : *T*:

```
((a :: x) @ l2) @ l3 = (a :: (x @ l2)) @ l3          by def of @
                     = a :: ((x @ l2) @ l3)          by def of @
                     = a :: (x @ (l2 @ l3))          by hypothesis
                                                     (and substitution)
                     = (a :: x) @ (l2 @ l3)          by def of @
```

So by lazy-list induction (l1 @ l2) @ l3 = l1 @ (l2 @ l3) for any l1, l2, l3 of type *T* list.

Similarly for bintrees, we can use **lazy-bintree induction** which says that to prove that P (t) holds for all t : T bintree, including partial and infinite bintrees, where P is an *admissible* predicate, it is sufficient to show that:

(1) P (Ω) holds;

(2) P (Lf a) holds for all a : T;

(3) P (t1 /\ t2) follows from the assumption that P (t1) and P (t2) hold for any t1, t2 : T bintree.

In the next chapter, we look at alternative programming techniques for use with non-lazy languages, and in Chapter 10 we return to a more formal treatment of the partial values denoted by expressions involving Ω which also provides the foundations for establishing proof rules like fixed point induction.

8.6 Bibliographic remarks

Lazy evaluation was proposed as a programming language feature by Henderson and Morris (1976) and independently by Friedman and Wise (1976). However, a similar mechanism was investigated for the lambda calculus and called *call by need* by Wadsworth (1971). This was implemented by Turner for the functional language SASL (Turner, 1976). Hughes (1984) gives some further examples showing the importance of lazy evaluation for abstraction. Fixed point induction and admissibility are discussed in more detail in Paulson (1987) and Bird (1976). Other information about proofs of functional programs may be found in Gordon *et al.* (1978), Turner (1982) and Bird (1984a, b). I derived the lazy dictionary from a Prolog program using difference lists described in Sterling and Shapiro (1986).

EXERCISES

8.1 If a data type is introduced with a single constructor as in:

```
datatype cint = C of int
```

then the patterns of the form C(n) are still regarded as refutable in Miranda. Explore the consequences of this decision and what differences there might be if such patterns were regarded as irrefutable. Note, that in SML, it is possible to remove references to constructors with no alternatives after type checking. However, SML is strict and definitions like the following are not particularly useful:

```
datatype t = C of t
val rec inft = C (inft)
```

8.2 Improve the definition of leavesof to avoid use of @ by passing an extra parameter (cf. Exercise 5.27). Does this have any consequences for the lazy characteristics of eqleaves? Evaluate:

eqleaves (Lf (3 * 2)) (Lf (3 + 3) /\ (Lf EL /\ ET))

using the improved definition of leavesof.

8.3 What would you expect to happen when from is defined in a strict language by:

```
fun from n = n :: from (n + 1)
```

8.4 What conditions must be placed on f to make the following equivalences true for all expressions E_1, E_2, E_3?

f (**if** E_1 **then** E_2 **else** E_3) = **if** E_1 **then** f (E_2) **else** f (E_3)

8.5 Using the data type:

```
datatype ctree = C0 | C1 of ctree | C2 of (ctree × ctree)
```

give recursive definitions of the infinite ctrees represented by the graphs in Figure 8.10. (Note that t4 is non-rational (Colmerauer, 1982) having an infinite number of distinct subtrees. It can be constructed by first defining a function make : ctree → ctree so that t4 = make C0.) Why are t1 and t3 indistinguishable ctrees?

8.6 Derive the value of:

front 5 (map double (leavesof infbt1))

given as [12, 12, 12, 12, 12] in the text.

8.7 Define a function:

polyvals : int list → int → int list

which, given a list of coefficients a0 :: a1 :: a2 :: a3 :: . . . and an integer value x, produces the list of values of the polynomials:

$$a0 :: (a0 * x + a1) :: (a0 * x^2 + a1 * x + a2) :: (a0 * x^3 + a1 * x^2 + a2 * x + a3) :: \ldots$$

8.8 Using polyvals from the previous exercise, construct a similar function polyderivs with the same type and which given the same input produces the values of the derivative polynomials, namely:

$$0 :: a0 :: (2 * a0 * x + a1) :: (3 * a0 * x^2 + 2 * a1 * x + a2) :: \ldots$$

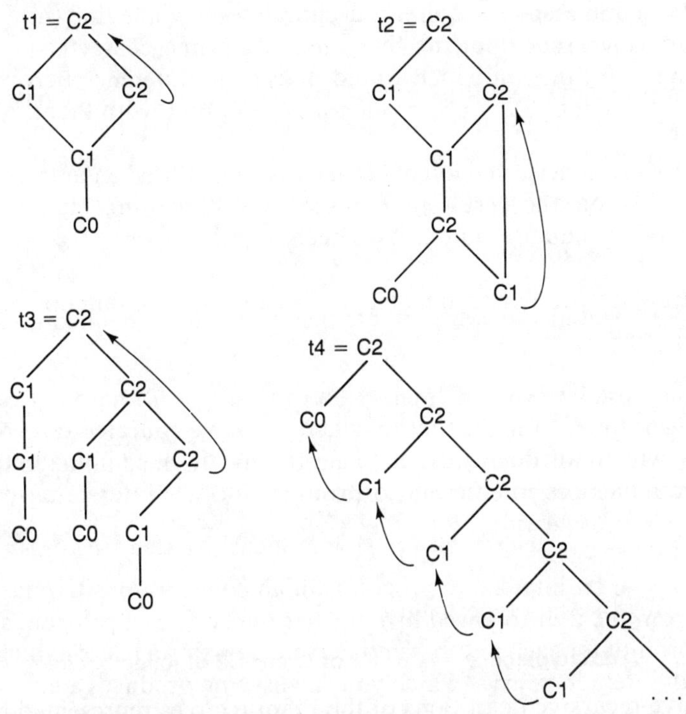

Figure 8.10 Some recursively definable ctrees (see Exercise 8.5) (assuming **datatype** ctree = C0 | C1 **of** ctree | C2 **of** (ctree × ctree)).

8.9 The eight queens problem requires finding a way to place eight queens on a chess board so that they cannot take each other (along rows, columns or diagonals). A placement of n queens in the first n columns could be represented by an int list of length n where each integer indicates the row where the queen for a particular column has been placed. Describe the list of solutions for n queens on an n by 8 board in terms of the list of solutions for n − 1 queens on an n − 1 by 8 board. Hence write a function which searches for a single solution for an n by 8 board assuming lazy evaluation.

8.10 (Turner). Write a program to produce the following (self referential and infinite) output:

```
line number 1 is:-
"line number 1 is:-"
line number 2 is:-
""line number 1 is:-""
line number 3 is:-
"line number 2 is:-"
line number 4 is:-
"""line number 1 is:-"""
```

8.11 Redefine choplines so that it accumulates a whole line (in reverse) and then sends out the line when a newline character is found. Write a function which would detect the difference between the two versions of choplines when it is composed with them.

8.12 Write a generic version of getnum which is passed a parameter f for acting on the resulting number and remaining character list produced after a number has been found.

8.13 Rewrite the definition of tellbin2 using the combinator repeated instead of alt.

8.14 Suppose we have an interaction of type (unit, β) interaction and we want to use it in a situation where we have collected data of type α which we do not wish to forget. Write a combinator which modifies the interaction to produce another interaction of type (α, $\alpha \times \beta$) interaction.

8.15 Design an interactive program which collects a positive integer n from the user followed by n further integers. The program should prompt for each number and finish by passing a list of n integers to an interaction main (which you can assume produces a final report and leaves ( ) as data). Modify the program so that the n integers can be confirmed or corrected by the user after they are entered, but before they are passed to main.

8.16 Redefine the lazy dictionary from Section 8.4.1 using an association list rather than a tree.

8.17 Prove that ones @ x = ones for any x : int list by fixed point induction.

8.18 Find some properties of lists proved by structural induction in Chapter 3 which are not true for either partial or infinite lists. Using Ω or otherwise, demonstrate some counterexamples. Conversely, prove those properties which you believe still hold by re-establishing them with lazy-list induction.

8.19 Prove that:

```
reflect (reflect t) = t
```

holds for all bintrees using lazy-bintree induction. (reflect was mentioned in Exercise 5.7 and gives the mirror image of a bintree.)

Chapter 9
Eager Evaluation

The more commonly used evaluation technique in programming languages has been 'call-by-value' which for functional languages is also called 'applicative reduction order' or 'eager evaluation'. With eager evaluation, arguments in a function application are evaluated before the function is applied. In this chapter we discuss restrictions and optimizations associated with eager evaluation.

9.1 Reasoning and eager evaluation

In the previous chapter, we used Ω to represent an expression whose value is completely undefined. With eager evaluation, functions are always strict. So, if we were to define:

fun K a b = a

then we would know that K 5 $\Omega = \Omega$. If we were to regard the definition of K as an equation holding for arbitrary a and b, then we could also deduce that K 5 Ω = 5 (substituting 5 for a and Ω for b). Hence, by transitivity and symmetry of equality, we could deduce that $5 = \Omega$ – a contradiction!

Clearly, then, we must modify our reading of the definition as a simple equation and interpret it as saying:

For all *defined* a and b ($a \neq \Omega$, $b \neq \Omega$),   K a b = a

But now we should check, before doing any substitutions, that these restrictions are satisfied.

This seems to be a very great loss for programming where optimization and correctness proofs involve transformations based on such substitutions, so why is eager evaluation even considered? The answer is that eager evaluation was used first historically and was much easier to implement and more efficient than any other order (with conventional implementation techniques). It is sometimes regarded as better to sacrifice the simplicity of a language in order to gain such efficiencies at runtime. Also, procedural languages involve side-effects which blend in much more readily with eager evaluation allowing the programmer to determine when any side-effects will be done.

It is important to study programming in a language with eager evaluation partly because there are many such languages around, partly because it enables us to study the possibilities of transforming programs by introducing side-effects to gain efficiency in the use of storage, and partly because optimization criteria are simpler. For current hardware and implementation techniques, eager evaluation is generally more efficient than lazy evaluation at runtime.

Eager evaluation is closely related to *innermost reduction order* where innermost subexpressions are evaluated first. However, there must be exceptions to innermost order as a general strategy of evaluation if recursive functions and conditionals are to be treated properly. The conditional has the properties:

if true **then** E_1 **else** $E_2 = E_1$
if false **then** E_2 **else** $E_2 = E_2$
if Ω **then** E_1 **else** $E_2 = \Omega$

for all expressions E_1 and E_2 including possibly Ω. In order that conditional expressions conform to these equational requirements, it is necessary to delay evaluation of the branches until after the test has been evaluated in case the evaluation of the unwanted branch causes failure or non-termination. So, conditionals must be evaluated differently to applications of functions defined by users and other primitives.

If we define or and & as in the previous chapter, then eager evaluation of expressions of the form E_1 or E_2 and E_1 & E_2 will require full evaluation of both E_1 and E_2 in each case. Indeed, in Standard ML, the user is encouraged to use some special constructions **andalso** and **orelse** in place of & and or (the latter functions not being built in). These constructions do not denote functions in ML but are abbreviations for conditional expressions that have the same delaying effect:

E_1 **andalso** E_2 abbreviates **if** E_1 **then** E_2 **else** false
E_1 **orelse** E_2 abbreviates **if** E_1 **then** true **else** E_2

We find that for eager evaluation:

false **andalso** Ω = **if** false **then** Ω **else** false
= false

but:

false & $\Omega = \Omega$

If we tried to create a function with this delaying effect by rewriting the definition of & using a conditional instead of pattern matching:

```
fun x and_also y = if x then y else false
```

then the new function would turn out to be strict (in SML) because the arguments E_1 and E_2 would always be evaluated before the conditional in an application of the form E_1 and_also E_2. In fact and_also would be exactly the same as &.

Similarly if we define:

```
fun cond x y z = if x then y else z
```

Then we would find that:

cond true E_1 $\Omega = \Omega$
cond false Ω $E_2 = \Omega$

The other exception to an innermost strategy is the evaluation of function bodies, which is not done before a function is applied.

9.2 Control over evaluation

9.2.1 Using conditionals

The exceptional treatment of conditionals provides us with the means to delay evaluation. Although functional programs abstract away from most aspects of control, the programmer can still influence the way in which a value is computed by writing expressions in different ways. If we have a non-lazy implementation of a functional language, we can still delay evaluation to a certain extent by the use of conditionals. Recall the example in the previous chapter where a function eqleaves was defined to compare two trees to see if they have the same leaves in the same order even if they are a different shape. With eager evaluation, the given definition can give rise to very wasteful computation by flattening both trees before comparing. We illustrate, here, how a different definition can be used to give better performance. This time eqleaves is defined in terms of an auxiliary function comparestacks which combines the action of flattening trees and comparing lists. The function comparestacks applies to two lists of trees (which we will refer to as forests) and determines whether or not the total lists of leaves from each forest (scanning the trees from left to right) are the same. Thus the function generalizes the original problem of determining leaf equality for two single trees and eqleaves is defined as the degenerate case of an application of comparestacks to two single-tree forests.

The more general function allows us to split the first tree whose leaves are to be found into two subtrees (unwinding the tree) so that the subtrees can be stacked up in the forest and inspected one at a time. In the definition there are six cases considered for the arguments of comparestacks which are discussed below:

```
fun eqleaves t1 t2 = comparestacks [t1] [t2]
and comparestacks [ ] [ ]      = true
  | comparestacks [ ] (a :: x) = false
  | comparestacks (a :: x) [ ] = false
  | comparestacks ((l /\ r) :: x) y = comparestacks (l :: r :: x) y
  | comparestacks x ((l /\ r) :: y) = comparestacks x (l :: r :: y)
  | comparestacks (Lf (a) :: x)  (Lf (b) :: y)
                                   = if a = b then comparestacks x y
                                               else false
```

If both lists are empty, then clearly the same leaves appear in each forest by default. On the other hand, in the two cases where only one list is empty, the non-empty list must contain at least one tree which will have at least one leaf, so the leaves in the two lists cannot be equal. The case where both lists are non-empty can be subdivided into three further cases.

When the first tree in the first list is not a leaf (and therefore has the form l /\ r with l and r representing its two subtrees), the total list of leaves of the forest (in the appropriate order) will be the same as the leaves of the first subtree followed by those of the second subtree followed by the leaves of the remaining trees. Thus comparestacks is recursively called with the partly unwound first tree, stacking l and r in front of the remaining trees in the list x. Similarly, in the case where the first tree in the second list is a compound tree there is a recursive call with the compound tree unwound by one level. This finally leaves the case where both of the first trees of the two lists are leaves. A simple comparison of these two leaves determines whether or not it is necessary to continue comparing the remaining trees in the two lists. When comparestacks is applied to two non-empty forests, the fourth case will repeatedly apply until the first forest begins with a leaf. At this point the fifth case will apply until the second forest also begins with a leaf and then the sixth case applies (causing a removal of the two leaves for continued comparison of the remaining forests or halting with result false). In essence, the comparison has been delayed by conditionals and the use of data structures (lists) to keep track of awaiting computations which can be thrown away when an inequality is discovered in the leaves. The gain in efficiency has been at the expense of complicating the original program.

Here is an illustration of an eager evaluation of the example we used in the previous chapter. This time, however, we assume the expression E_L evaluates to n : int and E_T evaluates to t : int bintree. This is because the trees to be flattened must be fully evaluated even though the intermediate lists are not:

```
eqleaves (Lf (3 * 2)) (Lf (3 + 3) /\ (Lf E_L /\ E_T))
  ... = eqleaves (Lf 6) (Lf 6 /\ (Lf n /\ t))
      = comparestacks [Lf 6] [(Lf 6 /\ (Lf n /\ t))]
      = comparestacks [Lf 6] [Lf 6, (Lf n /\ t))]
      = if 6 = 6 then comparestacks [ ] [(Lf n /\ t)]
                 else false
      = if true then comparestacks [ ] [(Lf n /\ t)]
             else false
      = comparestacks [ ] [(Lf n /\ t)]
      = false
```

Thus, although the expression E_T has to be evaluated fully to a bintree, t does not get flattened.

9.2.2 Delaying evaluation with functions

We have noted that function bodies are not evaluated until the function is applied. This means that the evaluation of any expression can also be delayed by embedding the expression within the body of a function, for example by making the expression the body of a function whose argument is a dummy, unused value. It is common practice to use the empty tuple ( ) : unit for this purpose. If we define, for some expression E of type T, say:

```
fun delay1 ( ) = E
```

then delay1 is a function of type unit → T. The application of delay1 to an appropriate argument (i.e. the empty tuple) will require the evaluation of E, but evaluation of delay1 itself just returns the function of type unit → T whose body is unevaluated. This provides a mechanism for simulating normal order evaluation (call by name) in a language which is evaluated eagerly. We illustrate this with the following (rather artificial) example. Suppose f is defined as follows:

```
fun f x y = if null x then [ ] else hd x :: y @ y
```

then f puts the head of the first list in front of two appended copies of the second list when the first list is not empty. With eager evaluation, a call such as f E_1 E_2 requires E_1 and E_2 to be fully evaluated before this operation is performed. Now consider the definition:

```
fun delayf xfun yfun = if null (xfun ( ))
                       then [ ]
                       else hd (xfun ( )) :: yfun ( ) @ yfun ( )
```

The function delayf is similar to f except that its arguments are expected to be functions of type unit → α list rather than α list. In the body of the function delayf, the arguments are applied to ( ) to obtain the actual lists whenever they are needed. Thus instead of evaluating f E_1 E_2 we could just as well evaluate:

```
delayf (fn ( ) => E1) (fn ( ) => E2)
```

which should produce the same result except that the evaluation of E_1 and E_2 is delayed in the latter case until the arguments to delayf are applied. In particular, if the first list (the value of E_1) is [ ] then E_2 is not evaluated at all. On the other hand, if E_1 does not evaluate to [ ], both E_1 and E_2 are evaluated twice (once for each application of xfun or yfun to ( ) where xfun = **fn** ( ) ⇒ E_1 and yfun = **fn** ( ) ⇒ E_2). This duplicated evaluation shows that we have simulated normal order evaluation but not lazy evaluation.

We can avoid repeated evaluation by careful use of local definitions as in the following version:

```
fun delayf' xfun yfun
  = let val x = xfun ( )
    in if null x
      then [ ]
      else let val y = yfun ( )
           in hd x :: y @ y end
    end
```

Note that the definition of y is nested within a branch of a conditional to avoid evaluation when the test is true. The value x is always calculated when delayf' is applied so we could just as well change the first parameter xfun back to a normal list parameter x for this example.

As another example consider:

```
fun condd x y z = if x then y ( ) else z ( )
```

This expects arguments of type bool, unit → α, unit → α respectively and applies at most one of its functional arguments. It follows that for any expressions E_1, E_2, E_3 of types bool, α, α respectively:

if E_1 **then** E_2 **else** E_3 = condd E_1 (**fn** ( ) ⇒ E_2) (**fn** ( ) ⇒ E_3)

and one of these expressions can be safely substituted for the other in the context of the above definition of condd.

9.3 Using functions to represent infinite objects

Another restriction of eager evaluation is that only functions can be defined recursively since eager evaluation of a recursive definition of a non-functional data structure will not terminate.

Infinite data structures can be modelled with eager evaluation by the use of functions which expand the structure bit by bit. That is, a data structure containing functions can represent an infinite object if application of the functions returns more information about the infinite object represented. A simple example is a tree represented by either a Nulltree or a Treenode consisting of the node information (label) and a function which produces the subtree indexed by x when applied to argument x. This allows both infinite branching (infinite width) when indices are integers as well as infinite depth in a tree. (Information could also be given at a node to indicate how many subtrees there are since it would take infinitely long to discover this information by inspection of the tree.) If α stands for the type of branches (argument type for the subtree function) and β for the type of node information, we can define:

```
datatype (α, β) inftree = Nulltree
                        | Treenode of β × (α → (α, β) inftree)
```

Then (bool, int) inftree is a type whose values are essentially binary trees with integer labelled internal nodes and with possibly infinite depth. They are binary, because the subtrees are indexed by values of type bool, namely true and false.

With this representation, a tree whose node label is 1, say, and whose left subtree is empty and whose right subtree is a copy of the original tree can be defined by:

```
val onestree
    = let fun onestreefn true  = Nulltree
            | onestreefn false = Treenode (1, onestreefn)
      in Treenode (1, onestreefn) end
```

Note that onestree itself is not defined recursively, even though the locally defined function onestreefn is. Had we tried to abbreviate the definition by substituting onestree for the body of the function definition in the false case, we would require a direct recursive definition of a non-functional object which would lead to non-termination (and is not allowed in SML).

9.3.1 Suspended lists (streams)

A similar use of delaying functions allows us to implement a form of **stream** in a non-lazy language. We may represent a stream not as a simple list, but instead as a data structure involving functions which we call a susplist (for **suspended list** since *stream* is used to mean something slightly different in SML). If we define:

```
datatype α susplist = Mksl of (unit → α × α susplist)
                    | Endsl

fun slCons a s = let fun f ( ) = (a, s)
                 in Mksl f end
fun slHd Endsl     = error "head of Endsl"
  | slHd (Mksl f)  = let val (a, s) = f ( )
                     in a end
fun slTl Endsl     = error "tail of Endsl"
  | slTl (Mksl f)  = let val (a, s) = f ( )
                     in s end
fun slNull Endsl    = true
  | slNull (Mksl f) = false
```

Then a (non-empty) susplist is represented as a function which produces a head and a tail when applied to ( ). The tail will be another susplist which is either empty or has another function which must again be applied to expand the structure further. The types of the above functions are:

```
Mksl   : (unit → (α × α susplist)) → α susplist
Endsl  : α susplist
slCons : α → α susplist → α susplist
slHd   : α susplist → α
slTl   : α susplist → α susplist
slNull : α susplist → bool
```

and the last four are just the counterparts to the obvious list operations. Note that Mksl is a constructor which converts a function into a susplist. We can now define infinite suspended lists as in the following examples:

```
val ones = let fun f ( ) = (1, Mksl f)
           in Mksl f end
fun from n = let fun f ( ) = (n, from (n + 1))
             in Mksl f end
val nat = from 1
```

giving ones : int susplist, from : int → int susplist and nat : int susplist. Note that the following definition for from will not work under eager evaluation.

```
fun from n = slCons n (from (n + 1))
```

This is because functions like slCons are still strict and arguments are evaluated fully before a susplist is formed, so evaluation of from n requires an evaluation of from (n + 1) first, for each n.

We now define a function which forces evaluation of a susplist to produce the first n items along with the remaining susplist. The n items are returned as an ordinary list, and the function has type:

```
slforce : int → α susplist → (α list × α susplist)
```

This is defined by:

```
fun slforce 0 s = ([ ], s)
|   slforce n Endsl = error "slforce of Endsl"
|   slforce n (Mksl f)
            = let val (a, s1) = f ( )
                  val (x, s2) = slforce (n − 1) s1
              in (a :: x, s2) end
```

This function is useful in defining other functions and can be thought of as a combined front and drop because it returns the result of taking n items as well as the result of dropping n items. We can always define versions of front and drop (which we call slfront and sldrop) in terms of slforce:

```
fun slfront n s = fst (slforce n s)
fun sldrop n s = snd (slforce n s)
```

but if we calculated these separately, there would be much repeated computation. We should optimize expressions involving both slfront n s and sldrop n s to expressions involving just one occurrence of slforce n s and use fst and snd.

Combining these functions with the infinite susplist defined above, we can calculate for example:

```
slfront 5 ones = [1, 1, 1, 1, 1]
slfront 5 nat  = [1, 2, 3, 4, 5]
```

Another useful function is one which generates a susplist from other functions. Suppose we have an arbitrary function step : $\alpha \rightarrow \beta \times \alpha$. Starting with an initial value a0 : α, the function can be used to provide a value of type β and another value of type α. That is (b1, a1) = step a0. Similarly, a1 can be used to provide (b2, a2) and a2 can be used to provide (b3, a3) and so on. Thus the as are used to generate bs which can be collected. We can describe this process once and for all as a function returning a β susplist. However, we will generalize the situation slightly and assume we also have a predicate isend : $\alpha \rightarrow$ bool which we will use to terminate the generation of values (when isend ai = false). This means that the generating function which we call susplist takes a pair of functions (step, isend) as first argument and a starting value a0 : α as second argument. It has type:

susplist : $((\alpha \rightarrow \beta \times \alpha) \times (\alpha \rightarrow \text{bool})) \rightarrow \alpha \rightarrow \alpha$ susplist

and the definition is:

```
fun susplist (step, isend) a0
  = if isend a0
    then Endsl
    else let fun f ( ) = let val (a1, b1) = step a0
                         in (b1, susplist (step, isend) a1) end
         in Mksl f end
```

To illustrate the use of this generator, we will define a variation of from which stops when an integer satisfying a given predicate p is found:

```
fun fromuntil p a = let fun step n = (n, n + 1)
                    in susplist (step, p) a end
```

The locally defined function step : int → int × int just returns the current integer and the next one. This is used by susplist along with the supplied predicate and starting integer to create a susplist of integers from a up to the first integer satisfying p (or forever if no such integer can be found (≥a)). The type of fromuntil is:

```
fromuntil : (int → bool) → int → int susplist
```

This use of functional data objects really only simulates call by name and does not give the advantages of sharing results of evaluations automatically. For this reason, it may be useful to have some facility for lazy evaluation in an otherwise eager implementation. For example, Hope provides both a non-strict cons (for streams) as well as the strict cons for non-lazy lists, but this mixture in programs can be very hard to reason with.

In a language where non-functional side-effects are possible, we can, in a very disciplined way, update an unevaluated representation with an equivalent partly evaluated representation when this is discovered. Appendix 3 contains such an implementation of updating (lazily evaluated) lists using the procedural features of SML.

9.4 Some techniques for improving performance

9.4.1 Tail recursion optimization and accumulating parameters

Up to now, we have avoided saying too much about the efficiency of functional programs because, in general, program efficiency depends on language implementation factors (particularly evaluation order). Since sequential, eager evaluation has heen focused on in many implementations, a brief mention of a related optimization technique, which has received much attention, seems in order.

There is a particularly important form of recursive definition of a function where the recursively defined name appears only in special positions on the right-hand side of the definition. The form of definition is called **tail recursive** and the special positions are known as **terminal** or **tail positions** because they correspond to the last application to be evaluated in a sequential, eager evaluation. These positions are outermost on the right-hand sides of definitions or outermost in branches of conditionals. The importance of tail recursive definitions lies in the fact that there is a close correspondence between tail recursion and iterative loops in imperative languages and certain optimizations can be used in evaluating calls to functions which have tail recursive definitions. Roughly speaking, application of functions in tail positions can be implemented by direct jumps instead of the more sophisticated context switches needed for other function calls in most language implementations. Tail recursive definitions can thus be compiled directly into iterative loops which do not use a stack for context information and thus save space during evaluation. Figure 9.1 shows a comparison between a tail recursive computation, an iterative loop and a fully nested recursion. As an example, we note that the following definitions of length are *not* tail recursive:

```
fun length x = if null x then 0 else 1 + length (t1 x)
```

and (equivalently):

```
fun length [ ]       = 0
|   length (a :: x) = 1 + length x
```

because in each case, the recursive call of length is subordinate to the addition operation. On the other hand:

```
fun alength (x, n) = if null x then n else alength (tl x, n + 1)
```

and (equivalently):

```
fun alength ([ ], n)     = n
|   alength (a :: x, n) = alength (x, n + 1)
```

are tail recursive. It can easily be checked that for all lists x:

```
fun length x = alength (x, 0)
```

so we can compute the length of a list using a function defined either tail recursively or non-tail recursively. This shows why it is the definition itself which determines tail recursiveness and not the function denoted.

The above example also illustrates an important technique for converting recursive definitions into a tail recursive form by the introduction of additional arguments to a function which are often referred to as **accumulating parameters**. Frequently the operations being 'stacked up' for application to the result of a recursive call of a function could be applied in a different order so that the recursive call comes at the end. For example, in summing the integers in a list, with the function defined by:

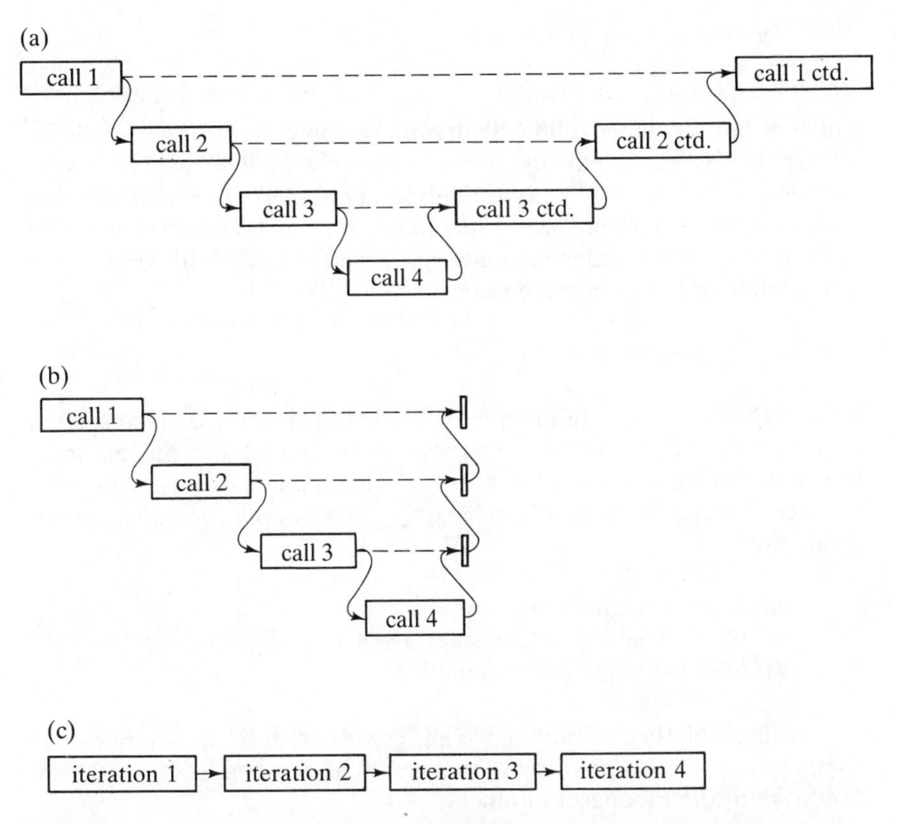

Figure 9.1 Tail recursion and loops: (a) a nesting of four recursive calls of a function where computation is continued after return from an inner call; (b) the semi nesting of a tail recursive computation – the inner call is the last step of each recursive call; (c) four iterations of a loop correspond to the optimized tail recursive calls of (b).

```
fun sumlist [ ]       = 0
|   sumlist (a :: x) = a + sumlist (x)
```

the first item of a non-empty list must be added to the result of summing the items in the tail of the list so the addition will be performed after the recursive call of sumlist. Similarly, all the additions to be performed will be stacked up and done only after the end of the list is reached. However, by using an extra parameter we could easily keep a running total rather than a stack of values. Since arguments are computed before calls to functions, then passing the running total as an argument (the accumulating parameter) would mean that computation need not be stacked up but could be done before the recursive call. Thus we could use:

```
fun accsum (a :: x, n) = accsum (x, a + n)
|   accsum ([ ], n)    = n
```

which is tail recursive. The first argument component of accsum is an integer list whose elements are successively added to the second argument component (the accumulating parameter). The final value of the accumulating parameter is immediately returned when the end of the list is reached so in order to sum a list we call accsum with zero as the initial value of the second argument:

```
fun sumlist x = accsum (x, 0)
```

This method of getting tail recursion for list operations is encapsulated once and for all in the tail recursive definition of the higher order function accumulate given in Chapter 2. Rather than repeating the method for each function such as sumlist, length, . . . we simply use accumulate to define them:

```
val length  = let fun count1 n a = n + 1
              in accumulate count1 0 end
val sumlist = accumulate plus 0
```

Accumulating parameters can greatly reduce the amount of computation needed to obtain the result as we can show with the definition of the Fibonacci numbers:

```
fun fibnum 0 = 0
|   fibnum 1 = 1
|   fibnum n = fibnum (n - 1) + fibnum (n - 2)
```

With this definition, it will take time exponential in n to evaluate fibnum n because recursive calls of earlier values will be excessively repeated. On the other hand, the following definition will compute in linear time:

```
fun fastfib n          = accfib (0, 1, n)
and accfib (a, b, 0) = a
|   accfib (a, b, n) = accfib (b, a + b, n - 1)
```

Here accfib carries forward two previous Fibonacci numbers to compute the next one as it counts down from n to 0 with its parameters. (This is analogous to a procedural solution with a loop – the accumulating parameters correspond to the use of additional variables in the loop which are updated on each iteration.) To prove the program is correct, we should show that for all $n \geq 0$:

```
fibnum n = fastfib n
```

This is done by generalizing the goal and establishing that for n, m ≥ 0:

```
accfib (fibnum n, fibnum (n + 1), m) = fibnum (n + m)
```

using induction on m. The result then follows as a special case and we leave the details as an exercise for the reader. Exercise 9.11 suggests a general purpose 'memo-izing' function which encapsulates a similar transformation for many problems of this nature needing the accumulation of results.

9.4.2 Continuation methods

In an earlier exercise (Exercise 5.29) we indicated another method for removing list append operations by introducing an extra parameter. The extra parameter is not used to accumulate the result but to provide a continuation for the result – a list which is to be appended to the normal result. The example given was an operation to flatten a tree. From the simple version:

```
fun flatten Empty = [ ]
|   flatten (Tr (t1, a, t2)) = flatten t1 @ [a] @ flatten t2
```

which involves many append operations, we derive this version:

```
fun flatten' t = flattenwith t [ ]
and flattenwith Empty x = x
|   flattenwith (Tr (t1, a, t2)) x
                      = flattenwith t1 (a :: flattenwith t2 x)
```

which involves no append operations. The list supplied as an extra parameter to flattenwith is to be appended to the list forming the flattened tree. Thus for an empty tree, this list is returned as the result. For a non-empty tree, the left subtree has to be flattened and appended with a continuation list which can be passed as an argument to flattenwith. This continuation list is formed by flattening the right subtree with the original continuation list (x) and then consing the node value a on the front. We can prove by induction on t that:

```
flattenwith t x = flatten t @ x
```

and hence deduce that flatten′ t = flatten t.

Similar techniques can be used for scanning other forms of tree but the technique of passing a continuation parameter is quite general and it need not be a list which is passed. In the most general form, the continuation is a function to be used on the result of the processing or to be used to construct further continuations. Furthermore, when there may be more than one course of action to take after processing an object, we can pass several continuation parameters. A classic example of this is when we are parsing. Instead of having a parsing function return a result of the form α possible, we can modify the function to take two continuation parameters which describe what is to be done in the successful and failure cases respectively. Thus if parseA is a parser for non-terminal A, success is the continuation to be used when an A is found, failure is the continuation to be used if no A is found and s is some incoming sequence of tokens, we write:

```
parseA success failure s
```

The type of these values would thus be of the form:

```
s : token list
failure : token list → result
success : (resultA × token list) → result
parseA : ((resultA × token list) → result)
            → (token list → result) → token list → result
```

(resultA would be the type of object produced on finding an A, whereas result is the type of the final object produced from a complete parse. This final result is entirely dependent on the nature of the continuations which could produce anything at all.)

As in Chapter 6, we explain how to write parsers of this form by explaining how to write some basic parsers and how to combine parsers to build new parsers. As an example of a basic parser, we could define isa which, given a particular token t as well as continuations (success and failure) and a token sequence s, checks to see if the next token in the sequence is t and then continues accordingly:

```
fun isa t success failure [ ] = failure [ ]
  | isa t success failure (t' :: s) = if t = t'
                                      then success (t', s)
                                      else failure (t' :: s)
```

Thus isa: $\alpha^{=} \rightarrow ((\alpha^{=} \times \alpha^{=}\ \text{list}) \rightarrow \beta) \rightarrow (\alpha^{=}\ \text{list} \rightarrow \beta) \rightarrow \alpha^{=}\ \text{list} \rightarrow \beta$.

Corresponding to '|' we will have a union of parsers (cf. ⟨|⟩ in Chapter 6) defined as:

```
fun union p1 p2 success failure = p1 success (p2 success failure)
```

This simply says that the parser union p1 p2 when supplied with two continuations (success and failure) is just the same as p1 supplied with the same success continuation, but a different failure continuation. The new failure continuation is the parser p2 supplied with the original success and failure continuations. The (most general) type of union is:

$$\text{union} : (\alpha \rightarrow \beta \rightarrow \gamma) \rightarrow (\alpha \rightarrow \delta \rightarrow \beta) \rightarrow \alpha \rightarrow \delta \rightarrow \gamma$$

A more complicated parser builder corresponds to sequences of parsers (cf. ⟨&⟩ in Chapter 6):

```
fun sequence p1 p2 success failure s0
  = let fun success1 (r1, s1)
              = let fun success2 (r2, s2) = success ((r1, r2), s2)
                    fun failure2 s = failure s0
                in p2 success2 failure2 s1 end
    in p1 success1 failure s0 end
```

Once again, the parser sequence p1 p2 when supplied with continuations and a token list (s0) is the same as the parser p1 supplied with a modified success continuation and same failure continuation (and s0). The new success continuation (success1) should receive a result r1 and token list s1. It passes s1 on to be used by the parser p2 with two new continuations. The success continuation for p2 first pairs the result r1 with any result it is passed and then calls the original continuation success. The failure continuation for p2, when supplied with a token list s ignores it, and calls the original failure continuation with the original token list (s0). The most general type of sequence is horrendous (we resort to using 'a, 'b, . . . , 'j for type variables):

```
sequence : (('a × 'b → 'c) → ('d → 'e) → 'd → 'f)
           → ('g × 'h → 'i) → ( 'j → 'e) → 'b → 'c)
           → (('a × 'g) × 'h → 'i) → ('d → 'e) → 'd → 'f
```

We can define an editing function to modify the result of a parser (cf. modify in Chapter 6) simply by altering the success continuation:

```
fun edit f p1 success failure
      = let fun success1 (r, s) = success (f r, s)
        in p1 success1 failure end
```

The parser edit f p1 when supplied with continuations is defined to be p1 with a modified success continuation which turns a result r into f r before calling the original success continuation.

Finally, we might define two particular continuations which we would supply to a parser initially. For making a success continuation we could use finish g:

```
fun finish g (r, [ ]) = r
  | finish g (r, s) = error ("end of input expected but found " ^ g s)
```

Here, the parameter g is used to form an error message when there are remaining unparsed tokens. Thus finish : (α list → string) → ($\beta \times \alpha$ list) → β. Similarly, for a final failure, we could simply use:

```
fun failfinish s = error "input not recognized"
```

(See Exercise 9.9.)

9.5 Introducing procedural components

If a fixed (sequential) call-by-value order of evaluation is specified for a functional language, it is feasible to consider an 'extension' to the language to include imperative commands (with side-effects). Although we have to view programs in a different way when such features are introduced, the behaviour of programs and parts of programs not using such features should be the same as before (otherwise the features are not an extension). Such mixed languages help us to understand and bridge the gap between procedural languages and functional languages and enable us to consider transformations from functional to procedural form. The semantics of such a mixed language is much more complex, but the finer control over storage and evaluation order can be used in optimizing programs for certain implementations. We will briefly discuss a few possibilities without going into detail.

9.5.1 Exceptions

One feature which is often considered useful is that of an **exception mechanism**. This can be used to escape from computations in which an error arises and to trap errors to continue with alternative computations without littering the program with extra tests. However, excessive use of exceptions can easily lead to the sort of 'spaghetti-code' associated with goto-like control. One can think of an exception mechanism as an implicit translation of function result types (α) to something like (α possible) with the addition of automatic handling of the failure case.

The continual need to check for and deal with 'unlikely' exceptional cases with ordinary conditionals and use of types like α possible throughout a program can be cumbersome in some circumstances, and an exception mechanism can put the raising and handling of exceptions into the background. The problem is that the exact order of evaluation of subexpressions needs to be known since the first exception encountered in evaluation will terminate normal evaluation. For example, if evaluation of E_1 and E_2 can both raise exceptions, we need to know the order of their evaluation in an application such as $(E_1\ E_2)$ so that we can determine which exception will be encountered first. With eager evaluation, E_1 is evaluated before E_2 and both are evaluated before the resulting function is applied to the resulting argument, so the exception in E_1 will be the one raised. Note that if the exception is in the body of the function described by E_1 it will not get evaluated when E_1 is evaluated but only when the resulting function is applied. In this case the exception in E_2 will be encountered first.

Standard ML has a rich exception mechanism which (at the time of writing) is likely to be replaced by a simpler more general one (Appel *et al.*, 1988). We have avoided using this non-functional feature of SML in this book except for the implementation of error given in the appendix.

9.5.2 References (storage cells) and assignments

The other main procedural feature that we can consider introducing is the **assignment statement** to change the contents of shared storage variables during a computation. As we indicated before, such an introduction dramatically changes the nature of the language forcing us to consider an evaluation as a sequence of actions which transform the state of storage variables as well as returning a result. Even though most evaluations do not have a side-effect we must consider them as identity transformations on the state for the sake of those actions which do change the state. Not only does the exact order of evaluation become important when side-effects are introduced, but also the details of when values are shared or copied. This is because an assignment to a copy of a storage variable will be quite different to an assignment to the original and so parameter copying mechanisms become significant in the evaluation of function applications. It is because of all these extra complexities that we feel programs should be written (at least initially) in a pure functional style. The introduction of side-effects into a program requires a sophisticated understanding of the evaluation mechanism and should only be used when the saving in storage space usage justifies it and a rigorous analysis has been carried out to establish the correctness of the resulting program. In particular, if correctness preserving transformation tools are available to guide a programmer who feels that a side-effect may enhance performance of a program, then it may be easier to justify the change. After all, a compiler is just such a tool, but direct compilation of the initial program may lead to a less efficient performance than compilation of a side-effecting program derived from the initial program by other correctness preserving transformations.

In recent years, denotational semantics (which we discuss in the next chapter) has shown us how to reduce most of the imperative constructs which are outside the applicative core to applicative equivalents. (See, for example, Bauer and Wossner (1982), Schmidt (1986).) Through this reduction, proof techniques and transformations on imperative programs can be discovered and explained in terms of much simpler operations in the applicative core. Part of the reason why transformations on imperative languages have proved difficult in the past lies in the fact that this core, while being of central concern in providing a formal meaning, has been excluded or partly excluded from the implemented language.

Standard ML can be considered as a procedural language because it does have primitives which form updatable storage variables along with an assignment operation. These are necessarily restricted because of the polymorphic type system. There is a type operator ref which has a single associated constructor (also denoted ref). The constructor ref can be applied to any value of a monotype T to produce a result of type T ref. This can be used to create updatable storage cells. For example, ref 5 is a storage cell containing 5. If we define:

```
val VarX = ref 5
```

then VarX is rather like (an initialized) program variable as found in most procedural languages. However, to get the contents we must use ! : α ref $\rightarrow \alpha$. We must write 1 + !VarX and not 1 + VarX to find the result of adding 1 to the contents of the cell variable. Then, of course, there is the non-functional assignment operator :=. To update destructively the contents of the cell VarX, we write:

VarX := E

where E is an expression of type int. The form VarX := E is considered to be an expression of type unit in SML, so such commands can be embedded anywhere in an expression to produce a side-effect and an object of type unit.

We have completely avoided this non-functional aspect of SML in this book (except for the implementation of lazy lists using side-effects given in the appendix). However, it seems necessary to use the procedural I/O primitives of SML in order to write interactive programs in such a non-lazy language. Some ways round this problem are suggested in the appendix.

EXERCISES

9.1 Go through the steps of an eager evaluation of eqleaves t (t /\ t) for t = ((Lf 3 /\ Lf 4) /\ Lf 5) /\ Lf 6.

9.2 How does the following definition of all behave for eager and lazy evaluation?

```
fun andc a b = a & b (that is andc is curried &)
fun all p x = reduce andc true (map p x)
```

9.3 Using the type (bool × int) inftree defined at the beginning of Section 9.3, define a function which for given n : int, produces a complete infinite tree (with no leaves) and n at each node. Similarly, define a complete infinite binary tree containing all possible bit strings (strings composed with digits "0" and "1") at the nodes (with "" at the top node).

9.4 Define some higher order susplist functions analogous to the ones used for lists.

9.5 Prove that fibnum n = fastfib n for all n ≥ 0.

9.6 Define hamming (see Section 8.2.6 and Figure 8.6) as an int susplist. You may find the following helpful:

```
fun fixpoint slfun = let fun f ( ) = slfun (Mksl f)
                     in Mksl f end
```

The function fixpoint : (α susplist → α susplist) → α susplist can be used to close a loop describing a susplist. First, the broken loop is described as a function slfun which when supplied with a susplist at the beginning of the loop produces a new susplist (at the end of the loop). The expression fixpoint slfun effectively ties the loop up so that the result and argument are identified. This result/argument is the value of fixpoint slfun.

9.7 Rewrite other examples from thc previous chapter using type susplist.

9.8 Redefine the quicksort algorithm using a continuation list parameter to avoid doing append operations.

9.9 Go through the parsers for commands described in Chapter 6 and adapt them to use the continuation method described here.

9.10 What would be the behaviour of parse : string → string defined by:

```
val p1 = union (isa "a")
               (edit (^) (sequence (isa "b") (isa "c")))
fun parse s = p1 (finish implode) failfinish
```

9.11 The function memo described below can be used to speed up computations where results of similar subcalculations are re-used, by remembering ('memo-izing') the results in an association list. It is used as follows.

Suppose that we wish to calculate a value of type β for any given value of type $\alpha^=$. First, we assume that there is a dependency ordering on values of type $\alpha^=$ expressed by a function (graph) g : $\alpha^= \rightarrow \alpha^=$ list. That is, if the result that needs to be calculated for some a : $\alpha^=$ depends on the results for a1, a2, a3 (say) then g a = [a1, a2, a3]. We also assume that this dependency is acyclic (no recursion).

Secondly, we assume that the calculation that needs to be done is expressed by a function combine which describes how the results for values like a1, a2, a3 should be combined to produce the result for a. In general, there may be a different function for each such a, so we parameterize on a : $\alpha^=$, giving:

combine : $\alpha^= \rightarrow \beta$ list $\rightarrow \beta$

Finally, when we come to do a calculation, we must supply not only a value a of type $\alpha^=$ (whose corresponding result of type β we want), but also a partial function done giving any known results (base cases or previously calculated results). This partial function has type $\alpha^= \rightarrow \beta$ possible so that it can terminate and report Fail if used on a value for which the result is not yet known (rather than being an error).

Putting all this together, the final calculation is performed by:

memo g combine (done, a)

which should return (done′, b). The value b : β is the result of the computation for a : $\alpha^=$, and done′ is an updated version of done containing any additional remembered results. Thus:

memo g combine : $(\alpha^= \times (\alpha^= \rightarrow \beta$ possible))
$\rightarrow (\beta \times (\alpha^= \rightarrow \beta$ possible))

Here is the full definition of memo. We use try to abbreviate memo g combine and the auxiliary function collect is similar to a map try but collects all the intermediate results by modifying the value of done″:

```
fun memo g combine
  = let fun try (done, a)
          = let fun cases (Ok b) = (done, b)
                  |   cases Fail
                        = let val (done′, y) = collect (done, g a)
                              val b = combine a y
                              val done″ = assoc [(a, Ok b)] done′
                          in (done″, b) end
            in cases (done  a) end
      and collect (done, [ ]) = (done, [ ])
        |   collect (done, a :: x)
                  = let val (done′, b) = try (done, a)
                        val (done″, y) = collect (done′, x)
                    in (done″, b :: y) end
    in try end
```

The exercise is to construct an appropriate g, combine and initial done in order to use memo in calculating (a) Fibonacci numbers, and (b) powers of n for some non-negative integer n.

Chapter 10
Denotational Semantics

This chapter introduces some formalism which allows us to give more precise descriptions of the values described by expressions in a functional language, and hence more detailed descriptions of the meaning of programs. This precision is necessary for reasoning about the correctness and equivalence of programs in subtle cases. In particular, we will need to be more precise in explaining when an expression is undefined and in explaining what sort of values can be described by expressions. We also aim to justify the claim that mathematical objects such as functions can be associated with recursive definitions without reference to some particular, underlying computation process. By providing a **denotational semantics** for a programming language we introduce mathematical values as the meanings denoted by each expression and program construct and thus obtain a precise definition of the programming language. This definition can be used in proving properties of programs and program equivalences. Furthermore the definition gives us an independent basis for judging the correctness of particular implementations of the language, since we can check to see how the result of an expression evaluation compares with the mathematical value described by the expression.

The phrase 'denotational semantics' derives from the use of mathematical objects as things denoted by programs and programming language constructs. An alternative to the denotational approach is **operational semantics** which involves an abstract model of how programs, expressions, definitions, etc. are evaluated. Although the evaluation mechanisms used in operational semantics are much more abstract than one would find in an actual implementation of a programming language, operational semantics are more 'concrete' than denotational semantics since the latter prescribe only what results are to be computed rather than how they are to be computed. For functional languages, an archetypal model for evaluation is provided by the lambda calculus which we look at in Chapter 12. (A third approach to describing the meaning of programs in a programming language is **axiomatic semantics** which involves logical assertions about the behaviour of programs. This approach is mainly suitable for procedural languages since most presentations of axiomatic semantics focus on axioms describing the effects of programs on state variables.)

Up to now, we have been somewhat lax in distinguishing between functional programs and the functions (or other values) denoted by the program, but it is very important to understand this distinction. In particular, it is necessary to make the distinction in order to discuss correctness preserving transformations which change the program without changing the meaning. Such transformations are important for optimization and program derivation (from specifications).

Much of the time, the meaning or value of an expression in a functional programming language is quite clear and can be determined from informal descriptions and definitions of the functions and constants involved in any expression. However, there will always be occasions when such definitions and descriptions are obscure and then we need to resort to more detailed formal descriptions. The extra mathematical detail is provided by a formal description of the semantics of the programming language.

The introduction of mathematical values corresponding to undefined or only partly defined expressions provides a first step for the construction of a denotational semantics for programs. Expressions which we expect to lead to non-terminating computations with no output can still be thought of as denotations of something; they denote a specially introduced value representing *undefined*. Using such explicit values, we can both explain the difference between strict and non-strict semantics as well as formalize the exact meaning of recursion (using the so-called *fixed point* theory of recursion).

We begin by discussing the basic concepts of denotational semantics, namely: partially defined values and their approximation ordering, domains of values and the construction of domains. These concepts are then brought together to give a formal definition of a lazy functional programming language. We conclude the chapter with a discussion of the fixed point theory of recursion.

10.1 Basic concepts

10.1.1 Partially defined values

Because we may write down arbitrary recursive definitions, we can easily give an incomplete definition of a function or other object. For example, if we define:

```
fun h x y = h y x
```

then the definition gives us no information about the value of h 3 4 (for example) other than the fact that it is equal to h 4 3 (which is also unspecified). It seems natural, therefore, to conclude that h x y is undefined for any x and y in the context of this definition. Similarly, expressions of the form error(s) for any string s were assumed to be undefined in previous chapters, so other functions defined in terms of such expressions may be undefined for some arguments yet defined for others. For example, in the context of the definition:

```
fun select n (a :: x) = if n = 1 then a else select (n − 1) x
  | select n [ ] = error "list select subscript out of bounds"
```

the expressions select 1 [ ] and select 5 [1, 2] are both undefined. However, as we noted in Chapter 8, some further rule for interpreting definitions is needed if we are to determine the value of expressions such as:

```
let fun g x = 5
in g (h 3 3) end
```

There are two main approaches that can be taken in the treatment of undefinedness. We could either say that an expression has no meaning if it (or a subexpression) is undefined, or we could introduce some default meaning – the mathematical value corresponding to undefined expressions mentioned above.

The problem with the first approach is that it is in general impossible to decide in a computable way whether or not an expression is defined and this rules out any hope of mechanically identifying and rejecting exactly those expressions which are meaningless before an attempt is made to evaluate them. Furthermore, this approach would be incompatible with our use of conditional expressions, requiring that both branches are defined regardless of which one is to be evaluated. We could not, for example, write:

```
if n = 0 then 1 else 100 div n
```

We do, however, use this approach up to a point if we reject expressions with type incompatibilities such as hd(6). We can describe in a computable way (using only the syntactic form) which expressions are correctly typed and which are not and then reject the latter as meaningless, thus avoiding the need for mathematical values representing ill-typed expressions. (A specific value such as wrong for ill-typed expressions may still be useful, however. In establishing the correctness of a type checking algorithm, for example, one can show that wrong cannot be expressed (denoted) by correctly typed expressions and therefore will not arise during an evaluation; see, for example, Milner (1978).) Those expressions which are correctly typed, but still not fully defined may lead to non-terminating computations when evaluated, but we can still reason about such expressions and it turns out to be convenient to adopt the second approach here. We introduce a value:

$\perp$ (pronounced *bottom*)

as the meaning of undefined (non-terminating) expressions. At this point, we should clarify the distinction between $\perp$ and Ω which we have used in earlier chapters. The former is a 'meaning' (i.e. semantic) object which we are including with our domain of values, whereas Ω was used to stand for an expression (i.e. a syntactic object) which happened to be undefined. Thus $\perp$ will be the meaning (value of) Ω. Introducing $\perp$ also allows us to be precise about the possible meanings of expressions with undefined subexpressions. If we let g stand for the function to be taken as the meaning of g in the context of the above local definition (**fun** g x = 5), then we may explain whether or not its definition implies that:

$g\,(\perp) = \perp$ or that $g\,(\perp) = 5$

(i.e. we can explain whether or not a strict or non-strict interpretation is to be assumed).

10.1.2 Values and domains

In order to provide a denotational semantics for a (monomorphically) typed programming language, we introduce sets of mathematical values which include, for example, the integers, boolean values, $\perp$, tuples of values and (total) functions on sets of values. These values constitute the possible meanings which can be denoted by expressions and programs. We introduce a collection of sets, one for each (mono-)type, so that there is a different domain of meanings for expressions of different types. The collections of values associated with a type are sets with some extra structure which enable us to interpret recursive definitions and also incomplete definitions. These sets with structure are called **domains**, and we will discuss the nature of this structure below.

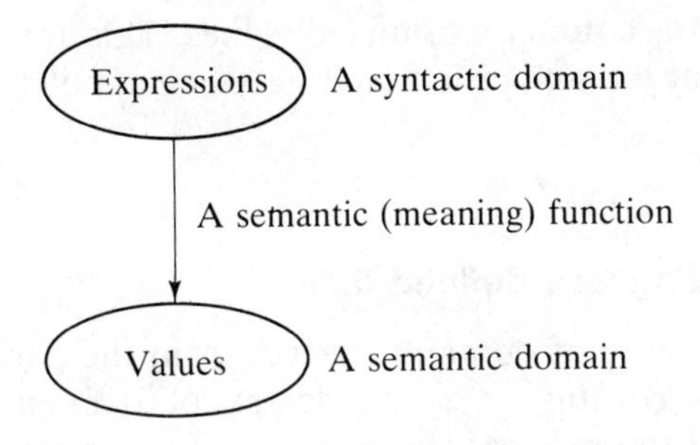

Figure 10.1 The semantic function formalizes meaning.

The expressions in a programming language and the domain of possible values they may denote are brought together with a **semantic function**. The semantic function maps each expression (regarded as a syntactic object) to a corresponding element of the domain of values and thus formalizes the meaning of expressions. This situation is depicted in Figure 10.1.

Polymorphic expressions present a further complication and there are different approaches to the semantics of polymorphism. We could think of polymorphic expressions as denoting several values (in different domains) rather than a single value. In this case, expressions but not values are considered to be polymorphic (see, for example, Wand (1984)). Another approach is to construct a single domain of mixed values. Scott (1976) showed how to construct complex domains including how to construct domains which satisfied certain equations. This allows us to describe the single mixed domain we want with subdomains corresponding to values of particular types.

With such a mixed domain of meanings, it is possible to give single values to polymorphic expressions; a value common to all the monotype instance domains. The subdomain of values associated with a polytype T will be the intersection of the subdomains of values associated with each monotype instance of T. To see why this should be so, consider the subdomain for type α list in a mixed domain. If an expression has type α list then it has instances of type T list for all types T. Thus if the expression denotes a single value in the mixed domain, that value must belong to every subdomain corresponding to T list for each type T. Hence the value belongs to the intersection of all these subdomains. For example, the value of [ ] is in the domain for α list and so is also in each of the domains for int list, bool list, ... etc. (In fact only the values [ ] and $\perp$ will be in this intersection domain associated with α list – any expression of type α list will denote one of these two values.)

We will discuss the construction of separate value domains appropriate for monotypes, below. We will then show how these can be embedded in a single domain of mixed values. This approach simplifies the explanation of the semantic functions when applied to polymorphic expressions.

10.1.3 Formalizing less-defined-than

Much of the structure of domains derives from the partial ordering of their elements according to some degree of definedness. With the introduction of $\perp$ to represent the meaning of an undefined expression, one might think that an expression is either undefined (with value $\perp$) or fully defined with some *normal* value. However, the situation is more subtle and interesting than this. For example, an expression may denote a function which is defined for some arguments and undefined for others, and we get a whole spectrum of degrees of definedness among such functions.

Similarly, lists and tuples and other structured values may have undefined components and so instead of just talking about whether a value is defined or not, we should talk about how much a value is defined and in particular when one value is more or less defined than another value.

We write $x \sqsubseteq y$ to indicate that x is less defined than (or equal to) y and to begin with we have $\perp \sqsubseteq x$ for all values x in a given domain. Clearly we also have the properties (for values x, y, z in some domain) (1) $x \sqsubseteq y$ and $y \sqsubseteq z$ implies $x \sqsubseteq z$, (2) $x \sqsubseteq x$, and (3) $x \sqsubseteq y$ and $y \sqsubseteq x$ implies $x = y$ which makes $\sqsubseteq$ a partial ordering of values. The ordering is not total, because we will have many incomparable values in general, such as 0 and 1 for which neither $0 \sqsubseteq 1$ nor $1 \sqsubseteq 0$ is the case. (The 'less-defined-than' ordering must not be confused with any other ordering which may be defined between values – such as the usual ordering of integers. This is the main reason for adopting the unusual notation $\sqsubseteq$ rather than $\leq$.)

In the sequel we will consider many different domains of values D, each with an ordering $\sqsubseteq_D$ and a least element $\perp_D$. We will usually just write these as $\sqsubseteq$ and $\perp$ if the domain is clear from the context.

For basic unstructured values such as 0, 1, . . . , true, false, only $\perp$ is less defined than each of them. If we let $\boldsymbol{Z}$ stand for $\{0, 1, -1, 2, -2, \cdots\}$ which is the set of 'normal' integer values, and $\boldsymbol{Z}_\perp = \boldsymbol{Z} \cup \{\perp\}$, then $\boldsymbol{Z}_\perp$ is the domain of values which can be denoted by an expression of type int and its elements are ordered by:

$$\text{(For all } d, d' \in \boldsymbol{Z}_\perp) \; d \sqsubseteq d' \text{ if and only if } d = \perp \text{ or } d = d'$$

Similarly, if we let $\boldsymbol{B}$ denote {true, false} then we can order $\boldsymbol{B}_\perp = \{\perp, \text{true}, \text{false}\}$, the set of possible meanings of values of type bool, in the same way as $\boldsymbol{Z}_\perp$. The domains $\boldsymbol{Z}_\perp$ and $\boldsymbol{B}_\perp$ are called flat domains because

Figure 10.2 The partial ordering of flat domains: (a) $\boldsymbol{Z}_\perp$; (b) $\boldsymbol{B}_\perp$.

values are either fully defined or totally undefined and the ordering appears (relatively) flat as depicted in the (Hasse-)diagram of Figure 10.2. The ordering $\sqsubseteq$ on unstructured values can be extended to structured values and then the ordering can become quite intricate. Consider, for example, the values representing pairs of values from some domain (e.g. $\boldsymbol{Z}_\perp$). Among the pairs, we have to consider not only 'normal pairs' like (0, 0), (0, 1) but also (⊥, 0), (⊥, 1), (0, ⊥), (⊥, ⊥). The Hasse-diagram in Figure 10.3 indicates part of the ordering we wish to associate with such pairs. The ordering can be defined by:

$(x, y) \sqsubseteq (x', y')$ if and only if $x \sqsubseteq x'$ and $y \sqsubseteq y'$

Functions between two domains D_1 and D_2 also have a natural ordering given by:

$f \sqsubseteq g$ if and only if $f(d) \sqsubseteq g(d)$ for all $d \in D_1$

This ordering reflects the relative definedness of each function on its arguments so that if g is more defined than f, then g produces results which are more defined or equal to the results produced by f (for each $d \in D_1$).

As an example, consider the case when $D_1 = D_2 = \boldsymbol{Z}_\perp$. If we write an expression E which describes a function of type int → int, then its meaning will be regarded as a total function (d, say) from $\boldsymbol{Z}_\perp \rightarrow \boldsymbol{Z}_\perp$. Note that the functions denoted by functional programs may be thought of as

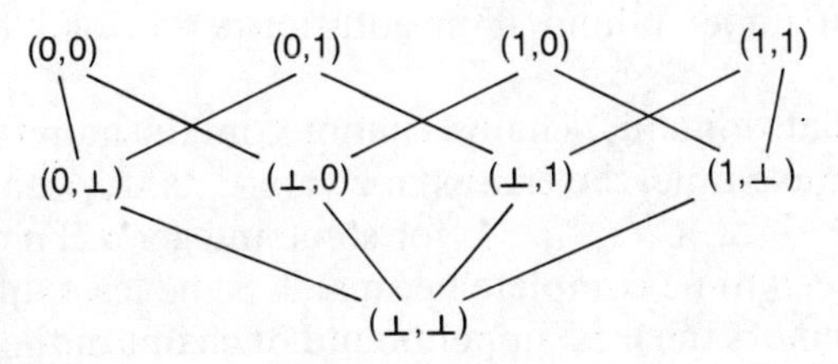

Figure 10.3 The partial ordering of some pairs – the ordering between pairs formed with 0, 1 and ⊥.

total functions rather than partial functions when $\bot$ is included as a value. It turns out to be more fruitful to model programs as total functions operating on possibly partial values rather than as partial functions operating on total values. In particular, if d is the above-mentioned function denoted by E, then $d(n) = \bot$ is our way of indicating that E is undefined for argument $n \in \boldsymbol{Z}_\bot$. Furthermore, for a lazy language, we can explicitly state whether or not the argument of the function needs to be evaluated by determining whether or not $d(\bot) = \bot$.

In a moment we will show how certain collections of functions between domains can themselves form a domain under the ordering described for functions.

10.1.4 Limiting values

An essential property of domains which we use in Section 10.4 is that limiting values of certain sequences of values exist in the domain. More precisely, a **chain** of values is a (denumerably infinite) sequence of domain elements each more defined than or equal to earlier elements in the sequence. So for $d_i \in D$ for $i = 1 \ldots$:

$$d_1, d_2, \cdots, d_n, \cdots$$

is a chain provided that:

$$d_1 \sqsubseteq d_2 \sqsubseteq \cdots \sqsubseteq d_n \cdots$$

We require domains to be **complete** which means that any chain must have a limiting value in the domain, which is technically known as a **least upper bound**. A least upper bound for a chain will be a value which is approximated by all elements of the chain and which is less defined than any other upper bound of the elements in the chain. So, for the example chain, d is an upper bound if:

$$d_i \sqsubseteq d \quad \text{for } i = 1 \ldots$$

and it is a least upper bound if in addition $d \sqsubseteq d'$ for all other upper bounds d'.

For the flat domains, chains cannot contain more than two distinct values. For example, the chains in $\boldsymbol{Z}_\bot$ are: $\bot, \bot, \bot, \cdots$, and sequences of the form $\bot, \bot, \cdots \bot, n, n, \cdots n, \cdots$ for some integer n. The flat domains are thus easily seen to be complete because $\bot$ is the least upper bound of the first chain and n is the least upper bound of chains of the second kind. The property becomes much more interesting in domains which have infinite ascending chains of values, and these are introduced by the function domain construction which we consider in a moment.

To summarize, a domain is a complete partial order (with a least element) – a 'CPO'. (In fact there are some other technical requirements for domains to satisfy, but the full description is beyond the scope of this book – see, for example, Plotkin (1982) or Scott (1982).)

10.2 Construction of domains

So far, we have introduced the flat domains $\boldsymbol{Z}_\perp$ and $\boldsymbol{B}_\perp$ corresponding to the basic types int and bool, respectively. We will introduce some standard ways of constructing new domains from given domains, so that we can describe the domains of values we want to associate with other monotypes (and also the domain constructions we want to associate with type operators). For example, we want to describe domains for $T_1 \times T_2$ and $T_1 \rightarrow T_2$ in terms of domains for T_1 and T_2. The domains we want to construct for these cases are called product and function domains respectively.

10.2.1 Product domains

This domain construction allows us to form the product of two (or more) domains. If D_1 and D_2 are domains, then we let:

$$D_1 \times D_2 = \{(d_1, d_2) \mid d_1 \in D_1 \text{ and } d_2 \in D_2\}$$

be the domain of pairs of values. This domain is naturally ordered by:

$$(d_1, d_2) \sqsubseteq (d_1', d_2') \text{ if and only if } d_1 \sqsubseteq d_1' \text{ and } d_2 \sqsubseteq d_2'$$

and the least element in $D_1 \times D_2$ is given by:

$$\perp_{D_1 \times D_2} = (\perp_{D_1}, \perp_{D_2})$$

where $\perp_{D_1}$ is the least element in D_1 and $\perp_{D_2}$ is the least element in D_2.

This product operation $\times$ on domains turns out to be exactly what we need for forming domains of pairs for types such as $T_1 \times T_2$ under non-strict semantics. So, if D_1 is the domain of T_1 values and D_2 is the domain of T_2 values, $D_1 \times D_2$ will be the domain of $T_1 \times T_2$ values with a non-strict tuple constructor. If d_1 is the value assigned to E_1 of type T_1 and d_2 the value assigned to E_2 of type T_2, (d_1, d_2) will be the value assigned to

(E_1, E_2) as one might expect. The distinction between $(d, \bot)$ and $\bot\ (= (\bot, \bot)$ in $D_1 \times D_2)$ when $d \neq \bot$ allows us to give a non-strict semantics to the pair constructor and also allows us to handle binary operations which are non-strict in some of their arguments. (We describe an alternative product domain construction suitable for use with strict semantics in a moment.)

For tuples of more than two components, we can construct domains such as $D_1 \times D_2 \times D_3 \times \cdots \times D_n$. In general if D_i are domains for types T_i $(i = 1 \cdots n)$ then $D_1 \times D_2 \times D_3 \times \cdots \times D_n$ will be the domain for type $T_1 \times T_2 \times T_3 \times \cdots \times T_n$. (We leave the generalization of the definition of the product domain for $n > 2$ as an exercise.)

For strict semantics we want to identify all tuples having an undefined component $(\bot)$ with $\bot$ itself. (This corresponds to the fact that with 'call-by-value' all components are evaluated before a tuple is formed and the undefinedness of a component means that the result of forming the tuple is undefined.) Thus it is convenient to introduce the domain constructor $\otimes$ so that:

$$D_1 \otimes D_2 = \{(d_1, d_2) \mid d_1 \in D_1 - \{\bot_{D_1}\} \text{ and } d_2 \in D_2 - \{\bot_{D_2}\}\} \cup \{(\bot_{D_1}, \bot_{D_2})\}$$

The domain $D_1 \otimes D_2$ is essentially $D_1 \times D_2$ with all pairs of the form $(d_1, \bot)$ and $(\bot, d_2)$ omitted (except for the case $(\bot, \bot)$) and the domains have the same ordering and least element as for the ordinary product construction $(\bot_{D_1 \otimes D_2} = (\bot_{D_1}, \bot_{D_2}))$. If d_1 is the meaning of E_1 and d_2 is the meaning of E_2 then the meaning of (E_1, E_2), with strict semantics, is defined as:

$\bot_{D_1 \otimes D_2}$, if $d_1 = \bot$ or $d_2 = \bot$ and

(d_1, d_2), otherwise

Analogously with the non-strict case we have, for domains $D_1, D_2, \ldots, D_n$:

$$D_1 \otimes D_2 \otimes \ldots \otimes D_n$$

and we leave the definition as an exercise for $n > 2$.

10.2.2 Function domains

Since certain functions between domains are also regarded as values, it is important that collections of such functions form a domain themselves for types such as $T_1 \rightarrow T_2$. The ordering of functions was indicated in Section 10.1.3 ($f \sqsubseteq g$ if and only if $f\ d \sqsubseteq g\ d$ for all d in the argument domain). However, many functions between domains are not computable, and we restrict our attention to functions satisfying properties which rule out some computationally 'badly behaved' ones. The first property is that of **monotonicity**.

Monotonicity of functions

The value $\perp$ is special in that we understand it as the meaning of undefined expressions of our programming language and, therefore, that no value may be produced when the expression is evaluated. A function between domains D_1 and D_2 such as d with the properties:

$$d(d') = \perp \text{ for some } d' \neq \perp \text{ in } D_1$$
$$d(\perp) = r \text{ for some } r \neq \perp \text{ in } D_2$$

could not arise as the meaning of any computable program. This is because the properties suggest that the program would be able to produce a result (r) if its argument is not defined (non-terminating) but be unable to produce a result if the argument is defined (d'), and this is clearly non-sense from a computational point of view. What we need to do, therefore, is exclude as a possible denotation those functions which produce more defined results with less defined arguments. This is achieved by requiring that all the functions we consider as possible meanings of programs preserve the 'less defined than' ordering. Thus all functions d denoted in programs will have the monotonic property that $d(x) \sqsubseteq d(y)$ whenever $x \sqsubseteq y$. As a simple illustration, consider a definition of a function of type int → int such as:

```
fun idint x = x + 0
```

the meaning of idint (*idint* say), can only be a strict function (with both a lazy and an eager interpretation) because we have that $idint(0) = 0$, $idint(1) = 1$, $\perp \sqsubseteq 0$ and $\perp \sqsubseteq 1$. By monotonicity, we know that $idint(\perp) \sqsubseteq 0$ and $idint(\perp) \sqsubseteq 1$ and since only $\perp$ is below 0 and 1 in $\mathbf{Z}_\perp$ we have $idint(\perp) = \perp$. On the other hand, k1 defined by:

```
fun k1 (x) = 1
```

can have both a strict extension:

$$k1_s(\perp) = \perp$$
$$k1_s(d) = 1 \text{ otherwise}$$

and a non-strict extension:

$$k1_n(d) = 1 \text{ for all } d \in \mathbf{Z}_\perp$$

both of which are monotonic, so we need to rely on the semantics of the programming language to tell us which is implied by the given definition of k1 (e.g. lazy or eager).

Continuity of functions

In Section 10.4 we will see why a further property of functions, namely **continuity**, is also important and why limits of increasing sequences of values (under $\sqsubseteq$) must always exist in domains for the purpose of understanding and giving a meaning to recursive definitions. Roughly speaking, continuity ensures that a function's behaviour on limiting (infinite) values is determined by its behaviour on finite approximations. This is necessary if the behaviour is to be computable (describable) by finite means.

More formally, we say a function is *continuous* if it maps the limiting value of any chain to the same value which is computed by first mapping each individual element of the chain to its corresponding result (thus forming a result chain) and then finding the limiting value of this result chain.

We will use the notation:

$$[D_1 \rightarrow D_2]$$

for the continuous functions from domain D_1 to D_2 and restrict our attention to such functions. In particular, we use $[D_1 \rightarrow D_2]$ as the domain of values of type $T_1 \rightarrow T_2$ where D_1 is the domain of values of type T_1 and D_2 is the domain of values of type T_2. (This is only when considering separate domains for each type. This interpretation of $T_1 \rightarrow T_2$ needs to be modified for polymorphism.) A related domain construction is one which forms the domain of the *strict* continuous functions from D_1 to D_2 (i.e. only those f in $[D_1 \rightarrow D_2]$ for which $f\,\bot = \bot$). This domain will be denoted:

$$[D_1 \rightarrow_{\bot} D_2]$$

10.2.3 Union of domains

Another useful domain construction is that of the **coalesced sum** or **union of domains** ($D_1 \oplus D_2$). This domain consists of the union of the values in each of the domains D_1 and D_2 with the two bottom elements $\bot_{D_1}$ and $\bot_{D_2}$ coalesced to form a single $\bot_{D_1 \oplus D_2}$. We assume the elements apart from the coalesced bottom element are labelled in some way so that their domain of origin (D_1 or D_2) can be determined uniquely. Figure 10.4(a) illustrates

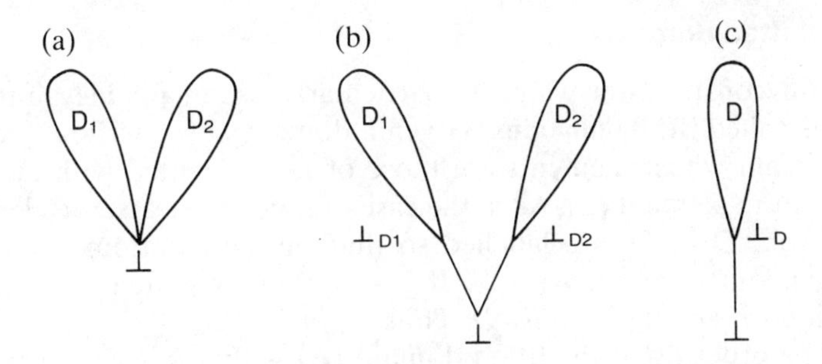

Figure 10.4 (a) The coalesced sum of D_1 and D_2 ($\bot = \bot_{D_1 \oplus D_2}$); (b) the separated sum of D_1 and D_2 ($\bot = \bot_{D_1 + D_2}$); (c) the lifted domain $L = D_\bot$ ($\bot = \bot_L = \bot_{(D_\bot)}$).

the ordering of elements in $D = D_1 \oplus D_2$ which is defined by:

$d \sqsubseteq d'$ (in $D = D_1 \oplus D_2$) if and only if either $d = \bot$ or else
d, d' both arise from the same D_i ($i = 1, 2$) and $d \sqsubseteq d'$ in D_i

Rather than give details of the labelling, we assume certain labelling and unlabelling functions for the union domain implicitly. In the general case, we write $D = D_1 \oplus D_2 \oplus \cdots \oplus D_n$ and leave the definition as an exercise for $n > 2$. Given such a union domain D where D_i is one of the summands, we often wish to refer to the (possibly labelled) version of some $d_i \in D_i$ as an element of D. We will write:

d_i *in* D

in this situation.

Union domains are used in explaining the semantics of concrete types introduced with several variants. For example, with a non-recursive type definition such as:

```
datatype T = c1 of T1 | c2 of T2
```

we associate a domain of the form $C_1 \oplus C_2$ with T where C_i are domains associated with the variants ci **of** Ti ($i = 1, 2$).

A different union of domains is the **discriminated sum** or **discriminated union of domains** ($D_1 + D_2$). This domain consists of the disjoint union of the values in each of the domains D_1 and D_2 (labelled as before), but with an additional bottom element ($\bot = \bot_{D_1 + D_2}$) which is distinct from the labelled values arising from $\bot_{D_1}$ and $\bot_{D_2}$ (see Figure 10.4(b)). However, we can derive this domain construction from a simpler one which we define next.

10.2.4 Lifted domains

A domain construction which is particularly useful for lazy interpretations is called **lifting domains**. Given a domain D, we write $D_\perp$ for the *lifted* domain whose elements are those of D augmented with an additional bottom element ($\perp$). As in the case of unions, we assume elements arising from D in $D_\perp$ are labelled so that the new bottom element is distinct and not confused with $\perp_D$. If $L = D_\perp$ then we write $d \text{ } in \text{ } L$ to mean the value in L arising from $d \in D$. Thus $\perp_D \text{ } in \text{ } L \neq \perp_L$.

The ordering of the lifted domain (L) is that inherited from the ordering of the original domain (D) along with the condition that $\perp_L \sqsubseteq d$ for all $d \in L$. (So $\perp_L \sqsubseteq (\perp_D \text{ } in \text{ } L)$ as shown in Figure 10.4(c).)

Note that we can now define:

$$D + E = D_\perp \oplus E_\perp$$

We also note that:

$$(D \times E)_\perp = D_\perp \otimes E_\perp$$

where D and E are domains.

When S is a set, we also wrote $S_\perp$ for the flat domain constructed from S which is akin to domain lifting (but S does not have a least element so it is not a domain). We will also abbreviate $S_\perp \otimes D_\perp$ as $(S \times D)_\perp$ by analogy with the domain equivalence mentioned above. If $C = (S \times D)_\perp$ (for domain D and set S) then elements of C are either $\perp_C$ or of the form $(s, d) \text{ } in \text{ } C$ for some $s \in S$ and $d \in D$.

We use lifting to embed (lazily evaluated) data structures in the domain of values so that we can give distinct values to expressions of the form C (Ω) and Ω where C is some constructor and (Ω) is an expression with value $\perp$. More precisely, we use a domain of the form $(S \times D)_\perp$ to represent data structures as illustrated by the following example. Using the **datatype** definition given above, we have that c1 is a constructor of type $T_1 \to T$. Suppose D_1 is the domain associated with type T_1, then we use $(\{c1\} \times D_1)_\perp$ as the domain of variants of type T constructed with c1. Thus if E is an expression which denotes $d \in D_1$ then (c1, d) represents the value (data structure) denoted by c1 (E). Here, we are using the constructor as a label which is attached to the argument as a pair. For convenience, we will allow ourselves to write:

c (d) instead of (c, d)

when this is not likely to cause confusion.

Now, we also have c2 : $T_2 \to T$ as the only other constructor for type T, so suppose D_2 is the domain of elements of type T_2. We want the domain of values of type T to be D where:

$$D = (\{\mathsf{c1}\} \times D_1)_\perp \oplus (\{\mathsf{c2}\} \times D_2)_\perp$$

With a little thought, one can see that when $D_2 = D_1$, this is, in fact, equivalent to:

$$D = (\{\mathsf{c1}, \mathsf{c2}\} \times D_1)_\perp$$

10.2.5 Recursive types and domain equations

In the above example using the union of domains for the meaning of concrete types, we explicitly exclude recursively defined types. We must now consider what the domain of values should be for a type such as the following:

datatype T = c0 | c1 **of** T

Intuitively we want values such as $\perp$, c0, c1(c0), c1(c1(c0)), $\cdots$. In the lazy case, we also want c1($\perp$), c1(c1($\perp$)), $\cdots$. In fact the lazy case is quite subtle because we also need 'infinite' values such as c1(c1(c1(c1($\cdots$)))) which will be the value of cycle1 defined by:

val rec cycle1 = c1 (cycle1)

For strict semantics, the meaning of cycle1 will just be $\perp$ and no 'infinite' values or partial values (other than $\perp$) arise. We actually want to construct domains D or D' which satisfy one of the following equations (or recursive definitions if you prefer):

(1) $D \equiv \{\mathsf{c0}\}_\perp \oplus (\{\mathsf{c1}\} \times D)_\perp$ $(\equiv \{\mathsf{c0}\}_\perp \oplus (\{\mathsf{c1}\}_\perp \otimes D_\perp))$ for the non-strict case, and

(2) $D' \equiv \{\mathsf{c0}\}_\perp \oplus (\{\mathsf{c1}\}_\perp \otimes D')$ for the strict case.

It was shown by Scott (1976) that such domain equations could be solved. We will not give the mathematical details necessary to demonstrate this here, but just state that the solutions do indeed contain exactly the values we intuitively want, and the ordering of the values for this example is indicated in Figure 10.5. In fact, in order to deal with polymorphic values, we need to embed all the values we are interested in into one single domain (**Val**). In the next section we define **Val** to include functions from [**Val** → **Val**], integers, boolean values, sequences (tuples) of elements in **Val** and data structures built with constructors applied to arguments in **Val**. Thus **Val** is defined (mutually) recursively and satisfies the equation given in Table 10.2.

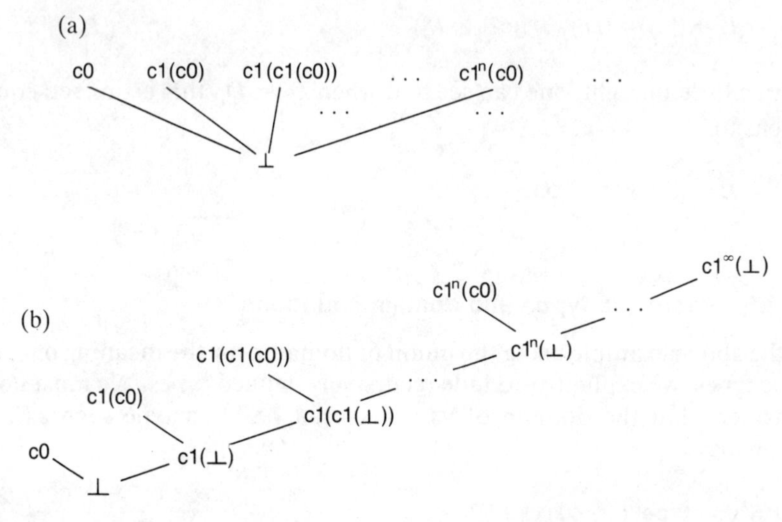

Figure 10.5 Values of type T defined by **datatype** $T = \text{c0} \mid \text{c1}$ **of** T: (a) domain for strict semantics; (b) domain for non-strict semantics.

10.2.6 Other domain constructions

Infinite unions are also possible, and a further domain which we will use in the sequel is:

$$\textbf{Tuples} = (\textbf{Val} \times \textbf{Val}) \oplus (\textbf{Val} \times \textbf{Val} \times \textbf{Val}) \oplus \cdots \oplus \textbf{Val}^n \oplus \cdots$$

where **Val** is our domain of values to be defined in a moment. The same conventions apply as in the case of finite unions. For example, if $d_1, d_2 \in \textbf{Val}$ then we can write (d_1, d_2) in **Tuples** for the pair considered as an element of the domain of tuples.

Finally, we will make use of a special domain of finite partial mappings from a set (S) to a domain (D). We will write $S \rightarrow_{\text{fin}} D$ for these mappings which we want to treat slightly differently from just functions. This particular construct will be used to express a domain of *environments* which associate values with variables. We will define:

$$\textbf{Env} = \textbf{Var} \rightarrow_{\text{fin}} \textbf{Val}$$

in the sequel, and describe the purpose of environments in the next subsection.

As well as being able to apply finite mappings to arguments (since mappings are functions), we can also calculate the finite set of elements from the argument domain for which a mapping produces a result. We will write *Dom* (m) for this finite set when m is such a mapping.

If S is a set and D a domain, then the empty mapping, written $\varnothing$, is an element of $S \rightarrow_{\text{fin}} D$ with $Dom\ (\varnothing) = \varnothing$ (i.e. the empty mapping has an empty domain set and therefore maps nothing in S to a value in D). We also write $[d/s]$ for the mapping in $S \rightarrow_{\text{fin}} D$ which maps s to d and nothing else. Thus $Dom\ ([d/s]) = \{s\}$. Finally, we write $m_1 + m_2$ for the mapping which behaves like m_2 whenever this maps an argument to a value in d but behaves like m1 otherwise. Thus $Dom\ (m_1 + m_2) = Dom\ (m_1) \cup Dom\ (m_2)$.

Note that we make a careful distinction between an element of S for which a mapping m produces no value in D (i.e. where the mapping is undefined) and a value which is mapped to $\perp_D$. In the latter case the mapping is defined but the value associated with the argument is the value in D representing non-termination.

To make $S \rightarrow_{\text{fin}} D$ into a domain, we should specify that $\varnothing$ is the bottom element and the ordering we are assuming is:

$m_1 \sqsubseteq m_2$ if and only if either $m_1 = \varnothing$ or
$Dom\ (m_1) = Dom\ (m_2)$ and $m_1\ (s) \sqsubseteq m_2\ (s)$ for all $s \in Dom\ (m_1)$

10.3 Semantics of a functional programming language

In providing a semantics for a programming language, we first define the syntactic domains of the various programming constructs. For example, we will have syntactic domains of expressions, patterns, definitions, etc. These are obviously interrelated, and this relationship is specified by the abstract syntax of the language. The next step is to specify the domains to be used for interpretation and finally define the semantic functions which map from the syntactic domains to the semantic domains. However, we need to introduce the concept of environment as well.

10.3.1 Environments

One of the principal requirements of denotational semantics is that the meaning of a syntactic construct is specified in terms of its immediate constituents (components). In order to do this, we need to take sub-expressions and talk about their meaning in isolation from the context in which they appear. Unfortunately, the context will generally contain the definition of identifiers used in the expression so the meaning of an isolated subexpression cannot simply be an element of the domain of values. For example, consider the meaning of the expression x + 3. Any value we associate with this expression must depend on the values we associate with the variables x and + (the expression could appear in a context in which + is redefined to have a different meaning from the standard one).

The solution is straightforward. We introduce the idea of an **environment** which is a mapping from variables to values. Thus an environment (ρ say) might map x to the integer value 5 and + to the normal addition function between integers. The value of x + 3 relative to ρ is then 8. In general, the meaning of an expression is a function from an environment to a value in the value domain (thus we formalize its context dependency).

We will write $\mathcal{Val}[\![E]\!]\rho$ for the value of E relative to ρ. (It is a standard convention to enclose syntactic objects such as E within $[\![\ ]\!]$ when we describe semantic functions. This serves two purposes. First, it prevents us from confusing the expressions we write to describe the semantic functions from the syntactic objects which we are defining a meaning for. Secondly, it helps to emphasize the fact that the syntactic object is to be thought of as a syntax tree, rather than a possibly ambiguous sequence of tokens. That is, we assume E is a parsed syntactic object.) Really, $\mathcal{Val}$ is just a higher order semantic function which when applied to an expression E produces a function which, when applied to environment ρ produces a final value for the expression E in environment ρ.

The meaning of a definition or collection of definitions can similarly be taken in isolation as a function from environments to environments. We will write $\mathcal{Def}\ [\![D]\!]\ \rho$ for the value of the definitions D relative to initial environment ρ, and this will be an environment which maps (binds) the newly defined variables to values. The new environment when combined with the original ρ provides the bindings used in subsequent evaluation of an expression introduced in the context of the definitions D.

The two main semantic domains we will use are **Env** (the domain of environments) and **Val** (the domain of values).

We now bring together all these elements of semantics in providing a formal definition of a functional language. This language is close to (but not identical with) a subset of Standard ML but unlike Standard ML it is given a non-strict semantics.

10.3.2 Syntactic domains

The abstract syntax of the language is given in Table 10.1. We have excluded some derived forms which are taken as being equivalent to one of the above forms. For example, in definitions, simultaneous bindings of the form:

$$P_1 = E_1 \textbf{ and } P_2 = E_2 \textbf{ and } \ldots P_n = E_n$$

Table 10.1 The abstract syntax (syntactic domains) (see text for simultaneous value bindings and function binding forms – datatype definitions are discussed in next chapter).

Syntactic domains:

Var	(variables ranged over by V, V_0, $\cdots$ – denumerable set)
Con	(constructors ranged over by C, C_0, $\cdots$ – denumerable set)
Exp	(expressions ranged over by E, E_0, $\cdots$)
Def	(definitions ranged over by D, D_0, $\cdots$)
Pat	(patterns ranged over by P, P_0, $\cdots$)

Abstract syntax:

Forms of expression (E)	V	(variable)
	C	(constructor)
	$E_1\ E_2$	(application)
	$(E_1, E_2, \ldots, E_n)$	(tuples ($n \geq 2$))
	if E_1 **then** E_2 **else** E_3	(conditional)
	let D **in** E **end**	(qualified)
	fn $P_1 \Rightarrow E_1 \mid \cdots \mid P_n \Rightarrow E_n$	(abstraction, $n \geq 1$)
Forms of definition (D)	**val** $P = E$	(non-recursive)
	val rec $P = E$	(recursive)
	$D_1\ D_2$	(sequence)
	local D_1 **in** D_2 **end**	(local)
Forms of pattern (P)	V	(variable)
	C	(constant)
	$(P_1, P_2, \ldots, P_n)$	(tuple, $n \geq 2$)
	$C\ P$	(construction)

are equivalent to the single binding:

$$(P_1, P_2, \ldots, P_n) = (E_1, E_2, \ldots, E_n)$$

so we only present the semantics for the latter form which is a special case of $P = E$, where P is a pattern and E is an expression. Similarly (as in Standard ML), function definitions involving pattern matched parameters and possibly curried parameters (introduced by **fun**) are equivalent to ordinary definitions introduced by **val rec**. For the case of a single function definition, the equivalence can be stated as:

$$\begin{array}{ll} \textbf{fun} & \mathsf{f}\ P_{11} \cdots P_{1n} = E_1 \\ \mid & \mathsf{f}\ P_{21} \cdots P_{2n} = E_2 \\ \cdots & \\ \mid & \mathsf{f}\ P_{m1} \cdots P_{mn} = E_m \end{array}$$

is equivalent to:

$$\begin{aligned}\textbf{val rec } \mathsf{f} = \textbf{fn } V_1 \Rightarrow \textbf{fn } V_2 \Rightarrow \cdots \textbf{fn } V_n \Rightarrow \textbf{fn } (&(P_{11}, \ldots, P_{1n}) \Rightarrow E_1 \\ &\mid (P_{21}, \ldots, P_{2n}) \Rightarrow E_2 \\ &\ldots \\ &\mid (P_{m1}, \ldots, P_{mn}) \Rightarrow E_m \\ &)\,(V_1, V_2, \ldots, V_n)\end{aligned}$$

where the variables $V_1, \ldots, V_n$ are new (not in any P_{ij} nor in any E_{ij} nor $\equiv$f). A similar but rather unwieldy equivalence can be stated for functions defined simultaneously but we omit the details.

We have excluded details of type definitions which are dealt with in the next chapter. We can assume that the parsed expression/definition/pattern has already been type checked and conforms to other syntactic restrictions such as:

(1) patterns must not contain repeated variables;
(2) there are no free variables (used but not defined) except for built in constants;
(3) constructor names in type definitions must all be distinct, etc.

We can then safely ignore type information in providing a semantics for (type-correct) expressions. A more sophisticated semantic definition might also give meanings to type definitions which could then be used to justify the process of type checking. (The interpretation of $E : T$ would be: the value denoted by E is in the subcollection of values denoted by the type T. Each monotype T denotes a subcollection of the values and polytypes denote the intersection of the subcollections denoted by each monotype instance of the polytype. Mathematically, these subcollections are known as 'ideals' and the intersection of ideals is also an ideal. Further details may be found in MacQueen and Sethi (1982).) For simplicity, we focus on the semantics of expressions and do not include the details of type semantics, treating type checking as just a syntactic constraint.

We assume that **Con** is an infinite set of constructor names distinct from any variables. Furthermore, we assume that **Con** is composed of disjoint sets $\textbf{Con}_0$ (used for constants) and $\textbf{Con}_1$ (used for constructors expecting an argument). This simplifies the description of the meaning of constructors since we want to treat the latter as functions and the former as just elements. We also assume that $\textbf{Con}_0$ includes all the boolean and integer constants (e.g. true, false 0, 1, ~1, . . . $\in \textbf{Con}_0$).

10.3.3 Semantic domains

We embed all values in one single domain (**Val**). **Val** is defined by the (mutually recursive) equations given in Table 10.2 and we assume the associated functions listed with it.

In addition to the domain **Val**, we have the domain **Env** of environments which is also defined in Table 10.2. An initial environment

Table 10.2 The semantic domains.

Semantic domains:

$\mathbf{Val} = \mathbf{Functions} \oplus \mathbf{Tuples} \oplus \mathbf{Constructions} \oplus \mathbf{Constants}$

where

$\mathbf{Functions} = [\mathbf{Val} \rightarrow \mathbf{Val}]_\perp$

$\mathbf{Tuples} = (\mathbf{Val} \times \mathbf{Val}) \oplus (\mathbf{Val} \times \mathbf{Val} \times \mathbf{Val}) \oplus \cdots \oplus (\mathbf{Val}^n) \oplus \cdots$

$\mathbf{Constructions} = (\mathbf{Con}_1 \times \mathbf{Val})_\perp$

$\mathbf{Constants} = (\mathbf{Con}_0)_\perp$

($d, d_0, \cdots$ range over **Val**)

$\mathbf{Env} = \mathbf{Var} \rightarrow_{\text{fin}} \mathbf{Val}$

($\rho, \rho_0, \cdots$ range over **Env**)

($\mathbf{Bool} = \boldsymbol{B}_\perp = \{\text{true, false}\}_\perp$)

($\mathbf{Int} = \boldsymbol{Z}_\perp = \{0, 1, \tilde{}1, \cdots\}_\perp$)

($\mathbf{Con}_0$ includes $\boldsymbol{Z}$ and $\boldsymbol{B}$)

Useful functions:

$apply : \mathbf{Val} \rightarrow \mathbf{Val} \rightarrow \mathbf{Val}$

$\quad \text{apply}\ d\ d_1 = f\ d_1$, if $d = f$ *in* **Functions** *in* **Val** ($f \in [\mathbf{Val} \rightarrow \mathbf{Val}]$)

$\quad = \perp$, otherwise

$sel_{n,i} : \mathbf{Val} \rightarrow \mathbf{Val}$ ($n \geq 2, 1 \leq i \leq n$)

$\quad sel_{n,i}(d) = d_i$, if $d = (d_1, \ldots, d_n)$ *in* **Tuples** *in* **Val**

$\quad = \perp$, otherwise

$argof : \mathbf{Val} \rightarrow \mathbf{Val}$

$\quad argof(d) = d_1$, if $d = (C, d_1)$ *in* **Constructions** *in* **Val**

$\quad = \perp$, otherwise

$isa_C : \mathbf{Val} \rightarrow \mathbf{Bool}$ ($C \in \mathbf{Con}_1$)

$\quad isa_C(d) = \text{true}$, if $d = (C, d_1)$ *in* **Constructions** *in* **Val**

$\quad = \text{false}$, if $d = (C_1, d_1)$ *in* **Constructions** *in* **Val** ($C \neq C_1$)

$\quad = \text{false}$, if $d = C_0$ *in* **Constants** *in* **Val**

$\quad = \perp$, otherwise

$isconst_C : \mathbf{Val} \rightarrow \mathbf{Bool}$ ($C \in \mathbf{Con}_0$)

$\quad isconst_C(d) = \text{true}$, if $d = C$ *in* **Constants** *in* **Val**

$\quad = \text{false}$, if $d = C_0$ *in* **Constants** *in* **Val** ($C \neq C_0$)

$\quad = \text{false}$, if $d = (C_1, d_1)$ *in* **Constructions** *in* **Val**

$\quad = \perp$, otherwise

binding certain variables to particular primitives (elements of **Val**) such as the addition operator an equality test, etc., could also be given, but we do not include such details here.

The domain **Val** is designed for non-strict interpretation of constructors. In particular, **Constructions** is a lifted domain, and $\times$ (rather than $\otimes$) is used for products in the domain of **Tuples**.

Associated with the domain **Val** we have the following functions:

(1) $sel_{n,i}$ for all $n > 1$ and $1 \leq i \leq n$. These are used to select components of tuples in **Val**.

(2) *argof* is used to retrieve the argument of a constructor in a construction. For example:

$$argof((C, d) \text{ in } \mathbf{Constructions} \text{ in } \mathbf{Val}) = d$$

(3) isa_C for each C in Con_1 finds out if a value d is a construction formed with C, and returns an element of {true, false, $\perp$}. It returns false if d is a constant or a construction with a different constructor.

(4) $isconst_C$ for each C in $\mathbf{Con}_0$ are similar to isa_C but compare with elements of **Constants** rather than **Constructions**.

(5) *apply* explains what value is produced when one value (d) is applied to another (d'). If d is in **Functions** then this is simply the application of the function to argument d as you would expect. This includes the case when $d = \perp$ which produces $\perp$ as result.

One particular consequence of using a single value domain that should be noted concerns our understanding of function types. Previously, we indicated that an expression of type $T_1 \to T_2$ would denote a function in $[D_1 \to D_2]$ where D_i is the domain of values of type T_i ($i = 1, 2$). With our single domain, this statement must be modified.

Although we are not presenting a formal definition of the semantics of types, we observe that the value of an expression of type $T_1 \to T_2$ will actually be a function in **Functions** = [**Val** $\to$ **Val**] (which is embedded in **Val**). Thus if D_1 are the values of type T_1 and D_2 are the values of type T_2 the intuitive meaning of the type $T_1 \to T_2$ is the set of values in **Functions** which produce values in D_2 when applied to values in D_1. Such a function will also produce values in **Val** when applied to arguments in **Val** outside D_1. However, we don't care what these might be, because a correctly typed program would not allow a function to be used on values outside the appropriate subdomain.

10.3.4 Semantic functions

The main semantic function is $\mathcal{V}al$ which applies to expressions and environments to produce a value in **Val**. We also make use of $\mathcal{D}ef$ to

Table 10.3 The semantic functions.

$\mathcal{V}al$	: **Exp** → **Env** → **Val**
$\mathcal{D}ef$	: **Def** → **Env** → **Env**
$\mathcal{M}atchEnv$	: **Pat** → **Val** → **Env**
$\mathcal{M}atchTest$	: **Pat** → **Val** → **Bool**

interpret definitions and $\mathcal{M}atchEnv$ and $\mathcal{M}atchTest$ to formalize pattern matching. The functionality of these is given in Table 10.3.

We write $\mathcal{V}al[\![E]\!]\rho$ for the value of expression E relative to environment ρ and similarly $\mathcal{D}ef[\![D]\!]\rho$ stands for the changes in the environment ρ produced by definitions D (these changes are a small environment which can be added to ρ to obtain a resulting environment for interpreting qualified expressions). $\mathcal{M}atchEnv[\![P]\!]d$ stands for the additional environment obtained by binding variables in the pattern P to appropriate parts of the value d (assuming d matches the pattern P). $\mathcal{M}atchTest[\![P]\!]d$ is a boolean value (possibly $\perp$) giving information on whether or not the value d matches the pattern P.

We now present the semantic definitions by describing the semantic functions for each of the possible forms for the syntactic arguments. These semantic equations which formalize meanings for our functional language are summarized in Tables 10.4, 10.5 and 10.6.

$\mathcal{V}al$

The meaning of expressions is given by $\mathcal{V}al$ according to the following cases. The value of a variable (relative to environment ρ) is determined by the environment, so:

$$\mathcal{V}al[\![V]\!]\rho = \rho(V)$$

The value of a constant constructor (in $\mathbf{Con}_0$) is itself:

$$\mathcal{V}al[\![C_0]\!]\rho = C_0 \ (in\ \textbf{Constants}\ in\ \textbf{Val})$$

and the value of a constructor in $\mathbf{Con}_1$ is a function which produces a construction:

$$\mathcal{V}al[\![C]\!]\rho = f(in\ \textbf{Functions}\ in\ \textbf{Val})$$
$$\text{where } f(d) = (C, d)\ (in\ \textbf{Constructions}\ in\ \textbf{Val})$$

The value of an application $(E_1\ E_2)$ (relative to ρ) is defined in terms of the values of E_1 (relative to ρ) and E_2 (relative to ρ). The first value is interpreted as a function and this is applied to the second value according to the cases given in the definition of apply (see Table 10.2):

Table 10.4 The definition of $\mathcal{Val}$.

Semantic equations for $\mathcal{Val}$:

$$
\begin{array}{ll}
\mathcal{Val}\,[\![V]\!]\,\rho & = \rho\,(V) \\
\mathcal{Val}\,[\![C]\!]\,\rho & = C \text{ in } \textbf{Constants} \text{ in } \textbf{Val} \ (C \in \textbf{Con}_0) \\
\mathcal{Val}\,[\![C]\!]\,\rho & = f \text{ in } \textbf{Functions} \text{ in } \textbf{Val} \ (C \in \textbf{Con}_1) \\
 & \quad \text{where } f(d) = (C, d) \text{ in } \textbf{Constructions} \text{ in } \textbf{Val} \\
\mathcal{Val}\,[\![E_1\ E_2]\!]\,\rho & = \text{apply}\,(\mathcal{Val}\,[\![E_1]\!]\,\rho)\,(\mathcal{Val}\,[\![E_2]\!]\,\rho) \\
\mathcal{Val}\,[\![(E_1, \ldots, E_n)]\!]\,\rho & = (\mathcal{Val}\,[\![E_1]\!]\,\rho, \ldots, \mathcal{Val}\,[\![E_n]\!]\,\rho) \text{ in } \textbf{Tuples} \text{ in } \textbf{Val} \\
\mathcal{Val}\,[\![\textbf{if } E_1 \textbf{ then } E_2 \textbf{ else } E_3]\!]\,\rho & \\
 & = (\mathcal{Val}\,[\![E_2]\!]\,\rho, \text{ if } \mathit{isconst}_{\mathrm{true}}\,(d) = \text{true} \\
 & = (\mathcal{Val}\,[\![E_3]\!]\,\rho, \text{ if } \mathit{isconst}_{\mathrm{false}}\,(d) = \text{true} \\
 & = \bot, \text{ otherwise} \\
 & \quad \text{where } d = \mathcal{Val}\,[\![E_1]\!]\,\rho \\
\mathcal{Val}\,[\![\textbf{let } D \textbf{ in } E \textbf{ end}]\!]\,\rho & = (\mathcal{Val}\,[\![E]\!]\,(\rho + \rho') \\
 & \quad \text{where } \rho' = \mathcal{Def}\,[\![D]\!]\,\rho \\
\mathcal{Val}\,[\![\textbf{fn } P_1 \Rightarrow E_1 \,|\, \cdots \,|\, P_n \Rightarrow E_n]\!]\,\rho & \\
 & = f \text{ in } \textbf{Functions} \text{ in } \textbf{Val} \\
 & \quad \text{where} \\
 & \quad f\,d = \mathcal{Val}\,[\![E_1]\!]\,\rho_1, \text{ if } \mathit{test}_1 = \text{true} \\
 & \qquad = \mathcal{Val}\,[\![E_2]\!]\,\rho_2, \text{ if } \mathit{test}_1 = \text{false and } \mathit{test}_2 = \text{true} \\
 & \qquad \ldots \\
 & \qquad = \mathcal{Val}\,[\![E_n]\!]\,\rho_n, \text{ if } \mathit{test}_i = \text{false } (1 \le i < n) \text{ and} \\
 & \qquad\quad \mathit{test}_n = \text{true} \\
 & \qquad = \bot, \text{ otherwise} \\
 & \qquad\quad \text{where } \rho_i = \mathcal{MatchEnv}\,[\![P_i]\!]\,d \quad (1 \le i \le n) \\
 & \qquad\quad \text{and } \ \mathit{test}_i = \mathcal{MatchTest}\,[\![P_i]\!]\,d \quad (1 \le i \le n)
\end{array}
$$

$$\mathcal{Val}\,[\![E_1\ E_2]\!]\,\rho = \mathit{apply}\,(\mathcal{Val}\,[\![E_1]\!]\,\rho)\,(\mathcal{Val}\,[\![E_2]\!]\,\rho)$$

The value of a tuple $(E_1, \ldots, E_n)$ (relative to ρ) is just the tuple of values of each component (relative to ρ), considered as an element of **Val**:

$$\mathcal{Val}\,[\![(E_1, \ldots, E_n)]\!]\,\rho = (\mathcal{Val}\,[\![E_1]\!]\,\rho, \ldots, \mathcal{Val}\,[\![E_n]\!]\,\rho) \ (\text{in } \textbf{Tuples} \text{ in } \textbf{Val})$$

The value of a conditional (relative to ρ) is determined by the value of the test (relative to ρ). If this produces true in **Val**, then the result is the value of the first branch and if it produces false in **Val**, then the result is the value of the second branch. In any other case (including when the value of the test is $\bot$) the value of the conditional is $\bot$:

$$
\begin{aligned}
\mathcal{Val}\,[\![\textbf{if } E_1 \textbf{ then } E_2 \textbf{ else } E_3]\!]\,\rho &= \mathcal{Val}\,[\![E_2]\!]\,\rho, \text{ if } \mathit{isconst}_{\mathrm{true}}\,(d) = \text{true} \\
&= \mathcal{Val}\,[\![E_3]\!]\,\rho, \text{ if } \mathit{isconst}_{\mathrm{false}}\,(d) = \text{true} \\
&= \bot, \text{ otherwise} \\
&\quad \text{where } d = \mathcal{Val}\,[\![E_1]\!]\,\rho
\end{aligned}
$$

The value of a qualified expression (relative to ρ) is the value of the main expression relative to a modified environment. The modified environment is ρ augmented with the environment defined by the qualifying definitions (defined in terms of $\mathscr{D}ef$ and ρ):

$$\mathscr{V}al\,[\![\textbf{let}\ D\ \textbf{in}\ E\ \textbf{end}]\!]\,\rho = \mathscr{V}al\,[\![E]\!]\,(\rho + \rho') \quad \text{where } \rho' = \mathscr{D}ef\,[\![D]\!]\,\rho$$

Finally, we consider the value of an abstraction. Rather than launching into the most general case, we consider a simple case to explain the basic idea. We would expect the meaning of an abstraction of the form **fn** $V \Rightarrow E$ (relative to ρ) to be an element of **Functions** = [**Val** → **Val**] considered as an element of **Val**. That is:

$$\mathscr{V}al\,[\![\textbf{fn}\ V \Rightarrow E]\!]\,\rho = f\ \textit{in}\ \textbf{Functions}\ \textit{in}\ \textbf{Val},\ \text{where } f \cdots$$

Now, we describe the function f according to the result produced for any d ∈ **Val**. We do not consider separate cases for d (e.g. when d = ⊥), which means that we are using a lazy (non-strict) interpretation. We simply define f by:

$$f(d) = \mathscr{V}al\,[\![E]\!]\,(\rho + [d/V])$$

Thus the result is the value of the body of the abstraction relative to the environment ρ augmented with the mapping (binding) of parameter V to actual argument d.

For the more general case, we have to consider a match with more complex patterns and possibly several cases in the abstraction. The full details are given in Table 10.4 in terms of *MatchEnv* and *MatchTest* which are described below.

One consequence of the definitions so far is that:

$$\mathscr{V}al\,[\![(\textbf{fn}\ V \Rightarrow E)\ E_1]\!]\,\rho = \mathscr{V}al\,[\![E]\!]\,(\rho + [d/V]) \text{ where } d = \mathscr{V}al\,[\![E_1]\!]\,\rho$$

which we leave as an exercise to prove.

MatchEnv and *MatchTest*

The semantic function *MatchEnv* produces an environment from a pattern P and a value $d \in$ **Val**. The environment *MatchEnv* $[\![P]\!]d$ will map any variables occurring in P to the corresponding components of d assuming that d matches against the pattern P. For example, if d has the form c1 (c2, c3 (c4)) and P has the form c1 (x, y) then the resulting environment should be [c2/x] + [c3 (c4)/y]. (We have omitted the full descriptions of the values with '*in* **Val**', etc.)

Table 10.5 Definitions of *MatchEnv* and *MatchTest*.

Semantic equations for MatchEnv and MatchTest:

$$\mathit{MatchEnv}\,[\![V]\!]\,d = [d/V]$$
$$\mathit{MatchEnv}\,[\![C]\!]\,d = \varnothing$$
$$\mathit{MatchEnv}\,[\![C\ P]\!]\,d = \mathit{MatchEnv}\,[\![P]\!]\,(\mathit{argof}\ d)$$
$$\mathit{MatchEnv}\,[\![(P_1, \ldots, P_n)]\!]\,d = (\mathit{MatchEnv}\,[\![P_1]\!]\,d_1) + \cdots + (\mathit{MatchEnv}\,[\![P_n]\!]\,d_n)$$
$$\text{where } d_i = \mathit{sel}_{n,i}\,(d)\ (\mathrm{i} = 1 \cdots \mathrm{n})$$

$$\mathit{MatchTest}\,[\![V]\!]\,d = \mathrm{true}$$
$$\mathit{MatchTest}\,[\![C]\!]\,d = \mathit{isconst}_C\,(d)$$
$$\mathit{MatchTest}\,[\![C\ P]\!]\,d = \mathit{isa}_C\,(d)\ \mathit{andalso}\ \mathit{MatchTest}\,[\![P]\!]\,(\mathit{argof}\ d)$$
$$\mathit{MatchTest}\,[\![(P_1, \ldots, P_n)]\!]\,d = (\mathit{MatchTest}\,[\![P_1]\!]\,d_1)\ \mathit{andalso} \cdots \mathit{andalso}\ (\mathit{MatchTest}\,[\![P_n]\!]\,d_n)$$
$$\text{where } d_i = \mathit{sel}_{n,i}\,(d)\ (\mathrm{i} = 1 \cdots \mathrm{n})$$

$\mathit{andalso} : \mathbf{Bool} \times \mathbf{Bool} \rightarrow \mathbf{Bool}$
true $\mathit{andalso}\ b = b$
false $\mathit{andalso}\ b =$ false
$\perp\ \mathit{andalso}\ b = \perp$

The related function *MatchTest* checks to see if a value d matches a pattern P and returns a boolean value. To be precise, it returns an element of $\mathbf{Bool} = \boldsymbol{B}_\perp = \{\mathrm{true}, \mathrm{false}, \perp\}$ since the checking may fail to terminate. For example, if P is c1 (x, y) and d is $\perp$, then $\perp$ should be the result of $\mathit{MatchTest}\,[\![P]\!]d$. If, on the other hand, d is c1 ($\perp$, $\perp$), then $\mathit{MatchTest}\,[\![P]\!]d$ should be true and $\mathit{MatchEnv}[\![P]\!]d$ should be $[\perp/\mathrm{x}] + [\perp/\mathrm{y}]$. The full definitions of *MatchEnv* and *MatchTest* are given in Table 10.5 and we discuss them briefly below.

When the pattern is a variable, *MatchTest* produces true regardless of the value d (which may even be $\perp$) and *MatchEnv* produces the simple environment which maps the variable to the value d. When the pattern is a constant C, *MatchTest* uses $\mathit{isconst}_C$ to check that d is indeed the same constant (and may return $\perp$ if d is $\perp$). *MatchEnv* just returns the empty environment for a constant pattern. When the pattern has the form of a constructor applied to an argument pattern ($C\ P$), *MatchTest* similarly uses isa_C to check that d is constructed in the same way, and continues to check that *argof* d matches P in the successful case. *MatchEnv* just produces the environment formed by matching *argof* d against P. The last case for a pattern is a tuple of patterns. *MatchTest* proceeds to test each of the component patterns in turn against the values $\mathit{sel}_{n,i}\,(d)$. No test is made to check that d is a tuple of length n since we rely on type checking for such a check. Furthermore, this ensures that (x1, . . . , xn) successfully matches $\perp$ and the environment $[\perp/\mathrm{x}\,1] + \cdots + [\perp/\mathrm{xn}]$ is returned by *MatchEnv* in this case. Note that the patterns in a tuple are compared one at a time from left to right, and comparison stops when a false is returned. This has significance for the degree to which d must be defined in order to produce false in a pattern match rather than $\bot$. This 'left to right' scan is encapsulated in the definition of the function *andalso* which we have defined so that:

$$\mathsf{false}\ \mathit{andalso}\ \bot = \mathsf{false}$$

The environment returned by $\mathcal{M}atchEnv$ when the pattern is a tuple is simply the addition of all the bindings produced by matching the components. The fact that variables are not repeated in patterns ensures that the component environments have disjoint domains.

$\mathcal{D}ef$

Turning now to the meaning of definitions, we define $\mathcal{D}ef$ by cases for the form of the definitions. The meaning of a definition is also given relative to an environment ρ and produces a new environment. The new environment records only the new bindings described by the definitions and not the bindings already in ρ.

Before discussing the base cases, we consider compound definitions which are either sequences of definitions or definitions with local definitions. In a sequence D_1, D_2, the definition D_1 is interpreted relative to some given environment ρ and is used to produce an additional environment ρ_1. Then the definition D_2 is interpreted in the augmented environment $(\rho + \rho_1)$ to produce another environment ρ_2. The final environment returned from the sequence is $\rho_1 + \rho_2$ which includes all the new bindings, without those from the original ρ:

$$\begin{aligned}
&\mathcal{D}ef\ [\![D_1\ D_2]\!]\ \rho = \rho_1 + \rho_2 \\
&\qquad\qquad\qquad\qquad \text{where } \rho_2 = \mathcal{D}ef\ [\![D_2]\!]\ \rho_1 \\
&\qquad\qquad\qquad \text{where } \rho_1 = \mathcal{D}ef\ [\![D_1]\!]\ \rho
\end{aligned}$$

The meaning of a definition with a local definition is very similar except that the environment formed from the local definitions (ρ_1) is not returned with those formed from the main definitions:

$$\begin{aligned}
&\mathcal{D}ef\ [\![\textbf{local}\ D_1\ \textbf{in}\ D_2\ \textbf{end}]\!]\ \rho = \rho_2 \\
&\qquad\qquad\qquad\qquad\qquad\qquad \text{where } \rho_2 = \mathcal{D}ef\ [\![D_2]\!]\ \rho_1 \\
&\qquad\qquad\qquad\qquad\qquad\qquad\qquad\qquad \text{where } \rho_1 = \mathcal{D}ef\ [\![D_1]\!]\ \rho
\end{aligned}$$

For the base cases, the simplest is when the definition is a single (non-recursive) value binding with a pattern P and expression E. We use $\mathcal{M}atchTest$ to check that the value of E (relative to ρ) matches P and use

$\mathcal{M}atchEnv$ to calculate the new environment when the result is true:

$$\mathcal{D}ef \,[\![\textbf{val } P = E]\!]\, \rho = \mathcal{M}atchEnv \,[\![P]\!]\, d, \text{ if } \mathcal{M}atchTest \,[\![P]\!]\, d = \text{true}$$
$$\text{where } d = \mathcal{V}al \,[\![E]\!]\, \rho$$
$$= \varnothing, \text{ otherwise}$$

We are now left with the most difficult case of all, a definition with recursive bindings. For the sake of simplicity, we will cheat a little here and allow ourselves to describe recursively the environment which is to be formed by such a definition. In the next section, we discuss how a non-recursive description of the same object can be constructed.

The meaning of a definition with a recursive binding of pattern P to expression E is very similar to the previous, non-recursive, case. The difference lies in the environment relative to which the expression E is to be evaluated. In the non-recursive case, this was just the given environment ρ, but for a recursive definition, the ρ needs to be modified by augmenting it with the new environment which is to be returned as the final result. Thus, we use the result ρ' in a recursive description of ρ':

$$\mathcal{D}ef \,[\![\textbf{val rec } P = E]\!]\, \rho = \rho'$$
$$\text{where (recursively)}$$
$$\rho' = \mathcal{M}atchEnv \,[\![P]\!]\, d, \text{ if } \mathcal{M}atchTest \,[\![P]\!]\, d = \text{true}$$
$$= \varnothing, \text{ otherwise}$$
$$d = \mathcal{V}al \,[\![E]\!]\, (\rho + \rho')$$

An alternative description which postpones our difficulty with recursion is to assume a primitive function called *fix* with the property that $fix\ f = f\,(fix\ f)$. We will show in the next section that this allows us to convert recursive bindings into non-recursive ones using the equivalence:

$$\textbf{rec } P = E \equiv P = \text{fix } (\textbf{fn } P \Rightarrow E)$$

If we assume that the recursive binding is an abbreviation for the equivalent non-recursive form, then we can dispense with a separate semantic description for the recursive case. However, we do have to explain why the equivalence holds (which we do in the next section).

This completes the semantic definitions for $\mathcal{D}ef$ which are summarized in Table 10.6. Some further consequences that can be shown are that:

$$\mathcal{V}al \,[\![\textbf{let val } V = E_1 \textbf{ in } E \textbf{ end}]\!]\, \rho = \mathcal{V}al \,[\![E]\!]\, (\rho + [\mathcal{V}al \,[\![E_1]\!]\, \rho / V])$$

and, with an appropriate definition of the substitution of E_1 for free occurrences of V in E (written $E\,[E_1/V]$ – see Chapter 12), that:

Table 10.6 Definition of $\mathscr{D}ef$.

Semantic equations for $\mathscr{D}ef$:

$$\mathscr{D}ef\,[\![D_1\ D_2]\!]\,\rho = \rho_1 + \rho_2$$
$$\text{where } \rho_2 = \mathscr{D}ef\,[\![D_2]\!]\,(\rho + \rho_1)$$
$$\text{where } \rho_1 = \mathscr{D}ef\,[\![D_1]\!]\,\rho$$

$$\mathscr{D}ef\,[\![\textbf{local}\ D_1\ \textbf{in}\ D_2\ \textbf{end}]\!]\,\rho = \rho_2$$
$$\text{where } \rho_2 = \mathscr{D}ef\,[\![D_2]\!]\,\rho_1$$
$$\text{where } \rho_1 = \mathscr{D}ef\,[\![D_1]\!]\,\rho$$

$$\mathscr{D}ef\,[\![\textbf{val}\ P = E]\!]\,\rho = \mathscr{M}atchEnv\,[\![P]\!]\,d, \text{ if } \mathscr{M}atchTest\,[\![P]\!]\,d = \mathsf{true}$$
$$\text{where } d = \mathscr{V}al\,[\![E]\!]\,\rho$$
$$= \varnothing, \text{ otherwise}$$

$$\mathscr{D}ef\,[\![\textbf{val rec}\ P = E]\!]\,\rho = \rho'$$
$$\text{where (recursively)}$$
$$\rho' = \mathscr{M}atchEnv\,[\![P]\!]\,d \text{ if } \mathscr{M}atchTest\,[\![P]\!]\,d = \mathsf{true}$$
$$= \varnothing, \text{ otherwise}$$
$$d = \mathscr{V}al\,[\![E]\!]\,(\rho + \rho')$$

$$\mathscr{V}al\,[\![E]\!]\,(\rho + [\mathscr{V}al\,[\![E_1]\!]\,\rho/V]) = \mathscr{V}al\,[\![E\,[E_1/V]]\!]\,\rho$$

We omit proofs here.

We have made some simplifications since this is intended as an illustration of some of the semantic concepts one might find in a formal definition of a functional language. For example, the meaning of types can be made more explicit as part of the semantics (see MacQueen and Sethi (1982)).

10.4 Recursion and fixed point theory

10.4.1 Recursive definitions

A recursive definition is not a true mathematical definition without some theory like the fixed point theory because it does not ‘explain’ the object being defined in terms of already familiar objects (since recursive definition may be circular). Instead we should view recursive definitions as equations which we hope have unique solutions. This is analogous to the way that we might regard x = 6 as a solution to the equation x = 20 − 3x in algebra. For example, the recursive definition:

```
fun sumto n = if n < 1 then 0 else n + sumto (n − 1)
```

is supposed to define sumto to be the unique function from integers to integers which adds up all the numbers from 1 to n (for given argument

$n > 0$) and is 0 if the argument is 0 or negative. The same function can in fact be defined non-recursively as:

```
fun sumto n = if n < 1 then 0 else (n * (n + 1)) div 2
```

but it is not at all obvious that a non-recursive description can always be found for a function defined by recursion. In general, we need some way of reasoning about recursive definitions to ensure that ordinary functions can be associated with them as appropriate solutions. (This corresponds to the manipulation of $x = 20 - 3x$ to deduce $4x = 20$ and hence $x = 5$.) Problems arise, however, with equations which might appear to have no solutions, e.g.:

```
fun f (x) = f (x) + 1
```

or many solutions, as in:

```
fun f (x) = f (x)
```

For a more subtle example, consider the following equation:

```
fun f (x) = if x = 0 then 1 else f (x − 2)
```

The following functions over the integers augmented with $\perp$ (i.e. in $[\boldsymbol{Z}_\perp \rightarrow \boldsymbol{Z}_\perp]$) all satisfy this last equation:

(1) the function (g, say) which produces result 1 for all integer arguments and also if the argument is $\perp$;
(2) the function (h, say) which produces 1 if the argument is an even non-negative integer and 2 for all other arguments except $\perp$ which produces $\perp$; and
(3) the function (u, say) which produces 1 for even, non-negative integer arguments and $\perp$ for all other arguments.

Most people reading the definition of f above would regard it as a description of the (partial) function we have called u since no information regarding odd numbers and negative numbers can be deduced from the equation. The presumption that negative and odd numbers produce 1 (as in g) or 2 (as in h) seems unfounded, and so the 'natural' interpretation is the 'least defined' function which is consistent within (i.e. which satisfies) the equation. The solution u has the property that it is less defined than any other solution (producing $\perp$ at least as often as any other solution) and it agrees with all other solutions when it is defined (producing an integer). The fixed point theory of recursion formalizes the construction of such a least solution to be associated with any recursive definition and incidentally establishes the uniqueness and existence of the least solution.

Before proceeding, we should explain where the phrase, 'fixed point', comes from.

10.4.2 Fixed points

Given a recursive definition **fun** f (x) = E where E is some expression involving possibly f and x, we noted earlier that this can be rewritten as:

val rec f = **fn** x ⇒ E

(which makes it clear that it is f we are defining). Furthermore, the right-hand side of the definition is an expression (**fn** x ⇒ E) which may involve f and can be re-expressed as a function of f in the form F (f) so we can consider our equation as being of the form:

f = F (f)

For example, we can re-express the recursive definition of factorial in the form of the equation:

```
fact = FACT (fact)
```

where FACT is an operation on functions defined by:

```
val FACT = fn g ⇒ (fn x ⇒ if x = 0 then 1 else g (x − 1) * x)
```

The usual definition of fact can be obtained from this version by simply expanding FACT (fact) according to the definition of FACT. That is:

```
FACT (fact) = fn x ⇒ if x = 0 then 1 else fact (x − 1) * x
```

Note that FACT can be regarded as the transformation needed to convert the left-hand side to the right-hand side of the above equation and the identifier fact does not itself occur in the definition of FACT which is non-recursive.

Any equation of the form f = F (f) (where F is not itself defined in terms of f) can now be seen as a statement that f should be unaffected by F. That is, f should be a fixed point of F, and any fixed point of F is a solution (for f) of the equation f = F (f).

The diagrams in Figure 10.6 show various ways of viewing the recursive definition of fact and its relationship to FACT.

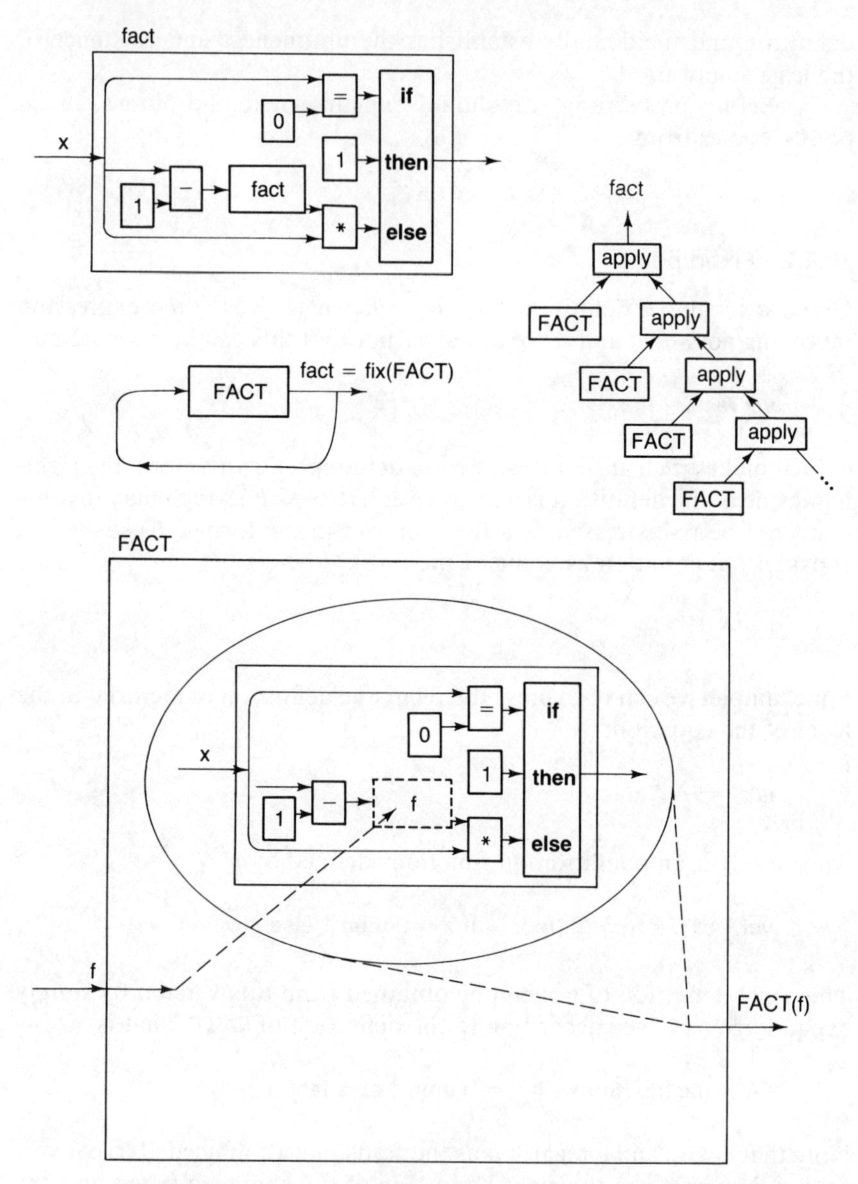

Figure 10.6 The relationships between FACT and fact.

The fixed point theory of recursion explains how we can find fixed points for a function like F, and pick out a unique, most natural one, namely the least defined one. Such a fixed point is then taken to be the real meaning of f intended by the recursive description. In fact, the least fixed point can be found by considering a chain of better and better approximations, starting with the least defined function.

Consider the following sequence of non-recursive definitions:

val $fact_0$ = **fn** x ⇒ Ω
val $fact_1$ = **fn** x ⇒ **if** x = 0 **then** 1 **else** $fact_0$ (x − 1) * x
val $fact_2$ = **fn** x ⇒ **if** x = 0 **then** 1 **else** $fact_1$ (x − 1) * x
...
...
val $fact_i$ = **fn** x ⇒ **if** x = 0 **then** 1 **else** $fact_i$ − 1 (x − 1) * x
...

The meaning $fact_i$ of each $fact_i$ is a function in $[Z_\perp \to Z_\perp]$ and each of the functions agree where they are defined. Furthermore, each $fact_{i-1}$ is more defined than the preceding $fact_j$ $(j < i)$, giving a chain of increasing function values (according to the definition of ⊑ for functions):

$fact_0\ z$ $= \perp$ for all $z \in Z_\perp$
$fact_1\ z$ $= 1$, if $z = 0$
$= \perp$, for all other $z \in Z_\perp$
$fact_2\ z$ $= 1$, if $z = 0$ or $z = 1$
$= \perp$, for all other $z \in Z_\perp$
$fact_3\ z$ $= 1$, if $z = 0$ or $z = 1$
$= 2$, if $z = 2$
$= \perp$, for all other $z \in Z_\perp$
$fact_4\ z$ $= 1$, if $z = 0$ or $z = 1$
$= 2$, if $z = 2$
$= 6$, if $z = 3$
$= \perp$, for all other $z \in Z_\perp$
...

Note, also, that each $fact_i$ is expressed in terms of $fact_{i-1}$, (for $i > 0$) and we have $fact_i = FACT\ (fact_{i-1})$ using the previous definition of FACT. This means that:

$$fact_i = FACT\ (FACT\ (\ldots FACT\ (\Omega) \ldots)) = FACT^i(\Omega)$$

Clearly, the function we want as the meaning of fact, satisfying the equation:

$$fact = FACT\ (fact)$$

is approximated by each of the $fact_i$, and should exist as a limiting value in the domain. The notion of limit is therefore important here.

10.4.3 Limits and continuous functions

Each fact_{i+1} described above denotes a more defined function than fact_i, being defined on more and more arguments (but always a finite number). The limit of this chain of functions exists in $[\boldsymbol{Z}_\perp \rightarrow \boldsymbol{Z}_\perp]$ and is defined for all non-negative integers. This limit is the factorial function (extended to produce $\perp$ for negative or undefined arguments). Each fact_i corresponds to an expansion of the recursive definition of fact up to a nesting of i inner recursive calls by substitution, and then replacing the i + 1th call by Ω to cut off the potentially infinite nesting at a finite depth. Recursion is our mechanism for describing infinitary things in a finite way. Arbitrarily good approximations may be obtained by 'unravelling' the recursion, even though we cannot deal with the completely unravelled (infinite) expression. We think of the recursively defined factorial function as equivalent to some sort of infinite 'expression':

fn x ⇒ **if** x = 0 **then** 1 **else** (^) (x − 1) ∗ x

where the arrow indicates a subexpression which is to be regarded as a copy of the entire 'expression'. This 'expression' is, essentially:

FACT (FACT (FACT (. . . FACT (. . . . . .) . . .)))

which can also be represented as a graph as in Figure 10.6.

Although infinite expressions are not introduced as part of the programming language, they are implicitly introduced by recursive definitions. However, by dealing directly with meanings in a domain we can speak of infinite values because of the existence of limit elements in domains. In general we give a meaning to a recursively defined f by finding a solution to its defining equation f = F (f) as follows. We take F (the meaning of F) and use it to construct the sequence of functions (which form a chain):

$$f_0 = \perp$$
$$f_1 = F f_0$$
$$f_2 = F f_1 = F(F\perp)$$
$$\ldots$$
$$f_i = F(F(F(F\ldots(\perp)\ldots))) = F^i(\perp)$$

The limit of such a chain always exists in domains as the least upper bound of the chain and is usually written as $\bigsqcup\{f_i \mid i = 0, 1, 2, \cdots\}$ or equivalently:

$$\bigsqcup\{F^i(\perp) \mid i = 0, 1, 2, \cdots\}$$

This leads us to another crucial point about computable functions and, indeed, any other infinitary data object: they can only be described as limits of finite approximations. Clearly if we wish to operate on such an infinitary object, within the programming language, we can only do so by dealing with its finite approximations. In any particular computation, we can only discover a finite amount of information about an infinite object so there will be some finite approximation which will be indistinguishable from the infinite object in each case. For example, in computing fact 6 each of the functions $FACT^{i}(\perp)$ for $i > 6$ will produce the correct answer when applied to 6. All infinite computable objects will be the limit of a sequence of finite approximations and to calculate the result of applying a function to an infinite object we must rely on calculations involving finite approximations to the argument. These calculations give us approximations of the final result.

We use the property that:

> When a computable operation (such as F) is applied to an infinitary object the result is equal to the limit of all the values obtained by applying the function to the approximations.

This is exactly the restriction placed on functions by continuity. Thus, for example, if $\{d_i \mid i = 1, \cdots\}$ is any chain of values then:

$$F(\bigsqcup \{d_i \mid i = 1, \cdots\}) = \bigsqcup \{F(d_i) \mid i = 1, \cdots\}$$

This allows us to establish the fixed point theorem, as discussed in the following section.

10.4.4 The fixed point theorem

By only dealing with continuous functions, it can be shown that suitable models exist so that all relevant chains of approximations do indeed have limits in our domains. Furthermore, the limit of chains such as those described above are the fixed points of the equations used to generate them. That is, if:

$$lim = \bigsqcup \{F^{i}(\perp) \mid i = 0, 1, 2 \cdots\}$$

then:

$$F(lim) = lim$$

This is easily shown to follow from the continuity of F:

$$\begin{aligned} F(lim) &= F(\bigsqcup \{F^{i}(\perp) \mid i = 0, 1, \cdots\}) \\ &= \bigsqcup \{F(F^{i}(\perp)) \mid i = 0, 1, \cdots\} \text{ by continuity} \\ &= \bigsqcup \{F^{i+1}(\perp) \mid i = 0, 1, \cdots\} \\ &= \bigsqcup \{F^{j}(\perp) \mid j = 1, \cdots\} \text{ changing the variable to } j = i + 1 \\ &= lim \end{aligned}$$

The last step follows since the missing $F^0(\bot)$ in the sequence is just $\bot$ and can easily be added back in without affecting the limit.

Furthermore, *lim* is less defined than any other solution of f = F (f) so if $F(d) = d$ for some d in the domain on which F is defined then $lim \sqsubseteq d$. This follows by considering first that:

$$F^0(\bot) = \bot \sqsubseteq d$$

Secondly, for any $i \geq 0$:

$$F^i(\bot) \sqsubseteq d$$

implies that:

$$\begin{aligned} F^{i+1}(\bot) = F(F^i(\bot)) &\sqsubseteq F(d) \text{ (by monotonicity)} \\ &= d \text{ (by assumption)} \end{aligned}$$

So by induction $F^i(\bot) \sqsubseteq d$ for all $i \geq 0$. This makes d an upper bound of the sequence:

$$\{F^i(\bot) \mid i = 0, 1, \cdots\}$$

By definition, *lim* is a least upper bound and thus $lim \sqsubseteq d$.

The previous two proofs involving F hold for any continuous function on domains and this establishes the **fixed point theorem** for domains:

> All continuous functions g on a domain have least fixed points which can be found as the least upper bound of the sequence:
>
> $$\{g^i(\bot) \mid i = 0, 1, \cdots\}$$

We will refer to this least upper bound as *fix g* in the sequel.

We have seen that the limit (least upper bound) *fix F* of the chain $\{F^i(\bot) \mid i = 0, 1, \cdots\}$ both satisfies the original equation (recursive definition) and is also the least solution. Hence *fix F* is the appropriate meaning for f defined by f = F (f). What is perhaps rather surprising is that the operation of finding the fixed point can itself be described as a program fix. This fix is the same primitive introduced in Chapter 1 to convert the recursive local definition:

let val rec $V = E$ **in** E' **end**

into the non-recursive:

let val V = fix (**fn** $V \Rightarrow E$) **in** E' **end**

Clearly with fix as a primitive denoting *fix*, recursive definitions are no longer (theoretically) needed. But *fix* can be defined in terms of pure function applications rather than assumed as a primitive. The following rather obscure looking function (usually written as Y) comes from the lambda calculus (see Chapter 12):

```
fun Y F = let fun g f = F (f f)
          in g (g) end
```

and has the property that Y F = F (Y F), so Y F is a fixed point of F (in fact it is the least fixed point). Unfortunately, as it stands, this expression cannot be given a proper type in Milner's polymorphic type system. The self application of f in (f f) requires f to have both type α and $\alpha \rightarrow \beta$ (with the same α in both cases) but types T for which $T \equiv T \rightarrow T'$ cannot be directly handled (as we discuss in the next chapter). A simple solution is to introduce a type operator and data constructor for converting between the types $T \rightarrow T'$ and T so that they need not be identified:

```
datatype α coded = Encode of ((α coded) → α)
```

(Thus T' coded will represent the required T and any Encode f of type T automatically gives us a value f of type $T \rightarrow T'$ and vice versa.) We can now define:

```
fun fix F = let fun g (Encode f) = F (f (Encode f))
            in g (Encode g) end
```

and then fix has polytype $(\alpha \rightarrow \alpha) \rightarrow \alpha$. A slight variant of fix is required for non-lazy implementations to ensure that fix F terminates under call-by-value. The variant fix′, given by:

```
fun fix′ F = let fun g (Encode f) x = F (f (Encode f)) x
             in g (Encode g) end
```

works without lazy evaluation, but its type is less general:

$$((\alpha \rightarrow \beta) \rightarrow (\alpha \rightarrow \beta)) \rightarrow (\alpha \rightarrow \beta)$$

This means that fix′ can only be used to find fixed points which are functions and not other data values (hence the restriction, in non-lazy implementations, that recursive definitions may only be used to introduce functions).

It is an instructive exercise to show that:

```
fix F = F(fix F)
```

by expanding the definition of fix.

Although the above examples emphasized the recursive definition of functions, we may also understand infinite lists as limits of finite approximations. For example, the infinite list of ones which we defined by:

```
val rec ones = 1 :: ones
```

can be seen as the limit of the sequence of 'partial lists' ⊥, 1 :: ⊥, 1 :: (1 :: ⊥), · · · . In fact ones denotes the least fixed point given by:

```
fix (fn x => 1 :: x)
```

Having defined chains and limits in this chapter, we are now in a position to give a more precise definition of the term 'admissibility' which we used in Chapter 8. A predicate P mapping elements of some domain D to {true, false} is **admissible** if the set of values of x (in D) for which $P(x)$ is true contains all the limits of any chains in the set. (The set is said to be *chain complete.*) For an admissible predicate, therefore, it is sufficient to establish that the predicate holds for all the elements of a chain in order to show that the predicate holds for the limit of the chain (which need not be an element of the chain). (Note that we say a *formula* is admissible, if it denotes an admissible predicate.)

10.5 Summary

This chapter on semantics has been included to show that a formal treatment of partial values and recursion is possible. It also illustrates how ambiguities in a programming language description can be resolved.

For more information about denotational semantics, the reader should refer to Schmidt (1986) which deals with semantics for programming languages in general and not just functional languages. (Note that Schmidt uses a slightly different definition of domain which does not necessarily include a bottom element. The domains described here correspond to his 'pointed domains'.) Further references are Gordon (1979), Tennent (1976), Stoy (1977, 1982) and Milne and Strachey (1976).

For more information about the fixed point theory of recursion and proofs about computable functions, see, for example, Paulson (1987) – which also gives an introduction to domain constructions – Bird (1976) and Manna (1974). For other introductions to domain theory see, for example, Scott (1982) and Plotkin (1982).

Recently, a complete formal definition of Standard ML has been published (Harper *et al.*, 1987) using **natural semantics**. This form of semantics is more operational (less abstract) than denotational semantics and describes how expressions are evaluated and type checked. This seems to be a more natural way of describing a language with non-functional features (side-effects and exception handlers) such as Standard ML.

In the next two chapters, we deal with type checking and evaluation, respectively.

EXERCISES

10.1 Define $D_1 \times D_2 \times \cdots \times D_n$, $D_1 \otimes D_2 \otimes \cdots \otimes D_n$, $D_1 \oplus D_2 \oplus \cdots \oplus D_n$ and $D_1 + D_2 + \cdots + D_n$, for $n > 2$.

10.2 Show that $(\{c1\} \times D)_\perp \oplus (\{c2\} \times D)_\perp \equiv (\{c1, c2\} \times D)_\perp$ when $c1 \neq c2$.

10.3 Show that:

$$\mathcal{V}al\ [\![(\mathbf{fn}\ V \Rightarrow E)\ E_1]\!]\rho = \mathcal{V}al[\![E]\!](\rho + [d/V]) \text{ where } d = \mathcal{V}al[\![E_1]\!]\rho$$

10.4 Show that:

$$\mathcal{V}al\ [\![\mathbf{let\ val}\ V = E_1\ \mathbf{in}\ E\ \mathbf{end}]\!]\ \rho = \mathcal{V}al\ [\![E]\!]\ (\rho + [\mathcal{V}al\ [\![E_1]\!]\ \rho/V])$$

10.5 Show that:

$$\mathcal{D}ef\ [\![\mathbf{let}\ D_1\ D_2\ \mathbf{in}\ E\ \mathbf{end}]\!]\ \rho = \mathcal{D}ef\ [\![\mathbf{let}\ D_1\ \mathbf{in\ let}\ D_2\ \mathbf{in}\ E\ \mathbf{end\ end}]\!]\ \rho$$

10.6 Show that:

$$\begin{aligned}&\mathcal{V}al\ [\![\mathbf{if}\ E_1\ \mathbf{then}\ E_2\ \mathbf{else}\ E_3]\!]\ \rho\\ &\quad = \mathcal{V}al\ [\![(\mathbf{fn}\ \mathsf{true} \Rightarrow E_1 \mid \mathsf{false} \Rightarrow E_3)\ E_1]\!]\ \rho\end{aligned}$$

10.7 Define a domain **Val**′ similarly to **Val** but suitable for a strict interpretation. Indicate where the changes would be made to the semantic functions to allow for a strict interpretation.

10.8 Define a combined version of *MatchTest* and *MatchEnv* which performs both actions at the same time. It should return a 'possible' **Env** which could be modelled as an element of:

$$\mathbf{Env} \oplus \{\mathsf{FAIL}\}_\perp$$

10.9 Show that:

$$\mathsf{fix}\ \mathsf{F} = \mathsf{F}\ (\mathsf{fix}\ \mathsf{F})$$

by expanding the definition of fix.

10.10 Show that fix I (where I is the identity operator) denotes the totally undefined function.

Chapter 11
Type Checking and Type Inference

In this chapter, we formalize the notion of correctly typed expressions and indicate how a type inference algorithm can be constructed for deducing the types of expressions from the types of primitive operations. (The first account of such an algorithm was given by Hindley (for the lambda calculus) and it was later reinvented by Milner.) As we have already noted, using Milner's type system, a polymorphic expression can have many types, but can be given a most general (principal) type such that all its types are instances of this principal type. A type inference algorithm should produce the principal type of an expression or report failure for any expression which cannot be given a type.

The purpose of describing the algorithm here is not just to provide a more detailed account of the type system we are using, but also to provide an example of the derivation of an interesting and complex algorithm with a functional presentation. (In the literature, the type inference algorithm is usually implemented using a non-functional program, and its purely functional implementation illustrates some further functional programming methods.)

11.1 Type inference systems

We separate out two different problems:

(1) Specifying formally what expressions have what types, and
(2) Constructing an algorithm either to check that an expression has a particular type or to infer a most general type for an expression.

Following Damas and Milner (1982), Cardelli (1985) and Damas (1985) we introduce a type inference system which specifies the relationship between expressions and types (i.e. solving problem (1)). This provides the basic definition of which expressions have which types and is a useful stepping stone for the derivation of an algorithm for the related problem (2). The type inference system consists of rules stating the single step deductions or inferences that can be made in showing that an expression has a type. It thus abstracts away from the problem of deciding which inference steps should be taken next in an attempt to find the most general type and leaves a framework for talking about all the possible inferences.

For example, one of the rules states that:

IF E_0 can be shown to have type bool
AND E_1 can be shown to have type T
AND E_2 can be shown to have type T
THEN **if** E_0 **then** E_1 **else** E_2 can be shown to have type T

This rule can be used in proving that a given expression has a particular type. It can also be adapted as part of an algorithm to check types automatically (which amounts to an automatic theorem prover for the inference system). For example, if the algorithm is required to check that an expression of the form **if** E_0 **then** E_1 **else** E_2 has type T, it should check that E_0 has type bool, that E_1 has type T and that E_2 has type T.

Alternatively, we can adapt the rule as part of an algorithm which automatically infers types for expressions. If such an algorithm is to find the type of an expression of the form **if** E_0 **then** E_1 **else** E_2, it should infer the types of the three subexpressions producing, say, $E_0 : T_0$, $E_1 : T_1$ and $E_2 : T_2$ and also check that T_0 is equivalent to bool and T_1 is equivalent to T_2. In a polymorphic system, *is equivalent to* means *has an instance in common with* rather than *is identical to*. Thus, if the requirements are satisfied and T is the most general common instance of T_1 and T_2 that can be found, then the algorithm can report success with T as the type of the conditional.

We look at the derivation of such algorithms after considering the rules themselves, and variations of the rules.

11.1.1 Assumptions

In the rules we should add that 'can be shown to have type' is relative to a set of assumptions (A) about the types of the variables and constructors occurring in an expression. In the above rule, A should be the same set of assumptions in each case, but this will not be the situation with all the rules. A more succinct notation for expressing the above rule is thus:

$$\frac{A \vdash E_0 : \text{bool} \qquad A \vdash E_1 : T \qquad A \vdash E_2 : T}{A \vdash (\textbf{if } E_0 \textbf{ then } E_1 \textbf{ else } E_2) : T}$$

where A stands for a set of assumptions such as $x : T$ where x is a variable (or constructor) and T is a type expression. The statement below the horizontal line follows from the statements above the line and $A \vdash E : T$ should be read as 'E has type T given the assumptions A'.

Assumptions are similar to the environments (which we introduced in the previous chapter) but associate types rather than values with variables and constructors. There are three different but essentially equivalent ways of viewing assumptions. We can think of them as:

(1) finite mappings from variables and constructors to types (similar to our treatment of environments); or

(2) sets of pairs of the form (x, T) where x is a variable or constructor and T is a type such that there are no two pairs (x, T) and (x, T') with $T \neq T'$; or

(3) lists of pairs of the form (x, T). In this case, any ambiguity is resolved by stating that the first occurrence of a pair with a given x overrides any others in the list.

The first two are really the same since a mapping is defined as a set of pairs with the stated property. The third view is a less abstract representational view. Which view we choose makes little difference in what follows. We use $A + A'$ to mean the assumptions A' along with those in A but overriding any conflicting assumptions in A. (We leave it as an exercise to define $+$ using each of the three views described above.) We also use $[x : T]$ to denote the single assumption that x has type T and nothing to denote an empty collection of assumptions as in $\vdash E : T$. Finally, to express that T is the type associated with x by assumptions A, we will write $A\ (x) = T$.

11.1.2 A monomorphic type inference system

Before dealing with a polymorphic type system, we present the rules for a monomorphic type system (without type variables). The types we assume

Table 11.1 A monomorphic type inference system.

VAR	$A \vdash V : T \quad \text{when } A\,(V) = T$
CON	$A \vdash C : T \quad \text{when } A\,(C) = T$
APP	$\dfrac{A \vdash E : T' \rightarrow T \qquad A \vdash E' : T'}{A \vdash E\,E' : T}$
TUP	$\dfrac{A \vdash E_1 : T_1 \qquad A \vdash E_2 : T_2 \;\ldots\; A \vdash E_n : T_n}{A \vdash (E_1, E_2, \;\ldots,\; E_n) : T_1 \times T_2 * \ldots \times T_n}$
COND	$\dfrac{A \vdash E_1 : \mathsf{bool} \qquad A \vdash E_2 : T \qquad A \vdash E_3 : T}{A \vdash \textbf{if } E_1 \textbf{ then } E_2 \textbf{ else } E_3 : T}$
LET	$\dfrac{A \vdash E' : T' \qquad A + [V : T'] \vdash E : T}{A \vdash \textbf{let val } V = E' \textbf{ in } E \textbf{ end} : T}$
ABS	$\dfrac{A + [V : T'] \vdash E : T}{A \vdash \textbf{fn } V \Rightarrow E : T' \rightarrow T}$

for the moment are generated by type operators including those for function and product types:

$$\_\!\rightarrow\!\_ \quad \textit{and} \quad \_\!\times\!\_ \quad \textit{and} \quad \_\!\times\!\_\!\times\!\_ \quad \textit{and} \quad \cdots$$

starting from some type constants including int and bool. Any other type operators (such as _ list) can be added without affecting what follows.

The inference rules are fairly self explanatory and presented in Table 11.1. Note that we have not considered patterns other than variables in definitions and we have only dealt with definitions of the form **val** $V = E$ in the rule LET. Abstractions are restricted to single cases with variables in the rule ABS. The more complex cases will be dealt with later.

The rules VAR and CON are really axioms stating that variables and constructors can be shown to have the type indicated in the assumptions. We can think of them as rules with no premisses above the line and a proviso written to the side:

$$\frac{}{A \vdash V : T} \qquad (\text{when } A\,(V) = T)$$

or we could make the proviso a premiss as in:

$$\frac{A\,(V) = T}{A \vdash V : T}$$

and then give additional rules which allow us to derive $A\ (V) = T$ formally. (This is largely a matter of taste, but see Exercise 11.3.)

In the rule ABS, we see that an abstraction can be shown to have type $T' \rightarrow T$ (assuming A) whenever the body can be shown to have type T under the assumptions A augmented with the assumption that the bound variable has type T'. We say that the assumption $[V : T']$ is 'discharged' when we use the rule and it is because of rules like this that the assumptions are made explicit and carried around at each stage in a proof. In any particular proof, we may well want to introduce additional assumptions about parameter types, temporarily, and rules such as ABS allow us to remove the additional assumptions when we have finished with them. Similarly, the LET rule discharges an assumption $[V : T']$ which can be added to A when showing that the main expression of a qualified expression has a type T. Note also that the expression bound to the variable V has to be shown to have the same type as the one introduced as an assumption for the variable's type. The repeated type shows a constraint between types of subexpressions (as in the case of APP and COND as well).

Let us illustrate this system by carrying out a proof that:

fn x ⇒ x : int → int

from no assumptions. Thus our goal is really to show that:

⊢ **fn** x ⇒ x : int → int

Since the expression is an abstraction, we clearly want to use the ABS rule. This states that the required result follows if we can show that:

[x : int] ⊢ x : int

Here, we have taken A to be the empty set of assumptions so that A + [x : int] ≡ [x : int]. Now the new goal is simply an instance of the axiom VAR since [x : int] (x) = int, and the proof is complete.

We usually lay out a proof as a tree indicating which rules are used at each step, so we summarize this proof as:

```
          ——————————————— VAR
        [x : int] ⊢ x : int
    ——————————————————————— ABS
    ⊢ fn x ⇒ x : int → int
```

This particular proof is a simple sequence, but in general it will look like a tree because rules like LET and APP and COND have more than one premiss above the line. For example, here is a proof that:

$[3 : \text{int}] \vdash$ **let val** f = **fn** x ⇒ x **in** f 3 **end** : int

The tree has the final result at the bottom and axioms at the leaves (at the top):

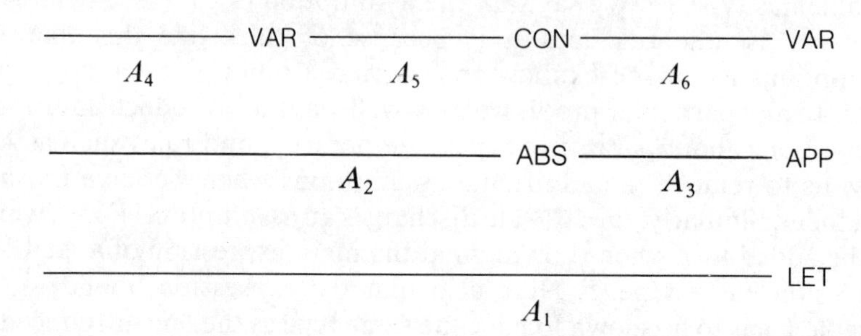

(using abbreviations $A_1, \ldots, A_6$ for the assertions involved, in order to fit the tree on the page: A_1 is $[3 : \text{int}] \vdash$ **let val** f = **fn** x ⇒ x **in** f 3 **end** : int; A_2 is $[3 : \text{int}] \vdash$ **fn** x ⇒ x : int → int; A_3 is $[3 : \text{int}] + [\text{f} : \text{int} \to \text{int}] \vdash \text{f } 3 : \text{int}$; A_4 is $[3 : \text{int}] + [\text{x} : \text{int}] \vdash \text{x} : \text{int}$; A_5 is $[3 : \text{int}] + [\text{f} : \text{int} \to \text{int}] \vdash 3 : \text{int}$; and A_6 is $[3 : \text{int}] + [\text{f} : \text{int} \to \text{int}] \vdash \text{f} : \text{int} \to \text{int}$).

In fact, the tree was constructed from the bottom up and the rule to be used at each stage was then completely determined by the form of the current goal expression. Some exercises are included at the end of the chapter for the reader to practice such proofs and see how automatically they can be constructed.

In the next section we discuss the introduction of type variables which, at first, seems to inject the need for more intelligence in proof construction.

11.2 Polymorphism

A naïve approach to polymorphism would be to introduce type variables and allow the inference of $E : T'$ from $E : T$ whenever T' is an instance of T:

$$\frac{A \vdash E : T}{A \vdash E : T'} \qquad \text{(when } T' \text{ is an instance of } T\text{)}$$

However, such a rule leads to inconsistencies with our intuitive understanding of polymorphism when used in an unrestricted way. To see this, suppose that we have shown that:

$A \vdash$ **fn** $V \Rightarrow E : T_1 \to T$

where T_1 is a polymorphic type. We expect the abstraction to denote a function which can be applied to any argument whose type is an instance of T_1. Now, consider how we might have established the type of the abstraction using rule ABS. In showing that the body E has type T we would have assumed that $V : T_1$. So far, this all seems uncontentious, but now suppose that there are several occurrences of V in E. If we are allowed to assume that any instance type of T_1 can be used as the type of V, then we get into trouble. The trouble is that some instance types of T_1 which we may have been forced to use in such a proof may turn out to be incompatible with other instance types that an actual argument for the abstraction might have. Here is a case in point:

fn x ⇒ (succ x, not x)

Assuming that succ : int → int and not : bool → bool, we could show that the abstraction has type:

$\alpha \rightarrow$ (int × bool)

that is, provided we are allowed to use the assumption x : α to show x : int and x : bool where int and bool are instances of α. However, our instinct should tell us that the abstraction should not be typeable because an argument to the function would have to be both an integer and a boolean for a result to be produced. The type $\alpha \rightarrow$ (int × bool) would allow us to apply the abstraction to any argument (including a string or a function such as succ or not) and thus allow, for example, (succ "aa", not "aa") to get evaluated.

We definitely want to have some form of instantiation rule like the one mentioned in order for polymorphism to work, but we need a mechanism to restrict when instance types can and cannot be used. A similar analysis of let expressions:

let val $V = E'$ **in** E **end**

using the rule LET shows that we would be safe in using instances of the type of V in deriving a type for E. This time, the type of the expression E' which should be used as the type of V establishes a single type T_1 such that all occurrences of V can be safely assumed to have an instance type of T_1. For example, if we tried to type:

let val x = E' **in** (succ x, not x) **end**

using the same assumptions succ : int → int, not : bool → bool then E' would have to have type α (not an instance of type α). Thus succ, not, 3, etc. would all be ruled out. In fact only expressions equivalent to Ω which do not terminate on evaluation should have such a general type as α. This means that we are perfectly safe in accepting the 'let' expression when E' can be typed in the appropriate way because no runtime type error could occur.

It is for this reason that we do not treat:

let val $V = E'$ **in** E **end**

as an equivalent form to:

(**fn** $V \Rightarrow E$) E'

as far as type checking is concerned, although the two forms have the same behaviour (meaning) when they can both be typed. In the former version, the type of E' guides us in determining whether or not the whole expression can be typed, but in the latter version, we have to type check the abstraction independently of knowledge of the type of the argument E' which is much more restricting.

11.2.1 Generic variables and type schemes

We will treat polymorphic types of variables introduced in abstractions differently from those introduced in local definitions in order to gain generality in the polymorphism without compromising safety. Then, if a variable V is introduced in an abstraction (e.g. in **fn** $V \Rightarrow E$), all occurrences of V in the body must have the same type. The type variables in the type given to V are called **non-generic** and cannot be instantiated to instances. On the other hand, if V is introduced in a local definition (e.g. **let val** $V = E'$ **in** E **end**) then we can be more flexible and allow occurrences of V in E to have different instances of the polymorphic type given to E' and to V. (These instances may be restricted by other variables occurring in E' which have non-generic type variables.)

To formalize this distinction, we introduce **type schemes**. Type schemes have the form:

$$\forall\alpha_1 \forall\alpha_2 \cdots \forall\alpha_n . T$$

($\forall$ is called a quantifier and pronounced 'for all') where T is some polymorphic type possibly involving type variables α_i ($i = 1 \ldots n$) but not involving inner quantifiers. We will use S rather than T when we mean a type scheme rather than a type, but note that types are a special case of type schemes (allowing 0 quantifiers).

Type schemes are also called shallow types, and we should denote the true type of a variable by a shallow type. Thus (for example) the type of the identity operator I is more precisely captured by the scheme $\forall\alpha. (\alpha \to \alpha)$ rather than by the type $\alpha \to \alpha$. During the process of inferring types, we frequently use both quantified and unquantified forms, but non-shallow types such as:

$$(\forall\alpha.\alpha \to \alpha) \to (\forall\alpha.\alpha \to \alpha)$$

are excluded. This is non-shallow because a quantifier is nested within a sub-(type-)expression rather than at the top level. Although non-shallow types could be included in a type inference system, they are not included in Milner's system because efficient automatic inference algorithms are not known for the more general form.

In the specialization of a type scheme we can substitute particular types for a quantified variable, thus $\forall\alpha.(\alpha \to \alpha)$ can be specialized by substituting int for α in $\alpha \to \alpha$ to get the instance type int $\to$ int. However, this specialization will be restricted by the 'shallow type' constraint.

If we want to instantiate $\forall\alpha.(\alpha \to \alpha)$ with a type scheme for α such as $\forall\beta.\beta \to \text{int}$, then we cannot just substitute to get the non-shallow type:

$$(\forall\beta.\beta \to \text{int}) \to (\forall\beta.\beta \to \text{int})$$

instead we will have to form the slightly less general instance:

$$\forall\beta.(\beta \to \text{int}) \to (\beta \to \text{int})$$

which is shallow. This idea is formalized in the notion of **generic instance**.

11.2.2 Generic instances

If S and S' are type schemes, we say that S' is a generic instance of S and write:

$$S > S'$$

if S' is obtained from S by removing the quantifiers of S, substituting types for some or all of the previously quantified variables (in a consistent way) and then (possibly) adding quantifiers for any variables in the new expression, except when the variable already occurred free (unquantified) in the original type scheme S. The last restriction means that:

$$\forall\alpha.(\beta \to \alpha) > \forall\gamma.(\beta \to (\beta \times \gamma))$$

but *not*:

$$\forall\alpha.(\beta \to \alpha) > \forall\beta\forall\gamma.(\beta \to (\beta \times \gamma))$$

In the first case α has been replaced by $\beta \times \gamma$ and the quantifier $\forall\gamma$ has been introduced. The second case is similar, but the introduction of $\forall\beta$ causes the problem because β occurs unquantified in the original scheme $\forall\alpha.(\beta \rightarrow \alpha)$. We leave it as an exercise to write a rigorous definition of $>$ along with a definition of $FV(S)$ which we use to denote the set of free variables (unquantified variables) occurring in a type scheme S. Note that if T and T' are types (a special case of type schemes), then $T > T'$ if and only if $T \equiv T'$. We also use $FV(A)$ for assumptions A to mean the union of all the free type variables occurring in the types associated with (value) variables by A. For example, if:

$$A = [\mathsf{x} : \forall\alpha.(\alpha \rightarrow \beta)] + [\mathsf{y} : \forall\beta.(\mathsf{int} \times \beta \times \gamma)]$$

then $FV(A) = \{\beta, \gamma\}$.

In the inference system, we will also allow generalization of a type T to the scheme $\forall\alpha.T$ but this is restricted to the case where α does not already occur free (unquantified) in the assumptions. It turns out that non-generic type variables can be identified with the free type variables occurring in the assumptions (see Cardelli (1985)).

We are now in a position to present a polymorphic type inference system based on that of Damas and Milner (1982).

11.2.3 A polymorphic type inference system

We extend the possible forms of type to include type variables $\alpha, \beta, \gamma, \cdots$ (but we will not deal with equality types here). A type scheme is defined to be either a type or the quantifier $\forall$ with a type variable and another type scheme. Finally, the rules for the polymorphic type inference system are those summarized in Table 11.2, and we explain them below.

Once again, we have not covered all the forms of expressions we have previously been using. We discuss some extensions for pattern matching and type declarations later. The only differences for polymorphism are that:

(1) VAR and CON have been altered to allow for type schemes in the assumptions rather than just types (hence S instead of T).

(2) LET is similarly modified to allow a type scheme to be associated with the variable V, but ABS is not changed.

(3) Two new rules GEN and INST are introduced to allow a type to be generalized or given a generic instance under the stated restrictions.

Although APP, TUP and COND are not modified to use type schemes, we can derive scheme versions with combinations of INST and

Table 11.2 A polymorphic type inference system.

VAR	$A \vdash V : S$ when $A\,(V) = S$
CON	$A \vdash C : S$ when $A\,(C) = S$
APP (as before)	$\dfrac{A \vdash E : T' \rightarrow T \qquad A \vdash E' : T'}{A \vdash E\,E' : T}$
TUP (as before)	$\dfrac{A \vdash E_1 : T_1 \qquad A \vdash E_2 : T_2 \;\ldots\; A \vdash E_n : T_n}{A \vdash (E_1, E_2, \ldots, E_n) : T_1 \times T_2 \times \ldots \times T_n}$
COND (as before)	$\dfrac{A \vdash E_1 : \mathsf{bool} \qquad A \vdash E_2 : T \qquad A \vdash E_3 : T}{A \vdash \textbf{if } E_1 \textbf{ then } E_2 \textbf{ else } E_3 : T}$
LET	$\dfrac{A \vdash E' : S \qquad A + [V : S] \vdash E : T}{A \vdash \textbf{let val } V = E' \textbf{ in } E \textbf{ end} : T}$
ABS (as before)	$\dfrac{A + [V : T'] \vdash E : T}{A \vdash \textbf{fn } V \Rightarrow E : T' \rightarrow T}$
GEN	$\dfrac{A \vdash E : S}{A \vdash E : \forall\alpha . S}$ when $\alpha \notin FV\,(A)$
INST	$\dfrac{A \vdash E : S}{A \vdash E : S'}$ when $S > S'$

GEN with APP, COND or TUP. For example, to prove that:

$$\vdash \textbf{fn}\ \mathsf{x} \Rightarrow \mathsf{x} : \forall\alpha.\alpha \rightarrow \alpha$$

we first show that:

$$\vdash \textbf{fn}\ \mathsf{x} \Rightarrow \mathsf{x} : \alpha \rightarrow \alpha$$

(by analogy with the earlier proof that **fn** x ⇒ x : int → int) and then use GEN to get the required result.

For another example, suppose $A = [5 : \mathsf{int}] + [\mathsf{true} : \mathsf{bool}]$ and that we want to show:

$$A \vdash \textbf{let val}\ \mathsf{f} = \textbf{fn}\ \mathsf{x} \Rightarrow \mathsf{x}\ \textbf{in}\ (\mathsf{f\ true, f\ 5})\ \textbf{end} : \mathsf{bool} \times \mathsf{int} \qquad \textbf{(10.1)}$$

First we show that:

$$A \vdash \textbf{fn}\ \mathsf{x} \Rightarrow \mathsf{x} : \forall\alpha.\alpha \rightarrow \alpha \qquad \textbf{(10.2)}$$

with essentially the same proof as above (noting that $\alpha \notin FV\,(A)$). We then form $A' = A + [\mathsf{f} : \forall\alpha.\alpha \rightarrow \alpha]$ and show both the following intermediate results using VAR followed by INST in each case:

$$\dfrac{\dfrac{}{A' \vdash \mathsf{f} : \forall \alpha . \alpha \rightarrow \alpha}\,\text{VAR}}{A' \vdash \mathsf{f} : \mathsf{int} \rightarrow \mathsf{int}}\,\text{INST} \qquad \dfrac{\dfrac{}{A' \vdash \mathsf{f} : \forall \alpha . \alpha \rightarrow \alpha}\,\text{VAR}}{A' \vdash \mathsf{f} : \mathsf{bool} \rightarrow \mathsf{bool}}\,\text{INST}$$

Each of these can be used to show (along with CON, INST and APP) that:

$$A' \vdash \mathsf{f\ true} : \mathsf{bool} \qquad A' \vdash \mathsf{f\ 5} : \mathsf{int}$$

and these combine with TUP to give:

$$A' \vdash (\mathsf{f\ true,\ f\ 5}) : \mathsf{bool} \times \mathsf{int} \qquad \textbf{(10.3)}$$

Finally, (10.2) and (10.3) combine with LET to give the result (10.1).

Had we worked from the bottom up in this proof, we would again have been guided by the form of the expression. However, in general, one may need to look ahead to discover which instances of a polymorphic type scheme are going to be needed. The exact points where GEN and INST are used and which generalizations and instances to make are not obvious at first and one might have to proceed by trial and error. The derivation of an inference algorithm solves this problem, as we shall see later, and no backtracking search for a proof is actually necessary.

As an illustration of the difference between generic and non-generic variables, we claim (without proof) that:

$$A \vdash (\textbf{fn}\ \mathsf{f} \Rightarrow (\mathsf{f\ true,\ f\ 5}))\ (\textbf{fn}\ \mathsf{x} \Rightarrow \mathsf{x}) : T$$

cannot be derived from the above system for any type T with A as above. We leave it as an exercise for the reader to find where the difficulty lies.

An even more subtle example is the following expression:

(**fn** x ⇒ x x)

This cannot be typed with Milner's polymorphic type system either. The reason is that any type T that is assumed for x would have to satisfy an equation of the form $T = T \rightarrow T'$ and no finite type can be found to satisfy such an equation. (We are assuming that types are finitely generated from type operators, type constants and type variables so infinite types are not included.)

Before discussing the derivation of an inference algorithm, we consider additional rules to allow for recursive and simultaneous bindings.

11.2.4 Rules for recursion and simultaneous bindings

The extension of the rule LET to allow several, simultaneous bindings in the definition is trivial. We just extend the assumptions in the premiss for the main expression and extend the number of premisses to obtain:

$$\text{LET (n)}\ \frac{A \vdash E_1 : S_1 \ldots A \vdash E_n : S_n \quad A + [V_1 : S_1] + \ldots + [V_n : S_n] \vdash E : T}{A \vdash \textbf{let val } V_1 = E_1 \textbf{ and} \ldots \textbf{and } V_n = E_n \textbf{ in } E \textbf{ end} : T}$$

In contrast, the extension to recursive bindings is not so easy. For the non-recursive case, we added additional assumptions for the variables introduced by the definition in the premiss for the main expression E. In the recursive case we need to add similar assumptions for these variables in the other premisses since any of the V_i could occur in any of the E_j.

Before considering schemes, let us write down a version with just types. We want:

$$\text{LETREC (n)}\ \frac{A + A' \vdash E_1 : T_1 \ldots A + A' \vdash E_n : T_n \qquad A + A' \vdash E : T}{A \vdash \textbf{let val rec } V_1 = E_1 \textbf{ and} \ldots \textbf{and } V_n = E_n \textbf{ in } E \textbf{ end} : T}$$

where $A' = [V_1 : T_1] + \ldots + [V_n : T_n]$.

In fact, we need to restrict the types of the variables to ordinary types rather than schemes, because their variables should be non-generic throughout the premisses for the E_i. However, this restriction need not apply in the premiss for the main expression E. The final version of the rule allows schemes rather than types for the last premiss. Given A and $A' = [V_1 : T_1] + \ldots + [V_n : T_n]$, we allow any $A'' = [V_1 : S_1] + \ldots + [V_n : S_n]$ where each S_i is a generalization of T_i ($S_i > T_i$) which does not bind free variables in A. That is, $S_i = \forall \alpha_1 \ldots \alpha_m . T_i$ for any $\alpha_1, \ldots, \alpha_m$ not in $FV(A)$. (An explanation of this restriction is given later where we derive the rule from other rules and use the fixpoint operator to replace recursion.)

The final rule for recursive bindings can now be written as:

$$\text{LETREC (n)}\ \frac{A + A' \vdash E_1 : T_1 \ldots A + A' \vdash E_n : T_n \qquad A + A'' \vdash E : T}{A \vdash \textbf{let val rec } V_1 = E_1 \textbf{ and} \ldots \textbf{and } V_n = E_n \textbf{ in } E \textbf{ end} : T}$$

where $A' = [V_1 : T_1] + \ldots + [V_n : T_n]$
and $A'' = [V_1 : S_1] + \ldots + [V_1 : S_n]$
and $S_i > T_i$ such that the variables bound in S_i
are not in $FV(A)$ (i = 1 ... n)

11.3 Deriving an algorithm

11.3.1 A modified inference system

We noted earlier that it was the rules INST and GEN which seemed to prevent us from deriving proofs automatically. This was because they can be used at any point in the proof and arbitrary instances can be derived and arbitrary generalizations made (subject to the restriction on free variables occurring in the assumptions).

In fact, by looking carefully at the rules one can see that it should be possible to restrict oneself to proofs where INST is only used immediately after CON or VAR to obtain a type. Proofs then proceed with ordinary types on the right-hand sides and schemes only appear in the assumptions until a LET rule is to be used. We use GEN just before LET to obtain the most general possible scheme(s) for the defined variable(s) to be added to the assumptions. This takes away the choice of when to use the two rules and which generalization to make. If we can also take away the choice of which instances to use (with INST) we can derive an algorithm which is completely driven by the form of the expression being typed.

Before investigating this possibility, we present a modified inference system which forces the above restrictions upon us and dispenses with the rules INST and GEN. This is based on the example given in Clement (1987) where a proof that both the original and modified systems allow the same inferences of types to be made is given. To formalize the idea of 'the most general scheme' obtained from a type relative to some assumptions we introduce the notation $Gen\ (A,\ T)$. Formally:

$$Gen\ (A,\ T) = \forall\alpha_1 \ldots \forall\alpha_n\ .\ T \text{ where } \{\alpha_1, \ldots, \alpha_n\} = FV(T) - FV(A)$$

where $FV(T) - FV(A)$ is the set of free (type) variables in T, which are not free variables of types in A. Thus if $S = Gen\ (A, T)$ then all the (non-generic) variables in T are made generic in S except when they are already non-generic in A. In Table 11.3 the new rules are presented. We have only given the single definition case again for LET′, but simultaneous bindings are again a trivial generalization and a new rule for recursive bindings is:

$$\text{LETREC}'\ (n)\ \frac{A + A' \vdash E_1 : T_1 \ldots A + A' \vdash E_n : T_n \qquad A + A'' \vdash E : T}{A \vdash \textbf{let val}\ V_1 = E_1\ \textbf{and} \ldots \textbf{and}\ V_n = E_n\ \textbf{in}\ E\ \textbf{end} : T}$$

$$\text{where } A' = [V_1 : T_1] + \ldots + [V_n : T_n]$$
$$\text{and } A'' = [V_1 : Gen\ (A,\ T_1)] + \ldots + [V_n : Gen\ (A,\ T_n)]$$

We will follow a small proof in this system to show how a type may be inferred automatically. Suppose we want to discover the (most general) type of:

```
(fn x => x) 5
```

Table 11.3 Modified type inference system.

VAR′	$A \vdash V : T$	when $A(V) = S > T$
CON′	$A \vdash C : T$	when $A(C) = S > T$
APP (as before)	$\dfrac{A \vdash E : T' \to T \quad A \vdash E' : T'}{A \vdash E\,E' : T}$	
TUP (as before)	$\dfrac{A \vdash E_1 : T_1 \quad A \vdash E_2 : T_2 \quad \ldots \quad A \vdash E_n : T_n}{A \vdash (E_1, E_2, \ldots, E_n) : T_1 * T_2 * \ldots * T_n}$	
COND (as before)	$\dfrac{A \vdash E_1 : \text{bool} \quad A \vdash E_2 : T \quad A \vdash E_3 : T}{A \vdash \textbf{if } E_1 \textbf{ then } E_2 \textbf{ else } E_3 : T}$	
LET′	$\dfrac{A \vdash E' : T' \quad A + [V : S] \vdash E : T}{A \vdash \textbf{let val } V = E' \textbf{ in } E \textbf{ end} : T}$	where $S = Gen(A, T')$
ABS (as before)	$\dfrac{A + [V : T'] \vdash E : T}{A \vdash \textbf{fn } V \Rightarrow E : T' \to T}$	

from the assumption [5 : int]. Then, we need to construct a proof whose final statement is of the form:

$$[5 : \text{int}] \vdash (\textbf{fn } x \Rightarrow x)\ 5 : T$$

where T is yet to be determined. This final statement can only be derived using the rule APP as in:

$$\frac{[5 : \text{int}] \vdash (\textbf{fn } x \Rightarrow x) : T' \to T \qquad [5 : \text{int}] \vdash 5 : T'}{[5 : \text{int}] \vdash (\textbf{fn } x \Rightarrow x)\ 5 : T}\ \text{APP}$$

where T' and T are both to be determined. The second premiss can only be derived using CON′ and furthermore we must have int $> T'$ which forces $T' =$ int. Similarly, the first premiss must be derived with ABS:

$$\frac{[5 : \text{int}] + [x : T'] \vdash x : T}{[5 : \text{int}] \vdash (\textbf{fn } x \Rightarrow x) : T' \to T}\ \text{ABS}$$

and the premiss of this must be derived with VAR′ giving the constraint $T' > T$ and hence $T = T' =$ int. The proof is complete and $T =$ int has been inferred.

As a longer example, consider finding a type for:

fn f ⇒ **if** true **then** f true **else** true

assuming [true : bool]. We start with the goal:

[true : bool] $\vdash$ **fn** f $\Rightarrow$ **if** true **then** f true **else** true : T

where T is unknown and, by looking at the form of the expression, we see that we must use ABS to get new goals and constraints. The new goal is:

[true : bool] + [f : T_1] $\vdash$ **if** true **then** f true **else** true : T_2

and we have the constraint that $T = T_1 \rightarrow T_2$.

Let us abbreviate [true : bool] + [f : T_1] by A. The next rule to use is clearly COND which gives us three premisses. The first one is:

$A \vdash$ true : bool

which is easily derived by CON′ with the constraint that bool > bool (which is always the case). The second premiss is:

$A \vdash$ f true : T_2

and by using APP, we get further goals:

$A \vdash$ f : $T_3 \rightarrow T_2$ and $A \vdash$ true : T_3

With VAR′ and CON′ these give us, respectively, the constraints:

$T_1 = T_3 \rightarrow T_2$ and $T_3 = \text{bool}$

Finally, going back to the third premiss of the conditional we have:

$A \vdash$ true : T_2

which, by using CON′, gives $T_2 = \text{bool}$. Once again the proof is complete and the constraints give us:

$T_3 = T_2 = \text{bool}$,
$T_1 = T_3 \rightarrow T_2 = \text{bool} \rightarrow \text{bool}$,
$T = T_1 \rightarrow T_2 = (\text{bool} \rightarrow \text{bool}) \rightarrow \text{bool}$

Note that in these inferences, we used T, T_1, . . . as meta type-variables standing for unknown types and these unknown types may involve ordinary type variables such as α, β, . . . and so on. There is a conceptual distinction between meta variables which we use (outside the system) to stand for any type and type variables which are part of the type system and also stand for any type. However, we can conveniently borrow ordinary type variables for use as meta type-variables to simplify the development of an algorithm. This merely means that we allow ourselves to convert the rules to forms involving α, β, ... as in:

$$\frac{A \vdash E : \alpha \rightarrow \beta \qquad A \vdash E' : \alpha}{A \vdash E\,E' : \beta}\ \text{APP}$$

A derivation of Milner's algorithm from rules similar to the ones we have used is described by Cardelli (1985). We discuss our own version of the algorithm which is presented in a purely functional form here.

The algorithm is to work on some initial assumptions A and an expression E, and has to produce a most general type for E which can be inferred from the rules. The key tool needed to implement an automatic inference algorithm is a **unifier** which solves constraints to find most general solutions.

11.3.2 Unification

The unifier is based on a standard algorithm first defined by Robinson (1965). Robinson's algorithm was originally introduced to unify expressions for resolution theorem proving and is at the core of implementations of logic languages like PROLOG.

In this application, the unifier is given two types and finds a most general substitution for the variables occurring in the types which produce a common instance type, thus unifying (making equivalent) the two types. For example, the two types:

$$\alpha \rightarrow \alpha \quad \textit{and} \quad \beta \times \text{int} \rightarrow \gamma$$

are compatible and can be unified with the substitution:

$$(\beta \times \text{int})\ \textit{for}\ \alpha \qquad \textit{and} \qquad (\beta \times \text{int})\ \textit{for}\ \gamma$$

giving the unified type $(\beta \times \text{int}) \rightarrow (\beta \times \text{int})$. A substitution of $\text{int} \times \text{int}$ for α and $\text{int} \times \text{int}$ for γ and int for β also unifies the above types, but it is a less general unifier and the resulting unified type is an instance of the most general one that can be obtained (namely, $(\beta \times \text{int}) \rightarrow (\beta \times \text{int})$). In contrast, the types:

$$\alpha \rightarrow \alpha \qquad \text{and} \qquad (\beta \times \text{int}) \rightarrow \text{bool}$$

cannot be unified because no substitution of types for type variables will work.

The unifier always returns a most general substitution when one exists and reports failure otherwise (i.e. it always terminates). Failure occurs either when two types are incompatible, or when a variable would have to be identified with a type expression involving the same variable. This latter sort of failure is the 'infinite type' problem. It arises, for example, in attempting to unify the types:

$$\alpha \rightarrow \alpha \qquad \text{and} \qquad (\beta \times \text{int}) \rightarrow \beta$$

The unifier will fail with these types because there is no finite type which is a common instance of both. (This is sometimes referred to as the 'occurs check problem'. It is sometimes ignored in PROLOG implementations because it is costly to perform, but it is necessary for correct behaviour with finite expressions.)

The problem of which instance of a type scheme to use with the rules VAR′ and CON′ is solved by use of the unifier. We take the most general possible instance type of the type scheme associated with a variable or constructor in the assumptions when we use VAR′ or CON′. However, subsequent analysis of expressions where the variable or constructor occurs may indicate that the type is too general and that a more specific instance should have been used. Instead of having to backtrack and repeat the inference with this more specific instance, we can just make a substitution in all the assumptions so that the original instance is converted to the more specific instance. This effectively specializes our original inference steps all in one go, so they do not need to be repeated. Similarly, when new (value-)variables are introduced by abstractions and definitions, we add to the assumptions a type which may involve type-variables which at a later stage need to be specialized. When the type variables are non-generic, this specialization needs to be retrospectively introduced in the original assumptions. Again this is done by a substitution which avoids the need to repeat any of the intermediate inference steps.

We will use the previous example:

fn f ⇒ **if** true **then** f true **else** true

with the assumption [true : bool] to show how the unifier is used to obtain the substitution. In order to find the type of the expression (appealing to rule ABS), we need to introduce an assumption about f and analyse the body. We will introduce a new type variable (not occurring elsewhere in the assumptions) and our new assumptions will be:

[true : bool] + [f : α]

When we have finished analysing the body obtaining type T (say), the overall type returned will be $T' \rightarrow T$ where f : T' in our assumptions. Note that because the analysis of the body may have required substitutions, it need not be the case that $T' = \alpha$.

The analysis of the body (which is a conditional) begins with an analysis of the test which will in fact return bool without any substitutions being made. This result is *unified* with bool to make sure that it is a boolean test. The unification of bool and bool is clearly successful and returns the empty substitution (i.e. the identity substitution which leaves variables as they are). The next step is to analyse the left and right branches of the conditionals. These are done one at a time, so that if any substitutions are made to the assumptions in analysis of the left branch, the modified assumptions are used in the analysis of the right branch. Finally, when both branches have been analysed producing types T_1 and T_2 (say), we unify T_1 and T_2. This either fails (in which case there is a type error) or produces a substitution which is applied to the assumptions. The substitution is also applied to either T_1 or T_2 to produce the resulting type of the body T.

In this particular example, analysis of the left branch produces a new type β but a substitution of bool $\rightarrow \beta$ for α will have been made. (This is the result of unifying α with bool $\rightarrow \beta$ when the occurrence of f is analysed.) Analysis of the right branch will produce type bool with no substitutions. Finally, unification of β and bool produces the substitution bool for β, and the type of the body is thus bool. The type of the whole abstraction will be (bool → bool) → bool which is derived from $\alpha \rightarrow$ bool with the substitutions bool $\rightarrow \beta$ for α and then bool for β.

We now present details of the algorithm, beginning with the representations of the sorts of objects we need to manipulate.

11.3.3 Representing types and substitutions

In Table 11.4 we give some (SML) type definitions along with some associated functions which can be used to represent types and substitutions and we also describe the unification algorithm. Types are either type variables or type operators with a list of argument types. Constant types such as int and bool are represented as type operators with an empty list of argument types.

Substitutions are represented as functions from type variables to types. We make them abstract for convenience and safety. The only operations we need to use with substitutions are:

```
emptySub : substitution
newSub : typeVar → typeExp → substitution
substitute : substitution → typeExp → typeExp
compose : substitution → substitution → substitution
```

Table 11.4 Types, substitutions and a unifier.

```
(* ------------TYPES------------ *)

datatype typeVar = Alpha of int
fun next (Alpha n) = Alpha (n + 1)

datatype typeExp = TypeOp of string × typeExp list
                 | TypeVar of typeVar

val bool       = TypeOp ("bool", [ ])
val int        = TypeOp ("int", [ ])
fun arrow t1 t2 = TypeOp ("arrow", [t1, t2])
fun tuple tlist = TypeOp ("tuple", tlist)

fun occurs i (TypeVar j) = i = j
|   occurs i (TypeOp (s, tlist)) = exists (occurs i) tlist
fun isTypeVar (Typevar i) = true
|   isTypeVar other       = false

(* ------------SUBSTITUTIONS------------ *)

abstype substitution = SUB of typeVar → typeExp
with
        val emptySub = SUB TypeVar; ( * identity substitution * )
        fun newSub i t = SUB (assoc [(i, t)] TypeVar)
        fun substitute (SUB f) (TypeVar i) = f i
        |   substitute subs (TypeOp (s, tlist))
                      = TypeOp (s, map (substitute subs) tlist)
        fun compose sub1 (SUB f) = SUB (substitute sub1 ∘ f)
end;

(* ------------UNIFIER------------ *)

fun unify (TypeVar i) t2
        = if occurs i t2 then if isTypeVar t2
                              then emptySub
                              else error "infinite type"
                         else newSub i t2
|   unify t1 (TypeVar i) = unify (TypeVar i) t1
|   unify (TypeOp (s1, tlist1)) (TypeOp (s2, tlist2))
        = if s1 = s2 then unifyall tlist1 tlist2
                     else error ("type mismatch " ^ s1 ^ " and " ^ s2)
and unifyall [ ] [ ] = emptySub
|   unifyall (t1 :: tlist1) (t2 :: tlist2)
        = let val sub1 = unify t1 t2
              val newtlist1 = map (substitute sub1) tlist1
              val newtlist2 = map (substitute sub1) tlist2
              val sub2 = unifyall newtlist1 newtlist2
          in compose sub2 sub1 end
|   unifyall tl1 tl2 = error "TypeOps with wrong arg nos (tuples?)"
```

The first is just an identity substitution which maps type variables to themselves (as type expressions). The function newSub maps a given type variable to a given type expression and otherwise behaves like emptySub. substitute allows a substitution to be applied to all variables occurring in a type expression to produce a new type expression. Finally, compose allows one substitution to be applied to the result of another substitution. In compose sub1 sub2 var, sub2 is applied first and then sub1 is applied to the result.

Part of the reason this type is made abstract is that more efficient implementations can be considered, but we leave such modifications as exercises.

The unifier in Table 11.4 has type:

```
unify : typeExp → typeExp → substitution
```

We use error in the failure cases, but the algorithm could be modified to produce a substitution possible if recovery from failure is required.

11.3.4 Assumptions and states

The representation of assumptions is quite subtle as we explain below. An assumption should be thought of as something with the form:

$$[V_1 : S_1] + \cdots + [V_n : S_n]$$

where the S_i are type schemas and the V_i are (identifiers for) variables or constructors. This suggests a simple list of pairs as a representation. However, by ensuring that a type variable occurring in more than one S_i is either generic (bound by a ∀) at each occurrence or non-generic (free at each occurrence) we can record the generic information separately and replace the S_i by T_i. That is, we can represent an assumption with two components:

```
A = AS (pairs, non_gen)
```

where pairs has the form:

```
[(V1, T1), . . . , (Vn, Tn)]
```

and non_gen specifies which type variables occurring in the T_i are non-generic (the others being implicitly generic). In fact, although non_gen could be just a list of type variables, it turns out to be more convenient to take non_gen to be a list of type expressions such that the non-generic variables are all those occurring in the type expressions. The reason for this is that it makes the addition of new assumptions with or without generalizing them both quick and easy. For example, to add a new assumption [V : Gen (A, T)] to assumptions A = AS (pairs, non_gen) we simply construct:

```
AS ((V, T) :: pairs, non_gen)
```

By not changing the component non_gen, we implicitly make all the type variables in T generic unless they are forced to be non-generic according to non_gen. Conversely, if we want to add [V : T] as a new assumption, we construct:

```
AS ((V, T) :: pairs, T :: non_gen)
```

which makes all the type variables in T non-generic as well.

As an example consider:

```
AS (pairs, non_gen)
```

where

```
pairs = [(Id "f", TypeOp ("arrow",
                          [TypeVar (Alpha 1), TypeVar (Alpha 2)])),
         (Id "x", TypeVar (Alpha 3))
        ]
non_gen = [TypeOp ("arrow", [TypeVar (Alpha 2), TypeVar (Alpha 3)])]
```

The non-generic type variables are Alpha 2 and Alpha 3, so this represents:

$$[f : \forall\alpha_1.(\alpha_1 \rightarrow \alpha_2)] + [x : \alpha_3]$$

This is almost the final representation chosen for assumptions, but there is one more optimization which we use.

A standard technique for improving performance where a large data structure is to be continuously updated in a functional way is to keep the original data structure and record the modifications separately. The record of modifications is only used when we access the data structure to retrieve something from it.

In the main program, we will be repeatedly applying substitutions to all the types in the assumptions to obtain modified assumptions. Instead of actually performing these substitutions, we will keep a separate record of the substitutions that are to be performed (i.e. pending). When we retrieve the type of a variable or identifier, we apply the current substitution to the resulting type.

Thus if the current substitution is θ:

$$\text{AS}\ ([(V_1, T_1), \ldots, (V_n, T_n)], [T'_1, \ldots, T'_k])$$

abbreviates:

$$\text{AS}\ ([(V_1, \theta(T_1)), \ldots, (V_n, \theta(T_n))], [\theta(T'_1), \ldots, \theta(T'_k)])$$

(More accurately, if θ is represented by subs1 : substitution then θ (T) is calculated as substitute subs1 T.)

During the analysis of an expression, we need to refer to the (unsubstituted) assumptions which are passed as a single parameter of type assumption. In addition, we need to refer to the substitution to be made which is passed as a separate parameter (called the **state**). The reason for this separation is that the result of analysis does not affect the assumptions but may extend the substitution. A functional way to implement this is to have the analyser return the modified substitution as result along with a type. In recursive analysis of subexpressions, the substitutions are passed on and modified versions returned for subsequent analyses, but the (unsubstituted) assumptions may only be temporarily modified in subcalculations and are not returned.

Finally, we keep track of which variables have been used at any point in the analysis. This enables us to produce a new variable easily without checking if it already occurs anywhere in the assumptions. A record of the next unused type variable name is carried with the substitutions as part of the state parameter. Since the next available variable name can be modified during analysis (by using a new variable), the modified information must be passed back as a result. This is why the information is kept in the parameter 'state' with the substitution.

New variables are always used to replace the generic type variables when we look up the type of a (value-)variable in the assumptions so that any constraints applied to the new variables do not carry over to the generic ones (which are implicitly quantified). This replacement is done by freshinst which we leave as an exercise to implement. It has type:

```
freshinst : typeExp → assumptions → state → (typeExp × state)
```

returning a modified state along with the type expression. As an example of the use of freshinst, suppose that we have retrieved the type $\alpha_1 \rightarrow \alpha_2$ (from the assumptions) for some identifier. This type has yet to have the current substitution applied, so this is done (by rawType). Suppose the result is:

$$(\alpha_3 \rightarrow \text{bool}) \rightarrow (\alpha_3 \rightarrow \alpha_4)$$

Now freshinst has to use the non-generic type information in the assumptions to determine which of the type variables (α_3 and α_4) are generic. Suppose α_3 is generic but α_4 is not, then freshinst needs to create a new variable to replace any α_3 occurring in the type expression. If (according to the current state) the next unused variable is α_8, then we would get as the final type instance:

$$(\alpha_8 \rightarrow \text{bool}) \rightarrow (\alpha_8 \rightarrow \alpha_4)$$

and the resulting state would signify that the next unused type variable is now 9. As a word of warning, we should point out that only generic variables get replaced by fresh variables, and furthermore this is done in a consistent way so that a repeated generic variable is replaced by the same fresh variable throughout any particular type expression.

The abstract types for assumptions and states with associated functions are defined in Table 11.5. For assumptions we have:

```
addAssum : ident → typeExp → assumptions → assumptions
addGenAssum : ident → typeExp → assumptions → assumptions
lookup : ident → assumptions → typeExp
getNG : assumptions → typeExp list
emptyAssum : assumptions
```

which, respectively, add a new assumption, add a new generalized assumption, retrieve a type for an identifier (variable or constructor) and retrieve the list of types containing the non-generic variables. The value emptyAssum has no assumption bindings and no non-generic variables and all assumptions are created from this initial value. Note that substitutions must be used on the result of the retrieve operations.

For states we have:

```
newTypeVar : state → typeExp × state
extendSub : substitution → state → state
getSub : state → substitution
state0 : state
```

The first of these delivers the next unused type variable as a type expression along with a new state. The second updates the state with a new substitution (by composing the substitutions) and the third retrieves the substitution to apply it to a type expression. The value state0 contains an empty substitution and an initial unused type variable name.

Finally, the main function which uses states and assumptions together to get a fresh instance of the type associated with an identifier is newTypeInst. The other three functions are auxiliary to this:

Table 11.5 Assumptions and states.

```
(* ------------ ASSUMPTIONS ------------ *)

datatype ident = Id of string;

abstype assumptions
        = AS of (ident × typeExp) list (* Assumption bindings *)
                  × (typeExp list)        (* Non-Generic typeVars *)
with
        fun addAssum i t (AS (A, ng)) = AS ((i, t) :: A, t :: ng);
        fun addGenAssum i t (AS (A, ng)) = AS ((i, t) :: A, ng);
        fun lookup i (AS (A, ng)) = assoc A (fn x ⇒ error "Not Found.") i;
        fun getNG (AS (A, ng)) = ng;
        val emptyAssum = AS ([ ], [ ])
end;
(* ------------ STATES ------------ *)

abstype state
        = ST of substitution     (* Accumulated subs *)
                  × typeVar        (* Next New Generic *)
with
        fun newTypeVar (ST (subs, v)) = (TypeVar v, ST (subs, next v));
        fun extendSub newsub (ST (subs, v)) = ST (compose newsub subs, v);
        fun getSub (ST (subs, v)) = subs;
        val state0 = ST (emptySub, Alpha 0)
end;
(* -------- RETRIEVING TYPES, FRESH INSTANCES FOR GENERICS ------- *)

fun newTypeInst i assum state
        = freshinst (rawType i assum state) assum state

and rawType i assum state = substitute (getSub state) (lookup i assum)
and freshinst t assum state = (* EXERCISE *)
and generic assum state i
        = not (exists (occurs i ∘ substitute (getSub state))
                  (getNG assum));
```

```
newTypeInst : ident → assumptions → state → (typeExp × state)
rawType : ident → assumptions → state → typeExp
generic : assumptions → state → typeVar → bool
freshinst : typeExp → assumptions → state → (typeExp × state)
```

rawType returns the type expression and does the substitution, generic determines whether or not a variable is generic (using the assumptions and substitutions) and freshinst uses generic to calculate a type expression with fresh variable instances from the result of rawType.

Table 11.6 Expressions.

```
                    EXPRESSIONS, DEFINITIONS AND PATTERNS
datatype exp  = VAR of ident
              | CON of ident
              | APP of exp × exp
              | COND of exp × exp × exp
              | TUP of exp list
              | LET of defn × exp
              | ABS of pat × exp
and      pat  = PVAR of ident
and      defn = BIND of pat × exp;
                         EXTENSIONS FOR EXERCISES
                ......
                | ABS of (pat × exp) list
     and pat    = PVAR of ident
                | PCON of ident
                | PTUP of pat list
     and defn   = DEFSEQ of defn × defn
                | LOCAL of defn × defn
                | BIND of (pat × exp) list
                | RECBIND of (pat × exp) list
                | DATATYPE of typedef
                | ABSTYPE of typedef × defn
     and typedef = TD of (ident × typeVar list × variant list)
     and variant = CONSTANT of ident
                 | CONSTRUCTOR of ident × typeExp;
```

11.3.5 Expressions

The data types for expressions along with those for patterns and definitions are given in Table 11.6. The main type inference algorithm will be used on values of type expression. We have restricted abstractions, patterns and definitions to simple cases here, but indicate the more general forms which can be used in the exercises. Finally, we can define the main algorithm.

11.3.6 The inference algorithm

The type inference algorithm is called analyse and has type:

analyse : expression → assumptions → state → (typeExp × state)

As we noted earlier, the state is returned with the type expression for use in subsequent analyses after recursive applications of analyse. The algorithm is reproduced in Table 11.7. We leave it as an exercise to extend the algorithm to cover simultaneous and recursive bindings. Remember that new variables introduced in recursive definitions have to be given types with non-generic variables when analysing the right-hand sides (cf. the ABS case in the algorithm) but they can be made generic when analysing the main expression. Some example calculations using this algorithm are given in Appendix 5.

In the next section we outline some other extensions to the type inference rules to allow for patterns, pattern matching and other forms of definition.

11.4 Extensions for other SML constructs

11.4.1 Patterns and match cases

If we extend abstractions to allow several cases with more complex patterns (instead of just variables) for parameters, we need to ensure the following:

(1) Patterns do not contain repeated variables.

(2) All the patterns have the same type in a match.

(3) All the expressions have the same type in a match.

(4) The type of each expression is derived relative to assumptions about the types of the variables in the corresponding pattern.

We will take the first requirement for granted, in stating the following rule:

$$\text{ABS}\,(P)\;\frac{A + A_1 \vdash P_1 : T' \ldots A + A_n \vdash P_n : T' \quad A + A_1 \vdash E_1 : T \ldots A + A_n \vdash E_n : T}{(\mathbf{fn}\; P_1 \Rightarrow E_1 \,|\, \ldots \,|\, P_n \Rightarrow E_n) : T' \rightarrow T}$$

where each A_i involves assumptions about exactly those variables occurring in P_i and involves only types (not schemes) for $i = 1 \ldots n$

This rule is stated somewhat informally. We can, in fact, introduce additional rules to describe how assumptions (like A_i) can be derived from a given P_i and T' (in the context of some A) with a notation such as:

$$A \vdash (P_i : T') \Longrightarrow A_i$$

Such an extension is convenient for obtaining a rule system suitable for turning into an algorithm. For example, we might have a rule of the form:

Table 11.7 The main algorithm.

```
(* ------------ TYPE-INFERENCE (MAIN FUNCTION) ------------ *)
(* analyse : exp → assumptions → state → typeExp X state *)
fun analyse (VAR i) assum state = newTypeInst i assum state
|   analyse (CON i) assum state = newTypeInst i assum state
|   analyse (APP (e1, e2)) assum state
      = let val (funtype, state1) = analyse e1 assum state
            val (argtype, state2) = analyse e2 assum state1
            val (restype, state3) = newTypeVar state2
            val subs = unify (arrow argtype restype) funtype
        in (substitute subs restype, extendSub subs state3) end
|   analyse (COND (e1, e2, e3)) assum state
      = let val (testtype, state1) = analyse e1 assum state
            val sub1 = unify testtype bool
            val state2 = extendSub sub1 state1
            val (lefttype, state3) = analyse e2 assum state2
            val (righttype, state4) = analyse e3 assum state3
            val sub2 = unify lefttype righttype
        in (substitute sub2 righttype, extendSub sub2 state4) end
|   analyse (TUP elist) assum state
      = let val (tlist, state') = analyseall elist assum state
        in (tuple tlist, state') end
|   analyse (LET (BIND (PVAR i, e'), e)) assum state
      = let val (auxtype, state1) = analyse e' assum state
            val newassum = addGenAssum i auxtype assum
            val (maintype, state2) = analyse e newassum state1
        in (maintype, state2) end
|   analyse (ABS (PVAR i, e)) assum state
      = let val (argtype, state1) = newTypeVar state
            val newassum = addAssum i argtype assum
            val (restype, state2) = analyse e newassum state1
            val argtype' = substitute (getSub state2) argtype
        in (arrow argtype' restype, state2) end
and analyseall [ ] assum state = ([ ], state)
|   analyseall (e1 :: elist) assum state
      = let val (t1, state1) = analyse e1 assum state
            val (tlist, state') = analyseall elist assum state1
            val t1' = substitute (getSub state') t1
        in (t1' :: tlist, state') end
```

$$\frac{A \vdash P_1 : T' \Longrightarrow A_1 \;\ldots\; A \vdash P_n : T' \Longrightarrow A_n \quad A + A_1 \vdash E_1 : T \ldots A + A_n \vdash E_n : T}{(\textbf{fn } P_1 \Rightarrow E_1 | \ldots | P_n \Rightarrow E_n) : T' \rightarrow T}$$

We will discuss such rules in the next section.

Similarly, we can extend the rules LET and LETREC to allow for patterns (assuming single bindings for the moment):

$$\text{LET }(P)\ \frac{A \vdash E' : T' \qquad A + A' \vdash P : T' \qquad A + A'' \vdash E : T}{A \vdash \textbf{let val } P = E' \textbf{ in } E \textbf{ end} : T}$$

where A' involves assumptions about exactly those variables occurring in P and involves only types (not schemes) and A'' is a generalization of the types in A' to schemes such that no type variable already free in A is quantified

The conditions are somewhat cumbersome, but can be refined with a notation such as that suggested above for ABS along with use of Gen.

For the recursive case, we want a very slight change:

$$\text{LETREC }(P)\ \frac{A + A' \vdash E' : T' \qquad A + A' \vdash P : T' \qquad A + A'' \vdash E : T}{A \vdash \textbf{let val rec } P = E' \textbf{ in } E \textbf{ end} : T}$$

where A' involves assumptions about exactly those variables occurring in P and involves only types (not schemes) and A'' is a generalization of the types in A' to schemes such that no type variable already free in A is quantified

With these new rules, we can express certain equivalences via additional rules. For example, we could replace COND by:

$$\frac{A \vdash (\textbf{fn } \text{true} \Rightarrow E_2 | \text{false} \Rightarrow E_3)\, E_1 : T}{A \vdash \textbf{if } E_1 \textbf{ then } \mathrm{E}_2 \textbf{ else } E_3 : T}$$

We can replace rules for simultaneous definitions with:

$$\frac{A \vdash \textbf{let val } (V_1, \ldots, V_n) = (E_1, \ldots, E_n) \textbf{ in } E \textbf{ end} : T}{A \vdash \textbf{let val } V_1 = E_1 \textbf{ and} \ldots \textbf{and } V_n = E_n \textbf{ in } E \textbf{ end} : T}$$

We can also replace rules for recursive definitions using:

$$\frac{A \vdash \textbf{let val } P = \text{fix } (\textbf{fn } P \Rightarrow E') \textbf{ in } E \textbf{ end} : T}{A \vdash \textbf{let val rec } P = E' \textbf{ in } E \textbf{ end} : T}$$

when $A\,(\text{fix}) = \forall\alpha\,.\,(\alpha \rightarrow \alpha) \rightarrow \alpha$

Table 11.8 Rules for deriving assumptions from patterns.

$$A \vdash (V : T) \Longrightarrow [V : T]$$

$$\frac{A \vdash C : T}{A \vdash (C : T) \Longrightarrow \varnothing}$$

$$\frac{A \vdash (P_1 : T_1) \Longrightarrow A_1 \quad \ldots \quad A \vdash (P_n : T_n) \Longrightarrow A_n}{A \vdash ((P_1, \ldots, P_n) : T_1 \times \ldots \times T_n) \Longrightarrow A_1 + \ldots + A_n}$$

$$\frac{A \vdash (P : T') \Longrightarrow A' \quad A \vdash C : T' \rightarrow T}{A \vdash (C\,P : T) \Longrightarrow A'}$$

(the fixed point operator fix was discussed in the previous chapter). As pointed out in the previous chapter, function definitions introduced by **fun** (possibly with curried argument patterns and several cases), can be regarded as abbreviations for a **val rec** definition using abstractions. Thus we should also have a rule for this abbreviation. (This is left as an exercise.)

11.4.2 More general forms of definition

In order to deal with more general forms of definition, we introduce some new forms of rule which allow us to derive assumptions from definitions. We also want rules which allow us to derive assumptions from patterns given a type for the pattern. Similar (more general) rules are introduced in Clement (1987) and Harper *et al.* (1987) to which we refer the reader for further examples.

For patterns P we introduce rules of the form:

$$A \vdash (P : T) \Longrightarrow A'$$

which should be read as 'assumptions A' can be derived from P having type T (given assumptions A)'. These rules are listed in Table 11.8 where $\varnothing$ is used to denote the empty set of assumptions. These rules can then be used in rules for deriving assumptions from definitions with the form:

$$A \vdash D \Longrightarrow A'$$

Once such rules are introduced, we can reformulate the rules for qualified expression, but we leave that as an exercise. We define *Clos* (A, A') to be the assumptions formed from A' by generalizing each type to a type scheme using *Gen* (A, T). That is, we replace each $V : T$ or $C : T$ in A' with $V : Gen\ (A, T)$ or $C : Gen\ (A, T)$ respectively. The rules for definitions (apart from data type definitions which we discuss below) are given in Table 11.9.

Table 11.9 Rules for deriving assumptions from definitions.

$$\frac{A \vdash D_1 \Rightarrow A_1 \qquad A + A_1 \vdash D_2 \Rightarrow A_2}{A \vdash \textbf{local}\ D_1\ \textbf{in}\ D_2\ \textbf{end} \Rightarrow A_2}$$

$$\frac{A \vdash D_1 \Rightarrow A_1 \qquad A + A_1 \vdash D_2 \Rightarrow A_2}{A \vdash D_1\ D_2 \Rightarrow A_1 + A_2}$$

$$\frac{A \vdash E : T \qquad A \vdash (P : T) \Rightarrow A'}{A \vdash \textbf{val}\ P = E \Rightarrow Clos\,(A, A')}$$

$$\frac{A + A' \vdash E : T \qquad A \vdash (P : T) \Rightarrow A'}{A \vdash \textbf{val rec}\ P = E \Rightarrow Clos\,(A, A')}$$

Finally, we look at rules for data type definitions. We consider only single data type definitions and we do not treat the problem of type definitions being generative. Instead, we assume that distinct type operator names and distinct constructor names are used in each type definition occurring in a program, and type definitions are global (not nested within function bodies etc.). More general rules such as those described in Harper *et al.* (1987) can be used without such constraints being assumed.

We assume a type definition has the form:

datatype *TD*

where *TD* has the form:

$$(\alpha_1, \ldots, \alpha_n)\ t = C_1\ \textbf{of}\ T_1 \mid \ldots \mid C_m\ \textbf{of}\ T_m$$

where t is the new type operator name and n may be 0 when a simple type rather than a proper type operator is being introduced. We discuss the cases where **of** T_i may be omitted in a moment.

Such a type definition introduces assumptions about all the constructors which are to be polymorphic. In fact each C_i should be given a type scheme:

$$C_i : \forall\alpha_1 \ldots \forall\alpha_n \,.\, T_i \rightarrow (\alpha_1, \ldots, \alpha_n)\ t$$

This gives us the axiom (rule with no premisses):

$$A \vdash (\alpha_1, \ldots, \alpha_n)\ t = C_1\ \textbf{of}\ T_1 \mid \ldots\ C_m\ \textbf{of}\ T_m \Rightarrow [C_1 : S_1] + \ldots + [C_m : S_n]$$

where $S_i = \forall\alpha_1 \ldots \forall\alpha_n \,.\, T_i \rightarrow (\alpha_1, \ldots, \alpha_n)\ t$
for $i = 1 \ldots m$

This is to be used in conjunction with rule:

$$\frac{A \vdash TD \implies A'}{A \vdash \textbf{datatype } TD \implies A'}$$

Now, when any **of** Ti is missing for some i in a TD, we merely change the scheme S_i to:

$$S_i = \forall \alpha_1 \ldots \forall \alpha_n . (\alpha_1, \ldots, \alpha_n)\ t$$

The general case for simultaneous type definitions is left as an exercise as is the case for abstract type definitions.

EXERCISES

11.1 Define + for assumptions using each of the three representations of assumptions: functions, sets of pairs, lists of pairs.

11.2 Use the monomorphic type inference rules to prove that:

(1) [add : int × int → int] ⊢ **fn** x ⇒ add (x, x) : int → int

(2) [add : int × int → int] + [3 : int] ⊢ **let val** f = **fn** x ⇒ add (x, x)
in f (f 3) **end** : int

11.3 Use the representation of assumptions as lists to provide rules for the deduction of $A\ (V) = T$ according to cases for A.

11.4 Give inductive definitions (abstract syntax style) for the sets of monomorphic and polymorphic types as described in the chapter.

11.5 Use the polymorphic type system (Table 11.2) to show that:

[3 : int] ⊢ **let val** x = 3 **in let val** f = **fn** y ⇒ x **in** f x **end end** : int

11.6 Using the same inference system, infer a (most general) type (scheme) for:

let val B = **fn** g ⇒ **fn** h ⇒ **fn** x ⇒ g (h x) **in** B **end**

from no assumptions.

11.7 Give a formal definition of $>$.

11.8 What goes wrong in attempting to show:

$$[5 : \mathsf{int}] + [\mathsf{true} : \mathsf{bool}] \vdash (\mathbf{fn}\ \mathsf{f} \Rightarrow (\mathsf{f\ true, f\ 5}))\ (\mathbf{fn}\ \mathsf{x} \Rightarrow \mathsf{x}) : T$$

for any T?

11.9 Implement the abstract type substitutions using as a representation, (typeVar × typeExp) list.

11.10 Define the function:

freshinst : typeExp → assumptions → state → typeExp × state

which instantiates generic variables in a type to new variables, taking care to replace repeated variables with the same new variable and to leave non-generic variables as they are. The function should return the modified state with the resulting type since the next available new variable may be changed.

11.11 Give a rule for simultaneous data type definitions.

11.12 Can you suggest any way to handle abstract type definitions of the form:

abstype *TD* **with** *D* **end**

with the extended form of inference rules? (See Harper *et al.* (1987) for a solution.)

11.13 Extend the inference algorithm to deal with all the other cases suggested in comments in Table 11.6. You might prefer to deal with type definitions after doing all the other cases. Note that further operations might be needed for assumptions.

11.14 Modify the type inference system to deal with equality types.

Chapter 12
The Lambda Calculus and Combinators

In this chapter, we focus on a canonical functional language. We also look at the relationship between programs written in the notation we have been using up to now and programs in the canonical language. We finish the chapter by looking at the redundancy of variables in programs.

12.1 The lambda calculus

After removing all the inessential features of functional programs, we arrive at the syntactically very simple notation of the lambda calculus (λ-calculus). Although the lambda calculus is rather minimal in form, it is every bit as powerful as any other programming language for describing computations. It allows us to study implementation methods and constructions of languages in an extremely general framework, and many languages can be viewed as just extra dressing or *syntactic sugar* on top of the core lambda calculus (as shown by Landin (1964, 1965, 1966)).

Historically, the lambda calculus precedes the development of all programming languages and it was first formalized by Church (1941) in order to establish the limits of what was computable. Other formalisms, such as recursion equations, can be used to investigate and explain functional languages, but these are equivalent to the lambda calculus, about which there is extensive knowledge. See, in particular, Barendregt (1984) and Hindley and Seldin (1986) and the references cited there.

12.1.1 The syntax of the lambda calculus

The syntax of the lambda calculus can be given as follows, where C ranges over a set of constants, V ranges over a (denumerable) set of variables, E, E_1, E_2 range over the set of lambda terms (expressions):

$$E ::= C \mid V \mid (E_1\ E_2) \mid (\lambda\ V.E_1)$$

This says that an expression has one of the following forms:

(1) A constant (C);
(2) A variable (V);
(3) A **combination** involving the application of one expression (E_1) to another (E_2). The subexpression E_1 is referred to as the **operator** and E_2 is referred to as the **operand**;
(4) An **abstraction** involving a variable (V) and an expression (E_1). This can be thought of as 'that function of V which produces result E_1' and it corresponds to our earlier notation (**fn** $V \Rightarrow E_1$) for describing anonymous functions. The subexpression E_1 is referred to as the **body** of the abstraction and V is called the **bound variable** of the abstraction.

Some examples of lambda terms are:

$(\lambda v.\, v)$
$(\lambda v.(v\ (x\ y)))$
$((\lambda v.c)\ (x\ v))$
$(v\ ((x\ (\lambda v.(y\ v))\ x)))$

Here and below we use $v, x, y, z, f, g, \cdots$ as well as V for arbitrary variables (we also assume that distinct letters stand for distinct variables unless otherwise stated), $E, E_1, E_2, \cdots$ are used for arbitrary terms and a, b, c, . . . as well as C are used for arbitrary constants (but we revert to plus, times, true, false, 1, 2, $\cdots$ etc. for specific constants). Despite the minimal syntax we also drop some parentheses using the conventions:

$$E_1\ E_2\ E_3 \cdots E_n \text{ means } (((E_1\ E_2)\ E_3) \cdots E_n)$$

and

$$\lambda v.E_1\ E_2 \text{ means } (\lambda v.(E_1\ E_2))$$

Constant is used here in a slightly different sense to our previous use of the word. Here, *constant* is used to mean both constructors (uninterpreted function symbols) as well as primitives (function symbols standing for some basic, predefined operation) such as plus for integer addition. The set of constants used is arbitrary and might include basic values such as booleans and integers and basic functions such as arithmetic operators and pair, fst and snd (for structuring data). The *pure* lambda calculus involves no constants at all, and we show later how basic values and functions can be represented with pure lambda terms without constants. When we include constants, we have an *applied* lambda calculus which can be a more practical proposition for modelling programming languages.

The lambda calculus is untyped, so there are no type constraints restricting the formation of expressions. Imposing type constraints reduces the number of well formed expressions we work with and, although typed versions of the lambda calculus are also studied, we will not discuss them further here. (See, for example, Hindley and Seldin (1986).)

12.1.2 Bound and free variables and syntactic equivalence

We need to distinguish carefully between **bound** and **free** variables occurring in an expression. An occurrence of v inside E is said to be *bound* if it occurs within a subexpression of E with the form $\lambda v.E_1$ (i.e. within an abstraction binding v) and the occurrence is said to be *free* otherwise. We similarly say that v occurs free/bound in E if there is a free (respectively, bound) occurrence. Thus, for example, v occurs free in $v\,(x\,y\,v)$, it occurs bound in $\lambda v.v\,(x\,y\,v)$ and it occurs both bound and free in $v\,(x\,(\lambda v.y\,v)\,y)$. We also say that v is free in E or v is a free variable of E if there is at least one free occurrence of v in E.

We regard two terms as equivalent if they only differ in their bound variables. For instance, we regard the terms:

$\lambda x.x$ and $\lambda y.y$

as being equivalent. On the other hand, we must be careful to distinguish the terms:

$\lambda x.y\,x$ and $\lambda y.y\,y$

since one has a free occurrence of y (so its meaning will depend on y) and the other has no free variables. We could obtain the second of these two terms from the first by changing the bound variable x to y, but then we could not reverse the process. This shows that such a change is *unsafe* and the terms are not equivalent.

When two lambda terms E_1 and E_2 are (syntactically) equivalent we write $E_1 \equiv E_2$. This equivalence of terms can be formalized using the notion of α-rules (which are changes of bound variables). (See Exercise 12.1.)

12.1.3 Reduction rules

As well as the syntax of terms, the lambda calculus provides a behavioural explanation of terms in the form of **rewriting** or **reduction rules**. These rules express the steps which may be used in simplifying a term and we write them in the form:

$$E \longrightarrow E'$$

We also write $E \longrightarrow E'$ to mean that E can be reduced in one step to E' using one of the rules on E itself or a subexpression of E. We can express this more formally as follows:

$$E_1 \longrightarrow E_2 \quad \text{whenever } (E_1 \longrightarrow E_2) \text{ is an instance of a rule in } R \text{ (the set of rules)}$$

and:

$$\frac{E_1 \longrightarrow E_2}{E_1\, E \longrightarrow E_2\, E} \qquad \frac{E_1 \longrightarrow E_2}{E\, E_1 \longrightarrow E\, E_2} \qquad \frac{E_1 \longrightarrow E_2}{\lambda x.E_1 \longrightarrow \lambda x.E_2}$$

Here, the horizontal lines indicate that the statement below the line follows from the statement above the line. Thus, for example, if plus 3 2 $\longrightarrow$ 5 is a rule then:

$$(\lambda \text{x.times x x})\ (\text{plus 3 2}) \longrightarrow (\lambda \text{x.times x x})\ 5$$

For a non-pure lambda calculus, we will have rules for each of the primitive functions. We therefore split the set of constants into two disjoint sets: the **primitives** *Prim* which are constants c for which there is some rule of the form $c \cdots \longrightarrow \cdots$; and the **constructors** *Con* for which there is no such rule. In the pure lambda calculus, there are no constants and hence no rules for constants.

Apart from the rules introduced to explain primitive functions, the main rule for the lambda calculus is the (β) reduction rule. This is given by:

Beta reduction: $(\lambda v.E_1)\, E_2 \longrightarrow E_1\,[E_2/v] \qquad (\beta)$

where E_1 and E_2 stand for arbitrary terms, v is any variable and $E_1\,[E_2/v]$ means the term formed by substituting E_2 for free occurrences of v in E_1. (Note that the correct notion of **substitution** is surprisingly subtle so we formalize it carefully below rather than relying on a vague description.) The (β) rule says that an abstraction $\lambda v.E_1$ applied to argument E_2 can be reduced by taking the body of the abstraction and replacing occurrences of the bound variable (formal argument) by the actual argument. Any term matching the left-hand side of a rule is called a **redex** and, in particular, any expression of the form $(\lambda x.E)\ E_1$ is called a **β-redex.** Examples of β-reductions are:

$$(\lambda v.v)\ c \longrightarrow c$$
$$(\lambda v.x\ (v\ c)\ v)\ (a\ y) \longrightarrow x\ ((a\ y)\ c)\ (a\ y)$$
$$(\lambda v.c)\ (x\ v) \longrightarrow c$$
$$(\lambda v.v\ c)\ (\lambda x.x\ a) \longrightarrow (\lambda x.x\ a)\ c \longrightarrow c\ a$$
$$(\lambda x.\mathsf{plus}\ x\ 1)\ ((\lambda y.\mathsf{times}\ y\ y)\ 3) \longrightarrow \mathsf{plus}\ ((\lambda y.\mathsf{times}\ y\ y)\ 3)\ 1 \longrightarrow \mathsf{plus}\ (\mathsf{times}\ 3\ 3)\ 1$$
$$(\lambda x.\mathsf{plus}\ x\ 1)\ ((\lambda y.\mathsf{times}\ y\ y)\ 3) \longrightarrow (\lambda x.\mathsf{plus}\ x\ 1)\ (\mathsf{times}\ 3\ 3) \longrightarrow \mathsf{plus}\ (\mathsf{times}\ 3\ 3)\ 1$$

In the pure lambda calculus, we have only the (β) rule since there are no constants. However, there is another rule called (η) which can be introduced to capture our *extensional* view of functions. The phrase $\lambda\beta\eta$-calculus is sometimes used to distinguish this system from the $\lambda\beta$-calculus (without the (η) rule). The rule is:

Eta reduction: $\lambda v.E\ v \longrightarrow E$ provided v is not free in E (η)

This is a way of capturing the idea of functions being equal if they have the same external behaviour. Unfortunately, the rule does not fit in well when we have constants which we do not regard as functions. For example, we do not necessarily want:

$\lambda v.3\ v$ and 3

to be related. Such problems can be avoided with type constraints by restricting the η-rule to cases where E denotes a function.

12.1.4 Formalizing substitution

The process of substitution is not completely straightforward because of the need to avoid **name clashes.** When a variable is bound in an abstraction, the actual name is irrelevant to the meaning but just serves to identify the free occurrences in the body which are to become bound. If the choice of a bound variable causes problems during substitution, we would like to be able to change the bound variable to avoid a clash. Such changes are justified because we regard syntactically equivalent terms as different representations of the same abstract term so they should be interchangeable. These problems of name clashes can also be avoided by adopting a slightly more abstract notation which uses numerals to represent bound variables as suggested by De Bruijn (1972). This is discussed in Exercise 12.2.

In trying to define substitution, we must take care not to confuse free and bound variables. We note that any free variables of the term being substituted should remain free in the resulting term and should not become bound by unfortunate clashes with bound variables of the term being substituted into. For example, if we substitute $\lambda x.y\ x$ for x in $((\lambda z.x\ z)\ (\lambda x.x\ y))$ we get:

$$((\lambda z.x\ z)\ (\lambda x.x\ y))\ [\lambda x.y\ x/x] \equiv (\lambda z.(\lambda x.y\ x)\ z)\ (\lambda x.x\ y)$$

On the other hand, if we substitute the same term for the same variable in $((\lambda y.x\ y)\ (\lambda x.x\ y))$ (where the bound variable z has been changed to y), we do *not* want:

$$((\lambda y.x\ y)\ (\lambda x.x\ y))\ [\lambda x.y\ x/x]$$

to be equivalent to:

$$(\lambda y.(\lambda x.y\ x)\ y)\ (\lambda x.x\ y)$$

This is because a free y in $\lambda x.y\ x$ will have been accidentally captured by the binding λy in $((\lambda y.x\ y)\ (\lambda x.x\ y))$. To avoid this, $\lambda y.x\ y$ should be changed to $\lambda z.x\ z$ prior to the substitution which can then proceed as in the first example.

We can now give some formal definitions which make this precise. First, we can calculate the set of free variables of a term E, denoted $FV(E)$ as follows:

$$FV(v) = \{v\}$$
$$FV(c) = \{\ \}$$
$$FV(E_1E_2) = FV(E_1) \cup FV(E_2)$$
$$FV(\lambda v.E_1) = FV(E_1) - \{v\}$$

E is said to be *closed* if and only if $FV(E) = \{\ \}$. For example, $\lambda z.(\lambda x.z\ x)\ (\lambda y.y\ z)$ is closed.

Substitution is defined by cases on the term into which we are substituting. That is, the definition of $E'[E/v]$ is described in terms of the cases for E'. When E' is the variable v, the result is just E. When E' is any other variable or a constant, this is left unchanged and when E' is an application, we substitute in both subterms. Finally if E' is an abstraction, we consider separate cases for the parameter of the abstraction. If the parameter is the same as v, then the abstraction will be unaffected by the substitution because there cannot be any free occurrences of v in E'. Otherwise, if the parameter is distinct from all the free variables in E, we can simply substitute E in the body of the abstraction. Finally if the parameter occurs free in E, it must be changed to some y which does not occur free in E or E' and then we can substitute E in the modified body as in the previous case:

$$
\begin{aligned}
v\,[E/v] &\equiv E \\
x\,[E/v] &\equiv x \text{ when } x \not\equiv v \\
c\,[E/v] &\equiv c \\
(E_1E_2)\,[E/v] &\equiv (E_1\,[E/v])\,(E_2\,[E/v]) \\
(\lambda v.E_1)\,[E/v] &\equiv (\lambda v.E_1) \\
(\lambda x.E_1)\,[E/v] &\equiv \lambda x.(E_1\,[E/v]) && \text{when } x \not\equiv v \text{ and } x \notin FV(E) \\
&\equiv \lambda y.((E_1\,[y/x])\,[E/v]) && \text{when } x \not\equiv v \text{ and } x \in FV(E) \\
& && \text{and } y \notin FV(E_1E)
\end{aligned}
$$

In the last case, y can be chosen as any variable not occurring in either E or E_1 (free or bound) to simplify the process. From now on, we can identify equivalent terms and think of any concrete lambda term as just a representative for a class of equivalent terms. Thus changes of bound variables (when necessary) can be taken for granted. We continue to write $E \equiv E'$ for equivalent terms because we want to reserve the notation $E = E'$ for something else, as described in the next subsection.

12.1.5 Reduction sequences and equality

In this section, we look at the *global* properties of reduction and the related notion of equality of terms. The next few definitions and theorems concern **normal forms** and **confluence of reductions**. For these definitions, we assume we have an arbitrary collection of reduction rules, R, on lambda terms given in the form $(E_1 \longrightarrow E_2)$ which respect the syntactic equivalence of terms. We will use $\longrightarrow$ or $\longrightarrow_R$ to denote a reduction step using rules R. As special cases, we use $\longrightarrow_\beta$ for the system of rules consisting of the (β) rule on its own (with no rules for constants) and $\longrightarrow_{\beta\eta}$ for the system of rules consisting of the pair of rules (β) and (η) alone.

Definition **($\longrightarrow^*$)**

We define $E_1 \longrightarrow^* E_2$ to mean that E_2 can be obtained from E_1 by a finite (possibly empty) sequence of reduction steps using $\longrightarrow$.

More precisely, $\twoheadrightarrow^*$ is the smallest relation between terms satisfying the following:

$$E \twoheadrightarrow^* E \qquad \frac{E_1 \twoheadrightarrow E_2}{E_1 \twoheadrightarrow^* E_2} \qquad \frac{E_1 \twoheadrightarrow^* E_2 \quad E_2 \twoheadrightarrow^* E_3}{E_1 \twoheadrightarrow^* E_3}$$

These state respectively that: there is always a sequence of (zero) reductions from E to E; a single reduction is a reduction sequence; and if there is a sequence of reductions from E_1 to E_2 and also a sequence of reductions from E_2 to E_3 then there is a sequence of reductions from E_1 to E_3.

Now consider the following examples of reductions where $\twoheadrightarrow$ is $\twoheadrightarrow_\beta$:

(1) $(\lambda x.\text{plus } x \; 1) ((\lambda y.\text{times } y \; y) \; 3) \twoheadrightarrow^* \text{plus (times 3 3) 1}$

(2) $(\lambda x.x \; x)(\lambda x.x \; x) \twoheadrightarrow (\lambda x.x \; x) \; (\lambda x.x \; x)$

(3) $(\lambda x.x \; x \; x) \; (\lambda x.x \; x \; x) \twoheadrightarrow (\lambda x.x \; x \; x) \; (\lambda x.x \; x \; x) \; (\lambda x.x \; x \; x)$

(4) $(\lambda y.c) \; ((\lambda x.x \; x \; x) \; (\lambda x.x \; x \; x)) \twoheadrightarrow c$

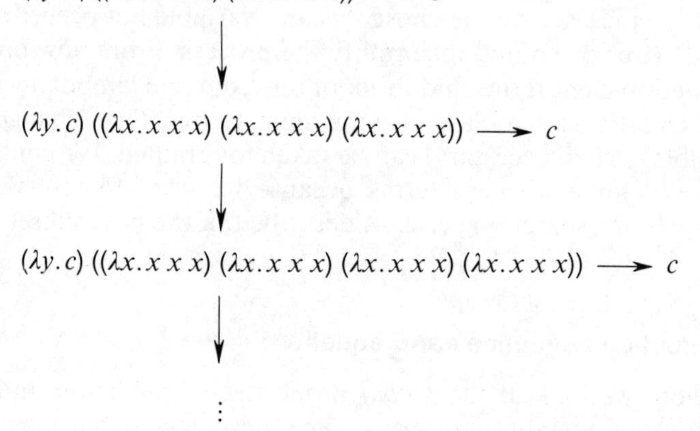

The first of these examples shows a complete reduction of a term with respect to $\twoheadrightarrow_\beta$ after two applications of (β). However, there are two different paths that may be taken depending on which *β-redex* is reduced first (as was shown in an earlier example). The second example shows that a term can be reduced to itself after a positive number of steps (one) and therefore that an infinite sequence of reduction steps is possible. Similarly, the third example can be extended to an infinite reduction sequence involving larger and larger terms. The fourth example demonstrates that a term can give rise to an infinite reduction sequence and yet every term in the sequence can be reduced (in one step) to a fully reduced form (c in this case) by choosing a different *redex*.

We will see below that for $\longrightarrow_{\beta}$ and $\longrightarrow_{\beta\eta}$ such fully reduced or *normal forms* are unique and always reachable from any point in a reduction sequence if they exist. This establishes three important facts about reduction with these rules:

(1) any reduction sequence terminating in a normal form will give the same result;

(2) not all reduction sequences end up at a normal form even if it exists; and

(3) backtracking is not necessary while reducing terms.

The third fact follows because having embarked on a particular reduction sequence we never have to go back to try alternatives since any normal form we can reach via alternative paths can also be reached from the current term.

Definition

We say that E is a **normal form** (with respect to $\longrightarrow$) if $E \longrightarrow^* E'$ implies $E \equiv E'$ (i.e. no simpler form can be obtained by reduction). We say that E *has a normal form* if there exists an E' such that $E \longrightarrow^* E'$ and E' is a normal form.

Definition

We say that $\longrightarrow$ is **confluent** (or $\longrightarrow$ has the Church-Rosser property) if: For all E, E_1, E_2 such that $E \longrightarrow^* E_1$ and $E \longrightarrow^* E_2$ there exists E_3 such that $E_1 \longrightarrow^* E_3$ and $E_2 \longrightarrow^* E_3$. Pictorially, we have:

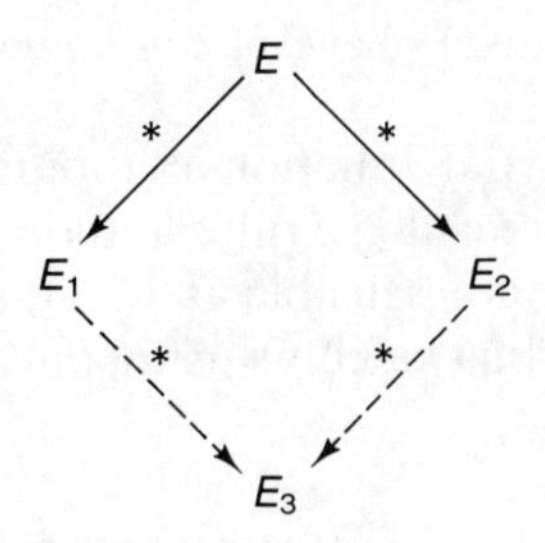

Theorem

If $\longrightarrow$ is confluent, then normal forms are unique (up to equivalence $\equiv$).

Proof The result follows directly from the definitions of normal form and confluence. Suppose E reduces to E_1 and also to E_2 which are both normal forms. By the confluence property, there exists an E_3 which the two normal forms both reduce to. Since normal forms only reduce to themselves, we must have $E_1 \equiv E_3 \equiv E_2$ and hence E_1 and E_2 are the same normal form.

Theorem (Church, Rosser)

$\longrightarrow_{\beta}$ and $\longrightarrow_{\beta\eta}$ are confluent.

Proof (See, for example, Hindley and Seldin (1986) or Barendregt (1984).)

Confluence is a fundamental property which we assume for functional programming. We rely on this when we evaluate programs by rewriting, knowing that we never have to 'backtrack' an evaluation. (This is also one of the main differences between functional and logic programming because, in general, logic programs search for solutions in a way which may well involve backtracking.)

It is easy to add rules for constants which ruin confluence and this must be avoided if we want to do functional programming. For example, a pair of rules such as:

$$\mathsf{c}\ E_1\ E_2 \longrightarrow E_1$$
$$\mathsf{c}\ E_1\ E_2 \longrightarrow E_2$$

could allow non-confluent reductions. Adding sensible rules to express the behaviour of primitive functions should not cause problems, however. A special case is where rules for constants are given in the form:

$$a\ b \longrightarrow \textit{constapply}\ (a, b) \text{ whenever } \textit{constapply}\ (a, b) \text{ is defined}$$

where *constapply* is a partial function mapping pairs of constants to closed terms. Such rules are called δ rules and do not destroy confluence. One way to ensure rules are sensible is by showing that they can be simulated in the pure lambda calculus using only (β). We give examples of this in Section 12.2.2.

Clearly we need to look at different strategies for reduction, since there are sometimes several different redexes to choose from at any stage. We do this in the next subsection, but first we just tie in the relationship between reduction and equality of terms.

For a given set of reduction rules $\longrightarrow$, there is a corresponding notion of equality given by: $E = E'$ if it is possible to get from E to E' by a finite sequence of steps using $\longrightarrow$ in either direction (i.e. reductions and inverse reductions). More formally:

Definition

$E = E'$ if there exists $E_1, E_2, \ldots, E_n$ such that $E \equiv E_1$, $E' \equiv E_n$ and for each i $(1 \leq i < n)$ either $E_i \longrightarrow^* E_{i+1}$ or $E_{i+1} \longrightarrow^* E_i$.

Theorem

If $\longrightarrow$ is confluent and $E = E'$ then there exists E'' such that $E \longrightarrow^* E''$ and $E' \longrightarrow^* E''$.

Proof This is proved by repeated application of the confluence property as indicated in Figure 12.1. If there is a path of reductions and inverse reductions from E to E' then we can break the path at the points where we change direction of reductions and use the confluence property to complete the diamonds. We leave the details of the proof as an exercise. (A formal proof involves induction on the number of changes of direction in the path.)

It follows that one way to show $E = E'$ is to reduce E and E' to see if they have a common form.

12.1.6 Reduction strategies

As we showed in the examples, there can be a choice of rules to apply (and/or a choice of redex) for a given term. We will consider some **reduction strategies** or **computation rules** which select the next reduction

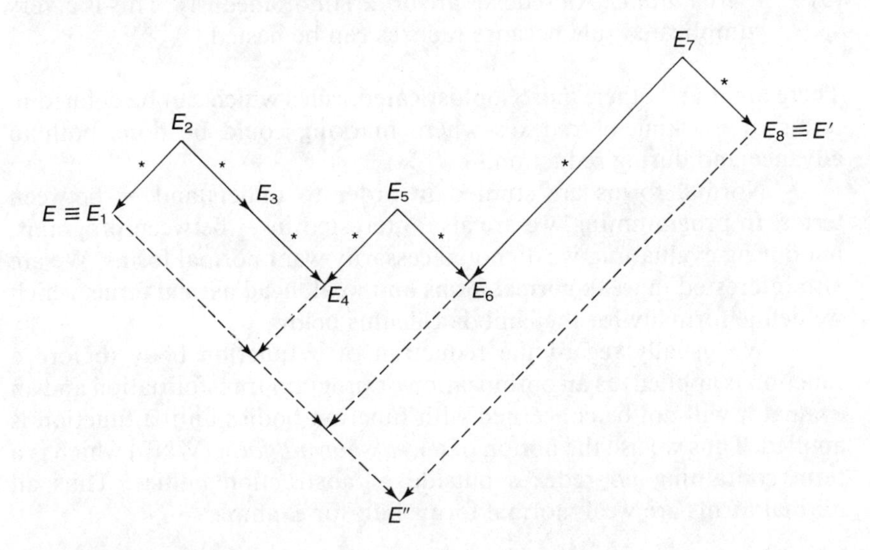

Figure 12.1 Repeated use of the confluence property.

step to be done at each stage in a reduction. We assume that $\longrightarrow$ is confluent from now on, so that different strategies cannot lead to different normal forms. However, we also saw examples where some reduction strategies never find a normal form even when it exists. If a strategy cannot be guaranteed to find normal forms when they exist, it is called *unsafe*; otherwise it is called *safe*.

For $\longrightarrow_{\beta}$ and $\longrightarrow_{\beta\eta}$ there is a simple safe strategy called *normal order* reduction and this can usually be modified to work when we add reasonable reduction rules for constants. Here are some example strategies for the pure lambda calculus and we indicate whether or not they are safe:

(1) *Leftmost-Outermost (Normal Order)* (safe): The next redex chosen to be done at each step is the one starting furthest to the left in the expression. When a β-redex is done, the argument need not be in normal form.

(2) *Leftmost-Innermost* (unsafe): So called because the chosen redex will be the one which finishes furthest to the left in the expression. This means that when a β-redex is chosen, both the abstraction and the argument will already be in normal form.

(3) *Parallel Outermost* (safe): All redexes which are not nested within another redex are chosen and done simultaneously. Note that the chosen redexes cannot overlap.

(4) *Parallel Innermost* (unsafe): All redexes which do not contain an inner redex are chosen and done simultaneously.

(5) *Fully Parallel:* All redexes are done simultaneously. This is a very complicated rule because redexes can be nested.

There are many other, more sophisticated, rules which can be defined in terms of marking of redexes where marking could be done both in advance and during reduction.

Normal forms are studied in order to understand = between terms. In programming, we are also interested in = between programs, but during evaluation, we do not necessarily want normal forms. We are also interested in **weak normal forms** and **weak head normal forms** which we define formally for the lambda calculus below.

We usually regard the reduction of a function body (before a function is applied) as an optimisation or program transformation and an evaluator will not be concerned with function bodies until a function is applied. Thus we use the notion of a *weak normal form* (WNF) which is a term containing no redexes outside of abstraction bodies. Thus all normal forms are weak normal forms but, for example:

$$\lambda x.(\lambda y.yx)(\lambda z.z)$$

is a weak normal form which is not a normal form. (Weak normal forms are sometimes referred to as values, but we avoid this term which we have used elsewhere in a more general sense.) A formal definition of a weak normal form for $\longrightarrow_\beta$ is a lambda term with one of the forms:

$$\lambda x.E \mid c\, M_1 \cdots M_n \mid v\, M_1 \cdots M_n$$

where E is an arbitrary term and M_i are weak normal forms. Furthermore, if we include the η-rule, we must also require that E is not of the form $E'\,x$ in the first case to ensure that an η-reduction is not applicable at the top level. When we have an applied lambda calculus with rules for some constants we must have that the n in the second form is less than the number of arguments (m) for each rule of the form:

$$c\, E_1 \cdots E_m \longrightarrow E$$

This ensures that $cM_1 \cdots M_n$ is not a redex.

Only constructors should be visible to a functional programmer at the top level, so we only see values with the abstractions hidden. The following reduction strategies are aimed at reducing terms to weak normal form rather than normal form:

(1) *Call by Name:* which is the same as leftmost outermost except that no redex inside an abstraction is chosen.

(2) *Call by Value* (eager evaluation): which is the same as leftmost innermost except that no redex inside an abstraction is chosen.

In addition to weak normal forms, there is another concept of **weak head normal form** (WHNF) introduced by Wadsworth (1976) which is useful for relating the denotational and operational semantics of the lambda calculus. In previous chapters, we have used the phrase 'normal order reduction' ambiguously to mean both normal order reduction to normal form, and also normal order reduction up to weak head normal form. To distinguish this latter reduction order, we will use the phrase **weak head normal order**. This is also related to *call by need* which was introduced by Wadsworth, predating the first implementations of lazy evaluation. Weak head normal forms are defined exactly as for weak normal forms except that the M_i can be arbitrary terms. This ensures that any such weak head normal form is either an abstraction or all subsequent reductions must be within the M_i and the head term (c or v) will not be affected. (Of course, the case with a variable v as head does not arise when we only consider closed terms.) In Chapter 8 we explained why in a lazy functional language terms should be reduced to weak head normal form. Subsequent evaluation of the M_i in a WHNF of the form

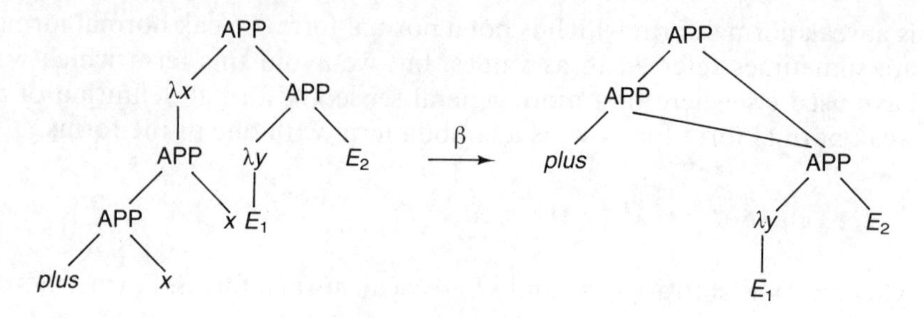

Figure 12.2 A reduction creating a shared subexpression.

c $M_1\, M_2 \cdots M_n$ may be demanded when that component of the WHNF is needed for printing or as the result of another function.

When considering the implementation of functional programs, we must concern ourselves with the representation of terms as well as the order of reduction so that we can be more explicit about whether or not a term is **copied** or **shared** during a reduction. When we represent terms as trees and graphs (rather than strings), we can differentiate between call by name (with copying) and *lazy evaluation* whereby a subgraph is shared instead of copied. The term **fully lazy** is used for evaluation strategies where no redex is ever duplicated by copying. Figure 12.2 illustrates how sharing in a β-reduction can save duplicating redexes. Combinations are represented by APP (apply) nodes with the operator and operand as left and right subtrees. Abstractions are represented as λ-nodes with the body as a subtree and constants and variables form terminal nodes of the tree (or graph). The figure shows the reduction of the outermost redex in a term of the form $(\lambda x.\,\mathsf{plus}\; x\, x)\,((\lambda y.\, E_1)\; E_2)$ to give $\mathsf{plus}\;((\lambda y.\, E_1)\; E_2)\;((\lambda y.\, E_1).E_2)$.

We will return to more detailed descriptions of evaluation and graph representations in the next chapter. In the next section, we look at the relationships between functional programs and lambda terms.

12.2 Translating programs to lambda terms

Various programming constructs can be directly translated into the lambda calculus. We illustrate this for some of the constructs we have been using. There are always several different possible translations, and we aim at a simple one rather than an efficient one. The translation of pattern matching seems to be the most complex aspect of the translation. Alternative translations should produce results which are equal with respect to $\longrightarrow$ where $\longrightarrow$ will be an extension of $\longrightarrow_{\beta\eta}$ with rules for some constants which we introduce below. This ensures that the 'meaning' or overall behaviour is preserved by the translation.

In the next chapter we look at a convenient way to evaluate lambda terms on a sequential machine, so the translation could be seen as a first step in implementing a functional language. For example, Ponder is a language with a compiler based on translation to lambda terms (and also combinators).

Following Hughes (1982) we describe a translation in terms of single steps with the form:

X **TRANS** Y

where X and Y are mixtures of program constructs and lambda terms. This means that X translates in one step to Y and a full translation to a lambda term is achieved by repeating such steps until no more can be done. (In contrast, Peyton-Jones (1987) presents direct descriptions of the results of translations. The stepwise description is more convenient for the language presented here.)

We assume that the programs being translated are correctly typed (so type checking is done before the translation).

12.2.1 Primitives

For each of the primitive functions of the programming language (such as +, *, <, =) we assume there is a corresponding constant (e.g. plus, times, less, eq) and appropriate reduction rules in the applied lambda calculus to which we are translating. We want (for example):

$E_1 + E_2$ **TRANS** plus E_1 E_2

$E_1 * E_2$ **TRANS** times E_1 E_2

$E_1 < E_2$ **TRANS** less E_1 E_2

$E_1 = E_2$ **TRANS** eq E_1 E_2

Note that the lambda calculus primitives have curried arguments since tuples are not built in to the lambda calculus. The corresponding reduction rules will have the form:

eq 0 0 ⟶ true

eq 0 1 ⟶ false

plus 3 5 ⟶ 8

etc.

12.2.2 Conditionals

We can translate conditionals using:

if E_1 **then** E_2 **else** E_3 **TRANS** if E_1 E_2 E_3

This treats conditionals as applications of the constant (primitive) if where the rules for if are given by:

$$\text{if true} \longrightarrow (\lambda x.\lambda y.x)$$

$$\text{if false} \longrightarrow (\lambda x.\lambda y.y)$$

As we noted in previous chapters, such a treatment of conditionals as applications of a primitive with three arguments must be modified if we are intending to use an unsafe reduction order to reduce the resulting lambda terms. An alternative approach for call by value is suggested in Exercise 12.6.

12.2.3 Local definitions

Next we deal with local definitions. We will assume that definitions (D) are either a sequence of definitions:

D_1 D_2

or have the form:

val B

where B are bindings with one of the following forms:

$P_1 = E_1$ **and** $\cdots$ **and** $P_n = E_n$
rec $P_1 = E_1$ **and** $\cdots$ **and** $P_n = E_n$

Later, we will also deal with parameterized definitions (including pattern matching) with the form:

fun $f\, P_{11} \cdots P_{1n} = E_1$
| $f\, P_{21} \cdots P_{2n} = E_2$
...
| $f\, P_{m1} \cdots P_{mn} = E_m$

(The form **local** D_1 **in** D_2 **end** for definitions is left as an exercise.)

Since the lambda calculus has only terms and not definitions, we do not attempt to translate definitions in isolation from the context of some expression. Each of the definition forms will appear as local definitions in a qualified expression of the form:

let D **in** E **end**

First, we will dispense with sequences of definitions occurring in such a context with the following translation step:

let D_1 D_2 **in** E **end** **TRANS** **let** D_1 **in let** D_2 **in** E **end end**

This just leaves the **val** forms to deal with. We postpone dealing with parameterized definitions (**fun** case) for a moment since this is rather messy when we allow curried definitions with several cases.

All the cases for bindings can be reduced to a single case of the form $P = E$ as we will show in a moment. Thus the main rule is for this case of a single ($n = 1$), non-recursive binding. We have:

let val $P = E_1$ **in** E_2 **end** **TRANS** (**fn** $P \Rightarrow E_2$) E_1

Note that we have introduced an abstraction with a pattern. Later, we will give translation steps to remove such patterns when they are not just single variables.

Now, we can reduce multiple simultaneous bindings ($n \geq 2$) to the single case by the use of tuples. We translate simultaneous bindings with:

$P_1 = E_1$ **and** $P_2 \cdots$ **and** $P_n = E_n$
TRANS
$(P_1, P_2, \ldots, P_n) = (E_1, E_2, \ldots, E_n)$

These tuples in patterns and expressions will also be removed by subsequent translation steps.

Now we only have to deal with (single) recursive bindings. For this case, we assume a constant fix with a reduction rule:

$$\text{fix } E \longrightarrow E\,(\text{fix } E)$$

and then:

rec $P = E_1$ **TRANS** $P = \text{fix}$ (**fn** $P \Rightarrow E_1$)

Thus recursion is translated into an application of a fixed point operator to an abstraction. (The justification for this was indicated in Chapter 10.)

12.2.4 Tuples

Tuples can be replaced by applications of primitive functions tuple_n for each $n \geq 2$:

$$(E_1, E_2, \ldots, E_n) \;\; \textbf{TRANS} \;\; \text{tuple}_n\, E_1\, E_2 \cdots E_n$$

Tupled patterns can be removed by introducing some uncurrying primitives (uncurry_n):

$$\textbf{fn}\,(P_1, P_2, \ldots, P_n) \Rightarrow E$$
$$\textbf{TRANS}$$
$$\text{uncurry}_n\,(\textbf{fn}\; P_1 \Rightarrow \textbf{fn}\; P_2 \Rightarrow \cdots \textbf{fn}\; P_n \Rightarrow E)$$

The action of these constants at runtime is described below using additional reduction rules. We also need constants for the projection functions which select the ith component of a tuple. We will write $\text{sel}_{n,i}$ for the constant which selects the ith component of an n-tuple. Now we want:

$$\text{sel}_{n,i}\,(\text{tuple}_n\, E_1\, E_2 \cdots E_n) \longrightarrow E_i$$
$$\text{uncurry}_n\, E_1\, E_2 \longrightarrow E_1\,(\text{sel}_{n,1}\, E_2)\,(\text{sel}_{n,2}\, E_2) \cdots (\text{sel}_{n,n}\, E_2)$$

Thus uncurry_n unpacks a tupled argument (E_2) and supplies the components as successive arguments for a curried function (E_1). There are no separate rules for the tuple_n which are constructors.

An alternative approach is to transform all tuples into pairs so that we only need the constants $\text{pair} \equiv \text{tuple}_2$, $\text{fst} \equiv \text{sel}_{2,1}$, $\text{snd} \equiv \text{sel}_{2,2}$ and $\text{uncurry} \equiv \text{uncurry}_2$. The transformation of tuples is then:

$$(P_1, \ldots, P_n) \;\; \textbf{TRANS} \;\; (P_1, (P_2, (\ldots, P_n)) \cdots) \text{ when } n > 2$$
$$(E_1, \ldots, E_n) \;\; \textbf{TRANS} \;\; (E_1, (E_2, (\ldots, E_n)) \cdots) \text{ when } n > 2$$
$$(E_1, E_2) \;\; \textbf{TRANS} \;\; \text{pair}\, E_1\, E_2$$

and the rules for the primitives fst, snd, and uncurry are:

$$\text{uncurry}\, E_1\, E_2 \longrightarrow E_1\,(\text{fst}\, E_2)(\text{snd}\, E_2)$$
$$\text{fst}\,(\text{pair}\, E_1\, E_2) \longrightarrow E_1$$
$$\text{snd}\,(\text{pair}\, E_1\, E_2) \longrightarrow E_2$$

We could perform some optimizations during translation, such as:

$$\text{sel}_{n,i}\,(\text{tuple}_n\, E_1\, E_2 \cdots E_n) \;\; \textbf{TRANS} \;\; E_i$$

(now seen as a translation rule rather than just a reduction rule). These effectively allow the corresponding reductions to be done at *compile time* (i.e. during translation) whenever possible.

12.2.5 Function definitions and abstractions

An abstraction where the pattern is a single variable can be translated to a lambda abstraction:

$$\textbf{fn}\ V \Rightarrow E \quad \textbf{TRANS} \quad \lambda V.E$$

However, this does not deal with abstractions with more complex patterns involving constructors and abstractions with several cases to be matched against. For this purpose, we introduce a constant match. However, this is only to simplify the explanation and occurrences of match will be removed by subsequent translations described in the next subsection. Abstractions of the form:

$$\textbf{fn}\ P_1 \Rightarrow E_1 | \cdots | P_n \Rightarrow E_n$$

where $n > 1$ or where $n = 1$ and P_1 is not a variable are translated as follows.

$$\textbf{fn}\ P_1 \Rightarrow E_1 | \cdots | P_n \Rightarrow E_n \quad \textbf{TRANS} \quad \lambda v.\mathsf{match}\,(P_1 \Rightarrow E_1 | \cdots | P_n \Rightarrow E_n)\ v$$

where v does not occur anywhere in the P_i or E_i and where $n > 1$ or $n = 1$ and P_1 is not a variable. (The simpler translation given above for the special case of **fn** $V \Rightarrow E$ should be used whenever possible.)

Turning to the translation of (curried) parameterized definitions with cases for pattern matching (**fun** definitions), first we should replace **fun** by **val rec**. So in a simultaneous (recursive) definition we want:

$$\textbf{fun}\ FB_1\ \textbf{and} \cdots \textbf{and}\ FB_n \quad \textbf{TRANS} \quad \textbf{val rec}\ FB_1\ \textbf{and} \cdots \textbf{and}\ FB_n$$

where FB_i stand for function value bindings (with parameters). (The **rec** can of course be omitted from the result if there are no actual recursive references in the definitions. A check to see if this were the case would be a useful optimization.) Each of these FB_i is then translated into ordinary value bindings (VB_i) without parameters. For the special case where all the parameters are variables, we can translate the bindings as follows:

$$f\,V_1 \cdots V_n = E \quad \textbf{TRANS} \quad f = \lambda V_1. \cdots \lambda V_n.E$$

In general, though, we will have to use match and the most complicated case is:

$$f\,P_{11} \cdots P_{1n} = E_1$$

$$\mid\; f\,P_{21} \cdots P_{2n} = E_2$$

$$\ldots$$

$$\mid\; f\,P_{m1} \cdots P_{mn} = E_m$$

TRANS

$$f = \lambda v_1.\lambda v_2.\cdots\lambda v_n.\text{match}\ ((P_{11}, \ldots, P_{1n}) \Rightarrow E_1$$
$$\mid (P_{21}, \ldots, P_{2n}) \Rightarrow E_2$$
$$\ldots$$
$$\mid (P_{m1}, \ldots, P_{mn}) \Rightarrow E_m$$
$$)\ (v_1, v_2, \ldots, v_n)$$

where the variables $v_1, \ldots, v_n$ are new (not in any P_{ij} nor in any E_i nor $\equiv f$).

12.2.6 Matches

The following translation steps show how the constant match can subsequently be removed by introducing a matchrule for each rule of a match. (We use *MATCH* to stand for matches of the form $P_1 \Rightarrow E_1 | \cdots | P_n \Rightarrow E_n$.) A matchfail, which indicates the failure of all patterns in a match, is also introduced. (The constant matchrule will be removed by subsequent translation steps, but matchfail will remain). The arguments for matchrule are, respectively: a pattern, an expression which represents the actual argument to match the pattern against, an expression which represents the result when the match is successful and an expression which represents the result when the match fails:

$$\text{match}\ (P \Rightarrow E \mid MATCH)\ E' \quad \textbf{TRANS} \quad \text{matchrule}\ P\ E'\ E\ (\text{match}\ MATCH\ E')$$
$$\text{match}\ (P \Rightarrow E)\ E' \quad \textbf{TRANS} \quad \text{matchrule}\ P\ E'\ E\ \text{matchfail}$$

Thus, if $P \Rightarrow E$ is the first rule case of a match and P matches E, then the result is simply E, but if the match case fails, then the result is formed using a match with the remaining rule cases. If this is the last rule of a match then all matches have failed and the result is simply matchfail. For example:

$$\text{match}\ (P_1 \Rightarrow E_1 \mid P_2 \Rightarrow E_2 \mid \cdots \mid P_n \Rightarrow E_n)\ E'$$

eventually translates to:

matchrule P_1 E' E_1
(matchrule P_2 E' E_2
(matchrule $\cdots$
$\cdots$
(matchrule P_n E' E_n
matchfail) $\cdots$))

Each matchrule can be expanded according to the form of the pattern for that rule and removed by the translation when patterns are reduced to the simplest forms (variables and constructors with no arguments). The cases for patterns are: variables (v), constructors with no arguments (k), constructors with an argument pattern ($c\ P$) and tuples of patterns:

matchrule v E_1 E_2 E_3 **TRANS** $(\lambda v.E_2)\ E_1$

matchrule k E_1 E_2 E_3 **TRANS** **if** (isconst k E_1) **then** E_2 **else** E_3

matchrule (c P) E_1 E_2 E_3 **TRANS**
if (isa c E_1) **then** (matchrule P (argof E_1) E_2 E_3) **else** E_3

matchrule ($P_1, P_2, \ldots, P_n$) E_1 E_2 E_3 **TRANS**
matchrule P_1 ($\text{sel}_{n,1}$ E_1) (matchrule P_2 ($\text{sel}_{n,2}$ E_1)
$\cdots$ (matchrule P_n ($\text{sel}_{n,n}$ E_1) E_2 E_3) $\cdots$) E_3) E_3

We omit the check for an argument tuple in the last rule, relying on type checking of the source program to ensure that this must be the case. This choice means that we are regarding tuples as irrefutable patterns. The additional constants are defined by:

isa c (c E) $\longrightarrow$ true
isa c (c' E) $\longrightarrow$ false when $c \not\equiv c'$
isa c k $\longrightarrow$ false
argof (c E) $\longrightarrow$ E
isconst k k $\longrightarrow$ true
isconst k k' $\longrightarrow$ false when $k \not\equiv k'$
isconst k (c E) $\longrightarrow$ false

We assume that k, k', c and c' range over the constructors in Con, which is the subset of constants for which there are no rules beginning with the constant (i.e. not primitive functions).

12.2.7 Patterns

To complete the translation, we now have to remove patterns from abstractions generated by other translation steps. We have already dealt with the case of a tupled pattern, and single variables after a **fn**. This leaves terms of the form **fn** $k \Rightarrow E$ for a constant k and **fn** $(c\ P) \Rightarrow E$ for a constructor c. By analogy with the way we treated matches, we see that we want:

fn $k \Rightarrow E$ **TRANS** $\lambda v.$**if** isconst $k\ v$ **then** E **else** matchfail
fn $(c\ P) \Rightarrow E$ **TRANS** $\lambda v.$**if** isa $c\ v$ **then** (**fn** $P \Rightarrow E$) (argof v)
else matchfail

We have included this detailed translation so that the reader can better appreciate why the lambda calculus is considered to be a canonical functional language. The complexity of our translation of pattern matching could be regarded as a problem; however, this complexity reflects the subtleties that pattern matching definitions entail.

Descriptions of other translations are given in Fairbairn and Wray (1986), Peyton-Jones (1987) and Harrison and Field (1988) where correctness and optimization are discussed in detail. In the next section, we consider the possibility of removing constants from the lambda calculus.

12.3 The pure lambda calculus

Perhaps surprisingly, we can represent constants (including primitive operations) within the pure lambda calculus. First, observe that all terms of the pure lambda calculus represent functions since they can always be applied to arguments. So we must think of appropriate functions to represent all the constants we want. We begin with a well known representation for the non-negative integers.

To motivate this representation, consider terms of the form:

$$f\,(f\,(f \cdots (f\,x) \cdots))$$

with n occurrences of f $(n \geq 0)$. We abbreviate such a term as $f^n x$. This expresses the application of f to x exactly n times. Now abstract such terms so that they are independent of any particular f and x to get $\lambda f.\lambda x.f^n x$ which expresses the idea of n-fold application. Such a term will be chosen as the representation for n abbreviated $\overline{n}$. In particular:

$$\overline{0} \equiv \lambda f.\lambda x.x$$
$$\overline{1} \equiv \lambda f.\lambda x.fx$$

We can now look for a suitable representation of the successor function succ, where succ $(n) = n + 1$. We define $\overline{\text{succ}}$ to be a lambda term with the property $\overline{\text{succ}}\ \overline{n} = \overline{n+1}$ (but we do not care what is produced when $\overline{\text{succ}}$ is applied to an expression which cannot be reduced to the form $\overline{n}$ for any n). Thus if:

$$\begin{aligned}\overline{\text{succ}}\ \overline{n} = \overline{n+1} &\equiv \lambda f.\lambda x.f^{n+1}x \\ &\equiv \lambda f.\lambda x.f(f^{n}x) \\ &\equiv \lambda f.\lambda x.f(\overline{n}\ f x)\end{aligned}$$

we clearly want:

$$\overline{\text{succ}} \equiv \lambda n.(\lambda f.\lambda x.f\ (n\,f\,x))$$

Similar reasoning leads to the definitions:

$$\begin{aligned}\overline{\text{add}} &\equiv \lambda n.\lambda m.\lambda f.\lambda x.n\,f\ (m\,f\ x) \\ \overline{\text{mult}} &\equiv \lambda n.\lambda m.\lambda f.n\ (m\ f)\end{aligned}$$

Now consider conditional expressions and boolean values. If we represent true and false by selector functions which, when applied to two arguments, respectively return the first and second, we get a particularly simple representation for if:

$$\begin{aligned}\overline{\text{false}} &\equiv \lambda x.\lambda y.y \\ \overline{\text{true}} &\equiv \lambda x.\lambda y.x \\ \overline{\text{if}} &\equiv \lambda x.x\end{aligned}$$

We shall check this representation for the $\overline{\text{true}}$ case:

$$\begin{aligned}&\overline{\text{if}}\ \overline{\text{true}}\ E_1\ E_2 \\ &\quad\equiv (\lambda x.x)(\lambda x.\lambda y.x)\ E_1\ E_2 \\ &\quad\longrightarrow (\lambda x.\lambda y.x)\ E_1\ E_2 \quad \text{(changing } y \text{ if necessary to avoid any name clash)} \\ &\quad\longrightarrow (\lambda y.E_1)\ E_2 \\ &\quad\longrightarrow E_1\end{aligned}$$

So $\overline{\text{if}}\ \overline{\text{true}}\ E_1\ E_2 = E_1$ as required.

With the same representation of true and false we illustrate a representation for the predicate iszero which asks if a non-negative integer is zero or not. The following definition is rather complex, but it is not difficult to check that it works:

$$\overline{\text{iszero}} \equiv \lambda x.x\ (\lambda y.\lambda z.\overline{\text{false}})\ (\lambda x.x)\ \overline{\text{true}}$$

We leave it as an exercise to show that:

$$\overline{\mathsf{iszero}\ \overline{0}} = \overline{\mathsf{true}}$$
$$\overline{\mathsf{iszero}\ \overline{n+1}} = \overline{\mathsf{false}}$$

Another problem is the representation of pairs, or more specifically the functions pair, fst and snd which satisfy:

$$\mathsf{fst}\ (\mathsf{pair}\ E_1\ E_2) = E_1$$
$$\mathsf{snd}\ (\mathsf{pair}\ E_1\ E_2) = E_2$$

One solution is to think of the object formed by pair E_1 E_2 as a function which when applied to a projection function returns either E_1 or E_2. Thus we choose:

$$\overline{\mathsf{pair}} \equiv \lambda x.\lambda y.\lambda f.f\ x\ y$$

The appropriate projection functions are $\overline{\mathsf{true}}$ and $\overline{\mathsf{false}}$ because:

$$\overline{\mathsf{pair}}\ x\ y\ \overline{\mathsf{true}} \longrightarrow^{*} \overline{\mathsf{true}}\ x\ y \equiv (\lambda x.\lambda y.x)\ x\ y \longrightarrow^{*} x$$
$$\overline{\mathsf{pair}}\ x\ y\ \overline{\mathsf{false}} \longrightarrow^{*} \overline{\mathsf{false}}\ x\ y \equiv (\lambda x.\lambda y.y)\ x\ y \longrightarrow^{*} y$$

The selectors fst and snd are simply defined to supply a pair with the corresponding projection function. If g stands for a pair of the form $\overline{\mathsf{pair}}\ x\ y$ then:

$$\overline{\mathsf{fst}} \equiv \lambda g.g\ \overline{\mathsf{true}} \equiv \lambda g.g\ (\lambda x.\lambda y.x)$$
$$\overline{\mathsf{snd}} \equiv \lambda g.g\ \overline{\mathsf{false}} \equiv \lambda g.g\ (\lambda x.\lambda y.y)$$

A complete proof that all the recursive (i.e. computable) functions can be represented in the pure lambda calculus is beyond the scope of this book, but we will give one more example, namely the representation of the fixed point or recursion operator (fix). We are looking for a term $\overline{\mathsf{fix}}$ with the property:

$$\overline{\mathsf{fix}}\ E = E\ (\overline{\mathsf{fix}}\ E)$$

for any lambda term E. As we have seen, such a term would allow us to simulate recursion using ordinary function application, so it is perhaps a little surprising that such a term exists. The *trick* in the construction lies in the use of self application which is unrestricted in the (untyped) lambda calculus. A solution drops out quite simply if one assumes that $\overline{\mathsf{fix}}\ E$ reduces to the form WW (for some W depending on E). You may like to try and discover a solution for yourself before looking at the solution given in Exercise 12.13. The solution given in the exercise is usually called Y, but it is by no means unique.

12.4 Combinators

In this section we show how abstractions and variables can be removed from programs to obtain even simpler forms which are built with a special class of constants which are called **combinators**.

12.4.1 Redundancy of abstractions and variables

If we consider lambda terms without any abstractions, we see that they must be entirely composed of (combinations of) constants and free variables. We call such terms **applicative forms** (AFs) and when they contain no variables, they are called **constant applicative forms** (CAFs). We will show that it is possible to convert lambda terms into AFs so that closed terms (programs) become CAFs. First, we consider how we have been using variables.

In the lambda calculus, the purpose of a variable like x is to mark positions in expressions in order that we may *abstract* the expression into a function by binding the variable in a lambda abstraction. This use directly corresponds to our use of parameters as an aid in function definitions. We saw in earlier chapters that it was sometimes possible to define a function without parameters (e.g. **val** $f = g \circ h$), but often, parameters were useful to help express the combination of function applications needed to produce the result.

Similarly, the (β)-reduction rule:

$$(\lambda x.E)\, E_1 \longrightarrow E\,[E_1/x]$$

clearly shows that the parameter (bound variable) is used in E to mark the places where the argument E_1 is to be substituted when we apply the abstraction. One might, therefore, ask the following question: is it always possible to describe a function without parameters? or, equivalently, is it always possible to construct a pure combination M such that M behaves like the abstraction $\lambda x.E$?

To say that M behaves like $\lambda x.E$ we mean that when it is applied to any expression E_1, say, we have that:

$$M\,E_1 = E\,[E_1/x] = (\lambda x.E)\,E_1$$

and of course we want to know if we can find such an M in a systematic way for any $\lambda x.E$. The answer is that it is always possible if we have primitives which can perform the action of distributing the argument to the appropriate places in the expression (i.e. the places marked by x in $\lambda x.E$. Perhaps surprisingly only two such primitives are necessary, namely S and K. Their action may be described by the following rules:

$$\begin{aligned} \mathsf{S}\ x\ y\ z &\longrightarrow (x\ z)\ (y\ z) \\ \mathsf{K}\ x\ y &\longrightarrow x \end{aligned}$$

So K behaves like $\lambda x.\lambda y.x$ and S behaves like $\lambda x.\lambda y.\lambda z.x\ z\ (y\ z)$. These special constants are called *combinators* and, in general, any constant defined by a rule with the form:

$$c\ x_1 \cdots x_n \longrightarrow M$$

where M is a pure combination of constants and arguments $x_1, \ldots, x_n$ is called a combinator.

Another combinator is I (the identity combinator) which corresponds to the lambda term $\lambda x.x$ and for which the rule is:

$$\mathsf{I}\ E \longrightarrow E$$

We can build I using S and K as follows: if we define $\mathsf{I} \equiv \mathsf{S}\ \mathsf{K}\ \mathsf{K}$ then we see that:

$$\begin{aligned} \mathsf{S}\ \mathsf{K}\ \mathsf{K}\ E &\longrightarrow \mathsf{K}\ E\ (\mathsf{K}\ E) && \text{by the rule for S} \\ &\longrightarrow E && \text{by the rule for K} \end{aligned}$$

Similarly any lambda-term or other combinator can be described as a pure combination using S and K, thus removing the need for lambda-abstraction and hence the need for variables. In particular, closed terms of the pure lambda calculus can be converted to combinations of just S and K and nothing else. This is a remarkable result, demonstrating that all programs can be described entirely by combinations of two primitives!

Although S and K are the only combinators we need in theory, there are some other useful combinators we shall be referring to later. For example, consider the combinator B which composes two functions (B is just prefix notation for $\circ$):

$$\mathsf{B}\ E_1\ E_2\ E_3 \longrightarrow E_1\ (E_2\ E_3)$$

This can be written as S (KS) K for consider:

$$\begin{aligned}\mathsf{S}\,(\mathsf{K}\,\mathsf{S})\,\mathsf{K}\,E_1\,E_2\,E_3 &\longrightarrow (\mathsf{K}\,\mathsf{S}\,E_1)\,(\mathsf{K}\,E_1)\,E_2\,E_3\\ &\longrightarrow \mathsf{S}\,(\mathsf{K}\,E_1)\,E_2\,E_3\\ &\longrightarrow (\mathsf{K}\,E_1 E_3)\,(E_2 E_3)\\ &\longrightarrow E_1\,(E_2\,E_3)\end{aligned}$$

Note that, because of our convention of left association, we have:

$$\mathsf{S}\,(\mathsf{KS})\,\mathsf{K}\,E_1\,E_2\,E_3 \not\equiv \mathsf{S}\,(\mathsf{KS})\,(\mathsf{K}\,E_1\,E_2)\,E_3$$

So only the S rule is applicable in the first line of this example.

Now take C defined by:

$$\mathsf{C}\,x\,y\,z \longrightarrow x\,z\,y$$

then C is equivalent to S (BBS) (KK).

12.4.2 An abstraction algorithm

We now demonstrate the above claims about S and K, by giving an abstraction algorithm which converts abstractions to AFs. To illustrate the method, recall that earlier we said that a (non-recursive) definition of the form **fun** $f\,x = E'\,x$ where E' does not involve x could be rewritten as **val** $f = E'$ thus dispensing with the need for the parameter. If the parameter x is distributed differently on the right-hand side, we need to re-express the right-hand side using functions to distribute x to the correct places so that it has the form $E'\,x$ for some E' not containing any free x. The abstraction algorithm shows us how to transform an arbitrary right-hand side E with respect to a given parameter x into such an E' with the property that $E'\,x = E$.

We will write ${}_x[E]$ for the combination E' obtained by abstracting out the variable x from E in this way. Actually, we assume that E is already an AF and then ${}_x[E]$ is the AF corresponding to the lambda term $\lambda x\,.\,E$. To deal with nested abstractions, we define ${}_{\mathsf{Abs}}[\_]$ which converts any term to an AF by converting each abstraction in turn, beginning with the innermost ones so that the body is always an AF.

The algorithms are defined by cases for E (the first case to apply is the one used in converting a term):

$$_x[E] \equiv \mathsf{K}\ E \text{ when } x \notin FV(E)$$
$$_x[x] \equiv \mathsf{I} \text{ (i.e. SKK)}$$
$$_x[E_1\ x] \equiv E_1 \text{ when } x \notin FV(E_1)$$
$$_x[E_1\ E_2] \equiv \mathsf{S}\ _x[E_1]\ _x[E_2]$$

There is no abstraction case of the form $\lambda v\,.\,E_1$ since this algorithm is only used on AFs E. Then, to remove all lambda abstractions from an arbitrary term, we can work from the innermost lambda abstraction outwards, converting $\lambda v\,.\,M$ to $_v[M]$:

$$_{\mathsf{Abs}}[x] \equiv x$$
$$_{\mathsf{Abs}}[E_1\ E_2] \equiv (_{\mathsf{Abs}}[E_1]\ _{\mathsf{Abs}}[E_2])$$
$$_{\mathsf{Abs}}[\lambda x.E] \equiv\ _x[_{\mathsf{Abs}}[E]]$$

Here are some examples:

$$_x[f\,x\,x] \equiv \mathsf{S}\ _x[f\,x]\ _x[x]$$
$$\equiv \mathsf{S}\ f\ \mathsf{I}$$

To find the CAF corresponding to the term $\lambda f.\lambda x.f\,x\,x$, we first calculate that:

$$_{\mathsf{Abs}}[\lambda f.\,\lambda x\,.\,f\,x\,x] \equiv\ _f[_x[f\,x\,x]]$$

and:

$$_f[_x[f\,x\,x]] \equiv\ _f[\mathsf{S}\ f\ \mathsf{I}] \equiv \mathsf{S}\ _f[\mathsf{S}\ f]\ _f[\mathsf{I}] \equiv \mathsf{S}\ \mathsf{S}\ (\mathsf{K}\ \mathsf{I})$$

We can check the result by calculating:

$$\begin{aligned} \mathsf{SS}\ (\mathsf{KI})\,f\,x &\longrightarrow \mathsf{S}\,f\,(\mathsf{K}\ \mathsf{I}\ f)\ x \text{ by the rule for S} \\ &\longrightarrow f\,x\ (\mathsf{K}\ \mathsf{I}\ f\,x) \text{ by the rule for S} \\ &\longrightarrow f\,x\ (\mathsf{I}\ x) \text{ by the rule for K} \\ &\longrightarrow^{*} f\,x\,x \text{ by the (derived) rule for I} \end{aligned}$$

For another example, consider the following term occurring in the definition of factorial (but with the variable f occurring free):

```
fn x ⇒ if x = 0 then 1 else f (x − 1) * x
```

After translation to lambda terms (along with a little optimization) such a definition might appear as:

```
λx . if (eq 0 x) 1 (times ( f (minus x 1)) x)
```

The x can be removed using the abstraction algorithm:

```
 x[if (eq 0 x) 1 (times x (f (minus x 1)))]
≡ S x[(if (eq 0 x) 1))] x[times x (f (minus x 1))]
≡ S (S x[if (eq 0 x)] x[1]) (S times S x[f (minus x 1)])
≡ S (S (S (K if) (eq 0)) (K 1)) (S times x[f (minus x 1)])
≡ S (S (S (K if) (eq 0)) (K 1)) (S times (S (K f) (S minus (K 1))))
```

This gives us a term without involving parameter x. However, a definition of factorial still involves a recursive reference to f, so if M abbreviates the resulting combination, we must rewrite the recursive definition **val rec** f = M using fix:

val f = fix (λf.M)

and then remove the λf. from this expression using the algorithm again (calculating $_{f}[M]$).

From a practical point of view, the resulting representations of programs are far too large (and therefore inefficient). Many improvements can be made by extending the set of combinators used as primitives. For example, we observe that when only one of the two expressions in a combination $E_1\ E_2$ involves free occurrences of x, the abstraction of x produces results of the form:

S (K E_1) M_2 or S M_1 (K E_2)

where $M_i \equiv {}_x[E_i]$. These can be rewritten as, respectively:

B E_1 M_2 and C M_1 E_2

Using this improvement on the factorial example, we get:

```
S (C (B if (eq 0)) 1) (S times (B f (C minus 1)))
```

The possibility of removing variables to obtain combinatory equivalents of lambda terms is a somewhat remarkable result first shown by Curry and Feys (1958). Its practical application to the implementation of functional languages was shown much later by Turner (1979a, b). Many further improvements have been suggested in the literature. In particular Hughes (1982) and also Johnsson (1984) show near optimal methods whereby the choice of combinators is derived from analysis of the program rather than determined in advance. On the other hand, fixing the set of combinators in advance allows the design of specific hardware for combinator evaluation (see, for example, Stoye *et al.* (1984)).

The next chapter makes use of some of the concepts and definitions used in this chapter to explain some practical functional programming language implementation methods.

EXERCISES

12.1 We can formalize $E_1 \equiv E_2$ as meaning E_1 and E_2 are α-interconvertible. Give a formal definition of α-conversion which involves a sequence of safe changes of bound variables in subexpressions of an expression.

12.2 (De Bruijn notation.) Since bound variables only serve to associate applied occurrences of a variable with the correct binding occurrence, we could replace them with some sort of pointer (from each applied occurrence to the associated binding occurrence). A particularly simple way to do this is to use an integer to point to the appropriate λ as described below.

In general, an applied occurrence of a bound variable will be nested within one or more abstractions. For example, in $\lambda x.(\lambda y.\lambda z.y\,7)\,9$ the applied occurrence of y is nested within the body of three abstractions. The innermost of these has bound variable z. The next one out has bound variable y (which is the binding occurrence we want to associate with the applied occurrence of y). Outside this is another abstraction with bound variable x.

We will remove all the binding occurrences of variables (leaving just the λs) and replace applied occurrences of bound variables by a $\#n$ where n is a numeral indicating how many surrounding λs there are between this occurrence and the correct binding λ for the variable. In the above example, there is one intermediate λ (namely $\lambda z.$) as we go up the levels of nested expressions before we find the first $\lambda y.$. Thus the example can be represented in the De Bruijn form as:

$$\lambda\,(\lambda\lambda\ \#1\ 7)\ 9$$

As a more complex example, we can convert:

$$\lambda y.(\lambda v.(\lambda z.\lambda x.y\ x\ z)\ (\lambda x.x\ v))\ y\ z$$

to:

$$\lambda\,(\lambda\,(\lambda\lambda\ \#3\ \#0\ \#1)\ (\lambda\ \#0\ \#1))\ \#0\ z$$

Note that the rightmost z was free so it remains as a variable in the result. The bound occurrence of v is converted to #1 (and not #3) because it is nested within one intervening abstraction of x before the associated abstraction of v. The other abstractions of x and z which occur textually between the $\lambda v.$ and v are not counted because these abstractions do not enclose the v and we are only counting the nested levels of λs. (Draw syntax trees for the example before and after the conversion.)

The main part of this exercise is to describe formally a conversion algorithm which generates the De Bruijn form from an arbitrary term. (Hint: Use an extra parameter which is a list of variables associated with enclosing λs and which is initially [ ].)

12.3 Define $BV(E)$, the set of bound variables of E by analogy with $FV(E)$.

12.4 Formalize the notion that a set of reduction rules on terms respect syntactic term equivalence.

12.5 Investigate all the possible reduction sequences (for $\longrightarrow_\beta$) starting with:

(a) (λx.plus x x) ((λy. times y y) (plus 5 5))
(b) (λg.g plus (g times (g plus 5))) (λf.λx.f x x)
(c) (λv.λf.f (f v)) ((λz.z z) (λz.z z)) ((λx.λy.x) 5)

12.6 Show that the rules for if ensure that:

if true E_1 $E_2 = E_1$
if false E_1 $E_2 = E_2$

Use the technique of delaying expressions by abstractions (e.g. making E into $\lambda x.E$ where $x \notin FV(E)$) to obtain a suitable translation of conditionals for call by value. Give the new rule appropriate for if in this case.

12.7 Translate the following into lambda terms:

(a) **let fun** f x = plus x x **in** f (f 3) **end**
(b) **let fun** f (x, y) = **if** less x 1 **then** y **else** f (minus x 1, g x y)
  and g x = times x
in f (z, y) **end**

12.8 In the text, translations were not given for definitions of the form:

local D_1 **in** D_2 **end**

It is necessary to deal with these in the context of a qualified expression (i.e. as the definition part of a **let** D **in** E **end**). Give sufficient translation rules to remove all such local definitions.

12.9 Prove that:

$$\overline{\mathsf{succ}\ \overline{n}} = \overline{n+1}$$
$$\overline{\mathsf{add}\ \overline{n}\ \overline{m}} = \overline{n+m}$$
$$\overline{\mathsf{mult}\ \overline{n}\ \overline{m}} = \overline{n*m}$$

(In fact $=$ can be replaced by $\rightarrow^*$ for these examples but this stronger result is not a necessary condition for the representation to be acceptable.)

12.10 Prove that $\overline{\mathsf{if}}\ \overline{\mathsf{false}}\ E_1 E_2 = E_2$.

12.11 Prove that:

$$\overline{\mathsf{iszero}}\ \overline{0} = \overline{\mathsf{true}} \qquad \overline{\mathsf{iszero}}\ \overline{n+1} = \overline{\mathsf{false}}$$

(remembering that $\overline{n+1}\ E_1\ E_2 \rightarrow E_1\ (\overline{n}\ E_1\ E_2)$).

12.12 Prove that:

$$\overline{\mathsf{fst}}\ (\overline{\mathsf{pair}}\ E_1\ E_2) = E_1 \qquad \overline{\mathsf{snd}}\ (\overline{\mathsf{pair}}\ E_1\ E_2) = E_2$$

12.13 Show that if:

$$\mathsf{Y} \equiv \lambda f.(\lambda x.f\ (x\ x))\ (\lambda x.f\ (x\ x))$$

then Y satisfies the fixed point finding property; that is:

$$\mathsf{Y}\ E = E\ (\mathsf{Y}\ E)$$

for any term E.

12.14 Show that:

$$\mathsf{Y}\ (\lambda f.(\lambda n.\ \overline{\mathsf{if}}\ (\overline{\mathsf{iszero}}\ n)\ \overline{1}\ (\overline{\mathsf{mult}}\ n\ (f\ (\overline{\mathsf{pred}}\ n)))\ \overline{3} = \overline{6}$$

where you may assume $\overline{\mathsf{pred}}\ \overline{n+1} = \overline{n}$.

12.15 Show that:

$$\mathsf{Y}' \equiv \lambda f.\ (\lambda g.\lambda x.f\ (g\ g)\ x)\ (\lambda g.\lambda x.f\ (g\ g)\ x)$$

is also a fixed point finder (compare Exercise 12.13).

12.16 Show C is equivalent to S (BBS) (KK).

12.17 Rewrite the abstraction algorithm to generate B and C directly.

12.18 Rewrite $\mathsf{Y} \equiv \lambda f.(\lambda x.f\ (x\ x))\ (\lambda x.f\ (x\ x))$ with S, K, B, C and I using the improved algorithm for abstraction.

12.19 Similarly use the algorithm to remove the parameters from the (non-recursive) definition:

```
fun zipop f x y = map f (zip pair x y)
```

12.20 Give graphical descriptions of the rules for the combinators S, K, I, C, B, Y (i.e. as graph rewriting rather than string rewriting rules – cf. Figure 12.2).

12.21 What types are allocated to S, K, C, B and I by the Milner-Hindley type inference algorithm? Can every combinator be typed?

Chapter 13
Implementation Techniques

In this chapter we outline some of the techniques for implementing functional languages. This is included because it can give some insight into efficiency issues in programming and also ties together some of the theoretical topics discussed in Chapters 10 and 12. We do not, however, cover implementation techniques in great detail and refer the reader to books devoted to the subject such as Peyton-Jones (1987) and Harrison and Field (1988) for more information.

We will be looking at practical ways in which the process of reduction in combination with the evaluation of primitive functions may be carried out on a conventional computer. There are several aspects to this problem, such as:

(a) *Representation:* This includes the representation of the expression during evaluation (code), the representation of values (especially function values) and the environment (see below).

(b) *Flow:* This includes the problem of which reduction to do next (i.e the evaluation order: calling by value/name/etc.) and parallelism.

(c) *Copying mechanism:* That is, the degree of sharing used during evaluation and the use of environments.

We are mainly interested in describing how the reduction process may be effectively simulated on an abstract machine which is simple enough to implement on any conventional computer. Consequently we will not be concerned with detailed representation and optimizations nor with other aspects of language implementation such as syntax analysis, memory management, runtime errors and error recovery.

Rather than just present a compiler and abstract machine for the target language, we will derive them (informally) from a simple interpreter.

13.1 A simple expression reducer

We have seen from Chapter 12 that lambda terms may be evaluated by a sequence of reduction steps terminating with an expression in (weak head) normal form or possibly not terminating at all. It is fairly easy to just write an interpreter which does this reduction in a completely naïve way. For example, here is an evaluator which reduces pure lambda terms using (weak) normal order (call by name):

$$\begin{aligned}&\mathit{evalN}\,[\![E_1\ E_2]\!] = \mathit{applyN}\,(\mathit{evalN}\,[\![E_1]\!])\,[\![E_2]\!]\\&\mathit{evalN}\,[\![E]\!] = [\![E]\!],\ \text{otherwise}\\&\mathit{applyN}\,[\![\lambda x.E']\!]\,[\![E]\!] = \mathit{evalN}\,(\mathit{substitute}\ x\,[\![E]\!]\,[\![E']\!])\\&\mathit{applyN}\,[\![E_1]\!]\,[\![E_2]\!] = [\![E_1\ E_2]\!],\ \text{otherwise}\end{aligned}$$

We have written $[\![$ and $]\!]$ around the syntactic objects we are evaluating to avoid confusion and we will not complete the definition of *substitute* because we will introduce a method which avoids substitutions in a moment. Note that arguments are not evaluated when a function is applied.

An evaluator to do reductions using call by value instead of call by name requires a small change in the first line to ensure that the argument is evaluated before the application is calculated:

$$\begin{aligned}&\mathit{evalV}\,[\![E_1\ E_2]\!] = \mathit{applyV}\,(\mathit{evalV}\,[\![E_1]\!])\,(\mathit{evalV}\,[\![E_2]\!])\\&\mathit{evalV}\,[\![E]\!] = [\![E]\!],\ \text{otherwise}\\&\mathit{applyV}\,[\![\lambda x.E']\!]\,[\![E]\!] = \mathit{evalV}\,(\mathit{substitute}\ x\,[\![E]\!]\,[\![E']\!])\\&\mathit{applyV}\,[\![E_1]\!]\,[\![E_2]\!] = [\![E_1\ E_2]\!],\ \text{otherwise}\end{aligned}$$

In addition to variables, applications and abstractions, expressions could also be constructors (uninterpreted constants). If we wish to add some primitive functions as constants then we can adapt applyV accordingly. We assume that we have a function of the form:

$$\mathit{applyPrim} : \mathit{constant} \rightarrow \mathit{expression} \rightarrow \mathit{expression}$$

which defines the behaviour of primitives and such that:

$$\mathit{applyPrim}\,[\![C]\!]\,[\![E]\!] = [\![C\ E]\!]$$

when C is a constructor. We then alter *applyV* so that:

$$\begin{aligned}&\mathit{applyV}\,[\![\lambda x\,.\,E']\!]\,[\![E]\!] = \mathit{evalV}\,(\mathit{substitute}\ x\,[\![E]\!]\,[\![E']\!])\\&\mathit{applyV}\,[\![C]\!]\,[\![E]\!] = \mathit{applyPrim}\,[\![C]\!]\,[\![E]\!]\\&\mathit{applyV}\,[\![E_1]\!]\,[\![E_2]\!] = [\![E_1\ E_2]\!],\ \text{otherwise}\end{aligned}$$

There are several points to note here. First, if we want to use *applyPrim* for the call by name evaluator, we have to take account of primitives being strict, and reduce arguments for primitives (but not arguments for constructors). Secondly, we are assuming that primitives take single arguments so we need constructors such as tuple_n to allow compound values to be built. Then if, for example, plus is a primitive, we want:

$$applyPrim\ [\![\text{plus}]\!]\ [\![\ \text{tuple}_2\ 6\ 5\ ]\!] = [\![11]\!]$$

An alternative approach, would be to assume primitives are curried, and to define *applyPrim* so that:

$$applyPrim\ [\![\text{plus } 6]\!]\ [\![5]\!] = [\![11]\!]$$

which means that the first argument needs to be an expression rather than just a constant. We leave such a modification as an exercise.

Note that with only tuples taking multiple arguments, the last case for *applyV* is only necessary to allow tuples to be collected as in:

$$applyV\ [\![\text{tuple}_n\ E_1 \cdots E_k]\!]\ [\![E]\!] = [\![\text{tuple}_n\ E_1 \cdots E_k\ E]\!]$$

with $k < n$. This is assuming that the expressions are derived from type correct programs so that applications of non-functions will not arise. (We show a more efficient way to deal with tuples later.)

As an illustration, we will adapt the above interpreter to a functional program written in ML notation. We first introduce a data type for the syntactic objects to be evaluated:

```
type ident = string
datatype constant = Prim of ident
                  | Num of int
                  | Constructor of ident
datatype expression = CON of constant
                    | VAR of ident
                    | APP of expression × expression
                    | ABS of ident × expression
```

We consider numbers to be special cases of constructors in order to use int as a representation, but booleans are just left as constructors (namely Constructor "true" and Constructor "false"). Note that APP (E_1, E_2) corresponds to $[\![E_1\ E_2]\!]$ and ABS (x, E') corresponds to $[\![\lambda x . E']\!]$. Similarly:

```
APP (APP (CON (Prim "plus"), CON (Num "6")), CON (Num "5"))
```

corresponds to ⟦plus 6 5⟧.

Now we can define the evaluator as:

```
fun evalV (APP (E1, E2)) = applyV (evalV E1) (evalV E2)
|   evalV E              = E
and applyV (ABS (x, E')) E = substitute x E E'
|   applyV (CON C) E     = applyPrim C E
|   applyV E1 E2         = APP (E1, E2)
and applyPrim . . .
and substitute . . .
```

We can extend these definitions to include more general forms of expression (such as qualified expressions and conditionals) to implement a functional language. In principle, we need only implement the lambda calculus and rely on a translation such as the one described in the previous chapter to convert other constructs to lambda terms. In practice, it is often more convenient to translate to some intermediate language (a half way house) and implement this. This gives us some flexibility in finding a combination of an efficient translation and an efficient interpreter.

In the rest of this chapter, we give higher level (abbreviated) descriptions of evaluators and translators and leave their conversion to actual programs as exercises.

In the next section we show how substitutions can be delayed and even avoided by implementing environments.

13.2 Using environments

13.2.1 Variables and environments

When we evaluate expressions involving abstractions and variables, we need to deal with the substitution of values for variables occurring in terms. A technique which allows us to provide for sharing and delaying of substitutions, is to use environments. An environment is just an association or binding of variables with values to be substituted for them in the evaluation of a subexpression. Thus when a free variable is encountered in the evaluation of an expression, its value may be found by looking it up in an environment. Qualified expressions with definitions such as:

let val $V = E'$ **in** E **end**

or equivalently applied lambda abstractions, such as:

$(\lambda V.E)\ E'$

require the evaluation of E with a new binding for V (namely the value of E′), so we will need to create new environments during evaluation. The value of an expression with free variables will be determined by the environment in which it is evaluated. For example, consider an environment *env1* in which:

x is bound to 3
y is bound to 4
z is bound to 2

In *env1* we would expect x + (y * z) to evaluate to 11. Similarly the expression:

let val x = x * x **in** x + (y * z) **end**

should evaluate to 17. This value is obtained by first evaluating x * x in *env1* and then creating a new environment *env2* which is the same as *env1* except for the new binding for x (the value of x * x). In *env2* we have:

x bound to 9
y bound to 4
z bound to 2

The expression x + (y * z) is then evaluated in *env2* giving the result 17.

We could just implement environments as functions (using assoc) but it would be better to use a non-functional, lower level implementation since we may well want to convert the implementation into a program in some much simpler (non-functional) language.

We will assume environments are formed from lists of pairs representing bindings and use:

bind : (ident × value) list → environment
++ : environment × environment → environment
lookup : ident → environment → value

to form a new environment from binding pairs, to combine two environments and to retrieve an associated value, respectively. (We will define what we mean by value, which is essentially a restricted form of expression, in a moment.) In *env1* ++ *env2*, the bindings of *env1* take precedence over those of *env2* (i.e. *env1* ++ *env2* corresponds to our $\rho_2 + \rho_1$ of Chapter 10). We leave the reader the exercise of filling in the details of environment implementation. We will also assume:

emptyenv = *bind* [ ] : environment

for an empty environment. So *env1* from the previous example might be written as:

env1 = *bind* [(x, 3), (y, 4), (z, 2)] ++ *emptyenv*

and *env2* would then be:

env2 = *bind* [(x, 9)] ++ *env1*

In a moment, we will adapt our evaluator to take an environment argument so that, for example:

evalV ⟦**let val** *V* = *E′* **in** *E* **end**⟧ *env* = *evalV* ⟦*E*⟧ (*bind* [(*V*, *d*)] ++ *env*)
where *d* = *evalV* ⟦*E′*⟧ *env*

This shows how the substitution information can be stored in the environment to delay doing the substitution. When we come across a variable during evaluation, we look up its substitution value in the environment, thus performing the substitution then:

evalV ⟦*V*⟧ *env* = *lookup V env*

For example, suppose x ∗x has been translated to times (pair x x) where pair ≡ $tuple_2$. Then an evaluation of this latter term in *env1* could proceed as follows:

evalV ⟦times (pair x x)⟧ *env1*
= *applyV* (*evalV* ⟦times⟧ *env1*) (*evalV* ⟦pair x x⟧ *env1*)
= *applyPrim* ⟦times⟧ (*applyV* (*applyV* ⟦pair⟧ (*evalV* ⟦x⟧ *env1*))
(*evalV* ⟦x⟧ *env1*))
= *applyPrim* ⟦times⟧ (*applyV* (*applvPrim* ⟦pair⟧ 3) 3)
= *applyPrim* ⟦times⟧ (*applyV* ⟦pair 3⟧ 3)
= *applyPrim* ⟦times⟧ ⟦pair 3 3⟧
= 9

13.2.2 Values

We use the word **value** for the result produced by reducing an expression. That is, a value is an expression in canonical form (which cannot be reduced further by the evaluator). In the case of the call by value evaluator, a value is a (weak) normal form such as:

⟦pair (c1 5) true⟧

Recall that weak normal forms are either abstractions or constants or constructors applied to weak normal forms. So a value will not contain a redex except possibly within the body of an abstraction (representing a function). In the value:

$[\![\text{pair } (\lambda V \,.\, E) \text{ true}]\!]$

E can be any expression.

On the other hand, for call by name, values will be weak head normal forms which are more general. Recall that *E* is in weak head normal form if it is either an abstraction (representing a function) or a constant or a constructor applied to an argument which need not be reduced. For example:

$[\![\text{c1 } E]\!]$

is a value (for call by name) for any expression *E*.

13.2.3 Closures

Now we have introduced environments, which contain suspended substitution information, we need to extend our representation of values. We want to allow a value to be a combination of an expression and an environment recording substitutions still to be done. Such a combination is usually called a **closure**. For example, if we evaluate c1 x using call by name with an environment *env* (binding x to *d*, say), then the result should be a closure formed from c1 x combined with *env* to record the substitutions still to be done. Since the argument to c1 is not evaluated, we want to avoid actually doing the substitutions, but we need to make the environment available with the result in case we need to evaluate the argument at a later stage. If we use call by value, then the argument does get evaluated, and x would be replaced by the value *d* giving the result c1 *d*. However, we still need to use closures for function bodies in call by value since the body does not get evaluated until the function is applied.

Consider a qualified expression such as:

let val f = λx . x ∗ z **in** *E* **end**

to be evaluated in an environment *env*. Clearly we need to bind f to a function value and, at first glance, one might think that the abstraction alone could be used as a representation for the function value. The flaw in this idea can be seen when one notes that the environment in which the function eventually gets applied need not be the same as the one in which it is defined. Free variables in the body (i.e. identifiers which are not parameters) such as z in the example above could then be misinterpreted (evaluated in the wrong environment). Allowing this would lead to a dynamic scope rule for variables, which we want to avoid. Many implementations of LISP use dynamic scope because this problem was not considered properly in early implementations and the 'dynamic' solution has perpetuated. More recent implementations such as Common LISP use static scope. To correct this and give static scope to variables, we represent functions with a closure containing an abstraction and an environment and we will write closures in the form:

Closure (*abstraction, environment*)

The evaluation of $\lambda V . E$ in *env* would then give:

$$evalV [\![\lambda V . E]\!]\ env = Closure\ ([\![\lambda V . E]\!], env)$$

The previous example of a qualified expression would then simplify to:

$$\begin{aligned} &evalV [\![\textbf{let val } \mathsf{f} = \lambda \mathsf{x} . \mathsf{x} * \mathsf{z} \textbf{ in } E \textbf{ end}]\!]\ env \\ &\quad = evalV [\![E]\!]\ (bind\ [(\mathsf{f}, d)] \mathbin{++} env) \\ &\quad\quad \text{where } d = Closure\ (\lambda \mathsf{x} . \mathsf{x} * \mathsf{z}, env) \end{aligned}$$

To summarize, we extend our definition of values to include closures. For call by value, we only ever have closures with abstractions, but for call by name we need more general closures of the form *Closure* (*expression, environment*).

For the moment, we will concentrate on call by value and return to consider call by name (and indeed lazy evaluation) afterwards.

13.2.4 A call by value reducer with environments

The following algorithm describes the call by value reduction of expressions with environments:

(1) $evalV [\![C]\!]\ env = C$
(2) $evalV [\![V]\!]\ env = lookup\ V\ env$
(3) $evalV [\![E_1\ E_2]\!]\ env = applyV\ (evalV[\![E_1]\!]env)\ (evalV[\![E_2]\!]env)$
(4) $evalV [\![\lambda V.E]\!]\ env = Closure\ ([\![\lambda V.E]\!], env)$
(5) $applyV\ (Closure\ ([\![\lambda V.E]\!], env))\ d = evalV [\![E]\!]\ (bind\ [(V, d)] \mathbin{++} env)$
(6) $applyV [\![C]\!]\ d = applyPrim [\![C]\!]\ d$
(7) $applyV [\![E]\!]\ d = [\![E\ d]\!]$ otherwise

We make the following comments on the algorithm: (1) Constants are fully evaluated already. (2) All variables should be bound to a value in the environment since programs should not contain free variables. Using an initial environment with 'predefined' variables bound to values would allow programs to contain such variables free, but we regard them as bound by implicit definitions. (3) Both the operator and operand of an application are reduced before applying the former to the latter. (4) Abstractions are converted to closures with the environment in which they are evaluated. (5) The application of a closure is carried out by forming a new environment from the environment in the closure (*env*) plus the binding of the parameter (V) with the actual argument (d). This new environment is then used to evaluate the body of the abstraction in the closure (E). (6) The application of primitives is carried out by *applyPrim* with the same definition as before but note that an argument could now be a closure. (7) *applyV* should be applied to a pair of values and the first should represent a function. This case should only be used in building up a tuple, and we show how to short-circuit this lengthy process in the next subsection.

13.2.5 Extensions

We will extend expressions to include tuples, qualified expressions (with simple definitions) and conditionals. With such an extension, we can allow less tortuous translations of functional programs from some high level language into the extended forms of expression in order to evaluate them. (As we saw in the previous chapter, some of the most difficult constructs to translate are pattern matching definitions and definitions with **local**, but we will not attempt to deal with these extensions here in order to keep the explanations relatively simple.)

Conditionals are particularly easy to include with the following modification to *evalV*:

$$
\begin{aligned}
evalV\,[\![\textbf{if}\ E_0\ \textbf{then}\ E_1\ \textbf{else}\ E_2]\!]\ env &= evalV\,[\![E_1]\!]\ env, \text{ if } d = [\![\mathsf{true}]\!]\\
&= evalV\,[\![E_2]\!]\ env, \qquad \text{otherwise}\\
&\quad \text{where } d = evalV\,[\![E_0]\!]\ env
\end{aligned}
$$

Turning to tuples, we have been assuming that:

$$(E_1, \ldots, E_n) \qquad \textbf{TRANS} \qquad \mathsf{tuple}_n\ E_1 \cdots E_n$$

where tuple_n is a constructor. If the target language of expressions is assumed to include tuples, we can dispense with this translation step and add the following to the definition of *evalV*:

$$evalV\,[\![(E_1, \ldots, E_n)]\!]\ env = (evalV\,[\![E_1]\!]\ env, \ldots, evalV\,[\![E_n]\!]\ env)$$

Furthermore, if the constructors tuple_n are not directly available in the original language, then we no longer have to allow for their application in the rules for *applyV* and *applyPrim*. We can therefore remove the last line in the definition of *applyV* (i.e. (7)). (We regard any missing cases in these definitions as implicit error cases.)

Next, we introduce qualified expressions with simple definitions, and consider simultaneous (non-recursive) bindings first. We define:

$$\begin{aligned} &evalV\,[\![\textbf{let val } V_1 = E_1 \textbf{ and} \cdots V_n = E_n \textbf{ in } E \textbf{ end}]\!]\ env \\ &\quad = evalV\,[\![E]\!]\,(bind\,[(V_1, d_1), \ldots, (V_n, d_n)] \mathbin{++} env) \\ &\qquad \text{where } d_1 = evalV\,[\![E_1]\!]\ env \\ &\qquad\qquad\quad \ldots \\ &\qquad\qquad\quad d_n = evalV\,[\![E_n]\!]\ env \end{aligned}$$

This is a relatively obvious extension to the evaluator and we leave it as an exercise for the reader to check that:

$$evalV\,[\![(\lambda V.E)\ E']\!]\ env = evalV\,[\![\textbf{let val } V = E' \textbf{ in } E \textbf{ end}]\!]\ env$$

using the above definitions.

For recursive bindings, if we want to avoid the use of fix and directly set up the appropriate environment (which may be much more efficient), we have to create a cyclic data object. If we evaluate an expression such as:

$$\textbf{let val rec } V = E' \textbf{ in } E \textbf{ end}$$

in an environment *env*, say, then we need to evaluate E in a new environment of the form:

$$newenv = bind\,[(V, d)] \mathbin{++} env$$

but the value d needs to be found using *newenv*:

$$d = evalV\,[\![E']\!]\ newenv$$

so d depends on *newenv* and *newenv* depends on d. For call by value, we expect that only functions can be defined recursively, and that d will be a closure. The environment in the closure should be *newenv*, and the closure should be stored in *newenv*, giving us a cyclic data object.

Since we would normally want to implement a functional language using a simpler language, we should illustrate how a cyclic data object can be set up without using a recursive definition (which would only be available as a method in a lazy functional language).

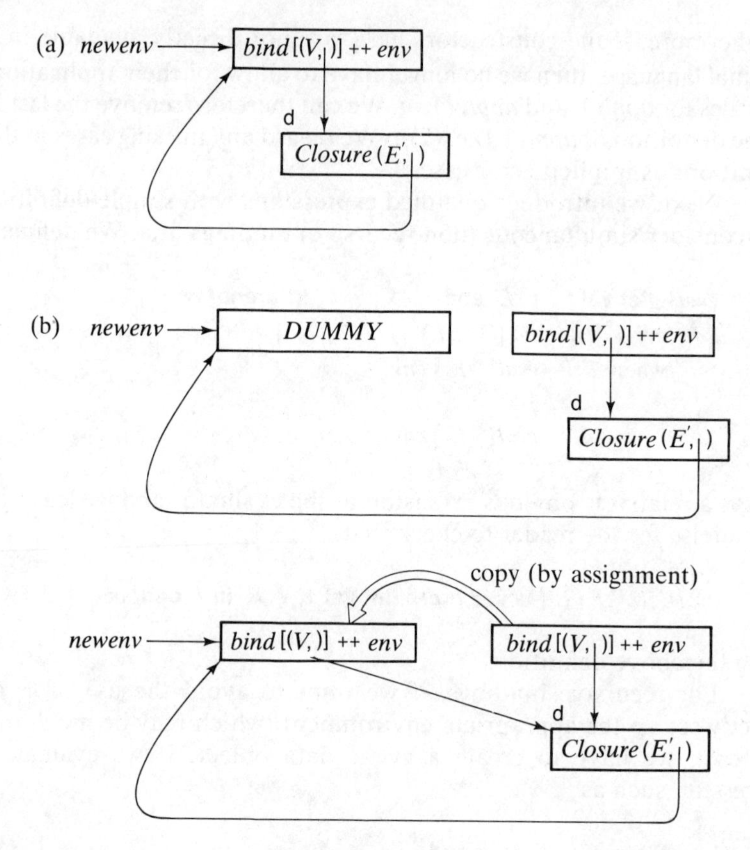

Figure 13.1 (a) A cyclic environment. (b) Two stage creation of the cyclic environment.

In procedural languages with side-effects, we assume that we can store data objects in memory cells and that we can store addresses of the cells of components instead of directly storing the component in a compound data object.

In order to set up a cyclic data object, we can use a 'dummy' cell with nothing or garbage in it (initially) as a component. When a compound object has been formed with this cell as a component, we can subsequently copy (a pointer to) the compound object into the contents of the component cell. Such an in-place update allows us to sequentially create cyclic objects in two phases. Figure 13.1(a) shows the structure of the environment we wish to create for the evaluation of the sub-expression E in our example, and Figure 13.1(b) shows the two-stage construction of the environment with a side effect. This has been referred to as 'tying knots'.

We add the following clause to deal with recursive bindings in auxiliary definitions, described using the (non-functional) imperative features of SML. (See Chapter 9 for a brief discussion of these.) We will assume that environments are updateable cells (references) created by bind and ++ ensuring that ++ does not copy the contents of its argument environment cells but shares references. For example, we could implement:

```
datatype bindstruct = Plus of (bindstruct ref × bindstruct ref)
                    | Bind of ((ident × value) list)
type environment = bindstruct ref
infix ++
  fun bind pairlist = ref (Bind pairlist)
  fun env1 ++ env2 = ref (Plus (env1, env2))
  fun lookup V env
    = let fun search (ref (Bind pl)) default = assoc pl default
          |   search (ref (Plus (e1, e2)) default
                = search e1 (search e2 default)
      in search env (fn V => error "unbound variable . . .") V end
  val emptyenv = bind [ ]
  fun UPDATENV env1 env2 = env1 := ! env2
```

Recall that evaluation of *ref d* creates a new cell (reference) with contents *d* and ! retrieves the contents of a cell such that ! (*ref d*) = *d*. The operator := causes a value to be assigned to a reference (returning ( ) as result). We will use *DUMMY* to denote some dummy initial contents for an environment which we intend to update. We could take *DUMMY* to be simply [ ] for example. The implementation also assumes that evaluation of *evalV* $[\![E_i]\!]$ *newenv* only makes copies of the reference *newenv* and does not access the contents (via *lookup*). This will be true if E_i is an abstraction and the resulting closure is formed with a pointer to the environment (i.e. a copy of the cell address rather than a copy of the contents).

Finally we observe that the definitions in the description of the environment are to be evaluated in the order they occur as in SML (call by value) so that the side-effects occur in the correct sequence:

```
evalV [[let val rec V₁ = E₁ and · · · Vn = En in E end]] env
   = (* SIDE EFFECT VERSION *)
     let val newenv = bind DUMMY
         val d₁ = evalV [[E₁]] newenv
          . . .
         and dn = evalV [[En]] newenv
         val SIDE_EFFECT = UPDATENV
                              newenv
                              (bind [(V₁, d₁), . . . , (Vn, dn)] ++ env)
     in evalV [[E]] newenv end
```

13.2.6 Conversion for lazy evaluation

When we use the call by name reducer, we need to allow closures with unevaluated expressions to occur more generally. Closures with arbitrary expressions (rather than just abstractions) are sometimes called **suspensions**. In order to achieve lazy evaluation, we also need to allow closures to be modified (in-place). This is because, when a closure gets evaluated, the closure needs to be replaced by the result to prevent future re-evaluation. Thus we extend values to also allow cells which can either contain a closure or a weak head normal form with (possibly) pointers to cells where component expressions might appear. (One way to implement this is to extend the type of expressions to allow both closures and references to closures in addition to normal expressions. The new forms of expression can then appear as subexpressions in other expressions (weak head normal forms).)

We use the assignment operator := to update a cell only when the two stored values (old and new) are different representations for the same thing. This shows that the side-effect is being used for efficiency purposes, and its omission would not affect any results:

(1) $evalL\ [\![C]\!]\ env = C$
(2) $evalL\ [\![V]\!]\ env = force\ (lookup\ V\ env)$
(3) $evalL\ [\![E_1\ E_2]\!]\ env = applyL\ (evalL\ [\![E_1]\!]\ env)\ (ref\,(Closure\ ([\![E_2]\!],\ env)))$
(4) $evalL\ [\![\lambda V.E]\!]\ env = ref\,(Closure\ ([\![\lambda V.E]\!],\ env))$
(5) $applyL\ (Closure\ ([\![\lambda V.E]\!],\ env))\ d = evalL\ [\![E]\!]\ (bind\ [(V,\ d)]\ ++\ env)$
(6) $applyL\ [\![C]\!]\ d = applyPrim\ [\![C]\!]\ d$
(7) $applyL\ [\![E_1]\!]\,[\![E_2]\!] = [\![E_1\ E_2]\!]$, otherwise
(8) *force d* = **case** !*d* **of**
 Closure ($[\![\lambda V.E]\!]$, *env*) ⇒ !*d*
 Closure ($[\![E]\!]$, *env*) ⇒ **let val** *SIDE_EFFECT*
  = *d* := *evalL* $[\![E]\!]$ *env*
 in !*d* **end**
 other ⇒ *other*
(9) *applyPrim* · · ·

The new version of *evalN* is called *evalL* (for 'lazy' evaluation) and applies to (ordinary) expressions to produce a weak head normal form. Values stored in the environment may be suspended values, so *force* is used to evaluate them and to update the cell with the result as well. Unsuspended values are left as they were by force and the first case in the definition of force is included to avoid repeatedly evaluating abstraction closures which are already evaluated.

The definition of *applyPrim* (which we omit) will involve applications of force to evaluate arguments for strict primitives, and, furthermore, will check that the result is not a suspension, applying *force* again if necessary.

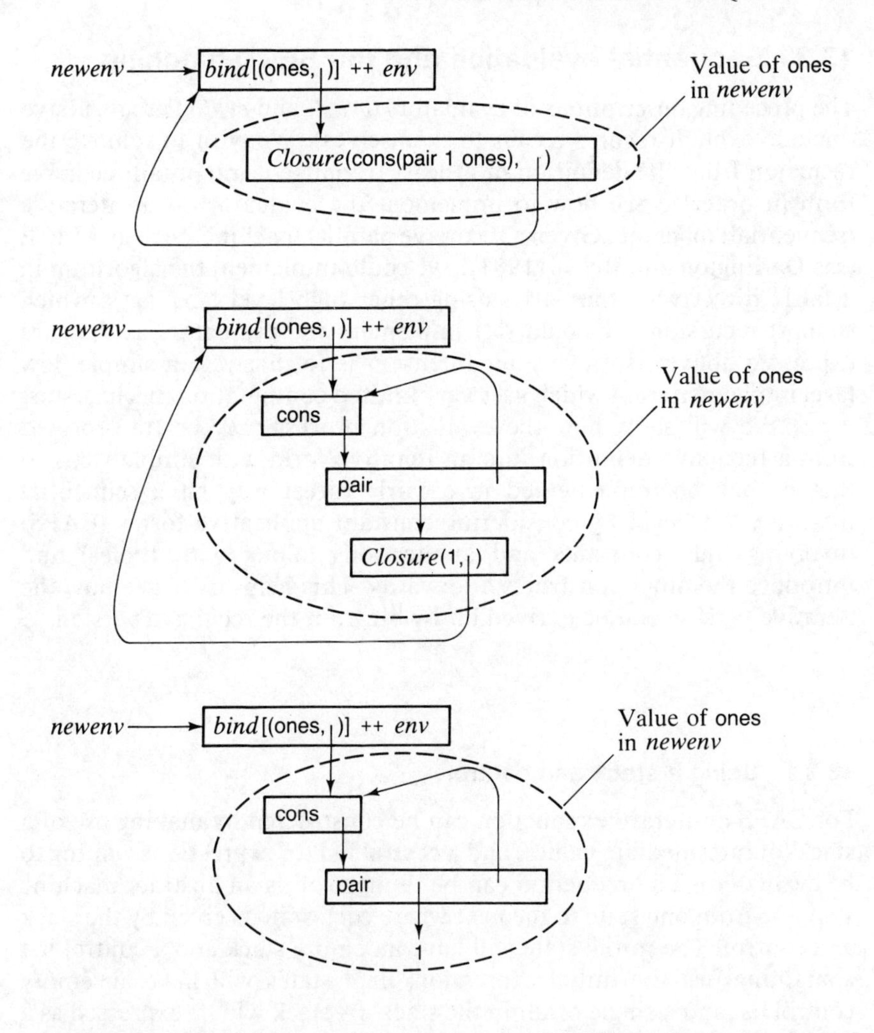

Figure 13.2 Transformation of a suspended value during lazy evaluation.

In Figure 13.2, we illustrate the transformation of a value (ones) stored in the environment as the evaluation of hd (tl ones) is calculated using the expression:

let val rec ones = cons (pair 1 ones) **in** hd (tl ones) **end**

evaluated in *oldenv*. We assume, for the example, that the environment contains the bindings created for the definitions:

hd = λx . **if** isa_cons x **then** fst (argof x) **else** matchfail
tl = λx . **if** isa_cons x **then** snd (argof x) **else** matchfail

13.3 Sequential evaluation and the SECD machine

The preceding descriptions of evaluators (*evalV* and *evalN*) are recursive (include explicit recursive calls to themselves). We wish to remove the recursion from the definition or at least trivialize it into a tail recursive form in order to see how to implement the evaluator on an iterative (sequential) machine. Given a recursive parallel machine, such as ALICE (see Darlington and Reeve (1981)), we could implement the algorithm in a fairly direct way. Similarly, using other high level languages, which support recursion, we could just implement the evaluators as they are expressed above. However, our intention is to illustrate a simple, low level implementation which uses very limited computation mechanisms.

We will show how the evaluation process may be transformed from a recursive definition into an iterative form with simple steps so that it may be implemented in a fairly direct way on a sequential machine. We begin by considering constant applicative forms (CAFS) involving only constants and applications (along with tuples) and introduce the other constructs afterwards. This helps us to see how the iterative version can be derived bit by bit from the recursive version.

13.3.1 Using a stack and control

For CAFS an iterative reduction can be constructed by making use of a **stack** (of intermediate values) and a **control list** (of expressions waiting to be evaluated). The reduction can be thought of as an abstract machine stepping from one state to the next where each state is given by the stack and control. The initial state will have an empty stack and a control list containing just the initial expression; final states will have an empty control list and a single result in the stack. (A stack will be expressed as a list of values.) We will use the symbol APP in the control list to represent an instruction to apply the function on the top of the stack to the argument just below it on the stack replacing both by the result. Similarly, for each $n \geq 2$ we introduce TUPLE n which is an instruction to build a tuple from n components on the stack. (This is just an implementation of our earlier optimization to save having to accumulate a tuple with n applications.)

The transitions of the abstract machine can be expressed by indicating the form of the stack and control before and after the transition:

$$s, c \vdash s', c'$$

The symbol $\vdash$ is traditional for representing a machine transition and should not be confused with our use of the same symbol for type inference systems in Chapter 11. We will use s to denote the stack and c to denote the control list (and use a and b for values). For example, if the head of the control is a constant we load it onto the stack:

$$s,\ C :: c \vdash C :: s,\ c$$

If the head of the control is an application, we replace it with three expressions on the control list:

$$s,\ (E_1\ E_2) :: c \vdash s,\ E_2 :: E_1 :: \mathsf{APP} :: c$$

It is usual to put the argument in front of the function to be evaluated first, but these could easily be reversed with a slight alteration to the rule for APP. If APP is found at the head of the control list we apply a function which will be above its argument on the stack:

$$a :: b :: s,\ \mathsf{APP} :: c \vdash r :: s,\ c \quad \text{where } r = \mathit{applyPrim}\ a\ b$$

If a tuple is at the head of the control list, we replace it by the list of component expressions followed by TUPLE n where n is the number of components. Thus:

$$s,\ (E_1, E_2, \ldots, E_n) :: c \vdash s,\ E_1 :: E_2 :: \ldots :: E_n :: \mathsf{TUPLE}\ n :: c$$

Finally, if TUPLE n is at the head of the control list we form a tuple with the n items on the top of the stack, thus:

$$a_n :: \ldots a_2 :: a_1 :: s,\ (\mathsf{TUPLE}\ n) :: c \vdash (a_1, a_2, \ldots, a_n) :: s,\ c$$

Note the reversal of the values on the stack so that the top item becomes the last component of the tuple.

As an example, we see how times (5, succ 9) gets evaluated step by step, assuming times and succ are primitives defined by *applyPrim*. We start with stack $s = [\ ]$ and $c = [\![\text{times (5, succ 9)}]\!] = \text{times (5, succ 9)} :: [\ ]$. We drop the $[\![$ and $]\!]$ around expressions from now on and hope that this does not cause confusion. We also use PAIR rather than TUPLE 2:

Starting with:	[ ],	times (5, succ 9) :: [ ]
⊢	[ ],	(5, succ 9) :: times :: APP :: [ ]
⊢	[ ],	5 :: succ 9 :: PAIR :: times :: APP :: [ ]
⊢	5 :: [ ],	succ 9 :: PAIR :: times :: APP :: [ ]
⊢	5 :: [ ],	9 :: succ :: APP :: PAIR :: times :: APP :: [ ]
⊢	9 :: 5 :: [ ],	succ :: APP :: PAIR :: times :: APP :: [ ]
⊢	succ :: 9 :: 5 :: [ ],	APP :: PAIR :: times :: APP :: [ ]
⊢	10 :: 5 :: [ ],	PAIR :: times :: APP :: [ ]
⊢	(5,10) :: [ ],	times :: APP :: [ ]
⊢	times :: (5,10) :: [ ],	APP :: [ ]
⊢	50 :: [ ],	[ ]

Result is: 50

A complete evaluation with such a machine can be described in terms of two functions, namely:

(1) *trans* (s, c) which produces the new stack and control (s', c') after a single step (transition), and

(2) *evalSC E* which iterates *trans* from the initial state $([\ ], E)$ until a final state is reached, that is:

$$
\begin{aligned}
&evalSC = unload \circ (while\ (non\ final)\ trans) \circ load\\
&load\ E = ([\ ], E)\\
&unload\ ([r], [\ ]) = r\\
&final\ (s, c) = null\ c
\end{aligned}
$$

Call by value is assumed because only evaluated expressions appear as arguments to functions on the stack. (We will only consider call by value in this section.)

13.3.2 Simple compilation

Instead of inspecting the expressions in the control list c and linearizing them during the computation, we can preprocess (compile) expressions into a control list of single instructions (i.e. a linear flow graph of instructions APP and LDC ('load constant') and TUPLE n) before starting the evaluation. We simply convert the expression into a reverse polish form and replace constants C by LDC C denoting the load instruction with its argument. An expression of the form $E_1\ E_2$ will be compiled to $c_2 @ c_1$ @ [APP] where c_i is the result of compiling subexpression E_i $(i = 1, 2)$. Tuples will be compiled by linking sequences of instructions for each component followed by a TUPLE n instruction:

$$\begin{aligned} &compile\ C &&= [\mathsf{LDC}\ C] \\ &compile\ (E_1\ E_2) &&= (compile\ E_2)\ @\ (compile\ E_1)\ @\ [\mathsf{APP}] \\ &compile\ (E_1, \ldots, E_n) &&= (compile\ E_1)\ @ \ldots @\ (compile\ E_n)\ @\ [\mathsf{TUPLE}\ n] \end{aligned}$$

For example, if times, 5 and 9 are constants then (using PAIR for TUPLE 2 again):

compile (times (5, 9))
= (*compile* (5,9)) @ (*compile* (times)) @ [APP]
= *compile* (5) @ *compile* (9) @ [PAIR] @ (*compile* (times)) @ [APP]
= [LDC 5] @ [LDC 9] @ [PAIR] @ [LDC times] @ [APP]
= [LDC 5, LDC 9, PAIR, LDC times, APP]

Although this gains nothing overall in terms of efficiency, it forms the basis of a compiler for more general expressions which we consider next.

13.3.3 Variables and environments

When abstractions and definitions (and hence variables) are introduced, we need to use environments as well as the stack and control to carry the information about substitutions (i.e. the environments provide the appropriate substitution value bound to a variable at each stage of an evaluation). The variables occurring in an expression will be interpreted as instructions to look up their value in the current environment. For example, we could have something of the form:

$$s, e, V :: c \vdash a :: s, e, c \quad \text{where } a = lookup\ V\ e$$

where a state is now represented as a triple of a stack (s), an environment (e) and a code list (c).

However, we will make another alteration at this point. A vast improvement in efficiency can be made by noticing that we can calculate the position of a variable in the environment while we are compiling expressions into linear form as a control list. Then at runtime, we can perform faster lookups by just selecting the appropriate component of the environment.

More specifically, we split environments (which were lists of variable value pairs) into separate lists of variables and lists of values. At compile time we only use lists of variables and translate a variable into a load instruction with a number indicating its position in the (compile time) environment. At runtime we just use lists of values for environments. A load instruction with an index number will cause the item at the indicated position in the environment to be loaded on to the stack.

The fact that this can be done is due to the static scope rules, and the introduction of index numbers to replace variables is exactly analogous to the translation of lambda terms to De Bruijn notation (see Exercise 12.2 from Chapter 12). The position of a variable in the compile time environment (which we call a namelist) corresponds to its 'depth' calculated from the number of variables introduced in definitions and abstractions which are in scope at the point where the variable occurs and within the scope of the binding occurrence of the variable.

During compilation we use namelist nl as an additional argument and compile any v to the instruction LD k where k is the position of V in *nl*. This is expressed by the rule:

$$compile\ V\ nl = [\mathsf{LD}\ k] \qquad where\ k = position\ V\ nl$$

and *position* is defined to return the position of the first occurrence of a variable name in a name list, e.g.:

$position\ V\ (V :: nl) = 1$
$position\ V\ (V' :: nl) = 1 + position\ V\ nl,$ if $V \neq V'$
(*position* V [ ] *is an error indicating an unbound variable*)

where we count the top variable as position 1 (this is often regarded as position 0 in the literature).

As an example, if we are compiling a subexpression which appears in a context where x, y, z have been introduced as bound variables (by definitions or abstractions), then the namelist could be [x, y, z]. If we come across a y, this will be translated to LD 2 because 2 = *position* y [x, y, z]. At runtime, the environment e will be a list of values such as $[a_1, a_2, a_3]$ and the instruction LD 2 causes the second item a_2 to be loaded on to the stack. This is expressed by:

$$s, e, (\mathsf{LD}\ k) :: c \vdash a :: s, e, c \quad \text{where } a = fetch\ k\ e$$

and *fetch* is just a more evocative name for the *select* function we defined for indexing into a list. We could also express this transition by:

$$s, a_1 :: \ldots :: a_k :: e, (\mathsf{LD}\ k) :: c \vdash a_k :: s, a_1 :: \ldots :: a_k :: e, c$$

This translation of variables is an important optimization because we only scan the body of a function once in compiling (thus doing the costly lookups/position finding of variables once for each variable occurrence). At runtime, a function can be applied many times and so the load instructions in the code for the body can be performed many times.

13.3.4 Abstractions

Abstractions will be translated into a single instruction which causes a closure to be formed at runtime. The instruction must have an argument containing the code list for the body of the abstraction, thus we introduce instructions of the form LDFUN c where c is a code list. (We can think of this code list as a jump address for the code of the function body.) When the instruction is executed, a closure is formed and placed as a single item on the top of the stack. The closure is constructed from the code list argument for LDFUN along with the environment from the machine state. Thus we have:

$$s, e, (\text{LDFUN } c') :: c \vdash \textit{Closure}\,(c', e) :: s, e, c$$

As with our earlier evaluators, a record of the environment at the time the function value is formed is necessary so that subsequent evaluation of the function body can take place in the correct environment. When a closure is applied to an argument, the code of the closure has to be evaluated not with the current environment but with one formed from the environment contained in the closure. In fact, the environment in the closure has to be extended to include the actual argument of the application as its top item. This corresponds to our binding the parameter to the actual argument when applying a closure in the previous versions of our evaluators.

The namelist (compile time environment) needs to be altered when we come across a new variable binding introduced by an abstraction (or definition) during the compilation. In order that variables are translated to the correct LD instructions, we must ensure that the compilation of the body of an abstraction is done using a namelist with the parameter on the top (= front). That is:

$$\begin{aligned} \textit{compile}\,(\lambda V.E)\; nl &= [\text{LDFUN } c] \\ &\quad \text{where } c = \textit{compile}\; E\; (V :: nl) \end{aligned}$$

Thus, for example:

$$\begin{aligned} \textit{compile}\,(\lambda \text{y.y})\; [\text{x, y, z}] &= [\text{LDFUN } (\textit{compile}\; \text{y } [\text{y, x, y, z}])] \\ &= [\text{LDFUN } [\text{LD } 1]] \end{aligned}$$

A closure on the top of the stack need not be immediately applied, since it could be transferred to the environment (as an argument to another function) or passed out to another environment (as the result of a function) or incorporated into another data object (e.g. as a component of a pair). Because of the way environments get used as parts of closures in this way, their use is not confined to the normal nesting which is associated with ALGOL-like stacks, but grow more like trees. Also, the fact that environments change temporarily (while subexpressions are evaluated) means that old environments need to be returned to.

13.3.5 Dumps

We will find that at certain points in an evaluation, the machine has to evaluate a subexpression using a different environment from the current one. For example, when a closure is to be applied to an argument, we need to install the (modified) environment from the closure temporarily. We also need to install the code from the closure (i.e. jump to the new code). However, this is also temporary, because when the evaluation of this code is complete, we have to continue where we left off (return) and go back to using the old environment and control. In order for this change to be done sequentially, a record of the old environment and code must be 'dumped' somewhere as part of the state data structure in order to be recovered when it is needed at later points. We use a fourth state component: the 'dump' to store return information and this gives us the final form of Landin's SECD machine (Landin, 1964). The states of a SECD machine are of the form of a quadruple:

A stack	(s)	a sequence of values
An environment	(e)	a sequence of values
A control list	(c)	a sequence of instructions (code)
A dump	(d)	another state (s', e', c', d')

The dump is used to store states which may be returned to later in a computation. Notice that we need to store a dump component in the dump so that a function can be called from within another function. There will be some initial empty dump from which computation starts, and we could think of a state as a list of s, e, cs if we prefer. That is:

(s_1, e_1, c_1, d_1)
where $d_1 = (s_2, e_2, c_2, d_2)$
    where $d_2 = (s_3, e_3, c_3, d_3)$
        where $d_3 = (s_4, e_4, c_4, d_4)$
            where d_4 is empty

Table 13.1 The SECD machine transitions.

	Stack	*Environment*	*Control*	*Dump*
	s	e	(LDC C) :: c	d
⊢	$C :: s$	e	c	d
	s	$a_1 :: \ldots a_k :: e$	(LD k) :: c	d
⊢	$a_k :: s$	$a_1::a_2::\ldots a_k::e$	c	d
	$a_1 :: \ldots a_n :: s$	e	TUPLE $n :: c$	d
⊢	$(a_n, \ldots, a_1) :: s$	e	c	d
	s	e	(LDFUN c') :: c	d
⊢	*Closure* $(c', e) :: s$	e	c	d
	$a :: s$	e	[ ]	(s', e', c', d')
⊢	$a :: s'$	e'	c'	d'
	Closure $(c', e') :: a :: s$	e	APP :: c	d
⊢	[ ]	$a :: e'$	c'	(s, e, c, d)
	$C :: a :: s$	e	APP :: c	d
⊢	$r :: s$	e	c	d
	where r = *applyPrim C* a			

could be represented by:

$$(s_1, e_1, c_1) :: (s_2, e_2, c_2) :: (s_3, e_3, c_3) :: [\ ]$$

In conventional compiling terms, such a list is usually referred as the **frame stack** or **dynamic chain**.

13.3.6 SECD transitions

The SECD machine was first described in Landin (1964) and a fuller description may be found there and in Henderson (1980) or Burge (1975). The transition steps for the machine are described in Table 13.1 and the compiler is defined in Table 13.2.

The introduction of the final dump component does not affect the transitions we have previously described, but only enters into the computation when functions are applied (and code from the closure is 'entered') and when such applications are returned from. The rules for these transitions are described below.

When a function body has been evaluated, the control list should be empty, the result should be at the head of the stack and the return information should be in the dump:

Table 13.2 Compiler for the SECD machine.

compile (C) *nl*	= [LDC C]
compile (V) *nl*	= [LD k] where k = position V *nl*
compile $(E_1\ E_2)$ *nl*	= *compile* E_2 *nl* @ *compile* E_1 *nl* @ [APP]
compile $(E_1, E_2, \ldots, E_n)$ *nl*	= c_1 @ c_2 @ . . . @ c_n @ [TUPLE n]
	where c_i = *compile* (E_i) *nl* (i = 1 . . . n)
compile $(\lambda V.E)$ *nl*	= [LDFUN c]
	where c = *compile* (E) $(V :: nl)$

$$a :: s, e, [\ ], (s', e', c', d')$$

The next state is the one from the dump but with the result attached to the stack:

$$a :: s', e', c', d'$$

A function is entered when a closure is found on the stack with the argument value below it, and APP is at the head of the control list, i.e. the stack, environment, control and dump have the following forms respectively:

$$(Closure\ (c', e')) :: a :: s, e, \text{APP} :: c, d$$

where c' is the body and e' the environment of the closure, a is the actual argument and s the rest of the stack. The next state will consist of an empty stack, a new environment and control formed from the closure and the dump will contain the return state:

$$[\ ], a :: e', c', (s, e, c, d)$$

The new environment is formed by adding the value to be bound with the parameter onto e' (i.e. the argument a from the stack). In c (the body) occurrences of the parameter will have been converted to instructions which will load a because of the way the namelist was modified in compiling the expression for the body.

Note that there is another rule for APP used when the top of the stack is a constant rather than a closure:

$$C :: a :: s, e, \text{APP} :: c, d$$

The rule says that the constant and its argument are to be replaced by the result of applying the former to the latter as determined by *applyPrim*, giving the new state:

$r :: s, e, c, d$ where $r = applyPrim\ C\ a$

Clearly a final state has an empty control and an empty dump and the result on the top of the stack, while the initial state will have an empty stack, dump and environment and the control compiled from the expression being evaluated.

13.3.7 Extensions

We include some interesting extensions for this basic version of the machine to make evaluation of conditionals and definitions more efficient.

Conditionals such as **if** E_0 **then** E_1 **else** E_2 may be compiled into a control list as follows: let E_i compile to give control lists c_i ($i = 0, 1, 2$), then append a new JOIN instruction at the end of c_1 and c_2. These latter two lists (pointers to them) are used as the two arguments of another new instruction SEL (= 'select') which is then appended onto c_0. That is, we get:

$compile$ (**if** E_0 **then** E_1 **else** E_2) nl
  $= c_0$ @ [(SEL c_1' c_2')]
   where $c_0 = compile\ E_0\ nl$
    and $c_1' = compile\ E_1\ nl$ @ [JOIN]
    and $c_2' = compile\ E_2\ nl$ @ [JOIN]

At runtime, the SEL instruction will be encountered after the evaluation of E_0 which will have left a boolean on the stack. The next step is to begin evaluation of either E_1 or E_2 depending on the boolean. That is we must jump to either c_1' or c_2' by installing the new code. However, the code after the SEL instruction must be returned to when we have finished, so we will dump it. The purpose of the JOIN instruction is to retrieve the dumped continuation code. Note that there is no need for the stack and environment to be dumped and retrieved along with the code in this case. We use '_' to indicate that the stack and environment components used are arbitrary and ignored, and the transitions are given by:

true :: s, e, (SEL c_1' c_2') :: $c, d \vdash s, e, c_1', (\_, \_, c, d)$
false :: s, e, (SEL c_1' c_2') :: $c, d \vdash s, e, c_2', (\_, \_, c, d)$
s, e, JOIN :: [ ], $(\_, \_, c, d) \vdash s, e, c, d$

In order to evaluate a non-recursive simultaneous definition, it is convenient to introduce instructions (APP n) for arbitrary $n \geq 1$ which will store n items (from below a function on the stack) in the environment.

APP is then synonymous with (APP 1). We then compile:

$$\begin{aligned} &\textit{compile}\ (\textbf{let val}\ V_1 = E_1\ \textbf{and} \ldots \textbf{and}\ V_n = E_n\ \textbf{in}\ E\ \textbf{end})\ nl \\ &\quad = c_1 @ \ldots @ c_n @ [(\text{LDFUN}\ c), (\text{APP}\ n)] \\ &\qquad \text{where} \\ &\qquad c_i = \textit{compile}\ E_i\ nl\ (i = 1 \ldots n) \\ &\qquad c = \textit{compile}\ E\ ([V_1, \ldots, V_n] @ nl) \end{aligned}$$

At runtime, the instruction APP n reverses n arguments from the stack onto the closure environment:

$$\begin{aligned} &\textit{Closure}\ (c', e') :: a_n :: \ldots :: a_1 :: s, e, (\text{APP}\ n) :: c, d \\ &\vdash \\ &[\ ], a_1 :: \ldots :: a_n :: e', c', (s, e, c, d) \end{aligned}$$

For a recursive definition, we could use the rather obscure (and inefficient) method of substituting a lambda term like:

$$\lambda f.(\lambda g.f\,(\lambda x.g\ g\ x))\ (\lambda g.f\,(\lambda x.g\ g\ x))$$

to represent Y. (Recall that $\lambda f.(\lambda g.f\,(g\ g))\ (\lambda g.f\,(g\ g))$ will not work properly with call by value.) However, it is much more efficient to introduce instructions DUM which puts Ω on the top of the environment and (RAP n) which is similar to APP n except that it in-place updates the environment before application of the function. For this to work, we need to assume that environments are cells which either contain bindings or a ++ of a pair of references to other environment cells, so that they can be updated by an assignment. We compile the recursive version as follows:

$$\begin{aligned} &\textit{compile}\ (\textbf{let val rec}\ V_1 = E_1\ \textbf{and} \ldots \textbf{and}\ V_n = E_n\ \textbf{in}\ E\ \textbf{end})\ nl \\ &\quad = \text{DUM} :: c_1 @ \ldots @ c_n @ [(\text{LDFUN}\ c), (\text{RAP}\ n)] \\ &\qquad \text{where} \\ &\qquad c_i = \textit{compile}\ E_i\ (\textit{addnames}\ [V_1, \ldots, V_n]\ nl)\ (i = 1 \ldots n) \\ &\qquad c = \textit{compile}\ E\ (\textit{addnames}\ [V_1, \ldots, V_n]\ nl) \end{aligned}$$

The differences are that DUM is added as a first instruction, APP n is replaced by RAP n, and each of the E_i are compiled relative to the extended namelist. We also use addnames rather than @ to extend the compile time environment. This is because the compile time environment should reflect the structure (shape) of the runtime environment and if we change the latter, a simple linear list for the former may not be appropriate. Details are left as an exercise.

At runtime, the effect of DUM is shown diagrammatically as follows:

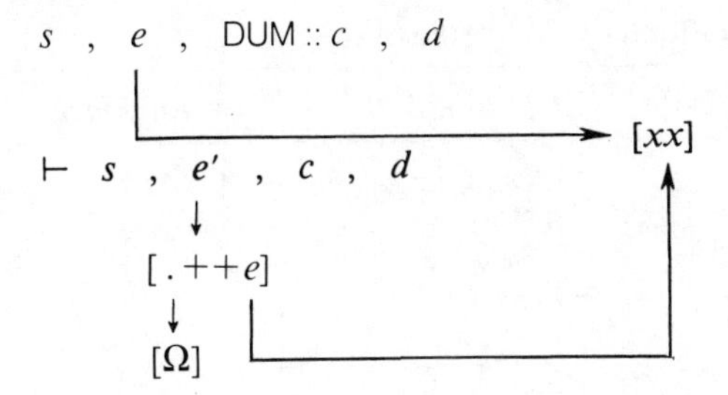

Then, when RAP n is about to be executed, the state should look like this

$Closure\,(c', e') :: a_n :: \ldots :: a_1 :: s\ ,\ e'\ ,\ (\text{RAP } n) :: c\ ,\ d$

[.++ e]

[Ω] [xx]

and the a_i will generally be closures with references to the same environment e'.

The next state is obtained by replacing Ω by the list of new values $[a_1, \ldots, a_n]$ and then entering the closure as for an APP n:

$[\,]\ ,\ e'\ ,\ c'\ ,\ (s,e,c,d)$

[.++ e]

[xx]

$[a_1, \ldots, a_n]$

The machine can also be specialized so that some of the constant operations (performed by *applyPrim*) are made into instructions. Thus we could change the compiler to produce, for example:

. . . :: PLUS :: . . . rather than . . . PAIR :: (LDC plus) :: APP :: . . .

so that at runtime we have:

$a :: b :: s, e, \text{PLUS} :: c, d \vdash r :: s, e, c, d$
where $r = a + b$

Similar more subtle changes can be made to allow closures to be applied to many arguments without forming a tuple by using APP n. However, this cannot be done if the tupled argument is passed around as a whole (e.g. to form the result of the application).

There is much scope for other optimizations (including the detection of tail recursion at compile time to generate more efficient code) but we will not go into this here (see Exercise 13.8).

Table 13.3 The (adapted) CAM transitions.

EnvStack	*Control*		*EnvStack*	*Control*
$a :: s$	(LDC C) :: c	$\vdash$	$C :: s$	c
$Env\ [a_1, \ldots, a_k, \ldots] :: s$	(LD k) :: c	$\vdash$	$a_k :: s$	c
$a :: s$	COPY :: c	$\vdash$	$a :: a :: s$	c
$a :: b :: s$	SWAP :: c	$\vdash$	$b :: a :: s$	c
$a_n :: \ldots :: a_1 :: s$	(TUPLE n) :: c	$\vdash$	$(a_1, \ldots, a_n) :: s$	c
$Env\ e :: s$	(LDFUN c') :: c	$\vdash$	$Closure\ (c', e) :: s$	c
$Closure\ (c', e) :: a :: s$	APP :: c	$\vdash$	$Env\ (a :: e) :: s$	c' @ c
$C :: a :: s$	APP :: c	$\vdash$	$r :: s$	c
			where $r = applyPrim\ C\ a$	

13.3.8 Other variations

The SECD machine can be adapted to support lazy evaluation with suspensions (see Henderson (1980)) and an extension of the machine to handle multi-programming with concurrent processes is described in Abramsky (1982). A highly optimized variant of the SECD called the FAM (= 'functional abstract machine') is described in Cardelli (1983) and has been used to implement Standard ML. This is a highly practical abstract machine which can be easily adapted to support various (call by value) functional languages.

The main feature of the optimization is that the formation of closures is done by collecting copies of those items in the environment that are actually referred to in the abstraction body rather than using a pointer to the entire environment. Although this copying takes more time, it means that the space occupied by extensions to environments and stacks can be reclaimed when they are finished with so that a conventional stack can be used.

The scheme chip (Sussman (1981) – see also Steele and Sussman (1978) and Sussman and Steele (1975)) can also be viewed as a hardware adaptation of the SECD machine.

Another, relatively new, abstract machine called the CAM (categorical abstract machine) was derived from a different starting point, but is clearly very similar to the SECD machine. We describe this briefly below and give details of the CAM transitions Table 13.3 along with a compiler in Table 13.4. The interested reader is encouraged to read Curien (1986) for a detailed account of the derivation of this machine. We just present a simplified version here and we have adapted the model slightly to illustrate the similarities with the SECD machine.

For the CAM, the stack and environment are combined and there are just two components in the state, namely: the control and the (environment/stack). Usually, if c is the code for some expression, and $Env\ (e)$ is an appropriate environment for the expression, then the state:

Table 13.4 A compiler for the (adapted) CAM.

compile (*C*) *nl*	= [LDC *C*]
compile (*V*) *nl*	= [LD *k*] where $k = position\ V\ nl$
compile (E_1 E_2) *nl*	= [COPY] @ *compile* E_2 *nl* @ [SWAP] @ *compile* E_1 *nl* @ [APP]
compile ($\lambda V.E$) *nl*	= [LDFUN *c*] where $c = compile\ (E)\ (V :: nl)$
compile ($E_1, \ldots, E_n$) *nl*	= [COPY] @ c_1 @ [SWAP, COPY] @ c_2 @ [SWAP, COPY] ... $c_{(n-1)}$ @ [SWAP] @ c_n @ [TUPLE *n*] where $c_i = compile\ (E_i)\ nl$

$$Env\ (e) :: s,\ c\ @\ c'$$

eventually transforms to:

$$r :: s,\ c'$$

where r' is the value of the expression in the given environment. Since the environment is consumed by the evaluation, there are two new instructions. One allows a stack item to be copied (COPY) and the other allows two items to be swapped around on the stack (SWAP). These are introduced by the compiler when several subexpressions need to be evaluated with the same environment.

Although there is no dump component, the APP instruction does require the appending of two control lists. The simplest way to avoid such a costly runtime calculation (which would copy the code in the first list) would be to introduce a dump component containing just a control continuation component. We leave the details as an exercise. We also leave it as an exercise for the reader to try out the compiler and transitions on some examples. Note that the initial stack must be:

$$Env\ [\ ] :: [\ ]$$

rather than just [ ].

13.4 Graph reduction

To support lazy evaluation, we have indicated that suspensions (updateable closures) can be used. Ideally, we should maximize the amount of sharing of values rather than copying during evaluation and also ensure that suspended values are updated whenever they are evaluated.

A limitation for sharing and updating is the presence of abstraction closures. When an abstraction closure is applied, we calculate the value of the body of the abstraction relative to an environment containing the actual argument of the application. This prevents us from using the result of the evaluation to update the closure, because the result generally depends on the actual argument.

It was shown in Chapter 12 that expressions could be converted to CAFs (constant applicative forms) without lambda abstractions thus removing bound variables and introducing some primitive combinators like S, K, I, C, B, Y, . . . etc. This means that instead of using the SECD machine, we would compile out the lambda abstractions and use a simpler machine to evaluate the resulting CAFs by reduction. Essentially, the conversion to combinators causes the environment to be replaced by a sequence of arguments to a CAF. The combinators then do the work of fetching values from an environment by distributing arguments to appropriate subexpressions in the CAF. (The CAM seems to do something very similar to this as well.)

Without lambda abstractions, subexpression of combinators can be treated as 'pure' code and evaluated in a context free manner. This has the important advantage that reductions can be done in place; that is, any subexpression can be directly replaced in memory by its reduced equivalent when it is evaluated. All the expressions sharing such a subexpression thus benefit from the evaluation which is only done once. Such in-place updating of an expression with an equal but simpler form should be contrasted with the haphazard updating produced by arbitrary assignment statements.

The representation of CAFs as cells with pointers to subexpressions means that the in-place updating involves only simple pointer changes. The structure representing an entire expression will be, in general, a graph rather than a tree, because subexpressions may be shared and pointed to cyclically to represent recursion (see Figures 13.3 and 13.4). The phrase **graph reduction** is thus used to describe this form of reduction.

In Turner (1979a, b) the combinator approach was shown to be a practical implementation technique for supporting lazy languages. Since then many improvements have been investigated including, most notably, **lambda lifting** and **super-combinators** (Hughes, 1982) and the **G machine** (Johnsson, 1984). Lambda lifting is a technique for finding specialized combinators which suit a particular program, and the G machine (graph machine) is a SECD-like machine which implements specialized combinators efficiently. This was used to implement Lazy ML and the implementation of Ponder is based on a similar abstract machine developed independently and described in Fairbairn (1985) and Fairbairn and Wray (1986). A hardware implementation of combinator reduction is also described in Clarke *et al.* (1980).

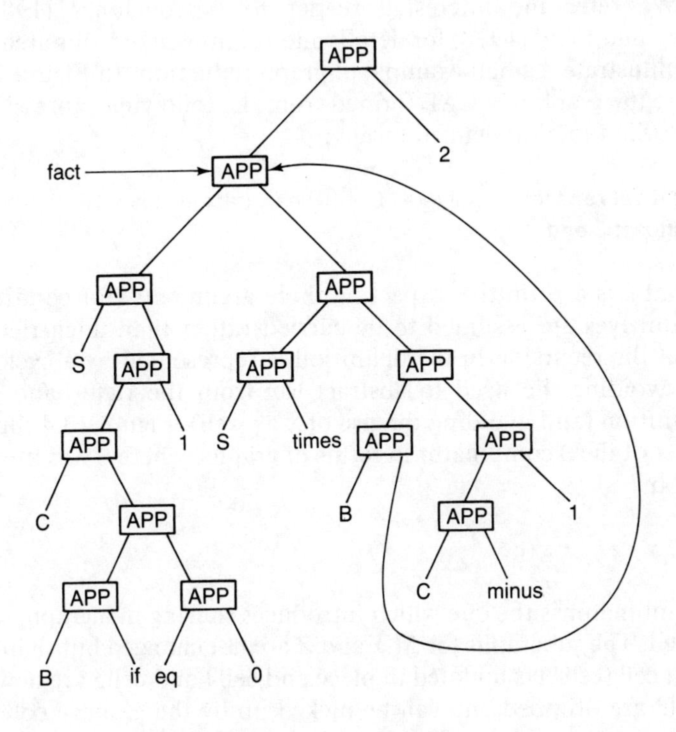

Figure 13.3 Graph of a CAF with value 2 factorial.

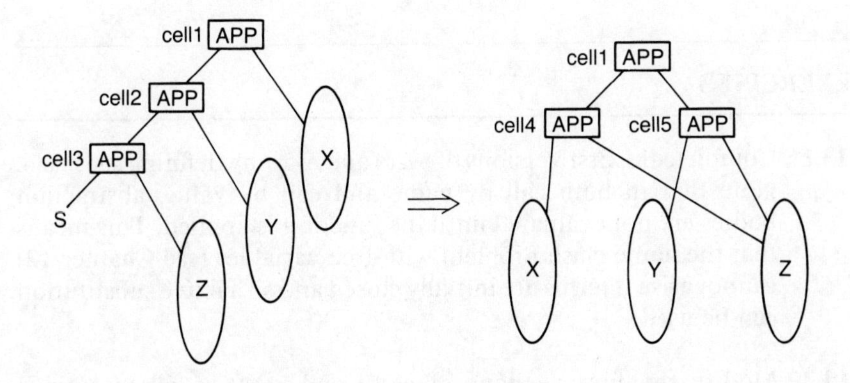

Figure 13.4 The action of combinator S as a graph rewriter.

We refer the interested reader to Peyton-Jones (1987) and Harrison and Field (1988) for details and recent work in this area. Below we just illustrate a small example of graph reduction. In Figure 13.3 we illustrate the graph of a CAF formed from the following expression with the factorial function defined locally:

```
let val rec fact = λx.if (eq x 0) 1 (times x (fact (minus x 1))
in fact 2 end
```

Note that if is a primitive expecting three arguments (for conditionals) and primitives are assumed to be curried rather than uncurried. Note also that the recursion in the definition is represented by a cycle in the graph, avoiding the need to abstract fact from the right-hand side of the definition (and avoiding the use of Y as well). Figure 13.4 illustrates the effect of the S combinator in terms of graphs, where S was previously defined by:

$$\mathsf{S}\ x\ y\ z \rightarrow x\ z\ (y\ z)$$

This combinator is the one which introduces sharing in a graph as it gets evaluated. The subgraphs for *X*, *Y* and *Z* are not changed but shared. The topmost cell (cell1) is updated in place and cell4 and cell5 are new. Cell2 and cell3 are dropped and can be picked up by the garbage collector if they are not components of other expressions (i.e. if they are not pointed to from elsewhere).

We leave it as an exercise for the reader to provide graph rewriting versions of B, C, K, I and Y and to use them to evaluate the graph for fact 2 by hand.

EXERCISES

13.1 Complete the first versions of evalN and evalV by defining substitute. Note that in both call by name and call by value, abstraction bodies are not evaluated until the function is applied. This means that the name clash problem with free variables (see Chapter 12) cannot arise if terms are initially closed and so a naïve substitution can be used.

13.2 Modify the first versions of evalN and evalV to allow curried primitives other than tuple_n, so that $m + n$ can be translated to plus m n instead of plus (m, n) or plus $(\mathsf{tuple}_2\ m\ n)$.

13.3 Implement environments using (a) a list of pairs of variable lists and value lists, (b) a pair consisting of a list of variable lists and a list of value lists. In each case give definitions for bind, ++ and lookup.

13.4 Compile and evaluate the following for both the SECD and the CAM:

times (5, succ 9)
(λx.times (x, succ x)) (succ 4)
(λx.λy.times (x, succ y)) (succ 4) 9
(λf.f (succ 4)) (λx.times (x, succ x))

13.5 Modify the compiler for the SECD machine to take an extra continuation parameter (initially [ ]) to avoid excessive @ operations in linking the code. Use the modified compiler to attach a final STOP instruction at the end of a program and a RETURN instruction at the end of code for a function body. Modify the SECD machine to allow for these instructions.

13.6 Modify the compiler and SECD machine to include primitive instructions such as PLUS, TIMES, . . .

13.7 What is the result of evaluation of a SECD program which denotes a function, such as:

let val rec f = λx.E **in** f **end**

13.8 In order to implement a tail recursion modification for the SECD, it is convenient to split APP into two separate actions. We introduce SAVE and ENTER as well as RETURN and RESTORE where:

s, e, SAVE :: c, d
⊢ s, e, c, (_, e, _, d)

Closure (c', e') :: a :: s, e, ENTER :: c, (_, e'', _, d'')
⊢ [ ], a :: e', c', (s, e'', c, d'')

a :: s, e, RETURN :: c, (s', e', c', d')
⊢ a :: s', e, c', (s', e', c', d')

s, e, RESTORE :: c, (s', e', c', d')
⊢ s, e', c, d'

Note that SAVE and RESTORE are inverses, so that we should be able to omit sequences such as SAVE, RESTORE. Finally, we introduce TAILAPPLY with the behaviour (described diagrammatically):

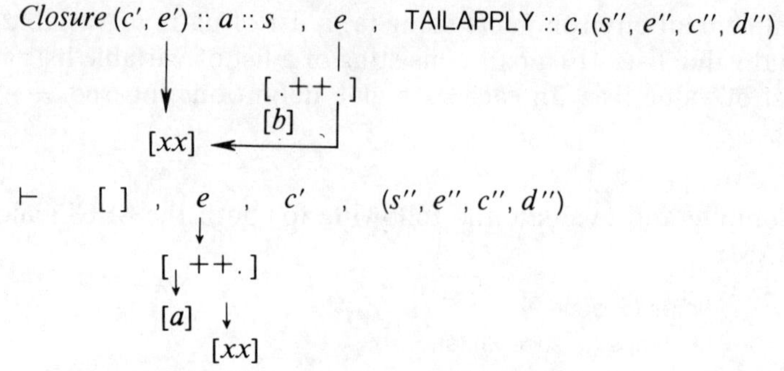

```
Closure (c', e') :: a :: s  ,  e  ,  TAILAPPLY :: c, (s'', e'', c'', d'')
          |                    |
          |          [.++.]    |
          ↓          [b]       |
        [xx]  ←----------------┘

⊢     [ ]  ,  e  ,  c'  ,  (s'', e'', c'', d'')
              ↓
          [↓ ++. ]
          [a]  ↓
              [xx]
```

Thus the existing environment is updated, and the state is not dumped on the call. Investigate ways of adapting the compiler to make use of these new instructions.

13.9 Introduce instructions DELAY and FORCE to create and evaluate suspensions (updateable closures) for a lazy SECD machine. Note that DELAY will be similar to LDFUN for a function with no arguments and FORCE will be similar to (APP 0) except for updating the suspension afterwards (see Henderson (1980) or Abramsky (1982) for a solution).

13.10 Introduce a dump component (d) for the CAM which contains only a control list and further dump (c', d') so that @ can be avoided in the rule for APP.

13.11 Using the following additional rule for the CAM:

$$a :: (Env\ b) :: s \quad \text{CONS} :: c \vdash Env\ (a :: b) :: s\ c$$

show that the following optimization for qualified expressions:

$$compile\ (\textbf{let val}\ V = E'\ \textbf{in}\ E\ \textbf{end})\ nl$$
$$= [\text{COPY}]\ @\ compile\ E'\ nl\ @\ [\text{CONS}]\ @\ compile\ E\ (V :: nl)$$

behaves correctly. That is, it has the same effect as:

$$compile\ ((\lambda V\,.\,E)\ E')\ nl$$

13.12 Use diagrams (cf. Figure 13.4 and Exercise 12.20) to go through the steps in the evaluation of fact 2 as given in Figure 13.3. Follow a normal order reduction by choosing the topmost leftmost redex in the graph at each step.

Chapter 14
Extending Functional Methods

This final chapter takes a brief look at some ways in which functional programming methods can be enhanced and extended. We select two areas in particular, where there is much current active research, namely: **non-determinism** (the introduction of non-determinism as another aid to abstraction); and **support for equational reasoning** (including extensions aimed at combining functional and logic programming).

14.1 Non-determinism

Non-determinism has often been used in computing as a convenient means of abstraction in several different ways. When specifying some desired behaviour of a program or system, it is sometimes useful to allow for several slightly different behaviours as acceptable implementations. Thus we may leave some aspects of the behaviour unspecified or constrained to fit one of several possible alternatives. As a very simple example, we might want a program to generate all the permutations of a list, where we are not concerned about the order in which the permutations are generated.

As another example of the use of non-determinism, consider the possibility of using several processors to 'race' each other for the production of a solution to a problem. We might have two different ways of obtaining a solution (i.e. two algorithms) and we want them both to be computed, so that we can take the answer from the first one to finish. Expressing such a computation will involve some form of non-determinism unless we are prepared to model details of execution speeds within the algorithm (which is likely to be highly impractical).

14.1.1 Non-determinism and referential transparency

One way to introduce non-determinism as a programming construct might be in the form of a primitive such as McCarthy's ambiguity operator amb. Informally, this can be used rather like a function of type $\alpha \times \alpha \to \alpha$ but provides the following behaviour. The value of an expression of the form:

$$E_1 \text{ amb } E_2$$

is either the value of E_1 or the value of E_2. This informal description of the meaning of amb leaves a lot of details to be filled in. For example, we need to know what values could be denoted by:

```
double (2 amb 3)
```

where double x = x + x. If we use the above property of amb we should be able to deduce that double 2 = 4 is a possible value as is double 3 = 6. However, we might also use a substitution to reason that:

```
double (2 amb 3) = (2 amb 3) + (2 amb 3)
```

which also allows 2 + 3 or 3 + 2 as solutions. Note that if call by value is used with amb, however, the result 5 would not be possible, since the ambiguity would be resolved in the argument before double gets applied. Furthermore, we would not get 5 as a result if we changed the definition of double so that double x = x * 2. In fact we have to be very careful in our reasoning since we want to avoid nonsense like:

$$2 = (2 \text{ amb } 3) = 3$$

These simple examples illustrate that the introduction of something like amb destroys the referential transparency of the programming language. This means that we lose the major advantages of using referentially transparent languages. We can no longer assume that we can substitute equals for equals in reasoning and calculating, and also the order of evaluation is significant which restricts potential for parallel evaluation. However, in order to design operating systems, the loss of referential transparency might be acceptable (especially if the loss can be localized).

There are other aspects of a non-deterministic primitive such as amb which need to be specified. For example, we might require that:

$$\Omega \text{ amb } E = E \quad \text{and} \quad E \text{ amb } \Omega = E$$

which gives an 'angelic' flavour to the operator. This is because undefined results would be avoided if possible. In contrast, a 'demonic' operator might be defined to produce $\perp$ whenever any one of its arguments is undefined. Both forms of operator (and other variations) turn out to have applications somewhere.

14.1.2 Non-determinism and multiprogramming

In Chapter 8 we mentioned how lazy evaluation allowed us to view functional programs as collections of processes passing data to each other, thus providing a suitable abstraction for dealing with concurrent systems without concern over interleaving problems. Communication between processes is expressed very naturally through the application of functions to arguments and through the sharing of values produced by subexpressions. Some examples of programs viewed as concurrent processes were given but to handle more complex examples we need to introduce non-determinism into the language.

Consider a process p with incoming data from other processes in a real-time system. The actual times of arrival of data will depend on the exact speeds of the processes, and we may require that p reacts to (or deals with) incoming data in the order it arrives. With only one input to a process, we are able to abstract away from complicated temporal concerns by using sequences (streams) to represent the order in which data values arrive. Similarly with more than one input to a process we can forget about temporal concerns provided that the output is uniquely determined by the ordering of data items on each incoming stream and not on their relative times of arrival on different streams. If the relative time of arrival between streams can affect the result, then the abstraction away from temporal concerns, by trying to consider p as a function, introduces non-determinism. That is, the result of applying the function corresponding to p to streams representing the data items arriving at p can produce any one of a collection of different results. If p receives the streams $a_1 :: a_2 :: \cdots$ and $b_1 :: b_2 :: \cdots$ and outputs a single stream of items *in the order in which they arrive*, then we may get as output any one of several possible streams such as:

$$a_1 :: a_2 :: b_1 :: a_3 :: a_4 :: b_2 :: \cdots \quad \text{or} \quad b_1 :: a_1 :: b_2 :: a_2 :: b_3 :: a_3 :: \cdots$$

Henderson (1982b) has shown how the introduction of a single non-deterministic primitive (interleave or MERGE) into a lazily evaluated functional language can prove sufficient for describing reasonably large operating systems. As a small example, Figure 14.1 contains a diagram for a very simple operating system ('sys6' in Henderson, 1982b). This system involves three main stream processing functions, namely edit, databasefun and run. edit receives a stream of editing commands and produces output for the screen, commands for the database and arguments for run which evaluates programs. The output from run is sent to databasefun and databasefun acts as a filestore, accepting commands for entering and retrieving items.

The stream functions $+_K$ and $+_D$ simply label items so that the function edit (receiving a mixed stream) can determine the source of each item in its input stream (K for keyboard and D for databasefun). Conversely, $-_D$ looks for items labelled for the database and removes the labels. It also throws away other items. Similarly, $-_S$ collects items intended for the screen and $-_R$ collects items intended for run.

The other stream function is the non-deterministic merge which allows two streams to be combined. Note that if we were to use an edit with two input streams, it would have to predict which stream it should expect its next input from and might hang if it made the wrong choice. By merging the streams, we isolate the problem of such choices to the operation MERGE itself.

Example operating systems like the one in Figure 14.1 are developed further in Jones (1983, 1984) and an alternative method is suggested in Stoye (1984). The advantage of Stoye's approach is that a single (infinitary) merge is assumed as part of the programming environment, acting like a mail delivery service. Programs themselves do not make use of any non-deterministic primitives, and so referential transparency is preserved for individual programs.

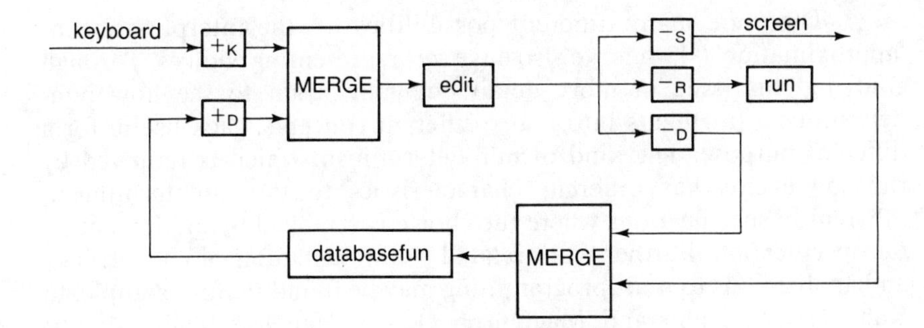

Figure 14.1 A simple operating system.

Note that we could define MERGE in terms of amb:

```
fun MERGE (a :: x) (b :: y) = (a :: MERGE x (b :: y))
                              amb
                              (b :: MERGE (a :: x) y)
  |  MERGE [ ] y = y
  |  MERGE x [ ] = x
```

assuming 'angelic' behaviour for amb to ensure that the choice is not made irrespectively of whether or not data is available on each stream. For example, we want (using Ω to represent an unavailable value):

$$\text{MERGE } \Omega \text{ dbaseout} = \text{dbaseout}$$

and:

$$\text{MERGE } (a :: \Omega)\ (b_1 :: b_2 :: \cdots) = b_1 :: \cdots :: b_n :: a :: b_{n+1} :: \cdots$$

for some $n \geq 0$.

Abramsky (1982) suggests the use of pattern matched equations which may overlap (i.e. ambiguous equations) for describing cooperating processes to be implemented in software or hardware. He also shows how the SECD machine can be extended to support the pseudo-parallel evaluation of these programs on a sequential machine.

Mathematically, non-determinism may be modelled by functions producing sets of results or sets of functions (one for each possible result) or relations between arguments and results rather than functions. In choosing the appropriate model we must take into account ⊥ as a possible outcome and this involves the construction of a suitable 'power domain' (corresponding to sets of elements from another domain) with an appropriate derived ordering of approximation (see, for example, Plotkin (1976), Smyth (1978), Abramsky (1983)).

There are many different possibilities for the interpretation of 'approximation' ($\sqsubseteq$) when we also have sets representing choices. Through studying this issue in more detail one may begin to see how non-determinism fragments into many different concepts, each useful for a different purpose. The kind of non-determinism which is removed by runtime events has different characteristics to the 'indeterminism' inherent in specifications where the choice is removed by implementing the specification. Further work related to the semantics of concurrency and applications to multiprogramming may be found in, for example, in Kahn (1974), Kahn and MacQueen (1977), Hennessy and Ashcroft (1976), Hennessy (1982), Park (1980), Abramsky (1982, 1983), Broy (1982, 1983), Holmstrom (1983) and Kaplan (1986).

14.2 Support for equational reasoning

14.2.1 Equational specifications and programs

Functional programs are sufficiently far removed from many implementation details that they can often be considered as specifications and the fact that they may also be run is an important bonus. The relative ease with which one functional program can be transformed into another, more efficient one shows how useful it is to have a unification of the language in which software requirements are specified with the language in which implementations are expressed. Unfortunately, definitions in the form we have used up to now are not adequate for a specification language on their own. Rather than specifying particular functions, we may wish only to describe properties, constraints and relationships between a group of functions and other abstract objects. Any particular group of objects which satisfy these requirements may be considered as a possible implementation.

The problem is, therefore, how to build a framework into which both general specifications as well as functional definitions can naturally be fitted so that transformations between them are straightforward. The use of equations to specify relationships seems the most natural choice as we mentioned in Chapter 7.

The equations needed to specify relationships between functions and other values are more general than those which we consider to be definitions in a functional language. We do not require such equations to be 'evaluated' as though they were left to right rewriting rules and a degree of ambiguity is acceptable if we do not wish to overspecify the possible implementations.

Equations can sometimes be used as rewriting rules without modifications and, provided that they satisfy the confluence property (see Chapter 12), they can be 'run' (evaluated) in the same way as the definitions in a functional program. There are also tools for helping to convert a collection of equations (a specification) into a suitable set of rewriting rules (a program) which may then be run.

In particular, we mention the Knuth-Bendix algorithm (Knuth and Bendix, 1970) which is a completion procedure for a set of equations. Given a set of equations which describe some constraints between functions, the algorithm produces (when it is successful) a set of rewriting rules which can be used to evaluate the functions. Note that simply considering the equations as left to right rewrite rules may be inadequate, as we illustrate with an example (taken from Huet and Oppen (1980)). Suppose we take the equations:

```
p (C, x) = x
p (n x, x) = C
p (p (x, y), z) = p (x, p (x, y, z))
```

These are in fact axioms for a group. They are satisfied by, for example, interpreting p as addition, n as negation and C as zero. If we just use the equations as rewrite rules (left to right):

```
p (C, x) ──► x
p (n x, x) ──► C
p (p (x, y), z) ──► p (x, p (y, z))
```

then we have lost the information that the equations were symmetric and evaluation may not be complete. Adding the inverses of the rules such as x ──► p (C, x) will not help here, because this is likely to lead to infinite evaluation sequences going round and round in circles. The Knuth-Bendix algorithm, on the other hand, helps us to complete the set of equations, so that evaluation using the equations as rewrite rules will produce 'normal forms' for any expression involving the functions p, x, C. In this example, the algorithm produces:

```
p (C, x) = x
p (n x, x) = C
p (p (x, y), z) = p (x, p (y, z))
p (n x, p (x, y)) = y
n C = C
p (x, C) = x
n (n x) = x
p (x, n x) = C
p (x, p (n x, y)) = y
n (p (x, y)) = p (n x, n y)
```

Note that the new equations are all consequences of the original equations.

Not only do the new equations allow us to evaluate expressions (i.e. they are a program for the original specification), they are also useful for answering questions about the original specification. Suppose we want to discover whether or not the specification implies that:

```
n (p (n C, C)) = p (C, C)
```

We can simply evaluate both sides of the equation (using the complete set of equations as rules) and get:

```
C = C
```

which is clearly true. Similarly, to discover if:

```
n (p (n C, C)) = p (C, Succ C)
```

where Succ is another function for which there are no rules (i.e. a constructor), we evaluate both sides of the equation to get:

```
C = Succ C
```

which is false since both sides are fully simplified and distinct.

Using equations like the above set as rewrite rules is not exactly the same as evaluation of functional programs given by pattern matching definitions. The extension to allow a richer form of left-hand side in defining equations is, however, perfectly possible and has been implemented in some programming languages. See in particular O'Donnell (1985) and Goguen and Tardo (1979).

14.2.2 Reasoning as a programming activity

The reduction of an expression E to a normal form N can also be viewed as a deduction of the fact that $E = N$. That is to say, functional program evaluation is a kind of theorem proving using equations. Bearing this in mind, we can consider what other forms of equational reasoning we might like to support in addition to straightforward evaluation.

For example, consider the following problem. We have designed a function flatten which produces a list of the node items in a tree in order (see Section 5.2.3) and is defined as follows:

```
fun flatten Empty = [ ]
|   flatten (Tr (t1, a, t2)) = flatten t1 @ (a :: flatten t2)
```

Then we can do an evaluation to show that:

```
flatten (Tr (Tr (Empty, 3, Tr (Empty, 6, Empty)), 7, Tr (Empty, 5, Empty)) =
    [3, 6, 7, 5]
```

Now suppose that we want to know which trees produce the same result when flattened. That is, we want to find all trees t which satisfy the property:

```
flatten t = [3, 6, 7, 5]
```

Note that we are effectively trying to invert the function flatten : α tree → α list. If this is a special case of a general problem which we frequently want to solve, we may well want to construct an inverse function:

```
unflatten : α list → α tree list
```

The result of the inverted function is given here as a list of trees since there will in general be more than one tree which flattens to a given list of node values. For example:

```
unflatten [1, 2] = [Tr (Empty, 1, Tr (Empty, 2, Empty)),
                    Tr (Tr (Empty, 1, Empty), 2, Empty)]
```

Unfortunately, a direct definition of the inverse is not particularly obvious. (Try defining it as an exercise.)

It would be a powerful extension to functional programming if there were tools to help solve problems such as the above automatically. These could be used in preference to constructing a direct functional program when a quick answer is needed in a specific instance and the functional program is not immediately available. Conversely, a program which needs to be run frequently and needs to be efficient may well be worth the effort of analysis for optimization. However, there may even be cases where an automatic search for a solution could be as efficient as a direct evaluation and could even be done dynamically, that is the problem to be solved might be generated during some normal function evaluation.

Careful analysis of a problem can often give insight into quick solutions or improved methods for solving the problem. In such situations, it is useful to have plenty of tools for reasoning about problems and experimenting with designs. In any case, a major activity of a 'programmer' should be in designing and reasoning about problems, correctness of designs, etc.

Functional and logic languages (see below) are seen by many as particularly advantageous in such areas where attention to correctness and reasoning is important and where facilities for abstraction are essential. In particular, the possibilities for rapid prototyping and derivation of efficient solutions by transformational techniques are enhanced by the use of such languages.

14.2.3 Logic programming

The style of logic programming proposed by Kowalski (1979) can be regarded as theorem proving with a restricted form of first order formulae. Proofs are developed automatically using a form of **resolution theorem proving** which relies heavily on the unification algorithm (Robinson, 1965; Martelli and Montanari, 1982). The unification algorithm is the same one we described in Chapter 11 for discovering information about types. Here, it is used to discover information about expressions (restricted to contain only constructors ('functors') and variables and without any higher order functions. The main language implemented in this way is PROLOG (see Clocksin and Mellish (1981)).

As a simple example, let us consider some logic programs for appending lists and flattening trees. Logic programs express relationships between data objects and may be used (when run) to deduce other relationships which may logically follow, or just to look up facts in the program. Relations rather than functions are the central concept, so the distinction between results and arguments is partly removed. This means that in principle, a logic program may be used in several ways – running in different directions depending on which arguments of a relation are regarded as input values and which are regarded as output values. Constructors such as Tr, Empty, [ ] and :: can be used in exactly the same way in logic programs as they are in functional programs. However, other functions are replaced by predicates describing relationships between arguments and results.

For example, instead of describing @ or append as a function of two lists, we use a predicate isappendof which describes a relationship between three lists. Informally isappendof (x, y, z) is true if and only if z is the list formed by appending y to the right of x, that is:

isappendof (x, y, z) is true if and only if x @ y = z is true

When we define this relationship formally as a logic program, we can use the program not only to deduce the value of z given x and y, but also to deduce x, given y and z, etc. Corresponding to the two cases in the recursive definition of a functional append, we have two clauses describing the relation. First, we may state that for any list x, isappendof ([ ], x, x) is true (i.e. the result of appending x onto [ ] is x). Secondly, for any lists x, y and z and item a, isappendof (a :: x, y, a :: z) is true if and only if isappendof (x, y, z) is true. These clauses may be written as follows:

```
isappendof ([ ], x, x).
isappendof (a :: x, y, a :: z) IF isappendof (x, y, z).
```

Each clause stands for a possible infinite collection of facts obtained by instantiating the parameter variables (a, x, y, z) with actual values. As well as being logical statements, though, the clauses may be given a procedural interpretation: we may read the second clause as a rule which says that in order to prove that isappendof (a :: x, y, a :: z) holds for some a, x, y and z (this is the goal), it is sufficient to prove that isappendof (x, y, z) holds (this is a subgoal). Similarly, in order to prove that isappendof ([ ], x, x) holds for some x, we need do nothing since it holds without any conditions. Sometimes a notation such as ⟶ is used instead of **IF** because we can regard the rule as a rewrite rule.

In order to describe tree flattening, we introduce some additional clauses for a predicate isflattenof:

```
isflattenof (Empty, [ ]).
isflattenof (Tr (x, a, y), z) IF isflattenof (t1, x1)
                              AND isflattenof (t2, x2)
                              AND isappendof (x1, a :: x2, z).
```

In general the clauses ('Horn clauses') may be written in the form:

$$A \textbf{ IF } A_1 \textbf{ AND } A_2 \ldots \textbf{ AND } A_n.$$

or just:

A.

where A and A_i are atomic clauses with the form of a predicate applied to arguments. Arguments may be (logical) variables, constants or constructors applied to arguments. (The form A. can be regarded as an abbreviation for A **IF** true.) Horn clauses are not as general as arbitrary sentences in first order logic, but most problems can be expressed in this restricted form which has the relatively fast implcmentation of deduction mentioned below.

To run a program we simply ask questions such as:

```
isappendof ([1, 2], [3], [ ])?
```

and the clauses are used to deduce the truth or falsity of the assertion in the question (in this case 'no' or 'false' is the reply).

More generally, questions containing free variables ('logical variables') are answered by establishing whether any values can be found to make the assertion in the question true and reporting any that are found. Thus:

```
isappendof ([l, 2], [3], ?z)?
```

produces the response z = [1, 2, 3] (we use a ? so that it is easy to spot the logical variables in a question). Similarly:

```
isappendof (?x, ?y, [1, 2, 3])?
```

can produce any or all of the responses:

```
(1) x = [ ]       and y = [1, 2, 3]
(2) x = [1]       and y = [2, 3]
(3) x = [1, 2]    and y = [3]
(4) x = [1, 2, 3] and y = [ ]
```

We illustrate the role that unification plays in discovering these solutions by tracing a small (PROLOG style) deduction. We will revert to an unabbreviated notation for lists writing Cons (1, Cons (2, Cons (3, [ ]))) instead of [1, 2, 3] for simplicity. During deduction, we keep a list of current goals and a record of the substitution produced by all the unifications performed so far. Furthermore, because PROLOG searches (in a depth first way), for solutions, we need to be able to return to points where there is a branch for a choice of computations (but we will not give all the details of how this can be done here).

At each step, the top goal in the goal list is matched against the left-hand sides of clauses (the expression to the left of the '**IF**' or '→'). There are two important points to note here. First, several left-hand sides may match, giving us a choice (and hence a branch point in the computation where we must return if we are to explore all possible paths). Secondly, the 'match' is more than just pattern matching as found in functional program evaluation but full unification. This is because variables may occur not only as parameters in the clauses, but also in the goal as logical variables. Once a left-hand side unifies with a goal, we replace the goal with the goal(s) on the right of the matching clause. The substitution for variables produced by a unification of a clause's left-hand side with a goal is applied to the new and remaining goals. (A record is also kept for the purpose of reporting final values discovered for variables in the original question.)

Each time a clause is used, new instances are chosen for the parameters (see below) to avoid accidental clashes. (This is similar to the use of instances of generic variables in the type inference algorithm described in Chapter 11.) Suppose our initial goal is:

```
isappendof (Cons (?x, [ ]), ?y, Cons (1, Cons (2, [ ])))?
```

We try to unify this with left-hand sides of each clause in the program. There are four clauses counting the two for isflattenof and the only one which unifies successfully is:

```
isappendof (Cons (a, x) y, Cons (a, z)) IF isappendof (x, y, z).
```

which we rewrite as:

```
isappendof (Cons (?1, ?2), ?3, Cons (?1, ?4)) IF isappendof (?2, ?3, ?4).
```

using fresh variable instances for the parameters in the clause. The substitution (most general unifier) produced by the unification maps:

```
?x to 1   ?2 to [ ]   ?3 to ?y   ?1 to 1   ?4 to Cons (2, [ ])
```

The replacement goals are obtained from the right-hand side of the clause (1 new goal and 0 remaining current goals) and using the substitution. This gives:

```
isappendof ([ ], ?y, Cons (2, [ ]))?
```

as our new goal (list). Following the same process, this unifies with the left-hand side of (a fresh instance of) the first clause for isappendof, say:

```
isappendof ([ ], ?5, ?5)
```

Unification gives a substitution which maps:

```
?y to Cons (2, [ ])   ?5 to Cons (2, [ ])
```

and this leaves no more goals. An empty goal list indicates success and we can report the final values of ?x and ?y, namely:

```
?x = 1   and   ?y = Cons (2, [ ])
```

In this example, there were no other choices of unifying clauses at each step, so there are no other solutions. A failed branch (with no solutions) arises when no left-hand side of a clause will unify with a goal, and when a branch has been explored to produce a result or failure, we go back to the most recent point in the computation where there was an untried choice (hence depth first search). From such a point we try the next choice after reinstating the goals and substitution associated with that point.

The interested reader might like to try a harder example such as:

```
isflattenof (?t, Cons (1, Cons (2, [ ])))?
```

as an exercise.

14.2.4 Functional and logic programming

Although logic programming is clearly an extension of functional programming in some respects, since we can reason about relationships which are not functional), it loses out on the limitation to first order functions and the loss of fast functional evaluation when a search is not necessary. The first drawback seems quite serious and extending unification to deal with higher order functions is only possible in a partial sense (see Huet (1975)).

On the other hand, the unification algorithm has been shown to be extendable to allow for function evaluation (see, for example, Gallier and Snyder (1987), Holldobler (1987)). This means that logic-style programming can be combined with first order functional programming relatively cleanly.

The problem with the basic unification algorithm is that it only performs a syntactic comparison of expressions which involve constructors and variables. If we introduce functions which can be evaluated, syntactic comparison becomes inadequate. For example:

f (x) and g (h (y))

do not unify in the syntactic sense, but if f (x) evaluates to g (h (x)) say, then the values denoted by the expressions should match, that is they match in a semantic sense.

We give a brief example below to illustrate how (evaluating) unification can be used to solve the 'unflatten' problem. We would like to evaluate flatten ?t = [3, 6, 5, 7] in order to discover information about the unknown value (or 'logic variable') ?t. (Again, we write ?t rather than just t to indicate that t is intended to be an unbound variable rather than something defined previously or an error.) Initially, we regard the problem as a collection of equations (a collection with one member in this case):

```
flatten ?t = Cons (3, Cons (6, Cons (5, Cons (7, [ ]))))
```

We regard the definitions of relevant functions as a collection of rewriting rules:

```
flatten Empty ──► [ ]
flatten (Tr (t1, a, t2)) ──► append (flatten t1, Cons (a, flatten t2))
append ([ ], x) ──► x
append (Cons (a, x), y) ──► Cons (a, append (x, y))
```

Now, the process of (extended) unification can be broken down into several rules for rewriting the set of equations. One important change is that instead of trying to unify two expressions in one go, we break it down into small steps matching a bit at a time. The choice of rule to use at each step is not always completely determined, which is why we have to allow for a search with some choices possibly leading to dead ends as before.

For the example, we begin by comparing the equation and the first rewrite rule which has the same function symbol on the left (i.e. a rule which matches as far as the first function symbol is concerned):

```
flatten ?t ──► Cons (3, Cons (6, Cons (5, Cons (7, [ ]))))
```

with:

```
flatten Empty ──► [ ]
```

We then replace the equation by two new equations, namely:

```
?t = Empty
Cons (3, Cons (6, Cons (5, Cons (7, [ ]))))= [ ]
```

These new equations are obtained by pairing the arguments of flatten on the two left-hand sides of the chosen equation and rewrite rule, and also pairing the two right-hand sides. In general:

$$f(E_1, \ldots, E_n) = E,\ OtherEqns$$

generates:

$$E_1 = E_1', \ldots, E_n = E_n',\ E = E',\ OtherEqns$$

when $f(E_1', \ldots, E_n') \longrightarrow E'$ is a rewrite rule.

The new first equation for our example (?t = Empty) can be 'solved' by identifying the variable and the value (replacing each occurrence of ?t by Empty and keeping a record of the binding for reporting any answers we might discover later). In general:

$$V = E,\ OtherEqns$$

generates:

$$OtherEqns\ [E/V]$$

provided V does not occur in E. Here $OtherEqns\ [E/V]$ means replace each occurrence of V by E in each equation in the collection *OtherEqns*. (At any stage we can of course turn an equation $E = E'$ into $E' = E$ to obtain a variable on the left before using the above **variable elimination rule.**)

In the example, we now have as our equation(s):

```
Cons (3, Cons (6, Cons (5, Cons (7, [ ])))) = [ ]
```

The left- and right-hand sides of this equation are expressions formed with distinct constructors (:: and [ ]) and this means that no solutions can be found by pursuing this branch of the search.

Returning to the original equation, we now try comparing the equation with the second rewrite rule for flatten. Since the rule contains parameter variables (t1, a and t2) we instantiate the rule to obtain a fresh instance with fresh parameter names, for example:

```
flatten (Tr (?1, ?2, ?3)) → append (flatten ?1, Cons (?2, flatten ?3))
```

This is because the parameters are implicitly quantified by a $\forall$ and the variable names used are arbitrary.

The comparison generates two equations:

```
?t = Tr (?1, ?2, ?3)
Cons (3, Cons (6, Cons (5, Cons (7, [ ]))))
= append (flatten ?1, Cons (?2, flatten ?3))
```

Once again we can use variable elimination on the first equation (since ?2 does not occur on the right-hand side). This leaves:

```
Cons (3, Cons (6, Cons (5, Cons (7, [ ]))))
= append (flatten ?1, Cons (?2, flatten ?3))
```

and we record that ?t is bound to Tr (?1, ?2, ?3).

After reversing the equation, we can compare the left-hand side with each of the rules for append and continue in this way. Eventually, some branches in the search should lead to an empty set of equations and the record of bindings will contain a solution for ?t in such cases.

Other rules which can be used are **term decomposition** where equations of the form:

$$f(E_1, \ldots, E_n) = f(E_1', \ldots, E_n')$$

are replaced by:

$$E_1 = E_1' \ldots E_n = E_n'$$

and **removal of trivial equations** where equations of the form:

$$E = E$$

are deleted. In addition there are two rules proposed by Holldobler which complete the set for dealing with recursive (infinite) objects created with lazy evaluation. For details, see Holldobler (1987).

The papers in DeGroot and Lindstrom (1986) contain much of the recent work on combining functional and logic programming. For other information concerning equational reasoning see, for example, O'Donnell (1977), Huet and Oppen (1980), Hoffman and O'Donnell (1982) and Thatte (1984, 1985, 1986), as well as papers in Jouannaud (1987) and Lescanne (1987). For examples of environments supporting equational reasoning see, for example, Lescanne (1983) and Dick (1987).

14.2.5 Other support for reasoning

Although PROLOG automates a fixed searching algorithm this can be controlled indirectly, for example by using 'cut' (see Clocksin and Mellish (1981)). However, as soon as it becomes necessary to do 'sophisticated' searches, the complex control structures of languages like PROLOG often become difficult to use and reason with. In such cases, a better approach using functional techniques is offered by the ML/LCF school. Using a functional language we may consider formulae, inference rules, theorems and proofs as data objects and, by means of higher order functions, strategies for finding proofs ('tactics') and means of combining strategies ('tacticals') may be defined, providing a better level of abstraction. The particular search strategy used in PROLOG implementations is just one such tactic for finding solutions (i.e. proving theorems). Also the strong-typing of ML provides security in that the logical soundness of proofs follows from the correct typing of objects claimed to be theorems. Abstract data types play a central role in the LCF approach. See Paulson (1987) for a recent book on LCF. (The early work is described in Gordon *et al.* (1978).)

14.3 Other developments

It would be impossible to mention all the many research activities related to functional programming in this book. There is other research which has not been mentioned which the author believes may well be significant for the development of functional programming in the near future. For example, there is much research related to the construction of specific hardware for supporting functional languages. There is also much research into techniques for transformational programming and combining programs with specifications. A specific development is the use of constructive mathematics in programming (Martin-Lof, 1982, 1984) which identifies specifications and types for applicative programs. Here, types are made powerful enough to provide a specification language. Although this necessarily means that type checking can no longer be fully automatic, it does allow a rich and natural form of specification language and has the potential for providing many program development tools. Also, it means that only totally defined programs need be considered (partial functions cannot be constructed). A programming language developed from this is Nuprl (Constable *et al.*, 1986).

When functional programming is viewed within the wider context of tools for developing correct and efficient software, it becomes more apparent that there is still much to be discovered and much to be gained by new discoveries.

Bibliography

Abramsky, S. (1982) *SECD-M: A Virtual Machine for Applicative Multiprogramming*, Computer Systems Laboratory, Queen Mary College, Univ. of London. See also Abramsky and Sykes (1985).

Abramsky, S. (1983) *On Semantic Foundations for Applicative Multiprogramming*, Computer Systems Laboratory, Queen Mary College, University of London.

Abramsky, S. and Sykes, R. (1985) 'SECD-M: A Virtual Machine for Applicative Programming'. In *Functional Programming Languages and Computer Architecture*, Lecture Notes in Computer Science (vol. 201), Springer-Verlag: Nancy, France.

ADJ (group of authors: Goguen, J.A., Thatcher, J.W., Wagner, E.G. and Wright, J.B.) (1975) *An Introduction to Categories, Algebraic Theories and Algebras*, IBM Technical Report PC 5369, Thomas J. Watson Research Center, Yorktown Heights, New York.

ADJ (group of authors: Goguen, J.A., Thatcher, J.W. and Wagner, E.G.) (1978a) 'An Initial Algebra Approach to the Specification, Correctness and Implementation of Abstract Data Types'. In *Current Trends in Programming Methodology,* vol. IV of R.I. Yeh (ed.) *Data Structuring*, Prentice Hall.

ADJ (group of authors: Thatcher, J.W., Wagner, E.G. and Wright, J.B.) (1978b) 'Data Type Specification: Parameterisation and the Power of Specification Techniques'. In *Proc. SIGACT 10th Symposium on Theory of Computing.*

Appel, A., MacQueen, D., Milner, R. and Tofte, M. (1988) 'Unifying Exceptions with Constructors in Standard ML', Report RCS-LFCS-88-55, Computer Science Department, University of Edinburgh, June 1988.

Augustsson, L. (1984) 'A Compiler for Lazy ML'. In *ACM Symp. on LISP and Functional Programming*, Austin, Texas, August 1984.

Backus, J. (1978) 'Can Programming Be Liberated from the Von Neumann Style? A Functional Style and its Algebra of Programs', *Communications ACM*, **21** (8), pp. 613–641.

Barendregt, H.P. (1984) *The Lambda Calculus, Its Syntax and Semantics*, North Holland. (First edition, 1981.)

Bauer, F.L. and Samelson, K. (1960) 'Sequential Formula Translation', *Communications ACM*, **3**.

Bauer, F.L. and Wossner, H. (1982) *Algorithmic Language and Program Development*, Texts and Monographs in Computer Science, Springer-Verlag.

Berlekamp, E.R., Conway, J.H. and Guy, R.K. (1982) *Winning Ways for your Mathematical Plays (Vol. 2)*, Academic Press.

Bird, R. (1976) *Programs and Machines (An Introduction to the Theory of Computation)*, Wiley.

Bird, R.S. (1984a) 'Using Circular Programs to Eliminate Multiple Traversals of Data', *Acta Informatica*, **21** (3), pp. 239–250.

Bird, R.S. (1984b) 'The Promotion and Accumulation Strategies in Transformational Programming', *ACM TOPLAS*, **6** (4).

Broy, M. (1982) 'A Fixed Point Approach to Applicative Multiprogramming'. In *Proceedings of Nato Summer School on Theoretical Foundations of Programming Methodology*, M. Broy and G. Schmidt (eds), Reidel, Munich, 1982.

Broy, M. (1983) 'Applicative Real-Time Programming'. In *Proc. 9th IFIP, Information Processing 1983*, pp. 259–264, North Holland.

Burge, W.H. (1975) *Recursive Programming Techniques*, Addison-Wesley.

Burn, G.L., Hankin, C.L. and Abramski, S. (1985) *The Theory and Practice of Strictness Analysis for Higher Order Functions*, Research Report 85/6, Department of Computing, Imperial College.

Burstall, R.M., MacQueen, D.B. and Sanella, D.T. (1980) *HOPE: An Experimental Applicative Language*, Internal report, Department of Computer Science, University of Edinburgh.

Burstall, R.M. and Goguen, J.A. (1980) 'The Semantics of CLEAR, A Specification Language'. In *Abstract Software Specification, Proceedings 1979*, D. Bjorner (ed.), Lecture Notes in Computer Science (vol. 86), Springer-Verlag.

Burstall, R.M. and Goguen, J.A. (1981) 'An Informal Introduction to Specification Using CLEAR'. In *The Correctness Problem in Computer Science*, R.S. Boyer and J.S. Moore (eds.), Academic Press.

Cardelli, L. (1983) 'ML under UNIX', *Polymorphism: The ML/LCF/Hope Newsletter*, **I** (3), December 1983.

Cardelli, L. (1984) 'Compiling a Functional Language', *1984 ACM Symp. Lisp and Functional Programming*, Austin, Texas, August 1984.

Cardelli, L. (1985) 'Basic Polymorphic Type Checking', *Polymorphism: The ML/LCF/Hope Newsletter*, **II** (1), January 1985. Also in *Science of Computer Programming*, **8** (2), 1987.

Cardelli, L. and Wegner, P. (1985) 'On Understanding Types, Data Abstraction and Polymorphism', *Computer Surveys*, **17** (4), December 1985.

Church, A. (1941) 'The Calculi of Lambda-Conversion'. In *Annals of Mathematical Studies No. 6*, Princeton University Press. (Reprinted in 1963 by University Microfilms Inc., Ann Arbor, Michigan.)

Clarke, T.J.W., Gladstone, P.J.S., MacLean, C.D. and Norman, A.C. (1980) 'SKIM – The S,K,I Reduction Machine'. In *Lisp Conference*, Stanford, 1980.

Clement, D. (1987) 'The Natural Dynamic Semantics of Mini-Standard ML'. In *TAPSOFT '87 Vol 2*, Lecture Notes in Computer Science, vol. 250, pp. 67–81; Springer-Verlag.

Clocksin, W.F. and Mellish, C.S. (1981) *Programming in Prolog*, Springer-Verlag.

Colmerauer, A. (1982) 'Prolog and Infinite Trees'. In *Logic Programming*, K.L. Clark and S.-A. Tarnlund (eds), Academic Press.

Constable, R.L. *et al.* (1986) *Implementing Mathematics in the Nuprl Proof Development System*, Prentice Hall.

Coppo, M. (1985) 'A Completeness Theorem for Recursively Defined Types'. In *12th ICALP Nafplion, Greece July 1985*, Lecture Notes in Computer Science (vol. 194), pp. 120–129, Springer-Verlag.

Curien, P.L. (1986) *Categorical Combinators, Sequential Algorithms and Functional Programming*, Research Notes in Theoretical Computer Science, Wiley.

Curry, H.B. and Feys, R. (1958) *Combinatory Logic* (*Vol. 1*), North Holland.

Damas, L. and Milner, R. (1982) 'Principal Type Schemes for Functional Programs'. In *Ninth ACM Symp. on Principles of Programming Languages*, pp. 207–212, Albuquerque NM.

Damas, L. (1985) *Type Assignment in Programming Languages*, PhD Thesis, University of Edinburgh (CST-33-85), April 1985.

Darlington, J. and Reeve, M. (1981) 'ALICE: A Multiprocessor Reduction Machine for the Parallel Evaluation of Applicative Languages'. In *ACM/MIT Conf. on Functional Languages and Parallel Architecture*, New Hampshire, 1981.

Darlington, J., Henderson, P. and Turner, D.A. (eds) (1982) *Functional Programming and Its Applications – An Advanced Course*, Cambridge University Press.

Darlington, J., Field, A.J. and Pull, H. (1985) *The Unification of Functional and Logic Languages*, Department of Computing Report DOC 85/3, Imperial College of Science and Technology, London University, February 1985.

De Bruijn, N.G. (1972) 'Lambda Calculus Notation with Nameless Dummies', *Inagationes Mathematicae*, (34), pp. 381–392.

DeGroot, D. and Lindstrom, G. (1986) *Logic Programming: Functions, Relations and Equations*, Prentice Hall.

Dick, A.A.J. (1985) *Introduction to ERIL* (*Equational Reasoning Interactive Laboratory*, Rutherford Appleton Laboratories, Chilton, Oxford.

Dijkstra, E.W. (1968) 'Goto Statement Considered Harmful', *Communications ACM*, **11** (3), pp. 147–149.

Dybjer, P. (1987) 'Inverse Image Analysis'. In *14th ICALP Karlsruhe, Germany July 1987*, Lecture Notes in Computer Science (vol. 267), pp. 21–30, Springer.

Ehrig, H. and Mahr, B. (1985) *Fundamentals of Algebraic Specification 1 – Equations and Initial Semantics*, Springer-Verlag.

Fairbairn, J. (1982) *Ponder and Its Type System*, University of Cambridge Computer Laboratory Technical Report No. 31, November 1982.

Fairbairn, J. (1984) *A New Type Checker for a Functional Language*, University of Cambridge Computer Laboratory Technical Report No. 53, 1984.

Fairbairn, J. (1985) *Design and Implementation of a Simple Typed Language Based on the Lambda Calculus*, University of Cambridge Computer Laboratory Technical Report No. 75, May 1985.

Fairbairn, J. (1986) *Making Form Follow Function: An Exercise in Functional Programming Style*, University of Cambridge Computer Laboratory Technical Report No. 89, June 1986.

Fairbairn, J. and Wray, S.C. (1986) 'Code Generation Techniques for Functional Languages'. In *ACM Symp. on Lisp and Functional Programming*, pp. 94–104, Cambridge, Mass.

Falkoff, A.D. and Iverson, K.E. (1986) *APL/360 User's Manual*, Thomas J. Watson Research Center, IBM, Yorktown, NY, July 1968.

Field, A.J. and Harrison, P.E. (1988) *Functional Programming*, Wokingham: Addison-Wesley.

Friedman, D. and Wise, D. (1976) 'CONS Should Not Evaluate Its Arguments'. In *Automata Languages and Programming*, pp. 257–284, Edinburgh University Press.

Futatsugi, K., Goguen, J.A., Jouannaud, J.-P. and Meseguer, J. (1985) 'Principles of OBJ2'. In *12th Annual Symposium on Principles of Programming Languages*, New Orleans, LA, 1985.

Gallier, J.H. and Snyder, W. (1979) 'A General, Complete E-Unification Procedure'. In *Lescanne (1987)*.

Goguen, J.A. and Tardo, J.J. (1979) 'An Introduction to OBJ: A Language for writing and Testing Formal Algebraic Specifications'. In *Reliable Software Conf. Proceedings*, R. Yeh (ed.), pp. 170–189, Cambridge, Mass.

Goguen, J.A. and Meseguer, J. (1983) *An Initiality Primer*. (Preliminary draft text).

Gordon, M., Milner, R., Morris, L., Newey, M. and Wadsworth, C. (1978) 'A Metalanguage for Interactive Proof in LCF'. In *Fifth Annual ACM Symposium on Principles of Programming Languages*, pp. 119–130, Tucson, AZ., January 1978.

Gordon, M.L. (1979) *The Denotational Description of Programming Languages*, New York: Springer-Verlag.

Guttag, J.V. (1975) *The Specification and Application to Programming of Abstract Data Types*, PhD Thesis, Toronto.

Guttag, J.V. (1982) 'Notes on Using Types and Type Abstraction in Functional Programming'. In *Functional Programming and Its Applications – An Advanced Course*, J. Darlington, R. Henderson and D.A. Turner (eds), Cambridge University Press.

Guttag, J.V., Horning, J.J. and Wing, J.M. (1985) *Larch in Five Easy Pieces*, Report 5, Digital Systems Research Center, Digital, Palo Alto, California, July 1985.

Guttag, J.V. and Horning, J.J. (1978) 'The Algebraic Specification of Abstract Data Types', *Acta Informatica*, **10**.

Harper, R., MacQueen, D. and Milner, R. (1986) *Standard ML*, Report ECS-LFCS-86-2, Computer Science Department, Edinburgh University, March 1986.

Harper, R., Milner, R. and Tofte, M. (1987) *The Semantics of Standard ML (Version 1)*, Report ECS-LFCS-87-36, Computer Science Department, Edinburgh University, August 1987.

Henderson, P. and Morris, J. (1976) 'A Lazy Evaluator'. In *Record, Third Symposium on Principles of Programming Languages*, pp. 95–103.

Henderson, P. (1980) *Functional Programming: Application and Implementation*, Prentice Hall International.

Henderson, P. (1982a) 'Functional Geometry'. In *ACM Symp. on Lisp and Functional Programming*, pp. 179–187, Pittsburgh.

Henderson, P. (1982b) 'A Purely Functional Operating System'. In *Functional Programming and Its Applications – An Advanced Course*, J. Darlington, P. Henderson and D.A. Turner (eds), Cambridge University Press.

Henderson, P., Jones, G.A. and Jones, S.B. (1983) *The Lispkit Manual*, Oxford University Computing Laboratory Programming Research Group PRG-32, 1983.

Hennessy, M. (1982) 'Powerdomains and Non-Deterministic Definitions'. In *Symp. on Programming*, Lecture Notes in Computer Science (vol. 137), Springer-Verlag.

Hennessy, M. and Ashcroft, E.A. (1976) 'The Semantics of Non-Determinism'. In *Proceedings ICALP 1976*, S. Michaelson and R. Milner (eds).

Hindley, J.R. and Seldin, J.P. (1986) *Introduction to Combinators and Lambda Calculus*, LMS Student Texts 1, Cambridge University Press.

Hoffman, C. and O'Donnell, M. J. (1982) 'Programming with Equations', *ACM Transactions on Programming Languages and Systems*, pp. 83–112.

Hogger, C.J. (1984) *Introduction to Logic Programming*, APIC Studies in Data Processing No. 21, Academic Press.

Holldobler, S. (1987) 'A Unification Algorithm for Equational Theories'. In *14th ICALP Karlsruhe, Germany July 1987*, Lecture Notes in Computer Science (vol. 267), pp. 31–41, Springer-Verlag.

Holmström, S. (1983) 'PFL: A Functional Language for Parallel Programming'. In *Declarative Programming Workshop*.

Huet, G. (1975) 'A Unification Algorithm for Typed Lambda-Calculus', *Journal of Theoretical Computer Science*, pp. 27–57.

Huet, G. and Oppen, D.C. (1980) 'Equations and Rewrite Rules – A Survey'. In *Formal Languages: Perspectives and Open Problems*, R. Book (ed.), Academic Press.

Hughes, J. (1982) *Graph Reduction with Super Combinators*, Technical Monograph PRG-28, Oxford University Computing Laboratory, June 1982.

Hughes, J. (1984) *Why Functional Programming Matters*, Report No. 16, Programming Methodology Group, University of Goteborg, November 1984.

Jenkins, M.A. (1983) *The Q'NIAL Reference Manual*, Queen's University Report, Kingston, Canada, December 1983.

Johnsson, T. (1984) 'Efficient Computation of Lazy Evaluation'. In *Proc. 1984 Symp. on Compiler Construction*, Montreal, 1984. (Also in *ACM Sigplan*, **19** (6), pp. 58–69, 1984.)

Jones, S.B. (1983) *Abstract Machine Support For Purely Functional Operating Systems*, Technical Monograph PRG-34, Programming Research Group, Oxford University, August 1983.

Jones, S.B. (1984) *A Range of Operating Systems Written in a Purely Functional Style*, Technical Monograph PRG-42, Computing Laboratories, Oxford University, September 1984.

Jouannaud, J.-P. (ed.) (1987) *Rewriting Techniques and Applications*, Lecture

Notes in Computer Science (vol. 202), Springer-Verlag, Dijon, France, May 1987.

Kahn, G. (1974) 'The Semantics of a Simple Language for Parallel Programming'. In *IFIP 74*, North Holland, 1974.

Kahn, G. and MacQueen, D. (1977) 'Coroutines and Networks of Parallel Processes'. In *IFIP 77*, B. Gilchrist (ed.), pp. 993–998, North Holland.

Kaplan, S. (1986) 'Rewriting with a Non-Deterministic Choice Operator'. In *ESOP'86, Saarbrucken*, Lecture Notes in Computer Science (vol. 213), Springer-Verlag.

Knuth, D.E. and Bendix, P.E. (1970) 'Simple Word Problems in Universal Algebra'. In *Computational Problems in Abstract Algebra*, J. Leech (ed.), pp. 263–297, Pergamon Press.

Kott, L. (1985) 'Unfold/Fold Program Transformations'. In *Algebraic Methods in Semantics*, M. Nivat and J.C. Reynolds (eds), Cambridge University Press.

Kowalski, R. (1979) *Logic for Problem Solving*, North-Holland.

Kreowski, H.-J. (1985) 'Recent Trends in Data Type Specification'. In *Proc. 3rd Workshop on Theory & Application of Abstract Data Types*, Informatik Fachsberichte 116.

Landin, P.J. (1964) 'The Mechanical Evaluation of Expressions', *BCS Computing Journal*, **6** (4), pp. 308–320, January 1964.

Landin, P.J. (1965) 'A Correspondence between Algol 60 and Church's Lambda Calculus', *Communications ACM*, **8** (3), pp. 89–101; 158–165.

Landin, P.J. (1966) 'The Next 700 Programming Languages', *Communications ACM*, **9** (3), pp. 157–166, March 1966.

Lescanne, P. (1983) 'Computer Experiments with REVE Term Rewriting Generator'. In *Proc. 10 ACM Symp. on Principles of Programming Languages*, pp. 99–108, Austin, Texas, 1983.

Lescanne, P. (ed.) (1987) *Rewriting Techniques and Applications*, Lecture Notes in Computer Science (vol. 256), Springer-Verlag, Bordeaux, France, May 1987.

MacQueen, D.B. and Sethi, R. (1982) 'A Semantic Model of Types for Applicative Languages'. In *ACM Symp. on Lisp and Functional Programming*, Pittsburgh, Penns., August 1982.

MacQueen, D.B. (1984) 'Modules For Standard ML'. In *1984 ACM Symposium on Lisp and Functional Programming*, pp. 198–207, Austin, Texas. (Also in Harper *et al.* (1986).)

MacQueen, D.B. (1986) 'Using Dependent Types to Express Modular Structure'. In *Proc. 13th ACM Symp. on Principles of Programming Languages.*

Manes, E.G. and Arbib, M.A. (1986) *Algebraic Approaches to Program Semantics*, Springer-Verlag.

Manna, Z. (1974) *Mathematical Theory of Computation*, McGraw-Hill.

Martelli, A. and Montenari, U. (1982) 'An Efficient Unification Algorithm', *ACM TOPLAS*, pp. 258–282.

Martin-Lof, P. (1984) 'Constructive Mathematics and Computer Programming'. In *Mathematical Logic and Programming Languages*, J.C. Shepherdson, and C.A.R. Hoare (eds), Series in Computer Science, Prentice Hall.

McCarthy, J. (1960) 'Recursive Functions of Symbolic Expressions and Their Computation by Machine', *Communications ACM*, **3** (4).

McCarthy, J., Abrahams, P.W., Edwards, D.J., Hart, T.P. and Levin, M.I. (1962) *LISP 1.5 Programmer's Manual*, MIT Press.

Meseguer, J. and Goguen, J.A. (1985) 'Initiality, Induction and Computability'. In *Algebraic Methods in Semantics*, M. Nivat and J.C. Reynolds (eds), Cambridge University Press.

Milne, R. and Strachey, C. (1976) *A Theory of Programming Language Semantics*, Chapman Hall.

Milner, R. (1978) 'A Theory of Type Polymorphism in Programming', *JCSS*, **17** (3), pp. 348–375, December 1978.

Milner, R. (1984) 'A Proposal for Standard ML'. In *ACM Symp. on Lisp and Functional Programming*, pp. 184–197, Austin, Texas, August 1984.

Milner, R. (1985) 'The Standard ML Core Language', *Polymorphism: The ML/LCF/Hope Newsletter*, **II** (2), October 1985. (Revised from Milner (1984). Also in Harper *et al.* (1986).)

More, T. (1981) *Notes on the Diagrams, Logic and Operations of Array Theory*, IBM Scientific Center Technical Report G320-2137, Cambridge, Massachusetts, September 1981.

Morris, J.H. (1973) 'Types are not Sets'. In *ACM Symp. on Principles of Programming Languages*, pp. 120–124, October 1973.

Mycroft, A. (1981) *Abstract Interpretation and Optimising Transformations for Applicative Programs*, PhD Thesis, University of Edinburgh.

Mycroft, A. and Nielson, F. (1983) 'Strong Abstract Interpretation Using Power Domains (Extended Abstract)'. In *Proc. 10th Int. Colloq. on Automata, Languages and Programming, Barcelona, Spain*, Lecture Notes in Computer Science (vol. 154), pp. 536–547, Springer-Verlag, July 1983.

Nivat, M. and Reynolds, J.C. (eds) (1985) *Algebraic Methods in Semantics*, Cambridge University Press.

O'Donnell, M.J. (1977) *Computing in Systems Described by Equations*, Lecture Notes in Computer Science (vol. 58), Springer-Verlag.

O'Donnell, M. J. (1985) *Equational Logic as a Programming Language*, MIT Press.

Park, D. (1980) *On the Semantics of Fair Parallelism*, Lecture Notes in Computer Science (vol. 86), Springer-Verlag.

Paulson, L. (1987) 'Logic and Computation', *Tracts in Theoretical Computer Science (2)*, Cambridge.

Pettorossi, A. and Skowron, A. (1987) 'Higher Order Generalisation in Program Derivation'. In *TAPSOFT '87, vol. 2*, Lecture Notes in Computer Science (vol. 250), Springer-Verlag.

Peyton-Jones, S.L. (1987) *The Implementation of Functional Languages*, Prentice Hall.

Plotkin, G.D. (1975) 'Call-by-name, Call-by-value and the Lambda Calculus', *Theoretical Computer Science*, **1**, pp. 125–159.

Plotkin, G.D. (1976) 'A Powerdomain Construction', *SIAM Journal of Computing*, **5**, pp. 452–486.

Plotkin, G.D. (1981) *A Structural Approach to Operational Semantics*, DAIMI F9-19, Computer Science Department Aarhus University, September 1981.

Plotkin, G.D. (1982) *The Category of Complete Partial Orders: A Tool for Making Meanings*, Postgraduate Lecture Notes, Computer Science Department, University of Edinburgh.

Reade, C.M.P. (1989) 'Balanced Trees – An Exercise in Rewriting and Proof', Computer Science Department Technical Report, Brunel University CSTR-89-2.

Reynolds, J.C. (1970) 'GEDANKEN – A Simple Typeless Language Based on Principles of Completeness and Reference Concepts', *Communications ACM*, **13** (5), pp. 308–319.

Richards, H. (1984) 'An Overview of ARC SASL', *ACM Sigplan Notices*, October 1984.

Robinson, J.A. (1965) 'A Machine-oriented Logic Based on the Resolution Principle', *ACM Journal*, **12**, pp. 23–41, January 1965.

Rosser, J.B. (1982) 'Highlights of the History of the Lambda-Calculus'. In *1982 ACM Symp. on Lisp and Functional Programming*, pp. 216–225, Pittsburgh, Penns, August 1982.

Sannella, D.T. and Wirsing, M. (1983) 'A Kernal Language for Algebraic Specification and Implementation', Lecture Notes in Computer Science (vol. 158), pp. 413–427, Springer-Verlag.

Schmidt, D.A. (1986) *Denotational Semantics – A Methodology for Language Development*, Allyn and Bacon.

Schönfinkel, M. (1924) 'Ueber die Bausteine der mathematischen Logik', *Math. Ann.*, **92**, pp. 305–316.

Scott, D.S. (1976) 'Data Types as Lattices', *SIAM Journal on Comp. Sci.*, **5** (3), pp. 522–587.

Scott, D.S. (1980) *Lecture Notes on a Mathematical Theory of Computation*, Programming Research Group Technical Report PRG-19, University of Oxford.

Scott, D.S. (1982) 'Domains for Denotational Semantics'. In *Proc. 9th ICALP*, Lecture Notes in Computer Science (vol. 140), pp. 577–613, Springer-Verlag.

Smyth, M.B. (1978) 'Powerdomains', *JCSS*, **16**, pp. 23–36.

Steele, G.L. and Sussman, G.J. (1978) *The Revised Report on SCHEME: A Dialect of LISP*, AI Memo 452, MIT Artificial Intelligence Laboratory, Cambridge, Mass, January 1978.

Sterling, L. and Shapiro, E. (1986) *The Art of Prolog*, MIT Press, Cambridge, Mass.

Stoy, J. (1977) *Denotational Semantics: The Scott-Strachey Approach to Programming Language Theory*, MIT Press, Cambridge, Massachusetts.

Stoy, J. (1982) 'Some Mathematical Aspects of Functional Programming'. In *Functional Programming and Its Applications – An Advanced Course*, J. Darlington, P. Henderson and D.A. Turner (eds), Cambridge University Press.

Stoye, W.R. (1984) *A New Scheme for Writing Functional Operating Systems*, University of Cambridge Computing Laboratory Report 56.

Stoye, W.R., Clarke, T.J.W. and Norman, A.C. (1984) 'Some Practical Methods for Combinator Reduction', *1984 ACM Symp. Lisp and Functional Programming*, Austin, Texas, August 1984.

Stoye, W.R. (1985) *Implementation of Functional Languages Using Custom Hardware*, PhD Thesis, University of Cambridge, Computing Laboratory Report 81.

Sussman, G.J. and Steele, G.L. (1975) *SCHEME: An Interpreter for Extended Lambda Calculus*, AI Memo 349, MIT Artificial Intelligence Laboratory, Cambridge, Mass, December 1975.

Sussman, G.J. (1981) 'Scheme-79-Lisp on a Chip', *IEEE Computer*, **14** (7), pp. 10–21, July 1981.

Tennent, R.D. (1976) 'The Denotational Semantics of Programming Languages', *Communications ACM*, **9** (8), pp. 437–453.

Thatte, S. (1984) *Demand Driven Evaluation with Equations*, University of Michigan, Computing Research Laboratory Report CRL-TR-34-84, August 1984.

Thatte, S. (1985) 'On the Correspondence Between Two Classes of Reduction Systems', *Information Processing Letters*, **20,** pp. 83–85.

Thatte, S. (1986) 'Towards a Semantic Theory for Equational Programming Languages'. In *ACM Conf. on Lisp and Functional Programming*, pp. 332–342, Cambridge, Mass., August 1986.

Thompson, S. (1986) *Writing Interactive Programs in Miranda*, Computing Laboratory Report 40, University of Kent at Canterbury.

Turner, D.A. (1976) *SASL Language Manual*, St Andrews University Technical Report, December 1976.

Turner, D.A. (1979a) 'A New Implementation Technique for Applicative Languages', *Software Practice and Experience*, **9**.

Turner, D.A. (1979b) 'Another Algorithm for Bracket Abstraction', *Journal of Symbolic Logic*, **44** (2), June 1979.

Turner, D.A. (1982) 'Recursion Equations as a Programming Language'. In *Functional Programming and Its Applications – An Advanced Course*, J. Darlington, P. Henderson and D.A. Turner (eds), Cambridge University Press.

Turner, D.A. (1985a) 'Miranda: A Non Strict Functional Language with Polymorphic Types'. In *Proceedings of the IFIP International Conference on Functional Programming Languages and Computer Architecture*, Lecture Notes in Computer Science (vol. 201), Springer-Verlag, Nancy, France, September 1985.

Turner, D.A. (1985b) 'Functional Programs as Executable Specifications'. In *Mathematical Logic and Programming Languages*, C.A.R. Hoare and J.C. Shepherdson (eds), Prentice Hall International Series in Computer Science.

Wadler, P. (1985) 'How to Replace Failure by a List of Successes'. In *Proc. IFIP Int. Conf. on Functional Programming Languages and Computer Architecture*, Lecture Notes in Computer Science (vol. 201), Springer-Verlag, Nancy, France, September 1985.

Wadsworth, C.P. (1971) *Semantics and Pragmatics of the Lambda Calculus*, PhD Thesis University of Oxford.

Wadsworth, C.P. (1976) 'The Relationship Between Computational and Denotational Properties for Scott's D Infinity Models of the Lambda Calculus', *Siam J. of Computing*, **5**, pp. 481–521.

Wagner, E.G., Bloom, S.L. and Thatcher, J.W. (1985) 'Why Algebraic Theories?' In *Algebraic Methods in Semantics*, M. Nivat and J.C. Reynolds (eds), Cambridge University Press.

Wand, M. (1984) 'A Types-as-Sets Semantics for Milner-Style Polymorphism'. In *Proc. ACM Conf. on Principles of Programming Languages*, pp. 158–164, Salt Lake City, Utah, 1984.

Wray, S.C. (1986) *Implementation and Programming Techniques for Functional Languages*, PhD Thesis University of Cambridge, Computing Laboratory Report 92, January 1986.

Zilles, S. (1974) *Algebraic Specifications of Abstract Data Types*, Project MAC Progress Report 11, pp. 28–52, MIT.

Appendix 1
The Syntax Used in Examples

Syntactic domains

Var	Variables ranged over by V, V_0, $\cdots$ – denumerable set
Con	Constructors ranged over by C, C_0, $\cdots$ – denumerable set
Exp	Expressions ranged over by E, E_0, $\cdots$
Def	Definitions ranged over by D, D_0, $\cdots$
Pat	Patterns ranged over by P, P_0, $\cdots$
Fbind	Function bindings ranged over by FB, FB_0, $\cdots$
TOp	Type operators ranged over by Top, Top_0, $\cdots$ – denumerable set
TVar	Type variables ranged over by α, α_0, $\cdots$ – denumerable set
TDesc	Type descriptions ranged over by TD, TD_0, $\cdots$
TCase	Type case (variant) ranged over by TC, TC_0, $\cdots$
Type	Type expression ranged over by T, T_0, $\cdots$

Syntactic forms

Forms of expression (E)

V	Variable
C	Constructor
$E_1\ E_2$	Application
$E_1\ V\ E_2$	Infix function application
$(E_1, E_2, \ldots, E_n)$	Tuples ($n \geq 2$)
if E_1 **then** E_2 **else** E_3	Conditional
let D **in** E **end**	Qualified
fn $P_1 \Rightarrow E_1 \mid \cdots \mid P_n \Rightarrow E_n$	Abstraction, $n \geq 1$
(E)	Bracketed

Forms of definition (D)

val $P_1 = E_1$ **and** $\cdots$ **and** $P_n = E_n$	Non-recursive, $n \geq 1$
val rec $P_1 = E_1$ **and** $\cdots$ **and** $P_n = E_n$	Recursive, $n \geq 1$
fun FB_1 **and** $\cdots$ **and** FB_n	Recursive functions, $n \geq 1$
$D_1\ D_2$	Sequence
local D_1 **in** D_2 **end**	Local
datatype TD_1 **and** $\cdots$ **and** TD_n	Data types, $n \geq 1$
abstype TD_1 **and** $\cdots$ **and** TD_n **with** D **end**	Abstract types, $n \geq 1$

Forms of pattern (P)

V	Variable
C	Constant
$(P_1, P_2, \ldots, P_n)$	Tuple, $n \geq 2$
$C\ P$	Construction
(P)	Bracketed

Forms of function binding (FB)

$V\ P_{1,1} \cdots P_{1,n} = E_1$
$\mid V\ P_{2,1} \cdots P_{2,n} = E_2$ (One form $m \geqslant 1$, $n \geqslant 1$)
$\cdots$
$\mid V\ P_{m,1} \cdots P_{m,n} = E_m$

Forms of type descriptions (TD)

$\alpha_1 \cdots \alpha_n\ Top = TC_1 \mid \cdots \mid TC_m$	$n \geq 0$, $m \geq 1$

Forms of type cases (TC)

C	New constant
C **of** T	New constructor

Forms of type (T)

$T_1 \cdots T_n\ Top$	Applied type operator, $n \geq 0$
α	Type variable
$\alpha^{=}$	Equality type variable

Appendix 2
Standard ML

The examples in this book have been written in Standard ML. We therefore collect some of the examples and present them as structures (see Chapter 7). In particular, we give a structure for a prelude of general purpose functions and structures for character pictures and the game of life (see Chapter 4). We also include a function for 'plotting coordinates' – for use with the game of life examples and a function which creates pictures of bintrees.

Note that the first definitions in the structure Prelude introduce the function error : string → α which we have used throughout the book as a standard way of signifying when an expression is undefined. The definition uses the exception mechanism in SML which we did not describe in the book because we preferred to use just error for raising exceptions. The line:

```
exception ex_undefined of string
```

defines a new exception name and type of value associated with it, and:

```
fun error str = raise ex_undefined str;
```

defines error as a function which whenever it is applied to a string aborts computation by raising an exception with the string as its associated value.

We also point out the use of a function with a side-effect in these examples. The function show : string → unit uses the output procedure to display a string at the terminal. This proved necessary with the particular implementation of SML which we were using in order to get escape sequences (e.g. newline characters) to be interpreted rather than displayed literally as they are at the top level. The use of show should be limited to use at the top level and for creating other display functions which should be similarly limited. For example, showpic : picture → picture is used to display pictures as a side-effect, but behaves like the identity function otherwise – it should not be used by functions which build pictures.

There are one or two other constructs used, which are part of SML but not described in this book. In particular: '**as**' and '_' are used in patterns – the former to name a compound construct while still matching components, and the latter as a 'wild card' or unnamed variable; **case** *E* **of** *MATCH* is equivalent to (**fn** *MATCH*) *E*; the symbol ';' is optional between definitions and '(*' along with '*)' are used to surround comments. (Comments explaining these examples have been removed – most are explained in the chapters where they were introduced.)

For further details about the language SML, including a description of the exception mechanism and the non-functional features such as assignments and I/O, consult Harper *et al.* (1986). For a formal definition of the full language, see Harper *et al.* (1987).

The implementation of SML used while this book was being written (and also used by students at Brunel University) was provided by Dave Mathews at University of Cambridge Computing Laboratory. There are other implementations available including: a version of Dave Mathew's Poly/ML System from Abstract Hardware Ltd. (Brunel University); a POPLOG version written at Sussex University and New Jersey ML from AT&T Bell Labs written by Dave MacQueen (and others).

```
(*******************************************
 *
 * PRELUDE (Some general purpose definitions)
 *
 *******************************************)

structure Prelude = struct

exception ex_undefined of string;
fun error str = raise ex_undefined str;

fun equal a b = a = b;

structure Combinator = struct
fun I x = x;
fun K x y = x;
fun C f x y = f y x;
fun W f x = f x x;
fun Y f = let fun fixf x = f (fixf) x in fixf end;
fun curry f a b = f (a, b);
fun uncurry f (a, b) = f a b;
fun pair a b = (a, b);
fun fst (x, y) = x;
fun snd (x, y) = y;
```

```
fun couple f g x = (f x, g x);
fun repeat f = let fun rptf n x = if n = 0 then x else rptf (n - 1) (f x);
                   fun check n = if n < 0 then error "repeat < 0" else n
               in rptf o check end
end; (* of Combinator *)
open Combinator;

structure Int = struct
fun plus (a : int) b = a + b;
fun times (a : int) b = a * b;
fun lessthan (a : int) b = b < a;
fun lesseq (a : int) b = b <= a;
fun greater (a : int) b = b > a;
fun greatereq (a : int) b = b >= a;
fun max (a : int) b = if a < b then b else a;
fun min (a : int) b = if a < b then a else b
end; (* of Int *)
open Int;

structure Bool = struct
fun non p = not o p;
fun ou p q x = p x orelse q x;
fun et p q x = p x andalso q x
end; (* of Bool *)
open Bool;

structure List = struct
fun assoc pairlist default arg
    = let fun search [ ]          = default arg
          |   search ((a, b) :: x)= if arg = a then b else search x
      in search pairlist end;


fun foldleft f = let fun foldf a [ ] = a
                     |   foldf a (b :: x) = foldf (f a b) x
                 in foldf end;
val accumulate = foldleft;
fun foldright f a x = accumulate (C f) a (rev x);
fun zip f = let fun zf (a :: x) (b :: y) = f a b :: zf x y
                |   zf [ ] [ ] = [ ]
                |   zf _ _      = error" zip with different lengthed lists"

            in zf end;
fun splice f = let fun sf (a :: x) (b :: y) = f a b :: sf x y
                   |   sf x [ ] = x
                   |   sf [ ] x = x
               in sf end;
fun filter p = let fun consifp x a = if p a then a :: x else x
               in rev o accumulate consifp [ ] end;
```

```
fun exists p = let fun existsp [ ] = false
                     | existsp (a :: x) = if p a then true
                                                  else existsp x
               in existsp end;
val all = non o exists o non;
fun member x a = exists (equal a) x;
fun contains x y = all (member y) x;
fun null [ ] = true
  | null _   = false;
fun hd (a :: x)  = a
  | hd [ ]       = error "hd of [ ] is undefined"
and tl (a :: x)  = x
  | tl [ ]       = error "tl of [ ] is undefined";
fun cons a x     = a :: x;
fun append x y= x @ y;
  infix 5 upto;
fun n upto m = if n > m then [ ] else n :: (n + 1 upto m);
val revonto = accumulate (C cons);
val reverse = revonto [ ];
fun link llist = rev (accumulate revonto [ ] llist);
fun linkwith (front, sep, back) l
  = let fun f [ ] = [back]
          | f [a] = [a, back]
          | f (a :: x) = a :: sep :: f x
    in link (front :: f l) end;
val pairlists = zip pair;
fun copy n x = repeat (cons x) n [ ];
val sumlist = accumulate plus 0;
val prodlist = accumulate times 1;

fun maxlist (a :: x) = accumulate max a x
  | maxlist [ ]      = error "maxlist of [ ] is undefined";
fun maxposlist x  = accumulate max 0 x;
fun transpose [ ] = [ ]
  | transpose x   = if exists null x
                    then [ ]
                    else (map hd x) :: transpose (map tl x);
val length = let fun count n a = n + 1
             in accumulate count 0 end;
val drop = repeat tl;
fun split n = if n < 0
              then error "negative subscript error (split failed)"
              else let fun shunt 0 x1 x2       = (rev x1, x2)
                         | shunt n x1 (a :: x2) = shunt (n - 1) (a :: x1) x2
                         | shunt _ _ _
                           = error "list subscript error (split failed)"
                   in shunt n [ ] end;
```

```
fun front n x = fst (split n x);
fun back n x = drop (length x - n) x;
fun select n = hd o (drop (n - 1));
fun sublist n m x = front m (drop (n - 1) x)
end; (* List *)
open List;

structure String = struct
fun concat s1 s2 = s1 ^ s2;
fun show x = output (std_out, x);
fun stringwith (front, sep, back) sl
  = let fun f [ ] = [back]
          |   f [a] = [a, back]
          |   f (a :: x) = a :: sep :: f x
     in implode (front :: f s1) end;
fun spaces n = implode (copy n " ");
fun newlines n = implode (copy n "\n");
fun sless (s : string) s' = s' < s;
fun slesseq (s : string) s' = s' <= s
end; (* String *)
open String

end; (* of struct Prelude *)
```

```
        structure Charpics = struct

(**********************************************************
ABSTRACT TYPE PICTURE (In structure Charpics using Prelude)
 **********************************************************)

        local open Prelude; infix upto in

        abstype picture = Pic of int * int * string list
        with
          fun mkpic linelist
             = let val d = length linelist;
                   val shape = map size linelist;
                   val w = maxposlist shape;
                   fun addspaces line = let val a = size line in
                                          if a < w then line ^ spaces (w - a)
                                                   else line
                                        end;
                   val checkedlines = map addspaces linelist
               in Pic (d, w, checkedlines) end;

          fun depth (Pic (d, _, _)) = d;
          fun width (Pic (_, w, _)) = w;
```

```
fun linesof (Pic (_, _, sl)) = sl;
val nullpic = Pic (0, 0, [ ]);
fun padside n (pic as Pic (d, w, sl))
   = if n <= w then pic
                 else Pic (d, n, map (fn s => s ^ spaces (n - w)) sl);
fun padbottom n (pic as Pic (d, w, sl))
   = if n <= d then pic
                 else Pic (n, w, sl @ copy (n - d) (spaces w));
fun rowwith fsb piclist
   = let val d' = maxposlist (map depth piclist);
         val blocks = map (linesof o padbottom d') piclist;
         fun mkline n = stringwith fsb (map (select n) blocks);
         val sl' = map mkline (1 upto d');
         val w' = if null sl' then 0 else size (hd sl')
      in Pic (d', w', s1') end;

val row = rowwith ("", "", "");

fun colwith (f, s, b) piclist
   = let val w' = maxposlist (map width piclist);
         val flines = map (implode o (copy w')) (explode f);
         val slines = map (implode o (copy w')) (explode s);
         val blines = map (implode o (copy w')) (explode b);
         val sl' = linkwith (flines, slines, blines)
                         (map (linesof o padside w') piclist);
         val d' = length sl'
      in Pic (d', w', sl') end;

val column = colwith ("", "", "");

fun indent n (pic as Pic (d, w, sl))
   = if n < 1 then pic
               else Pic (d, w + n, map (concat (spaces n)) sl);

fun lower n (pic as Pic (d, w, sl))
   = if n < 1 then pic
               else Pic (d + n, w, copy n (spaces w) @ sl);

fun table [ ] = nullpic
|    table piclistlist
       = let fun mkrect piclistlist (* makes sure each list has same length *)
                = let val sizerows = map length piclistlist;
                      val maxrow = maxposlist sizerows;
                      fun addnulls len piclist
                         = if len < maxrow
                           then piclist @ (copy (maxrow-len) nullpic)
                           else piclist
                   in zip addnulls sizerows piclistlist end;

             val newpics = mkrect piclistlist;
```

```
          val picwidths = map (map width) newpics
          val colwidths = map maxposlist (transpose picwidths);
          val picrowlists = map (zip padside colwidths) newpics;
          val tablerows = map (rowwith ("|", "|","|")) picrowlists;
          fun dashes n = implode (copy n "_");
          val sep = stringwith ("+","+", "+") (map dashes colwidths);
          val sl' = linkwith ([sep], [sep], [sep]) (map linesof tablerows);
          val d' = length sl';
          val w' = size (hd sl')
               in Pic (d', w', sl') end;

fun frame picture = table [[picture]];

fun header s pic = colwith ("", "~", "") [mkpic [s], pic];

fun showpic picture
  = (show (stringwith ("", "\n", "\n") (linesof picture)); picture);

fun paste n m pic1 pic2 (* n, m may be negative, pic2 goes over *)
                        (* pic1 at n rows down and m chars in    *)
  = if n < 0 then paste 0 m (lower (~n) pic1) pic2 else
    if m < 0 then paste n 0 (indent (~m) pic1) pic2 else
    let val pic1' = padbottom (n + depth pic2)
                              (padside (m + width pic2) pic1);
        fun spliceat n f x y = if n < 1
                               then splice f x y
                               else hd x :: spliceat (n - 1) f (tl x) y;
        fun overlay a b = b;
        fun stringop line line' = implode (spliceat m overlay
                                                    (explode line)
                                                    (explode line'));
        val sl' = spliceat n stringop (linesof pic1') (linesof pic2);
        val w' = if null sl' then 0 else size (hd sl');
        val d' = length sl'
    in Pic (d', w', sl') end;

fun cutfrom pic n m a b
             (* n, m, a, b may be negative, a picture of size a deep *)
             (* and b wide is cut from pic starting at n rows down   *)
             (* and m chars in                                        *)
  = if n < 0 then cutfrom (lower (~n) pic) 0 m a b   else
    if m < 0 then cutfrom (indent (~m) pic) n 0 a b else
    if a < 0 then cutfrom pic (n + a) m (~a) b       else
    if b < 0 then cutfrom pic n (m + b) a (~b)       else
    let val pic' = padbottom (n + a) (padside (m + b) pic);
        fun edit str = implode (sublist (m + 1) b (explode str));
        val newsl = map edit (sublist (n + 1) a (linesof pic'))
    in Pic (a, b, newsl) end

end (* of abstract type picture *)

end (* of local *)
end (* of Charpics *);
```

```
(****************************************************
* A structure containing definitions for the game of life        *
****************************************************
type generation
val mkgen          : (int * int) list -> generation
val alive          : generation -> (int * int) list
val mk_nextgen_fn : ((int * int) -> (int * int) list) -> (generation -> generation)
*----------------------------------------------------
    generation is an abstract type with operations mkgen and alive and mk_next-
    gen_fn.
    mkgen produces a generation from an arbitrary list of coordinates (integer
    pairs) for live squares.
    alive produces the list of coordinates of live squares of a generation
    in lexical order (with no repetitions).
    mk_nextgen_fn can be used to produce a nextgeneration function of type
    generation → generation. It should be supplied with an argument function
    which calculates the neighbours of a coordinate. For example, if you first define
        neighbours : (int * int) -> (int * int) list
    Then you can define
        val nextgen = mk_nextgen_fn (neighbours)
    This allows you to experiment with different neighbour functions (usually 8
    neighbours possibly modified with wraparound or cutoff at some upper and
    lower limits).
****************************************************)


structure Life = struct
  local (********* AUXILIARY DEFINITIONS *********)
    val filter = Prelude.filter;
    val length = Prelude.length;
    val member = Prelude.member;
    val revonto = Prelude.revonto;
    fun lexordset [ ] = [ ]
    |    lexordset (a :: x) = lexordset (filter (lexless a) x) @ [a] @
                              lexordset (filter (lexgreater a) x)
    and lexless (a1 : int, b1 : int) (a2, b2)
          = a2 < a1 orelse (a2 = a1 andalso b2 < b1)
    and lexgreater pr1 pr2 = lexless pr2 pr1;
    fun collect f list
      = let fun accumf sofar [ ] = sofar
            |   accumf sofar (a :: x) = accumf (revonto sofar (f a)) x
        in accumf [ ] list end;
    fun occurs3 x
      (* finds coords which occur exactly 3 times in coordlist x *)
      = let fun f xover x3 x2 x1 [ ] = diff x3 xover
            |   f xover x3 x2 x1 (a :: x)
```

```
        if member xover a then f xover x3 x2 x1 x else
        if member x3 a then f (a :: xover) x3 x2 x1 x else
        if member x2 a then f xover (a :: x3) x2 x1 x else
        if member x1 a then f xover x3 (a :: x2) x1 x else
                              f xover x3 x2 (a :: x1) x
     and diff x y = filter (not o member y) x
  in f [ ] [ ] [ ] [ ] x end


in (* * * * * * * * * * MAIN DEFINITIONS FOLLOW * * * * * * * * * *)

abstype generation = GEN of (int * int) list
 with
   fun alive (GEN livecoords) = livecoords
   and mkgen coordlist = GEN (lexordset coordlist)
   and mk_nextgen_fn neighbours gen
     = let val living = alive gen
           val isalive = member living
           val liveneighbours = length o filter isalive o neighbours
           fun twoorthree n = n = 2 orelse n = 3
           val survivors = filter (twoorthree o liveneighbours) living
           val newnbrlist = collect (filter (not o isalive) o neighbours) living
           val newborn = occurs3 newnbrlist
       in mkgen (survivors @ newborn) end
 end

end (* of local *)
end (* of Life *);
```

The following function can be adapted for use with the game of life (see Chapter 4).

```
(* - - - - - - - - - - - - - - - - - - - - - - - - - - - - - - - - - - - - - - - - - - - - *

 A function to plot coordinates as a list of strings plot: (int * int) list -> string list
 This will NOT work for negative coordinates and also assumes the coordinate
 list to be in lexicographic order with no repetitions (as produced by
 alive : generation -> (int * int) list)

* - - - - - - - - - - - - - - - - - - - - - - - - - - - - - - - - - - - - - - - - - - - - *)

local
  val spaces = Prelude.spaces;
  val xstart = 0 and ystart = 0;
  fun markafter n string = string ^ spaces n ^ "0";
  fun plotfrom (x, y) (* current position *)
               str    (* current line being prepared - a string *)
               ((x1, y1) :: more) (* coordinates to be plotted *)
```

```
    = if x = x1
      then (* same line so extend str and continue from y1 + 1 *)
              plotfrom (x, y1 + 1) (markafter (y1 − y) str) more
      else (* flush current line and start a new line *)
              str :: plotfrom (x + 1, ystart) "" ((x1, y1) :: more)
  |   plotfrom (x, y) str [ ] = [str]

in

fun plot coordlist = plotfrom (xstart, ystart) "" coordlist

end;
```

Finally, we give some operations on bintrees with a function to create a picture from a bintree.

```
(* BINARY TREES AND PICTURES *)

local
  val copy = Prelude . copy; val stringofint = . . . (see p. 31)
  open Charpics
in

(* type definition *)

datatype 'a bintree = Lf of 'a
                    |  / \ of 'a bintree * 'a bintree;
infix / \;

(* some higher order operations for bintrees *)

fun btreeop f g = let fun btfg (Lf x) = f x
                        |  btfg (t1 / \ t2) = g (btfg t1, btfg t2)
                  in btfg end;

fun btreemap f = btreeop (Lf ∘ f) (op / \);

(* a function for making pictures of trees *)

fun btreepic leafpicfun
  = let
      fun joinpics ((p, n1), (p', n1'))
        = let val n = width p;
              val dashn = (n − n1 + n1');
              val dashn2 = dashn div 2;
              val dashn1 = dashn × dashn2 − 1;
              val newn1 = n1 + dashn1 + 1;
              val line1 = implode (copy newn1 " " @ ["|"]);
              val line2 = implode (copy n1 " " @ [" . "] @
                                   copy dashn1 "−" @ ["^"] @
                                   copy dashn2 "−" @ [" . "]);
              val arms = mkpic [line1, line2];
              val newpic = column [arms, rowwith ("", "", " ") [p, p']]
          in (newpic, newn1) end;
```

```
    fun doleaf x
      = let val p = leafpicfun x;
            val n = width p;
            val n1 = n - n div 2 - 1;
            val arm = mkpic [implode (copy n1 "" @ ["|"])]
        in (column [arm, p], n1) end;

    fun picof t = let val (p, n) = btreeop doleaf joinpics t
                  in p end
    in
      picof
    end;
    end (* of local *);

(* intpic makes pictures of integers *)

fun intpic (n : int) = mkpic [implode ["(", stringofint n, ")"]];

(* tree1 and tree2 are example trees *)

val tree1 = ((((Lf 3 /\ Lf 4) /\ (Lf 5 /\ (Lf 6 /\ Lf 7))) /\ Lf 8) /\ Lf 9);
val tree2 = tree1 /\ tree1;

(* They can be pictured by e.g. *)

val picoftree2 = btreepic intpic tree2
```

Appendix 3
Lazy Lists in Standard ML

This appendix contains a functor (MakeLazy) which creates lazy lists and lazy list operations for a given type. Because the implementation uses references and side-effects, polymorphic lazy lists cannot be defined.

To create a structure Lazyint of operations for lazy integer lists, use:

```
structure Lazyint = MakeLazy (struct type t = int end)
```

```
( ***********************************************************
 SOME OPERATIONS FOR DEFINING AND MANIPULATING
 LAZY LISTS
 These definitions use some features of SML not mentioned in this
 book such as exceptions, raise, case _ and as
 *********************************************************** )

signature TYPE = sig type t end;
signature LAZY = sig
                     type t
                     type lazylist
                     exception lHd : unit
                     exception lTl : unit
                     val delay : (unit -> lazylist) -> lazylist
                     val fixpoint : (lazylist -> lazylist) -> lazylist
                     val force : lazylist -> lazylist
                     val lCons : t -> (lazylist -> lazylist)
                     val lHd : lazylist -> t
                     val lNil : lazylist
                     val lNull : lazylist -> bool
                     val lTl : lazylist -> lazylist
                     val lazy : (('a -> t *'a) * ('a -> bool)) -> 'a -> lazylist
                     val open_lazylist_in : (string -> t) -> (string -> lazylist)
                 end;
```

```
functor MakeLazy (T : TYPE) : LAZY =
struct
    type t = T.t
    exception lTl
         and lHd

    datatype lazylist = Ptr of hidden ref
         and hidden = Cons of t * lazylist
                    | Susp of (unit -> lazylist)
                    | Nil

    fun newptrto h = Ptr (ref h)
    fun contents (Ptr (ref h)) = h
    fun forcecontents (Ptr (ref (Susp f))) = forcecontents (f ( ))
    |   forcecontents (Ptr (ref other))    = other
    fun force (p as Ptr r) = (r := forcecontents p; p) (* returns pointer to a *)
                                                   (* Cons or Nil not Susp *)

   val lNil = newptrto Nil
   fun lCons a x = newptrto (Cons (a, x))
   fun lTl x    = case contents x
                   of Cons (_, y) => y
                   |  Nil         => raise lTl
                   |  Susp f      => Tl (force x)
   fun lHd x   = case contents x
                   of Cons (a, _) => a
                   |  Nil         => raise lHd
                   |  Susp f      => lHd (force x)
   fun lNull x  = case contents x
                   of Cons _      => false
                   |  Nil         => true
                   |  Susp f      => lNull (force x)
   fun delay unittolazy = newptrto (Susp unittolazy)
   fun fixpoint llfun = let val (fixpt as Ptr box) = newptrto Nil
                            fun new ( ) = llfun fixpt
                        in (box := Susp new; fixpt) end

   fun lazy (next, isend)
      = let fun mklazy x = delay (fn ( ) => if isend x
                                             then lNil
                                             else let val (hd, tl) = next x
                                                    in  lCons  hd  (mklazy  tl)
                                                    end)
        in mklazy end
```

```
fun open_lazylist_in convert (file : string)
    = let fun nextitem strm = (convert (input (strm, 1)), strm)
      in lazy (nextitem, end_of_stream) (open_in file) end

end (* of struct and functor MakeLazy *);

(*******************************************************************
 NOTE THAT the construct delay (fn ( ) => LAZYLISTEXP) can be
 used where just LAZYLISTEXP might cause an infinite loop under call
 by value.
 *******************************************************************)
```

Appendix 4
Miranda

Miranda is a lazily evaluated language, but otherwise has much in common with SML. Some of the differences of syntax are mentioned below, and we present some examples for comparison. Miranda is described in Turner (1985) and is available from Research Software Limited, 23 St Augustines Road, Canterbury CTI IXP, England, email: mira-request @ ukc.ac.uk.

The indentation is significant in the examples, since it is used to determine the scopes of definitions in a natural way. Programs are just (mutually recursive) collections of definitions (without keywords like **fun** or **val** or **and**, but with auxiliary definitions introduced by **where**). Comments follow || to the end of the line in the examples below.

Conditionals are covered by qualifications to definitions. Thus:

```
f x = E1, B
    = E2, otherwise
```

corresponds to the SML **fun** f x = **if** B **then** E_1 **else** E_2.

The symbols : and :: are switched in Miranda, so the former is 'cons' and the latter is used for 'has type'.

The append operation is ++ and # is the length function (for lists).

$[T]$ is written for the type T list, i.e. lists of values of type T, and (T_1, T_2, T_3) is written instead of $T_1 \times T_2 \times T_3$.

The symbol '.' is used for composition of functions.

Reals and integers share a single type num, and the function entier :: num → num can be used to ensure that a number is an integer by rounding down if necessary.

Infix function symbols can be used in sections and are curried. Thus (+) :: int → int → int and (+) 3 5 = 3 + 5.

Strings are lists of characters, and characters are written with single quotes. Thus "abc" ≡ ['a', 'b', 'c'] ≡ 'a' : 'b' : 'c' : [ ].

Lists are indexed from 0, and the function !n when applied to integer n and list x returns the nth item in the list (the head being the 0th term).

The first example concerns Pascal's triangles:

```
|| PASCALS TRIANGLE IN MIRANDA

|| The entire pascal triangle represented as an infinite list of [int]:

pascal = iterate nextline [1]
iterate f x = x : iterate f (f x)
nextline x = splice (+) x (0 : x)

|| A function to display n lines of the triangle with a triangular shape:

laypascal n
   = triangle indent (take n pascal)
     where indent = (n - 1) * step
intwidth = 5
step = (intwidth + 1) div 2

triangle i [ ] = [ ]
triangle i (a : x) = layline i a ++ newlines 2 ++ triangle (i-step) x

layline i a = copy i ' ' ++ [ch | m <- a; ch <- (' ' : pad intwidth m)]
|| auxiliary functions

pad width int || pads the string rep of an integer to width
            = copy (width - # string) ' ' ++ string
              where
              string = show (entier int)

copy n a = a : copy (n - 1) a, n > 0
         = [ ]                , otherwise

newlines n = copy n '\n'

splice f (a : x) (b : y) = f a b : splice f x y
splice f [ ] y = y
splice f x [ ] = x

|| EXAMPLE
|| Miranda laypascal 5
||
||                  1
||
||               1     1
||
||            1     2     1
||
||         1     3     3     1
||
||      1     4     6     4     1
```

The next example is a definition of (an abstract type of) character pictures in Miranda. Abstract types are specified by giving the signature, and the implementation is described by giving a representation type and definitions of the operations in the signature. Note that picture == (num, num, [[char]]) is equivalent to the SML type abbreviation **type** picture = int × int × string list. Thus the abstract type is identified with its implementation type (and conversion constructors need not be used).

```
abstype picture
with mkpic :: [[char]] -> picture
     width :: picture -> num
     depth :: picture -> num
     linesof :: picture -> [[char]]
     nullpic :: picture
     padside :: num -> picture -> picture
     padbottom :: num -> picture -> picture
     rowwith :: ([char], [char], [char]) -> [picture] -> picture
     row :: [picture] -> picture
     column :: [picture] -> picture
     colwith :: ([char], [char], [char]) -> [picture] -> picture
     indent :: num -> picture -> picture
     lower :: num -> picture -> picture
     paste :: num -> num -> picture -> picture -> picture
     cutfrom :: picture -> num -> num -> num -> num -> picture
     table :: [[picture]] -> picture
     frame :: picture -> picture
     header :: [char] -> picture -> picture
     showpicture :: picture -> [char]
picture == (num, num, [[char]])
mkpic linelist = (n, m, checkedlines)
                 where
                 n = # linelist
                 shape = map (#) linelist
                 m = maxposlist shape
                 checkedlines = map addspaces linelist
                 addspaces x = x ++ spaces (m - a), a < m
                             = x , otherwise
                               where a = # x

padbottom a (n, m, p) = (n, m, p), a <= n
                      = (a, m, p ++ rep (a - n) (spaces m)), a > n

padside a (n, m, p) = (n, m, p), a <= m
                    = (n, a, map (++ spaces (a - m)) p), a > m
```

```
depth (n, m, p)  = n
width (n, m, p)  = m
linesof (n, m, p) = p

rowwith fsb plist = (n′, m′, p′)
                    where
                    n′ = maxposlist (map depth plist)
                    newpiclines = map (linesof . padbottom n′) plist
                    p′ = [catwith fsb (map (!n) newpiclines)
                              | n <- [0 . . . n′ − 1]]

                    m′ = 0, p′ = [ ]
                       = # (hd p′), otherwise

row = rowwith ("", "", "")

colwith (f, s, b) plist = (n′, m′, p′)
                          where
                          m′ = maxposlist (map width plist)
                          newpics = map (padside m′) plist
                          flines = map (rep m′) f
                          slines = map (rep m′) s
                          blines = map (rep m′) b
                          p′ = catwith (flines, slines, blines)
                                       (map linesof newpics)
                          n′ = # p′

column = colwith (" ", "", " ")

nullpic = (0, 0, [ ])

table [ ] = nullpic
table plistlist = (n, m, p)
                  where
                  p = catwith ([sep], [sep], [sep]) (map linesof tablerows)
                  n = # p
                  m = # (hd p)
                  tablerows = map (rowwith ("|", "|", "|")) picrowlist
                  newpics = mkrect plistlist
                  picrowlist = map (zip padside columnwidths) newpics
                  columnwidths = map maxposlist (transpose picwidths)
                  picwidths = map (map width) newpics
                  sep = catwith ("+", "+", "+")
                                (map dashes columnwidths)
```

```
dashes n = rep n '-'

mkrect plistlist = zip addnulls sizes plistlist
                   where
                   sizes = map (#) plistlist
                   longest = maxposlist sizes
                   addnulls n x = x ++ rep (longest_n) nullpic

paste n m pic1 pic2 = paste 0 m (lower (neg n) pic1) pic2, n < 0
paste n m pic1 pic2 = paste n 0 (indent (neg m) pic1) pic2, m < 0
paste n m pic1 pic2
   = (d, w, p) ,n ≥ 0 & m ≥ 0
     where
     pic1' = padbottom (n + depth pic2) (padside (m + width pic2) pic1)
     stringop = spliceat m overlay
     p = spliceat n stringop (linesof pic1') (linesof pic2)
     d = # p
     w = 0, p = [ ]
       = # (hd p), otherwise

overlay a b = b

cutfrom pic n m a b = cutfrom (lower (neg n) pic) 0 m a b, n < 0
cutfrom pic n m a b = cutfrom (indent (neg m) pic) n 0 a b, m < 0
cutfrom pic n m a b = cutfrom pic (n + a) m (neg a) b, a < 0
cutfrom pic n m a b = cutfrom pic n (m + b) a (neg b), b < 0
cutfrom pic n m a b
   = (a, b, p) ,otherwise
     where
     p = map (sublist (m + 1) b) (sublist (n + 1) a (linesof pic'))
     pic' = padbottom (n + a) (padside (m + b) pic)

indent a pic = pic, a < 1
indent a (n, m, p) = (n, m + a, map (spaces a ++) p)

lower a pic = pic, a < 1
lower a (n, m, p) = (n + a, m, rep a (spaces m) ++ p)

frame pic = table [[pic]]
header str pic = colwith ("", "~", "") [mkpic [str], pic]
showpicture (n, m, lines) = catwith ("", "\n", "\n") lines

||EXAMPLES
example = mkpic ["this is", "an", "example"]
example2 = table [[example, example], [example], [nullpic, example]]
example3 = cutfrom (paste 3 7 example2 example2) 1 3 10 20

||GENERAL OPS
catwith (front, sep, back) listlist = front ++ sb listlist
                                      where
                                      sb [a] = a ++ back
                                      sb (a : x) = a ++ sep ++ sb x
                                      sb [ ] = back
```

```
zip f = zf
        where zf [ ] y = [ ]
              zf x [ ] = [ ]
              zf (a : x) (b : y) = f a b : zf x y
splice f = spf
        where spf [ ] y = y
              spf x [ ] = x
              spf (a : x) (b : y) = f a b : spf x y
spliceat n f x y = splice f x y, n < 1
                 = hd x : spliceat (n - 1) f (tl x) y, otherwise

maxposlist x = max (0 : x)
sublist n a x = take a (drop (n - 1) x) || indexing from 1 not 0 here
```

Appendix 5
Examples of Type Analysis

These examples illustrate the algorithm as described in Chapter 11. For readability and compactness of notation, we use the following abbreviations:

(1) Expressions being analysed will be written in concrete syntax and enclosed in double brackets ⟦ and ⟧ rather than with the constructors indicated in type Expression. Thus:

⟦**fn** x ⇒ x⟧ means ABS (PVAR (Id "x"), VAR (Id "x"))

⟦(I, f x)⟧ means TUP [CON (Id "I"), APP (VAR (Id "f"), VAR (Id "x")]

(2) Similarly we write types in the usual concrete syntax:

α_n means either Alpha n or TypeVar (Alpha n)

depending on the context (whether the type variable is being used as a type expression or just as a type variable), and:

$T_1 \rightarrow T_2$ means TypeOp ("arrow", $[T_1, T_2]$)

(3) Substitutions will be written as θ, θ_1 . . . and we use ∅ for emptySub, $[T_1/\alpha_{n_1}, T_2/\alpha_{n_2}, \ldots T_k/\alpha_{n_k}]$ for a substitution mapping α_{n_i} to T_i $(i = 1 \ldots k)$ and α to α for other type variables α.

(4) Assumptions will be written in their concrete form:

AS (id_type_list, type_list)

where id_type_list give the bindings and type_list is used for the non-generic information. Similarly states will be written as:

ST (θ, n) for some substitution θ and $n \geq 1$

The empty collection of assumptions is of course AS ([ ], [ ]) and the usual starting state is ST (∅, 1).

Example 1

(**fn** x ⇒ x) with no assumptions:

analyse ⟦**fn** x ⇒ x⟧ (AS ([ ], [ ])) (ST (∅, 1))

> newTypeVar (ST (∅, 1))
> = (α_1, ST (∅, 2))

> analyse ⟦x⟧ (AS ([(x$_1$, α_1)], [α_1])) (ST (∅, 2))
> = (α_1, ST (∅, 2))

= ($\alpha_1 \rightarrow \alpha_1$, ST (∅, 2))

Example 2

(**fn** x ⇒ x) (**fn** x ⇒ x) with no assumptions:

analyse ⟦(**fn** x ⇒ x) (**fn** x ⇒ x)⟧ (AS ([ ], [ ])) (ST (∅, 1))

> analyse ⟦**fn** x ⇒ x⟧ (AS ([ ], [ ])) (ST (∅, 1))
> = ($\alpha_1 \rightarrow \alpha_1$, ST (∅, 2))

> analyse ⟦**fn** x ⇒ x⟧ (AS ([ ], [ ])) (ST (∅, 2))
> = ($\alpha_2 \rightarrow \alpha_2$, ST (∅, 3))

> newTypeVar (ST (∅, 3))
> = (α_3, ST (∅, 4))

> unify (($\alpha_2 \rightarrow \alpha_2$) $\rightarrow \alpha_3$) ($\alpha_1 \rightarrow \alpha_1$)
> = [$\alpha_2 \rightarrow \alpha_2 / \alpha_3$, $\alpha_2 \rightarrow \alpha_2 / \alpha_1$] (= θ_1, say)

> θ_1 (α_3) = $\alpha_2 \rightarrow \alpha_2$

= ($\alpha_2 \rightarrow \alpha_2$, ST ($\theta_1$, 4))

Example 3

(**let val** f = **fn** x ⇒ x **in** f f **end**) with no assumptions:

analyse ⟦**let val** f = **fn** x ⇒ x **in** f f **end**⟧ (AS ([ ], [ ])) (ST (∅, 1))

> analyse ⟦**fn** x ⇒ x⟧ (AS ([ ], [ ])) (ST (∅, 2))
> $= (\alpha_1 \rightarrow \alpha_1$, ST (∅, 2))

> analyse ⟦f f⟧ (AS ([(f, $\alpha_1 \rightarrow \alpha_1$)], [ ])) (ST (∅, 2))
>
> Let as1 = AS ([(f, $\alpha_1 \rightarrow \alpha_1$)], [ ])
>
> Note [ ] for non-generics in assumption as1 means that α_1 is regarded as generic.
>
> > analyse ⟦f⟧ as1 (ST (∅, 2))
> > $= (\alpha_2 \rightarrow \alpha_2$, ST (∅, 3))
>
> > analyse ⟦f⟧ as1 (ST (∅, 3))
> > $= (\alpha_3 \rightarrow \alpha_3$, ST (∅, 4))
>
> > newTypeVar (ST (∅, 4))
> > $= (\alpha_4$, ST (∅, 5))
>
> > unify $((\alpha_3 \rightarrow \alpha_3) \rightarrow \alpha_4)\ (\alpha_2 \rightarrow \alpha_2)$
> > $= [\alpha_3 \rightarrow \alpha_3/\alpha_2, \alpha_3 \rightarrow \alpha_3/\alpha_4]$ (= θ_2, say)
>
> > $\theta_2(\alpha_4) = \alpha_3 \rightarrow \alpha_3$
>
> $= (\alpha_3 \rightarrow \alpha_3$, ST ($\theta_2$, 5))

$= (\alpha_3 \rightarrow \alpha_3$, ST ($\theta_2$, 5))

Example 4

(**fn** f $\Rightarrow$ **if** true **then** f true **else** true) assuming true : bool:

analyse ⟦**fn** f $\Rightarrow$ **if** true **then** f true **else** true⟧ (AS ([(true, bool)], [ ])) (ST ($\varnothing$, 1))

newTypeVar (ST ($\varnothing$, 1))
= (α_1, ST ($\varnothing$, 2))

analyse ⟦**if** true **then** f true **else** true⟧ (AS ([true, bool), (f, α_1)], [α_1])) (ST ($\varnothing$, 2))

Let as2 = AS ([true, bool), f, α_1)], [α_1]
Note [α_1] for non-generics in as2 means f has a non-generic type var α_1 in its type.

analyse ⟦true⟧ as2 (ST ($\varnothing$, 2))
= (bool, ST ($\varnothing$, 2))

unify bool bool
= $\varnothing$

analyse ⟦f true⟧ as2 (ST ($\varnothing$, 2))

analyse ⟦f⟧ as2 (ST ($\varnothing$, 2))
= (α_1, ST ($\varnothing$, 2)) $\leftarrow \alpha_1$ Not instantiated to new var because α_1 is non-generic in as1.

analyse ⟦true⟧ as2 (ST ($\varnothing$, 2))
= (bool, ST ($\varnothing$, 2))

newTypeVar ST ($\varnothing$, 2)
= (α_2, ST ($\varnothing$, 3))

unify (bool $\rightarrow \alpha_2$) α_1
= [bool $\rightarrow \alpha_2/\alpha_1$] (= θ_3, say)

$\theta_3(\alpha_2) = \alpha_2$

= (α_2, ST (θ_3, 3)) Note α_2 inherits non-genericity because non-generics are now all TypeVars in $\theta_3(\alpha_1)$ = bool $\rightarrow \alpha_2$.

analyse ⟦true⟧ as2 (ST (θ_3, 3))
= (bool, ST (θ_3, 3))

unify α_2 bool
= [bool/α_2]

$\theta_4 =$ compose [bool/α_2] θ_3 = [bool/α_2, bool $\rightarrow$ bool/α_1]

$\theta_4(\alpha_2)$ = bool

=(bool, ST (θ_4, 3))

$\theta_4(\alpha_1)$ = bool $\rightarrow$ bool

= ((bool $\rightarrow$ bool) $\rightarrow$ bool, ST (θ_4, 3))

Solutions to Selected Exercises

Chapter 1

1.1

```
fun abs n = if n < 0 then ~n else n
```

1.2 There is no single right answer to the problem. Clearly when $n \geq 0$, $m > 0$ we want $(n \text{ div } m) * m + (n \text{ mod } m) = n$ to hold where:

$$0 \leq n \text{ mod } m < m.$$

Standard ML specifies that the above equation holds for all n and all $m \neq 0$ where *either* $0 \leq \text{mod } m < m$ *or* $m < n \text{ mod } m \leq 0$. This means that the remainder (n mod m) has the same sign as m and is always smaller in magnitude than m.

1.3

```
fun sumbetween (m, n) = let val (s, d) = sumdiff (m, n)
                        in (s * (d + 1)) div 2 end
```

1.4 Assuming $m \geq 0$:

even (double m)	= even (m + m)	(by definition of double)
	= even (2 * m)	(using m + m = 2 * m)
	= (2 * m) mod 2 = 0	(by definition of even)
	= (2 * m + 0) mod 2 = 0	(using 2 * m = 2 * m + 0)
	= 0 = 0	(given property of mod)
	= true	

1.5 (a) Assuming m is a well defined integer:

```
m + if m = 0 then n else n − m
= m + if m = 0 then n − m else n − m
= m + (n − m)
= n
```

(b) Note that when m = n then m = avepair (m, n) and also avepair (m, n) = (m + n) div 2, so we get:

```
if m = n then m else
if m < n then avepair (m, n) else (m + n) div 2
    = (m + n) div 2
```

(c) Assuming s2 is a well-defined string:

```
size (if s1 = s2 then s1 ^ s2 else s1 ^ s1)
    = size (if s1 = s2 then s1 ^ s1 else s1 ^ s1)
    = size (s1 ^ s1)
    = 2 * size s1
```

Note that in (a) and (c) assumptions are made about some of the component values which do not appear in the simplified version. These equations do not hold without such assumptions.

1.6

```
for n ≥ 0  size (stringcopy (n, s)) = n * size s
```

1.7

```
sumg 4 = sumg (4 − 1) + g 4
       = (sumg 3) + g 4
       = (sumg 2 + g 3) + g 4
       = sumg 1 + g 2 + g 3 + g 4
       = sumg 0 + g 1 + g 2 + g 3 + g 4
       = g 0 + g 1 + g 2 + g 3 + g 4
```

1.8

```
local
        fun fact0 n = if n = 0 then 1 else n * fact0 (n − 1)
in
        fun fact n = if n < 0 then error "neg arg for fact"
                                else fact0 n
end
```

(The **local** ... **in** ... **end** construct is just used to hide the auxiliary definition of fact0 – see Section 1.6.2.)

1.9

```
local
        fun binrepnat 0 = "0"
        |   binrepnat 1 = "1"
        |   binrepnat n = binrepnat (n div 2) ^ binrepnat (n mod 2)
in
        fun binrepint n = if n < 0 then "~" ^ binrepnat (~ n)
                                   else binrepnat n
end
```

1.11

```
fun power (m, 0) = 1
|   power (m, n) = m * power (m, n − 1)
```

is a simple but non-robust definition which will loop for negative n. A robust version is given by:

```
local
        fun   power' (m, 0) = 1
        |     power' (m, n) = m * power' (m, n − 1)
in
        fun   power (m, n) = if n < 0
                             then error "power (m, n) with n < 0"
                             else power' (m, n)
end
```

1.12

```
fun product (m, n) = if m = n then m
                     else m * product (m + 1, n)
```

This version counts up from the lower bound. It is also possible to count down from the upper bound or to use the midpoint as suggested in Exercise 1.24. It is left as a further exercise to make this definition robust.

1.13 A (non-robust) version of the new sumg which we call sumrangeg is defined by:

```
fun sumrangeg (m, n) = if m = n
                       then g m
                       else g m + sumrangeg (m + 1, n)
```

A 'binary chop' version (see Exercise 1.24) could be defined by:

```
fun sumrangeg (m, n)
    = if m = n then g m else
        let val midpt = (m + n) div 2
        in sumrangeg (m, midpt) + sumrangeg (midpt + 1, n)
        end
```

As a further exercise, you should try this latter definition out by expanding sumrangeg (7, 10), for example.

1.14 One method is to define an auxiliary function ming : int × int × int → int so that ming (x, a, b) finds the smallest value of g (x, y) for $a \leq y \leq b$ then we can define minvalgh (x) = ming (x, 0, h (x)) as a special case, for example:

```
fun ming (x, a, b) = if a = b
                     then g (x, b)
                     else minpair (g (x, a), ming (x, a + 1, b))
fun minvalgh (x) = ming (x, 0, h (x))
```

In this definition of ming we use minpair to compare g (x, a) with the minimum in the rest of the range (a + 1 to b). A 'binary-chop' technique, as explained in the previous exercise, could also be used to split the range. (This is left as a further exercise.)

1.15

```
fun posgcd (m, n)
    = if m < n then posgcd (n, m) else
        let val r = m mod n
        in if r = 0 then n else posgcd (n, r)
        end
```

1.16 Using the definition:

```
fun stringcopy (0, s) = ""
  | stringcopy (n, s) = stringcopy (n - 1, s) ^ s
```

We try induction on $n \geq 0$ to prove

stringcopy (m + n, s) = stringcopy (m, s) ^ stringcopy (n, s)
for all $m \geq 0$

(Note that using the robust version of stringcopy, we would first prove the result for the auxiliary stringcopy0.)

When n = 0:

```
stringcopy (m + 0, s) = stringcopy (m, s)
                      = stringcopy (m, s) ^ ""
                      = stringcopy (m, s) ^ stringcopy (0, s)
```

When n = k + 1:

```
stringcopy (m + (k + 1), s)= stringcopy (m + (k + 1) − 1, s) ^ s
                             by definition
                           = stringcopy (m + k, s) ^ s
                           = (stringcopy (m, s) ^(stringcopy (k, s)) ^s
                             by induction hypothesis
                           = stringcopy(m,s)^(stringcopy(k,s)^s)  (*)
                           = stringcopy (m, s) ^ stringcopy (k + 1, s)
                             by definition (k + 1 − 1 = k)
```

Thus by induction, the result follows for all n ≥ 0. Note that we used the associativity of ^ in the step (*), i.e. that (s1 ^ s2) ^ s3 = s1 ^ (s2 ^ s3).

For the second proof, we use induction on m to show that:

```
stringcopy (m * n, s) = stringcopy (m, stringcopy (n, s))
```

for all n ≥ 0.

When m = 0:

```
stringcopy (0 * n, s) = stringcopy (0, s) = ""
                      = stringcopy (0, stringcopy (n, s))
```

When m = k + 1:

```
stringcopy ((k + 1) * n, s) = stringcopy ((k * n) + n, s)
                            = stringcopy (k * n, s) ^ stringcopy (n, s)
                              by the previous proof.
                            = stringcopy (k, stringcopy (n, s)) ^
                                                       stringcopy (n, s)
                              by induction hypothesis
                            = stringcopy (k + 1, stringcopy (n, s))
                              using the definition of stringcopy
```

So by induction the result follows for all m ≥ 0.

1.17 If we take the definition of gcd given in the chapter then:

```
even 0 & even 0 = true & true = true
```

but even (gcd (0, 0)) is undefined. With the modified interpretation of 'greatest', we should take gcd (0, 0) = 0 since 0 is the 'greatest' divisor of 0. All other properties of gcd which we described will still be true, and the given equivalence will hold as well.

1.18 If windowint (w, s) is calculated for $w < 0$, it is equivalent to stringcopy (w, "*") according to the definition and hence undefined by the definition of stringcopy. (The error message will be "stringcopy with neg int".)

1.21 We use the following ordering for argument pairs of *non-negative* integers:

$$(a', b') \prec (a, b) \text{ if } a' < a \text{ or } (a' = a \text{ and } b' < b)$$

This is a well founded ordering with least pair (0, 0).

Now we show ack (a, b) is defined for all $a \geq 0$ and $b \geq 0$ by complete induction with this ordering. We have to show that ack (a, b) is defined whenever ack (a′, b′) is defined for all $a' \geq 0$ and $b' \geq 0$ such that $(a', b') \prec (a, b)$.

We consider cases for the definition of ack (a, b). Either:

(a) $a = 0$, in which case ack (a, b) is defined and equal to $b + 1$; or

(b) $a > 0$ and $b = 0$, in which case ack (a, 0) = ack (a − 1, 1) which is defined by our inductive hypothesis since $(a - 1, 1) \prec (a, 0)$; or

(c) $a > 0$ and $b > 0$, in which case [ack (a, b) = ack (a − 1, ack (a, b − 1))] Now ack (a, b − 1) is defined by hypothesis since $(a, b - 1) \prec (a, b)$ and we let k = ack (a, b − 1). Similarly ack (a − 1, k) is defined by hypothesis since $(a - 1, k) \prec (a, b)$, so ack (a, b) is defined.

Hence by complete induction ack (a, b) is defined for all $a \geq 0$ and $b \geq 0$.

1.23 Here is one possible definition which uses a parameter (n) for an auxiliary function search, beginning with $n = 0$. At each step, $(n + 1)^2$ is calculated to see if it exceeds the original value m whose introot is sought:

```
fun introot m = let fun search (n) = if (n + 1) * (n + 1) > m
                                     then n
                                     else search (n + 1)
                in search 0 end
```

The recalculation of squares can be simplified by noting that:

$$(n + 2)^2 = (n + 1)^2 + 2n + 3$$

and using an additional parameter (nextsq) to keep a record of $(n + 1)^2$:

```
fun introot m = let fun search (n, nextsq) =
                        if nextsq > m
                        then n
                        else search (n + 1, nextsq + 2 * n + 3)
                in search (0, 1) end
```

In fact, the value of (2 * n + 3) can be recorded at each step by another parameter to remove all multiplications from the calculation. This last refinement is left as a further exercise.

1.24

```
fun product (m, n) = if m = n then m else
                     let val midpt = (m + n) div 2
                     in product (m, midpt) * product (midpt + 1, n)
                     end
```

1.25

```
fun power (m, 0) = 1
  | power (m, n) = if even n
                   then square (power (m, n div 2))
                   else square (power (m, n div 2)) * m
```

We assume **fun** square n = n * n here, and have not made the function robust for negative n.

1.26 Using 'product' defined in Exercise 1.12 (and also Exercise 1.24) we can simply define:

```
fun P (n, r) = product (n - r + 1, n)
```

Note that calculating (fact n) div (fact (n − r)) is extremely inefficient when n and r are not both very small.

1.27

```
fun g (x) = let val x = x + 1 in x * x end
fun f (x, y) =
        let val x = x + y in
           if let val x = y div 2 and y = x + y in x > y end
           then let val z = x * x in x * z end
           else x + y
        end
```

1.28 50 and 24.

1.29

	Scope of V_1	Scope of V_2
(a)	E_2, E	E
(b)	E	E_1
(c)	E	E
(d)	E_1, E_2, E	E_1, E_2, E
(e)	E_2, E	E_2, E
(f)	E_1, E_2, E	E
(g)	E_1, E_2, E	E_1
(h)	E	E_1, E_2
(i)	E_1, E_2, E	E_2, E
(j)	E_1, E_2, E	E_1, E_2

If $V_1 \equiv V_2$:

	Scope of first V_1	*Scope of second* V_1 $(= V_2)$
(a)	E_2	E
(b)	E	E_1
(c)	[Illegal	]
(d)	[Illegal	]
(e)	None	E_2, E
(f)	E_1, E_2	E
(g)	E_2, E	E_1
(h)	E	E_1, E_2
(i)	E_1	E_2, E
(j)	E	E_1, E_2

These assume V is distinct from V_1 and V_2.

There are many other cases to consider when $V \equiv V_1$ or $V \equiv V_2$. As one example we take:

```
let fun V1 (V) = E1 and V2 (V) = E2 in E end
```

If $V \equiv V_1$ then occurrences of V in E_1 will refer to the parameter V not the function V_1, so the scope of V_1 is just E. Similarly, if $V_2 \equiv V$ then the scope of the function V_2 is just E, and the scope of the parameter V is E_2 (for the second defining occurrence) and E_1 for the first defining occurrence. (If $V_1 \equiv V_2$, the whole expression is illegal regardless of V.)

1.30 The simplest way is to use **local** as follows:

```
local
        fun f x = E1
        and g y = E2
        and h z = E3
in
        val f = f
        and g = g
end
```

Alternatively, we can define a pair of functions simultaneously:

```
val (f, g) = let
                  fun f x = E1
                  and g y = E2
                  and h z = E3
             in (f, g) end
```

1.31 (a) Always true.

(b) Always true.

(c) Not true in general, but true when E imports no variables from D_1.

(d) Not true in general, but true when D_1 and D_2 export distinct variables.

(e) Always true.

Chapter 2

2.1 Such a function could be applied to any pair of values for which the first and second components have the same type. Using the rather contrived definition:

```
fun f (x, y) = if 5 < 3 then (5, x) else (3, y)
```

we would have $f : \alpha \times \alpha \rightarrow \text{int} \times \alpha$. Note that the conditional constrains the parameters x and y to have the same type. If we simplified the definition to:

```
fun f (x, y) = (3, y)
```

we would have $f : \alpha \times \beta \rightarrow \text{int} \times \beta$ giving f a more general type.

2.2 The argument pattern for the first case of the definition of f indicates that the argument type is a triple with an integer as third component. Thus, initially, we deduce:

$$[f : \alpha \times \beta \times \text{int} \rightarrow \gamma]$$

Now, the result for the first case is a (the first parameter) so the result type γ must be the same as α, giving:

$$[f : \alpha \times \beta \times \text{int} \rightarrow \alpha]$$

Turning to the second case of the definition of f, we see that the second component of the argument appears as a test in a conditional, so it must have type bool:

$$[f : \alpha \times \text{bool} \times \text{int} \rightarrow \alpha]$$

Finally, the use of the string concatenator $\hat{}\ : \text{string} * \text{string} \rightarrow \text{string}$ suggests that the type of a (α) is string, so:

$$f : \text{string} \times \text{bool} \times \text{int} \rightarrow \text{string}$$

Similar reasoning with the second definition gives:

$$g : \alpha \times (\alpha \times \alpha \rightarrow \alpha) \times \text{int} \rightarrow \alpha$$

2.3

Firstly

$$\dfrac{\dfrac{\dfrac{\text{int is a type constant}}{\text{int is a type}} \quad \dfrac{\alpha \text{ is a type variable}}{\alpha \text{ is a type}}}{\text{int} \rightarrow \alpha \text{ is a type}} \qquad \dfrac{\text{bool is a type constant}}{\text{bool is a type}}}{(\text{int} \rightarrow \alpha) \rightarrow \text{bool is a type}} \qquad (1)$$

Secondly

$$\cfrac{\cfrac{\cfrac{\beta \text{ is a type variable}}{\beta \text{ is a type}} \quad \cfrac{\alpha \text{ is a type variable}}{\alpha \text{ is a type}}}{\beta \to \alpha \text{ is a type}} \quad \cfrac{\text{int is a type constant}}{\text{int is a type}}}{(\beta \to \alpha) \times \text{int is a type}} \quad (2)$$

From (1) and (2) we obtain:

$$\cfrac{(1) \quad \cfrac{(2) \quad \cfrac{\alpha \text{ is a type variable}}{\alpha \text{ is a type}}}{((\beta \to \alpha) \times \text{int}) \to \alpha \text{ is a type}}}{((\text{int} \to \alpha) \to \text{bool}) \to (((\beta \to \alpha) \times \text{int}) \to \alpha) \text{ is a type}}$$

2.4 (a)

$$\cfrac{\text{double} : \text{int} \to \text{int} \quad \cfrac{\cfrac{\text{I} : \alpha \to \alpha}{\text{I} : \text{int} \to \text{int}} \quad 5 : \text{int}}{(\text{I } 5) : \text{int}}}{\text{double } (\text{I } 5) : \text{int}}$$

(b) **Firstly**

$$\cfrac{\cfrac{\text{double} : \text{int} \to \text{int} \quad 5 : \text{int}}{\text{double } 5 : \text{int}} \quad \cfrac{\text{not} : \text{bool} \to \text{bool} \quad \text{true} : \text{bool}}{\text{not true} : \text{bool}}}{(\text{double } 5, \text{not true}) : \text{int} \times \text{bool}} \quad (1)$$

From (1) we obtain

$$\cfrac{\cfrac{\text{I} : \alpha \to \alpha}{\text{I} : (\text{int} \times \text{bool}) \to (\text{int} \times \text{bool})} \quad (1)}{\text{I } (\text{double } 5, \text{not true}) : \text{int} \times \text{bool}}$$

(c)

$$\cfrac{\cfrac{\text{I} : \alpha \to \alpha}{\text{I} : (\alpha \to \alpha) \to (\alpha \to \alpha)} \quad \text{I} : \alpha \to \alpha}{\text{I}(\text{I}) : \alpha \to \alpha}$$

Note that a more rigorous treatment of typing polymorphic expressions is given in Chapter 11, where similar trees are used (but a record of the types of variables is kept to ensure consistency in assumptions).

2.5 Induction on n ≥ 0:

Case n = 0:

```
sumbetween (0, 0) = (0 + 0) * (abs (0 − 0) + 1) div 2
                  = 0 div 2
                  = 0
sum I 0 = I 0 = 0
```

Case n = k + 1:

```
sumbetween (0, k+1) = (0+k+1) * (abs (0 − (k+1)) + 1) div 2
                    = (k + 1) * (k + 2) div 2
                    = ((k + 1) * k + (k + 1) * 2) div 2
                    = ((k + 1) * k) div 2 + (k + 1)
```

(This last step uses the fact that (m + 2 * n) div 2 = m div 2 + n for m, n ≥ 0.)

```
sum I (k + 1) = sum I k + I (k + 1)
              = sum I k + (k + 1)
              = sumbetween (0, k) + (k + 1) (by induction
                                             hypothesis for k)
              = ((0 + k) * (abs (0 − k) + 1)) div 2 + (k + 1)
              = (k * (k + 1)) div 2 + (k + 1)
              = sumbetween (0, k + 1)        (as shown above)
```

So, by induction sum I n = sumbetween (0, n) for all n ≥ 0.

2.6

```
local
        fun sigma' g m n = if m = n then g m else
                             let val midpt = (m + n) div 2
                             in sigma' g m midpt +
                                sigma' g (midpt + 1) n
                             end
in
        fun sigma g m n = if n < m then sigma' g n m
                                    else sigma' g m n
end
```

Note that the auxiliary function was a 'binary chop' to calculate the required answer, but assumes that m ≤ n. The main function just swaps the integers m and n if n ≤ m and then uses sigma' to do the calculation.

We leave it as a further exercise to show that this function has the required properties.

2.7 Define **fun** both f (x, y) = (f x, f y) and **fun** duplicate x = (x, x) then:

```
(or) ∘ (both not) = not ∘ (&)
(&) ∘ (both not) = not ∘ (or)
not ∘ not = (I : bool → bool)
(&) ∘ duplicate = (I : bool → bool)
(+) ∘ duplicate = times 2
(or) ∘ duplicate = (I : bool → bool)
size ∘ (^) = (+) ∘ both size
```

2.8 The function duplicate: $\alpha \rightarrow \alpha \times \alpha$ defined by:

```
fun duplicate x = (x, x)
```

has the property that:

```
swappair ∘ duplicate = duplicate
```

Any function f whose type is an instance of $\alpha \rightarrow$ unit × unit will also satisfy:

```
swappair ∘ f = f
```

e.g. **fun** f x = (( ), ( )) (or **val** f = K (( ), ( ))).

2.9

```
fun least p n = if p n then n else least p (n + 1)
fun answer p = least p 0
```

(Thus answer becomes a function which might be named, more appropriately, 'first'.)

2.10 For example:

```
local
        fun min g (x, a, b) = if a = b
                              then g (x, b)
                              else minpair (g (x, a), min g (x, a+1, b))
in
        fun minval g h x = min g (x, 0, h (x))
end
```

2.11

```
fun sum g n
    = let
          fun countpos (acc, count) = count ≥ 0
          fun next (acc, count) = (acc + g count, count − 1)
      in
          fst (loopwhile countpos next (0, n))
      end
```

2.12 A general function could be defined by:

```
fun binchop' (f, a) (0, x) = a
|   binchop' (f, a) (n, x) = let
                                 val halfans = binchop' (f, a)
                                                        (n div 2, x)
                             in
                                 if even n
                                 then f halfans halfans
                                 else f x (f halfans halfans)
                             end
```

which could then be made robust, defining:

```
fun binchop (f, a) (n, x) = if n < 0 then error "binchop with neg. arg."
                                     else binchop' (f, a) (n, x)
```

2.13 $(\alpha \to \beta) \times (\alpha \to \gamma)$ is isomorphic to $\alpha \to (\beta \times \gamma)$. If we define:

```
fun both (f, g) a = (f a, g a)
fun split f = let fun f1 a = fst (f a)
                  fun f2 a = snd (f a)
              in (f1, f2) end
```

Then:

both : $((\alpha \to \beta) \times (\alpha \to \gamma)) \to (\alpha \to (\beta \times \gamma))$
split : $(\alpha \to (\beta \times \gamma)) \to ((\alpha \to \beta) \times (\alpha \to \gamma))$

and:

both $\circ$ split = I
split $\circ$ both = I

2.14

```
fun C f b a = f a b
```

C : $(\alpha \to \beta \to \gamma) \to (\beta \to \alpha \to \gamma)$

2.15

```
fun curry f a b = f (a, b)
```

curry : $(\alpha \times \beta \to \gamma) \to (\alpha \to \beta \to \gamma)$

```
fun uncurry f (a, b) = f a b
```

uncurry : $(\alpha \to \beta \to \gamma) \to ((\alpha \times \beta) \to \gamma)$

2.16

$E_1 + E_2$
$(E_1 +)\, E_2$
$(+\, E_2)\, E_1$
$(+)\, (E_1, E_2)$
plus $E_1\, E_2$
curry $(+)\, E_1\, E_2$
uncurry plus (E_1, E_2)

Clearly $(^{-}E_1)$ is a dangerous notation for a function of type int $\to$ int used as in $(^{-}E_1)\, E_2$ because it looks like the negative of E_1, i.e. $(\tilde{}E_1)$ which has type int.

2.18

```
fun cond1 p c x = if p x then c x else x
fun cond2 p c1 c2 x = if p x then c1 x else c2 x
fun loopwhile p c x = cond1 p (loopwhile p c ∘ c) x
```

This last definition throws up an interesting problem which cannot be fully explained until Chapter 8. If we 'cancel' the occurrences of parameter x we get:

```
fun loopwhile p c = cond1 p (loopwhile p c ∘ c)
```

but this definition will cause an infinite evaluation to be started whenever loopwhile is applied to some p and c.

2.19 If we define:

```
fun forcount n m c s
    = if n > m then s
                 else forcount (n + 1) m c (c (n, s))
```

then the parameter c has type (int × $\alpha \rightarrow \alpha$) instead of ($\alpha \rightarrow \alpha$). The first component of the argument pair for c is the value of the count variable, and the second component is the state. If the count variable is global, then it will already be part of the state. Assuming the state has the form (i, s), we could define:

```
fun globalforcount n m c (i, s)
                  = forcount' m c (n, s)
and forcount' m c (n, s)
              = if n > m then (n, s)
                         else let val (n', s') = c (n, s)
                              in forcount' m c (n + 1, s)
                              end
```

This allows the count variable n to be changed to n′, but the next iteration still uses n + 1. The only modification necessary to allow the count variable to be modified for subsequent iterations is to replace the n + 1 by n′ + 1.

2.20

```
fun repeatuntil p c = (loopwhile (non p) c) ∘ c
fun loopexit c1 p c2 = (loopwhile (non p) (c1 ∘ c2)) ∘ c1
```

2.21

```
K = curry fst
```

2.22

```
(K I) : β → α → α
(K I) b a = a
i.e. K I = curry snd
```

2.23

```
(let fun f x = 3 + x in f end) 5
  = (let val f = fn x ⇒ 3 + x in f end) 5
  = (fn x ⇒ 3 + x) 5
  = 3 + 5
  = 8
```

2.24 For example:

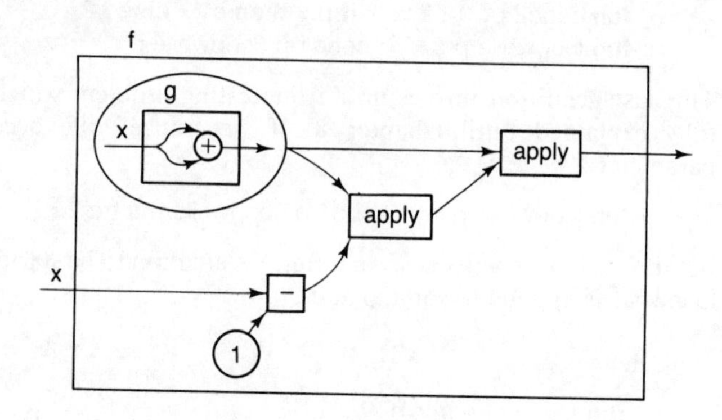

2.27

```
fun posequalfun f g = let fun search n = if f n = g n
                                         then search (n + 1)
                                         else false
                      in search 0 end
```

This function has an even more general type than that required, namely:

$$(\text{int} \rightarrow \alpha^{=}) \rightarrow (\text{int} \rightarrow \alpha^{=}) \rightarrow \text{bool}$$

To test for negative differences as well, we interweave two searches:

```
fun equalfun f g = let fun possearch n =
                         if f n = g n
                         then negsearch (~ (n + 1))
                         else false
                       and negsearch n =
                         if f n = g n
                         then possearch (~n)
                         else false
                   in possearch 0 end
```

It is not possible to test if two functions are equal in a computable way which is guaranteed to be defined for all cases. See Hoare and Allison (1972) for a discussion of such limitation theorems.

2.29 Clearly the expression has an undefined subexpression, namely 3 div 0, but we would expect the expression to be evaluated as:

if false **then** 3 div 0 **else** 3
  = 3 (according to the rules given for conditionals)

This shows that we cannot assume that expressions with undefined components are undefined. Recursive definitions also rely on the fact that not all subexpressions are evaluated.

2.30

B_1 **orelse** $B_2 \equiv$ **if** B_1 **then** true **else** B_2
B_1 **andalso** $B_2 \equiv$ **if** B_1 **then** B_2 **else** false

2.31 In a strict language:

```
cond (3 = 4) (3 div 0) 3
```

would be undefined whereas we want:

(**if** 3 = 4 **then** 3 div 0 **else** 3) = 3

In a lazy language, everything is alright and both expressions produce 3.

Chapter 3

3.1

```
[5, 8] : int list
5 :: 8 is a type error
[(5, 8)] : (int × int) list
[[5], [8]] : (int list) list
([5], [8]) : (int list) × (int list)
5 ::[8] : int list
(5, [8]) : int × (int list)
[5, [8]] is a type error
[5 :: [8]] : (int list) list
```

3.2 Using higher order functions:

fun copy n a = repeat n (cons a) [ ]

Using ZF notation:

fun copy 0 a = [ ]
| copy n a = [a | i ∈ 1 upto n]

3.3

```
f : bool → (bool → bool) → bool → bool
g : int → (int × int) → ((int list) × int)
h : int → int list
```

3.7

select : int → α list → α

This function selects an item from a list at a given index. When $0 < n \leq m$:

select n $[a_1, \ldots, a_m] = a_n$

For other arguments, select is undefined (giving error reports).

sublist : int → int → α list → α list

This function returns the sublist of a given list starting at a given index and of a given length.

When $0 < n$ and $0 < m$ and $n + m \leq k$:

select n m $[a_1, \ldots, a_n, \ldots, a_{n+m-1}, \ldots, a_k] = [a_n, \ldots, a_{n+m-1}]$

(Note the result has length m.)

When m = 0, select n 0 x = [ ] provided that length $x \geq n - 1$ and $n > 0$. For other arguments, select produces an error message.

3.8 For example:

```
fun back n x = rev (front n (rev x))
```

or

```
fun back n x = drop (length x − n) x
```

3.9

```
fun innerproduct = zip times
```

3.11

```
fun accufun f a g x y = if x > y then a
                        else accufun f (f a (g x)) (x + 1) y
fun reducefun f a g x y = if x > y then a
                          else f (g x)
                                 (reducefun f a g (x + 1) y)
```

Note that we have the relationships (for x ≤ y):

```
accufun f a g x y = accumulate f a (map g (x upto y))
reducefun f a g x y = reduce f a (map g (x upto y))
```

which could also be taken as definitions. We could also take y as a specification of the length rather than the upper-bound of the range (as for sublist described in Exercise 3.7) which requires a simple modification of the definitions.

3.12

```
fun (p et q) x = if p x then q x else false
et : (α → bool) × (α → bool) → (α → bool)
```

Note that **fun** (p et q) x = p x & q x is also possible but slightly different for a strict language (see Exercise 2.30 of Chapter 2).

3.14 The definitions of filter and map should have the form:

```
fun filter p x = reduce (consif p) [ ] x
fun map f x = reduce (conswith f) [ ] x
```

where consif and conswith have yet to be defined. We want:

```
fun consif p a x = if p a then a :: x else x
fun conswith f a x = f a :: x
```

(Note that conswith f = cons ∘ f.)

3.15

```
fun reducemap g a f [ ] = a
  | reducemap g a f (b :: x) = g (f b) (reducemap g a f x)
```

3.16 We need to define an appropriate nextsp function so that:

```
fun sumprod x = accumulate nextsp (0, 1) x
```

That is, we want:

```
fun nextsp (s, p) a = (a + s, a * p)
```

3.17 In a lazy language, such equivalences for the reduce case are true. In a strict language, use of reduce (or accumulate) will cause p to be applied to every item in the list, whereas the given definitions can terminate earlier. For example:

all positive [3, ~2, . . .] = false (regardless of the ". . .")

3.22

```
fun merge [ ] y = y
|   merge x [ ] = x
|   merge (a :: x) (b :: y) = if a < b then a :: merge x (b :: y)
                                        else b :: merge (a :: x) y

fun mergepairs (a :: b :: x) = merge a b :: mergepairs x
|   mergepairs other = other

fun repeatmerge [ ] = error "repeatmerge [ ]"
|   repeatmerge [a] = a
|   repeatmerge other = repeatmerge (mergepairs other)

fun mergesort [ ] = [ ]
|   mergesort x = repeatmerge (initialize x)
and initialize x = map singleton x
```

The initialization maps singleton across the list where singleton a = [a] to form a list of lists of length one. This can be improved to chop up the list into 'runs' of increasing integers, for example:

initialize [5, 6, 3, 2, 7, 9, 8, 10] = [[5, 6], [3], [2, 7, 9], [8, 10]]

but we leave this modification as a further exercise.

3.24 Taking the definition of upto as:

fun m upto n = **if** m > n **then** [ ] **else** m :: (m + 1) upto n

we would get 0 for sum g x when $x < 0$. It is useful to keep:

m upto (m − 1) = [ ]

but a more robust version of upto might be defined such that m upto n is an error if $n < m - 1$. In this case we would have different behaviour for sum.

3.26 We prove by induction on n that for all $n \geq 1$:

For all s, m such that $s \geq m * n$ and $m > 0$, summandsover m s n is defined and is a list containing exactly the ordered lists of length n with sum s and all items $\geq$ m.

Case $n = 1$:
If $m > 0$ and $s \geq m * 1$ (= m), then the only possible list of length 1 is clearly [s], and summandsover s m 1 is defined and equal to [[s]] as required.

Case n = k + 1 (for k ≥ 1):
Assume m > 0 and s ≥ m * (k + 1), then:

```
summands m s (k + 1) = [a :: x | a ∈ m upto (s div (k + 1));
                                  x ∈ m summands a (s − a) k]
```

Now for any a ∈ (m upto (s div (k + 1))), we have:

a > 0 and (s − a) ≥ a * k

and it follows from this and the induction hypothesis that:

summandsover a (s − a) k

is defined and is a list containing exactly those ordered lists with sum (s − a), length k and all items ≥ a. From this we can check that summands m s (k + 1) is also defined. The required lists for summands m s (k + 1) must have the form a :: x where a ≥ m and x is an ordered list of length k with sum (s − a) and all items ≥ a (i.e. x ∈ summandsover a (s − a) k).

The final step is to show that if a > s div (k + 1) then there are *no* lists with sum (s − a) and length k with all items ≥ a. Clearly if all items in such a list are ≥ a then the sum would be ≥ a * k > (s div (k + 1)) * k = s − (s div (k + 1)) > s − a. So no such lists exist and summandsover a (s − a) k = [ ]. The above result then follows by induction.

To show that summands s n is defined and produces all ordered lists of length n and sum s with items ≥ 1 when n ≥ 0, we just note that:

(a) When n = 0 or s < n then there are no such lists and summands s n is defined and equal to [ ] as required.

(b) Otherwise, summands s n is equal to summandsover 1 s n which is defined (since 1 > 0 and s ≥ 1 * n = n) and produces the required result.

To show that summandsover m s n = [copy n m] when s = n * m and m ≥ 0 and n ≥ 1, we again use induction on n ≥ 1.

Case n = 1:

summandsover m s 1 = [[s]] = [copy 1 s]

Case n = k + 1:

```
summandsover m s (k + 1) = [a :: x | a ∈ m upto (s div (k + 1));
                                      x ∈ summandsover a (s − a) k]
```

Now s = (k + 1) * m implies s div (k + 1) = m and m upto m = [m]. Since the only value of a is m, we can simplify the above list comprehension to:

[m :: x | x ∈ summandsover m (s − m) k]

But, s = (k + 1) * m implies (s − m) = k * m so by the induction hypothesis this list is equal to:

```
[m :: x | x ∈ [copy k m]]
```

which simplifies to:

```
[m :: copy k m]
= [copy (k + 1) m]
```

By induction, summandsover m s n = [copy n m] for all m ≥ 0, n ≥ 1 with s = n * m.

3.28 This function is predefined in Standard ML and denoted by '<' when used with strings. In order to define it for ourselves, we need to compare characters in the strings. We will assume we have a function prechar : string → string → bool such that for characters a, b (strings of length 1) prechar a b = true if b comes (strictly) before a in some extended alphabet (e.g. ASCII order), = false otherwise. We then define lexicalOrd so that lexicalOrd s1 s2 = true if s1 > s2 in the dictionary ordering of s1 and s2:

```
fun lexicalOrd s1 s2
      = lexOrdCharlists (explode s1) (explode s2)
and lexOrdCharlists [ ] [ ] = false
 |    lexOrdCharlists [ ] (b :: y) = false
 |    lexOrdCharlists (a :: x) [ ] = true
 |    lexOrdCharlists (a :: x) (b :: y) = if (prechar a) b then true else
                                           if (prechar b) a then false else
                                             lexOrdCharlists x y
```

Generalizing, we define lex by:

```
fun lex p [ ] [ ] = false
 |   lex p [ ] (b :: y) = false
 |   lex p (a :: x) [ ] = true
 |   lex p (a :: x) (b :: y) = if p a b then true else
                               if p b a then false else
                                 lex p x y
```

(Then lexOrdCharlists = lex prechar.)

3.29 See Appendix 4 for some hints on layout. The pascal function can be defined by:

```
fun pascal n = iterate (n − 1) nextline [1]
and nextline x = splice plus x (0 :: x)
```

The function splice was described in Exercise 3.10 and is similar to zip. The function iterate is similar to repeat but keeps a list of previous values. Thus:

```
fun iterate 0 f x = [x]
 |   iterate n f x = x :: iterate (n − 1) f (f x)
```

Chapter 4

4.4 This is quite a hard function to define. A version which only works if all coordinates are ≥ 0 is given in Appendix 2. This can easily be modified to work from a starting point other than (0, 0), and an appropriate starting point can be obtained by a prescan of the coordinates. However, there may be more elegant solutions.

Chapter 5

5.3 There are $4 * 13 = 52$ 'total' values of type card. (In Chapter 10 we discuss 'partial' values which are present in a lazy language, and there are many more of these than 'total' values of type card.)

5.4

```
fun power (Zero, m) = 1
|   power (Succ n, m) = numbmult (m, power (n, m))
```

5.5

```
fun countbasic (Basicpart partno) = 1
|   countbasic (Compoundpart (partno, clist))
                            = sumlist (map countcompound clist)
and countcompound (Quantity (part, quant))
                    = quant * (countbasic part)
```

5.7 Direct definitions are:

```
fun reflect (Lf a) = Lf a
|   reflect (t1 /\ t2) = reflect t2 /\ reflect t1
fun leavesof (Lf a) = [a]
|   leavesof (t1 /\ t2) = leavesof t1 @ leavesof t2
```

Using btreeop:

```
val reflect = btreeop (op /\ ∘ swappair) Lf
val leavesof = btreeop (op @) singleton
```

(where singleton a = [a], swappair (a, b) = (b, a)).

5.9 See Appendix 2.

5.12

```
datatype α graph = Graph of (α → α list) × (α → α → bool)
fun depthsearch (Graph (succ, eq)) p startnode
     = let fun find visited [ ] = Fail
           |    find visited (a :: x) = if memberwrt eq visited a
                                       then find visited x
                                       else if p a
                                            then Ok a
                                            else find (a :: visited)
                                                        (succ a @ x)
       in find [ ] [startnode] end
```

Note that memberwrt is a generalization of member defined by:

```
fun memberwrt eq [ ] a = false
|   memberwrt eq (b :: x) a = if eq a b then true
                                else memberwrt eq x a
```

5.15 We want associations to have type $\alpha^= \rightarrow \beta$ possible. We achieve this by starting with:

```
fun emptyassoc a = Fail
```

and associate new pairs with assoc after using:

```
fun convert [ ] = [ ]
|   convert ((a, b) :: x) = (a, Ok b) :: convert x
```

That is:

```
fun newassoc pairs default = assoc (convert pairs) default
```

Now we can define:

```
fun isdefined assocfun a = isOk (assocfun a)
and isOk (Ok a) = true
|   isOk (Fail) = false
```

5.16

```
fun assocall [ ] a' = [ ]
|   assocall ((a, b) :: x) a' = if a = a' then b::assocall x a'
                                 else assocall x a'
fun combine f g a = f a @ g a
```

Note that combine (assocall l1) (assocall l2) = assocall (l1 @ l2) should hold. We leave a proof of this as a further exercise.

5.18

```
datatype (α⁼, β) assocObj
         = Assoc of ((α⁼ × β) list → (α⁼, β) assoc Obj) × (α⁼ → β)
fun addassoc (Assoc (addpairs, look)) = addpairs
fun lookup (Assoc (addpairs, look)) = look
val newassoc = let fun mkAssoc (lookup)
                      = let fun addpairs x
                                  = mkAssoc (assoc x lookup)
                        in Assoc (addpairs, lookup) end
               in mkAssoc emptyassoc end
```

(where emptyassoc a = error "value not defined . . .").

5.25

```
fun mkforest Empty = [ ]
|   mkforest (Tr (l, a ,r)) = Vtree (a, mkforest l) :: mkforest r
fun mktree [ ] = Empty
|   mktree (Vtree (a, f1) :: f2) = Tr (mktree f1, a, mktree f2)
```

For example:

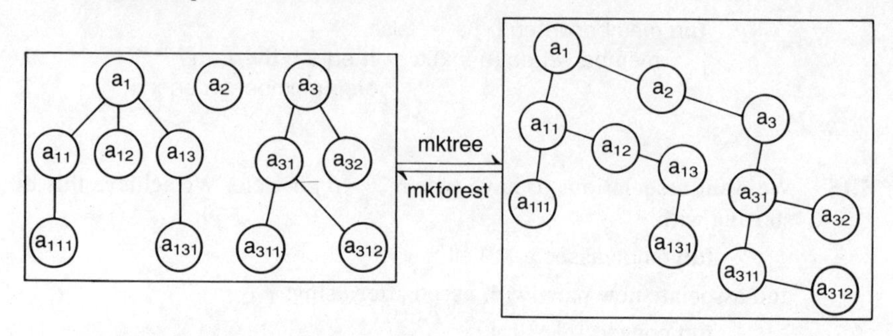

5.29 We show by induction on t : α tree that for all t : α tree

flattenwith t x = flatten t @ x for all x : α list

Case t = Empty:

flattenwith Empty x = x

and:

flatten Empty @ x = [ ] @ x = x

Case t = Tr (l, a, r):

```
flattenwith (Tr (l, a, r)) x = flattenwith l (a :: flattenwith r x)
  = flatten l @ (a :: (flatten r @ x))
    using the induction hypothesis with l and r
  = flatten l @ ((a :: flatten r) @ x)
  = (flatten l @ (a :: flatten r)) @ x
  = (flatten l @ [a] @ flatten r) @ x
  = flatten (Tr (l, a, r)) @ x
```

The result follows by induction. It follows that for all t : α tree:

flatten t = flatten t @ [ ] = flattenwith t [ ]

5.30

mkpair : $\alpha \rightarrow \beta \rightarrow (\alpha \rightarrow \beta \rightarrow \gamma) \rightarrow \gamma$
first : $((\alpha \rightarrow \beta \rightarrow \alpha) \rightarrow \gamma) \rightarrow \gamma$
second : $((\alpha \rightarrow \beta \rightarrow \beta) \rightarrow \gamma) \rightarrow \gamma$

```
first (mkpair a b) = mkpair a b K
                   = K a b
                   = a
second (mkpair a b) = mkpair a b KI
                    = KI a b
                    = b

fun eqpair pr1 pr2 = if first pr1 = first pr2
                     then second pr1 = second pr2
                     else false
```

eqpair : $((\alpha \rightarrow \alpha \rightarrow \alpha) \rightarrow \gamma^{=}) \rightarrow ((\alpha \rightarrow \alpha \rightarrow \alpha) \rightarrow \gamma^{=}) \rightarrow$ bool

This means that eqpair can only be applied to pairs where both components have the same type (more precisely, to pairs represented by functions whose type is an instance of $((\alpha \rightarrow \alpha \rightarrow \alpha) \rightarrow \alpha)$).

Chapter 6

6.5

```
datatype store = Store0
               | Update of (variable × value × store)
fun fetch (v, Store0) = Intval 0
|   fetch (v, Update (v', a, s)) = if v = v' then a else fetch (v, s)
```

6.10 We define:

```
fun mustfind a (Symbol x :: s) = if a = x
                                 then Ok (x, s)
                                 else error "... error report"
```

Then in definitions such as the one for ifcom in Table 6.3 we write:

```
ifcom s = (literal "IF"      ⟨&⟩ exp      ⟨&⟩
           mustfind "THEN"   ⟨&⟩ command  ⟨&⟩
           mustfind "ELSE"   ⟨&⟩ command     ) s
```

In fact, it would be better to have mustfind with an extra string parameter which is to be used in the error message, thus giving more information on what is missing.

6.11 With left recursive grammars, a parser following the structure would just loop. Following Burge (1976), we can define:

```
fun leftrecseq f A B x
  = let fun afterA Fail = Fail
        |   afterA (Ok (a, y)) = more a y
        and more a y =
            let fun afterB Fail = Ok (a, y)
                |   afterB (Ok (b, z)) = more (f(a, b)) z
            in afterB (B y) end
    in afterA (A x) end
```

which incorporates f to combine results as suggested.

Chapter 7

7.5

```
null_oil (nil_oil) = true
null_oil (insert_oil n x) = false
hd_oil (nil_oil) is undefined
hd_oil (insert_oil n nil_oil) = n
hd_oil (insert_oil n (insert_oil m x)) = if n < m
                                         then hd_oil (insert_oil n x)
                                         else hd_oil (insert_oil m x)

tl_oil (nil_oil) is undefined
tl_oil (insert_oil n nil_oil) = nil_oil
tl_oil (insert_oil n (insert_oil m x)) =
        if n < m
        then insert_oil m (tl_oil (insert_oil n x))
        else insert_oil n (tl_oil (insert_oil m x))
```

```
order [ ] = nil_oil
order (a :: x) = insert_oil a (order x)
```

These equations are constructed by choosing nil_oil and insert_oil as the basic constructing operations, and defining the other operations in terms of them.

Usually arguments of type ordintlist can be described as either nil_oil or insert_oil n y, but a further case analysis of y seems necessary for the equations defining hd_oil and tl_oil.

7.8 See Appendix 2 for definitions of the abstract types.

7.11 We suggest two different ways of specifying the operations for the extended version of intset. The equations for the original version treated memberset as an observer, and emptyset, insertset and removeset as primitive constructing operations. (No attempt was made to relate insertset and removeset except indirectly through the specification of the observer.) In the following set of equations, we treat subset, eqset, isemptyset and elements as additional observers, while regarding union, difference and intersection as additional primitive constructors:

```
memberset (union s1 s2) n = memberset s1 n or memberset s2 n
memberset (difference s1 s2) n = memberset s1 n
                                 & not (memberset s2 n)
memberset (intersection s1 s2) n = memberset s1 n
                                   & memberset s2 n
memberset emptyset n = false
memberset (insertset s m) n = m = n or memberset s n
memberset (removeset s m) n = if m = n then false
                                        else memberset s n
subset (union s1 s2) s = subset s1 s & subset s2 s
subset (difference s1 s2) s = subset s1 (union s2 s)
subset (intersection s1 s2) s = subset s1 (union (difference s1 s2) s)
subset emptyset s = true
subset (insertset s1 n) s2 = memberset s2 n & subset s1 s2
subset (removeset s1 n) s2 = subset s1 (insertset s2 n)
eqset s1 s2 = subset s1 s2 & subset s2 s1
isemptyset s = subset s emptyset
```

The specification of elements uses some auxiliary list operations described below:

```
elements (union s1 s2) = merge' (elements s1) (elements s2)
elements (difference s1 s2) = (elements s1) -- (elements s2)
elements (intersection s1 s2) = common (elements s1) (elements s2)
elements emptyset = [ ]
elements (insertset s n) = insert' n (elements s)
elements (removeset s n) = remove1 n (elements s)
```

merge′ should combine two ordered lists into a single ordered list, removing any common elements.

-- is the difference between two lists (preserving order of elements).

common should produce the elements common to two ordered lists (preserving the order).

insert′ should place an integer in the appropriate position of an ordered list only if the integer is not already in the list.

remove1 should remove a given integer from an ordered list, returning the original list if the integer is not present. (At most one occurrence need be removed as the list is assumed to contain no repetitions.)

The specification of image is somewhat harder. Here we choose to specify it indirectly in terms of list operations and elements:

```
image f s = accumulate insertset emptyset (map f (elements s))
```

i.e. we map f across the list of elements of s and then rebuild a set from the resulting list. Note that in each equation, one of the arguments to the operation being specified is strictly simpler on the right-hand side than on the left-hand side of the equation. (The same argument is simplified for each equation specifying the same function.)

An alternative specification follows, where we restrict the primitive constructors to just emptyset and insertset, defining all other operators in terms of these (ultimately):

```
memberset emptyset n = false
memberset (insertset s m) n = m = n or memberset s n
removeset emptyset n = emptyset
removeset (insertset s m) n = if m = n
                              then removeset s n
                              else insertset (removeset s n) m

union emptyset s2 = s2
union (insertset s1 n) s2 = insertset (union s1 s2) n
difference s1 emptyset = s1
difference s1 (insertset s2 n) = difference (removeset s1 n) s2
intersection s1 s2 = difference s1 (difference s1 s2)
isemptyset s = subset s emptyset
subset emptyset s2 = true
subset (insertset s1 n) s2 = memberset s2 n & subset s1 s2
eqset s1 s2 = (subset s1 s2) & (subset s2 s1)
elements emptyset = [ ]
elements (insertset s n) = insert′ n (elements s)
```

(where insert′ is the list operation described in the previous specification of intset)

```
image f s = accumulate insertset emptyset (map f (elements s))
```

Suggestions for implementations are not included in these selected solutions.

7.13 An obvious definition of type tree23 is:

```
datatype α tree23
             = E
             | Tr2 of α tree23 × α × α tree23
             | Tr3 of α tree23 × α × α tree23 × α × α tree23
```

However, it is surprisingly difficult to write rebalancing inserts and removes for such trees. One elegant solution to the problem is to add additional constructors which are used temporarily while rebalancing. For example, the following version deals with inserts only and uses an extra constructor Put: α tree23 × α × α tree23 → α tree23. Put nodes are created during an insert, but subsequently removed during rebalancing. The Put function descends to find the appropriate place to add a value (integer) and inserts the value as a Put node. On the way down, put replaces 2 and 3 nodes by tr2 and tr3 rebalancing functions. These either remove a Put node or bubble it up one level. Put nodes are removed when tr2 produces a 3-node (Tr3 instead of a Tr2). The main function insert23 uses checktop to deal with a Put bubbling up to the top:

```
datatype α tree23
         = E
         | Tr2 of α tree23 × α × α tree23
         | Tr3 of α tree23 × α × α tree23 × α × α tree23
         | Put of α tree23 × α × α tree23;
```

(We assume just integer 2-3-trees for simplicity, and restrict by using < : int × int → bool.)

```
fun put n E = Put (E, n, E)
 |  put n (Tr2 (t1, a, t2))
            = if n = a then Tr2 (t1, a, t2)   else
              if n < a then tr2 (put n t1, a, t2)   else
              (* n > a *)     tr2 (t1, a, put n t2)
 |  put n (Tr3 (t1, a, t2, b, t3))
            = if n = a then Tr3 (t1, a, t2, b, t3)   else
              if n = b then Tr3 (t1, a, t2, b, t3)   else
              if n < a then tr3 (put n t1 a, t2, b, t3)   else
              if n < b then tr3 (t1, a, put n t2, b, t3)   else
              (* n > b *)     tr3 (t1, a, t2, b, put n t3)
 |  put n other = error "put on un-normalized tree"
and tr2 (Put (t1, a, t2), b, t3) = Tr3 (t1, a, t2, b, t3)
 |  tr2 (t1, a, Put (t2, b, t3)) = Tr3 (t1, a, t2, b, t3)
 |  tr2 other                    = Tr2 other
and tr3 (Put (t1, a, t2), b, t3, c, t4)
            = Put (Tr2 (t1, a, t2), b, Tr2 (t3, c, t4))
 |  tr3 (t1, a, Put (t2, b, t3), c, t4)
            = Put (Tr2 (t1, a, t2), b, Tr2 (t3, c, t4))
 |  tr3 (t1, a, t2, b, Put (t3, c, t4))
            = Put (Tr2 (t1, a, t2), b, Tr2 (t3, c, t4))
 |  tr3 other  = Tr3 other
```

```
fun checktop (Put (t1, a, t2)) = Tr2 (t1, a, t2)
 |  checktop other = other

fun insert23 n t = checktop (put n t)
```

An extension of this method to deal with removals as well is somewhat more complex. Details of a solution can be found in Reade (1989).

7.14 The law can be replaced by the definition:

```
fun cons_oil (n, Cons_oil (m, x))
            = if n > m then cons_oil (m, cons_oil (n, x))
                       else Cons_oil (n, Cons_oil (m, x))
 |  cons_oil (n, Nil_oil) = Cons_oil (n, Nil_oil)
```

or more efficiently:

```
fun cons_oil (n, Cons_oil (m, x))
            = if n > m then Cons_oil (m, cons_oil (n, x))
                       else Cons_oil (n, Cons_oil (m, x))
 |  cons_oil (n, Nil_oil) = Cons_oil (n, Nil_oil)
```

Subsequently, all uses of Cons_oil in patterns can be left as they are, but all uses of Cons_oil outside of patterns should be replaced by cons_oil. For example, the definitions

```
val l1 = Cons_oil (2, Cons_oil (1, Nil_oil))
fun delete n Nil_oil = Nil_oil
 |  delete n (Cons_oil (m, x)) = if m = n
                                 then delete n x
                                 else Cons_oil (m, delete n x)
```

should be replaced by:

```
val l1 = cons_oil (2, cons_oil (1, Nil_oil))
fun delete n Nil_oil = Nil_oil
 |  delete n (Cons_oil (m, x)) = if m = n
                                 then delete n x
                                 else cons_oil (m, delete n x)
```

(Note that we have described a systematic change. In this particular example, the original definition of delete would still preserve the integrity of the type and the modification is redundant.)

Chapter 8

8.3 In SML such a definition is accepted and gives:

```
from : int → int
```

However, whenever from is applied to any integer, it loops without producing a result. This illustrates that in SML there is a difference between a function which is undefined (the definition causes a loop) and a defined function which has an undefined result whenever it is applied.

8.4 f must be strict, since if E_1 is Ω, the left-hand side gives f (Ω) and the right-hand side gives Ω.

8.5

```
val rec t1 = let val shared = C1 (C0)
             in C2 (C1 shared, C2 (shared, t1)) end
val t2 = let val rec shared1 = C1 (C2 (C0, shared2))
             and     shared2 = C1 (shared3)
             and     shared3 = C2 (shared1, shared2)
         in C2 (C1 shared1, shared3) end
val rec t3 = C2 (C1 (C1 C0), C2 (C1 C0, C2 (C1 C0, t3)))
```

For the definition of t4 we use make where:

```
fun make t = C2 (t, C2 (C1 t, make (C1 t)))
```

or better:

```
fun make t = let val t' = C1 t
             in C2 (t, C2 (t', make t')) end
```

then:

```
val t4 = make C0
```

Note that t1 and t2 are equal values, but t1 is just a convenient representation which shares a single diagram for a repeated subtree. There are infinitely many such diagrams for this value, but t1 is a minimal representation. The point is that one must be careful to distinguish between values and their representations as diagram – equality concerns equal values and never equal representations.

8.7 Here is one possible solution, based on the fact that the sequence can be expressed as:

```
a0 :: (a0 * x) + a1 :: (a0 * x + a1) * x + a2 :: · · ·
= zip plus (a0 :: a1 :: a2 :: · · · )
               (0 * x :: a0 * x :: (a0 * x + a1) * x :: · · · )
```

The first sequence is the list of coefficients and the second is the sequence of required outputs, each multiplied by x (with a preceding 0). This suggests the following diagram:

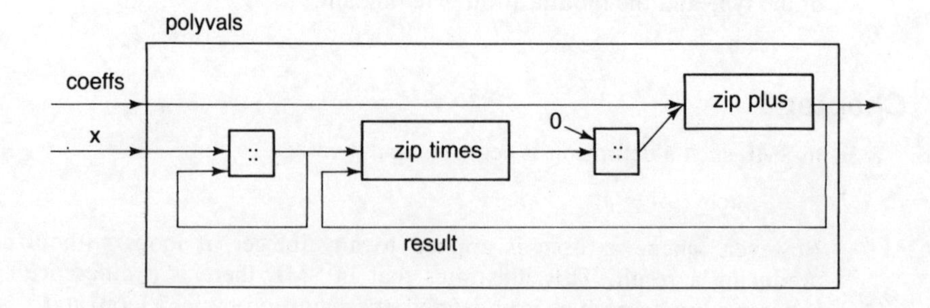

where we have expressed the multiplication by x as:

```
zip times (infx) result
```

where infx = x :: infx. (This is easier to draw a diagram for than map (times x) result.)

The definition is thus:

```
fun polyvals coeffs x
  = let val rec result = zip plus coeffs (0 :: zip times infx result)
        and     infx = x :: infx
    in result end
```

8.8 Again, we can rephrase the derivative sequence as the sum of 2 sequences:

$$\text{zip plus } (0 :: a0 :: a0 * x + a1 :: a0 * x^2 + a1 * x + a2 :: \cdots)$$
$$(0 * x :: a0 * x :: (2a0 * x + a1) * x :: \cdots)$$

The first sequence is the output of polyvals (see previous exercise) with a preceding 0, and the second sequence is the required output with each element multiplied by x, that is:

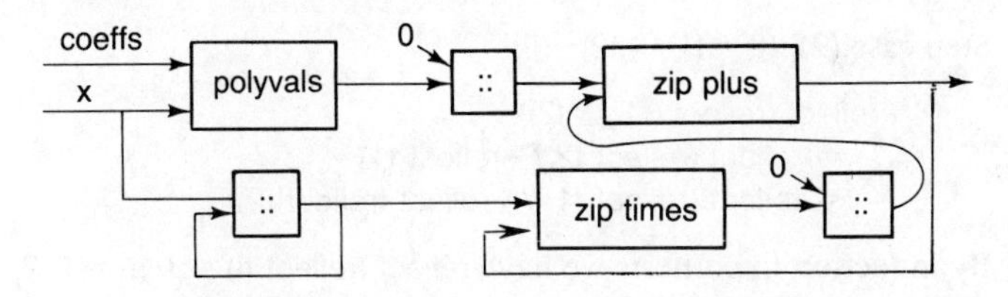

This can be seen as two applications of polyval:

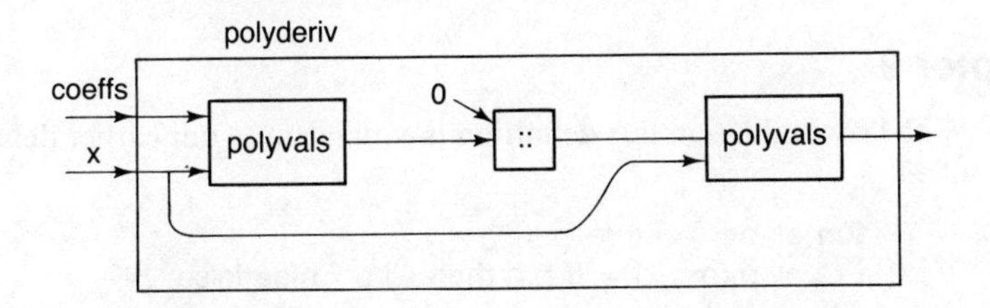

i.e.

```
fun polyderiv coeffs x = polyvals (0 :: polyvals coeffs x) x
```

8.17 Base case:

$$\Omega \mathbin{@} x = \Omega$$

since the definition of @ pattern matches on the first argument.

Step case:

Assuming that ones @ x = ones, we need to show that:

```
(1 :: ones) @ x = 1 :: ones
```

Now:

```
(1 :: ones) @ x = 1 :: (ones @ x) by definition of @
                = 1 :: ones       by hypothesis
```

Hence ones @ x = ones for all x : int list by fixed point induction (since the predicate P(y) defined as y @ x = y is admissible in y).

8.19 Using the definition:

```
fun reflect (Lf a) = Lf a
|   reflect (t1 /\ t2) = reflect t2 /\ reflect t1
```

we prove reflect (reflect t) = t (which is an admissible predicate on t) for all t : T bintree (for arbitrary type T) using lazy-bintree induction.

Base case, (t = Ω):

```
reflect (reflect Ω) = Ω as required
```

Step case (1), (t = Lf a):

```
reflect (reflect (Lf a)) = reflect (Lf a) = Lf a as required
```

Step case (2), (t = t1 /\ t2):

```
reflect (reflect (t1 /\ t2))
   = reflect (reflect t2 /\ reflect t1)
   = reflect (reflect t1) /\ reflect (reflect t2)
```

By induction hypothesis we have reflect (reflect ti) = ti (i = 1, 2) so reflect (reflect (t1 /\ t2)) = t1 /\ t2 as required.

Chapter 9

9.2 With lazy evaluation this definition is equivalent to our earlier definition of all:

```
fun all p [ ] = true
|   all p (a :: x) = if p a then all p x else false
```

which could also be written as:

```
fun all p [ ] = true
|   all p (a :: x) = p a & all p x
                   ( = andc (p a) (all p x))
```

However, with eager evaluation, the reduce definition is much less efficient since it will involve an application of p to all items of the list as well as a naïve conjoining of all the booleans afterwards, which could be avoided when a false is found. Furthermore different behaviour can be seen on partial lists. Take, for example:

```
all positive (~5 :: Ω)
```

Using the reduce definition of all, lazy evaluation gives false, but eager evaluation will not produce a result.

9.3

```
fun mkinftree n = let fun branch b = Treenode (n, branch)
                  in Treenode (n, branch) end
```

which is equivalent to (but more efficient than):

```
fun mkinftree n = let fun branch b = mkinftree n
                  in Treenode (n, branch) end
```

For the string tree, we define:

```
fun mkbittree s = let fun branch true  = mkbittree ("0" ^ s)
                      |   branch false = mkbittree ("1" ^ s)
                  in Treenode (s, branch) end
```

Then the required tree is:

```
mkbittree " "
```

9.6 The required slfun has the form:

```
fun slfun sl = slCons 1 (slmerge3 (slmap (times 2) sl)
                                  (slmap (times 3) sl)
                                  (slmap (times 5) sl))
```

Where slmap is the susplist version of map, and slmerge3 is defined analogously to merge3:

```
fun  slmerge sl1 sl2
   = let val  (hd1, tl2) = (slHd sl1, slTl sl1)
          and (hd2, tl2) = (slHd sl2, slTl sl2)
     in if hd1 < hd2 then slCons hd1 (slmerge tl1 sl2) else
        if hd2 < hd1 then slCons hd2 (slmerge sl1 tl2) else
                          slCons hd1 (slmerge tl1 tl2)
and slmerge3 sl1 sl2 sl3 = slmerge sl1 (slmerge sl2 sl3)
```

We then define:

```
val hamming = fixpoint slfun
```

9.8 Assuming integer lists, using lessthan : int → int → bool:

```
fun  quicksortwith [ ] y = y
|    quicksortwith (a :: x) y
        = let val  low  = filter (lessthan a) x
              and high = filter (non (lessthan a)) x
          in quicksortwith low (a :: quicksortwith high y)
          end
and quicksort x = quicksortwith x [ ]
```

9.10 parse would have type string list → string and is equivalent to:

```
fun parse ["a"] = "a"
  | parse ["b", "c"] = "bc"
  | parse ("a" :: some :: more)
        = error ("end of input expected but found"
                 ^ implode (some :: more))
  | parse ("b" :: "c" :: some :: more)
        = error ("end of input expected but found"
                 ^ implode some :: more))
  | parse other = error "input not recognized"
```

9.11 (a)

```
fun g n = [n - 1, n - 2]
fun combine n [fibn1, fibn2] = fibn1 + fibn2
  | combine n other = error "not possible"
fun done 0 = Ok (1)
  | done 1 = Ok (1)
  | done other = Fail
```

Then

```
fun memofib n = memo g combine (done, n)
```

(b) Using binary chop:

$$n^k = n^{k1} * n^{k2}$$

where k1 = k div 2, k2 = k − k1 for k ≥ 0. So:

```
fun g k = let val k1 = k div 2
          in [k1, k - k1] end

fun combine k [nk1, nk2] = nk1 * nk2
  | combine k other = error "not possible"
```

The function done is parameterized on the integer n for which powers are to be calculated:

```
fun done n 0 = Ok 1
  | done n 1 = Ok n
  | done n other = Fail
```

Then **fun** memopower n k = memo g combine (done n, k).

Chapter 10

10.2 The values of type $(\{c1\} \times D)_\perp$ are either $\perp$ or of the form c1 (d) for some $d \in D$ (writing c1 (d) instead of (c1, d)), and they are ordered by:

$\perp \sqsubseteq \perp \sqsubseteq$ c1 (d) for all $d \in D$
c1 $(d) \sqsubseteq$ c1 (d') if and only if $d \sqsubseteq d'$ in D

$(\{c2\} \times D)_\perp$ is similar, so the coalesced sum:

$(\{c1\} \times D)_\perp \oplus (\{c2\} \times D)_\perp$

has values:

$\perp$ or of the form c1 (d) $d \in D$
or of the form c2 (d) $d \in D$

and is ordered by:

$\perp \sqsubseteq \perp$
$\perp \sqsubseteq$ c1 (d) for all $d \in D$
$\perp \sqsubseteq$ c2 (d) for all $d \in D$
c1 $(d) \sqsubseteq$ c1 (d') if and only if $d \sqsubseteq d'$ in D
c2 $(d) \sqsubseteq$ c2 (d') if and only if $d \sqsubseteq d'$ in D

(and we never have c1 $(d) \sqsubseteq$ c2 (d') or c2 $(d) \sqsubseteq$ c1 (d')). This is exactly the structure of $(\{c1, c2\} \times D)_\perp$.

10.3

$$
\begin{aligned}
&\mathcal{Val}\,[\![(\textbf{fn}\ V \Rightarrow E_1)\ E_1]\!]\\
&\quad = apply\ (\mathcal{Val}\,[\![\textbf{fn}\ V \Rightarrow E]\!]\ \rho)\ (\mathcal{Val}\,[\![E_1]\!]\ \rho)\\
&= apply\ (f\ in\ functions\ in\ \textbf{Val})\ (\mathcal{Val}\,[\![E_1]\!]\ \rho)\\
&\qquad\qquad (\text{where } f\ (d) = \mathcal{Val}\,[\![E]\!]\ (\rho + [d/V])\\
&= f\ (\mathcal{Val}\,[\![E_1]\!]\ \rho)\\
&\qquad\qquad (\text{where } f\ (d) = \mathcal{Val}\,[\![E]\!]\ (\rho + [d/V])\\
&= \mathcal{Val}\,[\![E]\!]\ (\rho + [d/V]) \text{ where } d = \mathcal{Val}\,[\![E_1]\!]\ \rho
\end{aligned}
$$

10.4

$$
\begin{aligned}
&\mathcal{Val}\,[\![\textbf{let val}\ V = E_1\ \textbf{in}\ E\ \textbf{end}]\!]\ \rho\\
&\quad = \mathcal{Val}\,[\![E]\!]\ (\rho + \rho')\\
&\qquad \text{where } \rho' = \mathcal{Def}\,[\![\textbf{val}\ V = E_1]\!]\ \rho
\end{aligned}
$$

Now:

$$
\begin{aligned}
\mathcal{Def}\,[\![\textbf{val}\ V = E_1]\!]\ \rho &= \mathcal{MatchEnv}\,[\![V]\!]\ d, \text{ if } \mathcal{MatchTest}\,[\![V]\!]\ d = \text{true}\\
&\qquad\qquad \text{where } d = \textbf{Val}\,[\![E_1]\!]\ \rho\\
&= \phi \text{ otherwise}
\end{aligned}
$$

and:

$$
\begin{aligned}
&\mathcal{MatchTest}\,[\![V]\!]\ d = \text{true}\\
&\mathcal{MatchEnv}\,[\![V]\!]\ d = [d/V]
\end{aligned}
$$

so:

$$\mathcal{Def}\,[\![\textbf{val}\ V = E_1]\!]\ \rho = [d/V] \text{ where } d = \mathcal{Val}\,[\![E_1]\!]\ \rho$$

Putting this together gives:

$$
\begin{aligned}
\mathcal{Val}\,[\![\textbf{let val}\ V = E_1\ \textbf{in}\ E\ \textbf{end}]\!]\ \rho &= \mathcal{Val}\,[\![E]\!]\ (\rho + [d/V])\\
&\qquad \text{where } d = \mathcal{Val}\,[\![E_1]\!]\ \rho
\end{aligned}
$$

10.9 Using the definition:

```
fun fix F = let fun g (Encode f) = F (f (Encode f))
            in g (Encode g) end
```

we calculate that:

```
fix F = g (Encode g)       where g (Encode f) = F (f (Encode f))
      = F (g (Encode g))   where g (Encode f) = F (f (Encode f))
      = F (fix F)          as required
```

10.10 When F is I, the non-lazy definition reduces as follows:

```
fix I = let fun g (Encode f) x = I (f (Encode f)) x
        in g (Encode g) end
      = fn x => I (g (Encode g)) x
        where g (Encode f) x = I (f (Encode f)) x
```

Thus for any x:

```
fix I x = I (g (Encode g)) x   where g (Encode f) x = I (f (Encode f)) x
        = g (Encode g) x       where g (Encode f) x = I (f (Encode f)) x
        = I (g (Encode g)) x   where g (Encode f) x = I (f (Encode f)) x
        = g (Encode g)) x      where g (Encode f) x = I (f (Encode f)) x
```

This suggests that the calculation is not terminating. To prove this formally, we could show that:

g (Encode g) x $\sqsubseteq \Omega$ for all x : T

by fixed point induction (which means that g (Encode g) x is less defined, or equal to Ω which is completely undefined).

Chapter 11

11.3 With assumptions in the form of lists, A would have the form [ ] or $(V_1, T_1) :: A'$. The basic rule or axiom says that if an A has the form $(V, T) :: A'$ then $A(V) = T$:

$$\overline{((V, T) :: A')(V) = T}$$

The other rule we require is that this is unaltered by additional assumptions not involving V:

$$\frac{A(V) = T}{((V', T') :: A)(V) = T} \text{ when } V' \not\equiv V$$

11.8 Roughly, the parameter f gets a non-generic type variable, and this cannot be instantiated to a function type with argument types of both bool and int in the same context. In more detail, we will have an assumption, at some point, of the form:

[f : α] + A

and then we unify α with bool $\rightarrow T_1$, turning the assumption into:

[f : bool $\rightarrow T_1$] + A [bool $\rightarrow T_1/\alpha$]

Subsequently we need to unify bool $\rightarrow T_1$ with int $\rightarrow T_2$ which fails.

Chapter 12

12.1 We define ($\overset{\alpha}{\rightarrow}$) single α conversions by:

$\lambda x \,.\, E \overset{\alpha}{\rightarrow} \lambda y \,.\, E\,[y/x]$ provided y does not occur bound or free in E along with rules:

$$\frac{E_1 \overset{\alpha}{\rightarrow} E_1'}{E_1\, E_2 \overset{\alpha}{\rightarrow} E_1'\, E_2} \qquad \frac{E_2 \overset{\alpha}{\rightarrow} E_2'}{E_1\, E_2 \overset{\alpha}{\rightarrow} E_1\, E_2'} \qquad \frac{E \overset{\alpha}{\rightarrow} E'}{\lambda v \,.\, E \overset{\alpha}{\rightarrow} \lambda v \,.\, E'}$$

We then define $\overset{\alpha}{\leftrightarrow}$ to be the reflexive, symmetric, transitive closure of $\overset{\alpha}{\rightarrow}$, that is:

$E \overset{\alpha}{\leftrightarrow} E'$ if and only if there is some sequence:

$E_1 \ldots E_n\ (n \geq 1)$

where either $E_i \overset{\alpha}{\rightarrow} E_{i+1}$ or $E_{i+1} \overset{\alpha}{\rightarrow} E_i\ (1 \leq i < n)$

and E is the same as E_1 (syntactically identical to)
E' is the same as E_n

The required definition of syntactic identity modulo safe variable changes is then:

$E_1 \equiv E_2$ if and only if $E_1 \overset{\alpha}{\leftrightarrow} E_2$

12.2 The example given converts:

```
λy                                  λ
|                                   |
APP                                 APP
├── APP                             ├── APP
│   ├── λv                          │   ├── λ
│   │   └── APP                     │   │   └── APP
│   │       ├── λz                  │   │       ├── λ
│   │       │   └── λx              │   │       │   └── λ
│   │       │       └── APP    ==>  │   │       │       └── APP
│   │       │           ├── APP to  │   │       │           ├── APP
│   │       │           │   ├── y   │   │       │           │   ├── #3
│   │       │           │   └── x   │   │       │           │   └── #0
│   │       │           └── z       │   │       │           └── #1
│   │       └── λx                  │   │       └── λ
│   │           └── APP             │   │           └── APP
│   │               ├── x           │   │               ├── #0
│   │               └── v           │   │               └── #1
│   └── y                           │   └── #0
└── z                               └── z

λ–term                              De Bruijn form
```

Using informal notation, the algorithm can be described by:

convert′ varlist (V) = depthnumber varlist (V)

convert′ varlist (APP with children E_1, E_2) = APP with children (convert′ varlist E_1) and (convert′ varlist E_2)

convert′ varlist (λx over E) = λ over convert′ (x :: varlist) E

where depthnumber varlist var returns the location of var in the varlist, counting the first element of varlist as #0. If var is not present in the varlist, the variable is free so the function should return the variable itself. (An error signal would be more appropriate if we assume only closed terms are converted.) The main conversion is given by:

convert = *convert′* [ ]

12.3 $BV(x) = \{\ \}$
$BV(E_1\ E_2) = BV(E_1) \cup BV(E_2)$
$BV(\lambda v\,.\,E) = \{v\} \cup BV(E)$

12.4 A set of reduction rules respects syntactic equivalence if the reduction relation they generate (→) has the property that:

IF $E_1 \rightarrow E_2$ AND $E_1' \equiv E_1$ THEN $E_1' \rightarrow E_2'$

for some E_2' where $E_2' \equiv E_2$.

12.5 (a)

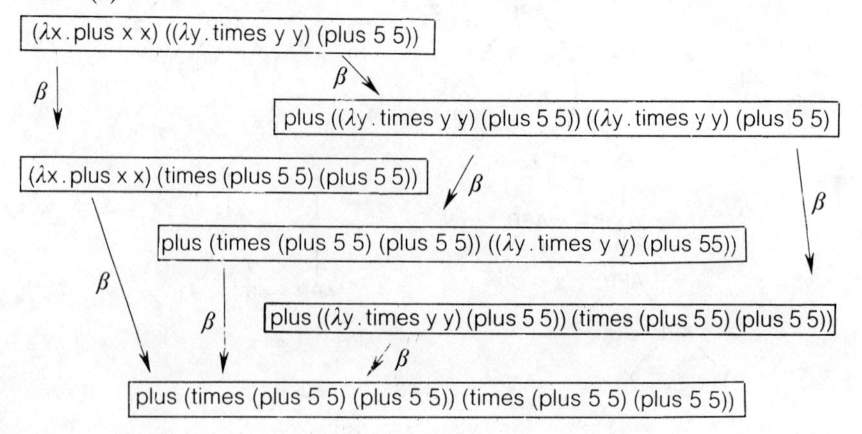

(b) Some of the possibilities are:

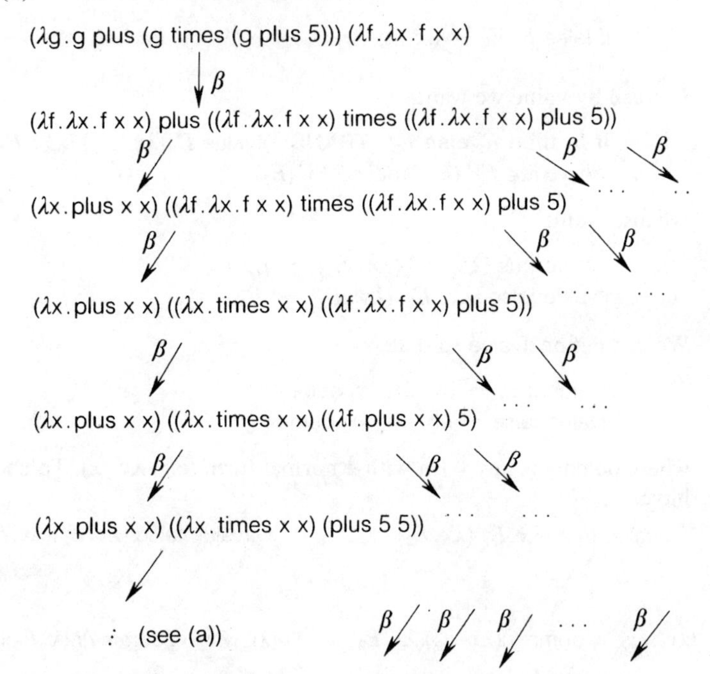

plus (times (plus 5 5) (plus 5 5)) (times (plus 5 5) (plus 5 5))

(This is in β normal form and all sequences end with this.)

(c)

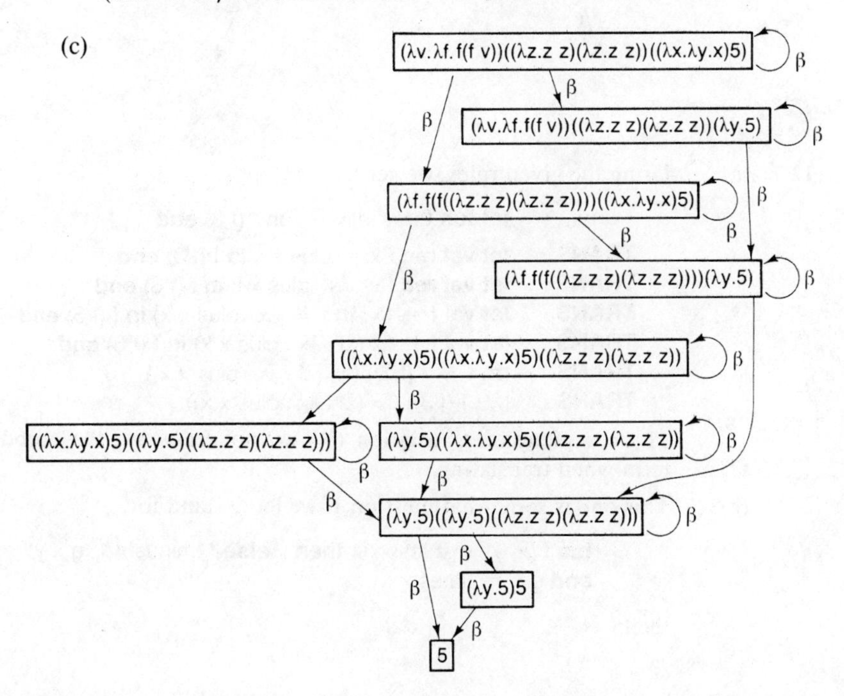

12.6

$$\text{if true } E_1\, E_2 \to (\lambda x\,.\,\lambda y\,.\,x)\, E_1\, E_2 \xrightarrow{\beta} (\lambda y\,.\,E_1)\, E_2 \xrightarrow{\beta} E_1$$

$$\text{if false } E_1\, E_2 \to (\lambda x\,.\,\lambda y\,.\,y)\, E_1\, E_2 \xrightarrow{\beta} (\lambda y\,.\,y)\, E_2 \xrightarrow{\beta} E_2$$

For call by value we want:

if E_1 **then** E_2 **else** E_3 **TRANS** ifvalue $E_1\,(\lambda x\,.\,E_2)\,(\lambda x\,.\,E_3)$
where $x \notin FV(E_1)$ and $x \notin FV(E_2)$

we also want:

ifvalue true $(\lambda x\,.\,E_2)\,(\lambda x\,.\,E_3) \to^* E_2$
ifvalue false $(\lambda x\,.\,E_2)\,(\lambda x\,.\,E_3) \to^* E_3$

We can define ifvalue so that:

ifvalue true $\to \lambda v_1\,.\,\lambda v_2\,.\,v_1$ dummy
ifvalue false $\to \lambda v_1\,.\,\lambda v_2\,.\,v_2$ dummy

where dummy is any term with a normal form (e.g. $\lambda x\,.\,x$). To check, we have:

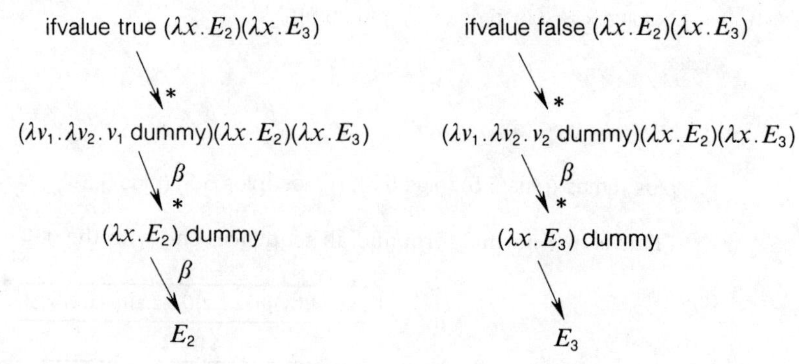

12.7 (a) Using the given rules, we get:

	let fun f x = plus x x **in** f (f 3) **end**
TRANS	**let val rec** f x = plus x x **in** f (f 3) **end**
TRANS	**let val rec** f = λx . plus x x **in** f (f 3) **end**
TRANS	**let val** f = fix (**fn** f ⇒ λx . plus x x) **in** f (f 3) **end**
TRANS	**let val** f = fix (λf . λx . plus x x) **in** f (f 3) **end**
TRANS	(**fn** f ⇒ f (f 3)) (fix (λf . λx . plus x x))
TRANS	(λf . f (f 3)) (fix (λf . λx . plus x x))

This completes the translation. (We are not *evaluating* the lambda term when translating.)

(b) This one is somewhat messier. If we let D stand for:

fun f (x, y) = **if** less x 1 **then** y **else** f (minus x 1, g x y)
and g x = times x

then:

```
D TRANS   val rec f (x, y) = if . . .
          and     g x = times x
  TRANS   val rec f = λv . match ((x, y) ⇒ if . . .) v
          and     g x = times x
  TRANS   val rec f = λv . matchrule (x, y) v (if . . .) matchfail
          and     g x = times x
```

which eventually gives:

```
val rec f = λv . (λx . (λy . (if . . .)) (sel2,2 v)) ((sel2,1 v)
    and g = λx . times x
```

The **if** . . . eventually translates to:

```
if (less x 1) (y) (f (pair (minus x 1) (g x y)))
```

So we now have D translated into the form:

val rec f = E_1
and g = E_2

(where E_1 and E_2 are fully translated). This then gives:

val rec (f, g) = (E_1, E_2)

and then:

val (f, g) = fix (**fn** (f, g) ⇒ (E_1, E_2))

The pair pattern can be translated further to get:

val (f, g) = fix (λv . (λf . (λg . pair E_1 E_2) ($sel_{2,2}$ v)) (($sel_{2,1}$ v))

which we will abbreviate to **val** (f, g) = E. Putting this in the original expression we get:

let val (f, g) = E **in** f (z, y) **end**

which eventually becomes:

(λv . (λf . (λg . f (z, y)) ($sel_{2,2}$ v)) ($sel_{2,1}$ v)) E

12.8 Definitions can have the following forms:

D_1 D_2
local D_1 **in** D_2 **end**
val P = E

(The previously given rules allow us to translate other forms into one of the above.)

Removal of local definitions by simple translation seems particularly difficult. However, the following (from Plotkin (1981)) could be used.

We introduce D_1 **AND** D_2 as another form of definition (temporarily) where we intend that D_1 and D_2 declare distinct variables. It is useful to define $DV(D)$ to mean the set of variables defined by D and in particular $DV(D_1$ **AND** $D_2) = DV(D_1) \cup DV(D_2)$. (Other cases are left as an exercise for the reader.)

The following equivalences can then be used to transform definitions, ultimately to produce the form **val** $P = E$, which can then be removed in the context of a **let** expression:

D_1 D_2 **TRANS local** D_1 **in** (D_2 **AND val** $P = P$) **end**
where $P = (x_1, x_2, \ldots, x_n)$
where $\{x_1, \ldots x_n\} = DV(D_1) - DV(D_2)$

local D_1 **in** D_2 **AND** D_3 **end TRANS**
(**local** D_1 **in** D_2 **end**) **AND** (**local** D_1 **in** D_3 **end**)

local D **in val** $P = E$ **end TRANS val** $P =$ **let** D **in** E **end**

(**val** $P_1 = E_1$) **AND** (**val** $P_2 = E_2$) ... **AND** (**val** $P_n = E_n$) **TRANS**
val $(P_1, P_2, \ldots, P_n) = (E_1, E_2, \ldots, E_n)$

12.11

$$\overline{\text{iszero}}\ \overline{0} \equiv (\lambda x.x\ (\lambda y.\lambda z.\overline{\text{false}})\ (\lambda x.x)\ \overline{\text{true}})\ (\lambda f.\lambda x.x)$$
$$\xrightarrow{\beta} (\lambda f.\lambda x.x)\ (\lambda y.\lambda z.\overline{\text{false}})\ (\lambda x.x)\ \overline{\text{true}}$$
$$\xrightarrow{\beta} (\lambda x.x)\ (\lambda x.x)\ \overline{\text{true}}$$
$$\xrightarrow{\beta} (\lambda x.x)\ \overline{\text{true}}$$
$$\xrightarrow{\beta} \overline{\text{true}}$$

$$\overline{\text{iszero}}\ \overline{n+1} \equiv (\lambda x.x\ (\lambda y.\lambda z.\overline{\text{false}})\ (\lambda x.x)\ \overline{\text{true}})\ \overline{n+1}$$
$$\xrightarrow{\beta} \overline{n+1}\ (\lambda y.\lambda z.\overline{\text{false}})\ (\lambda x.x)\ \overline{\text{true}}$$
$$\xrightarrow{\beta} (\lambda y.\lambda z.\overline{\text{false}})\ (\overline{n}\ (\lambda y.\lambda z.\overline{\text{false}})\ (\lambda x.x))\ \overline{\text{true}}$$
(by property of $\overline{n+1}$)
$$\xrightarrow{\beta} (\lambda z.\overline{\text{false}})\ \overline{\text{true}}$$
$$\xrightarrow{\beta} \overline{\text{false}}$$

12.18 First we calculate:

$$_{\text{Abs}}[\lambda x.f\ (x\ x)] = {}_x[f\ (x\ x)]$$
$$= B\ f\ {}_x[x\ x]$$
$$= B\ f\ (S\ I\ I)$$

Then:

$$_{\text{Abs}}[\lambda f.(\lambda x.f\ (x\ x))\ (\lambda x.f\ (x\ x))]$$
$$= {}_f[{}_{\text{Abs}}[\lambda x.f\ (x\ x)]\ {}_{\text{Abs}}[\lambda x.f\ (x\ x)]]$$
$$= {}_f[B\ f\ (S\ I\ I)\ (B\ f\ (S\ I\ I))] \text{ using the previous calculation}$$
$$= S\ {}_f[B\ f\ (S\ I\ I)]\ {}_f[B\ f\ (S\ I\ I)]$$
$$= S\ (C\ {}_f[B\ f]\ (S\ I\ I))\ (C\ {}_f[B\ f]\ (S\ I\ I))$$
$$= S\ (C\ B\ (S\ I\ I))\ (C\ B\ (S\ I\ I))$$

Note that calculating S (C B (S I I)) (C B (S I I)) F we first get C B (S I I) F (C B (S I I) F) which goes on to give F (C B (S I I) F (C B (S I I) F)).

12.19 Regarding the definition as:

$$\text{zipop} = \lambda f.\lambda x.\lambda y.\text{map f (zip pair x y)}$$

We see that we need to calculate:

$$\text{zipop} = {}_f[\,{}_x[\,{}_y[\text{map f (zip pair x y)}]]]$$

First:

$$\begin{aligned} {}_y[\text{map f (zip pair x y)}] &= \text{B (map f) } {}_y[\text{zip pair x y}] \\ &= \text{B (map f) (zip pair x)} \end{aligned}$$

Second:

$$\begin{aligned} {}_x[\text{B (map f) (zip pair x)}] &= \text{B (B (map f)) } {}_x[\text{zip pair x}] \\ &= \text{B (B (map f)) (zip pair)} \end{aligned}$$

Finally:

$$\begin{aligned} \text{zipop} &= {}_f[\text{B (B (map f)) (zip pair)}] \\ &= \text{C } {}_f[\text{B (B (map f))}] \text{ (zip pair)} \\ &= \text{C (B B } {}_f[\text{B (map f)}]) \text{ (zip pair)} \\ &= \text{C (B B (B B } {}_f[\text{map f}])) \text{ (zip pair)} \\ &= \text{C (B B (B B map)) (zip pair)} \end{aligned}$$

12.21

$$\begin{aligned} &\text{I} : \alpha \to \alpha \\ &\text{K} : \alpha \to \beta \to \alpha \\ &\text{S} : (\alpha \to \beta \to \gamma) \to (\alpha \to \beta) \to \alpha \to \gamma \\ &\text{B} : (\alpha \to \beta) \to (\gamma \to \alpha) \to \gamma \to \beta \\ &\text{C} : (\alpha \to \beta \to \gamma) \to \beta \to \alpha \to \gamma \\ &\text{Y} : (\alpha \to \alpha) \to \alpha \end{aligned}$$

(Assuming **fun** Yf = f (Yf).)

Chapter 13

13.1

```
fun substitute id E (APP E1 E2)
        = APP (substitute id E E1, substitute id E E2)
  | substitute id E (ABS (id', E'))
        = if id = id' then ABS (id', E')
                      else ABS (id', substitute id E E')
  | substitute id E (VAR id')
        = if id = id' then E else VAR id'
  | substitute id E (CON c) = CON c
```

This works properly when E contains no free variables.

13.4 We start with the namelist (*nl*) = [ ], but for the first example this is immaterial:

compile ⟦times (5, succ 9)⟧ *nl*
= *compile* ⟦(5, succ 9)⟧ *nl* @ *compile* ⟦times⟧ *nl* @ [APP]
= *compile* ⟦5⟧ *nl* @ *compile* ⟦succ 9⟧ *nl* @ [TUPLE 2]
@ *compile* ⟦times⟧ *nl* @ [APP]
= [LDC 5] @ (*compile* ⟦9⟧ *nl* @ *compile* ⟦succ⟧ *nl* @ [APP])
@ [TUPLE 2] @ [LDC times] @ [APP]

= [LDC 5, LDC 9, LDC succ, APP,
TUPLE 2, LDC times, APP]

Denoting this by C, the evaluation proceeds as follows:

[ ] [ ] C d_0
⊢ [5] [ ] [LDC 9, . . .] d_0
⊢ [9, 5] [ ] [LDC succ, . . .] d_0
⊢ [succ, 9, 5] [ ] [APP, . . .] d_0
⊢ [10, 5] [ ] [TUPLE 2, . . .] d_0
⊢ [(10, 5)] [ ] [LDC times, APP] d_0
⊢ [times, (10, 5)] [ ] [APP] d_0
⊢ [50] [ ] [ ] d_0 (result value is 50)

Omitting the next two examples, the last example compiles as:

compile ⟦(λf.f (succ 4)) (λx.times (x, succ x))⟧ *nl*
= *compile* ⟦λx.times (x, succ x)⟧ *nl* @
compile ⟦λf.f (succ 4)⟧ *nl* @ [APP]
= [LDFUN c_1, LDFUN c_2, APP]
where c_1 = *compile* ⟦ times (x, succ x)⟧ (x :: *nl*)
= [LD 0, LD 0, LDC succ, APP, TUPLE 2, LDC times, APP]
and c_2 = *compile* ⟦f (succ 4)⟧ (f :: *nl*)
= [LDC 4, LDC succ, APP, LD 0, APP]

This evaluates as follows:

[ ] [ ] [LDFUN c_1 . . .] d_0
⊢ [Closure (c_1, [ ])] [ ] [LDFUN c_2, APP] d_0
⊢ [Closure (c_2, [ ]), Closure (c_1, [ ])] [ ] [APP] d_0
⊢ [ ] [Closure (c_1, [ ])] c_2 d_1 where d_1 = ([ ], [ ], [ ], d_0)
⊢ [4] [Closure (c_1, [ ])] [LDC succ . . .] d_1
⊢ [succ, 4] · · · [APP . . .] d_1
⊢ [5] · · · [LD 0, APP] d_1
⊢ [Closure (c_1, [ ]), 5] [Closure (c_1, [ ])] [APP] d_1
⊢ [ ] [5] c_1 d_2 where d_2 = ([ ], [Closure (c_1, [ ])], [ ], d_1)
⊢ [5] [5] [LD 0, . . .] d_2
⊢ [5, 5] [5] [LDC succ, . . .] d_2
⊢ [succ, 5, 5] [5] [APP, . . .] d_2
⊢ [6, 5] [5] [TUPLE 2, . . .] d_2
⊢ [(6, 5)] [5] [LDC times, APP] d_2
⊢ [times, (6, 5)] [5] [APP] d_2
⊢ [30] [5] [ ] d_2
⊢ [30] [Closure (c_1, [ ])] [ ] d_1
⊢ [30] [ ] [ ] d_0 (result is 30)

13.5 We simply write:

$$\begin{aligned}
&\textit{compilecont}\ (C)\ nl\ c &&= \mathsf{LDC}\ C :: c\\
&\textit{compilecont}\ (V)\ nl\ c &&= \mathsf{LD}\ k :: c \text{ where } k = \textit{position}\ V\ nl\\
&\textit{compilecont}\ (E_1\ E_2)\ nl\ c &&= \textit{compilecont}\ E_2\ nl\\
& &&\quad (\textit{compilecont}\ E_1\ nl\ (\mathsf{APP} :: c))\\
&\textit{compilecont}\ (E_1, \ldots E_n)\ nl\ c &&= \textit{compilecont}\ E_1\ nl\\
& &&\quad (\textit{compilecont}\ E_2\ nl\\
& &&\quad \vdots\\
& &&\quad (\textit{compilecont}\ E_n\ nl\\
& &&\qquad (\mathsf{TUPLE}\ \mathsf{n} :: c)) \ldots)
\end{aligned}$$

$$\begin{aligned}
&\textit{compilecont}\ (\lambda V.E)\ nl\ c\\
&\qquad = (\mathsf{LDFUN}\ c_1 :: c)\\
&\qquad\quad \text{where } c_1 = \textit{compilecont}\ (E)\ (V :: nl)\ [\mathsf{RETURN}]
\end{aligned}$$

Then:

$$\textit{compile}\ (E)\ nl = \textit{compilecont}\ (E)\ nl\ [\mathsf{STOP}]$$

Note that there is a useful improvement which can be made in the abstraction case when the continuation (c) has the form APP :: c'. We know that the Closure is immediately applied and so we want:

$$\begin{aligned}
&\textit{compilecont}\ (\lambda V.E)\ nl\ (\mathsf{APP} :: c')\\
&\quad = \mathsf{KEEP} :: c_1 \text{ where } c_1 = \textit{compilecont}\ (E)\ (V :: nl)\ (\mathsf{DROP} :: c')
\end{aligned}$$

where:

$$\begin{array}{lllll}
 & \mathsf{a :: s} & \mathsf{e} & \mathsf{KEEP :: c} & \mathsf{d}\\
\vdash & \mathsf{s} & \mathsf{a :: e} & \mathsf{c} & \mathsf{d}
\end{array}$$

The **RETURN** has been replaced by a direct jump to the continuing code and **DROP** just removes the head of the environment to restore the state to the correct form when the code for E finishes.

13.7 The state will end up in the form:

$$[\mathsf{Closure}\ (c, e)]\quad e'\quad [\ ]\quad d_0$$

leaving a closure on top of the stack.

Defined Names and Symbols Index

Note: Symbols are in order of first appearance in the text. Entries in **bold** indicate key page references and references followed by (A2) indicate that entries appear in Appendix 2, etc.

General Index